JEWISH TRAVEL GUIDE 2002

International Edition

Published in association with the *Jewish Chronicle*, London

Editor

MICHAEL ZAIDNER

VALLENTINE MITCHELL
LONDON • PORTLAND, OR

First published in 2002 in Great Britain by
VALLENTINE MITCHELL & CO. LTD
Crown House, 47 Chase Side, Southgate
London N14 5BP

and in the United States of America by
VALLENTINE MITCHELL
c/o ISBS,
5824 N.E. Hassalo Street
Portland, Oregon 97213-3644

ISBN 0 85303 433 8
ISSN 0075 3750

Printed in Great Britain by
Creative Print and Design (Wales), Ebbw Vale

Contents

Publisher's Note

WE NEED YOUR ASSISTANCE TO KEEP THIS GUIDE UP TO DATE

The Editor and the Publishers have made every effort to ensure that this guide is as accurate and up to date as possible.

As in previous years, an update form is included the back of this book for those who become aware of additions they would like to be considered for inclusion. In addition, we would wish to be notified of any errors that may have occurred in the preparation of this book.

All information may be sent to us in London by post to the editor:

Vallentine Mitchell
Crown House
47 Chase Side
Southgate
London N14 5BP

Tel: +44(0)20 8920 2100
Fax: +44(0)20 8447 8548
E mail: jtg@vmbooks.com
Website: www.vmbooks.com

Please note that handwritten items are often not legible when sent by fax.

Potential advertisers or those who wish to stock and sell copies of the Jewish Travel Guide may use any of the above means to contact us for details of advertising rates and trade terms.

Foreword

For the person who wants to tap into Jewish heritage and Jewish culture there has never been a better time to travel the world. The people responsible for promoting destinations across Europe, the United States, South Africa, Asia, the Caribbean and even South America have realised that one of the most effective ways of marketing some of their more obscure cities and regions is to focus on their relevance to a particular ethnic group. And since Jews have been settling in different bits of the world since the dispersion, there are very few places which don't have something of interest to the Jewish traveller who wants to catch up on his past. Sometimes that past is, literally, buried – perhaps a historic Jewish cemetery, or the remains of a synagogue or a mikveh concealed beneath another more contemporary landmark; sometimes it is a synagogue which is long disused, or converted to some other use; sometimes the site of Jewish interest is nothing more than a street name or a single house, but nevertheless a testament to the indestructibility of some tiny segment of Jewry in some far-flung corner in the world. But whatever it is, it is very likely that some savvy marketing person has actually packaged a Jewish heritage tour in some way or another, by publishing some easy-to-follow itinerary, or by encouraging local tour companies to jump on the kosher bandwagon with accommodation and travel, or in some other way smoothing the path – literally – of the Jewish heritage traveller.

During the eight years in which I have been editing the travel section of the *Jewish Chronicle*, we have carried endless travel items which have featured Jewish heritage tours or packages. The Italians were among the first of the national tourist boards to spot the advantage of gathering information on their Jewish sites of interest, with a pocket-sized book called "Jewish Itineraries in Tuscany". This slim tome comprehensively covers the Jewish sites, remains and history of cities like Florence, Pisa, Siena and Livorno, as well as pretty little hilltop towns like Pitigliano which nestle in this delightful region. More recently, an Italian travel firm called ItalyItaly Enterprises has begun offering Jewish heritage tours, including guided tours with or without accommodation, capitalising on the Jewish interest in those enchanting Chiantishire towns. In Spain the tourist authorities of the western Spanish region of Caceres have put their Jewish heritage information into a modest little pamphlet which is nevertheless useful for anyone who wants to truffle out the sites of former synagogues, mikvehs and cemeteries in an area whose Jewish history is frequently overshadowed by that of the more famous towns of Gerona, Toledo and Grenada. The incredibly rich Jewish heritage of Alsace and its principal town of Strasbourg in eastern France has also been 'packaged' by the local tourist authorities so that anyone visiting can easily home in on the cities and sites which will yield the richest Jewish harvest, including synagogues, mikvaot, cemeteries, art, architecture and artefacts. All of which can be enjoyed along with the natural charm of this pretty region threaded with rivers and dotted with towns of elaborately decorated wooden houses.

The Turkish tourist authorities have also noted the value of Jewish heritage tourism, and arrange trips around the country's wild Eastern region to see the supposed birthplace of Abraham in Harran, the cradle of Judaism and Islam, through a tour and website called "Jewish Footprint". Down in South America, a guide to the Argentinian Jewish community's history and heritage can be found in a 300-page book called 'Shalom Buenos Aires', while Jewish organisations in the country can arrange special tours in the Mendoza region and in Buenos Aires itself.

Of course, no region of Europe has more in the way of Jewish interest than the group of Eastern bloc countries once coralled behind the Iron Curtain and virtually unknown to tourists. Poland – inevitably, mainly known for its death camps and ghettoes – is trying, through its heritage tourism packages, to emphasise the positive which exists in its history alongside the horror, highlighting through its Jewish sites in Warsaw, Lodz and Cracow, the almost 1,000 years when Poland was home to the greatest flowering of Ashkenazi culture, education and theology in Jewish history. Despite this, a city 'panorama' tour of Warsaw makes no attempt to gloss over Poland's complicity in genocide, pointing out the site of the infamous ghetto, of the Great Synagogue razed to the ground by the Nazis, and the Umschlagplatz, the gathering point from which Jews were put on trains for the death camps.

In many states of the former Soviet Union, synagogues and other sites of Jewish interest had fallen into disrepair or crumbled into utter oblivion. It is mainly only since the fall of the old Soviet empire that Jewish communities have begun to reclaim their buildings, and in some cases to restore them. The reality means that – in cities which, before the Second World War, held large Jewish populations – the tiny Jewish communities that arose from the ashes of the Nazi Holocaust, are painstakingly recreating their history in towns and streets from which Jews had all but vanished. As a new generation of Jews begins to consider its past – and the painful past of its parents and grandparents – it seems likely that heritage tourism to Eastern Europe will grow, eventually perhaps matching that to Central European cities like Prague and Budapest.

To a great degree, the growth in up-scale, i.e. expensive, Jewish heritage packages is a reflection of the higher visibility and greater affluence of the strictly Orthodox community across the world, primarily in the USA and Australia, but also in the UK, Continental Europe and Israel. The power of the "Orthodox Pound" means that strictly Observant Jews can now pick a spot almost anywhere on the face of the earth, and find that one of a small number of specialist operators is organising a kosher trip there. There is no longer any barrier to visiting China or India or Vietnam or Singapore if one of those mainly United States-based specialists has been there ahead of you, organising strictly kosher or strictly vegetarian cuisine, arranging Shabbat days off from touring, and – where relevant – introducing Jewish heritage sites into the itinerary. The scope of Jewish leisure travel – the lounging-beside-a-pool variety of holiday, as opposed to the more demanding museums-and-mausoleums type of travel – has also expanded due to the metamorphosis of the Jewish market.

From the 1930s to the 1960s, American Jews enjoyed long weekends and summer holidays at the kosher hotels in the Catskills or Miami, while British Jews headed off to the sprawling kosher seaside hotels of Bournemouth, Southport or St Anne's, and French and Belgian Jews took off for their own equivalent resorts. Growing prosperity in the late 1960s and 1970s encouraged people to travel further, but the range of kosher venues was always limited by the relatively small scale of the potential Orthodox market – the Italian resorts of Viareggio and Rimini had kosher dining rooms within their grand portals, while Switzerland had a trio of kosher hotels in Arosa, Lugano and Grindlewald. The assimilation and – paradoxically – the affluence, of the Jewish communities, together with the exponential growth in Israel's tourism industry spelled the death knell for those traditional European – and Catskill – kosher hotels. Middle class Jews, like other members of the growing middle classes, sought greater luxury and far greater variety. Destinations of choice for Jewish holidaymakers ranged across southern Europe, extending in the 1980s and 1990s to the USA and Canada, while Passover and school summer holidays were often spent in Israel at one of the growing numbers of increasingly luxurious hotels which dotted Israel's Mediterranean coast. Today the destinations are even more distant and exotic: Australia, New Zealand, the Pacific islands, the Far East, India and South America. Now, however, thanks to the growing Orthodox constituency, and a secular Orthodox Jewish renaissance – younger Jews who wear knitted kippot and opt for kosher-only venues – there are a large and increasing number of top-class resort properties throughout the USA and Europe which become kosher for specified periods – usually at festival times, like Passover and Succot – where like-minded Jews can relax and imbibe the atmosphere and kosher food and wine.

The pattern of travel to Israel has changed too. While the Anglo-Jewish community once took their Israel holidays almost exclusively in Tel Aviv, Netanya, Herzliya and Jerusalem, these days a very large proportion have switched their annual Israel vacation to Eilat, the country's Red sea paradise which boasts a magnificent range of hotels, from the Marrakesh-meets-Las

Vegas glitz of Herods and the glittering elegance of the Royal Beach, to the clean, cosy and functional Holiday Inn Express, and just about every level of accommodation in between. Israel's only truly purpose-built resort, fringing a horseshoe-shaped bay of clean, warm tropical waters flowing above a coral reef, Eilat has become a fixture on the North European Jewish holiday calendar for a spell of sunshine between October and April. In normal times, Israel's central resorts – Tel Aviv, Jerusalem, etc. – have competed vigorously against Eilat to maintain their share of the "ethnic" (i.e. Jewish) market, but during the period following the start of the 2000 Intifada, Eilat's distance from the nightly battles flickering across TV screens around the world has been a major factor in keeping Eilat travel in the ascendancy. Now, despite the lavish luxury and diversity of the hotels in the centre of the country – from five-star deluxe to cosy and charming B&Bs – and its myriad beautiful holy and historical sites – from the charm of tiny Galilee towns, with their recreated pioneer houses and hilltop restaurants, to the cobbled streets of Jerusalem crammed with five millennia of history and enough holy sites, museums, shops, galleries, gardens, parks and spectacular cityscapes to keep a visitor happy and busy for a month – Israel is facing a tough time keeping its tourism industry afloat. The Jewish communities around the world seem its best hope for survival as pilgrims and general tourists desert it in favour (in the wake of the September 11 terror atrocities in New York and Washington) of, literally, staying home or travelling only within their own national borders.

For those who do venture forth – and, inevitably, patterns of travel will ultimately return to something approaching the pre-September 11 status quo – there is also a whole gamut of new (or sometimes expanded and refurbished) Jewish museums across the world. These have been created, or extended and renovated, partly in a bid to capture Jewish tourism in a competitive market and partly with the more altruistic aim of commemorating some aspect of Jewish life, or marking a Jewish past or the Jewish contribution to the host city or country. The very newest and in many ways most significant, is the Jewish Museum in Berlin. Located in the Lindenstrasse, next to the old Prussian courthouse, the cold, modern structure by Polish-born American architecture Daniel Liebeskind was formally inaugurated in 2001, following an interregnum between the completion of the building in 1999 – during which time it was open to visitors – and its closure for 18 months for the exhibits to be put in place. This museum, described in the *Jewish Chronicle* by travel writer Jo Foley as "a building of such intense, impressive beauty that it stops the breath as it engages the brain", it is dedicated not just to the Holocaust, but to the whole history of Jews in Germany, and Berlin in particular. Possibly the only other Jewish museum to have had such a major impact in terms of both its architecture and its content in the past 20 years, is Washington's National Holocaust Museum, with its searing images and astonishing displays. For those in search of Jewish history in the United States, two new-ish museums in New York fulfil two purposes: the Tenement House on the Upper West Side – opened as a museum less than four years ago – recreates the experience of the early Jewish migrants to this great melting pot of a city, while the Museum of Jewish Heritage, which opened just over four years ago and used to sit in the shadow of the Twin Towers, details Jewish survival from the catastrophe of the Holocaust, and the Jewish immigrant community's contribution to the city.

Cape Town, the jewel in South Africa's crown, also has a brace of new Jewish museums. Both are located within the precincts of the city's Great Synagogue, one commemorating the Holocaust, and sensitively linking the experience of the Jews in Germany to the Blacks in Apartheid South Africa, the other recalling the history of South Africa's Jewish community.

Other European cities harbour great Jewish museums: Paris's Jewish Art and History Museum in the Marais, Vienna's Jewish Museum in Dorotheegasse, with its constant flow of high quality special exhibitions; and, of course, London's own much expanded and award-winning Jewish Museum, located on two sites – one at the Sternberg Centre in Finchley and the other striking Camden site, where the Jewish contribution to British life is reflected in a host of vibrant and imaginatively curated exhibitions.

In addition to Jewish heritage travel, kosher cruising has grown hugely in popularity – some of it with a Jewish cultural adjunct, some of it just an excuse to lap up the sun in infinite luxury (and with kosher cuisine) for a week or two. Jonah excepted, Jews have always enjoyed ships. The basic benefits of cruising – of being able to visit a whole range of cities and islands aboard a floating five-star hotel without having to pack and unpack more than once – has always appealed to the sybaritic traveller with an eye on simplicity and luxury. These advantages have, of course, always been supplemented by lavish on-board cuisine and, without meaning to sound like an inferior Jackie Mason, food is a not unimportant consideration for many Jews. The question of whether lots of Jews enjoyed cruising and therefore cruise lines introduced kosher food (or kosher-friendly menus), synagogues and sea-going Shabbat services, or whether the creation of these amenities attracted more Jews to cruising, is as perennial and unproductive as the-chicken-and-the-egg question. But it remains true that cruising is an increasingly popular Jewish activity, interestingly among a younger age group – the forty-something semi-empty-nesters rather than the traditional post-retirement couples. Apart from those amenities like kosher food (and strictly fish and vegetarian menus suitable for the Observant Jew), synagogues and Shabbat services, there are more specific semitic attractions. These include the

Kosher Cruise Collection from British-founded Orient Lines, which normally features more than a half-dozen itineraries with kosher cuisine, daily minyan, lectures on Jewish topics, and frequently places of specific Jewish interest at ports of call. Another highlight of the kosher cruise calendar is the annual "Festival of Jewish Music at Sea", which normally takes place in January, run by Celebrity Cruises, featuring a Jewish scholar-in-residence (last year Britain's Chief Rabbi Dr Jonathan Sacks), lectures, shiurim, daily services and concerts ranging from Cantorial and chasidic music to opera and klezmer. Which means that for Jews, even in our muted post-September 11 mood, the world is still our oyster … or more appropriately our fishball.

JAN SHURE
Travel Editor of the Jewish Chronicle
October 2001

Introduction

Another December; another *Jewish Travel Guide*. However, as in previous years, this is in no way merely a repeat of what was in an earlier edition with just a new cover. This year there have been again many changes. There are almost five hundred new establishments; whilst about the same number have been removed, either because they have closed, ceased to be kosher, or have not replied to our enquiries over the past few years and we have felt it appropriate to remove them rather than possibly inconvenience travellers. In addition, a substantial number of entries have, where appropriate, been updated.

At one time kosher restaurants just didn't change; somehow they seemed eternal. Restaurants like Blooms in the East End of London or Ratners in the Lower East Side of New York seemed to have always been in existence. Now life is different. Kosher restaurants open and close on a regular basis, just like any other business. It is the role of the Publisher of this Guide to meet this challenge, and to ensure that the information in it is as up to date and as accurate as is possible.

The year 2002 will be particularly important to all travellers to and within Europe. On 1 January 2002 a new currency will exist for twelve countries of the European Union. Details of this and how it will affect travellers are set out on page xii. We have also included, on page 380, details of International Access Dialling Codes which you will need when phoning home.

As in previous years the Editor wishes to draw your attention to the following:

It is the interest of all travellers, if they are uncertain, to consider checking in advance on the existence and the current kashrut status of an establishment before arranging a visit, particularly if any distance is involved. No responsibility can be accepted for any errors or omissions, or for any kashrut or other claims made by an establishment listed in this Guide.

The entries in this Guide have been kept as up to date as has been possible but the information is, of course, always liable to change. For this reason travellers are invited to get in touch with the Publisher after they make a trip in order to ensure they we aware of any significant changes to the entries in the Guide. All such notifications may be made in writing by post or email (jtg@vmbooks.com) or direct to our website (www.vmbooks.com).

Finally, I would like to once again thank Kim Knight without whose help and hard work this project would not have been completed on time.

MICHAEL ZAIDNER
December 2001

What the Euro (€) Means

Although the Euro was launched on 1 January 1999, it has for three years been of little significance to most of the world. No such thing as a Euro note or a fifty cent piece (there are 100 cents in a Euro) has yet been seen by the ordinary public. This is now all changing. With effect from 1 January 2002, the Euro and the cents will exist as physical notes and coins.

The twelve members of the European Monetary Union are:

Austria	Germany	Luxembourg
Belgium	Greece	The Netherlands
Finland	Ireland	Portugal
France	Italy	Spain

They all now have the same currency. There will be no need to change notes as one crosses borders and there will be no need to take multiple currencies if one is planning to travel throughout Europe.

There is a short transitional period, varying from country to country, during which both the existing national currencies and the Euro will circulate. During this period one can still spend existing money but one will receive all change in Euros.

Generally speaking, by 1 March 2002 all existing currencies will cease to be legal tender and will be withdrawn from circulation and only the Euro will be in use. 'Old' currency will, however, continue to be changeable at banks for a period of years, again varying from country to country.

As Euro bank notes will not be issued before 1 January 2002, and therefore will not yet have been handled or even seen, there are fears that counterfeit notes will be in circulation and one should be particularly careful in only accepting larger notes (the largest note, €500, will be equivalent to around £300 or $450) from banks or established retail stores and shops.

Travellers from outside Europe should be aware that there will be no change in the currencies of Denmark, Norway, Switzerland, Sweden or the United Kingdom. They are all unaffected by the change.

Generally speaking, most, but not all, of the overseas territories of those countries taking part in the Euro project are participating. As an example, while Reunion and Guadeloupe (both French) are affected, Aruba and the Dutch Antilles (both Dutch) are not. Advice should be taken from your travel agent or bank before going to one of these overseas territories.

Further information can be found on www.europa.eu.int/euro

Albania

There have been Jews living in the territory now known as Albania since Roman times and there are remains in Dardania (in the north of the country) of an ancient synagogue. The community was re-established by Jews from Iberia escaping the Spanish Inquisition in the fifteenth and early sixteenth centuries.

The number of Jews in Albania never increased significantly, and, in 1930, there were only 204 Jews in the country. However, this number was soon augmented by refugees escaping the Nazis. The local population was not, on the whole, hostile to the Jews and helped most of them to hide during the War when Italy, and then Germany, occupied the country.

The strict communist regime which followed the War led to the isolation of the Jewish community until the fall of communism. In 1991, almost the entire community (about 300) was airlifted to Israel. The few Jews who remained in Albania live in the capital, Tirana.

The Albanian–Israel Friendship Society will be happy to provide any further information.

GMT + 1 hour — Total Population 3,420,000
Country calling code (355) — Jewish Population Under 100
Emergency Telephone (Police - 24445) (Fire - 23333) (Ambulance - 22235)
Electricity Voltage 220

Tirana

Contact Information

Albanian–Israel Friendship Society
Rruga "Barrikatave" 226 (42) 22611

Algeria

Jews first settled in Algeria soon after the start of the Diaspora following the destruction of the Second Temple. A later influx occurred when Jews were escaping from Visigothic Spain.

In the twelfth and thirteenth centuries, Islamic conversion was forced on the Jews. Many Jews, however, crossed the Mediterranean from Spain during the time of the Inquisition, and these included some famous scholars. In 1830 the French occupied the country and, in due course, granted the Jews French citizenship.

Algerian Jews suffered anti-Semitism from both the local Muslim population and the wartime Vichy government. After the Allied landings in 1942, the anti-Jewish laws were slowly lifted. In the late 1950s, 130,000 Jews lived in Algeria, but after the civil war, which led to independence from France in 1962, most of the community moved to France, and some to Israel, leaving very few behind. The present-day community, centred in Algiers, has a synagogue but no resident rabbi.

GMT + 1 hour — Total Population 28,566,000
Country calling code (213) — Jewish Population Under 100
Emergency Telephone Electricity voltage 127/220

Algiers

Representative Organisations

Association Consistoriale Israélite d'Alger
6 rue Hassena Ahmed (2) 62-85-72

Synagogues

6 rue Hassena Ahmed (2) 62-85-72

Blida

Representative Organisations

Consistoire d'Algerie
29 rue des Martyrs (3) 49-26-57

Andora

Andorra

Andorra, which is governed by two co-princes: the Bishop of Urgel in Spain and the President of France, does not have a Jewish history.

There are currently however around fifteen Jewish families.

A synagogue was established in 1997 in Escaldes and is the first in Andorra's 1,100-year history. While its liturgy leans towards Sephardism it is also influenced by its Ashkenazi members.

There is a community centre in Escaldes.

GMT + 1 hour — Total Population 64,000
Country calling code (376) — Jewish Population Under 100
Emergency Telephone (Police - 825 225) (Fire and Ambulance - 118)

Contact Information

Dr David ben-Chayil or Dr David Bezold
Francesco B.P. 244, Andorra la Vella 333 567
Email: bezold@andorra.ad

For visits to the synagogue contact Isaac Benisty
Telephone 860 758

Argentina

The first Jewish arrivals (*Conversos*, or "secret Jews") came in the sixteenth and seventeenth centuries from Portugal and Spain. They assimilated quickly. A more significant Jewish immigration occurred in the middle of the nineteenth century, from Western Europe, and at the end of the nineteenth century many Jews arrived from Eastern Europe, taking advantage of the "open-door" policy towards immigrants. The new arrivals set up some Jewish agricultural settlements, under the auspices of the Alliance Israelita Universelle, and on the whole mixed with the local population.

The largest Jewish community is in Buenos Aires, with smaller communities in provincial centres. There are also some Jewish families remaining in the Jewish agricultural colonies, with Moiseville, Rivera and General Roca being the three most important.

There are Jewish newspapers, restaurants and other institutions. The Delegation of Argentine Jewish Associations (DAIA) represents all Jewish organisations at a political level.

GMT - 3 hours — Total Population 37,032,000
Country calling code (54) — Jewish Population 230,000
Emergency Telephone (Police - 101) (Fire - 100) (Ambulance - 107)
Electricity voltage 226

Bahia Blanca

Contact Information

Beit Jabad
Chiclana 763 8000 (291) 453-6582
Fax: (291) 456-5596

For details of Mikvah please phone.

Buenos Aires

The first recorded Jewish event in Buenos Aires was a wedding in 1860. Around 220,000 Jews live in Buenos Aires. There are fifty or so synagogues in the city and kosher food is widely available. The most interesting synagogues for visitors are in Once, although fewer Jews live there now.

Bakeries

Confitería Aielet
Aranguren 2911, Flores (11) 637-5419

Confitería Ganz
Paso 752, Once (11) 961-6918

Confitería Helueni
Tucumán 2620, Once (11) 961-0541

Confitería Mari Jalabe
Bogota 3228, Flores (11) 612-6991

Panadería Malena
Av. Pueyrredón 880, Once (11) 962-6290

Booksellers

Kehot Lubavitch Sudamericana
San Luis 3281 1186 (11) 865-0625
Fax: (11) 865-0625
Email: kehot@iname.com
Web site: www.kehot-lubavitch.com.ar

Librería Editorial Sigal
Av. Corrientes 2854 1193
(11) 861-9501; 865-7208; 962-1131
Fax: (11) 962-7931; 865-7208
Email: lib-sigal@cybergal.com
Web site: www. libreria-sigal.com

Contact Information

Asociacion Shuva Israel
Paso 557, Once (11) 962-6255

Beit Jabad Belgrano
O'Higgins 2358, Belgrano 1428 (11) 781-3848

Beit Jabad Villa Crespo
Serrano 69 (11) 855-9822

Chabad Lubavich Argentina
Agüero 1164, Flores 1425 (11) 963-1221

Congregacion Israelita de la Republica Argentina
Libertad 785, Centro
(11) 4372-2474/4371-8929/4374-7955/4372-0014
Fax: (11) 4372-2474

The total number of synagogues in Buenos Aires where there is a minyan at least Friday night and Shabbat morning exceeds fifty. Call any of the above numbers to locate the synagogue nearest you.

Embassy

Embassy of Israel
Avenida de Mayo 701-10° 1084
(11) 4345-6207/08
Fax: (11) 4345-6207
Email: cidipal@israel-embassy.org.ar

Groceries

Almacén Behar
Campana 347, Flores (11) 613-2033

Almacén Shalom
San Luis 2513, Once (11) 962-3685

Autoservicio Ezra
Ecuador 619, Once (11) 963-7062

Autoservicio Siman Tov
Helguera 474, Flores (11) 611-4746

Azulay,
Helguera 507, Flores

Battías,
Paso 706, Once

Kahal Jaredim
Argerich 386, Flores (11) 612-4590

Kaler,
San Luis 2810, Once

Kol Bo I,
Ecuador 855, Once (11) 961-3838

Kol Bo II,
Viamonte 2537, Once (11) 961-2012

Kol Bo Brandsen
Brandsen 1389, Barracas

Kosher Delights
La Pampa 2547, Belgrano (11) 788-3150

Kahal Jaredim
Argerich 386, Flores (11) 612-4590

La Esquina Casher
Aranguren 2999, Flores (11) 637-3706

La Tzorja,
Ecuador 673, Once (11) 961-1096

La Quesería,
Viamonte 2438, Once (11) 961-3171

Yehuda Kosher Foods
Moldes 2452, Belgrano (11) 637-1465

Kashrut Information

The Central Rabbinate of the Vaad Hakehillot
Ecuador 1110, Once (11) 961-2944
The Orthodox Ashkenazi Chief Rabbi of Argentina is Rabbi Shlomo Benhamu Anidjar.

Libraries

YIVO Library,
Pasteur 633, Third floor (11) 45-2474

Sociedad Hebraica Argentino
Sarmiento 2233 (11) 952-5570
Also has an art gallery.

Media

Newspapers

Comunidades
Die Presse
Kesher Kehilari
La Voz Judia
Mundo Israelita
Nueva Sion

Mikvaot

Helguera 270, Once (11) 612-0410
Moldes 2431, Belgrano (11) 4786-8046
Email: ajdut@netcomputer.com.ar

Museums

Museo Judio de Buenos Aires
Libertad 769 (11) 372-2474
Fax: (11) 372-2474
Email: adaszko@mail.retina.ar.
Hours: Tuesday and Thursday 4pm to 7pm.

Representative Organisations

DAIA (Political representative body of Argentine Jewry)
Pasteur 633, 7th Floor (11) 4952-8831; 4953-1781

Argentina

AMIA (Central Ashkenazi community)
Pasteur 633 (11) 953-9777; 953-2862
The community centre has now been reopened following the terror bomb attack in 1994.

Asociacion Israelita Sefaradi Argentina (AISA)
Paso 493 (11) 952-4707

Restaurants

Confiterie Helueni
Tucuman 2620, Once (11) 961-0541

Mama Jacinta
Tucuman 2580 C-P 4052 (11) 4962-9149
Fax: (11) 4962-7535
Supervision: Gran Rasino Josef Chehebar. Hours: 12.30-15.30 & 20.30-00.30..

Sucath David,
Tucuman 2349 (11) 4953-9656
Fax: (11) 4952-8878
Email: sucathdavid@sinectis.com.ar

Dairy

Soultani Café
San Luis 2601, Once (11) 961-3913

Meat

Al Galope,
Tucumán 2633, Once (11) 963-6888

Mama Jacinta,
Tucuman 2580 (11) 4962-9149

McDonald's,
Shopping Abasto, (Corrientes and Anchorena), Once
Supervision: Rav Oppenheimer - Ajdut Israel.
There are two McDonalds. Only one is kosher.

Synagogues

Ashkenazi Orthodox

Baron Hirsh,
Billinghurst 664 (11) 862-2624

Bet Rajel,
Ecuador 522 (11) 862-2701

Brit Abraham,
Antezana 145 (11) 855-6567

Etz Jaim,
Julian Alvarez 745 (11) 772-5324

Sinagoga Israelita Lituana
Jose Evaristo Uriburu 348 (11) 952-7968

Torah Vaaboda
Julian Alvarez 667 (11) 854-0462

Zijron le David
Azcuenaga 736 (11) 953-0200

Conservative

Beit Hilel,
Araoz 2854, Palermo (11) 804-2286

Colegio Wolfson, Comunidad Or-El
Amenabar 2972 (11) 544-5461

Comunidad Bet El
Sucre 3338 (11) 552-2365

Dor Jadash,
Murillo 649, Villa Crespo (11) 854-4467

Nueva Comunidad Israelita
Arcos 2319 (11) 781-0281

Or Jadash, Varela 850, Flores (11) 612-1171

German Orthodox

Ajdut Yisroel
Moldes 2449 (11) 4783-2831
Fax: (11) 4781-6725
Email: ajdut@netcomputer.com.ar

Progressive

Benei Tikva,
Vidal 2049 (11) 795-0380

Reform

Templo Emanu-El
Tronador 1455 (11) 552-4343
Fax: (11) 4555-4004
Email: kol_emanuel@name.com

Sephardi Orthodox

Aderet Eliahu
Ruy Diaz de Guzman 647 (11) 302-9306

Agudat Dodim,
Avellaneda 2874 (11) 611-0056

Bajurim Tiferet Israeil
Helguera 611 (11) 611-3376

Comunidad Sefaradi de Buenos Aires
Camargo 870 (11) 4855-9645
Fax: (11) 4855-9377
Email: acisba@continuidad.ar

Etz Jaim,
Carlos Calvo 1164 (11) 302-6290

Jaike Grimberg
Campana 460 (11) 672-2347

Kehal Jaredim
Helguera 270, Once (11) 612-0410

Od Yosef Jai,
Tucuman 3326 (11) 963-2349

Or Misraj,
Ciudad de la Paz 2555 (11) 784-5945

Shaare Sion,
Helguera 453 (11) 4637-5897
Fax: (11) 4637-1301
Email: editorial@shaaresion.org.ar
Web site: www.shaaresion.org.ar

Shaare Tefila
Paso 733 (11) 962-2865

Shalom,
Olleros 2876 (11) 552-2720

Shuba Israel,
Ecuador 627 (11) 862-0562
Sinagoga Rabino Zeev Gringberg
Canalejas 3047 (11) 611-3366
Sucath David,
Tucuman 2750 (11) 962-1091
Fax: (11) 962-1264
Email: perspect@satlink.com
Web site: www.judaicasite.com
Templo la Paz (Chalom)
Olleros 2876 (11) 552-6730
Yeshurun,
Republica de la India 3035 (11) 802-9310
Yesod Hadat,
Lavalle 2449 (11) 961-1615

Concordia

Contact Information

Beit Jabad Concordia
Entre Rios 212 3200 (45) 21-1934
Fax: (45) 21-7898

Cordoba

Contact Information

Jabad Lubavitch Cordoba
Sucre 1380, Barrio Cofico 5000 (351) 71-0223
Fax: (351) 411-9721
Email: jturk@elsitio.net

Groceries

Almacén, Sucre 1378, Barrio Cofico 5000
(351) 71-0223

Rosario

Contact Information

Beit Jabad Rosario
S. Lorenzo 1882 P.A. 2000 (341) 25-2899

Groceries

La Granja Kasher (341) 49-6210

Tucuman

Contact Information

Beit Jabad Tucuman
Lamadrid 752 4000 (381) 24-8892
Fax: (381) 248893
Email: jabadtucuman@amet.com.ar

Groceries

Almacén y Carnicería
9 de Julio 625 (381) 31-0227
Beit Jabad Tucuman
Lamadrid 752 4000 (381) 24-8892
Fax: (381) 248893
Email: jabadtucuman@amet.com.ar

Australia

The first Jews in Australia arrived with the first convict ships from the United Kingdom in 1788; and regular, organised worship started in the 1820s. The first free Jewish settler arrived with her husband, a deported convict, in 1816. The community grew in the nineteenth century, with the first synagogue being established in the mid-1840s. Events such as the gold rush and pogroms in Eastern Europe were catalysts for more Jewish immigration.

The Jewish contribution to Australian life has been prominent, with the commander of the ANZAC forces in the First World War being a practising Jew, Sir John Monash. The twentieth century saw some 7,000 Jewish refugees from Nazi Europe settling in Australia, and the community contains the largest percentage of Holocaust survivors in the world. They are a major influence on the present community, which is expanding and comparatively religious. There have also been two Jewish Governors-General.

The community is led by the Executive Council of Australian Jewry. Seventy-five per cent of primary and fifty-five per cent of secondary Jewish school children attend Jewish schools and there is a low level of inter-marriage. Melbourne has the largest community (42,000), with 35,000 in Sydney. There are Jewish newspapers, radio programmes of Jewish interest and museums on Jewish themes.

GMT + 7 to 10 hrs	Total Population 18,886,000
Country calling code (61)	Jewish Population 100,000
Emergency Telephone (Police, Fire and Ambulance - 000)	Electricity voltage 240/250

Australian Capital Territory

Canberra

Embassy

Embassy of Israel
6 Turrana Street, Yarralumla 2600 (262) 73-1309
Fax: (262) 73-4279
Email: israel.aust@embassy.net.au

Synagogues

The A.C.T. Jewish Community Synagogue
National Jewish Memorial Centre, cnr Canberra Ave & National Circuit, Forrest 2603 (262) 951-052
Fax: (262) 958-608
Web site: www.actjewish.org.au
Postal address: POB 3105, Manuka 2603

New South Wales

Newcastle

Synagogues

122 Tyrrell Street 2300 (49) 26-2820
Contact: Dr L.E. Fredman, 123 Dawson St, Cooks Hill, 2300 N.S.W.

Sydney

The first Jewish convict settlers were generally illiterate in both English and Hebrew, and there was no Jewish organisation until a Chevrah Kadishe was formed in 1817.

Most of Sydney's Jews are now settled outside the city in two suburban areas: the eastern suburbs, including Bondi, and the North Shore.

Bakeries

Carmel Cake Shop
14 O'Brien Street, Bondi
Supervision: NSW Kashrut Authority.

Booksellers

Gold's World of Judaica
9 O'Brien Street, Bondi 2026 (2) 9300-0495
Fax: (2) 9389-7345
Email: goldsyd@matra.com.au

Shalom Gift and Book Shop
323 Pacific Highway, Lindfield 2070 (2) 9416-7076
Fax: (2) 9416-7076

Butchers

Eilat, 173 Bondi Road, Bondi (2) 9387-8881
Supervision: NSW Kashrut Authority.

Hadassa, 17 O'Brien Street, Bondi (2) 9365-4904
Fax: (2) 9130-4760
Supervision: NSW Kashrut Authority.

Embassy

Consul General of Israel
37 York Street, Level 6 2000 (2) 9264-7933
Fax: (2) 9290-2259
Email: israsyd@acon.com.au

Hospital

Wolper Jewish Hospital
8 Trelawney Street, Woollahra (2) 9328-6077

Kashrut Information

Kosher Consumer Association
(2) 9337-6657
Fax: (2) 9371-0348

NSW Kashrut Authority
PO Box 7206, Bondi Beach 2026 (2) 9365-2933
Fax: (2) 9365-0933
Email: rabbig@ka.org.au
Web site: www.ka.org.au

Media

Newspapers

Australian Jewish News
146 Darlinghurst Road, Darlinghurst 2010
(2) 9360-5100
Fax: (2) 9332-4207
Email: valhadeff@jewishnews.net.au
Web site: www.ajn.net.au

Mikvaot

117 Glenayr Avenue, Bondi (2) 9130-2509

Museums

Sydney Jewish Museum
148 Darlinghurst Road, Darlinghurst 2010
(2) 9360-7999
Fax: (2) 9331-4245
Email: sydjmus@tmx.mhs.oz.au
Has won many awards for its work documenting Sydney's Jewish history and the Holocaust and has a kosher (dairy) restaurant.

Religious Organisations

Sydney Beth Din
166 Castlereagh Street, NSW 2000 (2) 9267-2477
Fax: (2) 9264-8871
Email: admin@greatsynagogue.org.au

Representative Organisations

Executive Council of Australian Jewry
146 Darlinghurst Road, Second floor,
Darlinghurst 2010 (2) 9360-5415
Fax: (2) 9360-5416
Email: ecaj@tig.com.au

Restaurants

Dairy

Red Tomato Café
50 Mitchell St, N Bondi 2026 (2) 9300-0707
Fax: (2) 9130-4477

Toovya the Milkman
379 Old South Head Road, North Bondi 2026
(2) 9130-4016
Supervision: NSW Kashrut Authority.
Not Cholov Yisrael. Vegetarian and vegan food. Eat in or take-away. Delivery to eastern suburbs, including to hotel room. Hours: Sunday to Thursday, 5 pm to 10 pm; Saturday, after Shabbat to midnight. Nearest metro: 387 bus from Bondi junction to the door.

Meat

Beaches Kosher Restaurant
11 O'Brien Street 2026 (2) 9365-5544
NSW Kashrut Authority

Café Maccabee
Corner Darlinghurst and Burton Street,
Darlinghurst (2) 9360-7999
Fax: (2) 9331-4245
Email: ceo@sjm.com.au

Lewis' Continental Kitchen
2 Curlewis Street, Bondi 2026 (2) 9365-5421
Fax: (2) 9300-0037
Email: lewis@acon.com.au
Web site: www.acon.com.au/lewis
Supervision: NSW Kashrut Authority Inc..
Glatt kosher.
Email: ceo@sjm.com.au

Savion Restaurant
38 Wairoa Ave (2) 9130-6357
Supervision: NSW Kashrut Authority.

The Pie Factory
Hall Street, Bondi Beach (2) 9130-6743
Fax: (2) 91306742
Supervision: NSW Kashrut Authority.
Also take-away.

Tibby's Kosher Restaurant at Jaffa
61-67 Hall Street, Bondi Beach 2026
(2) 9130-5051
Supervision: NSW Kashrut Authority.
Open Saturday to Thursday for dinner. Continental, Chinese, Sephardi and Israeli food. Glatt kosher.

Synagogues

Adath Yisroel
243 Old South Head Road, Bondi (2) 9300-9447

Australia / New South Wales

Bondi Mizrachi Synagogue
101/60 Blair Street, North Bondi 2026
(2) 9130-7221
Fax: (2) 9130-7221
Email: mizrachisydney@bigpond.com
Web site: mizrachi.org.au
Synagogue location is 339 Old South Head Road, Bondi 2026

Central Synagogue
15 Bon-Accord Avenue, Bondi Junction (2) 9389-5622

Coogee Synagogue
121 Brook Street, Coogee (2) 9315-8291

Cremorne & District
12a Yeo Street, Neutral Bay (2) 9908-1853
Fax: (2) 9908-1852

Great Synagogue
166 Castlereagh Street (2) 9267-2477
Fax: (2) 9264-8871
Email: admin@greatsynagogue.org.au
Web site: www.greatsynagogue.org.au
Houses the Rabbi L.A. Falk Memorial Library and the A.M. Rosenblum Jewish Museum. (Entrance for services: 187 Elizabeth Street.)

Kehillat Masada
9-15 Link Road, St Ives 2075 (2) 9988-4417
Fax: (2) 9449-3897
Email: kmasada@dingoblue.net.au

Illawarra Synagogue
502 Railway Parade, Allawah (2) 9587-5643
Email: georgefoster1@compuserve.com

Maroubra Synagogue (K.M.H.C.)
635 Anzac Parade, Maroubra 2035 (2) 9344-6095
Fax: (2) 9344-4298
Email: maroubrasyn@bigpond.com

North Shore Synagogue
15 Treatts Road, Lindfield (2) 9416-3710
Fax: (2) 9416-7659

Paramatta Synagogue
116 Victoria Road, Paramatta (2) 9683-5381

Sephardi Synagogue
40-42 Fletcher Street, Bondi Junction (2) 9389-3355
Fax: (2) 9369-2143

Shearit Yisrael
146 Darlinghurst Road, Darlinghurst 2010
(2) 9365-8770

South Head & District Synagogue
666 Old South Head Road, Rose Bay 2029
(2) 9371-7300
Fax: (2) 9371-7416
Email: admin@southhead.org
Web site: www.southhead.org

Strathfield & District Synagogue
19 Florence Street, Strathfield 2135 (2) 9642-3550
Fax: (2) 9642-4803

Western Suburbs Synagogue
20 Georgina Street, Newtown

Yeshiva,
36 Flood Street, Bondi (2) 9387-3822
Fax: (2) 9389-7652

Conservative

Temple Emanuel
7 Ocean Street, Woollahra 2025 (2) 9328-7833
Fax: (2) 9327-8715
Email: info@emanuel.org.au
Web site: www.emanuel.org.au
"Look forward to welcoming visitors from abroad."

Liberal

North Shore Temple Emanuel
28 Chatswood Avenue, Chatswood 2067
(2) 9419-7011
Fax: (2) 9413-1474
Email: nste@nste.org.au

Sefardim

Beth Yosef, Ground Floor, 243 Old South Head Road, Bondi

Tour information

(2) 9328-7604
For information about tours of Jewish Sydney, contact the Great Synagogue at the number listed above or Karl Maehrischel at this number.

Queensland

Brisbane

Community Organisations

Jewish Communal Centre
2 Moxom Road, Burbank 4156 (7) 3349-9749

Groceries

Tarlington Trading
(7) 3216-7505
Fax: (7) 3274-0058
Email: tarling@ribbonet.com.au

Mikvaot

Queensland Mikvah
46 Bunya Street, Greenslopes 4120 (7) 3848-5886

Religious Organisations

Chabad House of Queensland
43 Cedar Street, Greenslopes 4120 (7) 3848-5886
Fax: (7) 3848-5886
Email: kthomas@onenet.au

Synagogues

Brisbane Hebrew Congregation
98 Margaret Street 4000 (7) 3229-3412

Givat Zion
43 Bunya Street, Greenslopes 4000 (7) 3397-9025
Fax: (7) 3397-9025

South Brisbane Hebrew Congregation
46 Burya Street, Greenslopes 4120 (7) 3397-9025
Fax: (7) 3397-9025
Email: slatwall@ozemail.com.au

Progressive

Beit Knesset Shalom
13 Koolatah Street, Camp Hill 4152 (7) 3398-8843
Email: bks@hotmail.com

Gold Coast

Bakeries

Goldstein's Bakery
509 Olsen Avenue, Ashmore City 4214
(7) 5539-3133
Fax: (7) 5597-1064

Supervision: Rabbi Gurevitch, Gold Coast Hebrew Congregation.

Under the umbrella of the NSW Kashrut Authority. Challah and kosher breads available at fourteen stores along the Gold Coast, including Surfers Paradise shop. (Tel) 5531-5808.

Community Organisations

Association of Jewish Organisations
31 Ranock Avenue, Benown Waters 4217
(7) 5597-2222

Synagogues

Gold Coast Hebrew Congregation
34 Hamilton Avenue, Surfers Paradise 4215
(7) 5570-1851

Temple Shalom
25 Via Roma Drive, Isle of Capri 4217
(7) 5570-1716

South Australia

Adelaide

Bakeries

Bakers Delight
Frewville Shopping Centre, Glen Osmond Road

Groceries

Kosher Imports
c/o Hebrew Congregation,
13 Flemington Street, Glenside 5065 (8) 8338-2922
Fax: (8) 8379-0142
Email: jewish@ozemail.com.au
Web site: www.adelaidejewish.com

Kosher and Judaica products available.

Synagogues

Orthodox

Adelaide Hebrew Congregation
13 Flemington Street, Glenside 5065 (8) 8338-2922
Fax: (8) 8379-0142
Email: jewish@ozemail.com.au
Web site: www.adelaidejewish.com

Mikva on premises. Mailing address: PO Box 320, Glenside 5065.

Progressive

Beit Shalom
41 Hackney Road, Hackney 5000 (8) 8362-8281
Fax: (8) 8362-4406
Email: bshalom@senet.com.au
Web site: www.user.senet.com.au/~bshalom

Mailing address: PO Box 47, Stepney 5069.

Tasmania

Established as a penal colony in 1803. Jewish names first appeared in 1819, one being Ikey Solomons a famous Jewish convict who was said to be the model for Dickens' Fagin in *Oliver Twist*.

The community remained small. The Launceston Synagogue was closed in 1871 and not reopened until 1939.

Hobart

Contact Information

Jewish Centre
Chabad House, 93 Lord Street, Sandy Bay 7005
(3) 6223-7116
Fax: (3) 6223-7116

Contact in advance for Shabbat meals and mikva.

Synagogues

Progressive

Hobart Hebrew Congregation
PO Box 128B, Hobart 7000 (3) 6234-4720
Email: heards@bigpond.com

The oldest synagogue in Australia, having been consecrated in July 1845. Open 9.30 am and one Friday per month 6.15 pm. Other days by arrangement.

Launceston

Contact Information

Chabad House of Tasmania
5 Brisbane Street, Launceston 7250
(3) 6334-0705

For all enquiries please call or fax the Hon. Manager Mr Gershon Goldsteen at (3) 6344 9960 or email him at: hydronav@tassie.net.au

Australia / Tasmania

Synagogues

PO Box 66, St John Street 7250
(3) 6343-1143

The synagogue in St John Street is the second oldest in Australia, founded in 1846. It is shared by Reform and Orthodox congregation and still has the original "convict benches".

Victoria

Ballarat

Synagogues

211 Drumond Street North 3350 (353) 32-6330

Melbourne

With 42,000 Jews, Melbourne has the largest Jewish community in the country, and the largest Jewish school in the world (the Mount Scopus).

Bakeries

Big K Kosher Bakery
316 Carlisle Street,, Balaclava 3183 (3) 9527-4582
Supervision: Rabbi A.Z. Beck, Adass Israel.

Glicks Cakes and Bagels
330a Carlisle Street, Balaclava 3183 (3) 9527-2198
Supervision: Melbourne Kashrut.

Greenfield Cakes
7 Willow Street, Elsternwick (3) 9528-4261
Supervision: Rabbi A.Z. Beck, Adass Israel.
At same location is King David Kosher Meals on Wheels (Refuah), hospital meals, airline and TV dinners.

Haymishe Bakery
320 Carlisle Street, Shop 4 3183 (3) 9527-7116
Supervision: Rabbi A.Z. Beck, Adass Israel.

Kosher Delight Bakery
75 Glen Eira Road, Ripponlea (3) 9532-9994
Supervision: Rabbi A.Z. Beck, Adass Israel.

Lowy's Cakes & Catering
59 Gordon Street, Elsternwick (3) 9530-0246
Supervision: Rabbi A.Z. Beck, Adass Israel.

Meal-Mart
251 Inkerman Street, St Kilda 3182 (3) 9525-5077
Fax: (3) 9525-4230
Supervision: Rabbi A.Z. Beck, Adass Israel.
Pies, salads, pre-cooked and frozen foods.

Booksellers

Golds Book & Gift Company
3 - 13 William Street, Balaclava 3183 (3) 9527-8775
Fax: (3) 9527-6434
Email: info@golds.com.au
Web site: www.golds.com.au

Butchers

Continental Kosher Butchers
155 Glenferrie Road, Malvern 3144 (3) 9509-9822
Fax: (3) 9509-9099
Email: ckb@bigpond.net.au
Supervision: Rabbi J.S. Cohen and Rabbi M. Gutnick, Melbourne Kashrut.

Melbourne Kosher Butchers
251 Inkerman Street, East St Kilda 3182
(3) 9525-5077
Fax: (3) 9525-4230
Supervision: Rabbi A.Z. Beck, Adass Israel.
Sell other kosher products as well. Hours: Monday, 10 am to 5.30 pm; Tuesday to Thursday, 7 am to 5.30 pm; Friday, 7 am to 3 pm. Winter 2 pm.

Solomon Kosher Butchers
140-144 Glen Eira Road, Elsternwick 3185
(3) 9532-8855
Fax: (3) 9532-8896
Supervision: Rabbi Y.D. Groner, Agudas Chabad Kashrut Committee.
Hours: Monday to Thursday, 7 am to 5.30 pm; Friday, 7 am to 3 pm.

Yumi's Kosher Seafoods
29 Glen Eira Road, Ripponlea 3183 (3) 9523-6444
Fax: (3) 9532-8189
Email: yumis@bigpond.com
Supervision: Rabbi A.Z. Beck, Adass Israel.
Suppliers of kosher fresh fish.

Chocolate Shops

Kosher

Alpha Kosher Chocolates
17 William Street, Balaclava (3) 9527-2453
Australia's only kosher chocolate factory. Handmade chocolates of export quality. Visitors welcome. Open Sunday mornings.

Contact Information

Mizrachi Hospitality Committee
81 Balaclava Road, Caulfield 3161 (3) 9525-9833
Fax: (3) 9527-5665
Email: mizrachi@iprimus.com.au
Mailing address: PO Box 2247. Caulfield Junction. VIC 3161.

Delicatessens

E.S. Delicatessen
74 Kooyong Road, Caulfield 3161 (3) 9576-0804
Supervision: Melbourne Kashrut.

Eshel Take-Away Foods & Catering
59 Glen Eira Road, Ripponlea 3161 (3) 9532-8309
Fax: (3) 9532-8089
Supervision: Rabbi A.Z. Beck, Adass Israel.

Groceries

Benedikt Imports
40 Pakington Street, St Kilda 3182 (3) 9534-8192
Importers of kosher foods and wines.

Dainty Foods (Kravsz)
62 Glen Eira Road, Ripponlea 3183 (3) 9523-8463
Grocers/Importers.

Gefen Liquor Store
144 Chapel Street, Balaclava 3183 (3) 9531-5032
Fax: (3) 9525-7388
Hours: Monday to Thursday, 9 am to 5 pm; Friday, 9 am to 4 pm. Public transport access: #3 tram to corner of Carlisle and Chapel Streets or Sandringham line train to Balaclava Station.

Milecki's Balaclava Health Food
277 Carlisle Street, Balaclava 3183 (3) 9527-3350
Open every day except Shabbat and all Jewish holidays. Hours: 9 am to 9 pm. Close to rail station and on tram line.

Rishon Foods Party Ltd.
23 Williams Street, Balaclava 3183 (3) 9527-5142

Singers, 57 Kooyong Road, Caulfield 3162
(3) 9509-2387
Fax: (3) 9509-2387

Tempo Kosher Supermarket
391 Inkerman Street, St Kilda 3183 (3) 9527-5021
Manufacturers of a range of kosher foods, including cheese, butter and juice drinks.

Hotels

Quest Kimberley Caulfield
441 Inkerman Street, Balaclava 3183 (3) 9526-3888
Fax: (3) 9525-9691
Strictly Glatt kosher.

Judaica

The Antique Silver Co.
253 Carlisle Street, Balaclava 3183 (3) 9525-8480
Fax: (3) 9525-8479
Large selection of Judaica and ritual objects.

Libraries

Kadimah Jewish Cultural Centre & National Library
7 Selwyn Street, Elsternwick 3185 (3) 9523-9817
Hours: 9.30 am-2.30 pm

Makor Jewish Community Library
306 Hawthorn Road, South Cantfield 3162
(3) 9272-5611
Fax: (3) 9272-5629
Email: jlibrary@vicnet.net.au
Web site: www.vicnet.net.au/~jlibrary

Media

Newspapers

Jewish News, PO Box 1000, South Cantfield
Publish weekly newspaper.

Yidishe Geshefen
(3) 9532-7323
Fax: (3) 9523-0106
Jewish advertising monthly.

Mikvaot

Caulfield Mikva
9 Furneaux Grove, East St Kilda 3183
(3) 9528-1116/9525-8585
Contact: Mrs C Sofer.

Lubavitch Mikva
38 Empress Road, East St Kilda 3183 (3) 9527-7555
Fax: (3) 9525-8838
Email: ktrubin@wavenet.net.au

Museums

Jewish Holocaust Centre
15 Selwyn Street, Elsternwick 3185 (3) 9528-1985
Fax: (3) 9528-3758
Email: hc@sprint.com.au
Hours: Monday and Wednesday 10.00 am to 4.00 pm, Tuesday, Thursday and Friday 10.00 am to 2.00 pm, Sunday 11.00 am to 3.00pm.

Jewish Museum of Australia
26 Alma Road, St Kilda 3182 (3) 9543-0083
Fax: (3) 9543-0844
Email: info@jewishmuseum.com.au
Web site: www.jewishmuseum.com.au

Religious Organisations

Orthodox

Council of Orthodox Synagogues of Victoria
c/o Jetset House, 5 Queens Road 3000
(3) 9828-8000

Melbourne Beth Din
Synagogue Chambers, 572 Inkerman Road, North Caulfield 3161 (3) 9527-8337
Fax: (3) 9527-8072

Orthodox Rabbinate of Australia
ISB on Accord Avenue, Bondi Junction 2022
(2) 9389-5622
Fax: (2) 9389-5418

Rabbinical Council of Victoria
c/o Honorary Secretary, Rabbi Mordechai Gutnick, 7 Meadow St., East St Kilda 3183 (3) 9525-9542
Fax: (3) 9525-9546

Progressive

Victorian Union for Progressive Judaism
78 Alma Road, St Kilda 3182 (3) 9510-1488
Fax: (3) 9521-1229
Email: vupj@tbi.org.au

Australia / Victoria

Representative Organisations

Jewish Community Council of Victoria Inc.
306 Hawthorn Road, South Caulfield 3162
(3) 9272-5566
Fax: (3) 9272-5560
Email: jccv@netspace.net.au
Head body of Melbourne Jewish community.

Restaurants

Klein's Kosher Gourmet
19 Glen Eira Road, Ripponlea (3) 9528-1200

Dairy

Sheli's Coffee Shop
306 Hawthorn Road, South Caulfield (3) 9272-5607

Meat

Delishes Restaurant
8-10 Glen Eira Ave., Rippon Lea (3) 9523-1801
Kosher Express
263-265 Carlisle St, Balaclava (3) 9527-9911
Fax: (3) 9527-9922
Supervision: Mehadrin Melbourne.
Lamzini's,
219 Carlisle Street, St. Kilda (3) 9527-1283
Supervision: Melbourne Kashrut.

Synagogues

Kollel Beth Hatalmud
362a Carlisle Street, East St Kilda 3183
(3) 9527-6156
Fax: (3) 9527-8034
Email: kbt@blaze.net.au

Independent

Bet Hatikva Synagogue
233 Nepean Highway, Gardenvale 3185
(3) 9576-9755

Liberal

Bentleigh Progressive Synagogue
549 Centre Road 3204 (3) 9563-9208
Fax: (3) 9557-9880
Email: suzpol@techno.net.au

Leo Baeck Centre
33-37 Harp Road, East Kew 3102 (3) 9819-7160
Email: lbc@netspace.net.au
Web site: www.leobaeckcentre.org.au
PO Box 430 East Kew 3102
Temple Beth Israel
P O Box 128, St Kilda 3182 (3) 9510-1488
Fax: (3) 9521-1229
Email: info@tbi.org.au
Web site: www.tbi.org.au

Orthodox

Brighton Hebrew Congregation
132-136 Marriage Road, East Brighton 3187
(3) 9592-9179
Fax: (3) 9593-1682
Email: brightonshule@iprimus.com.au
Office hours: Monday to Friday 9 am-1 pm. PO Box 202 Bentleigh 3204. Visitors welcome.
Burwood Hebrew Congregation
38 Harrison Avenue 3125 (3) 9808-3120
Chabad House, Duver Heights (3) 9387-3822
Caulfield Hebrew Congregation
572 Inkerman Road, Caulfield 3161 (3) 9525-9492
Fax: (3) 9527-8463
Email: chcmelb@ozemail.com.au

Elwood Talmud Torah Congregation
39 Dickens Street, Elwood 3184 (3) 9531-1547
East Melbourne City Synagogue
Albert St 3002 (3) 9662-1372
Fax: (3) 9662-1843
Email: office@melbournecitysynagogue.com
Web site: www.melbournecitysynagogue.com
The oldest Shule building in Melbourne Australia, since 1877 at its present location. It is a tourist attraction classified by the National Trust and the only shule in the Central Business District.
Kew Synagogue
53 Walpole Street, Kew 3101 (3) 9853-9243
Fax: (3) 9853-1354
Email: kewshul@iprimus.com.au

Mizrachi,
81 Balaclava Road, Caulfield 3161 (3) 9525-9833
Fax: (3) 9527-5665
Email: mizrachi@iprimus.com.au
Communication: P O Box 2247, Caulfield Junction, VIC 3161.
Melbourne Hebrew Congregation
Cnr. Toorak & St Kilda Roads, S. Yarra 3141
(3) 9866-2255
Fax: (3) 9866-2022
Email: mhc@bigpond.com

Moorabbin & District Synagogue
960 Nepean Highway, Moorabbin 3189
(3) 9553-3845

North Eastern Malvern Chabad
Glenferrie Road, Malvern
South Caulfield Synagogue
47 Leopold Street, South Cantfield 3162
(3) 9578-5922
Fax: (3) 9578-5299

St Kilda Hebrew Congregation Inc.
12 Charnwood Grove, St Kilda 3182 (3) 9537-1433
Fax: (3) 9525-3759
Web site: www.stkildashule.org.au

The Sassoon Yehuda Sephardi Synagogue
79 Hotham Street, East St Kilda 3183 (3) 9527-8863
Email: amar@netspace.net.au
Sephardi Kiddush follows Saturday service.

Yeshiva Shule
92 Hotham Street, East St Kilda 3183 (3) 9522-8222
Fax: (3) 9522-8266

Tourist Sites

North Eastern Jewish War Memorial Centre Inc.
6 High Street, Doncaster 3108 (3) 9816-3516
Fax: (3) 9857-4430
Email: nejc@one.au

Western Australia

Perth

Delicatessens

Aviv Catering
The Jewish Centre, 61 Woodrow Avenue, Yokinea 6060 (8) 9276-6030
Fax: (8) 9276-6030
Supervision: Kashrut Authority of Western Australia.
Open 10am-2pm

Representative Organisations

Council of Western Australian Jewry
J.P. PO Box 763 6062

Synagogues

Jewish Community Centre of W.A.
Woodrow Avenue, Mt Yokine 6060 (8) 9276-8572
Fax: (8) 9276-8330
Email: peter@lennys.com.au

Northern Suburbs Congregation
4 Vernon Street, Noranda 6062 (8) 9275-5932

Perth Hebrew Congregation
Freedman Road, Menora 6050 (8) 9271-0539
Email: phc@theperthshule.asn.au
Web site: www.theperthshule.asn.au

Liberal

Temple David
34 Clifton Crescent, Mt Lawley 6050 (8) 9271-1485

Lubavitch

Chabad House
396 Alexander Drive, Dianella 6062 (8) 9275-4912

Austria

The arrival of Jews in this area of Europe (probably with the Romans) occurred more than a 1,000 years ago. The community was expelled from Austria between 1420 and 1421, but Jews were allowed to return in 1451. The Jews were granted their own quarter of Vienna in 1624, but were expelled again in 1670. The economy declined after the expulsion, and so they were asked to return.

It was not until 1782 that the situation became more stable when Joseph II began lifting the anti-Jewish decrees that his mother, Maria Theresa, had imposed on her Jewish subjects. The Jews received equal rights in 1848 and, in 1867, legal and other prohibitions were lifted.

Anti-Semitism did continue, however, and many influential anti-Semitic publications were available in Vienna and were keenly read by many people, including the young Adolf Hitler. After the First World War, Austria lost its empire (which included Czech lands and Galicia, which had a very large Jewish community), and the Jewish population fell accordingly. At the time of the Nazi take-over in 1938, 200,000 Jews lived in the country. Some 70,000 were killed in the Holocaust, the rest having escaped or hidden.

Today there are several synagogues in Vienna. The city has an active Ultra-Orthodox community and kosher food is available. Visitors to Vienna should not miss the new Jewish Museum, opened in 2001. It combines Rachel Whiteread's memorial, the museum of Medieval Jewish Life and the excavations of a medieval synagogue built around the middle of the 13th century.

GMT + 1 hour — Total Population 8,211,000
Country calling code (43) — Jewish Population 10,000
Emergency Telephone (Police - 133) (Fire - 122) (Ambulance - 144) — Electricity voltage 220

Baden

Cemeteries

Jewish Cemetery
Halsriegelstrasse 30 (2252) 85405
Contains some 3,000 graves. (Keys to be obtained at Tourist Information Centre, tel. (2252) 4453157.)

Synagogues

Grabengasse 14 (2236) 26383 or (2252) 45705
Services are held Shabbat mornings from May to September. Contact Dr Grossinger any time except Shabbos/holidays. Kosher catering possible. Event room (for 50 persons). Baden is R. Naftali Carlebach's last kehillah in Europe and the site of his distinguished sons R. Shlomo's z'tzal and R. Eliyahu Chaim's z'l Barmitzvah.

Edlach

A memorial to Dr Theodor Herzl, erected by the Viennese Jewish community, can be seen in the garden of the local sanatorium, where the founder of the Zionist movement died in 1904.

Eisenstadt

Cemeteries

Old Cemetery
The old cemetery, closed around 1875, contains the grave of Rav Meir Eisenstaat (Maharam Esh), who died in 1744. To this day it is the scene of pilgrimages, particularly on the anniversary of his death. Keys to the cemetery are with the porter of the local hospital, which adjoins the old cemetery.

Museums

Austrian Jewish Museum
Unterbergstrasse 6 (2682) 65145
Fax: (2682) 65145; 65144
Email: info@oejudmus.or.at
The museum now also comprises the restored private synagogue of Samson Wertheimer, Habsburg court Jew and Chief Rabbi of Hungary (1658–1724). The museum is open daily except Monday from 10 am to 5 pm. The Eruv Arch, spanning Unterbergstrasse, is at the end near the Esterhazy Palace. The road chain was used in former times to prevent vehicular traffic on Shabbat and Yom Tov.

Graz

Community Organisations

Synagogue and Community Centre
Synagogenplatz 1 (512) 712 4684

Innsbruck

Community Organisations

Community Centre
Sillgassse 15 (512) 586-892

Kobersdorf

Cemeteries

Jewish Cemetery
Waldgasse
The keys of the cemetery on the Lampelberg are with Mr Piniel, Waldgasse 25 (one of the two houses to the left of the cemetery) and Mr Grässing, Haydngasse 4.

Linz

Community Organisations

Community Centre
Bethlehemstrasse 26 (732) 779-805

Salzburg

The Salzburg community dates back to 803 when Archbishop Arno summoned a Jewish doctor to set up a practice in the town.

Community Organisations

Community Centre
Lasserstrasse 8 5020 (662) 875-665
Community synagogue and mikva are to be found at the same address.

Vienna

Vienna was in the past the most important centre for Central European Jews. From 180,000 Jews in the 1930s, there are about 1,000 Jews (mainly elderly) in Vienna today. Professor Freud's clinic is a popular attraction, and the Jewish Museum of Vienna gives much information on the history of the Jews.

Bakeries

Engländer
Hollandstrasse 10 1020 (1) 214-5617
Supervision: Rabbi Abraham Yonah Schwartz.

Bed & Breakfasts

Pension Lichtenstein
Grosse Schiffgasse 19 1020 (1) 216-8498
Fax: (1) 214-7690
Web site: www.pension-lichtenstein.at
The pension consists of "suites" . It is within walking distance of the old Jewish quarter of Vienna in one direction, and 5-20 minutes from some small synagogues and a kosher bakery in the other direction. Visits should be co-ordinated in advance as there is no front desk reception; the key is kept in the owner's office around the block.

Orthodox

Booksellers

Chabad-Simcha-Center
Hollandstrasse 10 1020 (1) 216-2924
Chai Vienna
Praterstrasse 40 1020 (1) 216-4621
Fax: (1) 216-4621

Butchers

B. Ainhorn
Stadtgutgasse 7 1020 (1) 214-5621
Supervision: Rabbi David Grunfeld.
Also supplies "Fast Food".
Rebenwurzel
Grose Mohrengasse 19 1010 (1) 216-6640
Supervision: Rabbi Chaim Stern.
Sephardi Butcher
Volkertmarkt 1020 (1) 214-9650

Cemeteries

Floridsdorfer Cemetery
Ruthnergasse 28 1210
Those wishing to visit must first obtain a permit from the community centre.
Rossauer Cemetery
Seegasse 9 1090
This is the oldest Jewish cemetery in Vienna, dating from the sixteenth century. It has now been restored after being devastated by the Nazis and is open daily from 8 am to 3 pm. Access is via the front entrance of the municipal home for the aged at Seegasse 9-11, but a permit must first be obtained from the community centre.
Vienna Central Cemetery
Simmeringer Haupstr.244 A-1110
(1) 531 04 904, 767 6252
The Jewish section (the only one still in use) is at Gate 4 and there is an older Jewish part at Gate 1.
Währinger Cemetery
Semperstrasse 64a 1180
Those wishing to visit must first obtain a permit from the community centre.

Austria

Contact Information

Jewish Community Centre
Seitenstettengasse 4 (1) 531 04104
Fax: (1) 531 04108
Email: office@ikg-wien.at

Jewish Welcome Service Vienna
Stephansplatz 10 1010 (1) 533-2730
Fax: (1) 533-4098
Email: jewish.welcome@verkehrsbuero.at
Web site: www.jewish.welcome.at
Open: Monday to Friday 9 am to 5.30 pm.

Documentation Centres

Documentation Centre of Austrian Resistance
Old City Hall, Wipplingerstrasse 8 1010
(1) 534-3601 779
Fax: (1) 534-3699 01771
Email: office@doew.at
Web site: www.doew.at
Hours of opening: Monday to Thursday 9 am to 5 pm.

Documentation Centre of Union of Jewish Victims of the Nazis
Salztorgasse 6 A-1010 (1) 533-9131
Fax: (1) 535-0397

Embassy

Embassy of Israel
Anton-Frankgasse 20 1180 (1) 476-460

Groceries

Gross-Import-Wien
Nicklegasse 1, A-1020 (1) 214-0607
Fax: (1) 214-7690

Koscherland,
Kleine Sperlgasse 7 (1) 212-8169

Kosher Supermarket & Shutnes Laboratory
Hollandstrasse 7 1020 (1) 269-9675
Supervision: Rabbi Abraham Yonah Schwartz.

Ohel Moshe
Hollandstrasse 10 A-1020 (1) 216-9675
Supervision: Rabbi Abraham Yonah Schwartz.

Rafael Malkov
Tempelgasse 6, Ferdinandstrasse 2 A-1020
(1) 214-8394

Vinothek Gross
Taborstrasse 15 1020 (1) 212-6299

Hotels

Hotel Stefanie
12 Tabor Strasse 1020 (1) 211-500
Fax: (1) 211-50160
Email: stefanie@schick-hotels.com
Web site: www.schick-hotels.com
Four-star hotel with kosher breakfast on request.

Media

Newspaper

Die Gemeinde (1) 531 04 271
Fax: (1) 531 04 279

Mikvaot

Agudas Yisroel
Tempelgasse 3 1020 (1) 214-9973

Machsike Haddas
Fleischmarkt 22 1010 (1) 512-5262

Monument

Nameless Library
Judenplatz
The monument opened in 2001 depicts shelves of 9,000 books with their spines turned to the inside. The names of the concentration camps in which Austrian Jews were killed are engraved around the base. Underneath the memorial one can view the ruins of a synagogue razed in 1421.

Museums

Jewish Museum of the City of Vienna
Dorotheergasse 11 A-1010 (1) 535-0431
Fax: (1) 535-0424
Email: info@jmw.at
Web site: www.jmw.at
Hours: Sunday to Friday, 10 am to 6 pm; Thursday, 10 am to 8 pm. Cafeteria and bookshop on site. The cafeteria is not under supervision.

Museum Judenplatz
Judenplatz 8 A-1010
Email: info@jmw.at
Web site: www.jmw.at
A memorial for the Austrian victims of the Holocaust. A place of rememberance was created that is unique in Europe. It combines Rachel Whiteread's memorial (see above) and the excavations of the medieval synagogue with the Museum on Medieval Jewish Life to form a commemorative whole. Opening hours: Sunday to Thursday 10 am to 6 pm. Friday 10 am to 2 pm. Special guided tours for groups by prior arrangement only.

Sigmund Freud Museum
Berggasse 19 1090 (1) 319-1596
Fax: (1) 317-0279
Email: freud-museum@t0.or.at
Web site: www.freud-museum.at
Hours: 9 am to 5 pm, July to September 9am - 6pm

Restaurants

Meat

Restaurant Alef - Alef
Seitenstettengasse 2, A-1010 (1) 535-2530

Snack Bar

Berl Ainhorn Koscher Fleisch und Imbiss
Gross Stadtgutgasse 7 1020 (1) 214-5621

Site

Mauthausen Memorial Site
(1) 723-82269
Fax: (1) 723-83696
Those wishing to visit the site should contact the Jewish Welcome Service.

Synagogues

Orthodox

Agudas Yeshurun
Riemergasse 9 1010

Agudas Yisroel
Grünangergasse 1 1010 (1) 512-8331

Agudas Yisroel
Tempelgasse 3 1020 (1) 214 9262

Machsike Haddas
GroBe Mohreng. 19 A-1020 (1) 216 0679

Misrachi, Judenplatz 8 1010 (1) 535-4153

Ohel Moshe
Lilienbrunngasse 19 1020 (1) 216-8864

Rambam Syn. im Maimonides Zentrum
Bauernfeldgasse 4 A-1190

Seitenstettengasse Synagogue
Seitenstettengasse 4 1010 (1) 531-040
Fax: (1) 531-04108
Email: office@ikg-wien.at
Web site: www.ikg-wien.at
Built in 1824-26 and partly destroyed during the Nazi period, this beautiful synagogue was restored by the community in 1988. For information about guided tours, contact the Community Centre offices.

Shomre Haddas
Glasergasse 17 1090

Sephardi Centre
Tempelgasse 7 1020 (1) 214 3097

Thora Etz Chayim
Grosse Schiffgasse 8 1020 (1) 214 5016

Progressive

Or Chadasch
Rosentalgasse 5-7/4/3 1140 (1) 967 1329
Fax: (1) 914 5245

Azerbaijan

Azerbaijan has a remarkable Jewish history, which can be better explored now that the country is independent from the Soviet Union. The Tats (mountain Jews) believe that their ancestors arrived in Azerbaijan at the time of Nebuchadnezzar. They lived in several mountain villages, and adopted the customs of their non-Jewish neighbours. They spoke a north Iranian language, known as Judeo-Tat, to which they had added some Hebrew words. The Soviets clamped down on their way of life after 1928, changing the alphabet of their language from Hebrew to Latin and then, in 1938, to Cyrillic. Some of their synagogues were also closed down. Zionist feeling is high, with almost 30,000 emigrating to Israel since 1989.

The other strand in Azerbaijan's Jewish population are the Ashkenazis who arrived in the nineteenth century from Poland and other countries to the west.

The community has some 10-15 organisations in Baku, the capital, including Zionist and youth groups. The largest synagogue in Baku is the Tat synagogue, but there are also Ashkenazi and Georgian synagogues. Synagogues are found in other towns.

GMT + 5 hours — Total Population 7,734,000
Country calling code (994) — Jewish Population 20,000

Baku

Embassy

Embassy of Israel
Stroiteley Prospect 1

Synagogues

Mountain Jews
Dmitrova Street 39 370014 (12) 892-232-8867

Ashkenazi
Pervomoskaya Street 271 (12) 892-294-1571

Kuba

Synagogues

46 Kolkhoznaya Street

Bahamas

Luis de Torres, the official interpreter for Columbus, was the first Jew in the Bahamas, as well as being one of the first Europeans there. He was a *Converso*, a 'secret Jew', who officially had converted to Catholicism, but who practised Judaism in private. The British arrived in 1620, and eventually gained control of the islands. Although there was a Jewish Attorney-General and Chief Justice in the islands in the eighteenth century, few Jews settled there until the twentieth century, coming from Eastern Europe and the UK after the First World War, and settling in Nassau, the capital.

There are approximately 100 Jewish residents in the Bahamas. However it is estimated that about 350,000 Jews visit the islands each year as tourists. There are congregations in Nassau and Freeport. Both cities have Jewish cemeteries, that in Nassau being the more historic.

GMT - 5 hours	Total Population 307,000
Country calling code (1242)	Jewish Population under 100
Emergency Telephone (Police, Fire and Ambulance - 919)	Electricity voltage 120

Freeport

Embassy

Consul General of Israel

362-4421

Synagogues

Freeport Hebrew Congregation
Luis de Torres Synagogue, East Sunrise Highway,
PO Box F-41761 373-2008
Email: don@coralwave.com

Services every Friday evening at 8.30 pm from September through April, as well as Community Sedar, Chanukah celebration and full-time certificated marriage officer.

Nassau

Synagogues

Progressive

Bahamas Jewish Congregation
PO Box CB-11002 363-2305

Barbados

Jewish history in Barbados starts in 1628, a year after the British first settled there. Jewish settlers came from Brazil, Surinam, England and Germany, and were mainly Sephardi. The first synagogue was established in Bridgetown (the capital) in 1654. Early settlers were engaged in cultivating sugar and coffee.

The Jewish population was well treated, and Barbados was the first British possession in which Jews were granted full political emancipation. Despite a largely favourable climate, the community suffered losses from hurricanes, which destroyed sugar plantations, and the Jewish population fell to 70 by 1848. By 1925, no Jews remained, but a new influx (30 families escaping Nazism) came shortly after.

The synagogue was restored in 1987, and postage stamps were produced which commemorated its restoration. The Jewish population remains small, but it was a group of Barbadian Jews who founded the Caribbean Jewish Congress. The Jewish cemetery, one of the oldest in the Americas, is now back in use.

GMT - 4 hours
Country calling code (1246)
Electricity voltage 110

Total Population 265,000
Jewish Population Under 100

Community Organisations

Barbados Jewish Community
PO Box 651, Bridgetown 427-0703
Fax: 436-8807

Caribbean Jewish Congress
PO Box 1331, Bridgetown 436-8163
Fax: 437-4992
Email: comphosting.sunbeach.net\cjc

Synagogue Restoration Project
PO Box 256, Bridgetown 432-0840
Fax: 432-2147
Email: altman@caribsurf.com
Local inquiries to Henry Altman, Little Mallows, Sandy Lane, St. James. Tel: 1246 132-6462

Synagogues

Nidhe Israel, Synagogue Lane 427 7611
Services are held Friday evenings at 7 pm at 'True Blue', Rockley New Road, Christ Church, during the summer, and at the synagogue at 7.30 pm in winter.

Have you any information for us?

Any comments you may have on this guide are always welcomed. Please do get in touch if you have any relevant information which you may feel will be of use to other travellers. Just send a quick email to jtg@vmbooks.com Alternatively you can use one of the other methods set out on page iv. Appropriate forms for this are also available at the back of the book.

Belarus

For the adventurous traveller, who has a keen interest in Jewish history, Belarus (also known as White Russia) makes an interesting and unusual destination. Situated on the western side of the former Soviet Union, this largely flat country borders Poland and Lithuania to the west, Ukraine to the south and Russia to the east. Belarus finally achieved independence in 1991, and within its present borders are many towns and villages of Jewish interest, such as Minsk, Pinsk and Grodno. One of the most famous villages in Belarus is Lubavitch, a hamlet in the far east of the country, near the Russian border, where the world-wide Lubavitch movement has its origins.

The majority of this region's Jews died in the Holocaust and although emigration to Israel is high, the community is slowly rebuilding itself after decades of Soviet control. Americans and Israelis are contributing rabbis to help in this revival, and Jewish schools have been set up. Yiddish is used far more here than in other parts of the former USSR.

GMT + 2 hours	Total Population 10,236,000
Country calling code (375)	Jewish Population 26,600
Emergency Telephone (Police, Fire and Ambulance - 03)	Electricity voltage 220

Baranovichi

Synagogues

39 Svobodnaya St.

Bobruisk

Synagogues

Engels St.

Borisov

Synagogues

Trud St.

Brest

Synagogues

Narodnaya St.

Gomel

Contact Information

Rosa Sorkina (23) 252-5808

Synagogues

13 Sennaya St.

Grodno

Contact Information

Misha Kemerov (15) 2313-798

Synagogues

Menorah Jewish Community PO Box 9

Minsk

Contact Information

Rabbi Nelly Shulman (17) 2660-0180
Email: nashulman@mail.ru

Embassy

Embassy of Israel
Partizanski Prospekt 6A 220002 (17) 2304-444

Memorial

This memorial devoted to 5,000 Jews killed by the Nazis on Purim 1942 was erected in 1946 and is the only one in what was the USSR devoted to the Holocaust which displays Yiddish writing.

Synagogues

22 Kropotkin Fstreet (17) 2558-270
13b Daumana Street

Progressive

Association of Progressive Jewish Congregations in Belarus
Per K Chyornogo 4, apt 18,
Simcha 220012 (17) 2846-089
Fax: (17) 2662-928
Email: simcha@open.by

Moghilev

Synagogues

1 2nd Krutoy La.

Orsha

Synagogues

Nogrin St.

Belgium

Jewish settlement in the area now called Belgium dates back to the thirteenth century, and suffered a similar fate to other medieval European Jewish communities, taking the blame for the Black Death and suffering expulsions. The Sephardim were the first to resettle in Belgium, mainly in Antwerp. After independence in 1830, conditions for the Jews improved and more Jews began to settle there. The diamond centre of Antwerp later developed rapidly, attracting many Jews from Eastern Europe.

By 1939, the Jewish population had grown to 100,000, a large proportion of whom were refugees hoping to escape to America. Some succeeded, but many became trapped after the German invasion. Some 25,000 Belgian Jews were deported and killed in the Holocaust. A national monument listing the names of the victims, stands in Anderlecht in Brussels.

The present Jewish population includes a large Chassidic community in Antwerp, where there are some thirty synagogues. There are also more than ten synagogues in Brussels. There are Jewish schools in Antwerp and Brussels, and Jewish newspapers.

GMT + 1 hour — Total Population 10,161,000
Country calling code (32) — Jewish Population 40,000
Emergency Telephone (Police - 101) (Fire and Ambulance - 101) — Electricity voltage 220

Antwerp

Seen by some as 'the last shtetl in Europe', Antwerp is a well-known Hassidic centre. Antwerp's Jewish population (15,000) has one of the highest numbers of Ultra-Orthodox in the Diaspora. Served by thirty synagogues (many of them small shtiebels), there are also kosher restaurants and food shops.

Bakeries

Gottesfeld,
Mercatorstraat 20 (3) 230-0003

Kleinblatt,
Provinciestraat 206 (3) 233-7513; 226-0018
Fax: (3) 232-0920

Steinmetz,
Lange Kievitstraat 64 (3) 234-0947

Booksellers

I. Menczer,
Simonstraat 40 (3) 232-3026

N. Seletsky,
Lange Kievitstraat 70 (3) 232-6966
Fax: (3) 226-9446

Stauber,
Van Leriusstraat 3 (3) 231-8031

Butchers

Berkowitz,
Isabellalei 9 (3) 218-5111

Farkas,
Lange Kievitstraat 66 (3) 232-1385

Fruchter,
Simonstraat 22 (3) 233-1811; 1557
Fax: (3) 231-3903

Kosher King,
Lange Kievitstraat 40 (3) 233-6749

Kosher King,
Isabellalei 7 (3) 239-4189

Mandelovics,
Isabellalei 96 (3) 218-4779

Moszkowitz,
Lange Kievitstraat 47 (3) 232-6349
Fax: (3) 226-0471

Contact Information

Machsike Hadass (Israelitische Orthodoxe Gemeente)
Jacob Jacobsstraat 22 (3) 233-5567

Shomre Hadass (Israelitische Gemeente)
Terliststraat 35 2018 (3) 232-0187
Fax: (3) 226-3123
Email: shomre-hadas@net4all.be
Web site: www.members.net4all.be/shomre-hadas

Delicatessens

Weingarten,
Lange Kievitstraat 124 (3) 233-2828

Groceries

Col-Bo,
Jacob Jacobsstraat 40 (3) 234-1212

Grosz-Modern,
Terliststraat 28 (3) 232-4626

Herzl & Gold,
Korte Kievitstraat 38 (3) 232-2365

Belguim

Stark,
Mercatorstraat 24 (3) 230-2520
Superette Lamoriniere
199 Lamboriniere Straat (3) 239-3110
Fax: (3) 281-3205
Super Discount
Belgielei 104-108 (3) 239-0666

Media

Newspapers

Belgisch Israelitisch Weekblad
Pelikaanstraat 106-108 2018 (3) 233-7094
Fax: (3) 233-4810
Email: biw@planetinternet.be

Mikvaot

Machsike Hadass
Steenbokstraat 22 (3) 239-7588
Shomre Hadass
Van Diepenbeeckstraat 42 (3) 239-0965

Museums

Plantin-Moretus Museum
Vrijdagmarkt (nr Groenplaats) (3) 233-0688
Open daily (except Monday). Contains examples of early Jewish printing, such as the famous Polyglot Bible.

Restaurants

Blue Lagoon, Lange Herentalsestraat 70
(3) 226-0114
Supervision: Machsike Hadass.
Also sell chocolates, contact R Suchowolski on 230-2871 or fax: 281-1702. Five minutes from Central station.
Garden of Eden
Plantin En Moretuslei 10 2018 (3) 281-4281
Fax: (3) 700-4034
Open: 12 pm-2 pm and 6 pm-10 pm.

Dairy

USA Pizza,
118a Isabellalei (3) 281-2300
Supervision: Machzikey Hadas.
Take away option.

Meat

Hoffy's,
Lange Kievitstraat 52 (3) 234-3535
Fax: (3) 226-0282
Email: hoffys@pandora.be
Jacob,
Lange Kievitstraat 49 (3) 233-1124

Synagogues

Orthodox

Hoofd synagoog
Oostenstraat 43 (3) 239-3038
Machsike Hadass
Jacob Jacobsstraat 22
(3) 232-0021
Fax: (3) 233-8797

Tour Information

Toerisme Antwerpen
Grote Markt 15 2000 (3) 232-0103
Fax: (3) 231-1937
Email: toerisme@antwerpen.be
Web site: www.dma.be

Arlon

Synagogues

Rue St Jean (63) 217-985
Established 1863. The secretary, J.C. Jacob, can be reached at 11 rue des Martyrs, 6700. A monument has been erected in the new Jewish cemetery to the memory of the Jews of Arlon deported and massacred by the Nazis.

Brussels

The capital of Belgian is less well endowed with kosher facilities than Antwerp, although there are 23,000 Jews living in the city. The headquarters of the European Union of Jewish Students is based there. The Anderlecht area has a monument to the Belgian Holocaust victims and a memorial to Jews who fought in the Belgian Resistance.

Bakeries

Bornstein,
62 rue de Suéde, St Gilles (2) 537-1679

Booksellers

Colbo,
121 rue du Brabant (2) 217-2620
Menorah,
12 Ave. J. Voldens 1060 (2) 537-5073

Butchers

Lanxner, 121 rue de Brabant 1030 (2) 217-2620
Supervision: Rabbinate of the Jewish Orthodox Community of Brussels.
Grocery: Jewish specialities, also Delicatessen. Hours: Sun, Mon, Fri 8.30 am to 13.00 pm. Tues 8.30 am to 18.00 pm. Wed-Thurs 8.30 am to 19.30 pm.

Community Organisations

Centre Communautaire Laic Juif
Yitzhak Rabin Center,
52 rue Hotel des Monnaies (2) 543-0270
Fax: (2) 543-0271
Email: info@cclj.be

Embassy

Embassy of Israel
40 Avenue de l'Observatoire 1180 (2) 373-5500

Groceries

Hod Taim,
Boulevard Jamar 51 (2) 527-1832

Media

Newspapers

Centrale,
91 Avenue Henri Jaspar (2) 538-8036
Monthly

Fax de Jerusalem
68 Avenue Ducpétiaux (2) 538-5673
Fax: (2) 534-0236
Email: alyabelgique@skynet.be

Weekly

Kehilatenou,
2 rue Joseph Dupont (2) 512-4334
Monthly

Regards,
52 rue Hotel des Monnaies (2) 538-4908
Fax: (2) 537-5565

Fortnightly

Mikvaot

Machsike Hadass
67a rue de la Clinique (2) 537-1439

Museums

Jewish Museum
74 Ave de Stalingrad 1000 (2) 512-1963
Fax: (2) 513-4859
Email: info@mjb.jmb.org

Hours: Mon-Thurs 12.00 - 5.00 pm. Sunday 10.00 am to 1.00 pm. Closed Friday, Saturday and Jewish holidays.

Religious Organisations

Communaute Israelite de Bruxelles
2 Rue Joseph Dupont 1000 (2) 512-4334
Fax: (2) 512-9237

Machsike Hadass (Communauté Israélite Orthodoxe de Bruxelles)
67a rue de la Clinique (2) 524-1486; 521-1289

Yechiva de Bruxelles
50 Ave Brugmann 1190 (2) 347-2143
Fax: (2) 347-2143
Email: bxlyechiva@hotmail.com

Restaurants

Chez Gilles
Rue de la Clinique 21 1070 (2) 522-1828
Open from 9 am - 5 pm

El Assado,
Roosendael 154 (2) 346-3487

Meat

Athenee Maimonide
Boulevard Poincarte 67 (2) 523-6336

El Assado,
154 Rue Roosendael

Site

National Monument to the Jewish Martyrs of Belgium
corner rue Emile Carpentier and rue Goujons, Square of the Jewish Martyrs, Anderlecht.
This monument commemorates the Jews of Belgium who were deported to concentration camps and killed by the Nazis during the Second World War. The names of all 23,838 are engraved on the monument.

Synagogues

Liberal

Communaute Israelite Liberale de Belgique - Beth Hillel
Avenue de Kersbeek 96 1190 (2) 332-2528
Fax: (2) 376-7219
Email: cilb.asbl@chello.be

Orthodox

Adath Israel
126 rue Rogier
Schaerbeek 1030 (2) 241-1664
Near City Center

Ahavat Reim
73 rue de ThySt Gilles (2) 648-3837

Beth Hamidrash
rue du Chapeau, Anderlecht (2) 524-1486

Beth Itshak
115 Ave du Roi 1060 (2) 538-3374; 520-1359

Communaute Israelite de Bruxelles
Rue de la Regence 32 1000 (2) 512-4334
Fax: (2) 512-9237

Maale, 11 Ave Messidor 1180 (2) 344-6094
Near City Center

Or Hahayim
77 rue P. Decoster 1190 (2) 344-2342

Sephardi

Communauté Sepharade de Bruxelles
47 rue du Pavillon 1030 (2) 215-0525
Fax: (2) 215-0242

Belgium

Charleroi

Community Organisations

Community Centre
56 rue Pige-au-Croly

Ghent

Contact Information

Jacques Bloch
Veldstraat 60 (9) 225-7085
Email: jbloch@compaqnet.be

The treasurer of the community will be happy to meet English-speaking visitors. As the community is a very small one, there is no permanent synagogue. Services are held on the High Holy Days.

Knokke

Synagogues

30 Van Bunnenlaan (50) 61-0372
Also has a Mikvah

Liège

Community Organisations

Community Centre
12 Quai Marcellis 4020

Museums

Musee Serge Kruglanski
19 rue L. Fredericq 4020 (43) 438-043
Fax: (43) 226-0234

Synagogues

19 rue L. Frédéricq 4020 (41) 436-106

Mons

Contact Information

SHAPE 7010 (65) 445-808; 444-809

Nearby, at Casteau, the International Chapel of NATO's Supreme Headquarters Allied Powers Europe, includes a small Jewish community, established 1951, that holds regular services. Call for further information.

Ostend

Synagogues

Van Maastrichtplein 3 (59) 511-622
Services during July and August. Inquiries to Mrs Liliane Wulfowicz, Parklaan 21, B-8400, (59) 802-405.

Waterloo

Synagogues

Communaute Israelite de Waterloo et du Brabant Sud (CIWABS)
140 Avenue Belle-Vue, 1410 Waterloo
(2) 354 6789

Regular Services Shabbat and Festivals; English speaking visitors very welcome.

Bermuda

Jews have lived in Bermuda since the seventeenth century, but the first formal congregation was not established until the twentieth century.

The resident Jewish population is very small, but the transient population (of tourists largely from the USA, Britain and Canada) is much greater. High holy-day services are normally held at the US Naval Air Station Chapel. Friday services are held, usually monthly, at the Unity Foundation, 75 Reid Street, Hamilton.

GMT - 4 hours — Total Population 64,000
Country calling code (1) — Jewish Population Under 100
Emergency Telephone (Police - 112) (Fire - 113) (Ambulance -115) — Electricity voltage 110

Hamilton

Community Organisations

Jewish Community of Bermuda
PO Box HM 1793 HM05 (441) 291-1785
Web site: www.jcb.bm

Bolivia

The history of the Jews of Bolivia dates back to the Spanish colonial period. *Conversos* (converts to Christianity who practised Judaism in secret) arrived with the Spaniards in the seventeenth century.

The main influx of Jews occurred in 1905, with immigrants from Eastern Europe, but the number entering Bolivia was much smaller than that going to other South American countries. In 1933 there were only some thirty Jewish families. At the end of the decade, however, there was a small increase in Jewish immigration as German and Austrian Jews fled from Europe. Ironically, the Jewish community did not grow very much, even though the government granted every Jew an entry visa.

Many Jews started to leave Bolivia in the 1950s because of political instability and the apparent lack of educational opportunities. The present-day community has a central organisation known as the Circulo Israelita de Bolivia.

GMT - 4 hours
Country calling code (591)
Emergency Telephone Electricity voltage 110/220

Total Population 8,239,000
Jewish Population 400

Cochabamba

Representative Organisations

Asociacion Israelita de Cochabamba
PO Box 349, Calle Valdivieso

Synagogues

Calle Junin y Calle Colombia, Casilla 349

La Paz

Synagogues

Circulo Israelita de Bolivia
Casilla 1545, Calle Landaeta 346, PO Box 1545
(2) 32-5925
Fax: (2) 34-2738
Representative body of Bolivian Jewry. All La Paz organisations are affiliated to it. Service Shabbat morning only.

Comunidad Israelita Synagogue
Calle Canada Stronguest 1846, PO Box 2198
Affiliated to the Circulo. Friday evening services are held here.

Tour information

Centro Shalom
Calle Canada Stronguest 1846

Santa Cruz

Community Organisations

Centro Cruceño
PO Box 469

Representative Organisations

WIZO, Castilla 3409

Bosnia-Hercegovina

Sephardi Jews were the first to arrive in the area, in the late sixteenth century. They established a Jewish quarter in Sarajevo, and this was home for poorer Jews until the Austrians conquered the land in 1878. It was the Turks, however, who emancipated the Jews in the nineteenth century when Bosnia-Hercegovina was under Ottoman rule.

When Bosnia-Hercegovina became part of the newly formed Yugoslavia, after the First World War, the community maintained its Sephardi heritage and joined the all-Yugoslav Federation of Jewish Religious Communities. The Jewish population numbered 14,000 in 1941. This number dropped sharply after the Germans conquered Yugoslavia.

After the War the survivors were joined by many who had decided to return. The Sephardi and Ashkenazi communities became unified. La Benevolencija, founded 100 years ago, is a humanitarian organisation which supported the community through its troubles and became well known in the early 1990s at the time of the civil war. After the Yugoslav civil war, many made *aliyah* to Israel, reducing the community still further.

GMT + 1 hour — Total Population 3,972,000
Country calling code (387) — Jewish Population 600
Emergency Telephone (Police - 664 211) (Fire - 93) (Ambulance - 94) — Electricity voltage 220

Sarajevo

Cemeteries

Kovacici

This historic Jewish cemetery is in town. Not far from the centre of town, on a hill called Vraca, there is a monument with the names of the 7,000 Jews from the area who fell victim to the Nazis.

Community Organisations

Sarajevo Jewish Community "La Benevolencija"
Hamdije Kresevljakovica 83 7100 (33) 663-472
Fax: (33) 663-473

Museums

Jewish Museum
Mulamustafe Baseskije Street
This historic museum, placed in the oldest synagogue in Sarajevo, with priceless relics dating back to the expulsion from Spain, is temporarily closed to the public.

Novi Hram
This gallery is also located in a former synagogue. The president of the community will gladly show visitors around.

Synagogues

Synagogue and Community Centre
Hamdije Kresevljakovica 59 (33) 663-472
Fax: (33) 663-473
Email: la_bene@soros.org.ba

Brazil

The first Jewish settlers in Brazil came with the Portuguese in 1500. They were mainly *Conversos*, escaping persecution in Portugal, and initially worked on the sugar plantations. In due course they played important roles as traders, artisans and plantation owners. The huge area that is called Brazil today was in the process of being conquered by the Dutch and the Portuguese. Two synagogues were opened in Recife during the 1640s and many Jews came from Holland. When the Dutch left Brazil in 1654 one of the terms of surrender allowed the Jews who had been on their side to emigrate. Many fled and some went on to found the first Jewish community in New York, then known as New Amsterdam. A seventeenth-century mikveh was discovered in 2000 in the basement of the Tsur Israel Synagogue in Recife.

With Brazilian independence in 1822, conditions became more favourable for Jews and many came from North Africa and Europe. The majority of Jews in Brazil today, however, originate from the immigration of East European Jews in the early twentieth century. From about 6,000 Jews in 1914, the community grew to 30,000 in 1930. After 1937 Brazil refused to allow Jewish immigrants into the country, but some limited immigration managed to continue despite the restrictions.

A central organisation was established in 1951 (the CONIB), and this includes 200 various Jewish organisations. Brazilian Jews live in an atmosphere of tolerance and prosperity, and assimilation is common.

There are synagogues in all the major cities.

GMT - 3 to - 5 hrs — Total Population 170,115,000
Country calling code (55) — Jewish Population 130,000
Emergency Telephone (Police - 147) (Fire - 193) (Ambulance - 192) — Electricity voltage 220/100

Amazonas

Manaus

Community Organisations

Grupo Kadima,
Rua Ramos Ferreira 596

Bahia

Salvador

Synagogues

Rua Alvaro Tiberio 60 (71) 3-4283
Community centre and Zionist organisation are at the same address.

Brasilia

Embassy

Embassy of Israel
Av. das Nacoes Sul, Lote 38
(61) 244-7675/244-7875
Fax: (61) 244-6129

Synagogues

ACIB,
Entrequadras Norte 305-306, Lote A (61) 23-2984
Community centre is at the same address.

Minas Gerais

Belo Horizonte

Contact Information

Lojinha do Beit Chabad
Av. Serzedelo Corrêa 276 (31) 241-2250

Mikvaot

Rua Rio Grande do Norte 477 (31) 221-0690

Representative Organisations

Associacão Israelita Brasileira
Rua Rio Grande do Norte 477 (31) 221-0690
Uniao Israelita de Belo Horizonte
Rua Pernambuco 326 (31) 224-6013

Synagogues

Av. Leonardo Malchez 630, Centro

Brazil / Minas Gerais

Congregacao Israelita Mineira
Rua Rio Grande do Norte 477 (31) 3224-2129
Fax: (31) 3224-2129
Email: cim@pib.com.br

Para

Belém

Community Organisations
Community Centre
Travessa Dr. Moraes 37

Synagogues
Eshel Avraham
Travessa Campos Sales 733
Shaar Hashamaim
Rua Alcipreste Manoel Theodoro 842

Parana

Curitiba

Community Club and Jewish Federation
Centro Israelita do Parana
Rua Mateus Leme 1431 80530 (41) 338-7575
Fax: (41) 338-7922

Synagogues

Orthodox

Francisco Frischmann
Rua Cruz Machado 126 (41) 224-5218
Fax: (41) 224-8172

Pernambuco

Recife

Community Organisations
Community Centre
Rua da Gloria 215

Synagogues
Rua Martins Junior 29

Rio de Janeiro

The old Jewish area is situated around Rua Alfandega. The country's first Ashkenazi Synagogue (Grande Templo Israelite) is an imposing building which was renovated in 1986.

Campos

Community Organisations
Community Centre
Rua 13 de Maio 52

Greater Rio de Janeiro

Butchers
Frigorifico
Rua Ronald Carvalho 265
Copacabana 22021-020
(21) 295-7341

Supervision: Rav Stauber.

Cultural Organisations
ASA - Associacao Sholem Aleichem
Rua Sao Clemente 155
Botafogo 22260 (21) 539-7740
Fax: (21) 266-1980
Email: asa@asa.org.br
Web site: www.asa.org.br

The institution is dedicated to promote cultural events (seminars, debates, video exhibitions, etc.).

Embassy
Consul General of Israel
Av. Copacabana 680 (21) 255-5432

Groceries
Kosher House
Rua Anita Garibaldi 37 lj. A, Copacabana (21) 255-3891

Mikvaot
Kehilat Yaakov
Rua Capelao Alvares da Silva 15
Copacabana 22041 (21) 2236-3922

Museums
Museu Judaico do Rio de Janeiro
Rua Mexico 90
Andar 20031-141 (21) 240-1598
Fax: (21) 240-1598
Email: museujudaico@vol.com.br
Web site: www.museujudaico.org.br

Representative Organisations
Confederacao Israelita de Brazil (Conib)
Avenida Nilo Pecanha 50 (21) 240-0034
Fax: (21) 240-2717
Organizaco Israelita do Estado do Rio de Janeiro
Rua Tenente Possolo 8
Rabinado do Rio de Janeiro
Rua Pompeu Loureiro 40 (21) 2256-3587
Fax: (21) 236-0249
Email: rabinatorio@aol.com

Restaurants
Cafeteria no Rabinato
Rua Pompeu Loureiro 40 Copacabana
(21) 236-0249

Hours: 10am to 5pm Sunday to Thursday.

Kosher House
Rua Anita Garibaldi 371Copacabana

Synagogues

Liberal

Associacão Religiosa Israelita
Rua General Severiano 170
Botafogo, 22290
(21) 2543-6320; 2542-5598
Fax: (21) 2542-6499
Email: ariadm@openlink.com.br

Orthodox

Agudat Israel
Rua Nascimento Silva 109,
Ipanema 22421
(21) 267-5567

Grande Templo Israelita
Rua Tenente Possolo 8, Centro, 20230
(21) 232-3656

Kehilat Yaakov
Rua Capelao Alvares da Silva
Copacabana 22041

Tours of Jewish Interest

Michel Mekler
Av. Graca Aranha 81/608Centro 20030
(21) 220-8817
Web site: www.orbita.starmedia.com/via/~caritur

Niteroi

Community Organisations

Centro Israelita
Rua Visconde do Uruguai 255,24030

Sociedade Hebraica
Rua Alvares de Azevedo 185, Icarai 24220

Petropolis

Religious Organisations

Machane Israel Yeshiva
Rua Duarte de Silveira 1246 25600 (242) 45-4952

Synagogues

Sinagoga Israelita Brasileira
Rua Aureliano Coutinho 48 25600

Rio Grande do Sul

Erechim

Synagogues

Av. Pedro Pinto de Souza 131

Passo Fundo

Synagogues

Rua General Osório 1049

Pelotas

Synagogues

Rua Santos Dumont 303

Porto Alegre

Butchers

Kosher Butcher
Rua Fernandes Vieira 518 (51) 250-441

Cultural Organisations

Instituto Cultural Judaico Marc Chagall - Projeto Memoria
Rua Dom Pedro II, 1220/sala 216 (51) 343-5748

Mikvaot

Rua Francisco Ferrer 170

Museums

Museu Judaico
Rua João Telles 329 (51) 226-0379

Religious Organisations

City Rabbinate
Rua Henrique Dias 73 (51) 219-649

Synagogues

Liberal

SIBRA,
Mariante 772 (51) 331-8133
Services on Shabbat only.

Orthodox

Beit Chabad,
Rua Felipe Camarão 748 (51) 330-7078
Daily services.

Centro Israelita Porto Alegrense
Rua Henrique Dias 73 (51) 228-1935
Daily services.

Linath Ha-Tzedek
Rua Bento Figueredo 55 (51) 332-1065
Daily services.

Poilisher Farband
Rua João Telles 329 (51) 226-0379
Daily services.

União Israelita Porto Algrense
Rua Dr Barros Cassal 750 (51) 311-6515
Fax: (51) 311-5886
Daily services.

Sephardi

Centro Hebraico Riograndense
Rua Cel. Machado 1008
Services on Shabbat only.

São Paulo

Campinas

Synagogues

Beth Yacob Campinas
Rua Barreto Leme 1203 (19) 231-4908

Guaruja

Synagogues

Beit Yaacov,
Av. Leomil 628 (13) 387-2033
Neve Itzhak,
Av. Leomil 950 (13) 386-3167

Mogi Das Cruzes

Community Organisations

Jewish Society
Rua Dep. Deodato Wertheimer 421 (11) 469-2505

São Jose dos Campos

Synagogues

Beit Chabad,
Rua Republica do Ira 91 (11) 3064-6322

Santo Andre

Synagogues

Beit Chabad,
Rua 11 de Junho 172 (11) 449-1568

Santos

Community Organisations

Club,
Rua Cons. Neblas 254 (132) 32-9016

Synagogues

Sinagoga Beit Jacob
Rua Campos Sales 137
Beit Sion,
Rua Borges 264

São Caetano do Sul

Synagogues

Sociedade Religiosa S. Caetano do Sul
Rua Para 67 (11) 442-3514

São Paulo

Bakeries

Buffet Mazal Tov
Rua Peixoto Gomide 1724 (11) 883-7614
Fax: (11) 3064-5208

Matok Bakery,
Rua P. João Manoel 709 (11) 3064-6668
Supervision: Rabbi I. Dichi.
Matok Bakery, Al. Barros 921 (11) 66-7514
Supervision: Rabbi I. Dichi.

Booksellers

Livraria Sêfer
Alameda Barros, 893 01232-001 (11) 3826-1366
Fax: (11) 3826-4508
Email: sefer@sefer.com.br
Web site: www.sefer.com.br
Bookseller and Judaica.

Butchers

Casa de Carnes Casher
Rua Fortunato 241 (11) 221-2240
Under supervision of Rabbi Elyahu B. Valt.
Mehadrin,
Rua S. Vicente de Paulo (11) 67-9090
Under supervision of Rabbi M.A. Iliovitz.
Mehadrin, Rua Prates 689 (11) 228-1771
Under supervision of Rabbi M.A. Iliovitz.

Embassy

Consul General of Israel
Rua Luis Coelho 308, 7th Floor
(11) 257-2111; 257-2814

Groceries

All Kosher,
Rua Albuquerque Lins 1170 (11) 825-1131
Amazonas,
Rua Amazonas 91 (11) 229-1336
Chazak,
Rua Afonsa Pena 348a (11) 229-5607
Chazak,
Rua Haddock Lobo 1002 (11) 3068-9093
Dom Bosco,
Rua Guarani 114 (11) 228-6105
Mazal Tov,
Rua Peixoto Gomide 1724 (11) 883-7614
Fax: (11) 3064-5208

Sta. Luzia,
Al. Lorena 1471 (11) 883-5844
Look for kosher section.
Zilanna,
Rua Itambé 506 (11) 257-8671

Media

Magazines

Morasha Magazine
Rua Dr Veiga Filho 547,
Higienopolis 01229-000 (11) 3662-2154
Fax: (11) 3030-5630
Email: morasha@uol.com.br
Web site: www.morasha.com

Newspapers

O Hebreu
Rua Cunha Gago 158 05421-000
(11) 3819-1616
Fax: (11) 3819-1616
Email: ohebrew@ohebrew.com.br
Web site: www.communidadejudaica.com/ohebrew
Monthly.

Resenha Judaica
Rua Antonio Carlos 582/5 (11) 255-8794
Weekly.

Tribuna Judaica
Rua Tanabi 299 05002-010
(11) 3871-3234/3873-3020/3862-9074
Fax: (11) 3871-3234
Email: tjudaica@uol.com.br
Weekly.

Mikvaot

Congregacao Mekor Haim
Rua Sao Vicente de Paulo 276 01229-010
(11) 3662-6238; 3826-7699
Fax: (11) 3666-6960
Email: revista_nascente@hotmail.com
Rua Chabad 60 01417-030
Email: chabad@chabad.org.br

Micre Taharat Menachem - Perdizes
Rua Dr. Manoel Maria Tourinho 261
(11) 3865-0615
By appointment only.

Orthodox

Beit Yaacov Synagogue
Rua Dr Veiga Filho 547,
Higienopolis 01229-000 (11) 3662-2154
Fax: (11) 3662-2154
Email: morasha@uol.com.br

Congregacao Monte Sinai
Rua Piaui 624, Higienopolis 01241-000
(11) 3824-9229
Fax: (11) 3824-9229
Email: cmsinai@sanet.com.br

Religious Organisations

Centro Judaico Religioso de Sao Paulo
(11) 220-5642
Office hours: 9 am to 1 pm weekdays.

Comunidade Israelita Ortodoxa de Sao Paulo
Kehilat Hacharedim, Rua Haddock Lobo 1091
(11) 282-1562; 852-9710
This community centre has two synagogues.

Restaurants

Meat

Hebraica Kosher Restaurant
Rua Hungria 1000
(11) 815-6788; 815-6980; 818-8831
Fax: (11) 815-6980
Supervision: Rabbi Elyahu B. Valt.
Buffet Mosaico inside the Hebraica São Paulo club.
Closed Mondays, open Saturday night 1 1/2 hours after Shabbat.

Kosher Center
Rua Corrèa de Melo 68 01123-020 (11) 223-1175
Fax: (11) 223-3721
Supervision: Rabbi M.A. Iliovitch Shlita of Kehal Hachareidim.
Restaurant and Bakery. Hours: Sun 9.00 am-4.00 pm. Mon-Thurs 8.00 am-6.00 pm. Fri 7.30 am-3.00 pm

Restaurant Beit Chinuch
Rua P. João Manoel 727 (11) 280-5111
Fax: (11) 280-4553
Email: lavne@uninet.com.br
Phone for directions and times.

Dairy

Kosher Pizza,
Rua padre Joao Manoel 881 (11) 3064-9022

Matok,
Av. Higienopolis 618 (11) 3823-2935
Third floor of Higienopolis Shopping Mall.

Meat

Bero,
Rua Pelxoto Gomide 2020 (11) 3086-2808
Reservations are preferred

Synagogues

Congregacao Mekor Haim
Rua Sao Vicente de Paulo 276 01229-010
(11) 3826-7699
Fax: (11) 3666-6960
Email: revista_nascente@hotmail.com

Beit Chabad Perdizes
Rua Dr. Manoel Maria Tourinho 261
(11) 3865-0615
By appointment only.

Brazil / São Paulo

Hasidic

Kehal Chassidim
Rua Mamore 597 (11) 224-0278

Hungarian

Adas Yereim, Rua Talmud Tora 86 (11) 282-1562; 852-9710

Liberal

Congregacao Israelita Paulista
Rua Antonio Carlos 653 (11) 256-7811
Fax: (11) 257-1446
Email: scrtgeral@dialdata.com.br
Web site: www.cip.sp.com.br

Orthodox

Beit Chabad Central
Rua Dr. Melo Alves, 580 01417-010
(11) 3060-9777
Fax: (11) 3060-9778
Email: chabad@chabad.org.br
Web site: www.chabad.org.br

Beit Itzchak
Rua Haddock Lobo 1279 (11) 3062-9710
Fax: (11) 881-3064, 0302

Beit Yaacov
Rua Dr Veiga Filho 547,
Higienopolis 01229-000 (11) 3662-2154
Fax: (11) 3662-2154
Email: morasha@uol.com.br

Kehal Machzikei Hadat
Rua Padre Joao Manuel 727 (11) 280-5111

Sinagoga Israelita Paulista – Beit Chabad
Rua Augusta 259 01305-000 (11) 258-7173

Progressive

Comunidade Shalom
Rua Coronel Joaquim Ferreira Lobo
195 04544-150 (11) 829-1477
Fax: (11) 828-9177

Sephardi

Templo Israelita Brasileiro Ohel Yaacov
Rua Abolicao 457 (11) 606-9982
Fax: (11) 227-6793

Travel Agencies

Carmel Tur, Rua Xavier de Toledo 121/10
(11) 257-2244

Sharontur,
Rua de Graca 235 (11) 223-8388
Fax: (11) 220 5036
Email: sharontur@sharontur.com.br
Web site: sharontur.com.br
Open: 8.00 am-6.00 pm. Closed Shabat (Saturday) & Sunday. International & domestic tickets. Car rental, exchange, hotel reservations. Languages spoken: English, Hebrew, Spanish. Contact person: Mr Dov Smaletz

Vertice,
Rua Sao Bento 545/10 (11) 3115-1970
Fax: (11) 3115-1970
Email: turismo@vertice.com.br

Sorocaba

Synagogues

Community Centre
Rua Dom Pedro II 56 (11) 31-3168

Bulgaria

Dating back to the Byzantine conquest, the community in Bulgaria was established by Greek Jews in Serdica (the capital of which is Sofia). The Jewish community grew when the Bulgarian state was founded in 681. Czar Ivan Alexander (1331-71) had a Jewish wife (who converted to Christianity).

The community has included eminent rabbinic commentators, such as Rabbi Dosa Ajevani and Joseph Caro, the codifier of the 'Shulchan Aruch', who escaped to Bulgaria after the expulsion from Spain. The various Jewish groups joined to form a unified Sephardi community in the late seventeenth century.

About 50,000 Jews lived in Bulgaria in 1939. Bulgaria joined the War on the side of Germany but despite much pressure from the Nazis, the government and general population refused to allow Bulgarian Jews to be deported. Only Jews from Macedonia and Thrace, then occupied by Bulgaria, were deported. Despite being saved, most of the community emigrated to Israel after the War. The ten per cent who remained were then under the control of the communists and had little contact with the outside world.

Since the fall of communism, the community has been reconstituted and now has synagogues in Sofia and Plovdiv. The community is ageing, although 100 children attend a Sunday school run by the Shalom Organisation, the central Jewish organisation for Bulgaria.

GMT + 2 hours — Total Population 8,225,000
Country calling code (359) — Jewish Population 3,000
Emergency Telephone (Police - 166) (Fire - 160) (Ambulance - 150) — Electricity voltage 220

Pazardjik

Community Organisations

Community Centre
Asson Zlatarov St. 26 (34) 28-364

Plovdiv

Libraries

Library and House of Culture
Vladimir Zaimov St. 20 (32) 761-376

Synagogues

Tsar Kalojan St. 15
In the courtyard of a large apartment complex.

Rousse

Synagogues

Community Centre
Ivan Vazov Sq. 4 (82) 270-540

Sofia

About half of Bulgarian Jewry lives in Sofia. The Great Synagogue of 1878 ranks among the largest of Sephardi synagogues.

Cemeteries

Jewish Cemetery
Orlandovtzi suburb
Take a tram (Nos 2, 10 or 14) to the last stop for this large Jewish cemetery.

Community Organisations

Social & Cultural Organisation of Bulgarian Jews
Shalom, Alexander Stambolisky St. 50 (2) 870-163
Publishes a periodical 'Evreiski Vesti' and a yearbook. It also maintains a museum devoted to "The Rescue of Bulgarian Jews, 1941–1944". At the same address are the offices of El Al, the Joint and the Jewish Agency.

Embassy

Embassy of Israel
1 Bulgaria Sq. NDK, 7th floor (2) 951-5029
Fax: (2) 952-1101

Religious Organisations

Central Jewish Religious Council
Ekzarh Josef St. 16 (2) 983-1273
Fax: (2) 985-5085
Email: isaksaiu@mail.orbitel.bg

Synagogues

Sofia Central Synagogue
Ekzarh Josef St. 16 (2) 983-1273
Fax: (2) 985-5085
Email: isaksaiu@mail.orbitel.bg
Adjacent to the synagogue is a museum dedicated to the history of Bulgarian Jewry.

Canada

The Jewish settlement of Canada began with the British expansion into Canada. In 1760, the Shearith Israel Synagogue was founded in Montreal and in 1832 Jews received full civil rights. In the 1850s the community began to spread from Montreal to Toronto and Hamilton.

The community grew throughout the early twentieth century, from 16,000 in 1900 to 126,000 in 1921. After the Second World War, Jewish immigration increased and by 1961 the population was 260,000.

The headquarters of the Canadian Jewish Congress is in Montreal. This is the main national organisation for Canadian Jewry, and the community is provided with a full range of services, with Jewish schools, yeshivot, newspapers and the unique (in the Americas) Montreal Jewish Library. There are also several kosher restaurants.

GMT - 3 to 8 hours — Total Population 31,147,000
Country calling code (1) — Jewish Population 362,000
Emergency Telephone (Police, Fire and Ambulance - 911) In remote areas, calls have to be made via the operator. — Electricity voltage 110

Alberta

Calgary

Bakeries

Susan's Kosher Bakery
131, 2515 - 90th Av. SW (403) 238-5300
Fax: (403) 238-3023
Supervision: Calgary Kosher.
Hours of operation: Sunday 10 am to 2 pm, Tuesday to Thursday 9 am to 6 pm, Friday 8 am to 4 pm (winter 8 am to 2 pm). Closed Mondays and Shabbat.

Delicatessens

Izzy's Kosher Meat Market
2515 90th Av. S.W. (403) 251-2552

Media

Newspapers

Jewish Free Press
8411 Elbow Dr. SW T2V 1K8 (403) 252-9423
Fax: (403) 255-5640
Email: jewishfp@cadvision.com

Religious Organisations

Calgary Rabbinical Council
(403) 253-8600
Fax: (403) 253-7915

Representative Organisations

B'nai Brith Canada
Western Region, 1607 90 Av. S.W. T2V 4V7
(403) 258 1848
Fax: (403) 258 1815

Calgary Jewish Community Council
1607 90th Av. S.W. (403) 253-8600
Fax: (403) 253-7915
Email: cjcc@jewish-calgary.com
Web site: www.jewish-calgary.com
The Council issues a booklet "Keeping Kosher in Calgary".

Restaurants

Karen's Cafe, Calgary Jewish Centre,
1607 90th Av. S.W. (403) 255-5311
Hours:Monday to Thursday, 10 am to 7 pm; Friday, 10 am to 1 pm. Closed on Sunday

Synagogues

Conservative

Beth Tzedec
1325 Glenmore Trail S.W.
T2V 4Y8 (403) 252-8319
Email: info@bethtzedec.ab.ca

Orthodox

Congregation House of Jacob-Mikveh Israel
1613-92nd Av., Jerusalem Rd. SW T2V 5C9
(403) 259-3230
Fax: (403) 259-3240
Email: hojmi@cadvision.com
Web site: www.cadivision.com/hojmi

Reform

Temple B'nai Tikvah
Calgary Jewish Centre, 1607
90th Av. S.W. T2V 4V7 (403) 252-1654
Fax: (403) 252-1709
Email: temple@cadvision.com

Edmonton

Media

Newspapers

Edmonton Jewish Life
10342 107th St. T5J 1K2 (780) 488-7276
Fax: (780) 487-4342
Email: ejlife@powersurfr.com

Edmonton Jewish News
#330, 10036 Jasper Av. T5J 2W2 (780) 421-7966
Fax: (780) 424-3951

Representative Organisations

Edmonton Jewish Federation
7200 156th St. T5R 1X3 (780) 487-0585
Fax: (780) 481-1854
Email: edjfed@netcom.ca
Contact Gayle Tallman, Exec. Director, for additional information.

Restaurants

Dairy

King David Pizza
West Edmonton Mall (780) 486-9020

Synagogues

Conservative

Beth Shalom
11916 Jasper Av. T5K 0N9 (780) 488-6333
Fax: (780) 488-6259
Email: bshalom2@telusplanet.net

Orthodox

Beth Israel
131 Wolf Willow Road T5T 7T7 (780) 482-2840
Fax: (780) 482-2470
Email: edbeth@telusplanet.net

Chabad Lubavitch
Westridge Shopping Centre (780) 486 7244
Fax: (780) 486 7243

Reform

Temple Beth Ora
7200 156th St. T5R 1X3 (780) 487-4817
Fax: (780) 481-1854
Email: bethora@planet.eon.net

Lethbridge

Synagogues

Orthodox

Beth Israel
914 15th Street South T1J 3A5 (403) 327-8621

British Columbia

Kelowna

Synagogues

Traditional

Beth Shalom Sanctuary
OJCC, 102-1 North Glenmore Road
V1V 2E2 (250) 862-2305
Fax: (250) 862-2365
Email: shalom@ojcc.net
Web site: www.ojcc.net
Shabbat services last Saturday of the month, 9.30 am.

Richmond

Bakeries

Garden City Bakery
#360-9100 Blundell Road (604) 244-7888
Supervision: Orthodox Rabbinical Council of British Columbia.

Kashrut Information

Orthodox Rabbinical Council of British Columbia
8080 Francis Road V6Y 1A4 (604) 275-0042
Fax: (604) 277-2225
Email: bckosher@direct.ca
Kashrut Director, Rabbi A. Feigelstock; Kashrut Administrator, Rabbi Levy Teitlebaum.

Synagogues

Conservative

Beth Tikvah
9711 Geal Road V7E 1R4 (604) 271-6262
Friday, 8 pm; Shabbat, 9.30 am. Wheelchair access.

Orthodox

Eitz Chaim
8080 Frances Road V6Y 1A4 (604) 275-0007
Fax: (604) 277-2225
Daily, 7 am and sunset; Shabbat, 9 am and sunset; Sunday, 9 am. Wheelchair access.

Surrey – White Rock

Community Organisations

White Rock/South Surrey Jewish Community Centre
PO Box 75186 V4A (604) 541-9995
Monthly Shabbat services. Wheelchair access.

Synagogues

Hasidic

The Centre for Judaism of the Lower Fraser Valley
2351 128th Street (604) 541-4111
Email: shfy@aol.com
Weekly Shabbat services. Wheelchair access.

Canada / British Columbia

Vancouver

Bed & Breakfasts

Mrs Levin's Kosher Bed & Breakfast
Apt 101, 2772 Spruce V6H 2R2 (604) 738-2457
Shulamit Mass
5434 Manson Street V5Z 3H1 (604) 266-8965

Cafeteria

Dairy

Cafe Sabra Too (Jewish Community Centre)
950 West 41st Avenue V5Z 2N7 (604) 257-5111
Supervision: Orthodox Rabbinical Council of British Columbia.
Take-out, eat-in and catering. Dairy, pareve (meat is take-out only). Hours: Monday to Thursday, 8.30 am to 8 pm; Friday, 8.30 am to 2 pm; Sunday, 10 am to 6.30 pm.

Contact Information

Jewish Federation of Greater Vancouver
950 West 41st Avenue, Suite 200
V5Z 2N7 (604) 257-5100
Fax: (604) 257-5119
Email: shalom_vancouver@ultranet.ca
Web site: www.shalomvancouver.org
Executive Director Daniella Givon.
Shalom BC
950 West 41st Avenue V5Z 2N7 (604) 257-5111
Fax: (604) 257-5119
Email: info@shalombc.org
Web site: www.shalombc.org
Jewish Information & Welcome Service, and Volunteer Centre. Publishes a "Guide to Jewish Life in British Columbia". Hours: Monday to Friday 10 am to 2 pm. Visitors welcome.

Media

Newspapers

Western Jewish Bulletin
301, 68 East 2nd Avenue V5T 1B1 (604) 689-1520
Fax: (604) 689-1525

Restaurants

Dairy

Chagall's @ JCC
950 West 41st Avenue (604) 263-7507
Fax: (604) 263-7507
Supervision: British Columbia Kosher Council.
Deliveries to Hotels - Pareve available on request.
Dairy, cafeteria style café and restaurant.
Sabra Kosher Bakery, Restaurant and Grocery
3844 Oak Street V6H 2M5 (604) 733-4912
Fax: (604) 733-4911
Supervision: Orthodox Rabbinical Council of British Columbia.
Take-out, eat-in and catering. Dairy, pareve (meat is take-out only). Hours: Monday to Thursday, 8:30 am to 8 pm; Friday, 8:30 am to 2 pm; Sunday, 10 am to 6:30 pm.
Surat Sweet,
1938 West 4th Avenue (604) 733-7363
Indian vegetarian - Gujarati style.

Meat

Omnitsky Kosher B.C.
5866 Cambie Street (604) 321-1818
Fax: (604) 321-1817
Email: omnitskykosher@aol.com
Web site: www.escape.ca/omnitsky.com
Supervision: Orthodox Rabbinical Council of British Columbia.
Fresh meats, poultry. Manufacturers of all beef delicatessen products under B.C.K.

Synagogues

Conservative

Beth Israel
4350 Oak Street V6H 2N4 (604) 731-1346
Fax: (604) 731-4989
Daily, 8 am (public holidays, 9 am) and 6 pm; Friday, 8:15 pm; Shabbat, 9:15 am and 6 pm; Sunday, 9 am and 6 pm. Wheelchair access.
Congregation Har El
North Shore Jewish Community Centre,
1305 Taylor Way, West Vancouver V7T 2Y7
(604) 925-6488
Fax: (604) 922-8245
Friday, 7 pm; Shabbat, 10 am (Seasonal). Visitors welcome.

Hasidic

Chabad Richmond
200-4775 Blundell Road, Richmond
Email: chabad@axionet.com
Chabad-Lubavitch
5435 Baillie Street V5Z 3M6 (604) 266-1313
Fax: (604) 263-7934
Email: chabadbc@axionet.com
Daily, 7 am and sunset; Shabbat, 10 am; Sunday, 9 am. Wheelchair access.

Jewish Renewal

Or Shalom
710 East 10th Avenue V5T 2A7 (604) 872-1614
Fax: (604) 872-4406
Email: orshalom@telus.net
Web site: www.orshalom.bc.ca
Family Kabbalat Shabbat and potluck dinner monthly; Shabbat 10 am. Wheelchair access.

Orthodox

Louis Brier Home
1055 West 41st Avenue V6M 1W9 (604) 261-9376
Daily mincha, 4.30 pm; Friday, 4.15 pm; Shabbat, 9 am. Wheelchair access.

Schara Tzedeck
3476 Oak Street V6H 2L8 (604) 736-7307
Fax: (604) 730-1621
Monday and Thursday, 7 am; Tuesday, Wednesday and Friday, 7.15 am; weekdays, sunset; Friday, 7.30 pm; Shabbat, 9 am and half hour before sunset; Sunday, 8.30 am.

Reform

Temple Shalom
7190 Oak Street V6P 3Z9 (604) 266-1957
Fax: (604) 266-7121
Monday and Wednesday, 7.15 am; Friday, 8.15 pm; Shabbat, 10 am. Also has a gift shop.

Sephardi Orthodox

Beth Hamidrash
3231 Heather Street V5Z 3K4
(604) 872-4222; 873-2371
Daily, 7 am; Shabbat, 9 am; Sunday and public holidays, 8.30 am; Friday, 5 pm; Shabbat, sunset.

Traditional

Burquest Jewish Community
720 6th St., PO Box 187, New Westminster
BC V3L 3C5 (604) 552-7221
Fax: (604) 552-7201
Email: info@burquest.org
Web site: www.burquest.org
Oneg Shabbat services second Friday of each month, 8 pm. Wheelchair access. Mailing address: PO Box 52552, 1136-2929 Barnet Hwy, Coquitlam, BC V3B 7J4, Canada.

Shaarey Tefilah
785 West 16th Avenue (604) 873-2700
Friday evening, call for time; Shabbat and Sunday, 9 am. Wheelchair access.

Victoria

Community Organisations

Victoria Jewish Community Centre
3636 Shelbourne Street (250) 477-7184
Fax: (250) 477-6283

Synagogues

Conservative

Emanu-El
1461 Blanshard V8W 2J3 (250) 382-0615
Thursday, 7 am; Shabbat, 9 am. Wheelchair access.

West Vancouver

Synagogues

Orthodox

Torat Hayim Community
491 Eastcot Road (604) 984-4168
Fax: (604) 984-4168
Email: info@hayim.com
Shabbat: 10.30 am followed by Kiddush

Manitoba

Winnipeg

Bakeries

City Bread
238 Dufferin Avenue R2W 2X6 (204) 586-8409

Goodies' Bake Shop
2 Donald Street R3L 0K5 (204) 489-5526

Gunn's
247 Selkirk Avenue R2W 2L5 (204) 586-6150

Butchers

Omnitsky's
1428 Main Street R2W 3V4 (204) 586-8271

Tuxedo Quality Foods
1853 Grant Avenue R3N 1Z2 (204) 987-3830
Frozen only

Communal Organisation

Asper Jewish Community Campus
C300 - 123 Doncaster Street R3N 1B2
(204) 477-7400
Fax: (204) 477-7405
Email: info@jewishwinnipeg.org
Web site: www.jewishwinnipeg.org
Home to Winnipeg Jewish Theatre, Canadian Jewish Congress and Jewish Heritage Centre.

Groceries

Bathurst Street Market
1570 Main Street R2W 5J8 (204) 338-4911

Canada / Manitoba

Media

Newspapers

Jewish Post & News
117 Hutchings Street R2X 2V4 (204) 694-3332
Fax: (204) 694-3916
Weekly English language newspaper.

Mikvaot

Community Mikvah
123 Doncaster Street R3N 2B1 (204) 477-7445
Mikva Chabad-Lubavitch
455 Hartford Avenue R2V 0W9 (204) 339-4761
Fax: (204) 586-0487
Email: aaltein@mbnet.mb.ca
Mailing address: 2095 Sinclair Street, Wpg.MB R2V 3K2.

Restaurants

Asper Jewish Community Campus Restaurant
123 Doncaster Street R3N 2B2 (204) 477-7418
Fax: (204) 477-7507

Bathurst Downstairs Deli
1570 Main Steet R2W 5J8 (204) 338-4911

Synagogues

Egalitarian Conservative

Beth Israel
1007 Sinclair Street R2V 3J5 (204) 582-2353
Congregation Shaarey Zedek
561 Wellington Crescent R3M 0A5 (204) 452-3711

Orthodox

Chevra Mishnayes
700 Jefferson Avenue R2V OP6 (204) 338-8503

Lubavitch Centre
2095 Sinclair Street R2V 3K2 (204) 339-8737

New Brunswick

Fredericton

Synagogues

Sgoolai Israel
Westmorland Street E3B 3L7 (506) 454-9698
Fax: (506) 452-8889
Email: samuels@unb.ca
For information on availability of kosher food, call Rabbi Yochanan Samuels: (506) 454-2717.

Moncton

Synagogues

Tiferes Israel
56 Steadman Street E1C 8L9 (506) 858-0258
Fax: (506) 858-0259
Email: tifisrl@nbnet.nb.ca
Mikva on premises.

Saint John

Museums

Saint John Jewish Historical Museum
29 Wellington Row E2L 3H4 (506) 633-1833
Fax: (506) 642-9926
Email: sjjhm@nbnet.nb.ca
Web site: www.sjjhm.tripod.com
May-mid Octoberr 10 am to 4 pm Monday to Friday. Also, during July and August, Sunday 1 pm to 4 pm or by appointment. This is the only Jewish museum in the Atlantic Provinces of Canada. There are eight display areas as well as library and archives. Guided tours available.

Synagogues

Conservative

Shaarei Zedek
76 Carleton Street E2L 2Z4 (506) 657-4790
Community centre on premises.

Newfoundland

Hebrew Congregation of Newfoundland & Labrador (Beth El)
Elizabeth and Downing Avenues A1C 5L4
(709) 737-6548
Fax: (709) 737-6995
Email: mpaul@mun.ca
Mailing address: P O Box 724, St. John's A1C 5L4, NF, Canada.

Nova Scotia

Glace Bay

Synagogues

Orthodox

1 Prince Street B1A 3C8 (902) 849-8605

Halifax

Community Organisations

Atlantic Jewish Council
5670 Spring Garden Road, Suite 508 B3J 1H6
(902) 422-7491
Fax: (902) 425-3722
Email: jgoldberg@theajc.ns.ca
Web site: www.theajc.ns.ca
Covers Nova Scotia, New Brunswick, Price Edward Island, Newfoundland and Halifax. Also at this address: Canadian Jewish Congress, Atlantic Region, Canadian Zionist Federation, United Jewish Appeal, Canadian Young Judea, Hadassah, Jewish National Fund, Atlantic Provinces Jewish Student Federation, Camp Kadimah, Regional Chaplaincy.

Media

Newspapers

Shalom Magazine
5675 Spring Garden Road, Suite 800 B3J 1H1
(902) 422-7491
Fax: (902) 425-3722
Email: jgoldberg@theajc.ns.ca

Synagogues

Conservative

Shaar Shalom
1981 Oxford Street B3H 4A4 (902) 423-5848
Fax: (902) 422-2580
Email: shaar.shalom@ns.sympatico.ca

Orthodox

Beth Israel
1480 Oxford Street B3H 3Y8 (902) 422-1301
Mikva on premises.

Sydney

Synagogues

Conservative

Temple Sons of Israel
P.O. Box 311, Whitney Avenue B1P 6H2
(902) 564-4650

Yarmouth

Contact Information

R & V Indiq
13 Parade Street B5A 3A5
Will be happy to provide details of the local Jewish community.

Ontario

Belleville

Synagogues

Conservative

Sons of Jacob
211 Victoria Avenue K8N 2C2 (613) 962-1433

Brantford

Synagogues

Orthodox

Beth David
50 Waterloo Street N3T 3R8 (519) 752-8950

Chatham

Synagogues

Conservative

Children of Jacob
29 Water Street N7M 3H4 (519) 352-3544

Cornwall

Synagogues

Beth-El
321 Amelia Street K6H 3P4 (613) 932-6373

Guelph

Synagogues

Traditional

Beth Isaiah
47 Surrey Street W. N1H 3R5 (519) 836-4338
Email: cgdk@aol.com
Full line of Kosher products at Ultra-519-763-3827.

Hamilton

Butchers

Hamilton Kosher Meats
889 King Street West L8S 1K5

Delicatessens

Westdale Deli
893 King Street West L8S 1K5 (905) 529-2605
Fax: (905) 529-2605

Media

Newspapers

Hamilton Jewish News
P.O. Box 7528, Ancaster L9G 3N6 (905) 648-0605
Fax: (905) 648-8388

Canada / Ontario

Representative Organisations

Hamilton Jewish Federation
1030 Lower Lions Club Road, Ancaster
L9G 3N6 (905) 648-0605
Fax: (905) 648-8350
Email: hamujajf@interlynx.net

Synagogues

Conservative

Beth Jacob
375 Aberdeen Avenue L8P 2R7 (905) 522-1351

Orthodox

Adas Israel
125 Cline Avenue S. L8S 1X2 (905) 528-0039
Fax: (905) 528-7497

Reform

Anshe Sholom
215 Cline Avenue N. L8S 4A1 (905) 528-0121
Fax: (905) 528-2994

Kingston

Community Organisations

B'nai B'rith Hillel Foundation
26 Barrie Street (613) 542-1120

Synagogues

Orthodox

Beth Israel
116 Centre Street K7L 4E6 (613) 542-5012
Fax: (613) 542-9071
Email: bethisrael@kingston.net

Reform

Temple Iyr Hamelech
331 Union Street West K7L 2R3 (613) 789-7022

Kitchener

Synagogues

Temple Shalom
116 Queen Street North N2H 2H7 (519) 743-0401

Traditional

Beth Jacob
161 Stirling Avenue South N2G 3N8 (519) 743-8422

London

Community Organisations

London Jewish Federation
536 Huron Street N5Y 4J5 (519) 673-3310
Email: admin@ljf.on.ca

There are no kosher establishments, but kosher frozen meat, prepared foods and select groceries are available at the local A&P, IGA North London market, and Loblaws Stores. Communal inquiries to Executive Director at the above number.

Media

Newspapers

London Jewish Community News
536 Huron Street N5Y 4J5 (519) 673-3310
Fax: (519) 673-1161
Email: susan.merskey@sympatico.ca

Synagogues

Conservative

Congregation Or Shalom
534 Huron Street N5Y 4J5 (519) 438-3081
Fax: (519) 439-2994

Orthodox

Congregation Beth Tefilah
1210 Adelaide Street North N5Y 4T6
(519) 433-7081
Fax: (519) 433-0616
Email: beth_tefilah@canada.com
Web site: www.execulink.com/~cbt/

Mikva on premises.

Reform

Temple Israel
651 Windermere Road N5X 2P1 (519) 858-4400
Fax: (519) 858-2070
Email: jwitts@julian.uwo.ca

Mississauga

Synagogues

Solel Congregation
2399 Folkway Drive L5L 2M6 (905) 820-5915
Fax: (905) 820-1956

Niagara Falls

Synagogues

Conservative

B'nai Jacob
5328 Ferry Street L2G 1R7 (416) 354-3934

North Bay

Synagogues

Orthodox

Sons of Jacob
302 McIntyre Street West P1B 2Z1 (705) 497-9288
Fax: (705) 497-9812
Email: martybrown@gosympatico.ca
Friday evening services.

Oakville

Synagogues

Reform

Shaarei-Beth El
186 Morrison Road L6J 4J4 (905) 849-6000
Fax: (905) 849-1134
Email: sbe@idirect.com
Web site: www.webhome.idirect.com/~sbe

Oshawa

Synagogues

Orthodox

Beth Zion
144 King Street East L1H 1B6 (905) 723-2353

Ottawa

Ottawa is the capital of Canada and its fourth largest city. The first Jewish settler came in 1858 when Ottawa was still known as Bytown. Ottawa has always been strongly traditional and has a growing community presently numbering around 13,000.

Bakeries

Rideau Bakery
1666 Bank St (613) 737-3355
Rideau Bakery
384 Rideau St (613) 234-1019

Embassy

Embassy of Israel
Suite 1005, 50 O'Connor Street
K1P 6L2 (613) 567-6450
Fax: (613) 237-8865

Religious Organisations

Vaad Ha'ir (Jewish Community Council)
151 Chapel Street K1N 7Y2 (613) 232-7306
Fax: (613) 563-4593
Vaad Hakashruth located here for all kashrut information.

Representative Organisations

Canadian Jewish Congress National Office
100 Sparks Street, Suite 650 K1P 5B7
(613) 233-8703
Fax: (613) 233-8748
Email: canadianjewishcongress@cjc.ca
Web site: www.cjc.ca
Publishes the "National Synagogue Directory". Contact to find out information on synagogues in the city to which you are travelling.

Restaurants

Dairy

Viva's,
Solway JCC, 21 Nadolny Sachs Private
(613) 798-9818

Synagogues

Conservative

Agudath Israel
1400 Coldrey Avenue K12 7P9 (613) 728-3501
Fax: (613) 728-4468

Orthodox

Beth Shalom Congregation
151 Chapel Street K1N 7Y2 (613) 789-3501
Beth Shalom West
15 Chartwell Avenue K2G 4K3 (613) 723-1800
Machzikei Hadas
2310 Virginia Drive K1H 6S2 (613) 521-9700

Reform

Temple Israel
1301 Prince of Wales Drive K2C 1N2
(613) 224-1802

Owen Sound

Synagogues

Conservative

Beth Ezekiel
3531 Bay Shore Road N4K 5N3 (519) 376-8774

Pembroke

Synagogues

Beth Israel
322 William Street K8A 1P3 (613) 732-7811

Peterborough

Synagogues

Conservative

Beth Israel, Waller Street (705) 745-8398

Canada / Ontario

Richmond Hill

Synagogues

Beth Rayim
9711 Bayview Avenue L4C 9X7 (905) 770-7639
The Country Shul
Carville Road and Bathurst Street (905) 770-4191

St Catharine's

Community Organisations

Community Centre
Newman Memorial Building (416) 685-6767

Synagogues

Reform

Temple Tikvah
83 Church Street, PO Box 484
L2R 3C7 (416) 682-4191

Traditional

B'nai Israel
190 Church Street L2R 4C4 (416) 685-6767
Fax: (416) 685-3100

Sudbury

Synagogues

Orthodox

Shaar Hashomayim
158 John Street P3E 1P4 (705) 673-0831

Thornhill

Booksellers

Israel's Judaica Centre
441 Clark Avenue West L47 6W7 (905) 881-1010
Fax: (905) 881-1016
Email: contact@israelsjudaica.com
Web site: www.israel.judaica.com

Also sells gifts.

Matana Judaica
248 Steeles Avenue West, #6 L4J 1A1
(905) 731-6543
Fax: (905) 882-6196

Also sells gifts.

Delicatessens

Marky's Delicatessen North
7330 Yonge Street L4J 1V8 (905) 731-4800
Wok'n'Deli
441 Clarke Avenue West L4J 6W7 (905) 882-0809

Restaurants

Dairy

My Zaidy's Pizza
441 Clark Avenue West L4J 6W8 (905) 731-3029

Meat

Miami Grill, 441 Clark Avenue (905) 709-0096
Supervision: COR.
Taste of Tikvah
7700 Bathurst Street (905) 771-0699
Supervision: COR.

Thunder Bay

Synagogues

Orthodox

Shaarey Shomayim
627 Grey Street P7E 2E4 (807) 622-4867
Email: phlab@baynet.net

Toronto

There have been one and a half centuries of organised Jewish life in Toronto since its start in 1849. The Jewish population increased significantly during the 1980s, and now Toronto is home to almost half of Canada's Jews. There is a good range of Jewish facilities in the city.

Bakeries

Bagels Galore
First Canadian Place M5X 1E1 (905) 363-4233
Carmel Bakery
3856 Bathurst Street (905) 633-5315
Dairy Treats Bakery
3522 Bathurst Street (416) 787-0309
Fax: (416) 787-1935

Richman's Kosher Bakery
4119 Bathurst Street (416) 636-9710
Fax: (416) 636-9614

Booksellers

Israel's Judaica Centre
897 Eglinton Avenue West
M6C 2C1 (905) 256-2858
Email: contact@israelsjudaica.com
Web site: www.israel.judaica.com
Negev Importing Co Ltd
3509 Bathurst Street M6A 2C5
(905) 781-9356 (Toll free: 1-888-618-9356)
Fax: (905) 781-0071
Email: negev_imp@hotmail.com

Community Organisations

Bernard Betel (Senior Centre)
1003 Steeles Avenue West M2R 3T6 (416) 225-2112
Fax: (416) 225-2097
Email: betelctr@idirect.com
Centre operates Conservative Synagogue - has two Sephardi congregations on site - Beth Yosef and Tehillat Yerushalayim.

Jewish Federation of Greater Toronto
4600 Bathurst Street, North York
M2R 3V2 (905) 635-2883
Fax: (905) 635-9565
Email: office@ujafed.org

Contact Information

Greater Toronto Area Jewish Information Service
4588 Bathurst Street, Suite 214, Willowdale
M2R 1W6 (416) 635-5600
Fax: (416) 636-5813
Email: jinfo@ujafed.org
Web site: www.jewishtoronto.net
Publishes a "Jewish Community of Services Directory" for Greater Toronto, as well as other Jewish publications.

Delicatessens

Marky's Delicatessen
280 Wilson Avenue, Downsview (905) 638-1081

Mati's Fallafel House
3430 Bathurst Street M6A 1C2 (905) 783-9505
Sells dairy products only.

Embassy

Consul General of Israel
180 Bloor Street West, Suite 700 M5S 2V6
(905) 640-8500
Fax: (905) 640-8555
Email: hasbara@idirect.com
Israel Government Tourist Office: 964-3784.

Gift Shop

Miriam's,
3007 Bathurst Street (416) 781-8261
Fax: (416) 781-8261

Media

Newspapers

Canadian Jewish News
10 Gateway Blvd, Suite 420, Don Mills
M3C 3A1 (905) 422-2331
Fax: (905) 422-3790

Jewish Tribune
15 Hove Street, Downsview
M3H 4Y8, (905) 633-6227
Fax: (905) 630-2159

Memorial

Holocaust Education & Memorial Centre
4600 Bathurst Street, Willowdale
M2R 3V2 (905) 635-2883

Museum

Silverman Heritage Museum
Baycrest Centre for Geriatric Care, 3560
Bathurst Street M6A 2E1 (905) 785-2500 Ext.2802
One of the few Judaica museums in Canada it has an active exhibit programme.

Religious Organisations

JEP/Ohr Somayach Centre
2939 Bathurst Street M6B 2B2 (905) 785-5899
Has a minyan.

Kashruth Council of Canada
4600 Bathurst Street, Ste 240
M2R 3V2 (416) 635-9550
Fax: (416) 635-8760
All enquiries about kashrut here.

Restaurants

Hakerem
3030 Bathurst Street, Willowdale
MB6 3B6 (416) 787-6504
Fax: (416) 787-6504

Dairy

Dairy Treats Cafe
3522 Bathurst Street M6A 2C6 (416) 787-0309
Fax: (416) 787-1935

Milk'n Honey
3457 Bathurst Street, Downsview
M6A 2C5 (905) 789-7651
Fax: (905) 789-4788

Pizza Tova,
3020 Bathurst Street (905) 781-1326
Supervision: COR.

Tov Li Pizza
5972 Bathurst Street, Willowdale
M2R 1Z1, (905) 650-9800

Meat

King Solomon's Table
3705 Chesswood Drive, Downsview
M3J 2P6 (416) 630-0666
Fax: (416) 630-4585
Open Monday to Thursday 12.00 noon to 10.00 pm. Sunday 4.00 pm to 10.00 pm. Closed Friday and Saturday. Kashrut: COR.

Marky's Delicatessen
6233 Bathurst Street, (just South of Steel)
(905) 227-0707
Supervision: Kashruth Council of Toronto.

The Chicken Nest
3038 Bathurst Street M6B 4K2 (905) 787-6378
Fax: (905) 222-6057

Windsor

Community Organisations

Jewish Community Council
1641 Ouellette Avenue N8X 1K9 (519) 973-1772

Media

Periodicals

Windsor Jewish Community Bulletin
Fax: (519) 973-1774

Synagogues

Orthodox

Shaar Hashomayim
115 Giles Blvd East N9A 4C1 (519) 256-3123
Fax: (519) 256-3124
Email: shaar@mnsi.net

Shaarey Zedek
610 Giles Blvd East N9A 4E2 (519) 252-1594

Reform

Congregation Beth-El
2525 Mark Avenue N9E 2W2 (519) 969-2422

Quebec

Montreal

1760 saw the arrival of the first Jews in Montreal as civilians attached to the British Army. In the 1920s and 1930s the Boulevard St-Laurent was equivalent to London's East End or New York's Lower East Side. There are now just over 100,000 Jews in the city. Twenty per cent of these are North African Sephardim.

Bakeries

Biscuit Adar, 5458 Westminister (514) 484-1198
Supervision: Vaad Ha'ir.

Boulangerie-Adir
6795 Darligton (514) 342-1991
Supervision: Vaad Ha'ir.

Cite Cashere, 4747 Van Horne (514) 733-2838
Supervision: Vaad Ha'ir.

Delice Cashere
4655 Van Horne (514) 733-5010
Supervision: Vaad Ha'ir.

Katzberg Home Bread and Cake Delivery
5355 Jeanne Mance (514) 273-4042
Supervision: Vaad Ha'ir.

La Biscuit Adar
1204 Beaumont (514) 343-0272
Supervision: Vaad Ha'ir.

Kleins Kosher Bakery
5540 Hutchison (514) 274-4633
Supervision: Vaad Ha'ir.

Kosher Quality Bakery
5855 Victoria (514) 731-7883
Fax: (514) 731-0205
Supervision: Vaad Ha'ir.
Hours: Sunday - Wednesday 6 am to 9 pm. Thursday 6 am to 10 pm. Friday 6 am winter 2 pm or summer 4 pm.

Montreal Kosher
7005 Victoria (514) 739-3651
Supervision: Vaad Ha'ir.

Montreal Kosher
2135 St. Louis, St. Laurent (514) 747-5116
Supervision: Vaad Ha'ir.

Montreal Kosher
2865 Van Horne, Wilderton Shopping Centre
(514) 739-3651
Supervision: Vaad Ha'ir.

New Homemade Kosher Bakery
6685 Victoria (514) 733-4141
Supervision: Vaad Ha'ir.

New Homemade Kosher Bakery
6915 Querbes (514) 270-5567
Supervision: Vaad Ha'ir.

New Homemade Kosher Bakery
5638 Westminister (514) 486-2024
Supervision: Vaad Ha'ir.

New Homemade Kosher Bakery
1085 Bernard W. (514) 276-2105
Supervision: Vaad Ha'ir.

Patisserie Chez Ma Souer
5095 Queen Mary (514) 737-2272
Supervision: Vaad Ha'ir.

Pita Royal, 5897 Van Horne (514) 488-9414
Supervision: Vaad Ha'ir.

Renfels Bakery
2800 Bates (514) 733-5538
Supervision: Vaad Ha'ir.

Booksellers

Kotel Book & Gift Store
6414 Victoria Avenue H3W 2S6 (514) 739-4142
Fax: (514) 739-7330

Rodal's Hebrew Book Store & Gift Shop
4689 Van Horne Avenue
H3W 1H8 (514) 733-1876
Fax: (514) 733-2373
Email: rodals@ican.net

Victoria Gift Shop
5875 Victoria Avenue H3W 2R6 (514) 738-1414

Community Organisations

Federation CJA
5151 ch, de la Côte Ste-Catherine
H3W 1M6 (514) 735-3541
Operates the Jewish Information and Referral Service (JIRS), Tel: 737-2221.

Jewish Community Council of Montreal
6333 Decarie, Suite 100
H3W 3E1 (514) 739-6363
Fax: (514) 739-7024
Email: semanuel@generation.net
Web site: www.mk.ca
Visitors requiring additional information about kosher establishments should contact the Vaad Ha'ir at the above numbers. Also apply to them for a list of kosher butchers, bakeries and caterers.

Embassy

Consul General of Israel
1155 Boulevard Rene Levesque Ouest,
Suite 2620 H3B 4S5 (514) 940-8500
Fax: (514) 940-8555
Email: cgisrmtl@videotron.net
Web site: www.israelca.org

Libraries

Jewish Public Library
5151 Côte Ste-Catherine Road
H3W 1M6 (514) 345-2627
Fax: (514) 345-6477
Email: c-stern@hotmail.com

Media

Newspapers

Canadian Jewish News
6900 Decarie Blvd, #341
H3X 2T8 (514) 735-2612

Restaurants

Exodus,
5395 Queen Mary (514) 483-6610
Supervision: Vaad Ha'ir.

Dairy

Bistrot Casa Linga
5095 Queen Mary H3W 1X4 (514) 737-2272

Cummings Jewish Centre for Seniors Cafeteria
5700 Westbury Avenue
H3W 3E8 (514) 342-1234
Fax: (514) 739-6899
Email: info@cummings-senior-centre.org
Supervision:

Foxy's,
5987A Victoria Avenue (514) 739-8777
Supervision: Vaad Ha'ir.

Pizza Pita,
5710 Victoria Avenue (514) 731-7482
Supervision: Vaad Ha'ir.
Pizza, pita and a variety of Milchig dishes. Open 9.30 am-11.30 pm daily, Saturday night until 2.30 am.

Tatty's Pizza
6540 Darlington (514) 734-8289
Supervision: Vaad Ha'ir.

Meat

Chez Babys,
Cote St. Luc Road
Supervision: Montreal Sephardic Vaad.

El Morocco II
3450 Drummond Street (514) 844-6888; 844-0203
Fax: (514) 844-1204
Email: elmorocco@spring.ca
Supervision: Vaad Ha'ir.
Open for lunch and dinner until 10 pm. Located downtown near hotels and boutiques.

Ernie's & Ellie's Place
6900 Decarie Blvd H3X 2T8 (514) 344-4444
Fax: (514) 344-0001
Supervision: Vaad Ha'ir.

Synagogues

Canadian Jewish Congress National Headquarters
Samuel Bronfman House,
1590 Docteur Penfield Avenue H3G 1C5
(514) 931-7531
Fax: (514) 931-0548
Email: mikec@cjc.ca
Contact to find out which of the many synagogues in Montreal is nearest.

Quebec City

Cemeteries

Beth Israel Ohev Sholom
Boulevard Rene Levesque, Sainte-Foy
(418) 658-6677
This is an official monument and historic site - 5 miles from the old centre.

Synagogues

Orthodox

Beth Israel Ohev Shalom
1251 Place de Merici G1R 1Y2 (418) 688-3277

Ste. Agathe-des-Monts

A resort in the Laurentian Mountains known as the "Catskills" of Montreal where members of the Montreal community spend their summer months.

Synagogues

House of Israel Congregation
31 Albert Street J8C 1Z6 (819) 326-4320
Fax: (819) 326-8558
Web site: www.houseofisrael.org

Saskatchewan

Moose Jaw

Synagogues

Conservative

Moose Jaw Hebrew Congregation
937 Henry Street S6H 3H1 (306) 692-1644

Regina

Synagogues

Orthodox

Beth Jacob
4715 McTavish Street S4S 6H2 (306) 757-8643
Fax: (306) 352-3499

Reform

Temple Beth Tikvah
Box 33048, Cathedral Post Office
S4T 7X2 (306) 761-2218

Saskatoon

Synagogues

Conservative

Agudas Israel
715 McKinnon Avenue S7H 2G2 (306) 343-7023
Fax: (306) 343-1244
Email: jewishcommunity@sk.sympatico.ca
Will be pleased to welcome visitors.

Cayman Islands

In addition to a very small permanent Jewish community there are a number of Jews who spend part of the year on the Islands.

GMT - 5 hours — Total Population 32,000
Country calling code (1345) — Jewish Population Under 100
Emergency Telephone (Police - 911) (Ambulance - 555) — Electricity voltage 110

Grand Cayman

Contact Information

Harvey DeSouza
PO Box 72 949-7739

Chile

The original Jewish settlers in Chile were *Conversos*. Rodrigo de Organos, a *Converso*, was the first European to enter the country in 1535. The Inquisition, however, curtailed the growth of the community.

The first legal Jewish immigration, albeit small, occurred only after Chile's independence in 1810. In 1914 the Jewish community numbered some 500, but this increased in the late 1930s with those refugees from Nazism who were able to avoid the strict immigration laws. Anti-Semitism, however, also grew, and the Comite Representativo was formed to respond to it.

There is an umbrella organisation and a large Zionist body in Chile. Most of the community is not religious, but some keep kosher and there are several synagogues in Santiago (the capital) and a few kosher shops. There are two Jewish schools and several Jewish newspapers are published.

GMT - 4 hours — Total Population 15,211,000
Country calling code (56) — Jewish Population 15,000
Emergency Telephone (Police - 133) (Fire - 132) (Ambulance - 131) — Electricity voltage 220

Arica

Community Organisations

Sociedad Israelita
Dr Herzl, Casilla 501

Iquique

Community Organisations

Comunidad Israelita
Playa Ligade 3263, Playa Brava

La Serena

Community Organisations

Community Centre
Cordovez 652

Rancagua

Community Organisations

Comunidad Israelita
Casilla 890

Santiago

The majority of Chilean Jews live in Santiago. The city has a couple of notable features in connection with its Jewish community. The Circulo Israelita Synagogue has an interesting stained glass design in its interior, and the "Bomba Israel" is a fire service, manned by volunteers who include a few rabbis. Two of their fire engines carry the Chilean and Israeli flags.

Embassy

Embassy of Israel
San Sebastian 2812, Casilla 1224 (2) 246-1570

Representative Organisations

Communal Headquarters (Comite Representativo de las Entidades Judias de Chile)
Miguel Claro 196 (2) 235-8669

Supermarket and Butchers

Meat

Kosher Deli, Americo Vespucio Sur 1301
(2) 251-3145
Supervision: Jabad.

Synagogues

Ashkenazi

Comunidad Israelita de Santiago
Serrano 214-218

German

Sociedad Cultural Israelita B'ne Jisroel
Portugal 810

Hungarian

Maze,
Pedro Bannen 0166 (2) 274-2536

Orthodox

Bicur Joilim,
Av. Matte 624
Jabad Lubavitch
Gloria 62, Las Condes (2) 228-2240
Jafets Jayim,
Miguel Claro 196

Sephardi

Maguen David,
Av. R. Lyon 812

Temuco

Community Organisations

Comunidad Israelita
General Cruz 355

Valdivia

Community Organisations

Community Centre
Arauco 136 E.

Valparaiso

Community Organisations

Comunidad Israelita
Alvarez 490, Vina del Mar (32) 680-373

China

Jews have been in China since the twelfth century. The largest established community of around 1,000 was in Kaifeng. The first Kaifeng synagogue was built in 1163.

The Treaty of Nanking 1842 opened Shanghai to trade. In 1845 Elias Sassoon pioneered the Jewish settlement of Shanghai. Many Baghdadi Jews followed and were under protection of the British government. In due course they were in the forefront of the development of the city. A second community was formed later, mainly by Russians and Poles fleeing religious persecution. The final influx was of refugees from Nazi oppression in the period 1933-39. Almost all the community left Shanghai after the Second World War.

A community was established again in 1999.

GMT + 8 hours	Total Population 1,284,485,000
Country calling code 86 (Hong Kong 852)	Jewish Population 2,500
Emergency Telephone (Police - 110) (Fire - 119)	Electricity voltage 220/240

Beijing

Embassy

Embassy of Israel
1 Jianguo Menwai Da Jia 100004
(10) 6505-2970/1/2
Fax: (10) 6505-0328

Hong Kong

Although there were some Jewish merchants trading out of Hong Kong over the centuries, the first permanent community consisted of Jews who came from Baghdad in the early nineteenth century. The first synagogue was not established until 1901, the early settlers preferring to organise communal events from their homes. The majority of the community were Sephardi, but Nazi persecution led to more Ashkenazi settlers arriving in Hong Kong, via Shanghai. Since the Second World War many Chinese Jews have emigrated through Hong Kong to Australia and the USA, although some have remained in Hong Kong. Following the reversion to Chinese control in mid-1997, the Jewish community is still thriving, and the mood is optimistic.

The Jews have contributed greatly to the building of the infrastructure of Hong Kong and, since the 1960s, many Western Jews, attracted by the success of this major financial centre, have made their homes there. The first communal hall was founded in 1905, but a new, multi-purpose complex (the Jewish Community Centre) has recently been opened, which is one of the most luxurious in the world. This centre includes everything from a library and a strictly kosher restaurant to a swimming pool and sauna.

Cemeteries

The Jewish Cemetery
Located in Happy Valley 2589-2621
Fax: 2548-4200

Community Organisations

Hong Kong Jewish Community Centre
One Robinson Place, 70 Robinson Road, Mid-Levels 2801-5440
Fax: 2877-0917
Email: csw@jcc.org.hk
Web site: www.jcc.org.hk

Two glatt kosher restaurants under the supervision of a full-time Mashgiach. Meals on Shabbat, take-away and delivery service available. Also houses banquet facilities, kosher supermarket, library, swimming pool, gymnasium and leisure facilities. A full programme of activities and classes. Visitors are welcome.

Cultural Organisations

The Jewish Historical Society of Hong Kong
2807-9400
Fax: 2887-5235

Publishes monographs on subjects of Sino-Judaic interest and maintains an archive. Information from Mrs Judith Green.

Embassy

Consul General of Israel
Room 701Admiralty Centre, Tower 2, 18 Harcourt Street 2529-6091
Fax: 2865-0220
Email: isrcons@asiaonline.net

Restaurants

Hong Kong Jewish Community Centre
One Robinson Place, 70 Robinson Road,
Mid-Levels 2801-5440
Fax: 2877-0917
Email: csw@jcc.org.hk
Web site: www.jcc.org.hk

Two kosher restaurants under full-time Mashgiach supervision. Meals on Shabbat, take-away and delivery service available.

Shalom Grill, 2/F Fortune House,
61 Connaught Road, Central
2851-6218; 2851-6300
Fax: 2851-7482
Email: darvick@darvick.com.hk

Glatt kosher restaurants under full-time Mashgiach supervision, Meals on Shabbat after services, take-away and delivery service available. There is also a kosher supermarket, Sunday-Thursday Lunch 12.30-2.30 pm. Dinner 6.30-9.30 pm. Friday 12.30-2.30 pm.

Synagogues

Orthodox

Chabad of Hong Kong
1A Kennedy Heights, Mid-levels 2523-9770
Fax: 2845-2772
Email: info@chabadhk.org
Web site: www.chabadhk.org

Wide range of programming and services available to overseas visitors.

Ohel Leah Synagogue
70 Robinson Road, Mid-Levels 2589-2621
Fax: 2548-4200
Web site: www.hkjew.com

Built in 1902 and carefully restored in 1998, the Orthodox Ohel Leah Synagogue known by some as the "crown jewel" of Asian Jewry still remains the region's most vibrant centre of Jewish religious activity. Classes, daily services, a Beth Din, and a mikveh operate on premises. Gourmet catered shabbat meals - Friday eve is by reservation and shabbat community kiddush luncheon is complimentary following services. Book nearby hotels at discounted rates through the synagogue office.

Zion Congregation
21 Chatham Road, Kowloon 2366-6364
Corner of Mody Road (opposite to Kowloon Shangri-La Hotel).

Sephardi

Beit Midrash Shuva Israel and Community Centre
2/F Fortune House, 61 Connaught Road,
Central 2851-6218; 2851-6300
Fax: 2851-7482
Email: darvick@darvick.com.hk

Daily Shacharil at 7.00 and Mincha-Ma'ariv fifteen minutes before sunset. Shabbat services are followed by Shabbat meals. Full day kollel.

Kaifeng

Museums

Kaifeng Museum
The Kaifeng Museum documents the ancient history of Kaifeng Jewry. The most significant artifact is a fifteenth century etched stone with inscriptions describing Kaifeng's Jewish history and customs from the times of Abraham.

Shanghai

Synagogues

Jewish Community of Shanghai
1277 Beijing Xi Lu 20th floor 200040
(21) 6289-9903
Fax: (21) 6289-9957
Email: sjcchina@usa.net
Web site: www.chinajewish.org

Shabbat services are held in the Portman Ritz Hotel.

Colombia

The first Jews in Colombia were *Conversos,* as was common in South America. However, they were soon discovered by the Inquisition when it was established in Colombia.

The next influx of Jews came in the nineteenth century, followed by mass immigration from Eastern Europe and the Middle East after 1918. Jews were banned from entering after 1939, but this restriction was eased after 1950.

The present community is a mixture of Ashkenazi and Sephardi elements, each having their own communual organisations. There are also youth and Zionist organisations. There is a central organisation for Colombian Jewry in Bogota (the capital).There are also Jewish schools and synagogues, and Jewish publications and radio programmes.

GMT - 5 hours | Total Population 42,321,000
Country calling code (57) | Jewish Population 5,650
Emergency Telephone (Police - 112) (Fire - 119) (Ambulance - 132) | Electricity 110/120

Baranquilla

Community Organisations

Centro Israelita Filantropico
Carrera 43, No 85-95, Apartado Aereo 2537
(53) 342-310; 351-197

Comunidad Hebrea Sefaradita
Carrera 55, No 74-71, Apartado Aereo 51351
(53) 340-054; 340-050

Bogota

Embassy

Embassy of Israel
Calle 35, No 7-25, Edificio Caxdax
(1) 245-6603; 245-6712

Media

Monthly

Menorah, Apartado Aereo 9081

Religious Organisations

Union Rabinica Colombiana
Tranversal 29, No 126-31 (1) 274-9069; 218-2500

Synagogues

Ashkenazi

Centro Israelita de Bogota
Transversal 29, No 126-31 (1) 274-9069
Kosher meals available by prior arrangement with Rabbi Goldschmidt, 218-2500.

German

Asociacion Israelita Montefiore
Carrera 20, No 37-54 (1) 245-5264

Orthodox

Congregacion Adath Israel
Carrera 7a, No 94-20 (1) 257-1660; 257-1680
Fax: (1) 623-2237
Mikva on premises.

Comunidad Hebrea Sefaradi
Calle 79, No 9-66 (1) 256-2629; 249-0372
Mikva on premises.

Jabad House,
Calle 92, No 10, Apt. 405
Rabbi's Tel:(1)257-4920.

Cali

Representative Organisations

Union Federal Hebrea
Apartado Aereo 8918 (2) 443-1814
Fax: (2) 444-5544
An umbrella organisation co-ordinating all Jewish activities in Cali.

Synagogues

Ashkenazi

Sociedad Hebrea de Socoros
Av. 9a Norte # 10-15,
Apartado Aereo 011652 (2) 668-8518
Fax: (2) 668-8521

German

Union Cultural Israelita
Apartado Aereo 5552 (2) 668-9830
Fax: (2) 661-6857

Sephardi

Centro Israelita de Beneficiencia
Calle 44a, Av. 5a Norte Esquina,
Apartado Aereo 77 (2) 664-1379
Fax: (2) 665-5419

Medellin

Community Organisations

Union Israelita de Beneficencia
Carrera 43B, No 15-150, Apartado Aereo 4702

Costa Rica

The first Jews arrived in Costa Rica in the nineteenth century from nearby islands in the Caribbean such as Jamaica. The next wave of immigrants came from Eastern Europe in the 1920s. Thereafter Costa Rica did not welcome new Jewish immigrants, and passed laws against foreign merchants and foreign land ownership. However, the Jewish community in Costa Rica established a communual organisation in 1930. There is a monthly newsletter, and a synagogue in San Jose. Most Jewish children attend the Haim Weizmann School, which has both primary and secondary classes.

It is interesting to note that the Costa Rican embassy in Israel is in Jerusalem and not Tel Aviv, where most other embassies are situated.

GMT - 6 hours	Total Population 4,023,000
Country calling code (506)	Jewish Population 2,500
Emergency Telephone (Police, Fire and Ambulance 911)	Electricity voltage 110/220

San Jose

Contact Information

Centro Israelita Sionista de Costa Rica
PO Box 1473-1000 233-9222
Fax: 233-9321

Embassy

Embassy of Israel
Edificio Centro Colon, Piso 11,
PO Box 5147-1000 221-60-11/221-64-44
Fax: 257-0867
Email: embofisr@sol.racsa.co.cr

Groceries

Little Israel Pita Rica
Frente a Shell, Pavas 290-2083
Fax: 296-4802
The only kosher bakery and mini-market in Costa Rica.

Hotels

Barcelo San Jose Palacio
Apdo 458-1150 220-2034; 220-2035
Fax: 220-2036
Email: Palacio@sol.racsa.co.cr
Hotel has separated kosher kitchen and its key in the mashgiach's (Rabbi Levkovitz) hands. The hotel is about a half hour walk to the synagogue.

Camino Real,
Prospero Fernandezy, Camino Real Boulevard
289-7000
Fax: 289-8930
Email: caminoreal@ticonet.co.cr
Hotel has new separated kosher kitchen, with the key in the Mashgiach's (Rabbi Levkovitz) hands.

Melia Confort Corobici
PO Box 2443-1000 232-8122
Fax: 231-5834
Email: melia.confort.corobici@solmelia.com
There is no separate kosher kitchen, but it is fairly close to the Orthodox synagogue. The hotel has two separate storage rooms for kosher cookware.

Synagogues

Shaarei Zion

Croatia

Jews were in the land now known as Croatia before the Croats themselves. The Croats arrived in the seventh century, the Jews some centuries before with the Romans: there are remains of a third-century Jewish cemetery in Solin (near Split).

The first Jewish communities were involved in trade with Italy across the Adriatic Sea, and also in trade along the River Danube. Their success was brief, however, and they were expelled in 1456, only returning more than 300 years later. The area became part of the newly formed Yugoslavia after the First World War, and the Jewish community became part of the Federation of Jewish Communities in Yugoslavia.

The Croatian Jews suffered greatly under the German occupation in the Second World War when the local *Ustashe* (Croatian Fascists) assisted the Germans. Despite their efforts, some Jews survived and even decided to rebuild their community when peace returned.

Today, after the civil war, there are synagogues in towns across the country. There are some Hebrew classes and newsletters are published. There are also many places of historical interest, such as Ulicia Zudioska (Jewish Street) in Dubrovnik.

GMT + 1 hour — Total Population 4,473,000
Country calling code (385) — Jewish Population 2,000
Emergency Telephone (Police - 92) (Fire - 93) (Ambulance - 94) — Electricity voltage 220

Dubrovnik

Synagogues

Zudioska Street 3

Zudioska means "Street of the Jews". This is the second oldest synagogue in Europe and is located in a very narrow street off the main street – the Stradun or Placa. The Jewish community office is in the same building. Zudioska Street is the third turning on the right from the town clock tower. There are about thirty Jews in the city. Tourists help to make up a minyan in the synagogue on Friday night and High Holy Days.

Osijek

Community Organisations

Brace Radica Street 13 (31) 211-407
Fax: (31) 211-407

The community building contains objects from the synagogue that was destroyed during the Second World War. The community numbers about 150 members and has two cemeteries. No regular services are held. A former building of the pre-war synagogue in Cvjetkova Street is a Pentecostal church today. There is a plaque at the site of the destroyed synagogue in Zupanijska Street.

Rijeka

Synagogues

Filipovieva ul. 9, PO Box 65 51000
(51) 425-156/336-032

The community numbers about sixty. Services are held in the well maintained synagogue on Jewish holidays.

Split

Community Organisations

Zidovski Prolaz 1 (21) 45-672

The synagogue at Split is one of the few in Yugoslavia to have survived the wartime occupation. The Jewish community numbers about 200. There is a Jewish cemetery, established in 1578. More information from the community offices at the above number.

Zagreb

Booksellers

Voice of the Jewish Communities of Croatia
Email: jcz@oleh.srce.hr

Community Organisations

Jewish Community of Zagreb
Palmoticeva Street 16, PO Box 986 (1) 434-619
Fax: (1) 434-638
Email: jcz@public.stce.hr

Before the War Zagreb had 11,000 Jews. There are now only about 1,500, but they remain very active in Jewish communal life. Services are held in the community building on Friday evenings and holidays.

Monuments

Central Synagogue
Praska Street 7
There is a plaque on the spot of this pre-war synagogue.

Mirogoj Cemetery
There is an impressive monument in this cemetery to the Jewish victims of the Second World War.

Cuba

The first Jew to set foot in Cuba (1492) was Luis de Torres. Although hundreds followed following the Spanish Inquisition, they were prohibited from practising their religion. This situation changed in 1898 following Cuba's liberation from Spain. With the end of Spanish colonial rule in that year, Jews from nearby areas, such as Jamaica and Florida, and Jewish veterans of the Spanish-American War began to settle in Cuba. A congregation was established in 1904. Later, Turkish Sephardim formed their own synagogue. The community was then augmented by immigrants from Eastern Europe who had decided to stay in Cuba, which was being used as a transit camp for those seeking to enter America. A central committee was established for all Jewish groups in the 1930s. Cuba clamped down on immigration at that time, and the story of the German ship *St Louis* (full of Jewish refugees) which was refused entry into Cuba, is well known.

About 12,000 Jews lived on the island in 1952. Havana had by far the largest community, and seventy-five per cent of the Cuban community was Ashkenazi. Although the Cuban revolution did not target Jews, religious affiliations were initially discouraged and many Jews emigrated (as did many non-Jews). The remaining community has synagogues and a Sunday school. Kosher food and Judaica are imported, mainly from Canada and Panama. Cuba broke off diplomatic relations with Israel in 1973, although in 1998/99 a number of Jews were allowed to emigrate to Israel.

GMT - 5 hours
Country calling code (53)
Emergency Telephone
(Police - 82 0116) (Fire - 81 1115) (Ambulance 404 551)

Total Population 11,201,000
Jewish Population 1,300
Electricity voltage 110/220

Havana

Synagogues

Conservative

Patronado de la Casa de la Comunidad Hebrea de Cuba
Calle 13 e I, Vedado (7) 32-8953
Modern community centre as well.

Orthodox

Hadath Israel
Calle Picota 52, Habana Vieja (7) 61-3495

Reform

The United Hebrew Congregation
Av. de los Presidentes 502
The Jewish cemetery is at Guanabacoa.

Cyprus

During the Roman Empire, Jewish merchants made their home on Cyprus. However, after a revolt that destroyed the town of Salamis, they were expelled. In medieval times, small Jewish communities were established in Nicosia, Limasso, and other towns; but the community was never large.

It is interesting to note that Cyprus was seen as a possible 'Jewish homeland' by the early Zionists. Agricultural settlements were established at the end of the nineteenth century, but they were not successful. Herzl himself tried to persuade the British government to allow Jewish rule over Cyprus in 1902, but met with failure.

Some German Jews managed to escape to Cyprus in the early 1930s. After the War, many Holocaust survivors who had tried to enter Palestine illegally were deported to special camps on the island. Some 50,000 European Jews were held there. Since the establishment of the State of Israel, the Jewish community on the island has become small, and the Israeli embassy serves as a centre for community activities.

GMT + 2 hours
Country calling code (357)
Emergency Telephone (Police, Fire and Ambulance - 112)

Total Population 756,000
Jewish Population Under 100
Electricity voltage 240

Nicosia

Community Organisations

Committee of the Jewish Community of Cyprus
PO Box 24784 1303 (2) 694758
Fax: (2) 662077
Email: amiyes@spidernet.com.cy
Contact Mrs Z. Yeshurun for information.

Embassy

Embassy of Israel
4 Grypari Street (2) 664195
Fax: (2) 666338
Email: israel@cytanet.com.cy

Czech Republic

Prague, the capital of this small central European country, has become a major tourist attraction. It is one of the few cities to actively promote its Jewish heritage, which dates from early medieval times. The oldest (still functioning) synagogue in Europe is there (the Altneuschul), as well as many other interesting Jewish sites.

After the first Jews arrived in the country in the tenth century, they suffered similar tragedies to those of other medieval Jewish communities - such as forced baptism by the Crusaders and expulsions - together with some tolerance. Full emancipation was attained in 1867 under the Hapsburgs. The celebrated Jewish writer, Franz Kafka, lived in Prague and did not neglect his Judaism, unlike many other Czech Jews who assimilated and intermarried.

The German occupation led to eighty-five per cent of the community (80,000 people) perishing in the Holocaust. Further difficulties were faced in the communist period after the War, but since the 1989 'Velvet Revolution', Judaism is being rediscovered. The community (mostly elderly) has several synagogues around the country, a kindergarten and a journal, and there are kosher restaurants in the old Jewish quarter in Prague.

GMT + 1 hour — Total Population 10,244,000
Country calling code (420) — Jewish Population 2,800
Emergency Telephone (Police - 158) (Fire - 150) (Ambulance - 155) — Electricity voltage 220

Boskovice

Museums

Medieval Ghetto

(501) 454601; 452077
Fax: (501) 452077
Email: museum@mas.cz

Seventeenth-century Jewish town, synagogue and cemetery.

Brno

Community Organisations

Community Centre

tr. Kpt. Jarose 3 60200 (5) 4524-4710
Fax: (5) 4521-3803
Email: zob@zob.cz
Web site: www.zob.cz

The community president can be reached at 77-3233.

Synagogues

Skorepka 13

Holesov

Museums

Schach Synagogue

Dating from 1650, this synagogue is now a museum. Open in the mornings. At other times the curator will show visitors around, if contacted. The old cemetery is close by.

Karlovy Vary (Carlsbad)

Once a very popular spa town. The beautiful synagogue, destroyed on *Kristallnacht*, is commemorated by a plaque on the wall of the Bristol Hotel.

Synagogues

Community Centre

Masaryka 39

Services, Friday evening and Shabbat morning.

Liberec

Synagogues

Community Centre

Matousova 21, Reichenberg 46001 (48) 510-3340

Each weekday 9 am-11 am.

Mikulov

Site

Only one synagogue, still being restored, remains of the many which flourished here when the town was the spiritual capital of Moravian Jewry and the seat of the Chief Rabbis of Moravia. The cemetery contains the graves of famous rabbis.

Olomouc

Synagogues

Community Centre

Komenskeho 7 (68) 522-3119

Czech Republic

Ostrava

Synagogues

Community Centre
Ceskobratrska 17 (69) 611-2389

Pilsen

Synagogues

Community Centre
Smetanovy Sady 5, Pilsen (19) 723-5749
Services Friday evenings. The Great Synagogue is now closed.

Polna

Museum

A museum was opened in 2000 in a reconstructed seventeenth century synagogue. It charts the spread of anti-Semitism in Central Europe.

Prague

Most of the Jews in the Czech Republic live in Prague, which has had a thousand-year history of Jewish settlement. The impact of the Jews in Prague has been great, the Golem has entered Prague folklore, and the Altneushul is the oldest functioning synagogue in Europe. The Jewish Quarter in the old town contains many historical sites.

Terezin is some forty miles from Prague and is easily visited. On the way is the town of Lidice, destroyed in June 1942 by the Nazis in retaliation for the assassination of Reinhard Heydrich.

Cemeteries

Old Jewish Cemetery
U Stare Skoly 1,3 11001 (2) 2171-1511
Fax: (2) 2481-9458
Email: office@jewishmuseum.cz
The oldest cemetery in Europe, containing the graves of such famous rabbis & scholars as Avigdor Karo (died 1439), Yehuda Low ben Bezalel (1609), David Gans (1613) & David Oppenheim (1736).

Contact Information

Jewish Town Hall
Maislova 18 1
Houses the Federation of Jewish Communities in the Czech Republic as well as the Shalom restaurant and the famous Hebrew clock.

Embassy

Embassy of Israel
Badeniho Street 2 7 (2) 333-25109
Fax: (2) 333-20092

Hotels

President Hotel
Namesti Curieovych 100 116-88 (2) 231-4812
Fax: (2) 231-8247
A few minutes walk from the old Jewish quarter.

Judaica art and souvenirs

Precious Legacy
Maiselova 16, Prague 1, Josefov (2) 232-1951
Fax: (2) 232-0398, 472-1068
Email: legacy_tours@oasanet.cz

Museums

Jewish Museum in Prague
U Stare Skoly 1,3 (2) 2481-9456
Fax: (2) 2481-9458
Email: office@jewishmuseum.cz
Web site: www.jewishmuseum.cz
In 2001 a new set of facilities were opened. The complex includes art restoration workshops, a library, and an exhibition hall. Reservation centre: Tel: 2231-7191. Fax: 2231-7181.

Restaurants

Casablanca,
Na Prikope 10 1 (2) 2423-1501

Dairy

Jerusalem,
Brehova 5 1 (2) 232-4729
Fax: (2) 232-4729
Supervision: Chabad Lubavitch Prague.
Sells a few groceries. Boxed lunches and Shabbat meals can be ordered.

Meat

King Solomon,
Siroka 8, Prague 1 (2) 248-18752
Fax: (2) 786-4664
Web site: www.kosher.cz

Synagogues

Orthodox

Altneuschul,
Cervena ul.7 1 (2) 231-0909
Dates back to 1275 and is the only one in Prague to hold regular services.

Jubilee Synagogue
Jerusalemska 7

Chabad Center Prague
3 Parizska Street, Prague 1 11000
(2) 232-0200 or 232-0896
Fax: (2) 232-0200 or 232-0896
Email: chabadprague@mbox.vol.cz
Web site: chabadprague.cz

Tours of Jewish Interest

Heritage Tours

(2) 472-1068

Precious Legacy Tours

Maiselova 16, Prague 1, Josefov (2) 232-0398

Fax: (2) 472-1068

Email: legacy_tours@oasanet.cz

Web site: legacytours@oasanet.cz

Wittmann Tours

Manesova 8, 120 00 Praha 2 (2) 2225-2472

Fax: (2) 2225-2472

Email: sylvie@wittmann-tours.com

Web site: www.wittmann.tours.com

Teplice

Synagogues

Community Centre

Lipova 25, Teplitz-Schönau (417) 26-580

Terezin

Museums

Theresienstadt

There is a new museum in the town dedicated to the Jews who were deported from Theresienstadt to Auschwitz. There is also a cemetery in which 11,250 individual and 217 mass graves and the crematorium are placed.

Usti Nad Labem

Community Organisations

Community Centre

Moskevska 26, Aussig (47) 520-8082

Denmark

Jews were allowed to settle in Denmark in 1622, earlier than in any other Scandinavian country. Thereafter, the community grew, with immigration largely from Germany. The Danish king allowed the foundation of the unified Jewish community of Copenhagen in 1684, and the Jews were granted full citizenship in 1849.

In the early part of the twentieth century many refugees arrived from Eastern Europe, and Denmark welcomed refugees from Nazi Germany. When the Germans conquered Denmark and ordered the Jews to be handed over, the Danish resistance managed to save 7,200 (ninety per cent of the community) by arranging boats to take them to neutral Sweden. Some Jews did, however, stay behind and were taken to the transit ghetto of Theresienstadt (Terezin), where many died.

After the War, most of the Jews returned, and there is now a central Jewish organisation based in Copenhagen. There are also homes for the elderly, synagogues and a mikva. Kosher food is available.

GMT + 1 hour
Country calling code (45)
Emergency Telephone (Police, Fire and Ambulance - 112)

Total Population 5,293,000
Jewish Population 9,000
Electricity voltage 220

Copenhagen

The vast majority of Danish Jews live in the capital which has a Jewish population of almost 9,000. The community centre contains most of the offices of the Jewish community, and three homes for the elderly are jointly run with the Copenhagen Municipality. The Great Synagogue and the cemetery dating from 1693 are interesting sites.

Bakeries

Mrs Heimann
3332-9443

Butchers

Kosher Delikatesse
87 Lyngbyvej 2100 3918-5777
Fax: 3918-5390

Community Organisations

Jewish Community Centre
Ny Kongensgade 6 1472 3312-8868
Fax: 3312-3357
Email: mt@mosaiske.dk

Embassy

Embassy of Israel
Lundevangsvej 4, Hellerup 2900 3962-6288
Fax: 3962-1938
Email: israel@pip.dknet.dk

Groceries

I. A. Samson
Roerholmsgade 3 1352 3313-0077
Fax: 3314-8277
Kosher grocery, provisions and delicatessen. Catering for groups, twenty persons plus.

Mikvaot

Jewish Community Centre
Ny Kongensgade 6 1472 3312-8868
Fax: 3312-3357
12 Krystalgade 1172 3393-7662; 3332-9443

Synagogues

Orthodox

Machsike Hadass
Ole suhrsgade 12 1354 3315-3117
Fax: 4396-9729
Email: machsike-hadas@subnet.dk
Web site: www.machsike-hadas.subnet.dk
Daily and Shabbat services.
12 Krystalgade 1172 3929-9520
Fax: 3229-2517
Daily and Shabbat services.

Hornbaek

A resort and seaside town where many members of the Copenhagen community spend the summer months or weekends. It is located on the area of the coast from which the Jewish community escaped in 1943.

Hotels

Kosher

Hotel Villa Strand
Kystvej 12 3100 2176-8680
Fax: 4596-9137

Synagogues

Granavenget 8 4220-0731
Open from Shavuot to Succot.

Dominican Republic

Dominican Republic

Jewish settlement in the Dominican Republic occurred comparatively late - the oldest Jewish grave dates back to 1826. Descended from central European Jews, the community was not religious and many married Christians. President Francisco Henriquez y Carvajal (1916) traced his ancestry back to the early Jewish settlers.

In 1938 the republic decided to accept refugees from Nazism (one of the very few countries of the world that did so freely), and even provided areas where they could settle. As a result, there were 1,000 Jews living there in 1943. This number declined as, once again, the Jewish community assimilated and married the local non-Jewish population. Despite this, many non-Jewish husbands, wives and children take part in Jewish events.

Two synagogues and a rabbi who divides his time between them are features of Jewish life. There is also a Sunday school in Santo Domingo and a bi-monthly magazine is produced. There is a small Jewish museum in Sosua.

GMT - 4 hours
Country calling code (1)
Emergency Telephone (Police, Fire and Ambulance - 999)

Total Population 8,495,000
Jewish Population 150
Electricity voltage 220/240

Santo Domingo

Embassy

Embassy of Israel
Av. Pedro Henriquez Urena 80 1404
(809) 542-1635; 542-1548

Representative Organisations

Consejo Dominicano de Mujeres Hebreas
PO Box 2189 (809) 535-6042
Fax: (809) 688-2058

Synagogues

Centro Israelita de la Republica Dominicana
Av. Ciudad de Sarasota 21 (809) 535-6042
Email: lalo@codetel.net.do

Sosua

Contact Information

Felix G. Koch (809) 571-2284
Welcomes all Jewish visitors.

Do you eat fish?

If so, there is a comprehensive list of kosher fish listed alphabetically by country on pages 381 to 384 which you should find useful on your travels.

Ecuador

As in most Latin American countries, *Conversos* comprised the earliest Jewish settlers in Ecuador. It was not until 1904 that East European Jews began to arrive, and numbers increased further following the Nazi take-over in Germany, as Ecuador granted refuge to more Jews than other neighbouring countries. About 3,000 Jews entered Ecuador in the 1930s. The Jewish population peaked in 1950 at 4,000, but this number declined owing to emigration. In recent years, some Jews have moved to Ecuador from elsewhere in South America.

There are no Jewish schools, but children do have access to Jewish education.

GMT - 5 hours — Total Population 12,646,000
Country calling code (593) — Jewish Population 1,000
Emergency Telephone (Police - 101) (Fire - 102) (Ambulance - 131) — Electricity voltage 110/120

Guayaquil

Synagogues

Community Centre
cnr. Calle Paradiso & El Bosque

Quito

Community Organisations

Communidad Judia Del Ecuador
Calle Roberto Andrade, OE3 580 y Jaime, Roldos
Urbanizacion Einstein (Carcelen) (9) (2) 828-452
Fax: (9) (2) 828-452
Email: aiq@uio.satnet

Embassy

Embassy of Israel
Av. Eloy Alfaro 969, Casilla 2463
(2) 547-322 & 548-431

Egypt

For more than two thousand years there has been a virtually continuous Jewish presence in the vicinity of Cairo and an even more ancient Jewish presence in Egypt is recounted in the Bible. After the exodus Jews returned to Egypt during the time of Alexander the Great and at that time the Ben Ezra Synagogue was built. The Bible was translated into Greek during that period. In the first century CE, the Jewish presence declined but a renaissance occurred with Moses Maimonides's arrival in Egypt in the twelfth century. Most of his books were written in Cairo and his yeshiva still exists in the Jewish quarter. From then on, the Jewish community expanded and flourished, especially with the arrival of refugees from pogroms and during the First and Second World Wars.

Before 1948 there were about 70,000 Jews in Egypt. The 1956 Suez War and the 1967 Six Day War encouraged Jewish emigration. At present, the community is small but the Jewish heritage (mostly synagogues classified as antiquities) represent an inestimable treasure worth visiting, as, for example, the recently restored Ben Ezra Synagogue, home of the world-famous Genizah of some 400,000 documents (the majority of which are now in Cambridge, England).

GMT + 2 hours — Total Population 68,470,000
Country calling code (20) — Jewish Population 200
Electricity voltage 220

Egypt

Alexandria

Synagogues

Eliahu Hanavi
69 Nebi Daniel Street, Ramla Station
(3) 492-3974; 597-4438

Cairo

The Jewish community in Cairo, has had a long and important history. The community has however declined in line with the rest of Egyptian Jewry. However, there are a number of interesting sites, such as the recently restored Ben Ezra Synagogue, where the Cairo Genizah used to be located.

Community Organisations

13 Rue Sabyl El Khazindar, Abbassieh
(2) 824-613 & 824-885
Web site: www.geocities.com

Embassy

Embassy of Israel
6 Ibn Malek St., Gizeh (2) 3610528
Fax: (2) 3610414
Email: isremcai@mail.rite.com

Synagogues

Ben-Ezra, 6 Harett il-Sitt Barbara,
Mari Girges, Old Cairo (2) 847-695

Meir Enaim,
55 No.13 Street, Maadi
Under the supervision of the Jewish Community of Cairo and can be visited on request.

Shaarei Hashamayim
17 Adli Pasha Street, Downtown Cairo (2) 749-025
Services are held on holidays. There is an interesting library across from the synagogue, which is only accessible with a key. Ask the guards.

El Salvador

The Jewish connection to El Salvador is not a strong one. It is believed that some Portuguese *Conversos* crossed the country a few hundred years ago. After that, some Sephardis from France moved to Chaluchuapa. Other Jews came from Europe, but in smaller numbers than those settling in other Latin American countries. There were only 370 Jews in 1976, and this number was reduced during the civil war, when many emigrated. Some returned, however, when the war was over.

An official community was set up in 1944 and a synagogue was opened in 1950.

El Salvador is one of the few countries to have an embassy in Jerusalem, rather than Tel Aviv.

GMT - 6 hours — Total Population 6,276,000
Country calling code (503) — Jewish Population 120
Emergency Telephone (Police, Fire, Ambulance - 123) — Electricity voltage 110

San Salvador

Embassy

Colonia Escalon
85 Av. Norte, No 619 238-770; 239-221

Synagogues

Conservative

23 Blvd. del Hipodromo 626,
Colonia San Benito 237-366
Friday evening services only.

Comunidad Israelita de El Salvador
Boulevard del Hipodromo 626,
1 Colonia San Benito, PO Box 06-182
263-8074
Fax: 264-5499
Services Friday, Shabbat Morning and Holy Days.

Estonia

Despite being the only country officially declared *Judenrein* (free of Jews) at the Wannsee conference in 1942, there is a Jewish community here today. The community has always been small, and is believed to have begun in the fourteenth century. However, most Jews arrived in the nineteenth century, when Czar Alexander II allowed certain groups of Jews into the area.

The first community was established in Tallin in 1830. By 1939, the community had grown to 4,500 and was free from restraints. After the Soviet and Nazi occupations in the Second World War the Jews returned, mainly from the Soviet Union. Now that Estonia is independent, the Jewish community is able to practise its religion freely.

GMT + 2 hours
Country calling code (372)
Emergency Telephone
(Police - 02 or 002) (Fire - 01 or 001) (Ambulance - 03 or 003)

Total Population 1,327,000
Jewish Population 2,000
Electricity voltage 220

Tallinn

Community Organisations

Jewish Community of Estonia
Karu Street 16, PO Box 3576 10507 (6) 62.30.34
Fax: (6) 62.30.34
Email: ciljal@icom.ee

Publishes a monthly, called "Hashaher", in Estonian and operates a radio programme on Radio 4 (Thursday 10.15 pm-11 pm). Information on vegetarian restaurants available.

Synagogues

Synagogue of Tallinn
Karu 16 EE10120 (2) 437-693
Email: jatskin@icom.ee
9 Magdalena Street, PO Box 3576 EE0090
(2) 55-7154

Ethiopia

The Falashas (Ge'ez for 'stranger', applied to the Ethiopian Jews) of Ethiopia became known world-wide in the early 1980s, when many were airlifted to Israel. The origins of the Beta Israel, as they call themselves, are unclear and little is known for certain. Historians have concluded that they may have become Jewish as early as the second or third century.

As the area became known to the West through nineteenth-century explorers, some Western Jews set up schools in the country. The Jewish population was believed to have been about 50,000 in 1934. After the establishment of Israel, more interest was taken in the Ethiopian community and the Ethiopian civil war was the catalyst for Operation Moses, when 10,000 people were airlifted to Israel in 1984–85. A further 15,000 left for Israel in 1991.

GMT + 2 hours
Country calling code (251)
Electricity voltage 220

Total Population 62,565,000
Jewish Population 100

Addis Ababa

Community Organisations

PO Box 50 (1) 111-725 & 446-471

Fiji

When Henry Marks, at the age of 20, moved to Fiji from Australia in 1881, he was the first recorded Jew on the island. Over the years, he developed a successful business across the region, and was later knighted.

Indian and other Jews later moved to Fiji but did not organise any official community. In recent years the Fiji Jewish Association has been created. The Israeli embassy organises an annual Seder.

GMT + 12 hours — Total Population 797,000
Country calling code (679) — Jewish Population Under 100
Emergency Telephone (Police, Fire, Ambulance - 000) — Electricity voltage 240

Representative Organisations

Fiji Jewish Association
PO Box 882, Suva
387-980
Fax: 387-946
Email: contex@is.com.fj

Finland

When Finland was occupied by Russia in the nineteenth century, many Jewish conscripts in the Russian Army settled in Finland after their discharge. They were still subject to several restrictions, but these ended after Finland's independence in 1917. In addition to these 'Cantonists', as they were known, immigrants came to Finland from Eastern Europe. Finland proved a safe haven, as the government refused to hand over Finnish Jews to the Nazis, despite being allied to Germany in its war with Soviet Russia.

The community is keen to preserve a sense of Jewish identity among the young generation, who are encouraged to experience Jewish life in Israel. The community is also keen to help other Jews in the newly independent Baltic states across the sea to the south of the country. There is a central body for Jewish communities, and kosher food is available. There are also a school and synagogues.

GMT + 2 hours — Total Population 5,176,000
Country calling code (358) — Jewish Population 1,100
Emergency Telephone (Police - 10022) (Fire and Ambulance - 112) — Electricity voltage 220

Helsinki

Some 900 Jews (the majority of the Jewish population in Finland) live in Helsinki. The community centre is next to the synagogue. There is also a Jewish cemetery containing an area dedicated to the Jews who fought in the Finnish Army in various wars, including the Russo-Finnish War.

Embassy

Embassy of Israel
Vironkatu 5A 00170
(9) 681-2020
Fax: (9) 135-6959
Email: postmaster@ilemb.pp.fi

Monument

A monument was unveiled in 2000 in a park opposite the harbour where Jewish refugees were deported in 1942 to Germany

Restaurants

Community Centre
Malminkatu 26
(9) 586-03121
Fax: (9) 694-8916
Email: hjc@hjc.pp.fi

Kosher Deli,
Malminkatu 24
(9) 685-4584
Fax: (9) 694-8916
Email: kosher.deli@hjc.pp.fi
Hours: Tuesday to Wednesday, 1 pm to 5 pm; Friday, 9 am to 2 pm.

Synagogues

Orthodox

Jewish Community Synagogue
Malminkatu 26 00100 (9) 586-0310
Fax: (9) 694-8916
Email: jc@hjc.pp.fi

Services Monday and Thursday morning, 7:45 am, other weekdays 8 am; Friday evening, 7 pm (summer), 5 pm (winter); Shabbat and Sunday mornings, 9 am.

Turku

Synagogues

Brahenkatu 17 (2) 231-2557
Fax: (2) 233-4689

The secretary is always pleased to meet visitors.

France

France now boasts the largest Jewish community in Europe. The Jewish connection with France is a long one: it dates back over 1,000 years as there is evidence of Jewish settlement in several towns in the first few centuries of the Jewish Diaspora. The community grew in early medieval times, and contributed to the economy of the region. Two great Jewish commentators, Rashi and Rabenu Tam, both lived in France. However, French Jewry suffered both from the Crusaders and from other anti-Semitic outbursts in the medieval period.

Napoleon's reign heralded the emancipation of French Jewry and, as his armies conquered Europe, the emancipation of other communities began. Despite this, incidents such as the Dreyfus Affair highlighted the fact that anti-Semitism was not yet dead. The worst case of anti-Semitism in France occurred under the German occupation, when some 70,000 Jews were deported from the community of 300,000. After the War, France became a centre for Jewish immigration, beginning with 80,000 from Eastern Europe, and then many thousands from North Africa, which eventually swelled the Jewish population to nearly 700,000.

The community is well served with organisations. Paris has 380,000 Jews alone, more than in the whole of the UK. There are many kosher restaurants, synagogues in many towns throughout the country, newspapers, radio programmes and schools in several cities. In Carpentras and Cavaillon there are synagogues which are considered to be national monuments.

GMT + 1 hour — Total Population 59,114,000
Country calling code (33) — Jewish Population 700,000
Emergency Telephone (Police - 17) (Fire - 18) (Ambulance - 15) — Electricity voltage 220

Agen

Synagogues

52 rue Montesquieu 47000 05.53.66.24.20

Tourist Site

rue des Juifs 47000
Site of the old ghetto of the fifteenth Century.
Museum of the deportation
rue Montesquieu 47000.

Aix-en-Provence

Butchers

Zouaghi, 7 rue de Sevigne, Bouches du Rhône 13100
04.42.59.93.94

Supervision: Grand Rabbinate of Marseille.

Synagogues

5 rue de Jerusalem 13100 04.42.26.69.39

Aix-les-Bains

Butchers

Berdah,
29 Av. de Tresserve 73100 04.79.61.44.11

Eurocach
Av. d'Italie 73100

Hotels

Kosher

Auberge de La Baye
Chemin du Tir-Aux-Pigeons, Savoie 73100
04.79.35.69.42

Strictly kosher. Tennis courts and swimming pool.

France

Mikvaot
Pavillon Salvador
rue du President Roosevelt 73100 04.79.35.38.08

Synagogues
Rue Paul Bonna 73100 04.79.35.28.08
Mikva on Premises

Amiens

Synagogues
38 rue du Port d'Amont 8000

Angers

Synagogues
12 rue Valdemaine 49100

Annecy

Synagogues
18 rue de Narvik 74000 04.50.67.69.37

Annemasse

Butchers
Yarden, 59 av de la Liberation, Gaillard 74100
04.50.92.64.05

Synagogues

Orthodox

8 rue du Docteur Coquart 74100

Antibes-Juan-les-Pins

Butchers
Berreche
12 av. Courbet 06160 04.93.67.16.77
Le Kineret
25 av. D l'Esterel 06160 04.92.93.16.01
Fax: 04.93.88.14.76

Restaurants
L'Alhambra, 12 bis, Avenue de l'Esterel
04.93.67.65.17
Le Relais de Belleville
47 Avenue Guy de Maupassant 06160
Maxime,
6 Bd de la Pinede 06160 04.92.93.99.40

Synagogues
Villa La Monada, 30 Chemin des Sables 06160
04.93.61.59.34

Arcachon

Synagogues

Orthodox

36 av Gambetta

Avignon

The first archaeological evidence of a Jewish presence dates from the fourth century. For years the Avignon Jewish population flourished and there were many Jewish scholars and writers who were born and lived there. The first Hebrew printing venture was attempted in Avignon in 1446 before Gutenberg's success in 1450.

Butchers
Cachere Royale
15 rue Chapeau Rouge 84000 04.90.82.47.50
Supervision: Grand Rabbinate of Marseille.
Eden,
25 rue Ninon Vallin 84000 04.90.85.99.95

Mikvaot
Vaucluse 04.90.86.30.30
Mme Cohen Zardi

Synagogues

Orthodox

2 Place de Jerusalem 84000 04.90.85.21.24
Fax: 04.90.85.21.24

Bar-le-Duc

Synagogues
7 Quai Carnot

Bayonne

Synagogues
35 rue Maubec 64100 05.59.55.03.95

Beauvais

Synagogues
Rue Jules Isaac 60000 03.44.05.46.90

Belfort

Community Organisations
27 rue Strolz 90000 03.84.28.55.41
Fax: 03.84.28.55.41
Publishes 'Notre Communaute' (quarterly)

Synagogues
6 rue de l'As-de-Carreau 90000 03.84.28.55.41
Fax: 03.84.28.55.41

Benfeld

Synagogues
7a rue de la Dime 67230 03.88.74.47.11

Besancon

Butchers
M. Croppet
18 rue des Granges 25000 03.81.83.35.93
Thursdays only.

Community Organisations
10 rue Grosjean 25000 03.81.80.82.82

Synagogues
23c Quai de Strasbourg 25000

Beziers

Synagogues
19 Place Pierre-Semard 34500 04.67.28.75.98
Operates a kosher food store.

Biarritz

Synagogues
Rue Pellot 64200
July, August and Yom Kippur.

Bischeim-Schiltigheim

Synagogues
9 Place de la Synagogue 67800 02.38.33.02.87

Bitche

Synagogues
28 rue de Sarreguemines 57230
Services, Rosh Hashana & Yom Kippur.

Bordeaux

Community Organisations
15 Pl. Charles-Gruet 33000 05.56.52.62.69

Mikvaot
213 rue Ste. Catherine 33000 05.56.91.79.39

Restaurants
Mazal Tov
137 cours Victor Hugo 33000 05.56.52.37.03

Synagogues
8 rue du Grand-Rabbin-Joseph-Cohen 33000
05.56.91.79.39

Boulay

Synagogues
Rue du Pressoir 57220 03.87.79.28.34

Boulogne-sur-Mer

Synagogues
63 rue Charles Butor 62200

Bouzonville

Synagogues
3 rue des Benedictins 57320

Brest

Synagogues
40 rue de la Republic 29200
Services, Friday, 7.30 pm.

Caen

Butchers
Boucherie Marcel
26 Rue de l'Engannerie 14000 02.31.86.16.25

Synagogues
46 Av. de la Liberation 14000 02.31.43.60.54

Caluire- et- Cuire

Synagogues
107 Av. Fleming 69300 04.78.23.12.37

Cannes

Butchers
Cannes Casher
9 rue Marceau 06400 04.93.39.85.08
Chez Sylvie
15 rue Mal. Joffre 06400 04.93.39.57.92

Community Centre
20 Boulevard d'Alsace 06400 04.93.38.16.54
Fax: 04.93.68.92.81

Groceries
Monoprix, Rue Marechal Fox
Has a comprehensive kosher section.
La Emounah
32 rue de Mimont 06400
Near the main synagogue.

Mikvaot
20 boulevard d'Alsace 04.93.99.79.03
Contact: Mme Annie Rebibo

Restaurants

Dairy

Pizza Dick
7 bis , rue de Mimont 06400 04.92.59.10.82

France

Meat

Le Tovel
3 rue du Dr Gerard Monod 06400 04.93.39.36.25

Synagogues

Chabad Lubavitch
22 Rue Commandant Vidal 06400 04.92.98.67.51
Fax: 04.92.98.81.29
Email: canorhabad@aol.com
Web site: www.jewish-cannes.com

Sephardi

20 Boulevard d'Alsace 06400 04.93.38.16.54
Fax: 04.93.68.92.81

Carpentras

Synagogues

Place de la Mairie 04.90.63.39.97
The Synagogue originally built in 1367 and the oldest in France was reconstructed in 1741-43 and again in 1959. The French government has declared it a historic site.

Tourist Site

Cathedral St Siffrein
The fifteenth-century door on the south side is where Jews had to go on their way to conversion and is known as "Porte des Juifs".

Cavaillon

The Jews originally lived in Rue Hebraique. The present synagogue, classified as a historical monument, was built in 1792.

Synagogues

04.90.76.00.34
Fax: 04.90.71.47.06

Tours of Jewish Interest

Musees de Patrimoine de Cavaillon
52 Place de Castil-Blaze 84300 04.90.76.00.34
Fax: 04.90.71.47.06

Chalon-sur-Saone

Synagogues

10 rue Germiny 71100

Chalons-sur-Marne

Synagogues

21 rue Lochet 51000

Chambery

Synagogues

44 rue St-Real 73000
Services, Friday, 7pm and festivals.

Chateauroux

Contact Information

Michel Touati
3 Allee Emile Zola, Montierchaume, Deols 36130
02.54.26.05.47

Clermont-Ferrand

Synagogues

6 rue Blatin 63000 04.73.93.36.59

Colmar

Community Centre

3 rue de la Cigogne 68000 03.89.41.38.29
Fax: 03.89.41.12.96
Kosher food can be purchased in the community centre on Wednesdays and Thursdays. Kosher restaurant; Wednesday noon during the school period.

Contact Information

Haut-Rhin 68000

Synagogues

3 rue de la Cigogne 68000 03.89.41.38.29
Fax: 03.89.41.12.96

Compiegne

Synagogues

4 rue du Dr.-Charles-Nicolle 60200

Deauville

Synagogues

14 rue Castor 14800 02.31.81.27.06

Restaurants

King J.J.
23 Rue Gambetta 14800 01.31.87.46.48

Dieuze

Synagogues

Av. Foch 57260

Dijon

Butchers

Albert Levy
25 rue de la Manutention 21000 03.80.30.14.42

Synagogues

5 rue de la Synagogue 21000 03.80.66.46.47
Mikva on premises.

Tourist Site

Archaelogical Museum
Has an important collection of old Jewish tombstones.

Dunkirk

Synagogues

19 rue Jean-Bart 59140

Elbeuf

Synagogues

29 rue Gremont 76500 02.35.77.09.11

Epernay

Synagogues

2 rue Placet 51200 03.26.55.24.44

Services, Yom Kippur only.

Epinal

Synagogues

9 rue Charlet 88000 03.29.82.25.23

Evian-les-Bains

Synagogues

Adjacent to 1 av. des Grottes, 74502
04.50.75.15.63

Eze-Village

Hotels

Hotel les Terrases d'Eze

Route de la Turbie 06360 04.92.41.55.55
Fax: 04.92.41.55.10

Supervision Nice Beth Din.

Faulquemont-Crehange

Synagogues

Place de l'Hotel de Ville 57380

Services, festivals & High Holydays only.

Forbach

Synagogues

98 Av. St.-Remy 57600 03.87.85.25.57

Frejus

Synagogues

Rue de Progres, Frejus-Plage 83600
04.94.52.06.87

Grenoble

Butchers

C. Cohen

19 rue de Turenne 38000 04.76.46.48.14

Groceries

Aux Delices du Soleil

49 rue Thiers 38000 04.76.46.19.60

David France

4 ave de Vizille 38000 04.76.70.49.15

Ghnassia

15 place Gustave Rivet 38000 04.76.87.80.90

Media

Radio

Radio 100

4 rue des Bains, Isère 38000 04.76.87.21.22

Synagogues

Rachi, 11 rue Maginot, Isère 38000
04.76.87.02.80
Fax: 04.76.87.27.14
Email: rabbin38@aol.com

Mikva at same address.

Synagogue and Community Centre

4 rue des Bains, Isère 38000 04.76.46.15.14

Grosbliederstroff

Synagogues

6 rue des Fermes 57520

Hagondange

Synagogues

Rue Henri-Hoffmann 57300

Haguenau

Synagogues

3 rue du Grand-Rabbin-Joseph-Bloch 67500
03.88.73.38.30

Hyeres

Synagogues

Chemin de la Ritorte 83400 04.94.65.31.97

Ingwiller

Synagogues

Cours du Chateau 67340

Insming

Synagogues

Rue de la Synagogue 57670

France

Izieu

Museums

The Izieu Children's Home
Bouches du Rhône 01300
recording 04.79.87.20.00;
booking 04.79.87.20.08
Fax: 04.79.87.25.01
Email: izieu@alma.fr
Web site: www.izieu.alma.fr

The Izieu Children's Memorial Museum is dedicated to the memory of forty-four children and their guardians, taken away on 6 April 1944 by the Gestapo under the command of Klaus Barbie. The Museum's mission is to defend dignity, justice and to contribute to the fight against all forms of intolerance. Two buildings can be visited: The House takes the visitors back to the everyday life of the children's home, the Barn presents the historical background through permanent and temporary exhibitions. Meetings, conferences and discussions are organized throughout the year.

La Ciotat

Synagogues

1 Square de Verdun 13600 04.42.71.92.56
Services, Friday 7 pm (Winter), 7.30 pm (Summer). Saturday 9am.

La Rochelle

Contact Information

Pierre Guedj
20 rue Chef de Ville 17000 05.46.67.38.91
Fax: 05.46.41.24.68

La Seyne-sur-Mer

Butchers

Elie Benamou
17 rue Batistin-Paul 83500 04.94.94.38.60

Synagogues

5 rue Chevalier-de-la-Barre 83501 04.94.94.40.28

Le Havre

Synagogues

38 rue Victor-Hugo 76600 02.35.21.14.59

Le Mans

Synagogues

4-6 Blvd. Paixhans 72000 02.43.86.00.96

Libourne

Synagogues

33 rue Lamothe 33500

Lille

Groceries

Monoprix
Shopping Centre Euralille, rue du Molinel 59000

Synagogues

5 rue Auguste-Angellier 59000
03.20.30.69.86 or 03.20.85.27.37
Mikva on premises.

Limoges

Synagogues

25-27 rue Pierre-Leroux 87000 05.55.77.47.26

Lorient

Synagogues

18 rue de la Patrie 56100
Services, Friday nights, festivals & Holy Days only.

Luneville

Synagogues

5 rue Castara 54300

Lyons

Media

La Voix Sepharade
317 rue Duguesclin 69007 04.78.58.18.74
Hachaar, 18 rue St Mathieu 69008 04.78.00.72.50
CIV News
4 rue Malherbe, Villeurbanne 69100
04.78.84.04.32
Radio Judaica Lyon (R.J.L.)
POB 7063 69341 04.78.03.99.20
FM 94.5

Mikvaot

Chaare Tsedek (N. African)
18 rue St Mathieu 69008 04.78.00.72.50
Rav Hida (N. African)
La Sauvegarde, La Duchere 69009
04.78.35.14.44
Orah Haim
17 rue Albert-Thomas, St-Fons 69190
04.78.67.39.78

Organisations

Beth Din, 34 rue d'Armenie, 3e 04.78.62.97.63
Fax: 04.78.95.09.47
Regional Chief Rabbi
13 Quai Tilsitt 69002 04.78.37.13.43
Fax: 04.78.38.26.57

Consistoire Israelite de Lyon
13 Quai Tilsitt 69002 04.78.37.13.43
Fax: 04.78.38.26.57
Email: acil@free.fr

Consistoire Israelite Sepharade de Lyon
Yaacov Molho Community Centre,
317 Rue Duguesclin 69007 04.78.58.18.74
Fax: 04.78.58.17.49

Restaurants

Le Jardin d'Eden
14 rue Jean Jaures, Villeurbanne 69002
04.72.33.85.65

Dairy

Le Pinocchio
5 Rue A. Boutin, Villeurbanne 69100
04.78.68.62.95

Lippo,
9 Rue Michel Servet, Villeurbanne 69100
04.78.84.15.00

Pizza Cach
13 Rue d'Inkerman, Villeurbanne 69100
04.72.74.44.98

Presto Pizza
61 Rue Gneuze, Villeurbanne 69100
04.78.68.08.41

Meat

Lippmann Henry
4 Rue Tony Tollet, Villeurbanne 69002
04.78.42.49.82
Supervision: Lyon Beth Din.

La Palmeraie
27 Rue des charmettes, Villeurbanne 69100
04.78.24.37.03

Croq Sandwiches
32 Crs Emile-Zola, Villeurbanne 69100
04.78.84.16.07

Mac David
28 Rue Michel Servet, Villeurbanne 69100
04.78.03.31.62

Synagogues

Orthodox

Grande Synagogue
13 qui Tilsitt 04.78.37.13.43
Fax: 04.78.38.26.57
Email: acil@free.fr

Sephardi

Neveh Chalom
13 rue Duguesclin 69007 04.78.58.18.54
Fax: 04.78.58.17.49

Macon

Synagogues

32 rue des Minimes 71000

Marignane

Synagogues

9 rue Pilote-Larbonne 13700

Marseilles

Bakeries

Erets, 205 rue de Rome, Bouches du Rhône 13006
04.91.92.88.73
Supervision: Grand Rabbinate of Marseille.

Avyel Cash
28 rue St Suffren, Bouches du Rhône 13006
04.91.87.95.25
Supervision: Grand Rabbinate of Marseille.

Le Parve
72 av. Alphonse Daudet, Bouches du Rhône 13013
04.91.66.95.16
Supervision: Grand Rabbinate of Marseille.

Atteia et Fils
19 Place Guillardet, Bouches du Rhône 13013
04.91.66.33.28
Supervision: Grand Rabbinate of Marseille.

L'Entremets
206 avenue de la Rose, Bouches du Rhône 13013
04.91.70.72.19
Supervision: Grand Rabbinate of Marseille.

Cacher Food
31 blvd Barry, Bouches du Rhône 13013
04.91.70.13.43
Supervision: Grand Rabbinate of Marseille.

Butchers

Zennou Raphael
20 marché Capucin, Bouches du Rhône 13001
04.91.54.02.54
Supervision: Grand Rabbinate of Marseille.

Chez David
9 blvd G. Ganay, Bouches du Rhône 13009
04.91.75.04.56
Supervision: Grand Rabbinate of Marseille.

Jamap,
13 place Mignard, Bouches du Rhône 13009
04.91.71.11.70
Supervision: Grand Rabbinate of Marseille.

Sebane
59 rue Alphonse Daudet, Bouches du Rhône 13013
04.91.66.98.76
Supervision: Grand Rabbinate of Marseille.

France

Embassy

Consul General of Israel
146 rue Paradis, Bouches du Rhône 13006
04.91.53.39.87
Fax: 04.91.53.39.94

Groceries

Av bon gout
28 rue St Suffren, Bouches du Rhône 13006
04.91.37.95.25
Emmanuel
93 avenue Clot Bey, Bouches du Rhône 13008
04.91.77.46.08
Raphael Cash
299 avenue de Mazargues,
Bouches du Rhône 13009 04.91.76.44.13
King Kasher
25 rue François Mauriac,
Bouches du Rhône 13010 04.91.80.00.01
Delicash
94 blvd Barry,
Bouches du Rhône 13013 04.91.06.39.04

Religious Organisations

Consistoire de Marseille
117 rue de Breteuil,
Bouches du Rhône 13006 04.91.37.49.64;
04.91.81.13.57
Fax: 04.91.37.83.90
Email: consistoire.israelile@wanadoo.fr

Restaurants

Meat

Erets, 205, rue de Rome,
Bouches du Rhône 13006 04.91.92.88.73
Supervision: Grand Rabbinate of Marseille.
Nathania
17 rue du Village,
Bouches du Rhône 13006 04.91.42.05.31
Supervision: Grand Rabbinate of Marseille.

Synagogues

Ohel Yaakov
20 Chemin Ste-Marthe 13014 04.91.62.70.42
Merlan,
La Cerisaie, Batiment G1 13014 04.91.98.53.92

Ashkenazi

8 Impasse Dragon 13006

Sephardi

Merkaz Netivot Chalom
27 blvd Bonifay 13004 04.91.89.40.62
Bar Yohai
171 rue Abbe-de-l'Epee 13005 04.91.42.38.19

Main Synagogue
117 rue Breteuil 13006 04.91.37.49.64
Fax: 04.91.37.83.89

There are over forty more synagogues in Marseilles. The Consistoire de Marseilles will supply details if required.

Beth Simha
31 av. Des Olives 13013 04.91.70.05.45

Melun

Synagogues

Cnr. rues Branly & Michelet 77003 01.64.52.00.05

Menton

Synagogues

Centre Altyner,
106 Cours du Centenaire 06500 04.93.35.28.29

Merlebach

Synagogues

19 rue St-Nicolas 57800

Metz

Butchers

Claude Sebbag
22 rue Mangin, Moselle 57000 03.87.63.33.50
Supervision: Chief Rabbi of Moselle.

Groceries

Atac,
23 rue de 20e Corps Américain, Moselle 57000
Galaries Lafayette
4 rue Winston Churchill, Moselle 57000
03.87.38.60.60

Religious Organisations

Rabbi Bruno Fizon
27/29 en Jurue, Moselle 57000 03.87.36.43.82

Synagogues

Adass Yechouroun
41 rue de Rabbin Elie-Bloch, Moselle 57000
Main Synagogue and Community Centre
39 rue du Rabbin Elie-Bloch, Moselle 57000
03.87.75.04.44

Montauban

Synagogues

12 rue St-Claire 82000 05.63.03.01.37

Montbeliard

Synagogues

Rue de la Synagogue 25200

Montpellier

Butchers

Eretz, 41 rue de Lunaret 34000 04.67.72.67.94

Community Organisations

Centre Communautaire et Cultural Juif
500 blvd d'Antigone 34000 04.67.15.08.76

Synagogues

Mazal Tov
18 rue Ferdinand-Fabre 34000 04.67.79.09.82
Ben-Zakai
7 rue General-Laffon 34000 04.67.92.92.07

Mulhouse

Synagogues

2 rue des Rabbins 68100 03.89.66.21.22
Fax: 03.89.56.63.49

Mikva on premises. The old cemetery is also worth a visit.

Nancy

Community Organisations

Communal Centre
19 blvd Joffre 54000 03.83.32.10.67

Museums

The Musee Historique Lorrain
64 Grand rue 54000
When Jewish buildings were plundered in 1944 only historical Jewish items in the museum survived.

Restaurants

Restaurante Universitaire
19 blvd Joffre 54000 03.83.32.10.67
Open weekdays at noon.

Synagogues

17 blvd Joffre 54000 03.83.32.10.67

Nantes

Synagogues

5 Impasse Copernic 44000 02.40.73.48.92
Mikva on premises.

Nice

Booksellers

Librairie Tanya
25 rue Pertinax 06000 04.93.80.21.74
Fax: 04.93.13.87.90
Email: librairie.tanya@wanadoo.fr

Butchers

Ghighi,
32, av. Georges Clemenceau 04.93.88.69.88
K'Gel
18, rue Dante 06000 04.93.86.33.01

Kashrut Information

04.93.85.82.06
A list of kosher butchers and bakers can be obtained from the Chief Rabbi.

Kosher Food

Mickael
37 Rue Dabray 06000 04.93.88.81.23
Riviera Cacher
11 Avenue Villermont 06000 04.93.92.92.00

Mikvaot

22 rue Michelet 06100 04.93.51.89.80

Museum

Chagall museum
Avenue Docteur Menard 06000 04.93.53.87.20
Fax: 04.93.53.87.39

Religious Organisations

Regional Chief Rabbinate of Nice, Cote d'Azur and Corsica
1 rue Voltaire 06000 04.93.85.82.06
Centre Consistorial
22 rue Michelet 06100 04.93.51.89.80
Publishes an annual calendar and guide to Nice and district.

Restaurants

Dairy

Le Leviathan, 1 ave Georges Clemenceau
04.93.87.22.64

Meat

L'Alliance
13, rue Andrioli 06000 04.93.44.11.94
Le Dauphin Bleu
22, av. Malaussena 06000 04.93.82.98.74

Synagogues

Main Synagogue
7 rue Gustave-Deloye 06000 04.93.92.11.38

Nimes

Community Organisations

5 rue d'Angouleme 30000 04.66.26.19.51

Synagogues

40 rue Roussy 30000 04.66.29.51.81
Mikva on premises.

Obernai

Synagogues

Rue de Selestat 67210

Orleans

Synagogues

14 rue Robert-de-Courtenay 45000 (to the left of the cathedral)
Information on services to be had from M. Attali, tel: 02-38621662.

Paris

The city of Paris is divided into districts (*arrondissements*) designated by the last two digits of the postcode. In the categories below, establishments are listed in numerical order according to the postcode (that is, -01, -02, -03 and so on).

The historic centre of Paris Jewish life is found in the Marais area (fourth *arrondissement*) although a synagogue stood on the Ile de la Cite before Notre Dame, Jews having lived in the city since Roman times. Another more central area is that around rue Richer (ninth *arrondissement*), which although not historic as such has many kosher restaurants of varying styles and prices.

A most important new site to be visited is the Musee d'art et d'histoire du Judaisme which opened in December 1998.

Bakeries

Korcarz,
29 rue des Rosiers 75004 01.42.77.39.47
Fax: 01.48.58.28.44
Supervision: Beth Din of Paris/Chief Rabbi Mordechai Rottenberg.

Mezel,
1 rue Ferdinand Duval 75004 01.42.78.25.01
Supervision: Beth Din of Paris.

Les Ailes
34 rue Richer 75009 01.47.70.62.53
Supervision: Beth Din of Paris.

Golan,
10 rue Geoffroy Marie 75009 01.48.00.94.71
Supervision: Beth Din of Paris.

Zazou,
20 rue du Faubourg Montmartre 75009
01.47.70.81.32
Supervision: Beth Din of Paris.

Douieb,
11 bis rue Geoffroy Marie 75009 01.47.70.86.09
Supervision: Beth Din of Paris.

Korcarz,
25 rue Trévise 75009 01.42.46.83.33
Supervision: Beth Din of Paris/Chief Rabbi Mordechai Rottenberg.

Nathan de Belleville
67 blvd de Belleville 75011 01.43.57.24.60
Supervision: Beth Din of Paris.

Mendez
3 Ter rue de la Présentation 75011 01.43.57.02.03
Supervision: Beth Din of Paris.

Contini
116 av. Simon Bolivar 75019 01.42.00.70.80
Supervision: Beth Din of Paris.

Charles Tr. Patissier
10 rue Corentin Cariou 75019 01.47.97.51.83
Supervision: Beth Din of Paris.

Mat'amim
17 rue de Crimée 75019 01.42.40.89.11
Supervision: Beth Din of Paris.

Medayo
71 rue de Meaux 75019 01.40.03.04.20
Supervision: Beth Din of Paris.

Kadoche
2 av. Corentin Cariou 75019 01.40.37.00.14
Supervision: Beth Din of Paris.

Le Relais Sucre
135 rue Manin 75019 01.42.41.20.98
Supervision: Beth Din of Paris.

Nani
104 blvd de Belleville 75020 01.47.97.38.05
Supervision: Beth Din of Paris.

Eliyor
21 rue Bisson 75020 01.43.49.12.66
Supervision: Beth Din of Paris.

Lilo
20 rue Desnoyer 75020 01.47.97.63.20
Supervision: Beth Din of Paris.

Butchers

Saada
17 rue des Rosiers 75004 01.42.77.76.22

La Rose Blanche
43 rue Richer 75009 01.48.24.84.65

La Charolaise Richer
51 rue Richer 75009 01.47.70.01.57

Charlot
33 rue Richer 75009 01.45.23.10.34

Berbeche
46 rue Richer 75009 01.47.70.50.58

Adolphe,
14 rue Richer 75009 01.48.24.86.33

Chez Jacques
19 rue Bouchardon 75010 01.42.06.76.13

Charly Halak B. Y.
51 rue Richard Lenoir 75011 01.43.48.62.26

Chez Andre
69 blvd de Belleville 75011 01.43.57.80.38

Chez Jojo
20 rue Louis Bonnet 75011 01.43.55.10.29

Chez Lucien
180 rue de Charonne 75011 01.43.70.59.29
Maurice Zirah
91 rue de la Roquette 75011 01.43.79.62.53
J V (Temim)
2 rue de Dr Goujon 75012 01.43.45.78.77
Boucherie Guy
266 rue de Charenton 75012 01.43.44.60.90
Berbeche
5 rue Vandrezanne 75013 01.45.88.86.50
Berbeche
6 rue du Moulinet 75013 01.45.80.89.10
Boucherie Claude
174 rue Lecourbe 75015 01.48.28.02.00
Kassab
88 blvd Murat 75016 01.40.71.07.34
Ste Delicatess
209 av. de Versailles 75016 01.44.40.07.59
Gm Levy
83 rue de Lonchamp 75016 01.45.53.04.24
Krief
104 rue Legendre 75017 01.46.27.15.57
Espaces Courses Elles
177 rue de Courcelles 75017 01.47.63.36.26
Berbeche
39 rue Jouffroy 75017 01.44.40.07.59
Emsalem
17 quai de la Gironde 75019 01.40.36.56.64
Berbeche
15/17 rue Henri Ribiere 75019 01.42.08.06.06
Aux Viandes Cacheres
6 av. Corentin Cariou 75019 01.40.36.02.41
Andre Manin
135 rue Manin 75019 01.42.38.00.43
Emsalem
18 rue Corentin Cariou 75019 01.40.36.56.64
Boucherie Smadja
90 blvd de Belleville 75020 01.46.36.25.36
Henrino
122 blvd de Belleville 75020 01.47.97.24.52

Embassy

Embassy of Israel
3 rue Rabelais 75008 01.40.76.55.00
Fax: 01.40.76.55.55
Email: info@amb-israel.fr

Groceries

Francois
45 rue Richer 75009 01.47.70.17.43
Doueib
11 bis rue Geoffroy Marie 75009 01.47.70.86.09
Le Haim
6 rue Paulin Enfert 75013 01.44.24.53.34
Chekel
14 av. de Villiers 75017 01.48.88.94.97
Supervision: Beth Din of Paris.
Also sells delicatessen and sandwiches. Hours: 9 am to 8 pm. Nearest Metro: Villiers. Near Champs-Elysées/Opéra.
Compt Pdts Alimentaires
111 av. de Villiers 75017 01.42.27.16.91
Chochana
54 av. Secretan 75019

Hotels

Hotel Touring
21 rue Buffault 75009 01.48.78.09.16
Fax: 01.48.78.27.74
Email: infos@hotel-touring.fr
Web site: www.hotel-touring.fr

Pavillon De Paris
7 rue de Parme 75009 01.55.31.60.00
Fax: 01.55.31.60.01
Email: mail@pavillondeparis.com
Web site: www.pavillondeparis.com

Hôtel Aida Opéra
17 rue du Conservatoire 75009 01.45.23.11.11
Fax: 01.47.70.38.73
Email: reservation@aida-opera.com
Supervision: Beth Din of Paris.
Kosher breakfast.

Hotel Geoffroy-Marie Opera
12 rue Geoffroy-Marie 75009 01.47.70.11.85
Fax: 01.42.46.09.36
Email: dizemgoffoperahotel@wanadoo.fr
Supervision: Beth Din of Paris.
Breakfast only

L'Hotel de Mericourt
50 rue de la Folie Mericourt 75011 01.43.38.73.63
Fax: 01.43.38.66.13
Email: demericourt.hotel@wanadoo.fr
Situated in an area with many kosher facilities.

Libraries

Library Judaica of the Seminaire Israelite de France
9 rue Vauquelin 75005 01.47.07.22.94
Visit only by appointment.

Mikvaot

176 rue du Temple 75003 01.42.71.89.28
The mikvah is located in the centre of Paris, near Place de la République, at the rear of the building. The staff is English-speaking.
19-21 rue Galvani 75017 01.45.74.52.80

Mayan Hai Source de Vie Haya Mouchka
2-4 rue Tristan Tzara 75018 01.40.38.18.29; 01.46.36.11.09
1 rue des Annelets 75019 01.44.84.05.36
For men and women. Telephone is an answer-machine, for women only.

Mikve Haya Mouchka
25 rue Riquet 75019 01.40.36.40.92
Fax: 01.40.36.88.90
75 rue Julien Lacroix 75020 01.46.36.39.20; 01.46.36.30.10
For men and women.

Monument

Memorial To The Unknown Jewish Martyr
Rue Geoffroy l'Assenier 17
The memorial is a tribute to the Jews who perished in the Holocaust. Erected in 1956 it contains the Archives of the Centre Documentation Juive Contemporaine. At the centre is an "eternal flame".

Museums

Musée d'art et d'histoire de Judaisme
Hotel de Saint-Aignan,
71 rue de Temple 75003 01.53.01.86.60
Fax: 01.42.72.97.47
Open Monday to Friday from 11 am to 6 pm and Sunday from 10 am to 6 pm.

Religious Organisations

Communauté Israélite Orthodoxe de Paris
10 rue Pavée 75004 01.42.77.81.51
Fax: 01.48.87.26.29

Restaurants

Dairy

Panini Folie
11 rue du Ponceau 75002 01.42.33.14.55
Supervision: Beth Din of Paris.
Contini, 42 rue des Rosiers 75004 01.48.04.78.32
Supervision: Beth Din of Paris.
Hamman Café
4 rue des Rosiers 75004 01.42.78.04.46
Supervision: Beth Din of Paris.
Cine Citta Café
7 rue d'Aguesseau 75008 01.42.68.05.03
Supervision: Beth Din of Paris.
Maestro Pizza
19 rue d'Anjou 75008 01.47.42.15.60
Supervision: Beth Din of Paris.
Casa Rina
18 Faubourg Monmartre 75009 01.45.23.02.22
Supervision: Beth Din of Paris.

King Salomon
46 rue Richer 75009 01.42.46.31.22
Supervision: Beth Din of Paris.

Dizengoff Café
27 rue Richer 75009 01.47.70.81.97
Supervision: Beth Din of Paris.
Open from 12.00 am to 10.30 pm.

Cine Citta Café
58 rue Richer 75009 01.42.46.09.65
Supervision: Beth Din of Paris.

Bistrot Blanc
52 rue Blanche 75009 01.42.85.05.30
Supervision: Paris Beth Din.

Le New's
56 av. de la République 75011 01.43.38.63.18
Supervision: Beth Din of Paris.

Cocktail Café
82 av. Parmentier 75011 01.43.57.19.94
Supervision: Beth Din of Paris.

Gin Fizz
157 blvd Serrurier 75019 01.42.00.51.28
Supervision: Beth Din of Paris.

Pizza Curial
44 rue Curial 75019 01.40.37.15.00
Supervision: Beth Din of Paris.

Meat

Juliette
14 rue Duphot 75001 01.42.60.18.05
Fax: 01.42.60.18.98
Supervision: Beth Din of Paris.

La Petite Famille
32 rue des Rosiers 75003 01.42.77.00.50
Supervision: Beth Din of Paris.

Centre Edmond Fleg
8 bis, rue de l'Eperon 75006 01.46.33.43.31
Supervision: Beth Din of Paris.

Sivane,
36 rue de Berri 75008 01.49.53.01.21
Supervision: Beth Din of Paris.

Zazou Burger
19 rue du Faubourg Montmartre 75009
01.40.22.08.33
Supervision: Beth Din of Paris.

Synagogue Beth El
4 rue Saulnier 75009 01.45.23.34.89
Supervision: Beth Din of Paris.
Shabbat meals by arrangement.

Berbeche Burger
47 rue Richer 75009 01.47.70.81.22
Supervision: Beth Din of Paris.

France / Paris

Georges de Tunis
42 rue Richer 75009 01.47.70.24.64
Supervision: Beth Din of Paris.
Le Gros Ventre
7/9 rue Montyon 75009 01.48.24.25.34
Supervision: Beth Din of Paris.
Chez David
11 rue Montyon 75009 01.44.83.01.24
Supervision: Beth Din of Paris.
Adolphe, 1
4 rue Richer 75009 01.47.70.91.25
Supervision: Beth Din of Paris.
Douieb,
11 bis rue Geoffroy Marie 75009 01.47.70.86.09
Supervision: Beth Din of Paris.
Mao Tsur
10 rue Geoffroy Marie 75009 01.47.70.62.53
Fax: 01.47.70.27.76
Supervision: Beth Din of Paris.
Les Ailes
34 rue Richer 75009 01.47.70.62.53
Supervision: Beth Din of Paris.
Dolly's Food
9 rue cité Riverain 75010 01.48.03.08.40
Supervision: Beth Din of Paris.
Les Cantiques
16 rue Beaurepaire 75010 01.42.40.64.21
Supervision: Beth Din of Paris.
Deliver.
Cash Food
63 rue des Vinaigriers 75010 01.42.03.95.75
Supervision: Beth Din of Paris.
Le Manahattan
231 blvd Voltaire 75011 01.43.56.03.30
Supervision: Beth Din of Paris.
Le Cabourg
102 blvd Voltaire 75011 01.47.00.71.43
Supervision: Beth Din of Paris.
Hours: 12 pm to 2.30 pm and 7 pm to 11 pm.
Le Lotus de Nissan
39 rue Amelot 75011 01.43.55.80.42
Supervision: Beth Din of Paris.
Yun-Pana
115 Boulevard Voltaire 75011 01.43.79.20.48
Supervision: Beth Din of Paris.
La Libanaise
13 rue des Sablons 75016 01.45.05.10.35
Supervision: Beth Din of Paris.
Fradji,
42 rue Poncelet 75017 01.47.54.91.40
Supervision: Beth Din of Paris.
Brasserie du Belvedere
109 av. de Villiers 75017 01.47.64.96.55
Supervision: Beth Din of Paris.
Nini
24 rue Saussier Leroy 75017 01.46.22.28.93
Supervision: Beth Din of Paris.
Darjeeling
1 bis, rue des Colonels Renard 75017
01.45.72.09.32
Fax: 01.45.72.03.27
Web site: www.darjeeling-ontable.com
Supervision: Chief Rabbi Mordechai Rottenberg.
Mille Delices
52 av. Secrétan 75019 01.40.18.32.32
Supervision: Beth Din of Paris.
La Muraille de Chine
44 rue d'Hautpoul 75019 01.42.01.20.30
Supervision: Beth Din of Paris.
Lumieres de Belleville
102 blvd de Belleville 75020 01.47.97.51.83
Supervision: Beth Din of Paris.
Auberge de Belleville
110 blvd de Belleville 75020 01.43.15.02.59
Supervision: Beth Din of Paris.
Chez François
5 rue Ramponeau 75020 01.47.97.40.06
Supervision: Beth Din of Paris.
Chez Rene et Gabin
92 blvd de Belleville 75020 01.43.58.78.14
Supervision: Beth Din of Paris.
Elygel,
116 blvd de Belleville 75020 01.47.97.09.73
Supervision: Beth Din of Paris.
Le Petit Pelleport
135 rue Pelleport 75020 01.40.33.13.17
Supervision: Beth Din of Paris.

Synagogues

Liberal

Union Liberale Israelite de France
24 rue Copernic 75016 01.47.04.37.27
Fax: 01.47.27.81.02
Email: communication@ulif.com
Web site: www.ulif.com

Masorti

Communaute Juive Massorti de Paris
8 rue George Bernard Shaw (off rue Dupleix) 75015
01.45.67.97.96
Fax: 01.45.56.89.79
Email: RuzieDr@aol.com
Web site: www.jtsa.edu/synagogues/adathsfr/
The Paris Jewish Masorti (Conservative) Community. Services Friday night 6.30 pm. Shabbat morning 10 am festivals and Rosh Chodesh.

Orthodox
15 rue Notre-Dame de Nazareth 75003
01.42.78.00.30
Fax: 01.42.78.05.18

Groupe Rabbi Yehiel de Paris
25 rue Michel-Leconte 75003 01.42.78.89.17

Netzach Israël Ohel Mordehai
5 rue Sainte-Anastase 75003

Adath Yechouroun
25 rue des Rosiers 75004 01.44.59.82.36

Oratoire Mahziké Adath Mouvement Loubavitch
17 rue des Rosiers 75004

Synagogue des Tournelles
21 bis rue des Tournelles 75004 01.42.74.32.65;
01.42.74.32.80
Fax: 01.40.29.90.27
Email: david-halim@septodont.fr

Synagogue Tephilat Israël Frank-Forter
24 rue du Bourg-Tibourg 75004 01.46.24.48.94

Fondation Roger Fleishmann
18 rue des Ecouffes 75004 01.48.87.97.86
14 place des Vosges 75004 01.48.87.79.45
Fax: 01.48.87.57.58

Agoudas Hakehilos Instit Yad Mordekhai
10 rue Pavée 75004 01.48.87.21.54
Fax: 01.48.87.21.59

A striking Art Nouveau synagogue designed by Hector Guimard, whose wife was Jewish, the creator of the world famous Metro entrances.

Séminaire Israélite de France
9 rue Vauquelin 75005 01.47.07.21.22
Fax: 01.43.37.75.92

Centre Rachi
30 blvd du Port-Royal 75005 01.43.31.98.20

Centre Edmond Fleg
8 bis rue de l'Epéron 75006 01.46.33.43.31

Houses the Union des Centres Communautaires (UCC), which can be contacted via the same telephone number. Their fax number is 01.43.25.86.19. Tikvaténou, the Jewish youth movement of the Consistoire, is also located here, Tel: 01.46.33.43.24; Fax: 01.43.25.20.59.

E.E.I.F.
27 av. de Ségur 75007 01.47.83.60.33

Hékhal Moché
218-220 rue du Faubourg St-Honoré 75008
01.45.61.20.25

Located behind the Golden Tulip Hotel.

France / Paris

Kollel Rav Lévy
37 blvd de Strasbourg 75009

Synagogue Berit Chalom
18 rue Saint-Lazare 75009
01.48.78.45.32; 01.48.78.38.80

Grande Synagogue de Paris
44 rue de la Victoire 75009
01.40.82.26.26 ext. 2773 or 01.45.26.95.36
Fax: 01.45.26.95.36
Email: grandesynaparis@col.fr
Web site: www.col.fr/grande-synagogue-paris

Rachi Chull
6 rue Ambroise-Thomas 75009 01.48.24.86.95

Centre Communataire De Paris
5 rue Rochechouart 75009 01.49.95.95.92
Fax: 01.42.80.10.66

Siège du Beth Loubavitch
8 rue Lamartine 75009 01.45.26.87.60
Fax: 01.45.26.24.37

Tiferet Yaacob
71 rue de Dunkerque 75009
01.42.81.32.17; 01.42.49.65.12

Adass Yereim
10 rue Cadet 75009
01.42.46.36.47; 01.48.74.51.78
Fax: 01.48.74.35.35

Nussach Ashkenez

Beth-El
3 bis rue Saulnier 75009 01.47.70.09.23
Fax: 01.45.23.15.75
Email: bethel@eboom.com

Beth-Israël
4 rue Saulnier 75009 01.45.23.34.89

UNAT La Fraternelle
13-15 rue des Petites-Ecuries 75010 01.42.46.65.02

Beth-Eliaou
192 rue Saint-Martin 75010 01.40.38.47.53
Fax: 01.40.36.41.95

Rav Pealim (Braslav)
49 blvd de la Villette 75010 01.42.41.55.44
4 rue Martel 75010
9 rue Guy-Patin 75010 01.42.85.12.74

A.U.J.
130 rue du Faubourg Saint-Martin 75010
01.40.05.98.34

Synagogue Don Isaac Abravanel
84-86 rue de la Roquette 75011 01.47.00.75.95

Ozar Hatorath Shoul
40 rue de l'Orillon 75011 01.43.38.73.40
Fax: 01.43.38.36.45

Ora Vesimha
37 rue des Trois-Bornes 75011 01.43.57.49.84

Ets Haim
18 rue Basfroi 75011 01.43.48.82.42

Adath Israël
36 rue Basfroi 75011 01.43.67.89.20

Oratoire de la Fondation Rothschild (Maison de Retraite)
76 rue de Picpus 75012 01.43.44.72.98
Fax: 01.43.44.71.39

Névé Chalom
29 rue Sibué 75012 01.43.42.07.70
Fax: 01.43.48.44.50

Chivtei Israel
12-14 Cité Moynet 75012 01.43.43.50.12
Fax: 01.43.47.36.78
Email: ravatlan@club-internet.fr

Merkaz Beth Myriam
19 rue Domrémy 75013 01.45.86.83.99
Fax: 01.45.86.83.99

Avoth Ouvanim
59 av. d'Ivry 75013 01.45.82.80.73
Fax: 01.45.85.94.39

6 bis villa d'Alésia 75014 01.45.40.82.35
Fax: 01.45.40.72.89

223 rue Vercingétorix 75014 01.45.45.50.51

Beith Chalom
25 villa d'Alésia 75014 01.45.45.38.71
Fax: 01.43.37.58.49

Ohel Mordekhai
13 rue Fondary 75015 01.40.59.96.56

Ohel Avraham
31 rue Montevideo 75016 01.45.05.66.73
Fax: 01.40.72.83.76

23 bis rue Dufrénoy 75016
01.45.04.94.00; 01.45.04.66.73

Beth Hamidrach Lamed
67 rue Bayen 75017 01.45.74.52.80

Centre Rambam
19-21 rue Galvani 75017 01.45.74.52.80

Synagogue ACIP
42 rue des Saules 75018 01.46.06.71.39
Fax: 01.46.06.71.39

Synagogue de Montmartre
13 rue Sainte-Isaure 75018 01.42.64.48.34

Pah'ad David
11 rue du Plateau 75019 01.42.46.47.03
Fax: 01.42.46.47.56

Synagogue Michkenot Israel
6 rue Jean-Nohain 75019 01.48.03.25.59
Fax: 01.42.00.26.87

Kollel Ysmah Moché
36 rue des Annelets 75019 01.43.63.73.94

Ohr Tora - AJJ
15 rue Riquet 75019 01.40.38.23.36
Fax: 01.40.36.42.23
Email: ajj@free.fr

Beth Loubavitch
25 rue Riquet 75019 01.40.36.93.90
Fax: 01.40.36.60.15

Beth Loubavitch
53 rue Compans 75019 01.42.02.20.35

Chaare Tora
1 rue Henri-Turot 75019 01.42.06.41.12
Fax: 01.42.06.95.47

Ohr Yossef
44-48 Quai de la Marne 75019 01.42.45.74.20
Fax: 01.40.18.10.74

Beth Chalom
11-13 rue Curial 75019 01.40.37.65.16; 01.40.37.12.54

Collel Hamabit
7 rue Rouvet 75019 01.40.38.13.59

Heder Loubavitch
25 rue des Solitaires 75019 01.42.02.98.95
Fax: 01.42.02.04.62

Ohaley Yaacov
11 rue Henri-Murger 75019 01.42.49.25.00

Rabbi David ou Moché
45 rue de Belleville 75019 01.40.18.30.63
Fax: 01.40.18.30.62

Synagogue Michkan-Yaacov
118 blvd de Belleville 75020 01.43.49.39.59

Synagogue Achkenaze & Sephardi
49 rue Pali Kao 75020 01.46.36.30.10

Beth Loubavitch
47 rue Ramponeau 75020 01.43.66.93.00

Synagogue Bet Yaacov Yossef
5 square des Cardeurs,
43 rue Saint-Blaise 75020 01.43.56.03.11

Maor Athora
16 rue Ramponeau 75020 01.47.97.69.42

Beth Loubavitch
93 rue des Orteaux 75020 01.40.24.10.60

Ohr Chimchon Raphaël
5 passage Dagorno 75020 01.46.59.39.02
Fax: 01.46.59.14.99

Paris Suburbs

Alfortville

Butchers

Tiness, 12 Etienne Dollet, Val-de-Marne
94140 01.49.77.95.79

Synagogues

Orthodox

1 rue Blanche, Val-de-Marne
94140 01.43.78.86.43

Antony

Butchers

A.B.C., 96 av de la Division Leclerc,
Hauts-de-Seine 92160 01.46.66.13.43

Synagogues

Orthodox

Community Centre and Synagogue
1 rue Sdérot, Angle 1,
Rue Barthélémy, Hauts-de-Seine
92160 01.46.66.19.17

Asnieres

Mikvaot

82 rue du R.P. Christian-Gilbert,
Hauts-de-Seine 92600 01.47.99.26.59

Synagogues

Orthodox

73 bis rue des Bas,
Hauts-de-Seine 92600 01.47.99.32.55

Athis-Mons

Synagogues

55 rue des Coquelicots,
Essonne 91200 01.69.38.14.29

Aulnay-Sous-Bois

Synagogues

80 rue Maximilien Robespierre,
Seine-Saint-Denis 93600 01.48.69.66.93

Bagneux

Bakeries

Princiane
1 rue de l'Egalité, Parc de Garlande,
Hauts-de-Seine 92220 01.47.35.90.77
Fax: 01.47.35.93.67
Email: princiane@princiane.com
Supervision: Beth Din of Paris. Orthodox Union.

Butchers

Isaac,
188 av Aristide Briand,
Hauts-de-Seine 92220 01.45.47.00.21

Bagnolet

Bakeries

Sonesta,
27 rue Adélaide Lahaye, Seine-Saint-Denis
93170 01.43.64.92.93
Fax: 01.43.60.51.26
Supervision: Beth Din of Paris.

Synagogues

Orthodox

15-17 rue D. Vienot, Seine-Saint-Denis 93170
01.43.60.39.93

Bobigny

Restaurants

Le Simane Tov
22-24 rue Henri Barbusse,
Seine-Saint-Denis 93000 01.48.43.79.00
Supervision: Beth Din of Paris.

Synagogues

Orthodox

11-13 rue Mathurin Renaud,
Seine-Saint-Denis 93000 01.48.32.68.86

Bondy

Synagogues

Maison Communautaire
28 av. de la Villageoise,
Seine-Saint-Denis 93140 01.48.47.50.79

Boulogne sur Seine

Bakeries

Ariel, 143 avenue J.B. Clément,
Hauts-de-Seine 92100 01.46.04.24.42
Supervision: Beth Din of Paris.

Groceries

Ednale,
28 rue Georges Sorel, Hauts-de-Seine 92100
01.46.03.83.37

Synagogues

Orthodox

43 rue des Abondances,
Hauts-de-Seine 92100 01.46.03.90.63
Fax: 01.46.03.90.63

Bussiere

Mikvaot

Domaines de Melicourt,
Seine-Saint-Denis 77750 01.60.22.54.85;
01.60.22.53.01

Champigny

Synagogues

Orthodox

Synagogue Beth-David
25 av. du Général-de Gaulle,
Val-de-Marne 94500 01.48.85.72.29

Charenton le Pont

Butchers

Mazel Tov
14 rue Victor Hugo,
Val-de-Marne 94220 01.43.68.41.23

Chelles

Synagogues

Orthodox

14 rue des Anémones,
Seine-et-Marne 77500 01.60.20.92.93

Choisy-le-Roi

Butchers

Chez Ilane
131 Marechal de Lattre de Tassigny,
Val-de-Marne 94600 01.48.52.27.74

Mikvaot

28 av. de Newbum,
Val-de-Marne 94600
01.48.53.43.70; 01.48.92.68.68

Synagogues

Orthodox

28 av. de Newburn,
Val-de-Marne 94600 01.48.53.48.27

Clichy-sur-Seine

Synagogues

26 rue de Mozart (Espace Clichy),
Hauts-de-Seine 92210 01.47.39.02.43

Créteil

Bakeries

Tov 'Mie
25 rue du Dr Paul Casalis,
Val-de-Marne 94000 01.48.99.00.39
Supervision: Beth Din of Paris.

La Nougatine
20 Esplanade des Abîmes,
Val-de-Marne 94000 01.49.56.98.56
Supervision: Beth Din of Paris.

Quick Chaud
26 allée Parmentier,
Val-de-Marne 94000 01.48.99.08.30
Supervision: Beth Din of Paris.
Caprices et Delices
5 rue Edouard Manet,
Val-de-Marne 94000 01.43.39.20.20
Supervision: Beth Din of Paris.
Les Jasmins de Tunis
C.C. Kennedy,
Val-de-Marne 94000 01.43.77.50.66
Supervision: Beth Din of Paris.

Butchers

La Charolaise Julien
Cte Commercial Kennedy,
Loge 13 rue Gabriel Peri, Val-de-Marne
94000 01.43.39.20.43
Boucherie Patrick
2 rue Edouard Manet, Val-de-Marne
94000 01.43.39.29.64

Mikvaot

Rue du 8 Mai 1945, Val-de-Marne 94000
01.43.77.01.70; 01.43.77.19.68

Restaurants

Meat

Prumo Cacher
17, allee du Commerce, Val-de-Marne
94000 01.49.80.04.25
Supervision: Beth Din of Paris.

Synagogues

Orthodox

Community Centre
rue du 8 Mai 1945, Val-de-Marne 94051
01.43.77.01.70; 01.43.39.05.20
Fax: 01.43.99.03.60

Enghien-les-bains

Mikvaot

47 rue de Malleville, Val-d'Oise 95880
01.34.17.37.11

Synagogues

Orthodox

47 rue de Malleville, Val-d'Oise 95880
01.34.12.42.34

Epinay

Butchers

Chalom, 90 av. Joffre, Seine-Saint-Denis 93800
01.48.41.50.64

Fontainebleau

Synagogues

Orthodox

38 rue Paul Seramy, Seine-et-Marne 77300
01.64.22.68.48

Fontenay sous Bois

Synagogues

79 blvd de Verdun, Val-de-Marne
94120 01.48.77.38.67

Mikvaot

Haya Mossia
177 rue des Moulins, Val-de-Marne
94120 01.48.77.53.90; 01.48.76.83.84

Fontenay aux Roses

Synagogues

Centre Moise Meniane
17 av. Paul-Langevin, Hauts-de-Seine
92660 01.46.60.75.94

Garges-les-Gonesse

Butchers

Chez Harry
1 rue J B Corot, Val-d'Oise 95140 01.39.86.53.81
Boucherie Berbeche
C C Pal de la Dame Blanche, Val-d'Oise
95140 01.39.86.42.06

Mikvaot

15 rue Corot, Val-d'Oise 95140 01.39.86.75.64

Synagogues

Orthodox

Maison Communautaire Chaare Ra'hamim
14 rue Corot, Val-d'Oise 95140 01.39.86.75.64

Issy-Les-Moulineaux

Synagogues

72 blvd Gallieni, Hauts-de-Seine
92130 01.46.48.34.49

La Courneuve

Synagogues

13 rue Saint-Just, Seine-Saint-Denis
93120 01.48.36.75.59

La Garenne-Colombes

Synagogues

Synagogue and Community Centre of Courbevoie / La Garenne-Colombes
13 rue L.M. Nordmann, Hauts-de-Seine
92250 01.47.69.92.17

La Varenne St-Hilaire

Synagogues

10 bis av. du chateau, Val-de-Marne
94210 01.42.83.28.75

Le Blanc Mesnil

Synagogues

65 rue Maxime-Gorki, Seine-Saint-Denis
93150 01.48.65.58.98

Le Chesnay

Mikvaot

39 rue de Versailles, Yvelines
78150 01.39.54.05.65; 01.39.07.19.19

Le Kremlin-Bicetre

Synagogues

Orthodox

41-45 rue J.F. Kennedy, Val-de-Marne
94270 01.46.72.73.64

Le Perreux Nogent

Synagogues

Synagogue-Nogent/Le Perreux/Bry-Sur-Marne
165 bis av. du Gal-de Gaulle,
Val-de-Marne 94170 01.48.72.88.65

Le Raincy

Mikvaot

67 blvd du Midi, Seine-Saint-Denis
93340 01.43.81.06.61

Synagogues

Orthodox

Maison Communautaire
19 allée Chatrian, Seine-Saint-Denis
93340 01.43.02.06.11

Le Vesinet

Mikvaot

29 rue Henri Cloppet, Yvelines
78110 01.30.53.10.45; 01.30.71.12.26

Synagogues

Orthodox

Maison Communautaire
29 rue Henri-Cloppet, Yvelines
78110 01.30.53.10.45

Les Lilas

Butchers

Boucherie Des Lilas
6 rue de la Republique, Seine-Saint-Denis
93260 01.43.63.89.15

Levallois Perret

Restaurants

Meat

Delicates Eden
102 rue Rivay, Hauts-de-Seine
92300 01.42.70.97.06
Supervision: Beth Din of Paris.

Maisons-Alfort

Mikvaot

92-94 rue Victor-Hugo, Val-de-Marne 94700
01.43.78.95.69

Massy

Mikvaot

Allée Marcel-Cerdan, Essone
91300 01.42.37.48.24

Synagogues

Orthodox

Allée Marcel-Cerdan, Essone
91300 01.69.20.94.21

Meaux

Synagogues

11 rue P. Barennes, Seine-et-Marne
77100 01.64.34.76.58

Meudon-La-Foret

Mikvaot

Rue de la Synagogue, Hauts-de-Seine
92360 01.46.32.64.82; 01.46.01.01.32

Synagogues

Orthodox

Maison Communautaire
Rue de la Synagogue, Hauts-de-Seine
92360 01.48.53.48.27

Montreuil

Bakeries

Le Relais Sucre
62 rue des Roches, Seine-Saint-Denis
93100 01.48.70.22.60
Supervision: Beth Din of Paris.

Nat Cacher
21 rue Gabriel Péri, Seine-Saint-Denis
93100 01.48.58.05.25
Supervision: Beth Din of Paris.

Korcarz,
134 bis rue de Stalingrad, Seine-Saint-Denis
93100 01.48.58.33.45
Supervision: Beth Din of Paris/Chief Rabbi Mordechai Rottenberg.

Butchers

Andre Volailles
62 rue des Roches, Seine-Saint-Denis
93100 01.48.57.57.17

Boucherie Andre
64 rue des Roches, Seine-Saint-Denis
93100 01.48.57.57.17

Synagogues

Orthodox

179 bis rue de Paris, Seine-Saint-Denis 93100

Montrouge

Butchers

Boucherie Vivo
2 rue Camille Pelletan, Hauts-de-Seine
92120 01.47.35.23.06

Mikvaot

Ismah-Israel
90 rue Gabriel-Péri, Hauts-de-Seine
92120 01.42.53.08.54

Synagogues

Orthodox

Centre Communautaire Regional Malakoff-Montrouge
90 rue Gabriel-Péri, Hauts-de-Seine
92120 01.46.32.64.82
Fax: 01.46.56.20.49

Neuilly

Butchers

Neuilly Cacher
2/6 rue de Chartres, Hauts-de-Seine
92200 01.47.45.06.06

Groceries

King David
14 rue Paul- Chatrousse, Hauts-de-Seine
92200 01.47.45.18.19

Restaurants

Meat

King David
14 rue Paul-Chatrousse, Hauts-de-Seine
92200 01.47.45.18.19
Supervision: Beth Din of Paris.
Deliver. Hours: 8 am to 10 pm.

Synagogues

Orthodox

12 rue Ancelle, Hauts-de-Seine
92200 01.46.24.49.15

Noisy Le Sec

Synagogues

Beth Gabriel
2 rue de la Pierre Feuillère, Seine-Saint-Denis
93130 01.48.46.71.79

Pantin

Bakeries

Crousty Cash
27 av. Anatole France, Seine-Saint-Denis
93500 01.48.40.89.74
Supervision: Beth Din of Paris.

Butchers

Levy Baroukh
5/7 rue Anatole France, Seine-Saint-Denis
93500 01.48.91.02.14

Restaurants

Dairy

Chez Jacquy
24 rue du Pré-Saint-Gervais, Seine-Saint-Denis
93500 01.48.10.94.24
Supervision: Beth Din of Paris.

Synagogues

Orthodox

8 rue Gambetta, Seine-Saint-Denis
93500 40.18.44.87.99

Ris-Orangis

Synagogues

Orthodox

1 rue Jean-Moulin, Essone 91130 01.69.43.07.83

Roissy-En-Brie

Mikvaot

Rue Paul-Cézanne, C.Cial Bois Montmartre,
Seine-et-Marne
77680 01.60.28.34.65; 01.60.29.09.44

Synagogues

Orthodox

Maison Communautaire
1 rue Paul-Cézanne, Centre Commercial Bois Montmartre, Seine-et-Marne
77680 01.60.28.36.38

Rosny-Sous-Bois

Synagogues

62-64 rue Lavoisier, Seine-Saint-Denis
93110 01.48.54.04.11
Fax: 01.69.43.07.83

Rueil Malmaison

Synagogues

6 rue René-Cassin, Hauts-de-Seine
92500 01.47.08.32.62

Saint Germain

Synagogues

Liberal

Kehilat Gesher (Franco-American)
10 rue de Pologne 78100 01.39.21.97.19
Email: rabbenutom@compuserve.com

Saint-Denis

Synagogues

Orthodox

51 blvd Marcel-Sembat, (next to the Gendarmerie),
Seine-Saint-Denis 93200 01.48.20.30.87

Saint-Leu La Foret

Mikvaot

2 rue Jules Vernes, Val-d'Oise
95320 01.39.95.96.90; 01.34.14.24.15

Synagogues

Orthodox

2 rue Jules Verne,
Val-d'Oise 95320 01.39.95.96.90
Fax: 01.39.95.72.13

Saint-Ouen-l'Aumône

Synagogues

Maison Communautaire
9 rue de Chennevières,
Val-d'Oise 95310 01.30.37.71.41

Sarcelles

Bakeries

Natania, 34 blvd Albert Camus,
Val-d'Oise 95200 01.39.90.11.78
Supervision: Beth Din of Paris.

Louis D'or
90 av. Paul Valéry, Val-d'Oise 95200 01.39.90.25.45
Supervision: Beth Din of Paris.

Zazou
C.C. les Flanades, Val-d'Oise 95200 01.34.19.08.11
Supervision: Beth Din of Paris.

Oh Delices
71 av. Paul Valéry, Val-d'Oise 95200 01.39.92.41.12
Supervision: Beth Din of Paris.

Butchers

Hazout
5 av. Paul Valery, Val-d'Oise 95200 01.39.90.72.95

Boucherie Du Coin
60 blvd Albert Camus, Val-d'Oise
95200 01.39.90.53.02

Mikvaot

Mayanot Rachel
14 av. Ch.-Péguy, Val-d'Oise 95200 01.39.90.40.17

Restaurants

Dairy

Marina
103 av. Paul-Valéry, Val-d'Oise
95200 01.34.19.23.51
Supervision: Beth Din of Paris.

Meat

Berbeche Burger
13 av. Edouard-Branly, Val-d'Oise
95200 01.34.19.12.02
Supervision: Beth Din of Paris.

Synagogues

Orthodox

Maison Communautaire
74 av. Paul-Valéry, Val-d'Oise 95200 01.39.90.59.59
Mikva on premises.

Sartrouville

Synagogues

Synagogue Rabbi Shimon bar Yohai et Rabbi Meir Baal Hannes
1 rue de Stalingrad, Yvelines
78500 01.39.15.22.57

Savigny sur Orge

Synagogues

1 av. de l'Armee Leclerc, Essonne
91600 01.69.96.30.90

Mikvaot

1 av. de L'Armée-Leclerc, Essonne
91600 01.69.24.48.25; 01.69.96.30.90

Sevran

Mikvaot

25 bis du Dr Roux, Seine-Saint-Denis
93270 01.43.84.25.40
Mikva Kelim.

Synagogues

Orthodox

Synagogue Mayan-Thora
25 bis rue du Dr Roux, BP. 111,
Seine-Saint-Denis 93270 01.43.84.25.40

St-Brice-Sous-Foret

Synagogues

Centre Communautaire Ohel Avraham
10 rue Pasteur, Val-d'Oise 95350 01.39.94.96.10

Stains

Synagogues

8 rue Lamartine (face n°2),
Clos St-Lazare, Seine-Saint-Denis
93240 01.48.21.04.12
Provisional address: 8 av. Louis Bordes (Ancien Conservatoire Municipal).

Thiais

Community Organisations

Community Centre Choisy-Orly-Thiais
Voie du Four,
128 av. du Marechal de Lattre de Tassigny,
Val-de-Marne 94320 01.48.92.68.68
Fax: 01.48.92.72.82

Trappes

Synagogues

Orthodox

7 rue du Port-Royal, Yvelines 78190
01.30.62.40.43

Versailles

Synagogues

10 rue Albert-Joly, Yvelines 78000 02.39.07.19.19
Fax: 02.39.50.96.34
Mikva on premises.

Villejuif

Bakeries

Eden Eclair
30 rue Marcel Gromesnil,
Val-de-Marne 94800 01.47.26.42.96
Supervision: Beth Din of Paris.

Synagogues

Orthodox

106 av. de Gournay, Val-de-Marne
94800 01.46.78.76.53

Villeneuve-la-Garenne

Mikvaot

42-44 rue du Fond-de-la Noue,
Hauts-de-Seine 92390 01.47.94.89.98

Synagogues

Orthodox

Maison Communautaire
44 rue du Fond-de-la-Noue,
Hauts-de-Seine 92390 01.47.94.89.98

Villiers-le-Bel-Gonesse

Mikvaot

1 rue Léon Blum, Val-d'Oise
95400 01.39.94.45.51; 01.34.19.64.48

Synagogues

Orthodox

1 rue Léon-Blum, Val-d'Oise
95400 01.39.94.30.49; 01.39.94.94.89

Villiers Sur Marne

Synagogues

30 rue Léon-Douer, B.P. 15, Val-de-Marne
94350 01.49.30.01.47
Fax: 01.49.30.85.40

Vincennes

Butchers

Boucherie Hayache
146 av. de Paris, Val-de-Marne
94300 01.43.28.16.04

Boucherie Des Levy
32 rue Raymond du Temple, Val-de-Marne
94300 01.43.74.94.18

Synagogues

Orthodox

Synagogue Sepharade
30 rue Céline-Robert, Val-de-Marne
94300 01.47.55.65.07

Synagogue Achkenaze
30 rue Céline-Robert, Val-de-Marne
94300 01.43.28.82.83

Vitry-sur-Seine

Synagogues

133-135 av. Rouget-de-l'Isle,
Val-de-Marne
94400 01.46.80.76.54; 01.45.73.06.58
Fax: 01.45.73.94.01

Yerres

Mikvaot

Beth Rivkah
43/49 rue R. Poincare, Essone
91330 01.69.49.62.74; 01.69.49.62.62
Fax: 01.69.79.27.70
Email: beth-rivkah@wanados.fr

Pau

Synagogues

8 rue des Trois-Freres-Bernadac
64000 05.59.62.37.85

Perigueuex

Synagogues

13 rue Paul-Louis-Courrier 24000 05.53.53.22.52

Perpignan

Butchers

Gilbert Sabbah
3 rue P.-Rameil 66000 04.68.35.41.23
Fax: 04.68.51.09.83

Cemeteries

Rivesaltes
66000
Near the camp from which thousands of Jews were deported to Auschwitz.

Synagogues

54 rue Francois Arago 66000

Phalsbourg

Synagogues

16 rue Alexandre-Weill 57370

Poitiers

Synagogues

1 rue Guynemer 86000

Reims

Synagogues

49 rue Clovis 51100 03.26.47.68.47

Rennes

Community Organisations

32 rue de la Marbaudais 35000 02.99.63.57.18
Services held. Telephone for times.

Roanne

Synagogues

9 rue Beaulieu 42300 04.77.71.51.56

Rouen

Synagogues

55 rue des Bons-Enfants 76100 02.35.71.01.44
The Jewish Youth Club can provide board residence for student travellers and holiday-makers.

Saint-Avold

Cemeteries

The American Military Cemetery
Contains many graves of Jewish servicemen.

Synagogues

Pl. Saint-Nabor 57500 03.87.91.16.16

Saint-Die

Synagogues

Rue de l'Eveche 88100
Services, festivals and Holy Days only.

Saint-Etienne

Synagogues

34 rue d'Arcole 42000 04.77.33.56.31

Saint-Fons

Synagogues

17 av. Albert-Thomas 69190 04.78.67.39.78

Saint-Laurent-du-Var

Synagogues

Villa 'Le Petit Clos', 35 av. des Oliviers 06700

Saint-Louis

Cemeteries

The Hegenheim Cemetary
This cemetery dates from 1673.

Community Organisations

19 rue du Temple 68300 03.89.70.00.48
Kosher products available.

Synagogues

3 rue de General Cassagnou 68300
Rue de la Synagogue 68300

Saint-Quentin

Synagogues

11 ter blvd Henri-Martin 03.23.08.30.72

Sarrebourg

Synagogues

12 rue du Sauvage

Sarreguemines

Synagogues

Rue Georges-V 57200 03.87.98.81.40
Mikva on premises.

Saverne

Synagogues

Rue du 19 Novembre 67700

Sedan-Charleville

Contains many graves of USA servicemen who fell in the last war.

Synagogues

6 av. de Verdun 08200

Selestat

Synagogues

4 rue St-Barbe 67600

Sens

Synagogues

14 rue de la Grande-Juiverie
89100 03.86.95.16.65

Strasbourg

With a Jewish population of 16,000, this city – contested by France and Germany throughout history – currently has an important Jewish community, with several kosher restuarants and butchers, and even a kosher vineyard. The earliest evidence of jewish life dates from 1188. A thirteenth-century mikva was recently discovered.

Bakeries

Crousty Cash
4 rue Sellénick, Bas-Rhin 67000 03.88.35.68.21

Booksellers

Librairie du Cedrat
15 rue de Bitche 67000 03.88.37.32.37
Fax: 03.88.35.63.11
Email: nfraenckel@aol.com
Also Judaica antiquities.
Librairie Du Cedrat
19 rue du Marechal-Foch 67000 03.88.36.38.39
Fax: 03.88.37.96.60

Butchers

Buchinger
63 rue du Faubourg de Pierre 67000 03.88.32.85.03
Buchinger
13 rue Wimpheling 67000 03.88.61.06.98
David,
20 rue Sellenick 67000 03.88.36.75.01

Groceries

Yarden,
3 rue Finkmatt 67000 03.88.22.49.76
Yarden,
13 Blvd. de la Marne 67000
03.88.60.10.10/Office 03.88.60.51.96
Fax: 03.88.61.71.11

Media

Newspapers

Echos-Unir
1a rue du Grand-Rabbin-Rene-Hirschler 67000
03.88.14.46.50
Fax: 03.88.24.26.69
Monthly publication.

Mikvaot

1a rue du Grand-Rabbin-Rene-Hirschler 67000
03.88.14.46.68

Museums

Musee Alsacien
23, quai Alsacien 03.88.35.55.36
Has a section on Jewish Art.

France

Musee Judeo-Alsacien
62a, Grand Rue, Bouxwiller 67330 03.88.70.97.17
Fax: 03.88.70.97.17

Religious Organisations

Regional Chief Rabbi
5 rue du General-de-Castelnau 67000
03.88.32.38.97
Fax: 03.88.25.05.65

Consistoire Israelite du Bas-Rhin
23 rue Sellenick 67000 03.88.25.05.75
Fax: 03.88.25.12.75
Email: cibr1@libertysurf.fr

Restaurants

Dizengoff Café
68, blvd Clemenceau 03.88.36.74.88
Autre Part
60, blvd Clemenceau 03.88.37.10.02
Restaurant Universitaire
ORT-Laure Weil, 11 rue Sellenick 67000
03.88.76.74.76
Fax: 03.88.76.74.74
Email: ort.strasbourg@ort.asso.fr
Le King
28 rue Sellenick 67000 03.88.52.17.71

Meat

Massada
7, rue Baldung Grien 03.88.35.43.43

Synagogues

There are in all more than fifteen synagogues in Strasbourg; the following are among the largest and oldest.

Synagogue de la Paix
1a rue du Grand-Rabbin-Rene-Hirschler 67000
03.88.14.46.50
Fax: 03.88.24.26.69
Email: cis@media-net.fr

Esplanade
17, rue de Nicosie 67000

Orthodox

Ets Hayim
7, rue Turenne 67000 03.88.24.38.36
Fax: 03.88.24.38.36
Email: etzhaim@free.fr

Vineyard

Kosher

Goxwiller, R. Koenig, 35 rue Principale 67000
03.88.95.51.93

Tarbes

Synagogues

Cité Rothschild
6 rue du Pradeau 65000

Thionville

Synagogues

31 av. Clemenceau 57100 03.82.54.47.89
Fax: 03.82.53.03.76

Toul

Synagogues

Rue de la Halle 54200

Toulon

Butchers

Fennech,
15 av. Colbert, Var 83000 04.94.92.70.39
Supervision: Grand Rabbinate of Marseille.
Abecassis
8 rue Vincent Courdouan, Var 83000 04.94.97.39.86
Supervision: Grand Rabbinate of Marseille.

Synagogues

184 av. Lazare Carnot 83050 04.94.92.61.05
Mikva on premises.

Toulouse

Butchers

Lasry,
8 rue Matabiau 31000 05.61.62.65.28
Ghenassia
11 blvd Larrament 31000 05.61.42.05.81
Cacherout Diffusion
37 blvd Carnot 31000 05.61.23.07.59
Maalem,
7 rue des Chalets 31000 05.61.63.77.39

Community Organisations

Community Centre
2 place Riquet 31000 05.61.23.36.54

Groceries

Novogel,
14 rue Edmund Guyaux 31200 05.61.57.03.19

Mikvaot

13 rue Francisque Sarcey 31000 05.61.48.89.84

Religious Organisations

Grand Rabbinat du Toulouse et des Pays de la Garonne - A.C.I.T.
2 place Riquet 31000 05.62.73.46.46
Fax: 05.62.73.46.47

Regional Chief Rabbi
17 rue Calvert 31500 05.61.21.51.14

Restaurants

Community Centre
2 place Riquet 31000 05.62.73.56.56

Synagogues

Chaare Emeth
35 rue Rembrandt 31000 05.61.40.03.88

Ashkenazi

Adat Yechouroun
3 rue Jules-Chalande 31000 05.61.62.30.19
Fax: 05.61.62.86.79

Sephardi

Palaprat
2 rue Palaprat 31000 05.61.21.69.56

Tours

Community Organisations

Community Centre
6 rue Chalmel 37000 02.47.05.59.07

Synagogues

37 rue Parmentier 37000 02.47.05.56.95

Troyes

Memorial

A statue of Rashi stands in place Jean Moulin.

Mikvaot

15 rue Brunneval 03.25.73.34.44

Synagogues

5 rue Brunneval
The only half-timbered shul in France.

Valence

Synagogues

1 place du Colombier 26000 04.75.43.34.43

Valenciennes

Synagogues

36 rue de l'Intendance 59300 03.27.29.11.07

Venissieux

Synagogues

10 av. de la Division-Leclerc 69200 04.78.70.69.85

Verdun

Synagogues

Impasse des Jacobins 55100

Vichy

Synagogues

2 bis rue du Marechal Foch 03200

Vittel

Synagogues

211 rue Croix-Perrot 88800
03.29.08.10.87

Open in July and August only.

Wasselonne

Synagogues

Rue des Bains 67310

Overseas Departments

Corsica

Contact Information

Jo Michel Reis
La Grande Corniche, Routes des Sanguinaires, Ajaccio
9521-5752.
There are between ten and fifteen families in the town.

Synagogues

3 rue du Castagno Bastia, Bastia 20200
Services Shabbat morning and festivals.

Guadeloupe

Synagogues

Bas du Fort, Gosier, Lot 1 (590) 90.99.09
The synagogue, community centre and restaurant/kosher store are all located here.

La Réunion

Contact Information

Leon Benhamou
(262) 29.05.45

Hotels

Kosher

Hotel Astoria
16 rue Juliette Dodu, St Denis 97400 (262) 20.05.58
Fax: (262) 41.26.30

Synagogues

Communauté Juive de la Réunion
8 rue de l'Est, St Denis 97400 (262) 23.78.33
High Holy Day services and communal seder held here.

France / Overseas Departments

Martinique

Synagogues

Kenafe Haarets
12 Anse Gouraud, Schoeler,
Fort-de-France 97233 (596) 61.71.36
Fax: (596) 61.66.71

A community centre is also located here, which supplies kosher food, plus a kosher meat restaurant.

Tahiti

Synagogues

Synagogue,
Rue Morenhouy, Quartier Fariipti (689) 41.03.92
Fax: (689) 41.03.92
Email: Acispo@mail.pf

Georgia

Georgia has had a very long history of Jewish settlement, dating back to two centuries before the destruction of the Second Temple, if the archaeological findings are correct. These earliest Jewish communities may have descended from Babylonian exiles.

Many Jewish organisations operate in the country, some of which are academic, such as the 'Georgian Jewish Society for Natural Science and Technology'. The Georgian Jews are also well informed about their religion, which is not usual in a former Soviet republic.

Synagogues are found in major towns, there is a school in Tbilisi (the capital) and there are some newsletters. It is worth noting that the non-Jewish population has traditionally been far less anti-Semitic than the populations of some other ex-Soviet republics.

GMT + 4 hours | Total Population 4,968,000
Country calling code (995) | Jewish Population 6,000
Emergency Telephone (Police - 02) (Fire - 01) (Ambulance - 03) | Electricity voltage 220

Akhaltsikhe

Synagogues

109 Guramishvili Street

Batumi

Synagogues

6 9th March Street

Gori

Synagogues

Chelyuskin Street

Kutaisi

Synagogues

12 Gapanove Street
Near the main square.

Onni

Synagogues

Baazova Street

Poti

Synagogues

23 Ninoshivili
Tskhakaya Street

Sukhumi

Synagogues

56 Karl Marx Street

Surami

Synagogues

Internatsionalaya Street

Tbilisi

Organisations

Jews of Georgia Assoc.
Tsarity Tamari Street 8 380012 (32) 234-1057

Synagogues

45-47 Leselidze Street

Ashkenazi

65 Kozhevenny Lane

Sephardi

Leselidze Street

Tshkinvali

Synagogues

Isapov Street

Tskhakaya

Synagogues

Mir Street

Vani

Synagogues

4 Kaikavadze Street

Germany

It may be a surprise to many that Germany comes immediately after France and the UK in the population table of Western European Jews. German Jews have contributed much to the culture of European Jews in general since their arrival in what is now Germany in the fourth century. The massive Jewish presence in Poland and other East European states stemmed from German Jews escaping persecution in the late Middle Ages. They took the early Medieval German language with them, which formed Yiddish, the old lingua franca of European Jews.

The Jews who stayed behind in Germany contributed towards Jewish and German culture, with the Reform movement starting in nineteenth-century Germany, and Heine and Mendelssohn contributing to German poetry and music respectively. The Enlightenment and modern Orthodoxy also began in Germany.

The rise of Nazism destroyed the belief that the German Jews were more German than Jewish. Many managed to escape before 1939, but 180,000 were killed in the Holocaust (of the 503,000 who lived in Germany when Hitler came to power). Following the events of 1933-45, it seems incredible that any Jew should want to live in Germany again. However, the community began to re-form, mainly immigrants from Eastern Europe, especially Russia. Now there are again Jewish shops in Berlin, and kosher food is once more available. There are many old synagogues which have been restored, and several concentration camps have been kept as monuments to history. There is also a great interest in Jewish matters among some of the non-Jewish younger generation.

Visitors to Berlin should try to visit the new Jewish Museum (officially opened in September 2001). It covers the history of German Jewry through the middle ages and up to the present. It revives the tradition of an earlier museum opened in 1933 before the Nazis came to power.

GMT + 1 hour
Country calling code (49)
Emergency Telephone (Police - 110) (Fire and Ambulance - 112)

Total Population 82,220,000
Jewish Population 92,000
Electricity voltage 220

Aachen

Representative Organisations

Bundesverband Jüdischer Studenten in Deutschland
Oppenhoffallee 50 (241) 75998

Alsenz

Site

Synagogue,
Kirchberg 1 (636) 23149
Fax: (636) 23149
Restored eighteenth-century synagogue.

Amberg

Community Organisations

Community Centre
Salzgasse 5 (962) 113140

Andernach

Mikvaot

Rhine Valley
This Rhine Valley town contains an early fourteenth-century mikva. Key obtainable from tourist office.

Annweiler

Tourist Sites

(623) 53333
The oldest cemetery in the Palatinate dating from the sixteenth century.

Augsburg

Community Organisations

Community Centre
Halderstr. 8 (821) 517985
There is a Jewish museum in the restored Liberal synagogue.

Bad Kissingen

Hotels

Eden Park
Rosenstrasse 5-7 97688 (971) 717-200
Fax: (971) 717-272

There is a restaurant on the premises that serves kosher food and traditional meals.

Bad Kreuznach

Community Organisations

Community Centre
Gymnasialstr. 11 (671) 26991

Bad Nauheim

Hotels

Accadia, Lindenstr. 15/Frankfurterstr. 22
(6032) 39068

Restaurants

Judische Gemeinde
Karlstr. 34 (6032) 5605 or 0171-9509084
Fax: (6032) 938956

In the Jewish Community Centre. Entry for restaurant from Friedensstr.

Synagogues

Judische Gemeinde
Karlstr. 34 (6032) 5605; 0171-9509084
Fax: (6032) 5605

Synagogue is in the Jewish Community Centre.

Baden-Baden

Synagogues

Werderstr. 2 76530 (722) 139-1021
Fax: (722) 139-1024

Bamberg

Community Organisations

Community Centre
Willy-Lessing-Str. 7 (951) 23267

Bayreuth

Community Organisations

Community Centre
Munzgasse 2 (921) 65407

Berlin

Jewish life is beginning to develop again in Berlin, formerly an important centre for German Jewry. There are many sites which testify to the tragedy that befell the community before and during the War, such as the ruined Oranienburgerstrasse Synagogue, which has been turned into a Jewish centre. The site of the Wannsee Conference, to the south-west of the city, (where the Holocaust was officially planned), has been turned into a museum.

Bed & Breakfasts

Guestrooms
Tucholskystrasse 40, Mitte 10117 (30) 281-3135
Fax: (30) 281-3122
Web site: www.adassjisroel.de

Synagogue and kosher restaurant in the house.

Booksellers

Literaturhandlung
Joachimstaler-Str. 13 10719 (30) 882-4250
Fax: (30) 885-4713

Butchers

Kosher Butcher
Goethestr. 61 10625
The butcher sells wine, sweets, and other things.
Opening hours: 10 am to 5 pm (Friday until 2 pm only).

Cemeteries

Adass Jisroel
Wittlicherstrasse 2, Weissensee 13088
(30) 925-1724

Established in 1880, this historic cemetery is used to this very day. Rabbi Esriel Hildesheimer, Rabbi Prof. David Zvi Hoffmann, Rabbi Eliahu Kaplan and many other wise and pious Jews are buried here.

Community Centre

Ignatz Bubis-Gemeindezentrum
Tucholskystrasse 40, Mitte 10117 (30) 281-3135
Fax: (30) 281-3122

Open daily, except Shabbat, from 11 am to 10 pm. Closes Friday two hours before Shabbat.

Community Organisations

Community Centre
Fasanenstr. 79-80, off the Kurfurstendamm
(30) 88028-250
Fax: (30) 88028-250

This has been built on the site of a famous synagogue, destroyed by the Nazis.

Judische Gemeinde zu Berlin
Joachimstaler Str 13 10719 (30) 88020-0
Fax: (30) 88028-150

Judischer Kulturverein (Jewish Cultural Association)
Oranienburgerstr. 26, Berlin-Mitte 10117
(30) 282-6669; 285-98052
Fax: (30) 285-98053
Email: jkv.berlin@t-online.de

Hours: Monday-Thursday 11 am to 5 pm, Friday 11 am to 2 pm and 1 hour before evening and Sunday events. Friday for Kiddush 6-9 pm (Summer 7 pm). (Entrance around the corner.)

Germany

Zentralrat der Juden in Deutschland
Tucholskystr. 9 10117 (30) 284-4560
Fax: (30) 284-45613
Email: zentralratdjuden@aol.com

Embassy

Embassy of Israel
Auguste-Viktoria Strasse 74-78 14193
(30) 89045-500
Fax: (30) 89045-555
Email: botschaft@israel.de
Web site: www.israel.de

Groceries

Kolbo,
Auguststrasse 77-78, Mitte 10117 (30) 281-3135
In addition to kosher food and wines, sifrei kodesh as well as general literature about Jewish subjects can be obtained here.

Platzl,
Passauer Str.4 10789 (30) 217-7506

Schalom Koschere Lebensmittel (Kosher shop)
Wielandstr. 43 10625
Opening hours: 10 am to 5 pm (Friday until 3 pm only in the winter).

Libraries

Jewish Community
Fassenstrasse 79 10623

Jewish Library
Oranienburger Str. 28 10117 (30) 880-28-427/429

Media

Magazine

Judisches Berlin
Fasanen Str. 79 10623 (30) 88028-260;88028-269
Fax: (30) 88028-266
Email: jued.berlin@jg-berlin.org
Monthly

Magazines

Judische Korrespondenz
Oranienburgerstr. 26, Berlin-Mitte 10117
(30) 282-6669; 285-98052
Fax: (30) 285-98053
Email: jkv.berlin@t-online.de
Monthly.

Newspapers

Allgemeine Judische Wochenzeitung
Postfach 04 03 69, Tucholskystrasse 9 10117
(30) 2844 5650
Fax: (30) 2844 5699
Email: ajw@Juedische-Presse.de
Fortnightly.

"Hadshot Adass Jisroel"
Tucholsky str. 40 10117 (30) 281-3135
Published by Adass Jisroel and obtainable through their offices (see above for number).

Museums

Jewish Museum
Lindenstrasse 9-14 10969 (30) 2599 3456
Fax: (30) 2599 3400
Email: n.bodermann@jmberlin.de
Web site: www.jmberlin.de
The building is now open and well worth visiting. There is a restaurant on the premises.

Restaurants

Meat

Restaurant Arche Noah
Fasanenstr. 79-80 10623 (30) 88-26138
Shabbat reservations and payment have to be arranged before beginning of Shabbat. The restaurant is located in the first floor of the community building. Opening hours: Daily 12 noon to 3.30 pm and 6.30 pm to 10.30pm.

Synagogues

Liberal

Pestalozzistr.
14, 1000 10625 (30) 313-8411

Orthodox

Adass Jisroel
Tucholskystrasse 40, Mitte 10117 (30) 281-3135
Fax: (30) 281-3122
Web site: www.adassjisroel.de
Established 1869. Rabbinate, kashrut supervision and mohel can all be reached at this number. Near its community centre, there is a guest house, a kosher restaurant and a shop which sells kosher products.

Joachimstaler Strasse 13,
Mitte 16719
Daily minyan

Tourist Information

Staatliches Israelisches Verkehrsbureau
Stollbergstrasse 6 15 (30) 883-6759
Fax: (30) 882-4093

Tourist Site

Jewish Culture Edition
Leo-Baeck-House, Tucholsky Street 9 10117
(30) 28445659
Fax: (30) 28445661
Email: Verlang@Judaicum.de

Bochum

Synagogues

Alte Wittener Str. 18 44803 (234) 361563
Fax: (234) 360187

Bonn/Bad Godesberg

Synagogues

Templestr.
2-4, cnr. Adenauer Allee 53113
(228) 213560
Fax: (228) 2618366

Braunschweig

Community Organisations

Community Centre
Steinstr. 4 (531) 45536

Museums

Braunschweigisches Landesmuseum
Abt. Judisches Museum, Burgplatz 1 D-38100
(531) 1215-0
Fax: (531) 1215-2607
Email: derda@landesmuseum-bs.de
Web site: www.landesmuseum-bs.de

Founded in 1746, this museum was formerly the oldest Jewish museum in the world. It was re-opened in 1987 under the auspices of the Braunschweigisches Landesmuseum. Hours Tuesday-Sunday: 10 am to 5 pm; Thursday 10 am to 8 pm.

Bremen

Synagogues

Schwachauser Heerstr. 117 (421) 498-5104
Fax: (421) 498-4944

Celle

Museums

Im Kreise 24 29221

Formerly a beautiful synagogue, it now houses travelling exhibits on various themes of Jewish history and of Jewish life in Celle where a community started between 1671 and 1691. There are now enough Jews in the town to form a minyan.

Chemnitz

Community Organisations

Community Centre
Stollberger Str. 28 (371) 32862

Coblenz

Community Organisations

Community Centre
Schlachthof Str. 5 (261) 42223

Cologne

Hotels

Leonet, Rubensstr. 33 (221) 236016

Restaurants

Meat

Community Centre
Roonstr 50, 50674 (221) 240-4440
Fax: (221) 240-4440

Phone in advance. Glatt kosher.

Synagogues

Roonstr. 50,, Köln 50674 (221) 921-5600
Fax: (221) 921-5609
Email: synagoge-koeln@netcologne.de
Web site: www.sgk.de

Daily services. There are a youth centre, Jewish museum and library at the same address.

Liberal

Judische Liberale Gemeinde
Stammheimer Str 22, Koln-Riehl 50735
(221) 287-0424
Fax: (221) 287-0424
Email: jlg.koeln@gmx.de

Darmstadt

Community Organisations

Community Centre
Wilhelm-Glassing-Str. 26 (6151) 28897

Dortmund

Representative Organisations

Landesverband der Judischen Gemeinden von Westfalen
Prinz-Friedrich-Karl-Str. 12 44135 (231) 528495
Fax: (231) 5860372
Email: lvjuedwest@aol.com

Synagogues

Prinz-Friedrich-Karl-Str. 9 44135 (231) 528497

Germany

Dresden

Representative Organisations

Landesverband Sachsen der Judischen Gemeinden K.d.o.R.
Bautzner Str 20 01099 (351) 804-5491;802-2739
Fax: (351) 804-1445

A memorial to the six million Jews killed in the Holocaust stands on the site of the Dresden Synagogue, burnt down by the Nazis in November 1938.

Synagogues

Fiedlerstr. 3 (351) 693317

Dusseldorf

Hotels

Gildors Hotel
Collenbachstr. 51 (211) 488005
Israeli owned.

Synagogues

Zietenstr. 50 (211) 469120
Fax: (211) 485156

Emmendingen

Synagogues

Juedische Gemeinde Emmendingen
Landvogtei 11, D-79312 (764) 571-989
Fax: (764) 571-980
Email: juedgemam@aol.com
Web site: www.juedgemen.de

Erfurt

Community Organisations

Community Centre
Juri-Gagarin-Ring 16 (361) 24964

Essen

Community Organisations

Community Centre
Sedanstr. 46 (201) 273413
Fax: (201) 287112

Essingen

Cemeteries

Largest cemetery in the Palatinate, where Anne Frank's ancestors are buried; sixteenth century. Key at the Mayor's Office.

Frankfurt-Am-Main

Butchers

Aviv Butchery & Deli
Hanauer Landstrasse 50 60314 (69) 433013
Fax: (69) 448064
Email: avivgmbh.kosherfood@rhein-main.net
Under the supervision of the Frankfurt Rabbinate.

Community Organisations

Community Centre
Westendstr. 43 (69) 74 07 21
Fax: (69) 746874
Email: jg.ffm@t-online.de
This community produces a magazine, "Judische Gemeinde-Zeitung Frankfurt".

Mikvaot

Judische Gemeinde
Westendstr 43 D-60325 (69) 740721
Fax: (69) 746874

Museums

Jewish Museum
Untermainkai 14-15, 60311 (69) 212-35000
Fax: (69) 212-30705
Email: info@juedischesmuseum.de
Web site: www.juedischesmuseum.de
Sunday, Tuesday to Saturday 10.00 am-5.00 pm.
Wednesday 10.00am-8.00pm. Closed Monday.

Representative Organisations

Zentralwohlfahrtsstelle der Juden in Deutschland
Hebelstrasse 6 60318 (69) 94 43 71-15
Fax: (69) 49 48 17
Email: zentrale@zwst.org

Restaurants

Sohar's,
Savignystrasse 66 60325 (69) 75 23 41
Fax: (69) 741 0116
Supervision: Rabbi Menachem Halevi Klein, Frankfurt Rabbinate.
Hours: Tuesday to Thursday and Sunday, 12 pm to 8 pm; Friday, 12 pm to Shabbat; Shabbat, 1:30 pm to 4 pm; Monday, closed. Special arrangements can be made by phone. Friday and Shabbat meals must be ordered in advance. Provides party service, airline catering and delivery to hotels. Fifteen-minute walk from synagogue, fair centre and main train station.

Synagogues

Beth Hamidrash West End
Altkanigstr. 27 (69) 723805
Baumweg 5-7 (69) 439381
Westend Synagogue
Freiherr-vom-Stein-Str. 30 (69) 726263
This is the city's main synagogue.

Tourist Information
Tourismus-und Congress GmbH
Kaiserstrabe 56 (69) 2123-8800
Fax: (69) 2123-7880 - Reservat

Freiburg

Community Organisations
Community Centre
Engels Strasse (761) 383096
Fax: (761) 382332
Services: Erev Shabbat in Summer 7.30 pm, in Winter 6.30 pm. Shabbat morning 9.30 am. Kosher Kiddush after services.

Friedberg

Tourist Sites
Judengasse 20
An ancient mikva, built in 1260 is located here. The town council has issued a special explanatory leaflet about it, and it is now scheduled as a historical monument of medieval architecture.

Fulda

Community Organisations
Community Centre
von Schildeckstr. 13 (66) 170252
Fax: (66) 147465
Services every Friday 6.30pm, every Shabat 9.00am

Furth

Community Organisations
Community Centre
Blumenstr. 31 (91) 177-0879

Tourist Sites
Julienstr. 2
There is a beautifully restored synagogue as well as a historic mikva.

Gelsenkirchen

Community Organisations
Community Centre
Von-der-Recke-Str. 9 (20) 923143 & 206628

Hagen

Community Organisations
Community Centre
Potthofstr. 16 (2331) 711-3289

Halle

Community Organisations
Community Centre
Grosse Markerstr. 13 (345) 233-110
Fax: (345) 233-1122
Email: jghalle@gmx.net

Hamburg

Community Organisations
Community Centre
Schaferkampsallee 27 20357 (40) 440-9440
Fax: (40) 410-8430

Synagogues
Hohe Weide 34 20253 (40) 440-9440
Mikvah on premises.

Hanover

Community Organisations
Community Centre
Haecklstr. 10 810472

Synagogues
Haecklstr. 10 810472

Heidelberg

Restaurants
College Restaurant
Theaterstr.9 (6221) 168-767
Kosher meals available (by arrangement and in advance - it is not open all year round) Monday to Friday at college restaurant, 100 yards from College of Jewish Studies situated at Friederichstrasse 9.

Herford

Community Organisations
Community Centre
Keplerweg 11 (52) 212039

Hildesheim

Synagogues
Jewish Community in Hildesheim
Postfach 10 07 07, Lower Saxony D31135
(512) 1704962
Fax: (512) 1704964
Rabbi Dr Walter Homolka is responsible for all Lower Saxony.

Hof

Community Organisations
Community Centre
An Wiesengrund 20 (92) 815-3249

Germany

Ichenhausen

Museums

Museum of Jewish History

Located in the fine baroque synagogue, not far from Ulm.

Ingenheim

Tourist Sites

Klingenerstr. 20

Sixteenth century cemetery can be visited. Key obtained from Klingenerstr. 20.

Kaiserslautern

Community Organisations

Community Centre

Basteigasse 4 (63) 169720

Karlsruhe

Community Organisations

Community Centre

Knielinger Allee 11 (72) 172035

Kassel

Community Organisations

Community Centre

Bremer Str. 9 (56) 112960

Konstanz

Community Organisations

Community Centre

Sigismundstr. 19 (75) 312-3077

Krefeld

Community Organisations

Community Centre

Wiedstr. 17b (21) 512-0648

Landau

Synagogues

Frank-Loebsches Haus, Kaufhausgasse 9 D-76829

(6341) 86472

Fax: (6341) 13294

Email: sabine.haas.landau.de

Leipzig

Community Organisations

Community Centre

Lahrstr. 10 (341) 291028

Lubeck

Synagogues

Synagogue & Community Centre

St Annen Str. 11 23552 (451) 798-2182

Fax: (451) 0451-798-2182

Supervised through the Hamburg community.

Magdeburg

Community Organisations

Community Centre

Graperstr. 1a (391) 52665

Mainz

Community Organisations

Community Centre

Forsterstr. 2 55118 (6131) 613990

Fax: (6131) 611767

Tourist Sites

Untere Zahlbacherstr. 11

The key to the twelfth century Jewish cemetery can be obtained at the 'new' Jewish cemetery.

Mannheim

Community Organisations

Community Centre

F 3-4 (621) 153974

Marburg an der Lahn

Community Organisations

Community Centre

Unterer Eichweg 17 (642) 132881

Michelstadt

Tourist Site

Michelstadt

The town has an old synagogue which is now a museum of both Judaism and Jewish history. It is open every day in the summer except Saturday.

Minden

Community Organisations

Community Centre

Kampstr. 6 (57) 123437

Monchengladbach

Synagogues

Community Centre

Albertusstr. 54 41363 (216) 23879

Fax: (216) 14639

Email: juedischegemeindemg@t-online.de

Monsey

Community Organisations

Community Centre
Klosterstr. 8-9 (25) 144909

Mulheim/Oberhausen

Community Organisations

Community Centre
Kampstr. 7 (20) 835191

Munich

Booksellers

Literaturhandlung
Fürstenstr. 17 80333 (30) 89-2800135
Fax: (30) 89-281601
Email: literaturhandlung@online.de

Community Organisations

Community Centre
Reichenbachstr. 27 (89) 202-4000
Fax: (89) 201-4604
Email: info@ikg-m.de

Meat/Groceries

Danel Feinkost
Pilgersheimerstrabe 44 81543 (89) 669-888
Fax: (89) 669-820
Email: danel@t-online.de

Danel Feinkost
Viktualien-Markt, Westenriederstrabe 9 80331
(89) 2280-0258

Museums

Judisches Museum Munchen
Maximilian Str. 36

Restaurants

Community Centre
(89) 202 38252
Run by the community centre at Reichenbachstrasse. Hours: 12 pm - 2.30 pm; 6 pm - 9 pm. Shabbat meals must be ordered by Friday noon. Closed Sunday; August.

Synagogues

Schwabing Synagogue (Schaarei Zion)
Georgenstr. 71 (89) 2602-3337
Fax: (89) 2602-3338
Friday evenings and Sabbath mornings only.
Possartstr. 15 (89) 474-440
Mikva on premises.
Reichenbachstr. 27 (89) 202-4000
Fax: (89) 201-4604
Mikva on premises.

Liberal

Beth Shalom (89) 8980-9373
Fax: (89) 8980-9374
Email: obeth.shalom@hagalil.com
Please ask for address and timetable.

Neustadt/Rheinpfalz

Community Organisations

Community Centre
Ludwigstr. 20 (63) 212652

Odenbach

Tourist Sites

(67) 532745
There is a historic synagogue with baroque paintings in this small village near Bad Kreuznach.

Offenbach

Community Organisations

Community Centre
Kaiserstr. 109 63065 (69) 820036
Fax: (69) 820026

Osnabruck

Community Organisations

Community Centre
In der Barlage, 41 49078 (54) 148420
Fax: (54) 143-4701
Kashrut information or visitors who wish to eat; kosher on Shabbat, please contact Rabbi Marc Stern at Tel: 49 541-48553.

Synagogues

Orthodox

Jewish Congregation Synagogue
In der Barlage, 41 49078 (54) 148420
Fax: (54) 143-4701

Tourist Sites

The Felix-Nussbaum House
Lotter Str 2 (541) 323-2207
Fax: (541) 323-2739
Email: jaehner@osnabrueck.de
About 20 minutes walk from the congregation

Paderborn

Community Organisations

Community Centre
Pipinstr. 32 (52) 512-2596

Germany

Potsdam

Community Organisations

Potsdam Community Centre

Heinrich-Mann-Allee 103 Haus 16 (331) 872018

Regensburg

Community Organisations

Community Centre

Am Brixener Hof 2 (94) 157093; 21819

Rulzheim

The key to the early nineteenth-century synagogue in this village near Karlsruhe is obtainable from the town hall.

Saarbrucken

Community Organisations

Community Centre

Lortzing Str. 8 66111 (68) 135152

Synagogues

Synagogengemeinde Saar

Lortzingstr 8 66111 (681) 910-380

Fax: (681) 910-38-13

Schwerin/Mecklenburg

Community Organisations

Judische Gemeinde zu Schwerin

Schlachterstr. 3-5 (38) 555-07345

Speyer

Tourist Sites

(62) 353332

This town contains the oldest (eleventh-century) mikva in Germany, Judenbadgasse. To visit it, obtain the key from the desk at the Hotel Trutzpfuff, in Webergasse, just around the corner, or contact Professor Stein at the Historical Museum.

There are some early nineteenth-century village synagogues in the wine-growing region of the Palatinate.

Straubing

Community Organisations

Community Centre

Wittelsbacherstr. 2 94315 (94) 211387

Stuttgart

Religious Organisations

Israelitische Religionsgemeinschaft Wurttembergs

Hospitalstr. 36 70174 (711) 228360

Fax: (711) 2283618

Restaurants

Meat

Schalom Kosher Restaurant

Hospitalstrasse 36 70174 (711) 294752

Supervision: Orthodox Rav of the Stuttgart community. Open during morning hours through to about 7.00pm except Mondays (when its closed). Located on the premises of the Stuttgart Jewish community centre.

Sulzburg

There is a beautifully restored early nineteenth-century synagogue here, some 20 miles from Freiburg. Keys are obtainable from the Mayor's office.

Trier

Community Organisations

Community Centre

Kaiserstr. 25 (65) 140530; 33295

Veitshoechheim

Located a few miles from Wurzburg is the town of Veitshochheim, which reconsecrated a pre-Second World War synagogue and opened as a Jewish Museum in March 1994. Originally built in 1730, the synagogue was the community centre for local Jews who had lived in the area for nearly 300 years, from 1644 to 1942, when the last Jews were deported from Veitshoechheim to the Nazi concentration camps.

In 1986 the stone fragments of the original interior, including the Bima and the Ahron Hakodesch, were discovered beneath the floor, where they had been buried in 1940. This find prompted local officials to transform the synagogue back to its original function and splendour, using photographs from the 1920s as a guide.

Museums

The Synagogue and Museum of Jewish Culture

Thuengersheimer Strasse 17, D- 97209

(931) 9802-764

Fax: (931) 9802-766

Email: museum@veitschoechheim.de

Web site: www.veitshoechheim.de

Recently restored. Museum hours: Thursday 3 pm to 6 pm, Sunday 2 pm to 5 pm.

Wachenheim

A large sixteenth-century cemetery, the key is available from the town hall. The first records of registration of Jews date from the year 831.

Wiesbaden

Restaurants

Communal Offices
Friedrichstr. 31-33 (611) 933303-0
Fax: (611) 933303-9

Synagogues

Friedrichstr. 31-33 (611) 933-3030
Fax: (611) 933-3039
Email: JG.WI@fonline.de

Worms

The original Rashi Synagogue, built in the eleventh century, and the oldest Jewish place of worship in Europe, was destroyed by the Nazis in 1938. After the Second World War, it was reconstructed and was reconsecrated in 1961. The building also contains a twelfth-century mikva and a Jewish musuem. There is also an ancient Jewish cemetery.

Wuppertal

Community Organisations

Community Centre
Friedrich-Ebert-Str. 73 (202) 300233

Wurzburg

There are old Jewish cemeteries in Wurzburg, Heidingsfeld and Hochberg.

Community Organisations

Community Centre
Valentin-Becker-Str. 11 97072 (93) 151190
Fax: (93) 118184

Also guest rooms for tourists; kosher meals available.

Mikvaot

Community Centre
Valentin-Becker-Str. 11 97072 (93) 151190
Fax: (93) 118184

Appointments to be made.

Synagogues

Community Centre
Valentin-Becker-Str. 11 97072 (93) 151190
Fax: (93) 118184

Tourist Sites

There are old Jewish cemeteries in Wurzburg, Heidingsfeld and Hochberg.

Gibraltar

The first Jewish people in Gibraltar were Sephardi, who had crossed over the border from Spain before the Inquisition began in the fourteenth century. Many more followed in the ensuing centuries.

When Britain took possession, Jews were banned, but later they were allowed in as traders and finally, in 1749, they were granted full permission to live there. The community began to flourish and the Jewish population, which now also included many North African Jews, rose to 2,000.

At the end of the Second World War, some of the community returned after being evacuated to Britain. There are now fairly good Jewish facilities, namely four synagogues, and newsletters. Gibraltar has had a Jewish prime minister and a Jewish mayor.

GMT + 1 hour — Total Population 25,000
Country calling code (350) — Jewish Population 600
Emergency Telephone (Police, Fire, Ambulance 999) — Electricity voltage 220/240

Bakeries

J. Amar,
47 Line Wall Road 73516

Butchers

A. Edery,
26 John Mackintosh Sqaure 75168
Fax: 42529

Gibraltar

Community Organisations

Managing Board of Jewish Community
10 Bomb House Lane 72606
Fax: 40487

Contact Information

Solomon Levy M.B.E. J.P
3 Convent Place, PO Box 190
77789; 42818, 78047 (home)
Fax: 42527
Email: slevy@gibnet.gi
The vice president of the Jewish community is happy to provide information for Jewish travellers.

Cultural Organisations

Jewish Social & Cultural Club
7 Bomb House Lane 79636
Email: asuissa@gibnet.gi
Mailing address: Avner Suissa, 20 Lime Tree Lodge, Montagu Gardens, Gibraltar.

Delicatessens

Uncle Sam's Deli
62 Irish Town 51236; 51226
Fax: 42516
Email: dabamick@gibnet.gi.com
Provides kosher groceries and wine. Catering and takeaway service. Full glatt kosher service. Fully licensed.

Embassy

Consul General of Israel
Marina View, Glacis Road, PO Box 141 77244

Groceries

I&D Abudarham
32 Cornwall's Lane 216 78506
Fax: 73249
Email: djabudar@gibnet.gi
Kosher wines, meats & poultry.

Hotels

The Rock Hotel
The hotel has kosher facilities (meat and dairy) and can cater for pre-booked groups of 10 or more. Kosher take-away food can also be delivery to a room.

Judaica

A.Cohen,
3 Convent Place, PO Box 190 52734
Email: sofergib@prontomail.com
Supplier of Mezuzot ,Tephilim and Shaatnez.

Mikvaot

12 Bomb House Lane 77658 & 73090
Fax: 72359

Restaurants

Jewish Club
Open daily from 10 am to 11 pm, except Shabbat, but arrangements can be made with this restaurant owner for Shabbat meals.

Leanse Restaurant
7 Bomb House Lane 41751
Kosher.

Synagogues

Abudarham
20 Parliament Lane 78506 78047
Fax: 42527

Etz Hayim
Irish Town 75955 75563
Fax: 42939

Nefusot Yehuda
65 Line Wall Road 73037

Shaar Hashamayim
19 Engineer Lane 78069 74030
Fax: 74029
Enquiries: Joseph de M. Benyunes PO Box 1474

Greece

After the Hellenistic occupation of Israel (the Jewish revolt during this occupation is commemorated in the festival of Hanukah), some Jews were led into slavery in Greece, beginning the first recorded Jewish presence in the country. The next significant Jewish immigration occurred after the Inquisition, when many Spanish Jews moved to Salonika, which was a flourishing Jewish centre until the German occupation in the Second World War.

By the early 1940s, the Jewish population had grown to over 70,000, with 45,000 living in Salonika. With typical thoroughness, the Nazis deported not only the Jews from the Greek mainland, but also many communities from the Greek islands, including Crete. A local rabbi was a key member of the Greek resistance in the north of the country, and many local Christians did protect their Jewish neighbours in Athens. After the War, many of the survivors emigrated to Israel.

Today, there are Sephardi synagogues in Greece and, in Athens, a community centre and a Jewish museum. There are Jewish publications and a library in the community centre. In Aegina, Corfu, and other Greek islands, ancient synagogues may be visited.

GMT + 2 hours — Total Population 10,645,000
Country calling code (30) — Jewish Population 5,000
Emergency Telephone (Police - 100) (Fire - 199) (Ambulance - 166) — Electricity voltage 220

Athens

Almost 3,000 Jews live in Athens. The community has access to a centre, contains a library, and offers the facilities to have a kosher meal. The Jewish museum in the centre of the city details the rise and tragic fall of Greek Jewry.

Kosher meals are served at the Athens Jewish Cultural Centre upon request (contact Mrs Rachel Sasson, Tel. (1) 213-3371. Delivery to hotels in Athens can also be arranged).

Embassy

Embassy of Israel
Marathonodromou Street 1, Paleo Psychico,
POB 65140 15452 (1) 671-9530

Museums

Jewish Museum of Greece
39 Nikis Str 10557 (1) 322-5582
Fax: (1) 323-1577

Open daily from 10 am to 2 pm except Saturday.

Representative Organisations

Central Board of the Jewish Communities of Greece
36 Voulis Street 10557 (1) 324-4315-18
Fax: (1) 331-3852
Email: hhkis@hellasnet.gr
Web site: www..kis.gr

Restaurants

Meat

5 Averof St 10433 (1) 520-2880
Fax: (1) 520-2881
Email: chabad@otenet.gr

Telephone for orders.

Synagogues

Sephardi

Beth Shalom
5 Melidoni Street 10553
(1) 325-2773; 2823; 2875
Fax: (1) 322-0761

Tourist Information

Community Office
8 Melidoni Street 10553 (1) 325-2875
Fax: (1) 322-0761
Email: israth@hellasnet.gr

Chalkis

Community Organisations

Community Centre
35 Kotsou Street 34100 (221) 80690

Kashrut Information

Community Centre
(221) 27297

Greece

Synagogues

36 Kotsou Street

This synagogue has been rebuilt and renewed many times on its original foundations. Tombstone inscriptions in the cemetery go back more than fifteen centuries. Only open on High Holy Days.

Corfu

Community Organisations

Community Centre

5 Riz. Voulephton St. 49100 (661) 45650
Fax: (661) 43791

Tourist Sites

Velissariou St. (661) 38802

There was an ancient synagogue and cemetery here, destroyed by the Nazis.

Ioannina

Community Organisations

18 Josef Eliyia St. 45221 (651) 25195

Contact: John Kalef-Ezra on 32390.

Larissa

Synagogues

Community Centre

29 Kentavron St. 41222 (41) 532 965

Rhodes

Synagogues

Khal Shalom Kadosh

1 Simmiou St., Dodecanese Islands (241) 29406

The synagogue belongs to the Jewish Community of Rhodes which counts 38 members. It was built around 1577 in the medieval City of Rhodes which used to be the Old Jewish Quarter. A photographic museum is functioning next to the synagogue. The synagogue is on the World Monuments Fund list of 100 most endangered sites. Tourists wishing to visit these sites should contact: Jewish Community of Rhodes, No. 5 Polydorou Str., Old City. Tel: (0030) 241-22364 or Fax (0030) 241-73039.

Salonika

At the turn of the twentieth century Salonika, then part of the Ottoman Empire, had a Jewish majority population and the official day off was Saturday.

Cultural Organisations

The Israelite Fraternity House

24 Vassileos Irakliou St. (31) 221030

Yad le Zikaron

24 Vassileos Irakliou St. (31) 275701

Libraries

The Centre for Historical Studies of Salonika Jews

24 Vassileos Irakliou St., 1st Floor (31) 223231
Fax: (31) 229069

Synagogues

Monastirioton

35 Sygrou Str. 54630 (31) 524968

Trikkala

Synagogues

Yad Lezicaron

24 Vassileos Irakliou Str. (31) 223231
15 Athanassiou Diakou St

Volos

Community Organisations

Xenophontos & Moisseos Streets 38333
(421) 25302
Fax: (421) 25302

Kashrut Information

20 Parodos Kondulaki

Synagogues

Xenophontos & Moisseos Streets

Open primarily on High Holy Days.

Tourist Sites

Holocaust Monument

Riga Ferreou Square.

Guatemala

Conversos were the first recorded Jews in the country, but, a few centuries later, the next Jewish immigration occurred with the arrival of German Jews in 1848. Later, some East European Jews arrived, but Guatemala was not keen to accept refugees from Nazism and, as a result, passed some laws which, although not mentioning Jews directly, were aimed against Jewish refugees.

Even though these laws were in place, in 1939 there were 800 Jews in Guatemala. After the War, an Ashkenazi community centre was built in 1965, but despite accepting some Jewish Cuban refugees, the community is shrinking owing to assimilation and intermarriage.

Most Jews live in Guatemala City, and others in Quetzaltenango and San Marcos. There is a Jewish school and kindergarten.

GMT - 6 hours
Country calling code (502)

Total Population 10,982,000
Jewish Population 1,500
Electricity voltage 110

Guatemala City

Communal Organisation

Communidad Judia Guatemalteca
Apartado Postal 502 (2) 311-975
Fax: (2) 325-683

Embassy

Embassy of Israel
13 Av. 14-07, Zona 10 (2) 371305

Synagogues

Ashenkenazi,
Centro Hebreo, 7a Av. 13-51, Zona 9 (2) 367643

Sephardi

Maguen David,
7a Av. 3-80, Zona 2 (2) 232-0932

Haiti

Christopher Columbus brought the first Jew to Haiti - his interpreter, Luis de Torres, a *Converso* who had been baptised before the voyage. Thereafter more Jews settled but the community was destroyed in the anti-European revolt of Toussaint L'Ouverture in 1804. A hundred or so years later, Jews from the Middle East and some refugees from the Nazis settled in Haiti, but many subsequently emigrated to Israel.

The remaining community has benefited from the help of the Israeli embassy, and services are held in the embassy or at a private address. There is no central Jewish organisation, and the community is too small to support other Jewish facilities.

GMT - 5 hours	Total Population 7,259,000
Country calling code (509)	Jewish Population Under 100
Emergency Telephone (Police - 114) (Ambulance - 118)	Electricity voltage 110

Port au Prince

Contact Information

Religious services are held at the home of the Honorary Consul, Mr Gilbert Bigio.

Honduras

During the Spanish colonial period, some *Conversos* did live in Honduras, but it was only in the nineteenth century that any significant Jewish immigration occurred. In the early twentieth century, refugees from Nazism followed a handful of immigrants from Eastern Europe. Honduras was one of the small number of countries to aid refugees from Nazism, and many Jews owe their lives to the help of Honduran consulates which issued visas in wartime Europe.

Tegucigalpa (the capital) contains the largest Jewish population, but the only synagogue in the country is in San Pedro Sula (services are held in private homes in Tegucigalpa). There is also a Sunday school and WIZO branch.

GMT - 6 hours	Total Population 5,820,000
Country calling code (504)	Jewish Population Under 100
Emergency Telephone (Police - 119) (Fire - 198) (Ambulance - 37 8654)	Electricity voltage 110/220

San Pedro Sula

Contact Information

530157

Services Friday and Shabbat at synagogue and community centre.

Tegucigalpa

Contact Information

315908

Services usually held in private homes. Contact secretary at above number.

Embassy

Embassy of Israel
Palmira Building, 5th Floor 324232; 325176

Hungary

There were Jews living in Hungary in Roman times, even before the arrival of the Magyars (ancestors of the present-day Hungarians). The Jews suffered during the Middle Ages, when there was some anti-Semitism, but conditions improved under Austro-Hungarian rule, and Judaism was recognised as being on a legal par with Christianity in 1896.

Hungary lost a considerable amount of territory after the First World War, and as a result many of its original Jewish communities (such as Szatmar) found themselves within other countries. Anti-Semitism reached a peak in March 1944, when, during the German occupation, most Jewish communities began to be transported to Auschwitz. A number of those who were deported survived when Auschwitz was liberated by the Red Army in January 1945.

After the War, Hungary had the largest Jewish community in central Europe. Inevitably, the community dwindled through emigration (especially after the 1956 uprising) and assimilation. Communism in Hungary was far more lenient than in other Warsaw Pact countries, and synagogues were allowed to operate. Since 1989, religious interest has increased, and the government has recently renovated the Dohany Synagogue, the second biggest synagogue in the world and the largest in Europe. The Jewish population is still the largest in the region, although most are not religious.

GMT + 1 hour — Total Population 10,036,000
Country calling code (36) — Jewish Population 80,000
Emergency Telephone (Police - 107) (Fire - 105) (Ambulance - 104) — Electricity voltage 220

Budapest

Once known in the nineteenth century as 'Judapest', this city contains the majority of Hungarian Jews. There are several functioning synagogues, from Orthodox to 'Neolog' (Hungarian Reform). The recently restored Dohány Synagogue was built to accommodate 3,000 in prayer.

Bakeries

Dob utca 20
Kacinczy utca 28
Opening hours are variable.

Embassy

Embassy of Israel
Fullank Utca 8, II 1026

Groceries

Koser Bott,
Nyar utcal (1) 322-9276
Kosher products, bread, etc.

The Orthodox Central Synagogue
VII, Kazinczy utca 27
Kosher milk and cheese are available here three mornings a week.

Hotels

Kosher

King's Hotel
Nagydiofa Utca. 25-27 1074 (1) 352-7675
Fax: (1) 352-7675
Strictly kosher hotel with a restaurant.

Media

Newspapers

Uj Elet (New Life)
Central Board Hotel

Mikvaot

VII Kazinczy utca 16

Museums

Hungarian Jewish Museum and Archives
Dohany u.2 1077 (1) 343-6756
Fax: (1) 343-6756
Email: bpjewmus@mail.c3.hu
Web site: www.c3.hu/~bpjewmus

Hungary

Organisations

Central Board of the Federation of Jewish Communities in Hungary
VII, Sip utca 12 (1) 342-1355
Fax: (1) 342-1790
Email: bzsh@mail.matav.hu

The Central Rabbinical Council
VII, Sip utca 12 (1) 142-1180
Rabbi Schweitzer is Chief Rabbi of Hungary and Director of the Rabbinical Seminary.

Restaurants

Central Kitchen & Food Distribution
IX, Pava utca 9-11

Meat

King's Hotel,
Nagydiofa Utca 25-27 (1) 352-7675
Supervision: Orthodox Community.

Synagogues

Dohany Street Synagogue
VII Dohany Utca 4-6
Built in 1859, it is the largest in Europe and the second largest in the world. In its grounds lie buried Hungarian Jewish victims of the Nazis. There is also a commemorative plaque to Hanna Senesh, the Jewish parachutist who was captured and tortured before being shot by the Nazis. A plaque commemorating Theodor Herzl, the founder of Zionism is in the Jewish Museum.

Heroes Synagogue
VII Wesselenyi utca 5

Orthodox

The Orthodox Central Synagogue
VII, Kazinczy utca 27 (1) 132-4331

Tourist Information

Jewish Information Service
(1) 166-5165
Fax: (1) 166-5165

Tours of Jewish Interest

Chosen Tours (1) 185-9499
Fax: (1) 166-5165
Tours of Jewish sites are provided by telephone arrangement.

Sopron

Museums

The Old Synagogue Museum
Uj utca 22-24 H-9400 (99) 311327
Fax: (99) 311347
Email: smuzeum@mail.c3.hu
A department of the Sopron Museum. A medieval synagogue restored as a museum in 1976. Open from 1 May to 1 October, daily between 9 am and 5 pm. Closed Tuesdays.

Synagogues

Orthodox

Jewish Orthodox
Tomolom utca 22 H-9400 (99) 313558

Tourist Sites

Uj utca 11
A second medieval synagogue which formerly housed the museum is undergoing restoration. The ruins of the 1891 synagogue, out of use since 1956, can be seen at Pap-ret H-9400.

The Neologue Cemetery
Dating from the nineteenth-century. There is a memorial wall dedicated to the 1,600 local victims of the Holocaust.

India

The Jewish population of India can be divided into three components: the Cochin Jews, the Bene Israel and the Baghdadi Jews. The Cochin Jews are based in the south of India in Kerala. This community can be further divided into Black (believing themselves to be the original settlers) and White (of European or Middle Eastern origin). Most of the community has emigrated, but there is still a synagogue in Cochin that is a major tourist attraction.

The Bene Israel believe they are descended from Jewish survivors of a ship wrecked on its voyage from ancient Israel. No reliable documentary evidence, however, exists to support this claim. More reliable evidence dates settlement around the tenth century. The Bene Israel follow only certain Jewish practices, such as kosher food and Shabbat, and also adhere to certain Muslim and Hindu beliefs; for example, they abstain from eating beef. In the eighteenth century, they settled in Bombay and now form the largest group of Indian Jews.

Baghdadi Jews, immigrants from Iraq and the other Middle Eastern countries, arrived in India in the late eighteenth century, and followed British Colonial rather than local custom. Many emigrated to Israel in the 1950s and 1960s.

During the Indo-Pakistan war of 1972, the leading Indian military figure was General Samuels. In 1999 Lt-Gen. J.F.R. Jacob was appointed Governor of the Punjab State.

There is a Central Council of Indian Jewry, based in Mumbai, where most of the Indian Jews live. Kosher food is available, and there are three Jewish schools in the city. Relations with Israel have recently improved and it is now a major trade partner.

GMT: +5 1/2 — Total Population 1,013,662,000
Country calling code (91) — Jewish Population 5,500
Electricity voltage 220

Cochin

Community Organisations

Association or Kerala Jews
Thekkumbhagom Synagogue,
Jews Street (484) 366-247; 362-454
Fax: (484) 363-747
Eliza Apts. GB 42/1651, Old Railway Station Rd.
Cochin

Contact Information

Inquiries,
Princess Street, Fort (484) 24228; 24988

Synagogues

Chennamangalam
Jew Street, Chennamangalam
Built in 1614 and restored in 1916, this synagogue has been declared a historical monument by the Government of India. A few yards away is a small concrete pillar into which is inset the tombstone of Sara Bat-Israel, dated 5336 (1576).

Paradesi,
Jew Town, Mattancherry 2
The only Cochin synagogue that is still functioning. Built in 1568.

Ernakulam

Tourist Sites

Kadavumbagom Synagogue
Built in 1200 and rebuilt in 1690.

Thekkumbagon Syndagogue
Built in 1580 and rebuilt in 1939.

Khamasa

Synagogues

Magen Abraham
Bukhara Mohalla, opp. Parsi Agiari 380001
(79) 535-5224

Kolkata

Representative Organisations

Jewish Association of Calcutta
1&2 Old Court House Corner (33) 224861
General inquiries to this telephone number.

Synagogues

Bethel Synagogue
26/1 Pollack Street

Magen David Synagogue
109a Peplabi Rash, Bihari Bose Road, 1,
(formerly Canning Street)

India

Neveh Shalome Synagogue
9 Jackson Lane, 1

Mala

Built in 1597; the synagogue building was handed over to the local authorities.

Mumbai

Mumbai is home to the majority of the remaining Indian Jews. There are three Jewish schools, and the Council of Indian Jewry is in the city. Thane, some twenty-two miles away, is where much of the community now lives.

Embassy

Consul General of Israel
50 Kailash, G. Deshmukh Marg, 26 (22) 386-2793

Kosher Food

ORT India
68 Worli Hill Estate, PO Box 6571 400018
(22) 496-2350; 8423; 8457
Fax: (22) 496-2350; 491-3203
Email: ortbbay@bom5.vsnl.net.in
Web site: www.ortindia.com

The Jewish Education Resource Centre provides kosher food from its bakery and kitchen to all travellers. ORT India also arranges conducted tours to places of Jewish interest in Mumbai and to ancient synagogues in the Konkan region of Maharashtra State.

Synagogues

Beth El Synagogue
Mirchi Galli, Mahatma Gandhi Road, Panvel 410206
Beth El Synagogue
Rewdanda, Allibag Tehsil, Raigad
Beth Ha-Elohim Syn
Penn
Etz Haeem Prayer Hall
2nd Lane, Umerkhadi 400009 (22) 377-0193
Gate of Mercy (Shaar Harahamim)
254 Samuel Street,
Nr Masjid Railway Station 400003 (22) 345-2991
This is the oldest Bene Israel synagogue in use in India, established in 1796 and known as the Samaji Hasaji Synagogue or Juni Masjid until 1896 when its name was changed to Shaar Harahamim.
Hessed-El Synagogue
Poynad, Alibag Tehsil
Knesseth Eliahu Synagogue
V.B. Ghandi Road (Forbes Street), Fort 400001
(22) 283-1502
Freddie Sofer welcomes visitors to join him for lunch after Shabbat service.
Kurla Bene Israel Prayer Hall
275 S. G. Barve Road (C.S.T. Road),
Kurla, West Bombay 400070 (22) 514-5014
Magen Aboth Synagogue
Alibag
Magen David Synagogue
J.J.Nagpada, Byculla 400008 (22) 300-6675
Magen Hassidim Synagogue
8 Mohammaed Shahid Marg, (formerly Moreland Road), Agripada 400011 (22) 309-2493
Rodef Shalom Synagogue
Sussex Road, Byculla 400027
Shaar Hashamaim Synagogue
Tembi Naka, opp. Civil Hospital, Thane 400601
(22) 853-4817
Shaare Rason Synagogue
90 Tantanpura Street, 3rd Road, Don Tad, Israel Mohalla, Khadak 400009
Shahar Hatephilla Synagogue
Mhasla
Tifereth Israel Synagogue
92 K. K. Marg, Jacob Circle 400011 (22) 305-3713

Tours of Jewish Interest

ORT India
68 Worli Hill Estate, PO Box 6571 400018
(22) 496-2350; 8423
Fax: (22) 364-7308
Email: jhirad@giasbm01.vsnl.net.in

The Travel and Tourism Department arranges tours in Bombay & Raighad District.

TOV Jewish India Tours
96 Penso Villa, 1st Floor, Mbraut Rd,
Shivaji Park 400028 (22) 445-0134
Fax: (22) 437-1700
Email: indoisr@hotmail.com

Tours of Jewish India.

New Delhi

Synagogues

Judah Hyam Synagogue
A/7 Nirman Vihar, Patparganj 110092
(11) 224-3136

The Judah Hyam Annexe houses a library and centre for Jewish and inter-faith studies.

Judah Hyam Synagogue
2 Humayun Road 110003 (11) 463-5500

Parur

Synagogues

Parur Synagogue
Built in 1165, the synagogue was rebuilt in 1616 by the local Jewish community with the help of David Kastiel, who was not a Paradesi Jew, but a man of local origin. Paradesi Jews were associated with Mattancherry and their synagogue was built in 1568.

Pune

Synagogues

Ohel David Synagogue
9 Dr Ambedekar Road 411001 (206) 132048
Email: oheldavid@ip.eth.net

Succath Shelomo
93 Rasta Peth 411011
Inquiries to Hon. Sec. 247/1 Rasta Peth, Trupti Apt., Pune 411011 or Dr S. B. David 9 Bund Garden Road, Pune 411001

Tours

Tov Jewish India Tours
Suite 205 Palace orchard complex, Splendour, Forest Hilss 411028 (200) 693-1488

Thane

Kashrut Information

Pearl Farm, A/1 Dhobi Alley, Sulabha, Maharashtra 400601 (22) 536-0539
Kosher goat meat and fish.

Iran

Iran, formerly known as Persia, has an ancient connection with Jews. The first Jewish communities in Persia date from the time of the First Temple. King Cyrus, the Persian king who conquered Babylon, allowed the Jews to return to Israel from their exile. Not all returned, however, and some settled in Persia. The Persian community grew over time, suffering oppression after the Islamic conversion in 642. Certain segments of the Jewish community also grew in wealth in early medieval times.

In the twentieth century, there was a brief period of hope for the Jews in Iran when the country became more western-oriented after 1925. However, the 1979 revolution quashed the hope for a more tolerant Iran, and many thousands of Jews decided to emigrate. Association with Zionism became a capital offence and a number of Jews have been executed since 1979. The Jews are seen as *dhimmi*, "subordinates" to Islam, and as such are allowed some religious practices, but are so closely watched that maintaining a Jewish life style is difficult. The tombs of Esther and Mordechai (from the Purim story) are in Hamadan, south-west of the capital Tehran. Iran currently has the largest Jewish community in the Middle East outside Israel.

Kosher food has become expensive and is difficult to obtain.

GMT + 3.5 hours	Total Population 67,702,000
Country calling code (98)	Jewish Population 18,000
Electricity voltage 220	

Isfahan

Synagogues

Shah Abass Street

Tehran

Synagogues

Haim,
Gavamossaltaneh Street

Meshedi,
Kakh Shomali Avenue, opp. Abrishami School

The Iraqi,
Anatole France Street

Tourist Sites

Jewish Quarter of Tehran, Mahalleh, off Sirus Avenue

Irish Republic

The first report of Jews in Ireland records that in 1079 'five Jews came over the sea'. The small community was expelled in 1290, along with the Jews from the rest of the British Isles. The community slowly grew again after Jews were allowed to return and a few *Conversos* settled in Dublin. There was never a strong community, however, and only in 1822 did a significant influx of Jews occur when immigrants came from England and Eastern Europe.

Immigration continued and large numbers arrived from the Russian Empire after 1881. Some settled in Ireland intentionally but others believed that they had landed in America, deceived by the ships' captains. In 1901, the community was 3,800 strong. The highest figure for the Jewish population of Ireland has been estimated at 8,000.

Robert Briscoe (1894-1969) who played an important role in the struggle for Irish independence was twice Lord Mayor of Dublin.

Currently, most Jews live in Dublin although that community is now shrinking.

GMT + 0 hours — Total Population 3,730,000
Country calling code (353) — Jewish Population 1,000
Emergency Telephone (Police, Fire , Ambulance 999) — Electricity voltage 220

Cork

Synagogues

10 South Terrace (21) 487-0413
Fax: (21) 487-6537
Email: rosehill@iol.ie

Services: For information contact Fred Rosehill (353) 21 487-0413.

Dublin

The centre of Irish Jewry, Dublin's position on the east coast meant that many Jews settled there in the flight from Eastern Europe in the nineteenth century. The Jewish Museum in Dublin, opened by the then President of Israel, Irish-born Chaim Herzog, in 1985 during a state visit to Ireland, gives much information on the town's Jewish history.

Dublin was also the home of possibly the world's most famous fictional Jew, Leopold Bloom of James Joyce's *Ulysses*.

Bakeries

Hemmingway's Deli
Ballsbridge Terrace 4

Rowan's Deli
Main Street, Rathfarnham 14

Delicatessens

The Big Cheese
St Andrew's Lane 2 (1) 671-1399
Fax: (1) 490-9917

Has a Kosher section and is open on Sunday Morning

Embassy

Embassy of Israel
Carrisbrook House, 122 Pembroke Road,
Ballsbridge 4 (1) 668-0303
Fax: (1) 668-0418
Email: info@embisrael.iol.ie

Mikvaot

Terenure Hebrew Congregation,
Rathfarnham Road (1) 490-5348

Museums

Irish Jewish Museum
3-4 Walworth Road 8 (1) 490-1857
Fax: (1) 490-1857

Open Tuesday, Thursday and Sunday. May to September 11 am to 3.30 pm; October to April 10.30 am to 2.30 pm. Group visits by arrangement. (1) 490-1857.

Religious Organisations

Board of Shechita
1 Zion Road 6 (1) 492-3751
Email: irishcom@iol.ie

The Chief Rabbinate of Ireland
Herzog House, 1 Zion Road 6 (1) 492-3751
Fax: (1) 492-4680
Email: irishcom@iol.ie

Synagogues

Orthodox

Machzikei Hadass
Rathmore Villas, Rear of 77 Terenure Road
North 6W (1) 492-3751
Email: machadass@jerusalemail.com
Web site: www.jpostmail.com/jpost/users/machadass

Terenure Hebrew Congregation
Rathfarnham Road, Terenure 6

The Jewish Home of Ireland
Denmark Hill, Leinster Road West, Rathmines,
Dublin 6 (1) 497-6258
Fax: (1) 497-2018
Email: thejewishhomeofirl@tinet.ie
Services are held Friday evening at start of Shabbat and Shabbat morning. Kosher meals may be had in the home's dining room. Forty-eight hours notice is required.

Progressive

7 Leicester Avenue, Rathgar,
Po Box 3059 6 (1) 490-7605
Email: djpc@ulps.org
Friday evening at 8.15 pm, first Sabbath in the month and Festivals at 10.30 am.

Israel

General Information

Israel, the Promised Land of the Bible, is today a modern, thriving, bustling and vibrant country. For centuries, the sites of many of the most stirring events in the history of mankind lay dormant beneath shifting sands and crumbling terraces, until the land was reclaimed by the People of Israel returning from exile. In today's Israel, cities, towns and villages, fertile farms and green forests, sophisticated industries and well-developed commercial enterprises have replaced barren hillsides, swamps and desert wilderness.

Climate

Israel enjoys long, warm, dry summers (April - October) and generally mild winters (November - March), with somewhat drier, cooler weather in hilly regions, such as Jerusalem and Safed. Rainfall is relatively heavy in the north and centre of the country with much less in the northern Negev and almost negligible amounts in the southern areas. Regional conditions vary considerably, with humid summers and mild winters on the coast; dry summers and moderately cold winters in the hill regions; hot, dry summers and pleasant winters in the Jordan Valley; and year-round semi-desert conditions in the Negev.

Languages

Hebrew, the language of the Bible, and Arabic, are the official languages of Israel. Hebrew, Arabic and English are compulsory subjects at school. French, Spanish, German, Yiddish, Russian, Polish and Hungarian are widely spoken. Local and international newspapers and periodicals in a number of languages are readily available. All street and most commercial signs are in Hebrew and English and often in Arabic.

Passports and Visas

Every visitor to Israel must hold a valid passport; stateless persons require a valid travel document with a return visa to the country of issue. Visitors may remain in Israel for up to three months from the date of arrival, subject to the terms of the visa issued. Visitors who intend to work in Israel must apply to the Ministry of the Interior for a special visa (B/1).

Electrical Appliances

The electric current in Israel is 220 volts AC, single phase, 50 Hertz. Most Israeli sockets are of the three-pronged variety but many can accept some European two-pronged plugs as well. Electric shavers, travelling irons and other small appliances may require adapters and/or transformers which can be purchased in Israel.

Health Regulations

There are no vaccination requirements for visitors entering Israel.

Pets: Dogs or cats accompanying visitors must be over four months old, inoculated against rabies and bear a valid official veterinary health certificate from the country of origin.

Accommodation

Kashrut

In Israel, kosher means under official rabbinical supervision. Most hotels (but not all) do adhere. Kosher restaurants, hotels and youth hostels are by law required to display a kashrut certificate.

Hotels

Israel has over 300 hotels, offering a wide choice of accommodation to suit all tastes, purposes and budgets, ranging from small, simple facilities to five-star luxury establishments, with prices varying according to grade and season. Hotel rates are quoted in US dollars and do not include the 15% service charge.

Kibbutz Hotels

The kibbutz (collective settlement) is an Israeli social experience, in which all property is collectively owned and members receive no salaries but are provided with housing, education for their children, medical services, social amenities and all other necessities. Most of the 280 kibbutzim throughout Israel are essentially agricultural settlements but many are moving to a more industrially orientated economy.

Several kibbutzim, mostly in northern and central Israel have established hotels on their premises providing visitors with a close view of this world-renowned lifestyle. They offer guests the opportunity of a relaxed, informal holiday in delightful rural surroundings. Some present special evening programmes about the kibbutz experience.

For further information and a special tour of Israel's kibbutzim and kibbutz hotels, contact any Israel Government Tourist Office (IGTO), or the tourist information offices (TIO) in Israel, or Kibbutz Hotels, I Smolinskin St., Tel Aviv. Tel.: 03-527 8085 Fax: 03-523 0527.

Youth Hostels

The Israel Youth Hostels Association (IYHA), affiliated with the International Youth Hostels Association, operates some 30 youth hostels throughout the country for guests of all ages. All offer dormitory accommodation and most also provide meals and self-service kitchen facilities. Some hostels also provide family accommodation for parents accompanied by at least one child. Individual reservations should be booked directly at specific hostels and group reservations with the IYHA.

The IYHA also arranges individual 14-, 21- or 28-day package tours, called 'Israel on the Youth Hostel Trail'. These include nights in any of twenty-five hostels with breakfast and dinner, unlimited bus travel, a half-day guided tour, free admission to National Parks, a map and other informative material.

For further information, contact the Israel Youth Hostels Association, I Shazar Street, 91060 Jerusalem, Tel: 02-655 8400, Fax: 02-655 8401.

Currency and Bank Information

The currency of Israel is the New Israeli Sheqel (NIS) (plural sheqalim). Each sheqel is divided into 100 agorot (singular agora). Bank notes circulate in denominations of NIS 200, 100, 50 and 20 sheqels and coins in denominations of 5 sheqels, 10 sheqels, 1 sheqel and 50 and 10 agorot. One may bring an unlimited amount of local and foreign currency into Israel in cash, travellers' cheques, letters of credit, or State of Israel Bonds. Foreign currency may be exchanged at any bank and at many hotels.

Most banks are open from Sunday to Thursday from 08.30 to 12.00, and from 16.00 to 18.00 on Sunday, Tuesday and Thursday. On the eve of major Jewish holidays, banks are open from 08.30 to 12.00. Bank branches in major hotels usually offer convenient additional banking hours.

Shopping

Colourful oriental markets and bazaars may be found in the old city of Jerusalem and in several other towns and villages. The unique variety of goods available includes handmade items of olive wood, mother-of-pearl, leather and straw, as well as hand-blown glass and exotic clothing. In all cities and towns there are shopping malls which are open from 08:00 until 22:00. There are duty-free shops at Ben Gurion, Eilat and Ovda International Airports.

Opening Hours:

Most shops are open daily, Sunday to Thursday, from 9:00 to 19:00, although some close for a mid-day break between 13:00 and 16:00. On Fridays and the eve of major Jewish holidays, shops close early in the afternoon. Some Muslim-owned establishments are closed on Fridays and some Christian shops on Sundays

Radio and Television

Radio programmes are broadcast daily in English, Arabic, French, Yiddish, Russian and other languages. There are three daily news programmes in English and French. Many programmes shown on Israeli TV are in English with Hebrew, Arabic and Russian subtitles.

The Israel Broadcasting Authority news in English is screened nightly on the first TV channel at 18.15.

Facilities for the handicapped

Many hotels and public institutions in Israel (including Ben Gurion International Airport) provide ramps, specially equipped lavatories, telephones and other conveniences for the handicapped.

Milbat, the Advisory Centre for the Disabled at Sheba Medical Center in Tel Aviv (Tel: 03-530 3739), will be pleased to answer visitors' questions.

The Yad Sarah Organization with branches located throughout Israel provides wheelchairs, crutches and other medical equipment on loan, free of charge (a small deposit is requested). For more specific information, contact the organization's main office in Jerusalem, Tel: 02-624 4242.

Travellers to Israel, especially those with specific medical/paramedical needs, can turn to Traveller Hotline operated by Ezer Mizion, the Israel Health Support Fund. This volunteer organization provides all paramedical information and needs free of charge to the traveller, via the International Office (02-537 8070) and Travellers Hotline (02-500 211). Transport and other arrangements can be organized prior to arrival and special inquiries/needs can be seen to while in Israel.

Organised Tours

Numerous organised tours, mostly in air-conditioned buses or minibuses, are conducted by licensed tour operators. Itineraries and prices are determined in accordance with the Ministry of Tourism guidelines to ensure a full sightseeing programme in maximum comfort. Half-day, full-day and longer tours are available, some combining air with road travel. Tours depart regularly from major cities as well as from popular resort areas during the peak season. All organized tours are accompanied by experienced, licensed multilingual guides identified by an official emblem bearing the words Licensed Tourist Guide.

Smaller groups may hire a licensed driver-guide and a special touring limousine or minibus, identified by the red Ministry of Tourism emblem.

Full details of itineraries, prices and schedules are available at travel agencies, tour companies, IGTOs and TIOs.

Major public institutions and organizations such as WIZO, Hadassah, universities and the Knesset (Parliament) conduct guided tours of their facilities. Walking tours of the larger cities are arranged by the municipalities.

Visitors should be aware that certain tourist sites such as the Tomb of the Patriachs and Jericho are now within the boundaries of the Palestinian Authority.

They should consult the local tourist offices in Israel concerning travel to those areas.

When visiting religious sites always take care to be modestly dressed.

Buses

Buses are the most popular means of urban and inter-city transport throughout Israel. The Egged Bus Cooperative operates nearly all inter-city bus lines and also provides urban services in most cities and towns. (The greater Tel Aviv area is serviced by the Dan Cooperative and independent bus companies operate in Beer Sheva and Nazareth.) Fares are reasonably priced and service is regular. Most bus lines do not operate on the Sabbath (Friday evening to Saturday evening) and on Jewish holidays. Students are eligible for discount fares on inter-urban bus routes on presentation of an International Student Card. Special monthly tickets are available for Dan and Egged urban bus lines. Overseas visitors can purchase Israbus passes valid on all Egged bus lines for periods of 7, 14, 21 and 30 days. Tickets can be obtained at any Egged bus station.

Traffic Regulations

A valid International Driving Licence is recognised and preferred, although a valid national driving licence is also accepted, provided it has been issued by a country maintaining diplomatic relations with Israel and recognising an Israeli driving licence.

Traffic travels on the right and overtakes on the left. Drivers coming from the right have priority, unless indicated otherwise on the road signs, which are international. Distances on road signs are always given in kilometres (1 km is equal to 0.621 miles).

The speed limit is 50 km (approx. 31 miles) per hour in built-up areas; 80-90 km (approx. 50-56 miles) per hour on open roads.

Special Programmes For Tourists

Plant a Tree With Your Own Hands

Tree-planting centres have been established by the Jewish National Fund at several locations throughout Israel. For a nominal contribution, visitors may plant trees and receive a certificate and pin to mark the event. For further information, contact the Jewish National Fund, PO Box 283,91002 Jerusalem, Tel: 02-670 7402 Fax: 02-624 11781 or 96 Hayarkon Street, 63432 Tel Aviv, Tel: 03-523 4367 Fax: 03-524 6084.

GMT + 2 hours — Total Population 6,201,000
Country calling code (972) — Jewish Population 4,882,000
Emergency Telephone (Police - 100) (Fire - 102) (Ambulance - 101)

Afula

Restaurants

La Cabania,
Ha'atzmaut Square (4) 659-1638

San Remo,
4 Ha'atzmaut Square (4) 652-2458

Akko

Hotels

Palm Beach
P.O. Box 2192 24101 (4) 981-5815
Fax: (4) 991-0434
Supervision: Kashrut by local rabbi.
Hotel, Restaurant and Convention Centre.

Kosher

Palm Beach Sport E Spa Hotel
Sea Shore 24101 (4) 987-7777
Fax: (4) 9910434
Email: palmbech@netvision.net.il
Web site: www.palmbeach.co.il

Museums

Akko Municipal Museum
Old City (4) 991-8251
Fax: (4) 981-6686

Restaurants

Vegetarian

Amirei Hagalil
Akko-Safed Road, nr. Moshav Amirim 20115
(4) 698-9815/6

Tourist Information

Eljazar Street, opposite Mosque (4) 177-022-7764; 999-1764

Youth Hostels

Acre Youth Hostel
(4) 991-1982
Fax: (4) 991-1982

Israel

Arad

Hotels

Arad,
6 Hapalmach Street (8) 995-7040
Fax: (8) 995-7272

Margoa,
Mo'av Street, POB 20 89100 (8) 995-1222
Fax: (8) 995-7778
Email: margoa@mail.inter.net.il
Supervision: Kushrut: Rabbinat Arad.

Nof Arad,
Moav Street (8) 995-7056
Fax: (8) 995-4053

Youth Hostels

Blau-Weis (8) 995-7150
This organisation is located in the centre of town.

Ashdod

Hotels

Miami, 12 Nordau Street (8) 852-2085
Fax: (8) 856-0573

Tourist Information

4 Haim Moshe Shapira Street, Rova Daled
(8) 864-0485/090

Avihail

Museums

Beit Hagedudim (History of Jewish Brigade W.W.I)
42910 (9) 882-2212
Fax: (9) 862-1619

B'nei Berak

Hotels

Wiznitz,
16 Damesek Elizier Street (3) 777-1413

Restaurants

Dairy

Dairy Capit,
34 Rabbi Akiv St (3) 579-6927

Beersheba

Hotels

Desert Inn,
Tuviyahu Av. (8) 642-4922
Fax: (8) 641-2722

Museums

Man in the Desert Museum
Situated five miles north-east of the city.

Negev Museum,
Ha'atzmaut Street, cnr of Herzl Street (8) 623-4438
Fax: (8) 623-9105

Tours of Jewish Interest

Bedouin Market
The market is held every Thursday but it has been affected negatively by tourism and modernization. Permanent Bedouin encampments can be seen south of town.

Caesarea

Hotels

Dan Caesarea Golf Hotel
PO Box 1120 30600 (4) 626-9111
Fax: (4) 626-9122
Email: caesarea@danhotels.com
Web site: www.danhotels.com

Restaurants

Caesarean Self Service
Paz Petrol Station (4) 633-4609

Dan

Museums

Natural History and Archaeology

Beit Ussishkin Nature Reserve
12245 (4) 694-1704
Fax: (4) 695-1480
Email: ussishkin@kdan.co.il

Dead Sea

Hotels

Caesar Premier
(8) 668-9666
Fax: (8) 652-0303
Contact the Caesar Group sales office in Tel Aviv for information, Tel: (03) 696-8383; Fax: (03) 696-9896.

Crown Plaza (8) 659-1919

Grand Nirvana
(8) 668-9444
Fax: (8) 668-9400
Email: info@nirvana.co.il

Hod (8) 658-4644

Hyatt Regency
(8) 659-1234

Moriah Gardens
(8) 659-1591
Fax: (8) 658-4238

Radisson Moriah Plaza
(8) 659-1591

Degania Alef

Museums

Beit Gordon
15120 (4) 675-0040
Fax: (4) 670-9514

Eilat

Hotels

Ambassador
Coral Beach, PO Box 390 88103 (8) 638-2222
Fax: (8) 638-2200
Email: info@ambassador.co.il
Web site: www.ambassador.co.il

Americana Eilat
PO Box 27, North Beach 88000 (8) 633-3777
Fax: (8) 633-4174
Email: info@americanahotel.co.il
Web site: www.americanahotel.co.il

Caesar,
North Beach (8) 630-5555
Fax: (8) 633-3497

Club-In Villa Resort
Rte. 90 (Eilat-Taba Road), Box 1505
Coral Beach 88000 (8) 633-4555
Fax: (8) 633-4519

Dalia,
North Beach (8) 633-4004
Fax: (8) 633-4072

Dan Eilat,
Promenade, North Beach (8) 636-2222
Fax: (8) 636-2333

Edomit,
New Tourist Center (8) 637-9511
Fax: (8) 637-9738

King Solomon's Palace
Promenade, North Beach (8) 633-3444
Fax: (8) 633-4189

Marina Club,
North Beach (8) 633-4191
Fax: (8) 633-4206

Orchid, Rte. 90 (Eilat-Taba Road),
Box 994 88000 (8) 636-0360
Fax: (8) 637-5323

Princess
Rte. 90 (Eilat-Taba Road),
Box 2323 88000 (8) 636-5555
Fax: (8) 637-6333

Radisson Moriah Plaza
Promenade, North Beach (8) 636-1111
Fax: (8) 633-4158

Red Rock,
North Beach (8) 637-3171
Fax: (8) 637-1705

Royal Beach,
North Beach (8) 636-8888
Fax: (8) 636-8811

Royal Garden
North Beach 88000 (8) 638-6666
Fax: (8) 638-6665
Email: cro@isrotel.co.il
Web site: www.isrotel.co.il

The Neptune Hotel
North Beach (8) 636-9369
Fax: (8) 633-4389

Restaurants

Café Royal,
King Solomon's Palace Hotel,
North Beach (8) 667-6111
Chinese Restaurant
Shulamit Gardens Hotel,
North Beach (8) 667-7515
Dolphin Baguette
Tourist Centre
Egged,
Central Bus Station (8) 667-5161
El Morocco,
Tourist Centre
Golden Lagoon
New Lagoona Hotel, North Beach (8) 667-2176
Halleluyah,
Building 9, Tourist Centre (8) 667-5752
Off the Wharf
King Solomon's Palace Hotel,
North Beach (8) 636-3439

Dairy

La Trattoria,
Radisson Moriah Plaza Hotel,
North Beach (8) 636-1111

Meat

El Gaucho,
Arrava Road. (Rte. 90) (8) 633-1549
Shipudei Habustan
The Dan Eilat Promenade (8) 636-2294
Tamarind
North Shore 88103 (8) 638-0000

Tours of Jewish Interest

Orionia (8) 667-2902
Pirate (8) 667-6549

Israel

Youth Hostels

Eilat (8) 637-0088

Galilee

Hotels

Kosher

Ayelet Hashahar
Upper Galilee, Katzrin 12200 (4) 693-2611
Fax: (4) 693-4777

Hacienda,
Ma'a lot (4) 957-9000
Fax: (4) 997-4404

Rakefet,
Mishgav, Western Galilee (4) 980-0403
Fax: (4) 980-0317

Museums

Bar-David Museum of Jewish Art
Kibbutz Bar'am, off Route 899 (4) 698-8295
Fax: (4) 698-7505
Web site: www.galil-elion.org.il

Sculpture Gallery for Peace and Co-existence
Kawkab Abu Elhija, Gush Segev,
Lower Galilee (4) 852-5251
Fax: (4) 852-9166
Email: bhagefen@netvision.il
Web site: www.haifa.gov.il/beit-hagefen/index

Tel Hai Sculpture Garden
Tel Hai, Upper Galilee Region (4) 694-3731
Fax: (4) 695-0697

The Museum of Photography
Tel Hai Industrial Park (4) 695-0769
Fax: (4) 695-0771
Web site: www.iscar.com

The Open Museum
Tefen Industrial Park, Migdal Tefen (4) 987-2977
Fax: (4) 987-2861
Web site: www.iscar.com

Restaurants

Lev Hagolan,
30 Dror. Street, Katzrin (4) 961-6643

Orcha,
Commercial Centre, Katzrin (4) 696-1440

Youth Hostels

Karei Deshe (Tabgha)
Yoram (4) 672-0601
Fax: (4) 672-4818

Eleven miles north of Tiberias.

Golan Heights

Leisure

Hamat Gader
The Golan Heights rise steeply fron the Sea of Galilee to the Mount Avital plateau. The Hamat Gader were thought to be the nicest spa baths in the whole Roman world, according to the Byzantine empress Eudocia. There are impressive ruins including the extensive Roman and Byzantine spa, which served as a grand bathing resort for six centuries, and an ancient synagogue. Four mineral springs and a freshwater spring emerge at Hamat Gader and so it is used today as a modern bathhouse. There is also an alligator farm where dozens of alligators and crocodiles can be seen lazing around.

Museum

The Golan Archeological Museum
Katzrin (4) 696-9636
Fax: (4) 696-9637

Nature Reserve

Gamla Nature Reserve
(4) 682-2282
Fax: (4) 682-2285

Fifteen kilometres southeast of Katzrin.

Restaurants

Hamat Gader Restaurant
(4) 675-1039

Gush Etzion

Restaurants

Cravings Café
Dekel Shopping Center, Efrat (2) 993-3188

Pizzeria Efrat
Te'ena Shopping Center, Efrat (2) 993-1630

Meat

The Oak Tree Restaurant
Judaica Center, Gush Etzion Junction (2) 993-4370
Fax: (2) 993-4949
Email: judaica1@netvision.net.il

Available for groups and events.

Tours of Jewish Interest

Gush Etzion Judaica Center
Gush Etzion Junction
(2) 993-4040; Tourism Dept. 993-8388
Fax: (2) 993-4949
Email: judaica1@netvision.net.ill
Web site: www.judaica.org.il

Display and sales hall that features the items of over 200 items of Israeli Judaica. Can be combined with a visit to Kibbutz Kfar Etzion to see an audio visual show that movingly describes the history of Gush Etzion.

Hadera

Museums

The Khan Museum
74 Hagiborim Street, POB 3232 38131
(4) 632-2330; 632-4562
Fax: (4) 632-2072
Hours: Sunday to Thursday, 8 am to 1 pm; Friday, 9 am to 12 pm; Sunday and Tuesday, 4 pm to 6 pm.

Haifa

Hotels

Kosher

Dan Carmel,
85 Hanassi Avenue (4) 830-3030
Fax: (4) 838-7504
Email: dancarmel@danhotels.com
Web site: www.danhotels.com

Dan Panorama,
107 Hanassi Avenue (4) 835-2222
Fax: (4) 835-2235
Email: panorama-haifa@danhotels.com

Dvir,
124 Yafe Nof Street (4) 838-9131
Fax: (4) 838-1068

Nof Haifa,
101 Hanasi Avenue (4) 835-4311
Fax: (4) 838-8810
Email: s1@actcom.co.il
Web site: nof-hotels.co.il

Shulamit
15 Kiryat Sefer Street 34676 (4) 834-2811
Fax: (4) 825-5206

Museums

Beit Pinchas Biological Insititute
124 Hatishbi Street (4) 837-2390
Fax: (4) 837-7019
Email: biolinst@netvision.net.il
Includes nature museum, zoo and botanical garden. Entrance via Gan Ha'em. Hours: Sunday to Thursday, Winter, 8 am to 4 pm, July to August, 8 am to 7 pm; Friday and holiday eves, 8 am to 2 pm; Saturday, 9 am to 5 pm; Winter, 9 am to 4 pm.

Israel Edible Oil Industry Museum
Shemen Factory, 2 Tovim Street,
POB 136 31000 (4) 865-4237
Fax: (4) 862-5872

Israel Railways Museum
Haifa East Railway Station (4) 856-4293
Fax: (4) 856-4310

Mane Katz Museum
89 Yafe-Nof Street 34641 (4) 838-3482
Fax: (4) 836-3482

Museum of Clandestine Immigration & Navy Museum
204 Allenby Street 35472 (4) 853-6249
Fax: (4) 851-2958
Open: Sunday-Thursday 08.30 am - 16.00 pm.

Museum of Haifa
26 Shabbtai Levy Street 33043 (4) 852-3255
Fax: (4) 855-2714
Email: haifa4@netvision.net.il
Web site: www.haifa.gov.il
Includes Museums of Ancient Art, Modern Art and Music & Ethnology. Hours: Sunday, Monday, Wednesday, Thursday, 10 am to 4 pm; Tuesday, 4 pm to 7 pm; Friday and holidays, 10 am to 1 pm; Saturday, 10 am to 2 pm.

Museum of Pre-History
124 Hatishbi Street, Entrance from Gan Ha'em
(4) 837-1833
Fax: (4) 855-2714

Reuben & Edith Hecht Museum
Haifa University 31905 (4) 825-7773
Fax: (4) 824-0724
Email: mushecht@research.haifa.ac.il
Web site: www.mushecht.haifa.ac.il
Hours: Sunday, Monday, Wednesday, Thursday, 10 am to 4 pm; Tuesday, 10 am to 7 pm; Friday, 10 am to 1 pm; Saturday, 10 am to 2 pm. Admission free. Kosher restaurant.

The Israel National Museum of Science, Planning and Technology.
The Historic Technion Building, Balfour Street, Hadar Ha carmel (4) 862-8111
Fax: (4) 867-9103
Email: museum@mustsee.org.il
Web site: www.mustsee.org.il

The National Maritime Museum
198 Allenby Road (4) 853-6622
Fax: (4) 853-9286
Hours: Sunday, Monday, Wednesday, Thursday, 10 am to 4 pm; Tuesday, 4 pm to 7 pm; Friday and holidays, 10 am to 1 pm; Saturday, 10 am to 2 pm.

Tikotin Museum of Japanese Art
89 Hanassi Avenue, Mount Carmel 34642 (4) 838-3554
Fax: (4) 837-9824
Hours: Monday, Wednesday, Thursday, 10 am to 5 pm; Tuesday, 10 am to 2 pm and 5 pm to 8 pm; Friday and holiday eves, 10 am to 1 pm; Saturday, 10 am to 2 pm.

University of Haifa Art Collection
University of Haifa, Mount Carmel (4) 824-0660
Fax: (4) 824-0309

Restaurants

Banker's Tavern
2 Habankim Street (4) 852-8439
Lunch only. Closed Shabbat.

Ben Ezra,
71 Hazayit Street (4) 884-2273
Egged,
Central Bus Station (4) 851-5221
Self-service.
Gan Rimon,
10 Habroshim Street (4) 838-1392
Lunch only.
Ha'atzmaut,
63 Derech Ha'atzmaut (4) 852-3829
Hamber Burger
61 Herzl Street (4) 866-6739
Hamidrachov,
10 Nordau Street (4) 866-2050
Paznon,
Hof Carmel (4) 853-8181
Rondo,
Dan Carmel Hotel, 87 Hanassi Blvd (4) 838-6211
Technion,
Neve Shaanan (4) 823-3011
Self service. Lunch only.
The Chinese Restaurant of Nof
Nof Hotel, 101 Hanassi Blvd (4) 838-8731
The Second Floor
119 Hanassi Blvd (4) 838-2020
Tsemed Hemed,
Herbert Samuel Square (4) 824-2205

Dairy

Milky Pinky (Milk Bar)
29 Haneviim Street (4) 866-4166
Wissotsky Tea House
2 Mahanaim, Carmel Centre

Meat

Mac David,
131 Hanassi Blvd (4) 838-3684
Mac David,
1 Balfour Street

Tourist Information

106 Sderot Hanassi (4) 837-4010
What's on in Haifa
(4) 864-0840

Tours of Jewish Interest

(4) 867-4342
Bahai shrine and gardens, Druse villages, Muchraka, the Moslem village of Kabair, the Carmelite monastery and Elijah's cave, Wednesday, 9.30 am.
(4) 867-4342
Mt Carmel, Druse villages, Kibbutz Ben Oren and Ein Hod artists' colony: Sunday, Monday, Tuesday, Thursday, Saturday, 9.30 am.

Youth Hostels

Carmel
(4) 853-1944
Fax: (4) 853-2516
Shlomi,
Hanita Forest (4) 980-8975

Hanita

Museums

Tower & Stockade Museum
Route 8990 (4) 985-9677
Fax: (4) 985-9677

Haon

Holiday Village

Kibbutz Haon,
Jordan Valley (4) 675-7555/6

Hazorea

Museums

Wilfrid Israel House of Oriental Art
(4) 989-9566
Fax: (4) 989-0942

Herzlia

Hotels

Dan Accadia,
Herzlia on Sea (9) 959-7070
Fax: (9) 959-7092
Email: danhtls@danhotels.co.il
Tadmor,
38 Basel Street (9) 952-5000
Fax: (9) 957-5124
Email: hotel@tadmor.co.il
The Sharon
Herzlia on Sea 46748 (9) 952-5777
Fax: (9) 956-8741
Email: hasharon@netvision.net.il
Web site: www.sharon.co.il

Museums

Herzlia Museum of Art
4 Habanim Street 46379 (9) 950-2301
Fax: (9) 950-0043
Email: herz_mus@netvision.net.il
Web site: www.adgo.co.il/herzliya_museum

Restaurants

Dona Flor,
22 Hagalim Blvd., Herzlia Pituach (9) 950-9669
Tadmor Hotel School
38 Basel Street 46660 (9) 952-5050
Fax: (9) 957-5124
Email: hotel@tadmor.co.il

Israel

Meat

Steak.com,
27 Rehov Maskit, Herzliya Pituah (9) 956-1145

Tourist Information

English-Speaking Residents Association
PO Box 3132 46104 (9) 950-8371
Fax: (9) 954-3781
Email: esra@trendline.co.il

Jaffa

Museums

The Antiquities Museum of Tel Aviv-Yafo (Jaffa Museum)
10 Mifratz Shlomo Street, Old Jaffa 68038
(3) 682-5375
Fax: (3) 681-3624
Part of Eretz Israel Museum Tel Aviv. Opening hours: Sunday-Thursday 9 am to 1 pm.

Tours of Jewish Interest

Tel Aviv-Yafo Tourism Association
Ramat Gan
Walk takes 2.5 hours, starting at Clock Square near Yefet Street, in the centre of Jaffa. Free.

Jerusalem

Accommodation Information

Good Morning Jerusalem
9 Coresh Street 94146 (2) 623-3459
Fax: (2) 625-9330
Email: gmjer@netvision.net.il
Web site: www.accommodation.co.il
Lists rooms and apartments available for tourists.

Bed & Breakfasts

Kosher

Le Sixteen
16 Midbar Sinai Street,
Givat Hamivtar 97805 (2) 532-8008
Fax: (2) 581-9159
Email: le16@le16-bnb.co.il
Web site: www.le16-bnb.co.il
Member of the Jerusalem Home Accommodation Association. Can provide guest studios with kosher dairy kitchenettes.

Contact Information

Jeff Seidel's Jewish Student Information Centre
5 Bet-El, Jewish Quarter, Old City (2) 628-2634
Fax: (2) 628-8338
Email: jseidel@jeffseidel.com
Web site: www.jeffseidel.com

Jewish Student Information Centre
Hebrew University Off-Campus Center,
5/4 Etzel Street, French Hill (2) 581-4939
Email: jseidel@netmedia.net.il

Guest House

Bet Shmuel
6 Shamma Street 94101 (2) 620-3473; 620-3465
Fax: (2) 620-3467
Single and family guest rooms with a capacity of 240 beds; conference facilities and banquet services; restaurant and coffee shop; international culture and education centre with a central location.

Holiday Village

Youth Recreation Centre Holiday Village
Yefei Nof, Jerusalem Forest (2) 641-6060

Hotels

Isrotel Tower Jerusalem
204 Jaffa Street 94383 (2) 500-7777
Fax: (2) 500-7772
Email: towerjerusalem@isrotel.co.il
Web site: www.isrotel.co.il

Ariel Hotel Jerusalem
31 Hebron Road (2) 568-9999
Fax: (2) 673-4066
Email: info@arieljrm.co.il
Walking distance from Old City.

Caesar,
208 Jaffa Road (2) 500-5656
Fax: (2) 538-2802
Email: caesarjm@netvision.net.il

Central,
6 Pines Street (2) 538-4111
Fax: (2) 5381-480

Four Points
4 Vilnai Street 96110 (2) 655-8888
Fax: (2) 651-2266
The hotel is located in the prestigious hotel area at the entrance to the city and is within walking distance of the Israel Museum and the Knesset.

Hyatt Regency Jerusalem
32 Lehi Street (2) 533-1234
Fax: (2) 581-5947
Email: hyattjrs@trendline.co.il
Web site: www.hyattjer.co.il

Inbal,
Liberty Bell Park, 3 Jabotinsky Street 92145
(2) 675-6666
Fax: (2) 675-6777
Email: rsv@inbal-hotel.co.il
Web site: www.inbal-hotel.co.il

Jerusalem Hilton
7 King David Street 94101 (2) 621-1111
Fax: (2) 621-1000

Jerusalem Tower
23 Hillel Street (2) 620-9209
Fax: (2) 625-2167
Email: jthotels@inisrael.com

King David
23 King David Street 94101 (2) 620-8888
Fax: (2) 620-8882
Email: kingdavid@danhotels.com

King Solomon,
32 King David Street (2) 569-5555
Fax: (2) 624-1174
Email: solhotel@netvision.net.il

Lev Yerushalayim
18 King George Street (2) 530-0333
Fax: (2) 623-2432

Menorah,
44 Jaffa Road (2) 622-3122
Fax: (2) 625-0707

Mount Zion,
17 Hebron Road (2) 568-9555
Fax: (2) 673-1425
Email: hotel@mountzion.co.il

Palatin,
4 Agripas Street (2) 623-1141
Fax: (2) 625-9323
Email: info@hotel-palatin.co.il
Web site: www.hotel-palatin.co.il

Radisson Moriah Plaza Jerusalem
39 Keren Hayessod Street 94188 (2) 569-5695
Fax: (2) 623-2411

Reich,
1 Hagai Street, Bet Hakerem (2) 652-3121
Fax: (2) 652-3120

Renaissance Jerusalem Hotel
Ruppin Bridge, at Herz Blvd 91033 (2) 659-9999
Fax: (2) 651-1824
Email: renjhot@netvision.net.il
Glatt kosher. Contact: Eli Velter.

Sheraton Jerusalem Plaza
47 King George Street (2) 629-8666
Fax: (2) 623-1667
Kosher Lamehadrin.

Windmill,
3 Mendele Street (2) 566-3111
Fax: (2) 561-0964

Museums

Ammunition Hill Memorial & Museum, Ramat Eshkol
Levy Eshkol Boulevard 91181 (2) 582-8442
Fax: (2) 582-9132

Bible Lands Museum Jerusalem
25 Granot Street, POB 4670 91046 (2) 561-1066
Fax: (2) 563-8228
Email: biblelnd@netvision.net.il
Web site: www.blmj.org
The home of one of the most important collections of ancient artifacts displaying rare works of art from the dawn of civilisation to the Byzantine period. Gift shop, special exhibitions,weekly lectures and concerts. Hours: Sunday, Monday, Tuesday, Thursday, 9:30 am to 5:30 pm; Wednesday, April to October, 9:30 am to 9:30 pm, November to March, 1:30 pm to 9:30 pm; Friday and holiday eves, 9:30 am to 2 pm; Saturday and holidays, 11am to 3 pm. Daily guided tours. Kosher restaurant. Daily English guided tours.

Herzl Museum,
Herzl Blvd, Mount Herzl (2) 651-1108

Israel Museum
Ruppin Blvd (2) 670-8985
Fax: (2) 563-1832
Web site: www.imj.org.il
Includes Bezalel National Museum, Samuel Bronfman Biblical & Archaeological Museum, Shrine of the Book & the Rockefeller Museum in East Jerusalem.

L.A. Mayer Museum for Islamic Art
2 Hapalmach Street 92542 (2) 566-1291/2
Fax: (2) 561-9802

Museum of Italian Jewish Art
27 Hillel Street 94581 (2) 624-1610
Fax: (2) 625-3480
Web site: www.itcham.org.il/museum/

Museum of Natural History
6 Mohilever Street (2) 563-1116
Fax: (2) 566-0666

Nahon Museum of Italian Jewish Art
27 Hillel Street 94581 (2) 624-1610
Fax: (2) 625-3840
Web site: www.jija.org
This special museum collects and preserves objects pertaining to the life of the Jews in Italy from the Middle Ages to the present day. The main attraction is the ancient synagogue of Conegliano Veneto, a township some 60 km from Venice relocated in its entirety to Israel. Hours: Sunday, Tuesday, Wednesday, 9 am to 5 pm, Monday, 9 am to 2 pm, Thursday, Friday 9 am to 1 pm. For guided tours contact the numbers above.

Old Yishuv Court Museum
6 Or Hayim Street 91016 (2) 628-4636
Fax: (2) 628-4636
The museum is located in the heart of the Jewish Quarter in the Old City of Jerusalem in a sixteenth-century building. It displays the story of the Jewish community from the periods under Ottoman rule, through the final days of the British Mandate. Hours: Sunday to Thursday, 9 am to 2 pm.

Israel

S.Y. Agnon's House
16 Joseph Klausner Street, Talpiot 93388
(2) 671-6498
Email: agnon-h@inter.net.il
Hours: Sunday to Thursday, 9 am to 1 pm.

Siebenberg House of Archaeological Museum
7 Hagittit Street, Jewish Quarter (2) 628-2341

The Chagall Windows at the Hadassah Medical School
The Hebrew University, Hadassah (2) 641-6333
Fax: (2) 641-6333

The Sir Isaac & Lady Wolfson Museum
Hechal Shlomo (4th Floor),
58 King George Street (2) 624-7112
Fax: (2) 623-1810

Tourjeman Post Museum
4 Hail Hahandassa Street (2) 628-1278
Fax: (2) 627-7061

Tower of David Museum of the History of Jerusalem
Jaffa Gate (2) 626-5333
Fax: (2) 628-3418
Email: shivuk@tower.org.il

Yad Vashem, The Holocaust Martyrs' and Heroes' Remembrance Authority
Har Hazikaron, PO Box 3477 91034 (2) 644-3400
Fax: (2) 644-3443
Email: general.information@yadvashem.org.il
Web site: www.yadvashem.org.il
Open 9 am to 5 pm Sunday-Thursday, 9 am to 2 pm Friday and eves of holidays, closed on Saturday and all Jewish holidays.

Organisations

Ezer Mizion "Help from Zion"
25 Yirmiyahu St., 91410 (2) 537-8070
Fax: (2) 538-3315
Email: ezer_m@netvision.net.il
Web site: www.ami.org.il
Opening hours are 7.30 am - 10.30 pm.

Travelers Aid of Israel
PO Box 2828 (2) 582-0126
Fax: (2) 532-2094
Email: wolfilaw@netvision.net.il
Legal counselling, social and human services, immigrant assistance, interest-free loans, stranded travellers, medical assistance, crime-victim assistance, homelessness, emergency assistance.

Yad Sarah
P.R. Department, Kiryat Weinbergl Blvd. 95141
(2) 644-4242
Email: infor@yadsarah.org.il
Web site: www.yadsarah.org.il
Yad Sarah home care organization lends, free against a returnable deposit, regular and high-tech medical rehab. equipment. Visitors in wheelchairs can use the Yad Sarah special transportation vans, at a low fee. By pre-arrangement you can have the van and driver waiting at Ben Gurion airport. Minimum two weeks notice please for this service. Yad Sarah has 85 branches in Israel.

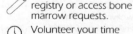

Religious Organisations

Israel Council of Young Israel
Heichal Shlomo Building,
58 King George Street 91072 (2) 623-1631
Fax: (2) 623-1363
Email: young-il@internet-zahav.net
Mailing address: PO Box 7306, 91072 Jerusalem, Israel. Office hours: Sunday through Thursday 9.00 am to 3.00 pm.

Restaurants

Casa Italiana
6 Yoel Salamon Street

Clafouti,
2 Hasoreg Street (2) 624-4491

Dagrill,
21 King George Street (2) 622-2922

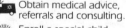

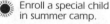

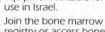

Feferberg's,
53 Jaffa Road (2) 625-4841
Pampa,
3 Rehov Yosef Rivlin (2) 623-1455
Ye Olde English Tea Room
68 Jaffa Road (2) 537-6595

Dairy

Bagel Nash,
14 Ben-Yehuda Street (2) 622-5027
Besograyim,
45 Ussishkin Street (2) 624-5353
Café Rimon,
4 Luntz Street (off Midrehov) (2) 624-3712
Chamomille,
6 Yoel Solomon Street (2) 625-2750
Dagim Beni,
1 Mesilat Yesharim Street (2) 622-2403
Daglicatesse,
1 Rachel Imenu (2) 563-2657
La Pasta,
16 Rivlin Street (2) 622-7687
Little Italy,
38 Keren Hayesod Street (2) 561-7638
Mamma Mia
38 King George Street 94262 (2) 624-8080
Fax: (2) 623-3336

Located in the centre of town in an old (1899) restored building. Air-conditioned. Hours: Sunday to Thursday, 12 pm to midnight, Friday 12 pm to 4 pm; Saturday, from the end of Shabbat.

Michael Andrew
12 Emil Bota (2) 624-0090
Of Course!,
Zion Confederation House,
Emile Botta Street (2) 624-5206
Off The Square
8 Ramban Street
Kosher Lamehadrin.
Poire et Pomme
The Khan Theatre, 2 Remez Square (2) 671-9602
Primus,
3 Yavetz Street (2) 624-6565
Rienzi,
10 King David Street (2) 622-2312
Rimon,
4 Lunz Street (2) 622-2772
Theatre Lounge
Jerusalem Theatre, 20 Marcus Street (2) 566-9351
Zeze,
11 Bezalel Street (2) 623-1761

Meat

Burger Ranch,
3 Lunz Street (2) 622-5935
Burger Ranch,
18 Shlomzion Hamalka Street (2) 622-2392
El Gaucho,
22 Rivlin Street (2) 624-1227
Fax: (2) 623-2660
El Marrakesh,
4 King David Street (2) 622-7577
El Morocco,
43 Yirmiyahu Street, Centre One (2) 500-1670
Fax: (2) 538-3496
Kinor David,
19 King David Street
Marvad Haksamim
16 King George Street
Marziano & Toledano
15 Rehov Yad Harutzim (2) 672-8672
Norman's Steak 'n Burger
27 Emek Refaim Street (2) 566-6603
Fax: (2) 673-1768
Email: rmjb@netvision.net.il
Web site: www.normans.co.il

American steakhouse. Reservations recommended. Easy walking distance from main hotels. Hours: Sunday to Thursday, 12 pm to 11 pm; Friday, closed; Saturday, from after Shabbat.

Rungsit,
2 Jabotinsky Street (2) 561-1757
Shaul's Shwarma Centre
14 Ben-Yehuda Street (2) 622-5027
Shemesh,
21 Ben-Yehuda Street (2) 622-2418
Shipodei Hagefen
74 Agrippas Street (2) 622-2367
Yemenite Step
12 Yoel Salamon Street (2) 624-0477
Yo-si Peking,
5 Shimon Ben-Shetach Street (2) 622-6893

Pizzerias

Pizzeria Rimini
7 Paran Street, Ramat Eshkol
Pizzeria Rimini
43 Jaffa Road (2) 622-5534
Pizzeria Rimini
15 King George Street (2) 622-6505
Pizzeria Trevi
8 Leib Yaffe Street (2) 672-4136

Vegetarian

Belinda,
20 King George Street (2) 624-5717
Chamomile,
6 Yoel Solomon St. (2) 625-2750

Israel

Vegetarian (K)

Village Green
33 Jaffa Street (2) 625-3065
Fax: (2) 625 3062

Take away

Synagogues

Two synagogues of interest, among the many are
Great Synagogue
60 King George Street
Yeshurun,
44 King George Street (2) 624-3942
Fax: (2) 622-4528
Email: netypjer@netvision.net.il

Tourist Information

ISSTA,
5 Eliashar Street (2) 622-5258
Ministry of Tourism
24 King George Street (2) 675-4811
Tourism Coordinator with the Palestinian Authority
Israel Ministry of Tourism, PO Box 1018, Jerusalem 91009 (2) 675-4903
Fax: (2) 624-0571
Email: zvin@tourism.gov.il

Tours of Jewish Interest

American P'eylim Student Union
10 Shoarim Street (2) 653-2131
Free tours of Jewish Quarter and free accommodation, in the hostel quarters.
Knesset (Parliament)
(2) 675-3416
Fax: (2) 561-1201
Sunday and Thursday 8.30 am and 2.30 pm
Society for the Protection of Nature in Israel: Israeli Nature Trails
13 Helen Hamalka Street 95101 (2) 624-4605
Fax: (2) 625-4953
Email: spnijeru@inter.net.il

Youth Hostels

Bet Bernstein
1 Keren Hayesod Street (2) 625-8286
Eighty rooms.
Davidka, 67 HaNevi'im Street, PO Box 37110
(2) 538-4555
Fax: (2) 538-8790
Seventy-five rooms; 4-6 bedded.
Ein Karem (2) 641-6282
Ninety-seven rooms. Ten minutes from the Louise Waterman-Wise Hotel in Bayit Vegan

Israel Youth Hostels Association
Youth Travel Bureau, Jerusalem International Convention Center, POB 6001, Jerusalem 91060
(2) 655-8442
Fax: (2) 655-8431
Email: iyha@iyha.org.il
Web site: www.iyha.org.il

There are thirty-one youth hostels in Israel for students, youth groups and adults, which are supervised by the Israel Youth Hostels Association (a member of the International Youth Hostels Federation). All hostels offer the standard facilities of dormitories, kosher dining rooms, etc. Most hostels also have a guest house section, with double and family rooms and private facilities. Most are air-conditioned.
Jerusalem Forest
(2) 675-2911
One hundred and forty rooms.
Moreshet Yahadut
(2) 628-8611
Old city; seventy-five rooms.

Kfar Giladi

Museums

Beit Hashomer
12210 (4) 694-1565
Fax: (4) 695-1505

Kfar Vitkin

Youth Hostels

Emer Hefer (9) 866-6032
Twenty-five miles north of Tel Aviv.

Kibbutz Harduf

Restaurants

Vegetarian Organic

Vegetarian Organic Restaurant
17930 (4) 905-9229
Fax: (4) 986-6835
Email: 986-1106

Kibbutz Yotvata

Leisure

Biblical Wildlife Reserve Hai Bar Arava
The reserve is situated thirty-seven miles north of Eilat. Biologoists have settled every breed of animal that is mentioned in the Bible. Animals include herd of Somalian wild asses, oryx antelope, ibex, ostriches, desert foxes, lynx, hyenas and the last desert leopard in the Negev, living out her days on the reserve. Guided tours start at 9 am and 10.30 am, noon and 1.30 pm.

Restaurants

Dairy

Dairy Restaurant

(8) 635-7449

Korazim

Holiday Village

Amnon Bay Recreation Centre

(4) 693-4431

Vered Hagalil Guest Farm

(4) 693-5785
Fax: (4) 693-4964
Email: vered@veredhagalil.co.il

Lod

Tourist Information

Ministry of Tourism

Ben Gurion International Airport (3) 971-1485

Lohamei Hagetaot

Museums

Ghetto Fighters' House, Holocaust & Resistance Museum

D.N. Western Gallilee 25220 (4) 995-8080
Fax: (4) 995-8007
Email: simstein@gfh.org.il
Web site: www.gfh.org.il

Hours: Sunday-Thursday 9 am to 4 pm. Friday 9 amto 1 pm. Saturday and holidays 10 am to 5 pm. Kosher dining room and cafeteria.

Maagan

Holiday Village

Maagan Holiday Village

Sea of Galilee 15160 (4) 665-4400
Fax: (4) 665-4455
Email: maaganhv@netvision.net.il

Maayan Harod

Youth Hostels

Hankin (4) 658-1660

Seven miles east of Afula.

Mahanayim

Tourist Information

Zomet Mahanayim (4) 693-5016

Moshav Shoresh

Hotels

Kosher

Shoresh Holiday Complex

Harey Yehuda (2) 533-8338
Fax: (2) 534-0262
Email: inifo@shoresh.co.il
Web site: www.shoresh.co.il

Nahariya

Leisure

Rosh Hanikra

Rosh Hanikra is situated four miles north of Nahariya, on the Lebanese border, and has an extensive system of caves which the sea has washed out of the soft chalk. There is also a lookout point with an adjacent restaurant which reveals a gorgeous panorama of the coast.

Hotels

Carlton,
23 Ha'agaaton Blvd (4) 992-2211
Fax: (4) 982-3771

Rosenblatt,
59 Weizmann Street (4) 992-0069
Fax: (4) 992-8121

Museums

Nahariya Municipal Museum

Hagaaton Blvd (4) 987-9863
Fax: (4) 992-2303

Restaurants

Cafe Tsafon,
10 Gaaton Blvd (4) 992-2567

Tourist Information

Israel Camping Union

PO Box 53 (4) 992-5392

Nazareth

Restaurants

Iberia,
Rassco Centre, Nazareth Elite (4) 655-6314

Nof Nazareth,
23 Hacarmel Street, Nazareth Elite (4) 655-4366

Israel

Negev

Restaurants

Bulgarian,
112 Keren Kayemet Street, Beersheba (8) 623-8504

Youth Hostels

Bet Noam,
Mitzpeh Ramon (8) 658-8433
Fax: (8) 658-8074

Bet Sara,
Ein Gedi (8) 658-4165
1.5 miles north of Kibbutz Ein Gedi on Dead Sea.

Blau-Weiss,
Arad (8) 995-7150
Centre of town.

Hevel Katif: Hadarom
(8) 684-7597
Fax: (8) 684-7680

For more detailed information, apply either to the Israel Youth Hostels Assoc. or to the nearest Israel Government Tourist Office.

Isaac H. Taylor
Masada (8) 658-4349
28 miles from Arad.

Netanya

Holiday Village

Kosher

Green Beach Holiday Village
(9) 865-6166
Fax: (9) 835-0075

Hotels

Arches
4 Remez Street 42271 (9) 860-9860
Fax: (9) 860-9866
Email: arches-hotel@correy.com

Galei Hasharon
42 Ussishkin Street 42273 (9) 834-1946
Fax: (9) 833-8128

Galil
26 Nice Blvd (9) 862-4455
Fax: (9) 862-4456

Ginot Yam
9 David Hamelech Street (9) 834-1007
Fax: (9) 861-5722

Goldar
1 Usishkin Street (9) 833-8188
Fax: (9) 862-0680
Email: order@goldar.co.il

Grand Yahalom
15 Gad Machnes Street (9) 862-4888
Fax: (9) 862-4890

Green Beach,
PO Box 230 (9) 865-6166
Fax: (9) 835-0075

Jeremy,
11 Gad Machnes Street (9) 862-2651
Fax: (9) 862-2651

King Koresh,
6 Harav Kook Street (9) 861-3555
Fax: (9) 861-3444

King Solomon,
18 Hamaapilim Street (9) 833-8444
Fax: (9) 861-1397

MacDavid,
7a Ha'atzmaut Street (9) 861-8711

Margoa,
9 Gad Machnes Street (9) 862-4434

Maxim,
8 King David Street (9) 862-1062
Fax: (9) 862-0190

Metropol Grand
17 Gad Machnes Street (9) 862-4777
Fax: (9) 861-1556

Orly,
20 Hamaapilim Street (9) 833-3091
Fax: (9) 862-5453

Palace,
N.L., 33 Gad Machnes Street (9) 862-0222
Fax: (9) 862-0224

Park,
7 David Hamelech Street (9) 862-3344
Fax: (9) 862-4029

Residence,
18 Gad Machnes Street (9) 862-3777
Fax: (9) 862-3711

The Seasons,
1 Nice Blvd (9) 860-1555
Fax: (9) 862-3022
Email: seasons@netmedia.net.il

Synagogues

Congregation Agudath Achim
45 Jabotinsky Street

Netanya Cultural Center
4 Raziel Street (9) 861-1687
Fax: (9) 861-7555
Email: Rina@netanya-cultural.co.il

New Synagogue of Netanya
7 MacDonald Street (9) 861-4591

Young Israel Congregation of North Netanya
39 Shlomo Hamelech Street (9) 862-1856

Tourist Information

Kikar ha'Atzmaut (9) 882-7286

Petach Tikva

Museums

Beit Yad Labanim
30 Arlozorov Street (3) 922-3450
Fax: (3) 922-3450

Qatzrin

Museums

Golan Archaeological Museum
(4) 696-9636
Fax: (4) 696-2412
Email: museum@golan.org.il

Ra'anana

Restaurants

Dana,
198 Achuza (9) 790-1452
Lady D,
158 Achuza (9) 791-6517
Limosa,
5 Eliazar Jaffe (9) 790-3407
Pica Aduma,
87 Achuza (9) 791-0508

Ramat Gan

Museums

Museum of Israeli Art
146 Abba Hillel Street 52572 (3) 752-1876
Fax: (3) 752-7377
Email: meirmusun@mail.inter.net.il
Pierre Gildesgame Maccabi Sports Museum
Kfar Hamaccabiah (3) 671-5729
Fax: (3) 574-6565
Email: lod@netvision.net.il
Yechiel Nahari Museum of Far Eastern Art
18 Hibat Zion Street (3) 578-1216
Fax: (3) 619-5837

Ramat Hanegev

Tourist Information

Zomet Mashabay Sadeh (8) 655-7314

Ramat Yohanan

Youth Hostels

Yehuda Hatzair
(4) 844-2976
Fax: (4) 844-2976

Eleven miles north-east of Haifa.

Rehovot

Museums

Havayeda - Science Through Fun Science Park
5 Yechezkai Habibi Street 76000 (3) 945-2949
Fax: (3) 945-2949
Web site: www.weizmann.ac.il

Weizmann House
Yad Haim Weizmann,
Marcus Sieff Blvd (3) 934-3230
Fax: (3) 934-3926
Web site: www.weizmann.ac.il

Restaurants

Rehovot Chinese Restaurant
202 Herzl Street (8) 947-1616

Rosh Hanikra

Youth Hostels

Rosh Hanikra (4) 998-2516
Near the grottos.

Rosh Pina

Youth Hostels

Hovevei Hateva
(4) 693-7086

Sixteen miles north of Tiberias

Safed

Hotels

Kosher

David,
Mount Canaan (4) 692-0062
Nof Hagalil,
Mount Canaan (4) 692-1595
Pisgah,
Mount Canaan (4) 692-0105
Rimon Inn,
Artists Colony (4) 692-0665/6
Ron,
Hativat Yiftah Street (4) 697-2590

Museums

Beit Hameiri Institute
(History & Heritage of Safed)
Keren Hayesod Street 13110 (4) 697-1307
Fax: (4) 692-1902

Israel Bible Museum
Citadel Hill (4) 699-9972
Fax: (4) 699-9972

Near Ron Hotel
Museum of Printing
Artists' Quarter (4) 692-3022

Israel

Tourist Information

50 Jerusalem Street (4) 692-0961/633

Youth Hostels

Bet Benyamin (4) 692-1086
Fax: (4) 697-3514

In southern part of town.

Tel Aviv

Accommodation Information

Kibbutz Hotels Chain: Head Office
1 Smolanskin Street,
PO Box 3193 61031 (3) 524-6161
Fax: (3) 527-8088
Email: batya@kibbutz.co.il
Web site: www.kibbutz.co.il

Contact Information

Jewish Student Information Centre
Tel Aviv University Off-Campus Center,
82/10 Levanon Street, Ramat Aviv
Email: jseidel@netmedia.net.il

Hotels

Adiv,
5 Mendele Street (3) 522-9141

Ambassador,
56 Herbert Samuel Street (3) 510-3993
Fax: (3) 517-6308

Armon Hayarkon
268 Hayarkon Street (3) 605-5271
Fax: (3) 605-8485

Avia,
Ben Gurion Intl Airport Area (3) 539-3333
Fax: (3) 539-3319

Basel,
156 Hayarkon Street (3) 520-7711
Fax: (3) 527-0005

Bell,
12 Allenby Street (3) 517-7011
Fax: (3) 517-4352

Carlton Tel Aviv
10 Eliezer Peri Street (3) 520-1818
Fax: (3) 527-1043
Email: request@carlton.co.il

City,
9 Mapu Street (3) 524-6253
Fax: (3) 524-6250

Dan Panorama,
Charles Clore Park (3) 519-0190

Dan Tel Aviv,
99 Hayarkon Street (3) 520-2525
Fax: (3) 524-9755
Email: dantelaviv@danhotels.com

Grand Beach,
250 Hayarkon Street (3) 543-3333
Fax: (3) 546-6589
Email: reservation@grandbeach.co.il
Web site: www.grandbeach.co.il

Synagogue on premises.

Howard Johnson - Shalom
216 Hayarkon Street (3) 524-3277
Fax: (3) 523-5895
Email: h_shlom@netvision.net.il

Maxim,
86 Hayarkon Street, PO Box 3442
63903 (3) 517-3721/5
Fax: (3) 517-3726

Metropolitan
11-15 Trumpeldor Street, 63803 (3) 519-2727
Fax: (3) 517-2626
Email: reserve@metrotlv.co.il
Web site: www.hotelmetropolitan.co.il

Ramat Aviv, 151 Namir Road (3) 699-0777
Fax: (3) 699-0997

Renaissance Tel Aviv
121 Hayarkon Street 63453 (3) 521-5555
Fax: (3) 521-5588
Email: reserv@renaissance-tlv.co.il

Sheraton Moriah
155 Hayarkon Street (3) 521-6666
Fax: (3) 527-1065
Email: shermor@inter.net.il

Sheraton Tel Aviv Hotel & Towers
115 Hayarkon Street (3) 521-1111
Fax: (3) 523-3322
Email: shtelviv@netvision.net.il

Tal,
287 Hayarkon Street (3) 542-5500
Fax: (3) 542-5501

Tel Aviv Hilton
Independence Park 63405 (3) 520-2222
Fax: (3) 527-2711
Email: fom_tel-aviv@hilton.com

Yamit Park Plaza
79 Hayarkon Street (3) 517-7111
Fax: (3) 517-4719
Email: yamit@netvision.net.il

Museums

Beit Bialik,
22 Bialik Street (3) 525-3403
Fax: (3) 525-4530

Ben Gurion House
17 Ben Gurion Blvd (3) 522-1010
Fax: (3) 524-7293

Eretz Israel Museum
2 Haim Levanon Street 69975 (3) 641-5244
Fax: (3) 641-2408

Hagana Museum
23 Rothschild Blvd 65122 (3) 560-8624
Fax: (3) 566-1208
Helena Rubenstein Pavilion for Contemporary Art
6 Tarsat Street (3) 528-7196
Jabotinsky Museum
38 King George Street 62398 (3) 528-7320
Fax: (3) 528-5587
Email: jabo@actcom.co.il
Web site: www.jabotinsky.org
Hours: Sunday to Thursday, 8 am to 4 pm.
Lehi Museum
8 Stern Street 66085 (3) 682-0288
Fax: (3) 681-9264
Museum of Jewish Ethnic Heritage
20 David Ha'melech Blvd, Lod (3) 923-4008
Fax: (3) 923-4008
Museum of the Jewish Diaspora (Beth Hatefutsoth)
Klausner Street, Ramat Aviv (3) 646-2020
Fax: (3) 646-2134
Email: bhmuseum@post.tav.ac.il
Web site: www.bh.org.il
Tel Aviv Museum of Art
27 Shaul Hamelech Blvd 61332 (3) 696-1297
Fax: (3) 695-8099
Hours: Monday and Wednesday 10 am - 4 pm, Tuesday and Thursday 10 am to 10 pm , Friday 10am to 2 pm and Saturday, 10 am to 4 pm Public transport: buses 9, 11 18, 28, 70, 82, 90, 91, 111. Parking facilities.

Restaurants

Hamakom,
1 Lilienbaum Street (3) 510-1823
Shaul's Inn,
11 Elyashiv Street, Kerem Hatemanim (3) 517-3303
Fax: (3) 517-7619
Supervision: Chief Rabbinate of Tel Aviv.
Oriental and Yemenite food. Popular and exclusive sections. Hours: 12 pm to 12 am.

Dairy

Apropo, Alexander Hotel,
3 Havakuk Street (3) 544-4442
Hungarian Blintzes
35 Yirmiyahu Street (3) 605-0674

Meat

China Lee, 102 Hayarkon Street (3) 524-6119
Olive Leaf,
Sheraton Tel Aviv Hotel and Towers,
115 Hayarkon Street (3) 521-9300
Fax: (3) 521-9301
Web site: www.sheraton-telaviv.com
Prestigious restaurant. Innovative cuisine with Mediterranean flavours.

Synagogues

Bilu,
122 Rothschild Blvd.
Great,
314 Dizengoff Street
Ihud Shivat Zion
86 Ben-Yehuda Street
Central European rite.
Tiferet Zvi,
Hermann Hacohen Street

Ashkenazi

Main Synagogue
110 Allenby Road

Progressive

Kedem,
20 Carlebach Street

Sephardi

Ohel Mis'ad,
5 Shadal Street

Tourist Information

Shop # 6108, 6th Floor, New Central Bus Station (3) 639-5660
Fax: (3) 639-5659
ISSTA, 109 Ben Yehuda Street
The Ministry of Tourism
6 Wilson Street (3) 556-2339
The Ministry of Tourism publishes a guide called 'The Best of Israel', detailing shops participating in the VAT refund scheme and recommended restaurants.

Travel Agencies

Interom Tourism Ltd
(3) 924-6425
Fax: (3) 579-1720

Tiberias

Hotels

Ariston,
19 Herzl Blvd (4) 679-0244
Fax: (4) 672-2002
Astoria,
13 Ohel Ya'akov Street (4) 672-2351
Fax: (4) 672-5108

Caesar,
103 The Promenade (4) 672-7272
Fax: (4) 679-1013

Carmel Jordan River
Habanim Street (4) 671-4444
Fax: (4) 672 2111

Gai Beach,
Derech Hamerchatzaot (4) 670-0700
Fax: (4) 679-2766

Galei Kinnereth
1 Kaplan Street (4) 672-8888
Fax: (4) 679-0260

Golan,
14 Achad Ha'am Street (4) 679-1901
Fax: (4) 672-1905

Kinar,
N.E. Sea of Galilee (4) 673-8888
Fax: (4) 673-8811
Email: kinarmamag@kinar.co.il

Lavi Kibbutz Hotel
Lower Galilee 15267 (4) 679-9450
Fax: (4) 679-9399
Email: lavi@lavi.co.il
Web site: www.lavi.co.il
Glatt Kosher, Shomer Shabbat.

Pagoda,
Lido Beach, PO Box 253 14102 (4) 672-5513
Fax: (4) 672-5518
Email: liz@kinneret.co.il
Open Sunday to Thursday 12.30-11.30pm. Saturday - opens for dinner only.

Quiet Beach,
Gedud Barak Street (4) 679-0125
Fax: (4) 679-0261

Tzameret Inn,
Plus 2000 Street (4) 679-4951
Fax: (4) 673-2444

Washington,
13 Zeidel Street (4) 679-1861
Fax: (4) 672-1860

Tourist Information

HaBanim Street, The Archaeological Park (3) 672-5666

Youth Hostels

Taiber (4) 675-0050
Fax: (4) 675-1628
Two-and-a-half miles south of Tiberias.

Zichron Ya'achov

Museums

Nili Museum & Aaronson House
40 Hameyasdim Street 30950 (4) 639-0120
Fax: (4) 639-0119

Restaurants

Dairy

Habayit Bayekev
Carmel Mizrachi Winery,
Rehov Hayayin (4) 629-0977

Tours of Jewish Interest

American P'eylim Student Union
10 Shoarim Street (4) 653-2131
Free tours of Jewish Quarter and free accommodation, in the hostel quarters.

Jerusalem Youth Centre
9 Shonei Halachot Street (4) 628-5623
Free accommodation.

Italy

Italy has an ancient connection with the Jews, and was home to one of the earliest Diaspora communities. Before the Roman invasion of ancient Israel, Judah Maccabee had a representative in Rome, and one of the reasons for the invasion was the Romans' desire to access the salt supply from the Dead Sea. There were Jewish communities in Italy after the destruction of the Second Temple, as Italy was the trading hub of the Roman Empire. After Christianity became the official religion in 313 CE, restrictions began to be placed on the Jewish population, forcing the community to migrate from town to town across the country.

In the medieval period, there was a brief flourishing of learning, but the Spanish conquered southern Italy in the fifteenth century, expelling the Jews from Sicily, Sardinia and, eventually, Naples. The first ever ghetto was established in Venice in 1516. Later in the century descendants of those expelled from Spain and Portugal arrived. Conquest by Napoleon led to the emancipation of Italian Jewry, and full equal rights were granted in 1870.

Ironically, the Italian Fascist party contained some Jewish members, as Mussolini was not anti-Semitic and, even under pressure from Hitler, did not instigate any major anti-Semitic policy. The situation changed after Germany's occupation of the north in 1943. Eventually, almost 8,000 Italian Jews were killed in Auschwitz, although the local population hid many of those who survived.

Today there is a central organisation which provides services for Italian Jews. There are kosher restaurants in Rome, Milan and other towns. There are also Jewish schools.

GMT + 1 hour	Total Population 57,298,000
Country calling code (39)	Jewish Population 35,000
Emergency Telephone (Police - 112) (Fire - 115) (Ambulance - 116)	Electricity voltage 220

Ancona

Community Organisations

Community Offices
Via Fanti 2 bis (071) 202638

Mikvaot

Via Astagno

Asti

Museums

Via Ottolenghi 8, Torino (0141) 539281

Synagogues

Via Ottolenghi 8, Torino

Bologna

Cafeteria

Comunita Ebraica Bologna
Via Gombruti 9 40123 (051) 232-066
Fax: (051) 229-474
Email: comebrbol@libero.it

Supervision: Rabbi Alberto Sermoneta.
Lunch Sunday to Friday; dinner Friday; closed mid-July and August.

Community Organisations

Comunita Ebraica Bologna
Via Gombruti 9 40123
(051) 232-066 & 227-931 (office of Rabbi)
Fax: (051) 229-474
Email: comebrbol@libero.it
Web site: www.menorah.it/ceb/indice.htm

Mikvaot

Mikveh Chaya Mushkah
Via Oreste Regnoli 17/1 (051) 623-0316

Museums

Museo Ebraico
Palazzo Pannolini, via Valdonica, 1/5,
40125 (051) 2911280
Fax: (051) 235430
Website: museoebraico.it

The Jewish Museum of Bologna is located in via Valdonica, in the area of the former ghetto. It was established as a means of conserving the Jewish cultural heritage that for centuries has been deeply rooted in Bologna and Emilia Romagna.

Synagogues

Via Mario Finzi

Italy

Casale Monferrato

Synagogues

Community Offices
Vicolo Salomone Olper 44 (0142) 71807
Fax: (0142) 76444
Email: qqcasale@mail.dex-net.com
Web site: www.menorah.it/qqcasale/indice.htm

The synagogue, built in 1595 is one of the most interesting in North Italy. It also contains a Jewish museum. Casale-Monferrato is on the Turin-Milan road, and can be reached by turning off it about thirteen miles beyond Chivasso. Casale may also be reached with tollway A26 (exit Casale north or south, whichever comes first). It is better to make advance appointments for visiting either the synagogue or Museum. Closed in the months of January, February and August.

Cuneo

Synagogue and Communal Office

Via Mondovi (0171) 692-007

A beautiful synagogue; parts dating from the fifteenth century. Services are now only held on Yom Kippur. In 1799 a special Purim was established after the synagogue was saved from destruction by a shell.

Ferrara

Community Organisations

Community of Ferrara
Via Mazzini 95 44100 (0532) 24 70 04
Fax: (0532) 24 70 04

Mikvaot

Via Mazzini 95 (0532) 24 70 04

Museums

Jewish Museum of Ferrara
Via Mazzini 95 44100 (0532) 21 02 28
Fax: (0532) 21 02 28
Email: museoebraico@comune.fe.it
Web site: www.comune.fe.it/museoebraico

Guided tours in English on Sunday to Thursday 10 am 11am 12 am. Closed on Fridays and Saturdays.

Synagogues

Via Mazzini 95 (0532) 24 70 33

Florence

Bakeries

Forno dei Ciompi
Piazza dei Ciompi (055) 241-256

Butchers

Bruno Falsettini
Mercato Coperto di S., Ambrogio (055) 248-0740
8 am to 10 am. Order in advance in advance specifying kosher.

Gionvannino,
Via dei Macci 106 (055) 248-0734
7.30 am to 1.00 pm. Order in advance specifying kosher

Community Organisations

Community Offices
Via L.C. Farini 4, Firenze 50121 (055) 245252
Fax: (055) 241811
Email: comebrfi@fol.it
Web site: www.fol.it/sinagoga

Open from Sunday to Friday from 9.30 am to 12.30 pm (Sunday closed in July and August).

Hotels

Regency,
Massimo D'Azeglio 3 (055) 245247
Fax: (055) 2346735
Email: info@regency-hotel.com
Web site: www.regency-hotel.com

Located in the square, near the synagogue.

Mikvaot

Via L.C. Farini 4, Firenze 50121 (055) 245252
Fax: (055) 241811
Email: comebrfi@fol.it
Web site: www.fol.it/sinagoga

Museums

Jewish Museum
Via L.C. Farini 4, Firenze 50121 (055) 245252
Fax: (055) 241811
Email: comebrfi@fol.it
Web site: www.fol.it/sinagoga

There is also a religious and artistic souvenir shop. Open Sunday - Thursday. Groups are kindly requested to book in advance. For further information and booking, please contact the Administation office.
(055) 2346054

Restaurants

Kosher vegetarian

Ruth's,
Via Farini 2/A (055) 248-0888
Bookings required for Shabbat meals and groups. Take-away.

Synagogues

Orthodox

Via L.C. Farini 4, Firenze 50121 (055) 245252
Fax: (055) 241811
Email: comebrfi@fol.it
Web site: www.fol.it/sinagoga

After service there is a public Kiddush. Services on Shabbat and holidays, not daily. The synagogue is open for tourists from Sunday to Thursday (hours vary). Groups should book in advance.

Via De Banchi (055) 212-474

After the service there is a public Kiddush. For the timetable of services ask in the Community Office.

Genoa

Community Organisations

Community Offices
Via Bertora 6 16122 (010) 839-1513
Fax: (010) 846-1006

Synagogues

Synagogue and Community Offices
Via Bertora 6 16122 (010) 839-1513
Fax: (010) 846-1006
Email: comgenova@tin.it

Every Friday and Shabbat morning.

Gorizia

Synagogues

Via Ascoli 19, Gradicia (03831) 532115

Leghorn

Butchers

Corucci,
Banco 25, Mercato Centrale, Livorno (0586) 884596

Mikvaot

Community Offices

Piazza Benamozegh 1, Livorno (0586) 896290

Museums

Jewish Museum
via Micali 21, Livorno (0586) 893361
Visits only by appointment.

Synagogues

Community Offices
Piazza Benamozegh 1, Livorno (0586) 896290
Fax: (0586) 896290

Mantua

Synagogues

Community Offices
Via G. Govi 11, Mantova (0379) 321490

Merano

Museums

Jewish Museum
Via Schiller 14 (0473) 236127
Fax: (0473) 237520

Hours: Tuesday and Wednesday 3 pm-6 pm. Thursday 9 am-12 am. Friday 3 pm-5 pm.

Synagogues

Community Offices
Via Schiller 14 (0473) 236127

Milan

Community Organisations

Community Offices
Sally Mayer 2 (02) 483-02806
Fax: (02) 483-04660

Documentation Centre

Contemporary Jewish Documentation Centre
Via Eupili 8 (02) 316338
Fax: (02) 336-02728

Groceries

Eretz,
Largo Scalabrini 5 (02) 423-6891
Fax: (02) 423-4753

Hours: 9 am to 7:30 pm. Buses, 50, 95, 13, 61, subway 1 (red), stop, Bande-Nere.

Mikvaot

Central Synagogue
Via Guastalla 19 (02) 551-2101
Fax: (02) 5519-2699

Persian

Angelo Donati Beth Hamidrash
Via Sally Mayer 4-6

Restaurants

Eshel Isroel,
Via Benvenuto Cellini 2 (02) 545-5076
Supervision: Rav G. H. Garelik.
Open weekdays.

Glat Kosher Beit Yoshef
via Montecuccoli 35 20146 (02) 4156199
Fax: (02) 41291105
Email: sissirattan@libero.it

Mifgash Jewish Center
via Montecuccoli 35 20146 (02) 4156199
Fax: (02) 41291105
Email: sissirattan@libero.it

Italy

Pizzeria Carmel
viale San Gimignano 10 (02) 416368
Fax: (02) 48512145
Supervision: Rav S. Behor.
Hours: 12 pm to 2:30 pm and 5:30 pm to 10:30 pm.
Nearest public transportation: buses 58, 61, 50, 95, subway 1.

Meat

Re Salomone,
Via Washington, 9 (02) 469-4643
Fax: (02) 43318049
Email: resalomone@tiscalinet.it
International meat restaurant with Mediterranean, Italian and oriental food and take-away.
Rey Solomon,
Calle Washington 9 (02) 469-4643

Synagogues

Beth Shlomo
Galleria Vittorio Emanuele,
(Via Ugo Foscolo 3.) 20121 (02) 8646-6118
Fax: (02) 2901-9561
Email: fweb.shlomo@bethshlomo.it
Web site: www.bethshlomo.it
Services are held on Friday evening, Shabbat, Sunday morning and Holy Days.
Central Synagogue
Via Guastalla 19 (02) 551-2101
Fax: (02) 5519-2699

Merkos L'Inyonei Chinuch
Via Carlo Poerio 35 20129 (02) 295-31213
New Home for Aged
Via Leone XIII (02) 498-2604
Services on Sabbaths and festivals. Kosher food available upon reservation.
New Synagogue
Via Eupili 8
Service on Sabbaths and festivals.

Lubavitch

Ohel Yacob,
Via Benvenuto Cellini 2 (02) 545-5076

Orthodox Sephardi

Via Guastalla 19 (02) 551-2029
Fax: (02) 551-92699
Rabbi Dr Laras is the Chief Rabbi.

Modena

Butchers

Macelleria Duomo
Mercato Coperto
(Covered Market), Stand 25 (059) 217269

Synagogues

Community Offices
Piazza Mazzini 26 (059) 223978

Naples

Synagogues

Community Offices
Via Cappella Vecchia 31, Napoli (081) 764-3480
Email: c.l.na@virgilio.it

Ostia Antica

Here can be found the partially restored excavated remains of a first-century synagogue built on the site of another one which stood there 300 years earlier. This is the oldest synagogue in Europe. Ostia Antica is near Leonardo da Vinci International Airport and about forty minutes by train from Rome (Termini or Pyramid stations). To reach the synagogue, cross the footbridge on leaving the station. The entrance to the excavations is straight ahead.

Padua

Mikvaot

Via S. Martino e Solferino 9, Padova (049) 871-9501

Synagogues

Community Offices
Via S. Martino e Solferino 9, Padova (049) 875-1106

Parma

Synagogues

Community Offices
Vicolo Cervi 4

Perugia

Synagogues

P. della Republica 77 (075) 21250

Pesaro

The remains of an old synagogue, built in the second half of the sixteenth century, is currently being restored by the town council. It is unusual as the Bimah is built on columns one storey above floor level. Pesaro was also the birthplace of Rossini.

Pisa

Synagogues

Community Offices
Via Palestro 24 (050) 542580
Services are held on festivals and Holy Days. During the week the resident beadle will be glad to show visitors round the synagogue, which is famed for its beauty. It is very near the Teatro Verdi.

Riccione

Hotels

Vienna Touring Hotel: The Hotel Nevada
(054) 160-1245
In the summer, kosher food is obtainable. Provides vegetarian food and particularly welcomes Jewish guests.

Rome

About half of Italian Jewry (some 15,000) live in Rome. As there has been such a long history of Jewish settlement, a Nusach Italki (Italian prayer ritual) has developed, which is practised in some synagogues in the town. Kosher restuarants and kosher food are available. Titus' Arch, depicting the destruction of Jerusalem by the Romans, is in the city, and Jews were forbidden to walk under it. The ghetto of Rome is behind the Great Synagogue. A visit to the ancient Jewish burial sites along the Appian Way is worth considering. Check tour arrangements with the Jewish Community offices, Tel: 580-3667.

Bakeries

Limentani Settimio
Via Portico d'Ottavia 1

Bed & Breakfasts

Pension Carmel
via Goffredo Mameli 11 00153 (06) 580-9921
Fax: (06) 581-8853
Email: reservation@hotelcarmel.it
Kosher pension situated in the old district of Trastevere, ten minutes from the main synagogue.

Butchers

Massari,
Piazza Bologna 11 (06) 429120
Sion Ben David
Via Filippo Turati 110 (06) 733358
Terracina,
Via Portico d'Ottavia 1b (06) 654-1364

Delicatessens

Kosher Bistrot
Terracina Angelo,
via Santa Maria del Pianto 68-69 (06) 686-4398
Supervision: Chief Rabbinate of Rome.

Embassy

Embassy of Israel
Via Michelle Mercati 14 00197 (06) 322-1541
Embassy of Israel to The Holy See
Via M. Mercati 12 00197 (06) 3619-8690
Fax: (06) 3619-8626

Groceries

Sabra,
Via S. Ambrogio 6

Media

Newspapers

Shalom,
Lungotevere Cenci 1 (06) 687-6816
Fax: (06) 686-8324
Email: shalom.mensile@flashnet.it
Web site: www.shalom.it
Monthly.

Mikvaot

Lungotevere Cenci (Tempio) 9

Museum

Museum of the Italian resistance
Via Tasso 145 (06) 700-3866
The museum was extended in 2001 with new displays dedicated to the fate of Roman Jews between 1938 and 1944.

Museums

The Jewish Museum
Lungotevere Cenci (06) 6840-0661
Fax: (06) 6840-0684
Email: romacer@tin.it
The main synagogue building contains a permanent exhibition covering the 2,000-year history of the Italian Jewish community. Another link with this long history is the Rome Ghetto almost adjoining. It can be reached by taking bus 170, H or 75, near the neighbouring Ponte Garibaldi. It is a maze of narrow alleys dating from Imperial Roman times, within which, until 1870 all Roman Jews were confined under curfew.

Religious Organisations

The Italian Rabbinical Council
Headquarters, Lungotevere Sanzio 9 (06) 580-3667; 580-3670

Representative Organisations

Unione Comunita Ebraiche Italiane (Union of Italian Jewish Communities)
Lungotevere Sanzio 9 (06) 580-3667; 580-3670
Fax: (06) 589-9569
Information on Italian Jewry, its monuments and history may be obtained from here.

Restaurants

La Taverna del Ghetto
Via Portico de Ottivia 8 (06) 880-9771
Simcha Labi,
Via Imperia 2, CAP 00161 (06) 4423--0332
Supervision: Chabad Rabbi.

Italy

Dairy

Yotvata,

Yotvata, Piazza Cenci 70 00186 (06) 6813-4481

Supervision: Chief Rabbinate of Rome.

Open at noon.

Meat

Da Lisa, via Foscolo (06) 77200460
Fax: (06) 70495456

Oriental Foods Kosher

Via Livorno, 8-10 (06) 440-4840
Fax: (06) 440-4840

Pizzerias

Zi Fenizia

via Santa Maria del Pianto 64-65 00186(06) 689-6976

The kashrut certificate is for meat - they do not use any cheeses in their pizzas.

Synagogues

Orthodox

The Great Synagogue

Lungotevere Cenci (Tempio) 9 (06) 684-00661
Fax: (06) 684-00684
Email: shalom.mensile@glashnet.it

Orthodox Ashkenazi

Via Balbo 33

Tours

Guides

G. Palombo,

Via val Maggia 7 (06) 810-3716; 993-2074

Ruben E. Popper

12 Via dei Levii (06) 761-0901
Fax: (06) 761-0901

Telephone number is afternoons only.

Senigallia

Synagogues

Via dei Commercianti

Siena

Synagogues

Vicolo delle Scotte 14 (0577) 284647

The committee has issued a brochure in English, giving the history of the community which dates back to medieval times. The synagogue dates from 1750. Services are held on the Sabbath and High Holy-days. Further information from Burroni Bernardi, Via del Porrione. M. Savini, via Salicotta 23. Tel: 283140 (close to the synagogue).

Spezia

Synagogues

Via 20 Settembre 165

Trieste

Community Organisations

Community Offices

Via San Francesco d'Assisi 19 34133
(040) 371466
Fax: (040) 371226

Chief Rabbi: Rav Dr Avraham Umberto Piperno. Tel: 3722681.

Synagogues

Via Donizetti 2 (040) 631898

Tour Information

Smile Service

via Martiri della Liberta' 17 34134 (040) 375-5638
Fax: (040) 375-5638
Email: smile@com.area.trieste.it

This service agency organises tours around the Jewish sites of Friuli Venezia-Giulia.

Turin

Booksellers

Biblioteca "E. Artom"

P.tta Primo Levi 12, Torino 10125 (011) 669-9097

Libreria Claudiana

Via Principe Toncmaso 1, Torino 10125
(011) 669-2458

Community Organisations

Community Centre

P.tta Primo Levi 12, Torino 10125 (011) 658-585

Groceries

Panetteria Bertino

Via B. Galliari 14, Torino 10125 (011) 669-9527

Mikvaot

P.tta Primo Levi 12, Torino 10125 (011) 658-585

Restaurants

Salomon e Augusto Segre - Jewish rest home

Via B. Galliari 13, Torino 10125 (011) 658-585

Only by reservation

Synagogues

P.tta Primo Levi 12, Torino 10125
(011) 658-585

Daily 6.50 am and sunset; Shabbat 9 am and half an hour before sunset (winter) or 6.30 pm (summer); on Shabbat (in winter) between Minchah and Maariv a Seudat Shelishit is held.

Tourist Site

Mole Atonellianta

Now the National Cinema Museum, it was originally built in the nineteenth century and was meant to be the grandest synagogue in Europe but was never completed.

Urbino

Synagogues

Via Stretta

Venice

Jews settled in Venice early in the tenth century and became an important factor in the economic life of the city. In 1516, however, the authorities banished the Jews to the Ghetto Nuovo (new foundry), district so establishing the first ghetto. The high walls surrounding the area still exist.

The fourteenth-century Jewish cemetery (the second oldest in Europe after the one in Worms) has recently been restored and was reopened in 1999 for guided tours (for details call the Jewish Museum).

Community Organisations

Community Offices

Cannaregio, Ghetto Nuovo 2899-30121
(041) 715-012
Fax: (041) 524-1862

Gift Shop

David's,

Ghetto Nuovo 2880

Jewish articles and religious appurtenances are available.

Mordehai Fusetti

Ghetto Nuovo 1219 (041) 714024

Jewish articles and religious appurtenances are available.

Guest House

Jewish Rest Home

Cannaregio 30121,
Ghetto Nuovo 2874 (041) 716002
Fax: (041) 714394

Kosher meals and accommodation can be had. Early booking is advised.

Hotels

Buon Pesce,

S. Nicolo 50., Ghetto Nuovo (041) 760533

Open April to October.

Libraries

Jewish Library and Archives "Renato Maestro"

30121 Venice, Cannaregio 2899 (041) 718833
Fax: (041) 5241862
Email: renatomaestro@libero.it

Mikvaot

Jewish Rest Home

Ghetto Nuovo 2874 (041) 715118

Museums

Jewish Museum

Cannaregio, Ghetto Nuovo 2902/B
(041) 715-359
Fax: (041) 723-007

Jewish Museum (Open Sunday through Friday from 10.00am to 4.30pm from October to May and from 10.00am to 7.00pm from June to September). Closed on Saturdays and Jewish holidays. Guided visits to the synagogues in English start every hour from the Jewish Museum. Sandwiches and drinks are available.

Restaurants

GAM-GAM

Bar Ristorante Ebraico

Sottoportico di Ghetto Vecchio,
Cannaregio 1122 (041) 715284
Fax: (041) 715284
Email: jewishvenice.org

Shabbat arrangements available. Open lunch and dinner. Glatt kosher.

Synagogues

Chabad

Cannaregio,
Ghetto Nuovo 2915 (041) 715284
Fax: (041) 715284
Email: jewishvenice.org

Shabbat arrangements available.

Schola Levantina

Ghetto Vecchio 1228 (041) 715-012

Shabbath services are held during winter. Friday about one hour before sunset and Saturday at 9.00am; on Saturday at 3.45pm (later in spring and summer). Tefillah Mincha and Seuda Shelishit.

Schola Spagnola

Ghetto Vecchio 1149 (041) 718-474
Fax: (041) 524-1862

Shabbath services are held here during summer. Friday about one hour before sunset and Saturday at 9.00am; on Saturday at 3.45pm (later in spring and summer). Tefillah Mincha and Seuda Shelishit.

Vercelli

Community Organisations
Community Offices
Via Oldoni 20

Synagogues
Via Foa 70

Verona

Community Organisations
Community Centre
Via Portici 3 (045) 800-7112
Fax: (045) 596627
Email: comebraica@libero.it

Synagogues
Via Portici 3

Viareggio

Contact Information
Mr Sananes
via Pacinotti 172/B (0584) 961-025
Private office: Tirreno Tour, 26 Viale Carducci, Tel: 30777, during daytime.

Sardinia

There is no Sardinian Jewish community today, but the island is of more than passing Jewish interest. In 19 CE, the Emperor Tiberius exiled Jews to Sardinia. There was a synagogue at Cagliari, the island's capital, at least as early as 599 CE, for in that year a convert led a riot against it. Sardinia eventually came under Aragonese rule, and when the edict of expulsion of the Jews from Spain was issued in 1492, the Jews of the island had to leave. Since then there has been no community.

Sicily

Although there are very few Jews in Sicily today, but there is a long and varied history of Jewish settlement on the island stretching back to at least the sixth century and possibly according to some scholars to the first or second centuries.

In 1282, Sicily came under Spanish rule. By the late Middle Ages, the community numbered 40,000. A century or so later, there was a wave of massacres of Jews, and another in 1474. These culminated in the introduction of the Inquisition in 1479, and the expulsion of the Jews in 1492.

Jamaica

During the time of Spanish colonisation, Jamaica witnessed many *Conversos* arriving from Portugal. After the British took over in 1655, many of these could again practise Judaism openly. Soon, other Jews, mainly Sephardim, followed from Brazil and other nearby countries. The community received full equality in 1831 (before a similar step was taken in England).

The Jews played an important role in Jamaican life, and in 1849 the House of Asembly did not meet on Yom Kippur! However, assimilation and intermarriage took their toll and in 1921 the Ashkenazi and Sephardi synagogues combined. There is now only one synagogue on the island, but there are remains of old synagogues in Kingston, Port Royal and other towns.

Community life includes WIZO, B'nai B'rith, and a school (the Hillel Academy). The community lost members after the Cuban revolution, because many feared a similar revolution in Jamaica. However, this was not the case.

GMT - 5 hours	Total Population 2,583,000
Country calling code (1)	Jewish Population 300
Emergency Telephone (Police - 119) (Fire - 110) (Ambulance - 110)	Electricity voltage 110

Kingston

Synagogues

Shaare Shalom

Duke Street & Charles Street (876) 927-7948
Fax: (876) 978-6240

Services, Friday, 5:30 pm (all year), Shabbat, 10 am; festivals, 9 am all year round.

Japan

After Japan became open to Western ideas and Westerners in the mid-nineteenth century, a trickle of Jewish immigrants from the Russian Empire, the UK and the USA began to make their homes there. The first Jewish community at Yokohama was founded in 1860. Many were escaping anti-Semitism and by 1918 there were several thousand in the country.

Individual Japanese, despite being allied to Nazi Germany, did not adopt the anti-Semitic attitude of the Nazis, and the Japanese consul in Kovno Lithuania even helped the Mir Yeshivah escape from occupied Europe in 1940.

The post-War American occupation of the country brought many Jewish servicemen, and the community was also augmented by Jews escaping unrest in China. In recent years, there have been some Jewish *gaijin*, or 'foreign workers'.

In Tokyo there is a synagogue, which provides meals on Shabbat, a Sunday school, and offices for the Executive Board of the Jewish Community of Japan, which is the central body.

GMT + 9 hours	Total Population 126,714,000
Country calling code (81)	Jewish Population 2,000
Emergency Telephone (Police - 110) (Fire and Ambulance - 119)	Electricity voltage 110

Japan

Hiroshima

Tourist Sites

Holocaust Education Centre
866 Nakatsuhara, Miyuki,
Fukuyama 720

(849) 558001
Fax: (849) 558001
Email: hecjpn@urban.ne.jp
Web site: www.urban.ne.jp/home/hecjpn/

Open Tuesday, Wednesday, Friday and Saturday, 10:30 am to 4:30 pm.

Kobe

Synagogues

Orthodox Sephardic

Ohel Shelomoh (Jewish Community of Kansai)
4-12-12 Kitano-cho,
Chuo-ku 650-0002

(78) 221-7236
Fax: (78) 242-7254
Email: j.yohay@seifu.ac.jp
Web site: chabonline.com/kobe

Shabbat meals; kosher provisions;mikvah by arrangement.

Nagasaki

There are now no known Jews living in Nagasaki, although when it was a centre for foreign trade in the mid-nineteenth century it had a community. The old Jewish cemetery is located at Sakamoto Gaijin Bochi. The site of the first synagogue in Japan is Umegasaki Machi.

Okinawa

While there is no native Jewish community on Okinawa, there are normally 200-300 Jews serving with the US military on the island. Regular services are conducted by the Jewish chaplain at Camp Smedley D. Butler, and visitors are welcome.

Tokyo

Community Organisations

Beth David Synagogue
8-8 Hiroo, 3-chome, Shibuya-ku 150

(3) 3400-2559
Fax: (3) 3400-1827
Email: jccmanager@gol.com
Web site: www.jccjapan.co.jp

Embassy

Embassy of Israel
3 Niban-cho, Chiyodaku (3) 3264-0911

Restaurants

Japan Jewish Community Center
8-8 Hiroo, 3-chome, Shibuya-ku 150

(3) 3400-2559
Fax: (3) 3400-1827
Email: jcc@crisscross.com

They sell prepared foods and kosher wine, as well as serve meals on Friday evening and Shabbat. Reservation strongly recommended.

Synagogues

Beth David Synagogue
8-8 Hiroo, 3-chome, Shibuya-ku 150

(3) 3400-2559
Fax: (3) 3400-1827

Services are held Friday evening at 6:30 pm (7 pm during summer); Shabbat morning, 9:30 am; and on Holy-days and festivals. Advance notification requested. Mikvah on premises.

Kazakhstan

Essentially this community began when the Soviets rescued several thousand Jews at the time of the Nazi invasion of the Soviet Union in 1941. Others joined after the War. The community is mainly based in Almaty, the former capital, and also in Chimkent. Some 2,000 Bukharan and Tat Jews also live in the country.

The central organisation is the Mitzvah Association, which heads various Jewish groups. It even has a chair on the All-Peoples Assembly of Kazakhstan. There is a high rate of emigration to Israel. There are synagogues in Almaty and Chimkent.

GMT + 6 hours	Total Population 16,223,000
Country calling code (7)	Jewish Population 10,000
Emergency Telephone (Police, Fire and Ambulance - 03)	Electricity voltage 220

Almaty

Community Centre
e 206 (raimbeka)
Tashkentskaya Street 480061 (3272) 439-358
Fax: (3272) 507-770
Email: synagogues@chabad.kz
Also includes a kosher butcher and store and mikva.

Synagogues
e206 (raimbeka)
Tashkentskaya Street 480061 (3272) 439-358
Fax: (3272) 507-770
Email: synagogues@chabad.kz

Astana

Synagogues
Prospect Republic 11 apt. 3 (3172) 286-923
Email: astanasynagogues@chabad.kz

Chimkent

Synagogues

Sephardi

Svobody Street, 47th Lane

Kenya

Kenya could have been the site of the first Jewish state for two thousand years as this offer was made to the Zionists in 1903. It was, however, rejected in 1905. There were some Jews living in Kenya at that time, and a synagogue was built in 1912. Many more Jews came here after the War as Holocaust survivors, and recently some Israelis have worked on a short-term basis in the country.

Kenya was an ally to Israel in its rescue of the Jews from Entebbe in Uganda. Jews have contributed much to the hotel industry and professional life of the country.

Regular services are held every Saturday in the Nairobi Hebrew Congregation, and there is a community centre next to the synagogue. The centre, the Vermont Memorial Hall offers educational and social events.

GMT + 3 hours	Total Population 30,080,000
Country calling code (254)	Jewish Population 400
Emergency Telephone (Police, Fire and Ambulance 999)	Electricity voltage 220/240

Nairobi

Community Organisations

Community Centre
Vermont Memorial Hall
Open Monday, Tueday, Friday 9 am to 1 pm; Wednesday 2.30 pm to 5.30 pm; Services Friday evening at 6.30 pm; Saturday morning at 8 am. All festivals. Kosher chickens available.

Synagogues

Nairobi Hebrew Congregation
cnr. University Way & Uhuru Highway,
PO Box 40990 (2) 222770, 219703

Kyrgyzstan

This central Asian ex-Soviet republic has only a short history of Jewish settlement. The community originated from migrants after the Russian Revolution and evacuees from the German advance into the Soviet Union in the Second World War. As a result, community members are almost all Russian speakers and are assimilated into the Russian minority of the country.

Before the collapse of the Soviet Union, there was no organised community. Following 1991, there is a synagogue in Bishkek (the capital), where there is also a Jewish library and an Aish HaTorah centre. The main umbrella group is the Menorah Society of Jewish Culture.

GMT + 5 hours — Total Population 4,699,000
Country calling code (996) — Jewish Population 2,500
Emergency Telephone (Police, Fire and Ambulance - 03)

Bishkek

Synagogues
193 Karpinsky Street

Latvia

The Jews in the medieval principalities of Courland and Livonia represent the earliest Jewish settlement in Latvia. Tombstones from the fourteenth century have been found. After the Russian take-over, Jews were only allowed to live in the area if they were considered 'useful', or had lived there before the Russians took control, because the area was outside the 'Pale of Settlement' that the Russian Empire had designated for the Jews.

The Jews contributed much to Latvia's development, but this was never recognised by the government, which tried to restrict their influence in business matters. Religious Jewish life, however, was strong. When the Nazis invaded Latvia, ninety per cent of the 85,000 Jews were systematically murdered by them and their Latvian collaborators.

The bulk of today's community originates from immigration into Latvia after the War, although 3,000 Holocaust survivors did return to Latvia. Before the collapse of communism, there was much Jewish dissident activity. There is a Jewish school and a Jewish hospital. There are some Holocaust memorial sites, in Riga (the capital), and also in the Bierkernieki Forest, where 46,000 Holocaust victims were shot.

GMT + 2 hours	Total Population 2,357,000
Country calling code (371)	Jewish Population 8,600
Emergency Telephone (Police - 02) (Fire - 01) (Ambulance - 03)	Electricity voltage 220

Daugavpils

Community Organisations

Jewish Community
Saules Street 47
Fax: (54) 8254-24658

Synagogues

Gogol Street
Suvorov Street

Liepaja

Community Organisations

Jewish Community
Kungu Street 21 (34) 25336

Rezhitsa

Synagogues

Kaleru Street

Riga

Cultural Organisations

Latvian Society for Jewish culture
Skolas 6 LV1322 (2) 289-580
Fax: (2) 821-494

Embassy

Embassy of Israel
Elizabetes Street 2 LV1340

Synagogues

Chabad Lubavitch Latvia
141 Lacplesa St., LV-1003 720 4022
Fax: 783 0444
Email: chabad@mailbox.riga.lv
Visitors welcomed for Shabbat and holiday meals. Take-out by order.

Riga Central Synagogue
6/8 Peitavas Street, L.V. 1050 721-0827
Fax: 722-1793
Hot kosher meals may be ordered in advance. Also has a mikveh.

Lithuania

The history of Lithuanian Jewry is as old as the state of Lithuania itself. There were Jews in the country in the fourteenth century, when Grand Duke Gedeyminus founded the state. The community eventually grew, and produced many famous yeshivas and great commentators, such as the Vilna Gaon. The community began to emigrate (particularly to South Africa) at the beginning of the nineteenth century; even so in 1941 there were still 160,000 Jews in the country. Ninety-five per cent of these were murdered in the Holocaust, by the local population as well as the Nazis.

The remaining post-War community included some who had hidden or had managed to survive by other means and some Jews from other parts of the Soviet Union. Interestingly, the Lithuanian Soviet Socialist Republic was more tolerant of Jewish activity than some of the neighbouring republics, such as Latvia. Now that Lithuania is independent, Jewish life is free once again.

The Lubavitch movement is present, and there are synagogues in Vilnius (known to many as Vilna), the capital, and Kaunas. There is also a school and it is possible to study Yiddish. There are tours available to show the old Jewish life in Lithuania. The grave of the Vilna Gaon can be visited, as well as Paneriai, otherwise known as Ponary, where thousands of Jews were shot during the Holocaust.

GMT + 2 hours — Total Population 3,670,000
Country calling code (370) — Jewish Population 4,400
Emergency Telephone (Police - 02) (Fire - 01) (Ambulance - 03) — Electricity voltage 220

Druskininkai

Community Organisations

Jewish Community
9/15 Sporto Street 54590

Kaunas

Community Organisations

Jewish Community
26 B Gedimino Street (7) 203717
Fax: (7) 7201135
Hours of opening: Sunday to Thursday 3 pm-6 pm

Synagogues

11 Ozheshkienes Street

Klaipeda

Community Organisations

Jewish Community
3 Ziedu Skersqatvis (6) 93758

Panevezys

Community Organisations

Jewish Community
6/22 Sodu Street 5300 (54) 68848

Shiauliai

Community Organisations

Jewish Community
24 Vyshinskio (1) 26795

Vilnius

Otherwise known as Vilna, this town used to be known as the 'Jerusalem of Lithuania'. There was a very important Jewish community in the town before the Holocaust. The town still has the largest community of Lithuanian Jews, and there are many sites of historical interest, including the Vilna Gaon's grave and the State Jewish Museum.

Bakeries

Matzah Bakery
39 Pylimo Street (2) 61-2523

Community Organisations

Jewish Community of Lithuania
Pylimo St. 4 2001 (2) 61-3003
Fax: (2) 22-7915
Email: jewishcom@post.5ci.lt
Web site: www.litvakai.mch.mii.lt
Opening hours: Monday to Friday 10 am-6 pm.

Cultural Organisations

The Israel Centre of Cultures and Art in Lithuania
4 Pylimo, 2nd Floor 2001 (2) 61-1736 or 652139

Museums
The Vilna Gaon Jewish State Museum
Pylimo 4, LT 2001 (2) 62-0730
Fax: (2) 22-7083
Email: jmuseum@puni.osf.lt
Holocaust exhibition and Museum administration, Pamenkalnio 12, The Tarbut School, Exhibitions and seat of Jewish Community. Opening hours Monday to Thursday 9 am to 5 pm and Friday 9 am to 4 pm.

Synagogues
Central Synagogue of Vilnius Chabad
12 Saltiniu g. St. 2006 (2) 250-387
Main Synagogue (Choral Synagogue)
39 Pylimo Street (2) 61-2523

Luxembourg

The small community in Luxembourg faced massacres and expulsions during medieval times and Jews only began to resettle here several hundred years later. Napoleon heralded the rebirth of the community when he annexed Luxembourg, and by 1823 a synagogue had been built, but the community remained small, although in 1899 another synagogue was built.

Later many refugees from the Nazis arrived in the country, bringing the number of Jews to nearly 4,000. After the Nazi take-over, 750 Luxembourg Jews were killed, but many others were saved by the local population.

The present community is generally prosperous and assimilated. The Consistoire Israelite, established by Napoleon, is recognised by the government as the representative of the community, and is also financed by the government. The Orthodox synagogue is situated fairly centrally in Luxembourg City.

GMT + 1 hour | Total Population 431,000
Country calling code (352) | Jewish Population 600
Emergency Telephone (Police - 113) (Fire and Ambulance - 112) | Electricity voltage 220

Esch-Sur-Alzette

Synagogues
52 rue de Canal
Minyan services held on Friday evenings.

Luxembourg City

Communal Organisation
Consistoire Israelite de Luxembourg
45 av. Monterey 2018 452914
Fax: 473772

Embassy
Consul General of Israel
38 BD Napoleon 1er L-2210 446-557
Fax: 453-676

Groceries
Calon,
rue de Reins 3

Kashrut Information
34 rue Alphonse munchen 2172 452366

Synagogues
45 av. Monterery 452914
Fax: 250430

Liberal
Chadash 316594
Email: j.bpreston@sl.lu

Macedonia

At the southern end of the former Yugoslavia, this new country has an ancient Jewish heritage dating back to Roman times. The Jews took advantage of the area's favourable commercial position, lying between Turkey and Western Europe, and the remains of a synagogue at Stobei dating back to the second and third centuries is evidence of a once thriving Jewish community.

Iberian Jews escaping the Inquisition settled in the area, and brought with them Sephardi customs and the Ladino language (based on Spanish). The fate of the 8,000 Macedonian Jews under Bulgarian occupation during the Second World War is in stark contrast to the fate of the Bulgarian Jews - the Macedonian Jews were deported to their deaths, yet the Bulgarian Jews were saved by the defiance of the king and the people. Only ten per cent of the Macedonian community survived, of whom many have emigrated to Israel.

Today's community is mainly based in the capital Skopje, but there are no synagogues and there is little access to Jewish life. However, the community does have contact with Jews in Serbia and Greece.

GMT + 1 hour	Total Population 2,024,000
Country calling code (389)	Jewish Population 100
Emergency Telephone (Police - 92) (Fire - 93) (Ambulance - 94)	Electricity voltage 220

Skopje

Community Organisations

Community Offices

Borka Talevski Street 24 (91) 237-543

Malaysia

Malaysia is a Muslim state, and the Jewish population is tiny, barely into double figures. There is, however, a Jewish cemetery on the island of Penang, in Georgetown in Jalan Yahudi (Jewish Street). The cemetery is looked after by Selvaraj Sundram, an Hindu. Decades ago the then vibrant Jewish community hired his great-grandfather to look after the site. His family has done so since; funds now being provided by an anonymous German. The Jews who today live on Penang originate from refugees from Russia. There was a synagogue, but it is now closed.

GMT + 8 hour	Total Population 10,359,000
Country calling code (60)	Jewish Population under100
Emergency Telephone (Police , Fire, Ambulance 999)	Electricity voltage 220

Malta

There is evidence of an ancient Jewish community on Malta, as archaeologists have discovered remains from 2,000 years ago. Malta fell into Arab hands in the early Middle Ages, when there were still a few Jews on the island. The island then changed to Sicilian hands and, in 1492, the Jews were expelled.

Between the sixteenth and eighteenth centuries, the island was used as a prison for Jewish captives of the Knights of St John. They were held for ransom, but managed to find time to build a synagogue. A synagogue in Spur Street Valetta, opened in 1912, was demolished in 1995 as part of a redevelopment scheme.

GMT + 1 hour	Total Population 373,000
Country calling code (356)	Jewish Population under100
Emergency Telephone (Police 191, Fire 199, Ambulance 196)	Electricity voltage 240

Birkirkara

Communal Organisation

P O Box 4 445924

Ta'xbiex

Synagogues

The Jewish Community of Malta

Flat 1, Florida Mansions, Enrico Mizzi St.

Email: jewsofmalta@digigate.net

Web site: maltesejewishcommunity.org

Morning services on the first and third Shabbat of each calendar month and on the first days of the main festivals. Visitors are welcome.

Mexico

Conversos were the first Jews in the country, and some achieved high positions in early Spanish colonial Mexico. As the Inquisition was still functioning here some 200 years after the sixteenth century, the number of Jewish immigrants was small. When Mexico became independent of Spain, Jews gradually began to enter the country, coming from German and other European communities.

It was during the twentieth century that most Jewish immigrants entered Mexico. There were both Ashkenazis and Sephardis, and they settled throughout the country. The communities grew on a parallel level, rather than together, with two languages, Yiddish and Ladino.

The current community is largely middle class and all the various factions come under the Comite Central Israelita. There are numerous synagogues and there are also kosher restaurants. The community is well equipped with Jewish schools and yeshivas.

GMT - 7 hours — Total Population 98,881,000
Country calling code (52) — Jewish Population 50,000
Emergency Telephone (Police, Fire and Ambulance 080) — Electricity voltage 110

Acapulco

Hotels

The Hyatt Regency
Costera Miguel Aleman 1 39869 (74) 69-1234
Fax: (74) 84-3087
Email: hyatta@netmex.com
The hotel has a synagogue and a mikva.

Restaurants

The Hyatt Regency
Costera Miguel Aleman 1 39869 (74) 69-1234
Fax: (74) 84-3087
Email: hyatta@netmex.com
Open only during the high season (generally Nov/Dec to March/April).

Cuernavaca

Synagogues

Madero 404 (73) 186-846
At the home for the elderly.

Guadalajara

Community Organisations

Comunidad Israelita de Guadalajara
Juan Palomar y Arias 651 (36) 416-463
Fax: (36) 427-168
Includes kosher restaurant, mikva and two synagogues. Phone in advance.

Mexico City

Despite the fact that the first *auto-da-fe* in which *Conversos* were burnt at the stake, it has been said that in 1550 there were more crypto-Jews in Mexico City than Roman Catholics. There are now many Jews, who represent the vast majority of Mexican Jewry. With twenty-three synagogues, and a number of kosher restuarants and Jewish schools, the city is well equipped with Jewish facilities. Polanco is a Jewish area in the city with some synagogues. The first synagogue, dating from 1912, is in the downtown area.

Butchers

Fuente de Templanza 17,
Tecamachalco
Mehadrin.

Carniceria Sary
Tecamachalco
Mehadrin.

Pollos Mugrabi
Platon 133, Polanco
Mehadrin.

Embassy

Embassy of Israel
Sierra Madre 215,
PO Box 11000 10 (5) 201-1500
Fax: (5) 201-1555

Groceries

Casa Amiga
Horacio 1719, Col. Polanco (5) 540-1455

Super Teca Kosher
Acuezunco 15,
San Miguel (5) 905-589-9823, 9860 or 3225

Media

Newspapers

CDI,
Centro Deportivo, Plaza de toros of Cuatro Caminos(5) 557-3000
Spanish weekly.

Di Shtime
Pedro Moreno 149 (5) 546-1720
Yiddish weekly.

Foro de Vida Judia en el Mundo
Aviacion Commercial 16,
Col. Polanco 15700 (5) 571-1114
Spanish monthly.

Kesher
Leibnitz 13-10,
Colonia Anzures CP 11590 (5) 203-0446
Fax: (5) 203-9084
Email: info@kesher.org.mx
Spanish bi-weekly.

La Voz de la Kehila
Acapulco 70, 2nd Floor (5) 211-0501
Spanish monthly.

Mikvaot

Bernard Shaw 110, Polanco (5) 203-9964
Av. de los Bosques 53, Tecamachalco (5) 589-5530
Platon 413 (5) 520-9569
Banos Campeche 58 (5) 574-2204

Tevila Cuernavaca
Priv. de Antinea 4,
Col. Delicias (5) 15 08 41; 18 16 55

Museums

The Holocaust Museum
Acapulco 70, Col Condesa (5) 211-051

Organisations

Comunidad Monte Sinai
Tennyson 134, Polanco (5) 280-6369
Fax: (5) 281-3969

Religious Organisations

Comite Central
(5) 520-9393; 540-7376

Comunidad Maguen David
Email: mdavid@ort.org.mx
Contact for any religious questions.

Jerusalem de Mexico
Anatore France 359,
Local C, Polanco (5) 531-2269

Restaurants

Meat

Aladinos
Ingenieros Militares 255 (5) 395-2959
Fax: (5) 395-9219

Hilarios
Cofre de Perote 244-B (5) 540-0453

Jewish Sport Center
Manuel Avila Camacho (5) 557-3000
Supervision: Rab. David E. Tabachnik.

O Grill/Kosher House
37 Polanco, Mexico City (5) 280-1638
Fax: (5) 280-1638

Restaurant Pini
Ejercito Nacional 458d
Supervision: Maguen David.

Sinai
Izazaga (between 5 de febrero and 20 de noviembre,
Near Pino Suarez (5) 709-4906
Supervision: Maguen David.

Synagogues

Agudas Achim
Montes de Oca 32, Condesa 06140 (5) 553-6430

Bet Midrash Tecamachalco
Fuente de Marcela 23,
Col. Tecamachalco (5) 251-8454

Beth Moshe
Tennyson No 134,
Col. Polanco 11560 (5) 280-6369 ;6375
Fax: (5) 281-3969
Email: monsinai@ort.org.mx

Beth Yehoshua
Fuente de San Sulpicio No. 16,
Col. Tecamachalco 53950 (5) 294-8617

Bircas Shumel
Plinio 311, Polanco (5) 280-2769

Cuernavaca
Prolongacion Antinea Lote 2, Delicias

Eliahu Elfasi
Fuente de Templanza 13,
Col. Tecamachalco (5) 294-9388
Shabbat services only.

Jajam Elfasi
Fuente Del Pescador 168, Col. Tecamachalco
Shabbat services only.

Kolel Aram Zoba
Sofocles 346, Col. Polanco (5) 280-2669; 4886;

Kolel Maor Abraham
Lafontaine 344, Col. Polanco (5) 545-2482

Mexico

Midrash Latorah
Cerrada de Los Morales 8,
Col. Polanco 11510 (5) 280-0875; 280-3526
Fax: (5) 280-5978

Rabbi Asher Zrihen, formerly of London, will be happy to welcome and assist visitors.

Nidche Israel
Acapulco 70, Condesa (5) 211-0575

Or Damesek
Seneca 343 (5) 280-6281

Ramat Shalom
Fuente del Pescador 35, Tecamachalco (5) 251-3854

Shaare Shalom
Av. de Los Bosques 53,
Tecamachalco (5) 251-0973

Shuba Israel
Edgar Alan Poe 43,
Col. Polanco (5) 545-8061 & 280-1036

Conservative

Bet El
Horacio 1722, Polanco los Morales (5) 281-2592
Fax: (5) 281-2467
Email: comunidad.betel@bigfoot.com

Beth Israel
Virreyes 114, Lomas (5) 520-8515
Fax: (5) 520-9559
Email: bethisrael@psi.net.mx

English-speaking.

Orthodox

Beth Itzhak
Eujenio Sue 20, Polence

Sephardi

Maguen David
Bernard Shaw 110, Polanco (5) 203-9964

Sephardi Synagogue
Monterey 359 (5) 564-1197;1367

Monterrey

Community Organisations

Centro Israelita de Monterrey
Canada 207, Nuevo León (83) 461-128
Includes a synagogue and mikva.

Tijuana

Contact Information

JCC Chabad House
Centro Social Israelita de Baja California,
Av. 16 Septiembre,
Baja California 3000 (66) 862-692; 862-693
Fax: (66) 341-532
Email: chabadtj@telnor.net

Synagogue and mikva on premises.

Synagogues

Tijuanua Hebrew Congregation
Amado Nervo 207, Baja California.

Moldova

Moldova used to be a Soviet Republic bordering Romania to the west and the Ukraine to the east. When the Jews first entered what is now Moldova, the area was known as Bessarabia, and was on an important trade route between Turkey and Poland. By the time of Russian rule in 1812, there was a permanent Jewish community. The Russians included the area in the 'Pale of Settlement', which held the majority of the Jewish population in their empire. By the end of the nineteenth century, there were over 200,000 Jews in the region. However, the twentieth century started with the infamous progrom in the capital Chisinev, where 49 Jews were killed and much damage was done to Jewish property. Emigration began to increase. The area fell under Romanian control between 1918 and 1940, but the community continued to lead a normal life until the Second World War, when many thousands of the pre-War community of over 250,000 were killed during the German occupation.

After the War, some survivors continued to live in Moldova, and Jews from other parts of the Soviet Union joined them. There is an umbrella society for Moldovan Jews, and there are synagogues and schools. The Lubavitch movement is active in building up religious life.

GMT + 2 hours
Country calling code (373)
Electricity voltage 220
Total Population 4,380,000
Jewish Population 6,500

Chisinau

Most of Moldova's Jews live in Chisinau. This city was the scene for two notorious progroms in 1903 and 1905.

Religious Organisations

Yeshiva of Chisinau
Sciusev 5 277001 (2) 274-362
Fax: (2) 274-331
Email: agudath@yeshiva.mldnet.com

Synagogues

Yakimovsky per. 8 277000 (2) 221-215
Aside from Jewish studies, a mikva and kosher food are on premises.

Teleneshty

Synagogues

4 28th June Street

Tiraspol

Contact Information

336-495
Fax: 322-208
Details of the Jewish Community from Dr Vaisman.

Monaco

Some French Jews lived in Monaco before 1939, and the government issued them with false papers during the War, thus saving them from the Nazis. This tiny country has also attracted retired people from France, North Africa and the UK.

There is an official Jewish body, the Association Culturelle Israelite de Monaco, and there is a synagogue, a school and a kosher food shop. Half of the total Jewish population are Ashkenazi and the other half are Sephardi, and sixty per cent of the community is retired.

GMT +1 hour
Country calling code (377)
Emergency Telephone (Police, Fire and Ambulance 080)
Total Population 30,500
Jewish Population 1,000
Electricity voltage 220

Monte Carlo

Communal Organisation

Association Culturelle Israelite de Monaco
15 Av. de la Costa 9330-1646

Synagogues

15 Av. de la Costa,
opp. Balmoral Hotel MC 98000 9330-1646
Services, Friday even. at 6.30 pm and Sat. morning at 8.45am and Sat. afternoon at 5.30 pm.

Morocco

There were Jews in Morocco before it became a Roman province (they first arrived after the destruction of the Temple in 587 BCE). The Jewish population has been settled in Morocco since the first century; the population increasing steadily due to several immigration waves from Spain and Portugal after the expulsion of Jews by the Inquisition in 1492.

Under Moslem rule, the Jews experienced a general climate of tolerance although they have suffered some persecution. During the Vichy period in the Second World War, Sultan Mohammed V protected the community. Almost 250,000 Jews have emigrated to Israel, Canada, France, Spain and Latin America, but they maintain strong links with the Kingdom.

Since ancient times, the Jewish community has succeeded in cohabiting harmoniously with the Berber and then with the Arab community. Today the present Jewish population is a living community, playing a significant role in Moroccan society - although they have declined in number.

GMT + 0 hours — Total Population 28,351,000
Country calling code (212) — Jewish Population 7,000
Emergency Telephone (Police and Ambulance - 19) (Fire - 15) — Electricity voltage 110/170

Agadir

Mikvaot

Av. Moulay Abdallah,
cnr. rue de la Foire (8) 842339

Organisations

Community Offices
Imm. Arsalane Av. Hassan II (8) 840091
Fax: (8) 822268

Synagogues

Av. Moulay Abdallah, cnr. rue de la Foire (8) 842339

Casablanca

Mikvaot

32 rue Officier de Paix Thomas (2) 276688

Organisations

Community Offices
Rue Abbou Abdallah al Mahassibi
(2) 270976 & 222861
Fax: (2) 266953

Restaurants

Americano
7 Place d'Aknoul
Aux Bon Delices
261 blvd Ziraoui, opp. Lycee Lyautey

Synagogues

Benisty
13 rue Ferhat Achad
Bennaroche
24 rue Lusitania
Em Habanim
14 rue Lusitania
Hazan
Rue Roger Farache
Ne'im Zemiroth
29 rue Jean-Jacques Rousseau
Temple Beth El
61 rue Jaber ben Hayane (2) 267-192

El Jadida

Organisations

Community Offices
PO Box 59

Essaouira (formerly Mogador)

Organisations

Community Offices
2 rue Ziri Ben Atyah

Synagogues

2 rue Ziri Ben Atyah

Fez

Contact Information

Mrs Danielle Mamane, La Boutique,
Hotel Palais - Jamai, Fez (5) 5562 2353
Email: boutique.palaisjamai@aim.net.ma
Mrs Mamane will be pleased to assist all Jewish visitors.

Mikvaot

Talmud Torah
rue Dominique Bouchery

Organisations

Community Offices
Rue Dominique Bouchery

Restaurants

Meat

Centre Maimonide
24 rue Zerktouni,
(adjacent to Hotel Splendide) (5) 620-593
Fax: (5) 659-412

Supervision: Local Rabbanut.

Synagogues

Beth El
rue de Beyrouth
Sadoun
ruelle 1, blvd Mohammed V.
Talmud Torah
Rue Dominique Bouchery

Kenitra

Mikvaot

58 rue Sallah Eddine

Organisations

Community Offices
58 rue Sallah Eddine

Synagogues

rue de Lyon

Marrakech

Mikvaot

Blvd Zerktouni (Gueliz) (4) 448-754
Fax: (4) 438-676

Contact: Mme Kadoch

Organisations

Community Offices
PO Box 515 (4) 448754

Restaurants

Le Sepharade
31 Lotissement Hassania, Gueliz (4) 43 98 09
Le Viennois Hotel Pulman Mansour Eddahbi
Av. de France, Marrakech (4) 339100

Synagogues

Beth-el
Blvd Zerktouni (Gueliz) (4) 448-754
Fax: (4) 438-676

Bittoun
Medina, rue Arset Laamach, Touareg
In course of renovation.
Rabbi Pinhas Ha Cohen
Medina rue Arset, Laamach (4) 389-798
Salat Laazama
Rue Talmud Torah, Mellah,
Hay Essalam (4) 403-798

Meknes

Mikvaot

5 rue de Ghana (5) 21968 or 22549
Tourists will be assisted if telephoning twenty-four hours in advance of their requests.

Synagogues

5 rue de Ghana (5) 21968 or 22549

Oujda

Organisations

Community Offices
Texaco Maroc, 36 blvd Hassan Loukili

Rabat

Mikvaot

3 rue Moulay Ismail

Organisations

Community Offices
1 rue Boussouni

Restaurants

Cercle de l'Alliance
3 rue Mellila (7) 72 76 79
The Menora
Villa 5, rue Er Riyad (7) 26 01 03

Synagogues

3 rue Moulay Ismail

Safi

Synagogues

Beth El
Rue de R'bat
Mursiand
Rue de R'bat

Tangier

Hotels

El Minzah (140)
85 rue de la Liberte (9) 935-885
Fax: (9) 934-546

La Grande Villa de France
Rue de Belgique
Les Almohade (150)
Av. des F. A. R.
Rambrant
Av. Pasteur (9) 378-7071
Rif
Av. d'Espagne

Mikvaot

Shaar Raphael
27 blvd Pasteur (9) 231304

Organisations

Community Centre
1 rue de la Liberte (9) 31633 or 21024

Morocco

Synagogues

Shaar Raphael
27 blvd Pasteur (9) 231304

Temple Nahon
Rue Moses Nahon

Tourist Sites

Rue des Synagogues, off rue Siaghines
There are a number of synagogues in the old part of the town in this street.

Tetuan

Organisations

Community Offices
16 rue Moulay Abbas

Synagogues

Benoualid
The old Mellah

Pintada
The old Mellah

Yagdil Torah
Adj. Community Centre

Mozambique

The small community in Mozambique originally consisted of South African Jews who were forced out of South Africa by President Kruger for supporting the British at the beginning of the twentieth century. The synagogue was opened in 1926, and there is a cemetery in Alto Maha. The biggest Jewish community is in Maputo.

GMT + 2 hours
Country calling code (258)
Emergency Telephone (Police - 119) (Fire - 198) (Ambulance - 117)

Total Population 17,796,000
Jewish Population Under 100
Electricity voltage 220

Maputo

Organisations

Jewish Community of Mozambique
Av. Tomas Nduda 235, PO Box 235 (1) 494413
Email: xero_servicos@mail.garp.co.mz

Myanmar (formerly Burma)

The first Jews came to Myanmar in the early eighteenth century from Iraq and other Middle Eastern countries. A synagogue was built in 1896. In the first years of the twentieth century Rangoon and Bassein both had Jewish mayors. The Jewish population swelled to 2,000 before 1939, but most of these fled to Britain and India before the Japanese invasion in the Second World War. Not many returned after the War (only a few hundred), and the community began to decline through intermarriage and conversion. The handful of remaining Jews are elderly and services are held only on the High Holy Days when a minyan is made up with help from the Israeli embassy.

There is also a tribe of Jews in the north of the country (the Karens), who have their own prayer houses and who believe that they are descended from the tribe of Menashe.

GMT + 6.5 hours
Country calling code (95)
Emergency Telephone In Yangon only
(Police - 199) (Fire - 191) (Ambulance - 192)

Total Population 45,922,000
Jewish Population Under 100
Electricity voltage 220/230

Yangon (formerly Rangoon)

Embassy

Embassy of Israel
49 Pyay Road (1) 222-290; 222-709; 222-201
Fax: (1) 222-463
Email: emisrael@datserco.com.mm

Synagogues

Musmeah Yeshua
85 26th Street (1) 75062

Namibia

Namibian Jewry began at the time when the country was a German colony, before the First World War. The cemetery at Swakopmund dates from that settlement. Keetmanschoop also had a congregation, but this no longer exists. The Windhoek synagogue is still in use, and was founded in 1924. Services are held on Shabbat and festivals.

South Africa provides some help for the community, such as a cantor on festivals, and the Cape Board of Jewish Education assists with Hebrew education. From approximately 100 Jewish families in the 1920s and 1930s, the number has dwindled.

GMT + 2 hours — Total Population 1,726,000
Country calling code (264) — Jewish Population 100
Emergency Telephone
(Police - 1011) (Fire - 2032270) (Ambulance - 2032276) — Electricity voltage 220/240

Windhoek

Synagogues

Cnr. Tal & Post Streets, PO Box 563

Nepal

Nepal has no Jewish history. It is however well visited by Israeli and other young Jewish tourists.

Each year a large Seder is organised by the Lubavitch movement. In 2000 approximately 1,000 attended at the Radisson Hotel.

GMT + 5.45 hour — Total Population 20,892,000
Country calling code (977) — Jewish Population under 100
Electricity voltage 220

Kathmandu

Embassy

Embassy of Israel — (1) 411 811
Bishramalaya House — Fax (1) 413 920
Lazimpat St — Email kathmandu@israel.org
GPO Box 371

Netherlands

Although some historians believe that the first Jews in Holland lived there during Roman times, documentary evidence goes back only to the twelfth century. The contemporary settlement occurred when Portuguese Marranos found refuge from the Inquisition in Holland. Religious freedom was advocated in the early seventeenth century and Jews contributed much to the Netherlands' 'golden age' of prosperity and power.

By the time of Napoleon, the community had grown to 10,000 (the largest in Western Europe), mainly due to incoming Jewish traders from Eastern Europe. The Jews were emancipated in 1796, but the community began to decline slowly during the nineteenth century. Of the 140,000 Jews (including 30,000 German Jewish refugees) in Holland in 1939, the Germans transported 100,000 to various death camps in Poland, but the local Dutch population tended to behave sympathetically towards their Jewish neighbours, hiding many. Anne Frank and her family are the most famous of the hidden Jews from Holland. Amsterdam witnessed a strike in February 1941, called as a protest against the Jewish deportations.

Today, there are three Jewish councils in the Netherlands, representing the Ashkenazi, Reform and Orthodox communities. There are many synagogues in Amsterdam, as well as synagogues in other towns. There are kosher restaurants in Amsterdam, which also has many historical sites - Anne Frank House, the Portuguese Synagogue, still lit by candlelight, and the Resistance Museum.

GMT + 1 hour — Total Population 15,786,000
Country calling code (31) — Jewish Population 30,000
Emergency Telephone (Police, Fire and Ambulance - 112) — Electricity voltage 220

Amersfoort

Synagogues

Drieringensteeg 2 (33) 720943

Amsterdam

The first Jews were said to have come to the city in 1598. It soon became the centre of the *Converso* Diaspora. The Jewish Historical Museum and the Anne Frank house are essential sites to visit. The Rijksmuseum contains a number of paintings of Jewish interest including 'The Jewish Bride' by Rembrant.

Bakeries

Thee Boom
Maasstraat 16 (20) 662-4827
Supervision: Amsterdam Jewish Community.

Thee Boom
Bolestein 45-47 (20) 642-7003
Supervision: Amsterdam Jewish Community.
Hours: Sunday - Friday 9 am - 5 pm, closed on Tuesday. Trams: 12, 25.

Booksellers

Joachimsthal's Boekhandel
Van Leijenberghlaan 116 1082 DB (20) 442-0762
Fax: (20) 404-1843
Email: joachims@xs4all.nl

Open Sunday to Thursday 9.30 am to 6 pm. Friday 9.30 am to 5 pm.

Samech Books
Gunterstein 69 (20) 642-1424
Fax: (20) 642-1424
Email: samech@dds.nl.

Butchers

Marcus, Rituel
Vuaa Lstraat 17 (20) 671-9881
Fax: (20) 642-6532

Supervision: Amsterdam Jewish Community.

Chocolate Shops

Chocolate shop Bonbon Jeannette
Hall Central Station Amsterdam,
Stationsplein 15 1012 AB (20) 421-5194
Fax: (20) 421-5194

Their bitter and dairy chocolates and bonbons are kosher and are sanctioned by the Chief Rabbinate for the Netherlands. Open daily, 8 am to 9 pm.

Delicatessens

Mouwes Koshere Delicatessan
Kastelenstraat 261 1082 (20) 661-0180

Hotels

Golden Tulip Amsterdam Centre
Stadhouderskade 7 1054 ES (20) 685-1351
Fax: (20) 685-1611
Email: info@gtacentre.goldentulip.nl

Hotel Doria
Damstraat 3 1012 (20) 638-8826
Fax: (20) 638-8726
Email: doria@euronet.nl

Kosher breakfast.

Hotel la Richelle
Holbeinstr 41 (20) 671-7971
Fax: (20) 671-0541

Kosher breakfast on request.

Jewish Library

Ets Haim Library - Livraria Montezinos
Mr. Visserplein 3 1011RD (20) 428-2596
Fax: (20) 428-2597
Email: biblio@etshaim.org

Open for research only Monday-Thursday 10 am-4 pm, Friday 10 am-12.30 pm.

Libraries

Bibliotheca Rosenthaliana
Singel 425 1012 WP (20) 525-2366
Fax: (20) 525-2311
Email: ros@uba.uva.nl

The Amsterdam University Library contains an extraordinary collection of Judaic and Hebrew writings given to the city in 1880 by the heirs of Lesser Rosenthal (1794-1868). The German occupation in the Second World War had severe repercussions for the Bibliotheca Rosenthaliana. The books were sent to Germany, where they were found by the Americans, and returned to Amsterdam in 1946. The collection now contains over 100,000 volumes, some dating back to the fifteenth century.

Media

Newspapers

Nieuw Israelietisch Weekblad
Rapenburgerstr. 109 1011 VL (20) 627-6275
Fax: (20) 624-2519
Email: niw@xs4all.nl
Web site: www.xs4all.nl/~niw

Mikvaot

Heinzestr. 3 (20) 662-0178/671-9393
Mr. Visserplein 3 (20) 625-6222

Netherlands

Museums

Anne Frank House
Prinsengracht 263 (20) 556-7100
Fax: (20) 620-7999
Web site: www.annefrank.nl

The original hiding place of Anne Frank, where she wrote her diary. Open daily from 9am to 7pm (April 1st to September 1st daily from 9am to 9pm. January 1st and December 25th 12 noon to 5pm). Last entry thirty minutes before closing time.

Jewish Historical Museum
Jonas Daniël Meÿerplein 2-4 1011 RH
(20) 626-9945
Fax: (20) 624-1721
Email: info@jhm.nl
Web site: www.jhm.nl

Housed in a complex of four former synagogues. Sandwich shop serving kosher food.. Open daily from 11am to 5pm. Group visits by arrangement.

The Resistance Museum
Plantage Kerklaan 61 (20) 620-2535
Fax: (20) 620-2960
Email: info@verzetsmuseum.org
Web site: www.verzetsmuseum.org

Open all year except 1January, 30 April and 25 December. Permanent Exhibition: From 10 May 1940 to 5 May 1945, the Netherlands were occupied by Nazi Germany. Almost every Dutch person was affected by the consequences of the occupation.

Religious Organisations

Ashkenazi Community Offices/Community Center
van der Boechorststr. 26, PO Box 7967 1008 AD
(020) 646-0046
Fax: (020) 646-4357
Email: info@nihs.nl
Web site: www.nik.nl

Restaurants

Mrs B. Hertzberger
Plantage Westermanlaan 9 1018 DK
(20) 623-4684

Five minutes from Portuguese Synagogue. Friday night and Shabbat meals only. Reservation in advance. Also lunchboxes for groups.

SEE FULL DETAILS ON PAGE 412.

Sandwichshop Sal. Meijer
Scheldestraat 45 1078 GG (20) 673-1313
Fax: (20) 642-9020
Supervision: Amsterdam Jewish Community.

Meat

Carmel
Amstelveensewag 224 1075 XT (20) 675-7636
Supervision: Amsterdam Jewish Community.
Hours: 12 pm to 11.30 pm, Sunday to Thursday. Cater Shabbat meals for groups if ordered in advance.
Transport: trams 6, 16, bus 15, 63, 170, 171, 172.

Jerusalem of Gold
Jodenbreestraat 148 1011 NS (020) 6250923
Fax: (020) 6415854
Web site: www.jerusalemofgold.homepage.com
Supervision: Amsterdam Jewish Community.
Hours: Noon to 10 pm daily.

Shabbes - Tisch
Brendele Hertzberger,
Plantage Westermanlaan 9 1018 DK
(20) 623-4684
Supervision: Rabbinate of The Netherlands.
Five minutes from Portuguese Synagogue. Friday night and Shabbath only. Reservations in advance.

Dairy

Museum Café
Jewish Historical Museum,
Jonas Daniel Meijerplein 2-4 (20) 626-9945
Fax: (20) 624-1721
Supervision: Amsterdam Jewish Community.
Hours 11 am to 5 pm daily.

Vegetarian

Bolhoed
Prinsengacht 60-62 (20) 626-1803
Hours: 12 pm to 10 pm daily. Serve organic vegetarian and vegan food.

Snack Bar

Vlaams Friteshuis (Vleminckx)
Voetboog Str. 33, (alleyway off Spui)
(020) 624-6075
This vendor sells only fries (chips), cooked in vegetable oil. A variety of sauces are available. The chips are served in a paper cone.

Synagogues

Buitenveldert
van der Boechorststr. 26,
PO Box 7967 1008 AD (20) 646-0046
Contact hours daily 9 am to 5 pm.
Kehilas Ja'Akow (E. Europe)
Gerrit van der Veenstraat 26 1077 ED
(20) 676-3602
Nidche Jisroel Jechanes
Nieuwe Kerkstr 149 (20) 676-6400
Fax: (20) 672-2973
Shabbat service at 9.30 hours.
Portuguese Jews' Congregation
Mr. Visserplein 3 1011 RD (20) 624-5351
Fax: (20) 625-4680
Email: pig-amsterdam@euronet.nl
This synagogue has been completely restored and is open from Sunday - Friday from 10 am to 4 pm. In August 2000 Hollands unique Sephardi Judaism collection was returned from safe keeping at The Hebrew University at Jerusalem.

Ashkenazi

Ashkenazi Rabbinate of Amsterdam
van der Boechorststr. 26,
PO Box 7967 (20) 646-0046
Fax: (20) 646-4357
Email: rabbinaat@nihs.nl
Contact hours Monday and 2 pm to 6 pm.
Beth Shalom Home for Aged
Kastelenstraat 80,
Amsterdam 1083 (20) 661-1516
Fax: (20) 661-2517
Chol Hamo'eed, Chanuka and Purim morning; Shabbat and Yomtov evening, morning, afternoon and evening. Open to the general public, meals can be arranged.
General Hospital Amstelveen (C.I.Z.)
Laan van de Helende Meesters 8,
Amstelveen (20) 347-4747
Fax: (20) 347-4917
Email: role@zha.nl.
The synagogue is a part of the 'Jewish Wing' of the General Hospital. Services: Saturday and Festival mornings. Open to the general public.

Liberal

Jacob Soetendorpstr. 8 1079 (20) 642-3562
Fax: (20) 442-0337
Email: ljgadam@ljg.nl
Web site: www.ljg.nl

Houses the Judith Druk Library and the Centre for Jewish Studies.

Orthodox

Gerard Doustraat Synagogue
Gerard Doustr. 238 (84) 675-0932
Fax: (84) 867-1626
Email: gd_sjoel@joods.nl
Web site: www.joods.nl/gd_sjoel
Services: Saturday and Festival mornings.
Raw Aron Schuster Sjoel
Jacob Obrechtplein
Daily services.

Sephardi

Portuguese Synagogue & Community Centre
Texelstr. 82 (20) 624-5351

Netherlands

Tourist Sites

Portuguese Jewish Cemetery
Kerkstraat 7, 1191 JB,
Ouderkerk aan de Amstel (20) 496-3498
Fax: (20) 496-5496
Email: bethaim@wxs.nl

Established 1614. One of the oldest Sephardic cemeteries still in use in Europe. Menasseh ben Israel is buried here, as are the parents of the philosopher Spinoza. Ten kilometres south-east of Amsterdam.

Arnhem

Synagogues

Pastoorstr. 17a (26) 442-5154

Liberal

Liberaal Joodse Gemeente Arnhem
Veluws Hof 24, Ermelo 3852 JJ (341) 557-860
Email: elisjewa@hetnet.nl

Breda

Synagogues

School Straat

Bussum

Synagogues

Kromme Englaan 1a (35) 691-4882

Delft

Synagogues

Beth Studentiem
Hillel House, Jewish Students Centre,
Technical University, Koornmarkt 9 (15) 212-0300

Eindhoven

Religious Organisations

Synagogue Inquiries
(40) 241-2710

Synagogues

H. Casimirstr. 23 (40) 751-1253

Enschede

Synagogues

Prinsestr. 16
(53) 432-3479; 435-3336; 435-1293; 434-4788
Fax: (53) 430-9725
Email: jmhartog@vromen.nl

Liberal

Liberal Congregation Inquiries
Haaksbergen (53) 435-1330

Groningen

Synagogues

Postbus 550 9700 AN (50) 312-3151
Email: NIG_Groningen@hotmail.com

Haarlem

Synagogues

Kenaupark 7 (23) 332-6899; 324-2051

Hilversum

Synagogues

Synagogue
Laanstr. 30 (35) 621-2044
Fax: (35) 624-3654
Email: ipor@wxs.nl

Inter-Provincial Chief Rabbinate also based at this address. Rabbi's J. S. Jacobs, S. Evers, A. L. Heintz and Rabbi S Spiero, Tel: 035-623-9238.

Leiden

Organisations

Jewish Students Centre
Levendaal 8 (71) 513-0382

Synagogues

Levendaal 14-16 2311 JL (71) 512-5793
Fax: (71) 512-5793

Maastricht

Synagogues

Capucijnengang 2
Est. 1840

Rotterdam

Synagogues

Joodse Gemeente Rotterdam
A B N Davidsplein 2 (10) 466-9765
Fax: (10) 467-5713

Mikva on premises.

Liberal

Mozartlaan 99
Postbox 91119 3007 (10) 218-0158
Fax: (10) 218-0322

Inquiries to Secretary on 010-461-3211

The Hague

Delicatessens

Jacobs
Haverkamp 220 (70) 347-4980
Fax: (70) 347-4980

Embassy
Embassy of Israel
Buitenhof 47 2513 AH (70) 376-0500
Fax: (70) 376-0555
Email: ambassade@israel.nl

Synagogues
Corn. Houtmanstraat 11,
Bezuidenhout 2593 RD (70) 347-0222
Fax: (70) 347-9002
Email: raabinaat-haag@zonnet.nl
Mikva on premises, appointments should be made twenty-four hours in advance by telephoning 350-7621.
Beis Jisroel
Doorniksestraat 152 2587 AZ (70) 358-6363
Fax: (70) 347-9002

Liberal
Liberal Synagogue
Prinsessegracht 26 (70) 365-6892
Fax: (70) 360-3883
Email: ljg-denhaag@hetnet.nl
Web site: www.ljgdenhaag.nl

Tourist Sites
Spinoza House
Paviljoensgracht
Spinoza House is of special interest, as is the eighteenth century Portuguese synagogue in the Prinsessegracht, which is now used by the Liberal congregation.

Tulburg

Synagogues
Liberal Synagogue Brabant
(70) 365-6893
Inquiries to 013-467-5566.

Utrecht

Bakeries
De Tarwebol
Zadelstr. 19 (30) 231-4887

Synagogues
Springweg 164 3511 VZ (30) 231-4742
Fax: (30) 272-2091
Email: heintz@globalxs.nl

Liberal
Liberal Synagogue
(20) 644-2619
Email: batja@hetnet.nl
Inquiries to 030-603-9343

Zwolle

Synagogues
Samuel Hirschstr. 8,
Postbox 1468 8001 (38) 211412

Netherlands Antilles

A Samuel Cohen served as an interpreter to the Dutch Army which captured Curaçao from the Spaniards in 1634. A congregation was founded in 1651. The Jews of Curaçao enjoyed excellent relations with the Dutch West India Company who owned the island until the end of the eighteenth century.

The Sephardi synagogue in Curacao established in 1732 is the oldest synagogue building in continuous use in the western hemisphere. It has, like the one in Paramaribo (Suriname), sand covering its floor because the synagogue is modelled on after the Tabernacle used in the Sinai desert during the forty years of exile. It is also a reminder of the days of the *Conversos* when sand was used to muffle sounds.

Curaçao also has the oldest existing Jewish cemetery in the western hemisphere.

GMT - 4 hours
Country calling code (599)
Emergency Telephone (Police - 114) (Ambulance - 112)

Total Population 207,000
Jewish Population 400
Electricity voltage 110/220

Netherlands Antilles

Aruba

Synagogues

Conservative

Congregation Beth Israel
Adriaan Lacle Blvd. #2, PO Box 5397,
Royal Plaza, Oranjestad (297) 823272
Fax: (297) 886264
Email: ledaneps@setarnet.aw

Curaçao

Embassy

Consul General of Israel
Blauwduifweg 5, Willemstad (9) 736-5068
Fax: (9) 737-0707
Email: midalya@ibm.net

Kashrut Information

There is no kosher restaurant in Curacao.However many kosher items may be purchased at the "food store" of the Congregation Shaarei Tsedek.

Museums

Jewish Cultural Historical Museum
Hanchi di Snoa 29, PO Box 322 (9) 461-1633
Fax: (9) 465-4141

Opening hours: Monday to Friday 9 to 11.45 am and 2.30 to 4.45 pm. If there is a cruise ship in port also on Sundays from 9am to noon. Closed on Shabbaths and Holy Days. On permanent display are a great many ritual, ceremonial and cultural objects, many of which date back to the seventeenth and eighteenth centuries and are still in use by adjacent congregation Mikve Israel-Emanuel (founded 1651, oldest in the Hemisphere).

Synagogues

Ashkenazi Orthodox

Congregation Shaarei Tsedek
Leliweg 1a, PO Box 498 (9) 737-5738
Fax: (9) 736-9546

Sephardi, Reconstructionist

United Congregation Mikve'Israel Emanuel
Hanchi di Snoa 29, PO Box 322 (9) 461-1067
Fax: (9) 465-4141
Email: info@snoa.com

Sabbath services are Friday at 6.30pm (second Friday in the month is a family service), Saturday at 10 am. Holy Day services at same times.

New Zealand

New Zealand Jewry is almost as old as the European presence in the country. The year 1829 marks the beginning of Jewish settlement, and Jews played a prominent role in the development of the country in the nineteenth century, especially in trading with Australia and Britain. The Auckland Jewish community was founded in 1841, followed by Wellington in 1843. There was also a Jewish prime minister, Sir Julius Vogel, in the nineteenth century.

British Jews emigrated to New Zealand in the twentieth century, but New Zealand restricted immigration from Nazi Europe.

Today the community has six synagogues, four on the North Island and two on the South Island. Auckland and Wellington have Jewish dayschools, and the "Kosher Kiwi Guide" is published in Auckland. There has been recent Jewish immigration from South Africa.

GMT + 12 hours	Total Population 3,862,000
Country calling code (64)	Jewish Population 4,800
Emergency Telephone (Police, Fire, Ambulance - 111)	Electricity voltage 230

Auckland

Bakeries

Manhattan Bagels
(9) 309-9098

Representative Organisations

Auckland Jewish Council
80 Webb St, Wellington (9) 384-4229
Fax: (9) 384-4229
Has a small shop selling kosher food.

Synagogues

Orthodox

Auckland Hebrew Congregation
108 Greys Avenue, PO Box 68-224 (9) 373-2908
Fax: (9) 303-2147
Email: office@ahc.org.nz
New Zealands largest selection of kosher goods. Open Wednesday to Friday 8.30 am to 3.30 pm. Sundays 9 am to 11 am

Progressive

Beth Shalom Progressive Synagogue
180 Manukau Road, Epsom 3 (9) 524-4139
Fax: (9) 524-7075
Email: bshalom@ihug.co.nz

Christchurch

Representative Organisations

Christchurch Jewish Council
(3) 358-8769

Synagogues

406 Durham Street (3) 365-7412
Fax: (3) 355-7982
Email: coxst@chch.planet.org.nz

Dunedin

Synagogues

Progressive Congregation
cnr. George & Dundas Streets

Wellington

Community Organisations

Wellington Jewish Community Centre
80 Webb Street (4) 384-5081
Fax: (4) 384-5081
Email: bethel@ihug.co.nz
There are no kosher restaurants in Wellington. Visitors who want kosher meals & kosher food should contact the centre office of the Community Centre or the Kosher Co-op, on 384-3136.

Delicatessens

Dixon Street Delicatessen
(4) 384-2436
Fax: (4) 384-8692
Not fully kosher but provides kosher challahs and various American & Israeli kosher foods.

Embassy

Embassy of Israel
Level 13, 111 The Terrace,
Equinox House, P O Box 2171 (4) 472-2368
Fax: (4) 499-0632
Email: israel-ask@israel.org.nz
Web site: www.webnz.co.nz/israel

Kosher Food

Kosher Co-op
80 Webb Street (4) 384-3136
Fax: (4) 384-5081
Email: clemclan@ihug.co.nz
Web site: www.go.to/koshernz
Open on Wednesday, Friday and Sunday for kosher meats, cheese and imported products. Goods can be sent anywhere in New Zealand.

Media

Newspapers

New Zealand Jewish Chronicle
PO Box 27-156 (4) 934-6077
Fax: (4) 934-6079
Email: mike@rifkov.co.nz
Monthly newspaper of local, Israeli and Jewish News.

Mikvaot

Wellington Jewish Community Centre
80 Webb Street (4) 384-5081
Fax: (4) 384-5081
Email: bethel@ihug.co.nz

Representative Organisations

Wellington Regional Jewish Council
54 Central Terrace 5 (4) 475-7622
Email: zwartz@actrix.gen.nz

Synagogues

Orthodox

Beth-El Synagogue
80 Webb Street (4) 384-5081
Fax: (4) 384-5081
Email: bethel@ihug.co.nz

Progressive

Temple Sinai
147 Ghuznee Street (4) 385-0720
Fax: (4) 385-0572
Email: temple@actrix.gen.nz

Norway

The only way Jews could enter Norway before the nineteenth century was with a 'Letter of Protection', as Danish control limited the amount of Jewish entry. The situation changed in the 1840s, when a Norwegian liberal poet, Henrik Wergeland, argued for the admission of Jews into the country, and the parliament eventually agreed. There were only some 650 Jews in the country after emancipation in 1891, mainly in Oslo and Trondheim. By 1920, the community numbered 1,457 and by the time of the Nazi invasion there were 1,800. Despite attempts by the Norwegian resistance to smuggle Jews to Sweden, 760 Jews were transported to Auschwitz, although 930 were able to reach Sweden. The Jewish survivors were joined after the War by Displaced Persons, especially invited by the Norwegian government.

The current situation forbids *shechita*, but there are no other restrictions on Jewish life. There is a synagogue in Oslo, and a kosher food shop. There is also a Jewish magazine. A home for the elderly was built in 1988. Trondheim, in the north of the country, has the northernmost synagogue in world.

GMT + 1 hour — Total Population 4,465,000
Country calling code (47) — Jewish Population 1,200
Emergency Telephone (Police - 112) (Fire - 110) (Ambulance - 113) — Electricity voltage 220

Oslo

Oslo is the major centre of Norwegian Jewry, with 900 Jews living in the capital. The Resistance Museum is of interest as is the Wergerland Monument in the Var Frisler Cemetery.

Embassy

Embassy of Israel
Drammensveien 82c, Oslo 0244 2244-7924
Fax: 2256-2183
Email: israel@online.no

Restaurants

Kosher Food Centre
Waldemar Thranesgt. 0171 2260-9166
Supervision: Rabbi Michael Melchior.
There are no kosher hotels or restaurants in Oslo but there is the Kosher Food Centre. Open 4 pm to 6 pm Tuesday and Thursday, and 12 pm to 2 pm on Friday. Closed Shabbat.

Synagogues

Det Mosaiske Trossamfund
Bergstien 13-15 0172 2269-6570
Fax: 2246-6604
Email: kontor@dmt.oslo.no

Tourist Sites

Ostre Gravlund Cemetary
There is a Jewish war memorial here.

Trondheim

Synagogues

Ark. Christiesgt. 1 7352-6568 or 4752-2030
Fax: 7353-1108
Email: palkom@online.no

The Worlds northernmost synagogue. The synagogue also has a museum.

Panama

Some Jews, most of them pretending to be Christians, came to Panama during colonial times. Panama was an important crossroads for trade and, as a result, many Jews passed through the country on their journeys throughout the region.

In 1849, immigrant Sephardic Jews in Panama founded the Hebrew Benevolent Society, the first Jewish congregation in the Isthmus. They came from the pious congregation of Netherland Antilles (Curacao) to settle in Panama.

Jews from Saint-Thomas (Virgin Islands) and Curacao founded in 1876 the Kol Shearith Israel Synagogue in Panama City, and in 1890 the Kahal Hakadosh Yangacob in Colon.

By the end of the First World War, a number of Middle Eastern Jews had settled in the country and founded the Israelite Benevolent Society Shevet Ahim. During the years of the Second World War, immigrants from Europe arrived at Panama, establishing Beth-El, the only Ashkenazi community in the country. The majority of Jewish community is Sephardi (around eighty per cent).

There have been two Jewish presidents in Panama, the only country - apart from Israel of course – where this has happened.

GMT - 5 hours
Country calling code (507)
Emergency Telephone (Police - 104) (Fire -103)

Total Population 2,677,000
Jewish Population 7,000
Electricity voltage 120

Panama City

Bakeries

Pita Pan
Plaza Bal Harbour, Paitilla 264-2786

Butchers

Ricuras de Esther
Calle 48, Urb. Marbella 265-7190
Supervision: Shevet Ahim.

Shalom Kosher
Plaza Bal Harbour, Paitilla 264-4411

Super Kosher
Calle San Sebastian, Paitilla 263-5254
Fax: 263-2067
Email: mzakay@skosher.com
Supervision: Shevet Ahim Rabinate.
Mailing Address POB 8242 Panama 7. Also Kosher supermarket, bakery and restaurant. Open from 8.30 am to 8.30 pm Sunday to Thursday. Friday until 4.30 pm

Chocolate Shops

Candies Bazaar
Via Argentina, 155 L-2 269-4857

Chocolatier
Calle 53, Urb. Marbella 264-4712
Fax: 223-1663
Email: chocolat@orbi.net

La Bonbonniere
Calle Juan XXIII, Paitilla 264-5704

Embassy

Embassy of Israel
Edificio Grobman, Calle Manuel Maria Icaza, 5th Floor 5 264-8257

Mikvaot

Beneficiencia Israelita Beth El
Calle 58E,, Urb. Obarrio 223-3383

Sociedad Israelita Shevet Ahim
Calle 44-27 225-5990
Fax: 227-1268

Organisations

Consejo Central Comunitario Hebreo de Panama
P O Box 3309 4 263-8411
Fax: 264-7936

Jewish Centre: Centro Cultural Hebreo De beneficiencia
Calle 50 Final, PO Box 7166, 5 5 226-0455
Fax: 226-0869
(K) Restaurant open daily for lunch and supper. Closed Saturdays.

Pizzeria

Pizzeria Italiana
Centro Cultural Hebreo de Beneficiencia, Calle 50 Final 226-0455
Fax: 226-0869

Panama

Restaurants

Restaurante Don Jacobo
Centro Cultural Hebreo de Beneficiencia,
Calle 50 Final 226-0455
Fax: 226-0869
Open daily for lunch and supper.

Dairy

Pita Pan
Plaza Bal Harbour, Paitilla 264-2786

Meat

Shalom Kosher
Plaza Bal Harbour, Paitilla 264-4411

Synagogues

Ashkenazi

Beneficiencia Israelita Beth El
Calle 58E, Urb. Obarrio 223-3383
Mikva on premises.

Orthodox Sephardi

Ahavat Sion
Calle Juan XXIII, Paitilla 265-1891
Daily Services. Mikva for women on premises.

Sociedad Israelita Shevet Ahim
Calle 44-27 225-5990
Fax: 227-1268
Daily services.

Reform

Kol Shearith Israel
Av. Cuba 34-16 5 225-4100

Paraguay

Jewish settlement in this land-locked country came late for this area of South America. The few who came over from Western Europe at the end of the nineteenth century rapidly assimilated into the general population. The first synagogue was founded early in the twentieth century by Sephardism from Palestine, Turkey and Greece. Ashkenazis arrived in the 1920s and 1930s from Eastern Europe and some 15,000 came to the country to escape Nazism, intending to move on into Argentina. Some of these settled in Paraguay.

Paraguay, in more recent times, accepted Jews from Argentina who were fleeing from the military regime.

Today there are three synagogues, a Jewish school and a Jewish museum in Asuncion. There is a high rate of intermarriage, but children of mixed marriages may receive a Jewish education.

GMT - 5 hours — Total Population 5,496,000
Country calling code (507) — Jewish Population 900
Emergency Telephone (Police, Fire, Ambulance - 00) — Electricity voltage 220

Asuncion

Embassy

Embassy of Israel
Calle Yegros No. 437 C/25 de Mayo, Edificio San Rafael, Piso 8, PO Box 1212 (21) 495-097; 496-043; 496-044
Fax: (21) 496-355

Organisations

Consejo Representativo Israelita de Paraguay
General Diaz, 657, PO Box 756 (21) 441-744
Fax: (21) 448-289

Synagogues

General Diaz, 657

Peru

The original Jewish population in Peru arrived with the first Europeans, as many *Conversos* were leaders in the Spanish Army which invaded the country in 1532. After the Inquisition was set up in 1570, the Jews were persecuted, and many were burned alive. From 1870, groups of Jews came over from Europe, but tended to disappear into the general population. In 1880, a group of North African Jews settled in Iquitos and worked in the rubber industry. More Jewish immigration occurred after the First World War, and later Nazi refugees entered the country. By the end of the Second World War the Jewish population had reached 6,000, but subsequently declined.

Almost all of the present Jewish population are Ashkenazi. Two Jewish newspapers are produced and most Jewish children go to the Colegio Leon Pinelo school, which is well known for its high standards. There is a cemetery at Iquitos built by the nineteenth-century community. The community is shrinking owing to intermarriage and assimilation.

GMT - 5 hours — Total Population 25,662,000
Country calling code (51) — Jewish Population 3,000
Emergency Telephone (Police - 105) (Fire -116) (Ambulance - 470 5000) — Electricity voltage 220

Lima

Caterer

Salon Majestic
Av. Bolivar 965, Pueblo Libre, 21 (2) 463-0031
Fax: (2) 461-8912
Supervision: Chief Rabbi Abraham Benhamu and Rabbi Efraim Zik.
Catering for special groups and parties by prior arrangement only.

Embassy

Embassy of Israel
Natalio Sanchez 125 6to Piso,
Santa Beatriz 1 (2) 433-4431
Fax: (2) 433-8925

Groceries

Minimarket Kasher
Av. Gral. Juan A. Pezet 1472,
San Isidro, 27 (1) 264-2187
Fax: (1) 264-2187
Email: rsapler@ec-red.com
Supervision: Rabbi Zik.
Hours of opening: Monday-Thursdat 9 am-6 pm, Friday 9 am-3pm.

Pharmax
Kosher items available.

Santa Isabel
Kosher items available.

Wong
Kosher items available.

Hotels

Hostal Regina
Av. 2 de Mayo 1421,
San Isidro, 27 (2) 441-2541; 442-8870
Fax: (2) 421-2044
Only a short walk to the Centro Sharon Synagogue.

Hotel Libertador
Los Eucaliptos 550,
San Isidro, 27 (2) 421-6680
Fax: (2) 442-3011
Only a short walk to the Centro Sharon Synagogue.

Kashrut Information

Chief Rabbi (2) 442-4505
Fax: (2) 442-8147
Email: abenhamu@mail.mba-sil.edu.pe
Rabbi Benhamu is the Chief Rabbi of Peru.

Rabbinate Rabbi Efraim Zik
Av. de Mayo 1815, San Isidro 27 (2) 214697
Email: efraimzik@hotmail.com
There is no kosher restaurant in Lima. Visitors who want kosher meals should contact the Mini Market Koshet, Tel: 511 2642187 at Av. Pezet 1472, San Isidro.

Media

Newspapers

J.T.A. - Publicationes Memora S. A.
Psje. Malvas 135, Brena, 5 (2) 425-0850
Fax: (2) 442-0534
Daily publication.

Peru

Shofar
Enrique Barron 1145, Santa Beatriz 1 (2) 471-1331
Fax: (2) 471-1331

Monthly.

Mikvaot

Union Israelita
Ave. Gral. Juan A. Pezet 1472,
San Isidro, 27 (2) 264-2187
Sociedad Israelita Sefardi; Beit Jabad.

Museums

Museum of the Inquisition
Junin 548, Lima 1 (2) 427-0365
Dungeon and torture chamber of the headquarters of the Inquisition for all Spanish South America from 1570 to 1820. On the right side of the Plaza Bolivar.

Organisations

Asociacion Judia de Beneficencia y Culto de 1870
Libertad 375, Miraflores 18
(1) 445-1089 or 445-5148
Fax: (1) 445-1089
Email: AJBC1870@terra.com.pe

Synagogues

Conservative

Asociacion Judia de Beneficencia y Culto de 1870
Jose Galvez 282, Miraflores 18
(2) 445-1089 or445-5148
Fax: (2) 445-1089
Email: fambrons@junin.itete.com.pe

Orthodox

Beit Jabad
Salverry 3095, San Isidro, 27 (1) 264-6060
Fax: (1) 264-5499
Email: chabadperu@unired.net.pe
Web site: www.lp.edu.pe/jabad
Synagogues (services daily), mikva, kosher food.

Centro Social y Cultural Sharon
Av. 2 de Mayo 1815, San Isidro, 27 (2) 440-0290
Fax: (2) 421-3684

Sociedad de beneficencia Israelita Sefardi
Enrique Villar 581, Santa Beatriz, 1 (2) 442-4505 or 471-7230
Fax: (2) 422-8147

Union Israelita del Peru
Av. Dos de Mayo 1815, San Isidro 27 (1) 421-3688
Fax: (1) 421-3684
Services are held at the Centro Sharon.

Tourist Sites

Pilatos House
Ancash 390, Lima 1
Seventeenth century private mansion, now used by the National Institute of Culture. On the 2nd floor was the synagogue of the *Converso* Jews.

Philippines Republic

Conversos who came with the Spanish in the sixteenth century were the first Jewish presence in the region. In the late nineteenth century, Western European Jews came to trade in the area, and after the Americans occupied the country in 1898, more Jews arrived from a variety of places, including the USA and the Middle East. The first synagogue was built in 1924. The Philippines accepted refugees from Nazism, but the Japanese occupied the islands during the War and the Jewish population was interned. After the War many of the community emigrated. However, a new synagogue opened in 1983, and services are also held in the US Air Force bases around the country.

GMT + 8 hours
Country calling code (63)
Emergency Telephone Electricity voltage 220

Total Population 75,967,000
Jewish Population 100

Manila

Embassy

Embassy of Israel
Trafalgar Plaza 23rd Floor, 105 H.V. dela Costa Street, Salcedo Village, Makati City 1200
(2) 892-5329/30/31/34
Fax: (2) 894-1027
Email: israelembphl@netasia.net
Postal address: POB 1697 MCPO, Makati Metro, Manila 1299.

Mikvaot

Jewish Association of the Philippines (Beth Yaacov Synagogue)
H. V. de la Costa Street, Salcedo Village,
Makati, Metro Manila 1200 (2) 815-0263, 0265
Fax: (2) 818-9990
By arrangement.

Synagogues
Jewish Association of the Philippines (Beth Yaacov Synagogue)
110 H.V. de la Costa corner Tordesillas West, Salcedo Village, Makati City, Metro Manila 1227
(2) 815-0263, 0265
Fax: (2) 840-2566
Email: jap.manila@usa.net
Services; Fri at 6.30 pm, Sat at 9.30 am.

Poland

After just five years of German occupation in the Second World War, the thousand-year-old Jewish settlement in Poland, one of the largest Jewish communities in the world, had been almost totally eradicated. Jews originally came to Poland, in order to escape anti-Semitism in Germany, in the early Middle Ages. They were initially welcomed by the rulers, and the Jews became significantly involved in the economy of the country.

Before the Second World War most Jews lived in the east and south of the country, under Russian and Austrian domination, respectively, until 1918. After 1918, Poland became an independent country once more, with over 3,000,000 Jews (300,000 in Warsaw.) The community continued to flourish before 1939, with Yiddish being the main language of the Jews. The community was destroyed in stages during the War, as Poland became the centre for the Nazi's destruction of European Jewry. After the War, the borders shifted again, and the 100,000 or so survivors mostly tried to emigrate. The few who remained endured several pogroms even after the events of the Holocaust.

Today the community is comparatively small, and most of the members are elderly, but there is a functioning synagogue in Warsaw and many Jewish historical sites are scattered throughout the country. The Polish Tourist Board publishes information about the Jewish heritage in Poland.

GMT + 1 hour — Total Population 38,765,000
Country calling code (48) — Jewish Population 5,000
Emergency Telephone (Police - 997) (Fire - 998) (Ambulance - 999) — Electricity voltage 220

Bialystok

Although there are only a few Jews living here now, before the Second World War it was more than sixty per cent Jewish, giving it the then highest concentration of Jews in any city in the world.

It is possible to visit the sites of a number of buildings of great Jewish interest.

Cemeteries
Wschodnis Street

Historic Site
Synagogue
Branickego Street

Bielsko-Biala

Organisations
Elzbieta Wajs, Ul Mickiewicza 26 43-300 (2) 22438

Bytom

Organisations
Ul Smolenia 4 41902 (3) 813510

Cracow

Booksellers
Jarden
2 Szeroka Street, Miodowa 41 (12) 217166

Cultural Festival
Jewish Culture Festival
(12) 429-2573
Email: office@jewishfestival.art.pl
The twelth annual Jewish Culture Festival will be held in Summer 2002 in the restored Jewish quarter of Kasimierz.

Galleries
Hadar
13 Florianska Street (12) 218992

Organisations
Judaica Foundation
U1 Rabina Meiselsa 17 (12) 423-5595
Fax: (12) 423-5034
Email: uwrussek@cyf-kr.edu.pl

Zwiakzek Wyznania Mojzeszowego
Ul Skawinska 2 (12) 662347

Poland

Restaurants

Meat

Na Kazimierzu
ul. Szeroka 39 31-053 (12) 229-644
Fax: (12) 219-909

Billed as the 'only kosher restaurant in Cracow and the south of Poland'. Hours: 12 pm to 12 am everyday. Traditional Shabbat courses are available on Shabbat.

Synagogues

Eizik Synagogue
18 Kupa Street 602 350 671 (Mobile)
Contact Sasha Pecaric.

Remuh
Ul Szeroka 40

Gliwice

Contact Information

Ul Dolnych Walow 9 44100 (32) 314797

Katowice

Contact Information

Ul Mlynska 13 40098 (32) 537742

Legnica

Contact Information

Ul Chojnowska 37 59220 (76) 22730

Lodz

Organisations

Jewish Chabad
(42) 331221, 336825

Jewish Congregation
Zachodnia 78 (42) 335156

Lublin

Once a major Jewish town in Eastern Europe, Lublin today has fewer than a hundred Jews. Pre-War Lublin was a centre for Torah study, and a large yeshivah was built only a few years before the Second World War, and is now used as a college. Majdanek Concentration Camp lies within the city's boundary, clearly visible from a major road leading south-east. There is a particularly moving memorial in the camp, consisting of the ashes from the camp's crematoria.

Contact Information

Ul Lubartowska 10 20080 (81) 22353

Rzeszow

Synagogues

ul. Bonicza, edge of Pl. Ofiara Getta

Szczecin

Contact Information

Ul Niemcewicza 2 71553 (91) 221674

Warsaw

Before the War, Warsaw had approximately 300,000 Jews. Now there are only a couple of thousand, mostly elderly. There are many sites that can be visited, such as surving fragments of the ghetto walls and 'A Memorial Route to the struggle and Martyrdom of the Jews 1940-43', known as 'Memory Lane'. The old Jewish cemetery, untouched by the Nazis, is very imposing, and is still in use. The Warsaw Ghetto fighters are included in the inscription on the Tomb of the Unknown Soldier in the centre of the city.

Embassy

Embassy of Israel
Ul I Kryzwickiego 24

Mikvaot

Nozyk Synagogue
6 Twarda Street
(22) 620-43-24 (ext 121) 620-06-76
Fax: (22) 620-10-37
Email: varshe@kehillah.jewish.org.pl
Contact Rachel Bookstein, tel: 620 34 96.

Monument

Monument to the Ghetto Heroes
Zamenhofa
Erected in 1948 this monument symbolises the heroic Ghetto defiance of the 1943 uprising.

Organisations

The Jewish Historical Institute
3/5 Tlomackie Street 00090 (22) 827-9221
Fax: (22) 827-8372
Email: zihinb@ikp.atm.com.pl

This establishment has a remarkable collection of Judaica. It includes a library of documents on the manuscripts stolen by the Germans from all over Europe.

Restaurants

Menora
Plac Grzybowski 2 (22) 203754

Nove Miasto Ecological Restaurant
Rynek Nowego Miasta 13/15 (22) 831-4379
Fax: (22) 831-4379
Web site: www.novemiasto.waw.pl

Panorama, Al Witsoa 31 (22) 642-0666
Salad Bar, Ul Tamka 37 (22) 635-8463

Synagogues

Nozyk Synagogue, Jewish Community of Warsaw, Union of Jewish Communities in Poland.
6 Twarda Street 00-950 (22) 6204324
Fax: (22) 6201037
Email: varshe@kehillah.jewish.org.pl
Supervision: The synagogue was renovated in 1977-83 and is well worth a visit. It is the only pre-War synagogue still standing in Warsaw.

Theatre

Jewish National Theatre
Plac Grzybowski 12/16
Performances are given in Yiddish.

Tours of Jewish Interest

Shalom Tours (22) 220-3037
Fax: (22) 220-0559

Wrocklaw

Museums

Historical Museum
Slezna Street 37 (71) 678236

Portugal

Portuguese Jewry had a parallel history to Spanish Jewry until the twelfth century, when the country emerged from Spain's shadow, and Jews worked with the Portuguese kings in developing the country. However, they were heavily taxed and had to live in special areas, although they were free to practise their religion as they pleased. As a result, the community flourished.

Persecution began during the period of the Black Death, and the Church was a key instigator of the riots which broke out against the Jews. After the Inquisition in neighbouring Spain, many Jews fled to Portugal, but were expelled in 1496. Many Jews converted in order to remain in the country and help with the economy. These became the Portuguese *Conversos* and some of their descendants are converting back to Judaism today.

Over the last century and a half, Jews have begun to re-enter the country, and many others used it as an escape route to America during the last war. Most of the community are Sephardi, and there is a Sephardi synagogue in Lisbon. There is also a central Jewish organisation which is a unifying force for Jews in the country.

GMT + 0 hours — Total Population 9,875,000
Country calling code (351) — Jewish Population 300
Emergency Telephone (Police, Fire and Ambulance - 115) — Electricity voltage 220

Algarve

Community Organisations

Jewish Community of Algarve
Rua Judice Biker 11-5°.,
Portimão 8500-701 (282) 416-710
Fax: (282) 416-515

Museums

Faro Jewish Cemetery and Museum
(282) 416-710
Fax: (282) 416-515
Only remaining vestige of the first post-Inquisition Jewish presence in Algarve. Open weekday mornings from 9:30 am to 12:30 pm. Situated opposite entrance to Faro Hospital. Enquiries to Ralf Pinto, Jewish Community of Algarve.

Belmonte

Organisations

Jewish Community of Belmonte
Apt. 18, Bairo de Santa Maina,
6250 Belmonte (275) 912465
Fax: (275) 912465

Lisbon

The Plaza Rossio, not far from the Royal Palace, housed the Inquisition. The building itself was destroyed in 1755 and the National Theatre of Dona Inana was erected in its place. There is a street in the Olfama, Lisbon's oldest district, called Rua de Judiaria.

Portugal

Community Organisations

Communal Offices
Rua Alexandre Herculano 59 1250 (21) 385-8604
Fax: (21) 388-4304

Embassy

Embassy of Israel
Rua Antonio Enes 16-4 1020-025 (21) 355-3640
Fax: (21) 355-3658
Email: israemb@mail.telepac.pt

Jewish Tours

Jewish Heritage Tours
Avenida 5 de Outubro, 321 1649-015
(217) 919-954
Fax: (217) 919-959
Email: fit.lisboa@space.pt
Web site: www.jewisheritage.pt
Tours to explore Jewish Ancestral roots in Portugal and to meet the descendants of the *Conversos*, the 'secret' Jews.

Kosher Meals

Mrs R. Assor
Rua Rodrigo da Fonseca 38.1'D (21) 386-0396
Fax: (21) 395-3725
Email: iassor@mail.telepac.pt
Kosher meals and delicatessen are obtainable if prior notice is given. For kosher meats, contact the communal offices.

Organisations

Jewish Club & Centre
Rua Rosa Araujo 10 (21) 572041

Synagogues

Jewish Community
Rua Alexandre Herculano 59 1250 (21) 385-8604
Fax: (21) 388-4304
Email: cilisboa@mail.telepac.nl
Tours for visitors. 10.00 am until 5 pm except Friday (until 1pm.) For groups please book in advance.

Ashkenazi

Avenida Elias Garcia
100-1'-1050

Oporto

Synagogues

Rua Guerra Junqueiro 340

Puerto Rico

The Jewish community in Puerto Rico is just over 100 years old; the first Jews arrived in 1898 after the beginning of American rule. During the Second World War, many Jewish-American servicemen went to the island, along with refugees from Nazism. A Jewish community centre dates from the early War years. After the War the community grew with the influx of Cuban and American Jews.

San Juan, the capital, has the largest Jewish population, and there are two synagogues.There is also a Hebrew school, held in the community centre. The first Chief Justice of Puerto Rico was Jewish.

GMT - 4 hours — Total Population 3,869,000
Country calling code (1) — Jewish Population 3,000
Emergency Telephone (Police - 343 2020) (Fire 343 2330) — Electricity voltage 120

San Juan-Santurce

Community Centre and Synagogue

Shaare Zedeck
903 Ponce de Leon Av.,
Santurce 00907 (787) 724-4157

Restaurants

Congregation Shaaree Torah
Del Parque Street, just before corner of Ponce de Leon
00914 (787) 724-1680
Fax: (787) 268-7679
Email: chabadpr@coqui.net
Kosher takeout available, call 787-727-2709.

Synagogues

Reform

Temple Beth Shalom
San Jorge Av. & Loiza St., Santurce 00907

Romania

Romanian Jewry was founded at the time the Romans gave the country its name and language. In the fifteenth century community life had begun to be organised and settlement had spread to the town of Iasi and some Moldavian towns. Jews were welcomed from Poland and other East European countries despite the opposition of the Church. Over the years, the community grew in size with further immigration, but emigration became the dominant factor after 1878 when the Treaty of Berlin, which demanded equal rights for Jews, was not implemented in Romania. Following Romania's acquisition of the large area of Transylvania from Hungary after 1918, the Jewish population increased once more. The Jews were finally emancipated, but harsh discriminatory decrees were passed in 1937, and Romania's alliance with Nazi Germany during the war led to 385,000 of the 800,000 Romanian Jews being killed in the Holocaust.

It is ironic that Romanian Jewry was able to function relatively normally under the harsh Ceausescu regime. He was the only Warsaw Pact leader not to sever relations with Israel in 1967, and he allowed Jewish practices to continue, even permitting the then Chief Rabbi, Dr Moses Rosen, to have a seat in the parliament. Emigration to Israel was also tolerated, as this was seen by Ceausescu as being advantageous to Romania. Post-1989, the community still has its central body, the Federation of Jewish Communities, and there are kosher cafeterias in several cities. The community is ageing, but many synagogues are still functioning, and there are also Jewish newspapers and a Yiddish theatre. The Choral Synagogue in Bucharest is of particular interest to visitors.

GMT + 2 hours	Total Population 22,327,000
Country calling code (40)	Jewish Population 11,500
Emergency Telephone (Police - 955) (Fire - 981) (Ambulance - 961)	Electricity voltage 220

Arad

Hotels

Hotel Astoria
Revolutiei 79-81 (57) 281-990

Hotel Parc
Bd. Dragulina 25 (57) 280-820

Organisations

Community Offices
10 Tribunal Dobra Street (57) 281310

Home for the Aged
22, 7 Episcopei Street

Restaurants

Ritual
22, 7 Episcopei Street (57) 280731

Synagogues

Muzeul Judetean
Piata George Enescu 1 (57) 280114

Neologa
10 Tribunal Dobra Street

Orthodox

12 Cozia Street

Bacau

Organisations

Community Offices
11 Alexandru cel Bun Street (34) 134714

Restaurants

11 Alexandru cel Bun Street

Synagogues

Avram A. Rosen Synagogue
31 V. Alecsandri Street

Cerealistilor
29 Stefan cel Mare Street

Botosani

Mikvaot

67 7 Aprilie Street

Organisations

Community Offices
220 Calea Nationala (31) 0315-14659

Restaurants

69 7 Aprilie Street (31) 0315-15917

Romania

Synagogues
Great
1a Marchian Street
Mare
18 Muzicantilor Street
Yiddish
10 Gh. Dimitrov Street

Brasov

Organisations
Community Offices
27 Poarta Schei Street (68) 143532

Restaurants
27 Poarta Schei Street (68) 144440

Synagogues
27 Poarta Schei Street

Travel Agents
International Tourism and Trade
Jozef Bem Str. 2,
Sf. Gheorghe 4000 (67) 316 375
Fax: (67) 351 551
Email: it&t@honoris.ro

PO Box: 1/152

Bucharest

Community Organisations
Federation of Jewish Communities of Romania
Str. Sf. Vineri 9-11, Sector 3 (1) 313-2538
Fax: (1) 312-0869
Email: asivan@pcnet.ro

Kosher supervision on 11 restaurants in the main Jewish communities of Romania.

Documentation Centre
Romanian Jewish History Research Centre
12 Juliu Barasch Street (1) 323-7246

Embassy
Embassy of Israel
6 Burghelea Street (1) 613-2634/5/6

Mikvaot
5 Negustori Street

Museums
Museum of the Jewish Community in Romania
3 Mamoulari Street (1) 615-0837
Hours: Wednesday and Sunday, 9 am to 1 pm.

Religious Organisations
Chief Rabbi of Romania
Strada Sf. Vineri 9 (1) 613-2538
Fax: (1) 312-0869

Representative Organisations
Federation of Romanian Jewish Communities
24 Popa Rusu Street (1) 211-8080
The Federation publishes a bi-monthly, 'Revista Realitatea Evreiasca'.

Restaurants
Jewish Community
18 Popa Soare Street (1) 322-4067
Fax: (1) 322-4067
Email: fcerdas@com.pcnet.ro
This restaurant is operated by the Jewish Community.

Synagogues
Choral Temple
Strada Sf. Vineri 9, Sector 3 (1) 313-1782
Fax: (1) 312-0869
Email: ccmailb@dial.kappa.ro

Credinta
48 Vasile Toneanu Street
Ieshua Tova
9 Nikos Beloiannis Street (1) 659-5675
Near the Lido and Ambassador hotels.

Sephardi
Great Synagogue
9-11 Vasile Adamache Street (1) 615-0846

Theatre
Jewish State Theatre
15 Iuliu Barash Str.,
Sector 3 74212 (1) 323-4530;4035
Fax: (1) 323-2746
Email: tes@dnt.ro
Web site: www.dnt.ro/users/tes

Cluj Napoca

Mikvaot
16 David Fransisc Street

Organisations
Community Offices
25 Tipografiei Street (64) 11667

Restaurants
5-7 Paris Street (64) 11026

Synagogues
Beth Hamidrash Ohel Moshe
16 David Fransisc Street
Sas Hevra
13 Croitorilor Street
Templul Deportatilor
21 Horea Street

Constanta

Organisations

Jewish Community Office and Cultural Club
3 Sarmisagetuza Street (41) 611598

Synagogues

Great Temple
2 C. A. Rosetti Street
Small
3 Sarmisagetuza Street

Dorohoi

Organisations

Community Office
95 Spiru Haret Street (31) 611797

Restaurants

14-18 Dumitru Furtuna Street

Synagogues

Great
4 Piata Unirii Street

Galati

Organisations

Community Office
9 Dornei Street (36) 413662

Restaurants

9 Dornei Street (36) 413662

Synagogues

Meseriasilor
11 Dornei Street

Iasi (Jassy)

Mikvaot

15 Elena Doamna Street

Organisations

Community Office
15 Elena Doamna Street (32) 114414

Restaurants

15 Elena Doamna Street (32) 1117883

Synagogues

Great
7 Sinagogilor Street
Schor
5 Sf. Constantin Street

Oradea

Mikvaot

5 Mihai Viteazu Street

Organisations

Community Office
4 Mihai Viteazu Street (59) 134843

Restaurants

5 Mihai Viteazu Street (59) 131383

Synagogues

Great
4 Mihai Viteazu Street
Neolog
22 Independentei Street

Piatra Neamt

Organisations

Community Office
7 Petru Rares Street (33) 623815

Synagogues

Leipziger
12 Meteorului Street
Old Baal Shem Tov
7 Meteorului Street
Old historical monument.

Radauti

Organisations

Community Office
11 Aleea Primaverii, Block 14, Apt.1 (30) 461333

Synagogues

Great
2, 1 Mai Street
Vijnitzer
49 Libertatii Street

Satu Mare

Satu Mare is the Romanian name for the town of Szatmar, where the famous Hassidic sect originated. It is in the north west of Romania, very near the border with Hungary. Before the First World War the town was in Hungary.

Organisations

Community Office
4 Decebal Street (61) 743783

Synagogues

Great
4 Decebal Street

Sighet

Organisations

Community Office
8 Basarabia Street (62) 511652

Romania

Synagogues
Great
8 Basarabia Street

Suceava

Organisations
Community Office
8 Armeneasca Street (30) 213084

Synagogues
Gah Chavre
4 Dimitrie Onciu Street

Timisoara

Mikvaot
55 Resita Street

Organisations
Community Office
5 Gh. Lazar Street (56) 132813

Restaurants
10 Marasesti Street (56) 136924

Synagogues
Cetate
6 Marasesti Street
Fabric
2 Splaiul Coloniei
Iosefin
55 Resita Street

Tirgu Mures

Organisations
Community Office
10 Brailei Street (65) 115001

Synagogues
21 Aurel Filimon Street

Tushnad

Hotels

Kosher

Olt Hotel
c/o Interom Tours 972-3924-6425
Fax: 972-3579-1720

Vatra Dornei

Organisations
Community Office
54 M Eminescu Street (30) 371957

Synagogues
Vijnitzer
14 Luceafarul Street

Russian Federation

Jews were not allowed to settle in Russia before the eighteenth century, and the few who did were later expelled by various Czars. After 1772, however Russia acquired a large area of Poland, in which lived a significant number of Jews. There were still restrictions against the Jews, but eventually they were allowed to settle in the 'Pale of Settlement', an area in the west of the Russian Empire. Between 1881 and 1914, 2,000,000 Jews emigrated from the Empire escaping anti-Semitism.

Jews were only allowed into Russia itself in the mid-nineteenth century, and by 1890 there were 35,000 Jews in Moscow. Most were expelled the following year. The community grew after the Second World War, drawing Jewish immigration from Belarus and Ukraine to cities such as Moscow and Leningrad. Birobidzhan (in the far East, near China) was a failed experiment which was intended to give the Jews their own 'Autonomous District', and those who moved there soon moved away. Under communism both religious practices and emigration to Israel were restricted; but since 1991 there has been a revival in Jewish learning. There are synagogues functioning in many cities, and there are now 100 Jewish schools. The major threat still comes from anti-Semitic right-wing groups, who are unfortunately increasing their activity.

GMT + 2 to 12 hours — Total Population 146,934,000
Country calling code (7) — Jewish Population 290,000
Emergency Telephone (Police - 02) (Fire - 01) (Ambulance - 03) — Electricity voltage 220

Astrakhan

Synagogues
30 Babushkin Street

Birobidjan

Birobidjan (the size of Belgium) was created in 1934 as a Jewish homeland in the wilds of Siberia. It was not a success and was effectively terminated in the 1940s. There has, however, now been a resurgence of interest in what was known as the Jewish Autonomous District.

Synagogues
9 Chapaev Street, Khabarovsk Krai

Bryansk

Synagogues
82 Lermontov Street
Narodov Vostoka Street

Lubavitch

Synagogue of Bryansk
27a Uritskovo Street 241000 (0832) 445-515

Derbent

Synagogues
94 Tagi-Zade Street

Lubavitch

Jewish Community of Derbent
23 Kandelaky Street 368600 (8724) 021-731

Ekaterinburg

Synagogues
18/2 Kirov Street, (formerly Sverdlovsk)
14 Kuibyshev Street, (formerly Sverdlovsk)

Irkutsk

Synagogues
17 Karl Liebknecht Street

Kazan

The capital of Tatarstan, an autonomous Russian republic, has 10,000 Jews, an Ort school, and its own Jewish newspaper.

Synagogues

Lubavitch

Synagogue of Kazan
15 Profsouznaya Street 420111 (8432) 329-743

Kostrama

Synagogues

Synagogue of Kostrama
16a Sennoi Peroulok 156026 (0942) 514-388

Krasnoyarsk

Synagogues

Synagogue of Krasnoyarsk
65 Surikova Street 660049 (3912) 223-615
Fax: (3912) 440-137
Email: jckras@hotmail.com

Kursk

Synagogues
3 Bolshevitskaya Street

Makhachkala

Synagogues
111 Yermoshkin Street

Moscow

Around 200,000 Jews now live in Moscow and, since the collapse of the USSR in 1991, the community has experienced a revival. The Choral Synagogue on Arkhipova Street, which was built in 1891 and was used during the Soviet regime, is again the focus of Jewish religious life. The Lubavitch movement has its own centre, and there has been an upsurge of interest in Jewish education.

Contact Information

Rabbi Pinchas Goldschmidt
Chief Rabbi of Moscow (95) 923-4788; 924-2424

Embassy

Embassy of Israel
Bolshaya Ordinka 56 (95) 230-6777
Fax: (95) 238-1346

Museums

Poliakoff Synagogue
Bolshaya Brennaya 6

Russia

Restaurants

Meat

King David Club
Bolshoi Spasoglinishchevsky per.
(Arkhipova St) 6, door code 77 (95) 925-4601
Fax: (95) 924-4243
Email: ail@ail.msk.ru
Supervision: Rabbi Pinchas Goldschmidt, Chief Rabbi of Moscow.
This kosher food centre serves as a glatt kosher restaurant and a mini hotel. Catering services are available as are lunchboxes.

Na Monmartre
Vetoshny per., 9 (95) 725-4797
Supervision: Rabbi Berl Lazar.
On the 5th floor of a modern shopping centre.

Synagogues

2nd Korenyovsky Lane, Moscow Oblast

Moscow Choral Synagogue
Bolshoi Spasoglinishchevsky per.
(Arkhipova St) 10 (95) 924-2424

Poliakoff Synagogue
Chabad Centre,
Bolshaya Brennaya 6 (95) 202-7696
Fax: (95) 202-7645

Lubavitch

Chabad Lubavitch
4 Novousushevsky Peroulok 103055 (95) 218-0001
Fax: (95) 219-9707
Email: lazar@glasnet.ru

Chabad Lubavitch Synagogue
6 Balshaya Bronya Street 103104 (95) 202-4530
Fax: (95) 291-6483

Darkei Shalom Synagogue
1 Novovladikinsky Peroulok 103055 (95) 903-0782
Fax: (95) 903-2218

Nalchik

Synagogues

73 Rabochaya Street, cnr. Osetinskaya

Nizhny Novgorod

Synagogues

Lubavitch

Nizhny Novgorod Synagogue
5a Gruzinskaya Street 603000 (8312) 336-345
Fax: (8312) 303-759

Novosibirsk

Synagogues

23 Luchezarnaya Street

Lubavitch

Synagogue of Novosibirsk
14 Koministisheskaya (3832) 210-698

Penza

Synagogues

15 Krasnaya Street

Perm

Synagogues

Kuibyshev Street
Pushkin Street

Rostov-na-Donu

Synagogues

Lubavitch

Synagogue of Rostov-na-Dou
18 Gazetny Peroulok 344007 (8632) 624-759
Fax: (8632) 624-119

Sachkhere

Synagogues

105 Tsereteli Street
145 Sovetskaya Street

Samara

Synagogues

3 Chapaev Street

Lubavitch

Jewish Community Center of Samara Synagogue
84B Chapaevskaya St 443099 (8462) 334-064
Fax: (8462) 320-242
Email: samara@fjc.ru
The community center has a mikvah, and a kosher lemihadrin kitchen.

Saratov

Synagogues

Posadskov Street
2 Kirpichnaya Street

Lubavitch

Synagogue of Saratov
208 Posadskovo Street 410005 (8452) 249-592

St Petersburg

With 100,000 Jews, St Petersburg is witnessing a Jewish revival similar to Moscow. There are opportunities to pray, learn and eat kosher; this was not the case (in general) before 1991 in the USSR. Americans and Israelis are the main instigators behind the revival, but St Petersburg Jewry is also eager to learn about religion, now that there is the freedom to do so.

Mikvaot

2 Lermontovsky Prospekt (812) 113-8974

Representative Organisations

St Petersburg Jewish Association
Ryleev St, 29-31, a/b 103 (812) 272-4113

Restaurants

Dining Room at Shamir School
Ligovskiy Prospekt 161-8 (812) 116-1003

Meat

8,K. Tomchaka Street (812) 327-5475

Synagogues

The Grand Choral Synagogue of St. Petersburg
2 Lermontovsky Prospekt 190121 (812) 114-4428
Fax: (812) 113-6209
Email: pewzner@synagogue.spb.su

This is the second street past the Mariinsky Opera & Ballet Theatre.

Tour Information

Zekher Avoteinu
Jewish Tourist and Genealogical Agency, Pr. Netakkustiv 6-57 195027 (812) 536-3843
Fax: (812) 175-1229
Email: zekhera@hotmail.com
Web site: www.zekheravoteinu.virtualave.net/index.htm

The centre carries out an exciting tour programme combining Jewish and general sightseeing in Russia and the former Pale of Jewish Settlement. It also does genealogical research for the families whose ancestors were from the Russian Empire. Representative in USA: 6801 19th Avenue, 4C, Brooklyn, NY 11204, USA. Tel: 1 718 236 6037.

Tshelyabinsk

Synagogues

Lubavitch

Synagogue of Tshelyabinsk
PO Box 16187 454091 (3512) 333-618
Fax: (3512) 332-468
Email: chabadural@mail.ru

Tula

Synagogues

15 Veresaevskaya Street

Vladikavkaz (formerly Ordzhonikidze)

Synagogues

Revolutsiya Street

Volgograd

Synagogues

Chabad of Volgograd
Novorosiyskaya 43 400087 (8442) 378-308
Email: volgograd@fjc.ru

Yekatrinburg

Synagogues

Lubavitch

Yekatrinburg Synagogue
118/93 Shekmana Street 620144 (3432) 236-440
Fax: (3432) 293-054

Singapore

As Singapore developed into an important south-east Asian trading centre in the mid-nineteenth century, some Jewish traders from India and Iraq set up a community there in 1841. A synagogue was built in 1878, and another in 1904. By the time of the Japanese occupation in the Second World War the community had grown to 5,000 and included some Eastern European Jews. The Japanese imprisoned the community and took their property. After the War, emigration to Australia and the USA reduced numbers, but in recent years Israelis who work in the country and other Jews have moved in. Ninety per cent of the community are Sephardi.

David Marshall, who had been a POW in Japan, returned to Singapore and in 1955 became Chief Minister.

One of the two synagogues is used regularly, and there is a mikva and a newsletter. The Sir Manasseh Meyer Community Centre is the hub of Jewish life. The Jewish community today is small and mainly composed of professionals.

GMT + 8 hours
Country calling code (65)
Emergency Telephone (Police, Fire, Ambulance 999)

Total Population 3,567,000
Jewish Population 300
Electricity voltage 220/240

Contact Information

Rabbi Abergel 737-9112
Email: mordehai@singnet.com.sg
Contact for more detailed information on the community and availability of kosher products.

Embassy

Embassy of Israel
58 Dalvey Road S-1025 235-0966
Fax: 733-7008

Representative Organisations

Jewish Welfare Board
Robinson Road, PO Box 474

Synagogues

Orthodox

Chesed-El
2 Oxley Rise S-0923 732-8832
Services, Monday only, Shacharit and Mincha/Maariv.

Maghain Aboth Synagogue
24/26 Waterloo Street 187950 337-2189
Fax: 336-2127
Email: jewishwb@singnet.com.sg
Daily and Shabbat services are held, except for Monday when services are held at Chesed-El Synagogue, 2 Oxley Rise, at 7.30 am. Because Singapore has equatorial times, Mincha/Maariv commences at 6.45 pm throughout the year. Shacharit: weekdays, 7.30 am, Friday night Shabbat meal served after evening service, Shabbat 9 am. Every Shabbat lunch is served for the community. Breakfast is currently served every morning after services. Mikvah is available for use. For details please contact 737 9112 Rabbi Mordechai Abergel. There are kosher meat, cheeses, wine and other grocery items on sale at the synagogue.

Slovakia

Slovakia has passed through the control of various countries over the centuries, finally gaining independence after the peaceful splitting of Czechoslovakia in 1992. Before 1918 the region was part of Hungary and many in southern Slovakia, near the Hungarian border, still speak Hungarian.

In 1939, the Jewish population in the Slovak area of Czechoslovakia numbered 150,000 but the Hungarians occupied the south of the country and assisted the Germans in deporting Jews to Auschwitz and other camps. Many survivors emigrated after the War, but some remained and are now rediscovering their Jewish heritage. Since independence, B'nai B'rith and Maccabi have been established, but anti-Semitism has re-emerged. There are kosher restaurants in Bratislava and Kosice, and Jewish education is available once more.

GMT + 1 hour
Country calling code (421)
Emergency Telephone (Police -158) (Fire - 150) (Ambulance - 155)

Total Population 5,387,000
Jewish Population 6,000
Electricity voltage 220

Bratislava

Known in German as Pressburg, Bratislava was a key centre of Judaism when Slovakia was under Hungarian rule before the First World War. Bratislava was especially famous for the number of Jewish scholars living there, including the Chatam Sofer. The preserved underground tomb of the Chatam Sofer and other rabbis is now a place of pilgramage.

Bed & Breakfasts

Chez David
Zamocka 13, Pressburg 81101
(7) 544-13 824; 544-16 943
Fax: (7) 544-12 642
Supervision: Rabbi Baruch Myers, the Jewish Religious Community.

Mikvaot

Zamocka 13, Pressburg 81101
(7) 544-13 824; 544-13 943
Fax: (7) 531-642

Museums

The Museum of Jewish Culture
Zidovska Street 81101 (7) 59349142/3/4
Fax: (7) 59349145
Contact person: Prof. PhDr. Pavol Mest'an Dr Sc.

Underground Mausoleum
Pressburg
Contains the graves of eighteen famous rabbis, including the Chatam Sofer. The key is available from the community offices.

Representative Organisations

Central Union of Jewish Religious Communities in the Slovak Republic
Kozia ul. 21 81447 (7) 5441-2167; 5441-8357
Fax: (7) 5441-1106
Email: uzzno@netax.sk

Restaurants

Meat

Chez David
Zamocka 13, Pressburg 81101
(7) 544-13 824; 544-16 943
Fax: (7) 544-12 642
Supervision: Rabbi Baruch Myers, the Jewish Religious Community. Take-away kosher food is obtainable here as well. (Open for lunch only.).

Synagogues

Heydukova 11-13, Pressburg
Services held Mon. Thursday–Saturday.

Galanta

Mikvaot

Partizanska 907

Synagogues

Partizanska 907
Daily services held.

Kosice

Restaurants

Community Centre
Zvonarska Ul 5, Kaschau 04001 (95) 622-1047

Synagogues

Puskinova Ul 3, Kaschau

Beth Hamidrash
Zvonarska Ul 5, Kaschau
Daily services held.

Piestany

Cemeteries

Old Cemetery
Janosikova Ul 606

Synagogues

Hviezdoslavova 59
Shabbat and festival services held.

Presov

Community Organisations

Community Centre
Okruzna 32 08001 (51) 77-31271
Fax: (51) 77-31271
Synagogue and museum on premises.

Trnava

Monument

Monument to Deportees
Halenarska Ul 32
In the courtyard of the former synagogue.

Synagogues

Kapitulska Ul 7

Slovenia

Maribor was the centre for medieval Jewish life in what is now Slovenia. Expulsion followed after the Austrian occupation in the late Middle Ages, but in 1867 the Jews in the Austrian Empire were emancipated and some returned to Solvenia. The community was never large. During the Second World War the members of the small Jewish community either escaped to Italy, fought with the Yugoslav partisans, or were deported.

There is a Jewish community in Slovenia which is connected to the Croatian community. There is one synagogue in Maribor which is classed as an historic monument and dates from the Middle Ages. There are also some sites from medieval times such as the cemeteries in Ljubljana (the capital) and Murska Sobota.

GMT + 1 hour	Total Population 1,986,000
Country calling code (386)	Jewish Population 100
Emergency Telephone (Police - 113) (Fire - 112) (Ambulance - 94)	Electricity voltage 220

Ljubljana

Community Organisations

Jewish Community of Slovenia
Trzaska 2 1000 (1) 4702-320
Fax: (1) 2521-836
Email: jss@siol.net

Synagogues 1101 (61) 315-884

South Africa

Although some believe that Jews were present in the country at around the time of the first European settlement in the area in the seventeenth century, the community only really began in the nineteenth century, when religious freedom was granted. In 1836 the explorer Nathaniel Isaacs published "Travels and Adventures in Eastern Africa", an important contemporary account of Zulu life and customs.

The year 1841 saw the first Hebrew Congregation in Cape Town, and the discovery of diamonds in the Transvaal later in the century prompted a wave of Jewish immigration.

The main immigration of Jews into South Africa occurred at the end of the nineteenth century when many thousands left Eastern Europe; the majority came from Lithuania (40,000 had arrived by 1910). Although the country did not officially accept refugees from the Nazis, about 8,000 Jews managed to enter the country after their escape from Europe.

Today the community is affluent and has good relations with the government. There is a South African Board of Deputies, and many international Jewish associations are present in the country. There are kosher hotels and restaurants, and Jewish museums. Kosher wine is produced at the Zaandwijk Winery.

GMT + 2 hour	Total Population 40,377,000
Country calling code ((27)	Jewish Population 80,000
Emergency Telephone	Electricity voltage 220/250
(Police - 1011) (Fire - 1022) (Ambulance - 10222)	

Eastern Cape

East London

Synagogues

Orthodox

Shar Hashomayim
Lukin Road (43) 722-2071

Reform

Belgravia Crescent

Kimberley

Synagogues

United Hebrew Institutions
20 Synagogue Street 8301 (531) 825-5652

Port Elizabeth

Museums

Jewish Pioneers' Memorial Museum
Raleigh Streetr cnr Edward Street (41) 373-5197
Fax: (41) 374-3612

Open between 10 am and noon every Sunday. The museum has a ramp for disabled for access via wheelchairs. It is also a National Monument. For further information visitors may phone Dr Sam Abrahams (041) 583 3671

Synagogues

Orthodox

Port Elizabeth Hebrew Congregation
Abraham Levy Centre, Barris Walk, Glendinningvale 6001 (41) 373-1332
Fax: (41) 374-3612
Email: peheb@xsinet.co.za

Progressive

Temple Israel
Upper Dickens Street (41) 373-6642

Free State

Bloemfontein

Religious Organisations

United Hebrew Institutions
Community Centre, 1 Dickie Clark Street,
PO Box 1152 (51) 436-2207
Fax: (51) 436-6447

Mornings.

Synagogues

1 Dickie Clark Street, Dan Pienaar,
PO Box 1152 (51) 436-2207
Fax: (51) 436-6447

Mikvah also available. Contact telephone number above.

Gauteng

Brakpan

Religious Organisations

Brakpan Synagogue
cnr. Victoria Avenue and Caendish
For further information phone Mr Waner, Tel: (011) 740-0903.

Johannesburg

The largest city in South Africa also has the largest Jewish community in the country. About seventy per cent of the country's Jews live there (a community of some 55,000) and the headquarters of many of South African Jewry's institutions are housed there. There are more than fifty synagogues in the city.

Bakeries

Friends Bakery
53 Ridge Road, Glenhazel (11) 440-5094
Fax: (11) 440-5096

Supervision: Johannesburg Beth Din.

Shirley's
114 William Road, Norwood (11) 728-0974
Fax: (11) 728-2807

Supervision: Johannesburg Beth Din.

Shula's
173 Oxford Road, Rosebank (11) 880-6989
Fax: (11) 880-6605

Supervision: Johannesburg Beth Din.

Bed and Breakfast

Gal Guest House
124 Third Avenue, Fairmount (11) 485-5006
Fax (11) 485-5518

Supervision: Johannesburg Beth Din.

Booksellers

Chabad House Books
Fairmount Shopping Centre, George Street,
Fairmount (11) 485-1957

Kollel Bookshop
Pick 'N' Pay Shopping Centre,
54 Sixth Ave., Gardens (11) 728-1822
Fax: (11) 728-1813

Butchers

Bolbrand Poultry Shoppe
74-76 George Avenue,
Sandringham 2192 (11) 640-4080
Supervision: Johannesburg Beth Din.

Gallo Manor Kosher Butchery
Morning Glen Shopping Centre, cnr. Braides & Kelvin Sts, Gallo Manor (11) 802-3539
Fax: (11) 802-6546
Supervision: Johannesburg Beth Din.

Gardens Kosher
cnr. Grant & 6th Avenue,
Norwood 2052 (11) 483-3357
Fax: (11) 728-1562
Supervision: Johannesburg Beth Din.

Maxi Discount Kosher Butcher
74 George Avenue, Sandringham 2192
(11) 485-1485; 485-1486
Fax: (11) 485-2991
Supervision: Johannesburg Beth Din.

Nussbaums
434 Louis Botha Avenue, cnr. Main St., Rouxville
(11) 485-2303
Fax: (11) 640-4663
Supervision: Johannesburg Beth Din.

Rishon Balfour
Checker Balfour Park, cnr. Louis Botha & Athol Sts, Highlands North (11) 786-9626
Fax: (11) 885-1996
Supervision: Johannesburg Beth Din.

Rishon Butchery
Balfour Park Shopping Centre, Atholl Road,
Balfour Park 2090 (11) 786-5396
Supervision: Johannesburg Beth Din.

Saveways Spar
Fairmount Shopping Centre, cnr. Sandler and Livingstone Sts, Fairmount (11) 640-6592
Fax: (11) 640-3057
Supervision: Johannesburg Beth Din.

Trevors
32 Merino Avenue, City Deep (11) 613-1808
Fax: (11) 613-1809
Supervision: Johannesburg Beth Din.

Community Organisations

Chabad House
27 Aintree Avenue, Savoy Estate,
Yeoville 2090 (11) 440-6600
Fax: (11) 440-6601
Email: chabad@chabad.org.co.za

Delicatessens & Bakeries

Feigel's Kosher Delicatessan
Shop 3, Queens Place, Kingswood Road,
Glenhazel 2192 (11) 887-1364
Supervision: Johannesburg Beth Din.

Feigel's Kosher Delicatessan
Bramley Gardens Shopping Centre,
Shop 1, 280 Corlett Drive (11) 887-9505/6
Fax: (11) 887-9507
Supervision: Johannesburg Beth Din.
Hours: Friday, 7:30 am to 4:30 pm; Sunday, 8 am to 1 pm; Monday to Thursday, 10 am to 5 pm.

Kosher King
74 George Avenue, Sandringham (11) 640-6234
Supervision: Johannesburg Beth Din.
Hours: Monday to Thursday, 8:30 am to 5 pm; Friday, 8 am to 3 pm; Sunday, 9 am to 1 pm.

Pick 'N Pay
Cnr. Grant Avenue & 6th Street,
Norwood (11) 483-3357
Fax: (11) 728-1562
Supervision: Johannesburg Beth Din.

Saveways Spar Supermarket
Fairmount Shopping Centre, cnr. Livingston St & Sandler Avenue, Fairmount 2192 (11) 640-3056
Fax: (11) 640-3057
Supervision: Johannesburg Beth Din.
Hours: Monday to Thursday, 8 am to 6 pm; Sunday and public holidays, 8 am to 1 pm.

Shirley's Bakery & Deli
442 Louis Botha Avenue,
Highlands North 2192 (11) 640-2629
Supervision: Johannesburg Beth Din.

Shoshana's Bakery
Stan Tech House, cnr. Cross Road and Queens Square, Glenhazel (11) 885-1039
Supervision: Johannesburg Beth Din.

Shula's
42 Kenmere Road, cnr. Hunter Street,
Yeoville (11) 487-1072
Supervision: Johannesburg Beth Din.

The Pie Works
74 George Avenue, Sea Point, Sandringham
2192 (11) 485-2447
Supervision: Johannesburg Beth Din.
Hours: weekdays, 8 am to 5 pm; Friday, to 4 pm; Sunday, to 2 pm.

The Pie Works
Shop 35 Greenhill Road,
Emmarentia 2195 (11) 486-1502
Fax: (11) 486-1527
Email: jossel@iafrica.com
Supervision: Johannesburg Beth Din.
Hours: Weekdays, 8 am to 5.30 pm; Friday to 4 pm; Sunday 9 am to 2 pm.

Libraries

Kollel Library
5 Water Lane, Orchards 2198 (11) 728-1308
Fax: (11) 728-8597

Media

Magazines

Jewish Affairs
Building 1, Anerley Office Park, 7 Anerley Road,
Parktown (11) 486-1434
Fax: (11) 646-4940
Email: sajbod@iafrica.com
Quarterly journal of the South African Jewish Board of Deputies.

Jewish Heritage
PO Box 3 7179, Birnham Park 2015 (11) 880-1830

Jewish Tradition
PO Box 46559, Orange Grove,
2119 Johannesburg, Yeoville (11) 648-9136
Fax: (11) 648-4014
Email: isaacrez@yebo.co.za
Publication of the Union of Orthodox Synagogues of South Africa.

South African Jewish Observer
PO Box 29189, Sandringham 2131 (11) 640-4420
Fax: (11) 640-4442
Publication of the Mizrachi organisation of South Africa.

The South African Jewish Times
Publico House, 30 Andries Street,
Wynberg (11) 887-6500
Fax: (11) 440-5364

Mikvaot

Adase Yashurun Mikvah
34 Fortesque Road, Yeoville (11) 648-6300
By appointment only. Phone Mrs Levy. (011) 648-6751

Glenhazel Mikvah (Ba'ar Rachel)
65 Nicholson Avenue, Glankay (11) 485-1555

Sandton Mikvah
211 Rivonia Road, Morningside (11) 883-4210

Religious Organisations

The Southern African Union for Progressive Judaism
357 Louis Botha Avenue,
Highlands North (11) 640-6614

Union of Orthodox Synagogues of South Africa
58 Oaklands Road, Orchards 2192 (11) 485-4865
Fax: (11) 640-7528
Email: jhb@uos.co.za
Beth Din located at same address and phone number.

Restaurants

Round the Corner
10 Dunnotter Street, Sydenham (11) 485-2585
Supervision: Johannesburg Beth Din.

Dairy

Brazilian Coffee Shop
Shop 174, Balfour Park Shopping Centre,
cnr. Athol Road, Highlands North (11) 440-8822
Fax: (11) 466-1876
Supervision: Johannesburg Beth Din.

Michelo's
3 Dunottar Street,
(off Louis Botha Ave) (11) 485-4626
Fax: (11) 615-3360
Supervision: Johannesburg Beth Din.

Shula's
173 Oxford Road, Rosebank 2196 (11) 880-6969
Fax: (11) 880-6605
Supervision: Johannesburg Beth Din.
Pareve and milk restaurant. Hours: Sunday to Thursday, 7 am to 11 pm; Friday, to 4 pm; Motzei Shabbat to 1 am.

Meat

D.J's Take Away
Balfour Park Shopping Centre, Shop No. 121,
Balfour Park 2090 (11) 440-1792
Supervision: Johannesburg Beth Din.

Marc Chagall's
Upper Level, Balfour Park Shopping Centre,
cnr. Athol Road, Highlands North (11) 786-0593
Fax: (11) 786-0594
Supervision: Johannesburg Beth Din.

Nandos
27 Aintree Avenue Savoy (11) 885-1496
Fax: (11) 885-1492
Supervision: Johannesburg Beth Din.
On The Square
Shop No. 7, Shell Court, cnr. Craddock Avenue & Baker Street, Rosebank 2196
(11) 880-4153; 447-4891
Supervision: Johannesburg Beth Din.
Hours: Sunday to Thursday, 10 am to 3 pm; 6 pm to 10 pm; Motzei Shabbat, 1 hour after Shabbat to 12 am.

Synagogues

There are more than 50 synagogues in Johannesburg. Please contact the approprite religious organisation for details (page 191).

Tour Information

Celafrica Tours
PO Box 357, Highlands North 2037 (11) 887-5262
Fax: (11) 885-3097
Email: celpro@hixnet.co.za
Web site: www.celafrica.com
The company specialises in kosher tours to southern Africa, for people needing kosher food and Shabbat arrangements.

Krugersdorp

Synagogues

Krugersdorp Synagogue
1 Cilliers Street, Monument (11) 954-1367
Fax: (11) 953-4905

Pretoria

Embassy

Israel Embassy & Consulate-General
3rd Floor, Dashing Centre, 339 Hilda St
Hatfield (12) 342-2693

Kashrut Information

Pretoria Council of BOD
(12) 344-2372
Fax: (12) 344-2059

Kosher Food

Pick 'N' Pay
Brooklyn Square Mall, Middle Street,
Muckleeneuk (12) 346-8680
Kosher prepacked food under the Johannesburg Beth Din
Spar
Groenkloof Plaza, George Stonar Drive,
Groenkloof (12) 346-5555
Kosher prepacked food under the Johannesburg Beth Din

Museums

Sammy Marks Museum
Swartkoppies Hall, Old Bronkhorstspruit 0001
(12) 802-1150
Fax: (12) 802-1292
Email: smarks@nfi.co.za
Hours of opening: Tuesdays - Sundays, 10 am-4 pm

Restaurants

JAFFA Old Age Home
42 Mackie Street, Baileys Muckleneuk 0181
(12) 346-2006
Fax: (12) 346-2008
Email: jaffa@smartnet.co.za
Hotel as well. Prior booking necessary. Kosher catering, resident mashgiach. Kosher meals available on request.

Synagogues

Orthodox

Adath Israel Centre
246 Schroder Stresst, Groenkloof (12) 460-7991
Fax: (12) 480-5911
Email: phc@netactive.co.za

Progressive

Temple Menorah
315 Bronkhorst Street, New Muckleneuk,
PO Box 1497 (12) 467-296

Springs

Synagogues

Springs Synagogue
40 Charterland Avenue, Selcourt (11) 818-2572

KwaZulu-Natal

Durban

Bed and Breakfasts

Beit Ya'akov
75 Windmill Road, PO Box 47314,
Greyville 4023 (31) 202-7275
Fax: (31) 202-7302
Email: koby@global.co.za
Run by family who are shomer mitzvot.

Butchers

Pick 'N Pay
Musgrave Centre, Berea 4001 (31) 201-4208
Bakery as well.

Community Organisations

Durban Jewish Club
44 Old Fort Road 4001 (31) 337-2581
Fax: (31) 337-9600
Email: mail@iua-ucf-kzn.co.za
Mailing address: PO Box 10797, Marine Parade 4056.

Representative Organisations

Council of KwaZulu-Natal Jewry
44 Old Fort Road 4001 (31) 337-2581
Fax: (31) 337-9600
Email: mail@iua-ucf-kzn.co.za
Mailing address: PO Box 10797, Marine Parade, 4056

Restaurants

Café Shalom
Durban Hebrew Congregation, cnr. Essenwood & Silverton Roads (31) 202-1205

Dairy

Café Shalom
Great Synagogue cnr. Silverton & Essenwood Roads, PO Box 50044, Musgrave Road 4062
(31) 202-1205
Fax: (31) 209-2925
Email: studycentre1@freemail.absa.co.za

Synagogues

Orthodox

Durban United Hebrew Congregation The Great Synagogue
Cnr. Essenwood & Silverton Roads,
PO Box 50044, Musgrave Road 4062
(31) 201-5177
Fax: (31) 202-8925
Email: shul@duhc.org.za

The Vryheid Memorial Shul
Cnr. Old Fort & Platfair Rds (31) 201-5177
Fax: (31) 202-8925

Progressive

Durban Progressive Jewish Congregation
369 Ridge Road (31) 208-6105
Fax: (31) 209-2429

Umhlanga

Contact Information

Chabad of Umhlanga
POBox 474 4320 (31) 561-2487
Fax: (31) 561-5845
Web site: www.chabadonline.com/kwazulu-natal
Open all hours. Regular minyanim especially Shabbat and Yomim Tovim. Ladies' mikva twenty minutes away. Kosher hospitality. For kosher tours in Southern Africa contact Shlomo on the above numbers.

Western Cape

Cape Town

Cape Town has approximately 17,000 Jews. A visit to the Campus comprimising the Gardens Synagogue (160 years old), the new South African Jewish Museum, the Albow Centre-housing the Holocaust Museum and the Gitlin Library-and the Cafe Riteve, is a must for Jewish visitors.

Bakeries

Checkers
Gallaria Centre, Regent Road, Sea Point
(21) 439-6159
Supervision: Cape Beth Din.

Shoprite Checkers
Main Road, Riverside Centre,
Rondebosch (21) 689-4563
Supervision: Cape Beth Din.

Butchers

Claremont Kosher Butchers and Deli
150 Main Road, Corner Oliver Sea Point, Claremont 7800 (21) 439-6909
Fax: (21) 439-6920
Email: adlercaz@hixnet.co.za
Supervision: Cape Beth Din.
Can deliver to your door.

Pick 'N Pay
Constantia Village (21) 794-5960
Supervision: Cape Beth Din.

Pick 'N Pay
Main Road, Claremont (21) 683-2724
Supervision: Cape Beth Din.
Prepacked with Beth Din sign only.

Pick 'N' Pay
Adelphi Centre, Main Road, Sea Point (21) 434-8987
Supervision: Cape Beth Din.

Shoprite
Rondebosch (21) 689-4563
Supervision: Cape Beth Din.

Delicatessens

Goldies Nosh Bar
64 Regent Road, Sea Point 8001 (21) 434-1116
Fax: (21) 438-3851
Supervision: Cape Beth Din.
Sit-down deli and take-away. Meat and pareve. Hours: Sunday to Thursday, 7 am to 8 pm; Friday, to 5 pm.

South Africa / Western Cape

Hotels

Kosher

The Belmont Shareblock
3 Holmfirth Road, Sea Point 8005 (21) 439-1155
Fax: (21) 434-9451
Supervision: Cape Beth Din.
Breakfast and Lunch only.

Kosher Food

Pick 'N' Pay
Centre Point Milnerton (21) 552-2057
Supervision: Cape Beth Din.
Prepacked with Beth Din sign only.

Reingold's Deli & Butchery
Plumstead (21) 762-8093
Supervision: Cape Beth Din.

Spar
Regent Road, Sea Point (21) 439-0913
Supervision: Cape Beth Din.
Prepacked with Beth Din sign only

Libraries

Jacob Gitlin Library
Albow Centre, 88 Hatfield Street 8001
(21) 462-5088
Fax: (21) 465-8671
Email: gitlib@netactive.co.za

Mikvaot

Arthur's Road Synagogue, Sea Point
(21) 434-3148; 439-8787

Museums

Cape Town Holocaust Centre
88 Hatfield Street, Gardens 8001 (21) 462-5553
Fax: (21) 462-5554
Email: ctholocaust@mweb.co.za
Web site: www.museums.org.za/ctholocaust

South African Jewish Museum
84 Hatfield Street, Gardens (21) 465-1546
Fax: (21) 465-0284
Email: info@sajewishmuseum.co.za
Web site: www.sajewishmuseum.co.za
Open Sunday - Friday. Shop and kosher café.

Representative Organisations

Cape Town Jewish Community Centre
87 Hatfield Street, Gardens 8001 (21) 464-6700
Fax: (21) 461-5805
Email: sajbd2@ctjc.co.za

Restaurants

Avron's Place Restaurant & Grill
307 Main Road, Sea Point (21) 439-7610
Fax: (21) 439-7599
Email: almeleh@netactive.co.za
Supervision: Cape Beth Din.

Café Riteve
88 Hatfield Street, Gardens (21) 465-1594
Fax: (21) 465-5980
Supervision: Cape Beth Din.

Meat

Goldies Bakery & Deli
66 Regent Road, Sea Point (21) 439-0628
Supervision: Cape Beth Din.

Kaplan Student Canteen
University of Cape Town (21) 650-2688
Fax: (21) 650-3064
Supervision: Cape Beth Din.
Lunches, take-away and orders. Meat and pareve.
Open Monday to Friday. Closed December/January for varsity holidays and during summer vacation.

Synagogues

Orthodox

Arthur's Road
31 Arthur's Road, Sea Point (21) 434-8680
Fax: (21) 434-8880

Camps Bay
Chilworth Road, Camps Bay (21) 438-8082
Fax: (21) 438-8082
Email: cbhc@netactive.co.za

Cape Town Hebrew Congregation
84 Hatfield Street, Gardens (21) 465-1405
Fax: (21) 461-7659
Email: cthc@mweb.co.za

Claremont Hebrew Congregation
Grove Avenue (at Morris Rd), P.O. Box 23035,
Claremont 7735 (21) 671-9007
Fax: (21) 683-3011
Email: clarshul@iafrica.com

Constantia
Old Rendal Road, Constantia 7806 (21) 713-1818
Fax: (21) 715-3110
Email: shul@chc.afrint.co.za
Web site: www.shul.org.za

Green & Sea Point Hebrew Congregation
10 Marais Road, Sea Point (21) 439-7543
Fax: (21) 434-3760
Email: gspheb@mweb.co.za

Milnerton
29 Fitzpatrick Road, Cambridge Estate
7441 (21) 551-0442
Fax: (21) 552-4285

Muizenberg
Camp Road, Muizenberg (21) 788-1488

Schoonder Street Shul
10 Yeoville Road, Vredehoek (21) 452-239
Fax: (21) 461-1510

Sephardi Hebrew Congregation
Weizmann Hall, 85 Regent Road, Sea Point
(21) 439-1962
Fax: (21) 439-9620
Email: rabbi@yebo.co.za

Wynberg Hebrew Congregation
5 Mortimer Road, Wynberg 7800 (21) 797-5029
Fax: (21) 761-4669

Reform

Temple Israel
Upper Portswood Road, Green Point (21) 434-9721
Fax: (21) 434-2400
Email: templect@iafrica.com

Oudtshoorn

Synagogues

United Hebrew Institutions
291 Buitenkant Street (44) 272-3068
Fax: (44) 272-3068

There is a Jewish section in the C.P. Nel Museum.

Paarl

Synagogues

New Breda Street (21) 872-4087
For further information phone Mr. Bloom (021) 872-6761.

South Korea

Before the Korean War (1950-53) there were a handful of Jews in the country who had escaped from Russia. During the Korean War a larger community came to South Korea as US Army soldiers. There is still an American detachment based in the country, and among them are some Jews. They have been joined by individuals coming to the country to work. Services are held at the US Army Base in Seoul, and the US Army has its own Jewish chaplain.

GMT + 9 hours — Total Population 45,314,000
Country calling code (82) — Jewish Population 150
Emergency Telephone (Police - 112) (Fire and Ambulance - 119) — Electricity voltage 110/220

Seoul

Synagogues

South Post Chapel
Building 3702, Youngsan Military Reservation
(2) 793-3728
Fax: (2) 796-3805

Civilians welcome to participate in all Jewish activities, inc. kosher le-Pesach sedarim, meals and services.

Spain

Spain has an ancient connection with the Jews, and the term 'Sephardi' originates from the Hebrew word for Spain. Beginning in Roman times, the Jews have suffered the usual cycle of acceptance and persecution, with a 'golden age' under the Islamic Moorish occupation which began in 711. Great Jewish figures arose from the Spanish community, such as Ibn Ezra and the Ramban. However, the situation changed when the Christians gained the upper hand and 'blood libels' began to circulate. In 1492, almost 100 years after a particularly violent period of persecution, the Jews were expelled from Spain. Many thousands were baptised but practised Judaism in secret (the *Conversos*), and many were caught and burnt at the stake.

Jewish life began again in the nineteenth century. The Inquisition ended in 1834 and by 1868 Spain had promulgated religious tolerance. Synagogues could be built after 1909, and Spain accepted many thousands of Jewish refugees before and during the Second World War. Angel Sanz-Briz alone helped to save thousands of Hungarian Jews by issuing 'letters of protection' and entry visas.

There has been a recent immigration from North Africa, and the community today has a central body, synagogues in several towns (including Torremolinos and Malaga). Rambam's synagogue in Cordoba can be visited, and there are several other old synagogues throughout the country.

GMT + 1 hour — Total Population 39,630,000
Country calling code (34) — Jewish Population 14,000
Emergency Telephone
(Police - 092 or 091) (Fire - 080) (Ambulance - 092) — Electricity voltage 220

Alicante

Organisations

Communidad Israelita
Apdo. 189, Playa de San Juan 03540
(96) 515-1572

Synagogues

Vila Carlota, 15 Urb Montivoli, Villajoyosa

Avila

The Mosen Rubi Church, on the corner of Calle Bracamonte and Calle Lopez Nunez, was originally a synagogue, built in 1462.

Barcelona

The ancient community of the city lived in the area of the Calle (from the Hebrew Kehilla) and the cemetery was in Montjuic ('Mountain of the Jews'). Most of the original tombstones are now in the Provincial Archaeological Museum.

Butchers

Carniceria|
Porvenir 24 (93) 200-3375
Supervision: Barcelona Rabanut.

Mikvaot

Porvenir 24 08071 (93) 200-6148, 8513

Organisations

Communidad Israelita de Barcelona
Porvenir 24 08071 (93) 200 6148
Fax: (93) 200 6148

Community Centre
Porvenir 24 08071 (93) 200-6148 or 8513
Kosher meals are available on request

Restaurants

Vegetarian

Self Naturista
Carrer de Santa Anna 11-17 08002 (93) 318 23 88
Fax: (93) 412 54 13

Synagogues

Orthodox

Communidad Israelita de Barcelona
Porvenir 24 08021 (93) 200-6148, 8513
The first synagogue to be built in Spain since the Inquisition.

Progressive

Communitat Jueva ATID de Catalunya

Castanyer 27, bajos 08022 (93) 417-3704
Fax: (93) 417-3704
Email: atid@arquired.es
Web site: www.atid.freeservers.com

Tour Information

Dominique T. Blinder

(93) 417-1191
Fax: (93) 417-1191
Web site: www.urbanculotors.com

Walk of the Call (Jewish Quarter) by a Jewish American architect. Vsits to other places of Jewish interest in Catalonia can also be arranged.

Travel Agencies

Jewish Travel Agency

Viajes Moravia, Consejo de Ciento 380
(93) 246-0300

Bembibre

The synagogue here was converted into a church.

Benidorm

Kashrut Information

(96) 522-9360

Besalu

The Juderia, one of the oldest in Catalonia, is by the River Fluviá. A mikva was recently discovered there.

Burgos

During the thirteenth century Burgos was the largest Jewish community in North Castile. The Juderia was in the area of the Calle Fernan Gonzalez.

Caceres

Between the thirteenth and fifteenth century, Jewish life flourished here, and in 1479 there were 130 families making up one quarter of the town's population. Part of the Juderia still exists. The San Antonio Church on the outskirts of the town is a thirteenth century former synagogue.

Ceuta

Kashrut Information

Calle Sargento Coriat 8

Synagogues

Calle Sargento Coriat 8

Cordoba

Tourist Sites

Calle de los Judios 20

This is an ancient synagogue (declared as a monument). Near by, a statue of Maimonides has been erected in the Plazuela de Maimonides. The entrance to the ancient Juderia is near the Almodovar Gate.

El Escorial

Libraries

San Lorenzo Monastry

The library of San Lorenzo Monastery contains a magnificent collection of medieval Hebrew Bibles and illuminated manuscripts. On the walls of the Patio of Kings, in the Palace of Philip II, are sculpted effigies of six kings of Judah.

Estella

The Jewish community here was one of the most important in the kingdom of Navarre. The Santa Maria de Jus Castillo Church was once a synagogue.

Gerona

The Jewish quarter of Gerona, known as the Call, is located in the heart of the old town. Its main street exists today, and it is known as Carrer de la Força. The Jewish Quarter of Gerona is one of the best-preserved to be found in Europe today.

During the Middle Ages, the Jewish community of Gerona achieved considerable importance. It was there that the most important Cabbala school in Western Europe was developed, largely under the guidance of Rabbi Mossé ben Nahman, or Ramban, perhaps its best known representative.

The Bonastruc ça Porta Center houses the Museum of Catalan-Jewish Culture and the Nahmanides Institute for Jewish Studies, on the site where the fifteenth- century synagogue was located.

In the municipal archives there is an important collection of fragments of Hebrew manuscripts dating from the thirteenth and fourteenth centuries. The Archaeological Museum contains more than twenty medieval gravestones with Hebrew inscriptions, found in the old Jewish cemetery.

Organisations

Patronat Municipal Call De Girona

c/ Sant Llorenc s/n 17004 (972) 21 67 61
Fax: (972) 21 67 61
Email: callgirona@grn.es
Web site: www.ajuntament.gi/el-call

The Catalan Museum of Jewish Culture. Temporary exhibitions on Jewish subjects. Guided tours.

Granada

The Juderia ran from the Corral del Carlon to Torres Bermejas.

Hervas

This village in the Gredos Mountains, 150 miles west of Madrid, has a well-preserved Juderia, which has been declared a national monument. Its main street has been renamed Calle de la Amistad Judeo Cristiana.

Madrid

About 3,500 Jews live in Madrid. A new synagogue was completed in 1968, and there is a community centre providing kosher food. The Prado has a number of paintings of Jewish interest.

Butchers

Elias Shoshanna
35 calle Viriato (91) 446-7847
Supervision: Harav ben Dahan, rabbi of the community.

Delicatessens

Department Store
El Corte Ingles, Castellana

Embassy

Embassy of Israel
Calle Velasquez 150,
7th Floor 28002 (91) 411-1357

Gift Shop

Kewn Shop, Sefarad II
Silva 8 28013 (91) 547-0722
Email: sefaradgalleries@bravored.com
Jewish religious articles.

Sefarad Handicrafts
Gran Via 54 (91) 548-2577, 547-6142
Fax: (91) 548-2577
Email: sefaradgalleries@bravored.com
Jewish religious articles.

Mikvaot

Calle Balmes 3 (91) 445-9843, 9835

Museums

Museo Arquelogico
Calle de Serrano 13
See casts of Hebrew inscriptions from medieval buildings.

Organisations
Community Centre
Calle Balmes 3 (91) 591-3131
Fax: (91) 594-1517
Email: cimsecretaria@terra.es

Restaurants
Community Centre
Calles Balmes 3 (91) 591-3131
Fax: (91) 594-1517
Email: cimsecretaria@teleline.es
For groups only.

Vegetarian
El Estragon
Pel de la Paja 10, Austrias 28005 (91) 365-8982

Synagogues
Calle Balmes 3 (91) 591-3131
Fax: (91) 594-1517
Email: cimsecretaria@terra.es
The capital's first synagogue since the expulsion of Jews in 1492 was opened in December 1968. The building also houses the Community Centre, as well as mikvah, library, classrooms, an assembly hall and the office of the community. Nearest underground station: Metro Iglesias.
Congregacion Bet El
Castello 77 28006 (91) 519-3227
Fax: (91) 662-3730
Email: betel_es@hotmail.com
Web site: www.members.xoom.com/betelspain/

Tourist Information
Ogicina Nacional Israeli de Turismo
Gran via 69, Ofic 801 28013 (91) 559-7903
Fax: (91) 542-6511

Malaga

Butchers
Carmiceria Kosher
Calle Somera 14 29001 (95) 260-4201

Mikvaot
Calle Somera 12 29001

Synagogues
Alameda Principal, 47,20.B 29001

Tourist Sites
There is a statue of the eleventh-century Hebrew poet, Shlomo Ibn-Gabirol, a native of Malaga, in the gardens outside the Alcazaba Castle, in the heart of the city.

Marbella

Bakeries
La Tahona (95) 282-2781

Groceries
Hipercor
El Corte Ingles, Puerto Banus
Joelle Kanner
(95) 277-4074
Kosher poultry and wine.

Media

Publications
Edificio Marbella 2000
Paseo Maritima
Focus
PO Box 145 29600
Community Journal

Organisations
Community Centre
Paseo Maritima

Synagogues
Beth El Synagogue
21 Calle Jazmines, Urbanizacion El Real,
Km 184 (95) 277-4074; 282-4983; 282-6649
Email: ikanner@vnet.es
About two miles from the town centre to the east. Services: Friday eve. (winter) 7.00pm, (summer) 8.30 pm; Shabbat morning & all festivals 10am. Kosher meals on request (also take out). Mikveh on premises.

Melilla

Kashrut Information
Calle General Mola 19, North Africa

Synagogues
Barrio Poligono
There are nine other synagogues in the Barrio Poligono. These are open on festivals and High Holydays only.
Isaac Benarroch
Calle Marina 7, North Africa
Jacob Almonznino
Calle Luis de Sotomayor 4, North Africa
Salama
Calle Alfonso XII 6, North Africa
Solinquinos
Calle O'Donnell, North Africa
Yamin Benarroch
Calle Lopez Moreno 8, North Africa

Mojacar

Tourist Information
Casa Shalom
c/- Granada 5, Apartado 641 04638 Fax: 472464

Spain

Montblanc

The Jewish quarter was in the Santa Clara district, where the church was once a synagogue.

Santiago de Compostela

The cathedral has twenty-four statues of biblical prophets framed in the so-called 'Holy Door'.

Saragossa

This city was once a very important Jewish centre. A mikva has been discovered in the basement of a modern building at 126-132 Calle del Coso.

Segovia

The Alcazar contains the sixteenth-century 'Tower of the Jews'. Calle de la Juderia Vieja and Calle de la Juderia Nueva are the sites of the medieval Jewish quarters, where the former synagogue now houses the Corpus Christi Convent.

Seville

The old synagogue, now the church of Los Venerables Sacerdotes, is in the Barrio de Santa Cruz. Seville Cathedral preserves in its treasures two keys to the city presented to Ferdinand III by the Jews. The Columbus Archives (Archives of the Indies), 3 Queipo de Llano Avenue, preserve the account books of Luis de Santangel, financier to King Ferdinand and Queen Isabella. There is a Jewish cemetery in part of the city's Christian burial ground in the Macarena district.

Synagogues

Comunidad Israelita de Sevilla
Calle Bustos Tavera 8 41003

Tarazona

The Juderia is near the bishop's palace. It is situated between the Conde and the Rue Alta.

Tarragona

Tarragona Cathedral, Calle de Escribanias Viejas. This has in its cloister a seventh-century stone inscribed in Latin and Hebrew. Some very old coins are preserved in the Provincial Archaeological Museum. The gate to the medieval Juderia still stands at the entrance to Calle de Talavera.

Toledo

Though it now has no established community, Toledo is the historical centre of Spanish Judaism. Well worth a visit are two ancient former synagogues, one of which is the El Transito (in Calle de Samuel Levi), founded by Samuel Levi, the treasurer of King Pedro I, in the fourteenth century. It has been turned by the Spanish government into a museum of Sephardi culture. The other, now the Church of Santa Maria la Blanca, is the oldest Jewish monument in Toledo, having been built in the thirteenth century. It stands in a quiet garden in what was once the heart of the Juderia, not far from the edge of the Tagus River. Also of interest is the house of Samuel Levi, in which El Greco, the famous painter, lived. The house is now a museum of his works.

Plaza de la Juderia, half-way between El Transito and Santa Maria la Blanca, was part of the city's two ancient Jewish quarters, where many houses and streets are still much as they were 500 years ago.

Torremolinos

Synagogues

Beth Minzi
Calle Skal La Roca 16 (95) 383952
Calle Skal La Roca is a small street at the seaward end of the San Miguel pedestrian precinct, almost opposite the Police Station. Sephardi and Ashkenazi services are held on Sabbath morning at 9.30am and Friday evening services are held at 6.30pm in winter and 8.30pm in summer.

Tortosa

The Museum of Santo Domingo Convent preserves the sixth-century gravestone of 'Meliosa, daughter of Judah of blessed memory'.

Tudela

The remains of the Juderia are near the cathedral. There is a memorial stone to the great Jewish traveller, Benjamin of Tudela author of *Book of Travels* (1172/3).

Valencia

Restaurants

Vegetarian

Buffet Chino Veg
Conde Altea 46 (96) 334-7061
La Lluna
San Ramon 23 (96) 392-214

Synagogues

Calle Asturias 7-4' (96) 334-3416
Services: Friday eve. & festivals.
Office
Calle Ingeniero Joaquin Belloch 46006 (96) 339901

Conservative

La Javura, Calle Uruguay 59,
pta 13 46007 (96) 380-2129
Web site: www.uscj.org/world/valencia
Tours of Jewish quarter. The synagogue is a room in a private home.

Orthodox - Sephardi

Comunidad Israelita de Valencia
Avenida Ingeniero Joaquin Beno,
lloch 29, 1-2a pta 46008.

Vitoria

The monument on the Campo de Judimendi commemorates the ancient Jewish cemetery. The town council undertook to take care of, and never to build over it.

Balearic Islands

Majorca

Majorca's Jewish population today numbers about 300, although fewer than a hundred are registered with the community. Founded in 1971, it was the first Jewish community in Spain to be officially recognised since 1435. The Jewish cemetery is at Santa Eugenia, some twelve miles from Palma.

Palma Cathedral containes some interesting Jewish relics, including a candelabrum with 365 lights, which was originally in a synagogue. In the 'Tesoro' room are two unique silver maces, over six feet long, converted from Torah *rimonim* brought from Sicily in 1493. The Santa Clara Church stands on the site of another pre-Inquisition synagogue. The Montezion Church was, in the fourteenth century, the Great Synagogue. In Calle San Miguel is the Church of San Miguel, which also stands on the site of a former synagogue. It is not far from the Calle de la Plateria, once a part of the Palma Ghetto.

Cemeteries

Santa Eugenia

Community Organisations

Comunidad Israelita de Mallorca
Apartado Correos 389 (971) 283799

Synagogues

Orthodox

Communidad Israelita de Mallorca (Jewish Community of Mallorca)
Palma de Mallorca 07014 (971) 283-799
Email: r_ajkatz@hotmail.com
Web site: www.fortunecity.com/victorian/coldwater/252
This synagogue was dedicated to the community in June 1987. Services are held on Fridays and Holy-days. A communal seder is also held. The community invites all congregants and guests to kiddush following the services.

Canary Islands

The first Jewish immigrants to the Canary Islands were *Conversos* from Spain seeking refuge from the Inquisition.

Las Palmas De Gran Canaria

Synagogues

Ap. Correos 2142, Holdings (928) 248497

Tenerife

Kashrut Information

General Mola 4, Santa Cruz,
Holdings 38006 (922) 274157
Welcomes all Jewish visitors.

Organisations

Comunidad Israelita de Tenerife
Holdings (922) 247296, 247246

Synagogues

Ap. De Correos 939 38001

Sri Lanka

Islamic and Samaritan legend relates that Adam came to the island after his expulsion from Eden and that Noah's Ark came to rest there. Solid evidence for Jewish settlement was recorded about 1,000 years ago by Muslim travellers. There was a small Jewish community when the Dutch took the island as a colony. This attracted Jews from southern India to the island because of the possibilities of trade.

There was a plan put forward when the island came under British rule for mass Jewish immigration. The Chief Justice, Sir Alexander Johnston appeared to consider the idea a serious one, but the British government did not act on it. A coffee estate was founded in 1841 near Kandy by Jews from Europe.

There is no communual organisation on the island. The Sri Lankans appear to be supportive of Israel, despite the government's official pro-Arab stance. Diplomatic relations with Israel were resumed in May 2000.

GMT + 5.5 hours
Country calling code (94)
Emergency Telephone
(Police - 433333) (Fire and Ambulance - 422222)

Total Population 17,500,000
Jewish Population Under 100
Electricity voltage 230/240

Colombo

Kashrut Information

82 Rosmead Place 7
(1) 695642
Fax: (1) 446543

Suriname

Suriname's Jewish community is a very old. The first Jews settled here in the seventeenth century, escaping from persecution in Brazil. Later Jews came Britain, after the country had passed into British hands. Suriname welcomed more Jewish refugees from the Caribbean, and when the country became a Dutch colony in 1668 there was an influx bringing Sephardi Jews from Amsterdam. Eventually, half the white population in the country was Jewish, and there was a 'Jodensavanne' (Jewish savannah) where the Jews owned large sugar plantations. They called the plantations by Hebrew names and built a synagogue in 1685. The community began to decline in the nineteenth century. Recently, many have emigrated to Israel.

Today, there are two synagogues in Paramaribo, the capital. The Ashkenazi synagogue, like the one in Curaçao, has a sandy floor, which is symbolic of the forty years in the desert and was also said to have muffled the footsteps of the *Conversos* as they carried out their Judaism in secret.

GMT - 3 hours
Country calling code (597)
Electricity voltage 110/220

Total Population 417,000
Jewish Population 200

Paramaribo

Kashrut Information

Commewijnestr. 21
(6) 400236
Fax: (6) 471154

Organisations

Suriname Jewish Community

Keizerstraat 82-84
(597) 400236/473896
Fax: (597) 402380/471154

Synagogues

Ashkenazi

Neveh Shalom
Keizerstr. 82
Services are held every Shabbat in each synagogue alternately.

Sephardi

Sedek Ve Shalom
Herenstr. 20
The entire contents of this eighteenth century synagogue are currently on 'long term loan' to the Israel Museum in Jerusalem. It is now being used as an Internet café.

Tourist Sites

Sights to see include Joden Savanah (Jewish Savanah), one of the oldest Jewish settlements in the Americas.

Sweden

Sweden was under the influence of the Lutheran church until the late eighteenth century and was opposed to Jewish settlement. Aaron Isaac from Mecklenburg in Germany, a seal engraver, was the first Jew admitted into the country, in 1774. The emancipation of Jews in Sweden was a slow process; Jews had limited rights, as they were designated a 'foreign colony'. After a gradual lifting of restrictions in the nineteenth century, Jews were fully emancipated in 1870, although the right to hold ministerial office was closed to them until 1951.

Emancipation heralded the growth of the community, and many Eastern European Jews found refuge in Sweden at the beginning of the twentieth century. The initial refusal to accept Jews fleeing the Nazis changed to sympathy as evidence for the Holocaust mounted, and in 1942 many Jews and other refugees were allowed into the country, followed, in 1943, by almost all of Danish Jewry. Sweden also accepted Hungarian, Czechoslovakian and Polish Jews after the War.

There is an Offical Council of Jewish Communities in Sweden, and many international Jewish groups, are represented. There are three synagogues in Stockholm, including the imposing Great Synagogue built in 1870. There are synagogues in other large towns. Although *shechita* is forbidden, kosher food is imported, and there are some kosher shops.

GMT + 1 hour
Country calling code (46)
Emergency Telephone (Police, fire and Ambulance - 112)

Total Population 8,910,000
Jewish Population 18,000
Electricity voltage 220

Boras

Organisations

Jewish Community of Boras & Synagogue
Varbergsvagen 21, Box 46 50305 (33) 124892
Email: s. rytz@vertextrading.se

Gothenburg

Groceries

Dr. Allards
gata 4 (31) 741-1545

Media

Radio

Thursdays at 9pm on 94.4 MHz.

Organisations

Jewish Community Centre and Community Offices
Ostra Larmgatan 12 S-411 07 (31) 177245
Fax: (31) 7119360
Email: kansli@judforsgot.o.se

Synagogues

Conservative

Ostra Larmgatan 12 S-411 07 (31) 177245
Fax: (31) 711-9360
Email: kansli@judforsgot.o.se

Orthodox

Storgatan 5

Sweden

Helsingborg

Organisations

Jewish Centre
Springpostgranden 4

Lund

Synagogues

Orthodox

Winstrupsgatan 1 (46) 148052
Services on festivals and High Holy-days only.

Malmo

Mikvaot

Kamrergatan 11 (40) 118860

Organisations

Jewish Community Centre
Kamrergatan 11,
Box 4198 20313 (40) 611 6460; 8860; 976043
Fax: (40) 234-469
Email: rabeli@alfa.telenordia.se

Synagogues

Orthodox

Foreningsgatan

Stockholm

Stockholm has a number of Jewish facilities. In addition the Raoul Wallenberg Park is worth a visit.

Embassy

Embassy of Israel
Torstenssongatan 4,
PO Box 14006 104 40 (8) 663-1465
Fax: (8) 662-5301
Email: israel.embassy.swipnet.se

Gift Shop

Menorah: Community Centre Shop
Judaica House, Nybrogatan 19, PO Box 5053 102 42
(8) 663-6580

Groceries

Kosherian Blecher & Co
Nybrogatan 19, PO Box 5053 102 42 (8) 663-6580
Fax: (8) 663-6580
Kosher groceries. Also offers cooked meals such as burgers, sausages, meat sandwiches etc. Delivery to group, hotels etc.

Kashrut Information

Rabbi Meir Horden
Community House, Wahrendorffsgatan 3B,
PO Box 7427 (8) 679-2900
Email: info@judiskacentret.a.se
Rabbi Meir Horden supervises kashrut in Stockholm. Look in to www.jf-stockholm.org/kosher for the latest updated information or contact the Jewish Community Centre (+46 8 587 85800).

Libraries

The Jewish Library
Wahrendorffsgatan 3,
PO Box 7427 103 91
(8) 587858 34
Fax: (8) 587-858 51
Email: judiska.biblioteket@jf-stockholm.org
Raoul Wallenberg Room also on premises, named after the Swedish diplomat who saved scores of thousands of Hungarian Jews from the Nazis, was arrested by the Russians in Budapest in 1945 and disappeared.

Media

Judisk Kronika
PO Box 5053 102 42 (8) 660-3872
Fax: (8) 660-3892
Email: judisk.kronika@swipnet.se

Menorah
PO Box 5053 102 42 (8) 667-6770
Fax: (8) 663-7676
Email: kh-uia@swipnet.se
Web site: www.menorah-sweden.com

Mikvaot

Community Centre
Judaica House, Nybrogatan 19 102 42
The Mikva is located in the Judaica House. To get in touch with Balanit, please contact the Jewish Community Centre (+46 8 587 85867).

Monument

The Holocaust Monument
Wahrendorffsgatan 3
The monument was opened in 1998 by King Carl XVI Gustaf of Sweden, and records over 8,000 holocaust victims who are relatives of Jews residing in Sweden.

Museums

Jewish Museum
Halsingegatan 2 (8) 318 404
Fax: (8) 318404
Email: info@judiska-museet.a.se
Web site: www.judiska-museet.a.se
Arranges exhibitions about the history of Swedish Jewry and is open every day, except Saturday, between noon and 4pm.

Organisations

Jewish Community Centre
Judaica House, Nybrogatan 19,
PO Box 5053 102 42 (8) 587-85867, 587-85870
Fax: (8) 667-3755
Email: info@jf-stockholm.org
Web site: www.jf-stockholm.org

Jewish Community of Stockholm
Wahrendorffsgatan 3,
PO Box 7427 103 91 (8) 5878-5800
Fax: (8) 5878-5858
Email: info@jf-stockholm.org
Web site: www.jf-stockholm.org
Open Monday to Thursday 9am-5pm Friday 9am-4pm (closed for lunch noon-1pm).

Restaurants

Community Centre
Nybrogatan 19 102 42 (8) 663-6566, 662-6686
Fax: (8) 667-3755
Email: info@judishacentret.a.se
Kosher lunches under Rabbi Meir Horden's supervision at the Community Centre are available during the summer. Dinners can be arranged at the Community Centre for groups. Contact Mr Ike Tankus. Tel: 647-4475, or email enkus@telia.com

Lao Wai
Luntmakargatan 74 (8) 673-7800
Supervision: Rabbi Meir Honden.

Mino's Café
Tegnergatan 36 (8) 30 77 42
Jewish North African Cuisine. All meats kosher but no kosher licence.

Synagogues

Masorti

Great Synagogue
Wahrendorffsgatan 3,
PO Box 7427 103 91 (8) 5878-5800
Fax: (8) 5878-5850
Email: kansli@jf-stockholm.org
Services: Monday, Thursday morning, Friday evenings & Saturday morning. Open to tourists Monday - Friday from 10 am till 2 pm.

Orthodox

Adat Jeshurun
Riddargatan 5, PO Box 5053 102 42 (8) 679-2900
Fax: (8) 663-6580
Daily services: Weekdays 7.45 am, Shabat 9 am, Sunday 8.30 am.

Adat Jisroel
St. Paulsgatan 13 118 46 (8) 679-2900
Daily Services: weekdays 7.30am, Shabbat 9.00am, Sunday 8.15am

Uppsala

Organisations

Jewish Students Club.
Dalgatan 15 (8) 125453

Switzerland

Swiss Jewry originated in the Middle Ages and their history followed the standard course of medieval European Jewry-working as money lenders and pedlars; being attacked by the local population (who accused them of causing the Black Death); then resettling a few years afterwards, only to be subsequently expelled.

By the late eighteenth century, when the Helvetic Confederation was formed, there were three small communities. Freedom of movement was allowed, and full emancipation was granted in 1866. Theodor Herzl held the first World Zionist Conference in Basle in 1897.

Although Switzerland accepted some refugees from Nazism, many were refused, and most of the new refugee Jewish population emigrated soon after the War. The community today has a central body, and is made up of various factions, from Ultra-Orthodox to Reform. The major towns have synagogues, and kosher meat is imported. There are several hotels with kosher facilities. Over half of the community live in the German-speaking area, the French-speaking area has the second largest number, and a small population is found in the southern, Italian-speaking area.

Switzerland has elected its first Jewish (and first female) president, Ruth Dreifuss.

GMT + 1 hour — Total Population 7,386,000
Country calling code (41) — Jewish Population 18,000
Emergency Telephone (Police - 117) (Fire - 118) (Ambulance - 144) — Electricity voltage 220

Switzerland

Arosa

Hotels

Levin's Hotel Metropol

(81) 377-4444
Fax: (81) 377-2100

Mikva on premises. Own kosher bakery.

Baden

Caterer

Atrium Hotel Blume
Kurplatz 4 5400 (56) 222-5569
Fax: (56) 222-4298
Email: atriumhotel_blume@bluewin.ch

Prepacked kosher meals on request

Synagogues

Israelitische Kultusgemeinde Baden
Parkstrasse 17 5400 (56) 221-5128
Fax: (56) 222-9447
Email: ikgb@dplanet.ch

Friday nights: Winter 6.30 pm; Summer 7.30 pm.
Shabbat and Festivals: mornings 8.45 am.

Basle

Bakeries

Bakery Schmutz
Austrasse 53 (61) 272-4765
IGB & IRG (61) 272-6365

Books and Judaica

Victor Goldschmidt
Mostackerstrasse 17 4051 (61) 261 61 91
Fax: (61) 261 61 23

Butchers

Genossenschaftsmetzgerei
Friedrichstrasse 26 4055 (61) 301-3493
Fax: (61) 381-6939

Supervision: Both Basel Rabbinates.
Also sells groceries and wine. Open 7.30am-12.00 noon, 3pm-6.00. Closed Friday afternoon.

Hotels

Hotel Euler
Centralbahnplatz 14 4002 (61) 275-8000
Fax: (61) 275-8050

Offers kosher meals on request. Has a synagogue and Mikva on the premises.

Media

Newspapers

Judische Rundschau Maccabi
Austr. 25 4009 (61) 206-6060
Fax: (61) 206-6060

Mikvaot

Thannerstrasse 60 (61) 301-2220
Eulerstr. 10 4051 (61) 301-6831

Museums

Jewish Museum of Switzerland
Kornhausgasse 8 4051 (61) 261-9514

Hours: Monday and Wednesday, 2 pm to 5 pm; Sunday, 11 am to 5 pm. Free entrance.

Restaurants

Restaurant Topas
Leimenstrasse 24 4051 (61) 206-9500
Fax: (61) 206-9501
Email: info@restaurant-topas.ch
Web site: www.restaurant-topas.ch

Supervision: Under the supervision of local rabbinical authority.
Hours: 11:30 am to 2 pm Sunday to Friday. 6:30 pm to 9 pm Sunday to Thursday. Friday night, Shabbat lunch and holidays by reservation before 2 pm of preceding day.

Synagogues

Israelitische Gemeinde Basel
Leimenstrasse 24 4003 (61) 279-9850
Fax: (61) 279-9851
Email: igb@igb.ch

Israelitische Religionsgesellschaft
Ahornstrasse 14 (61) 301-4898

Rabbi, Tel: 41-61-302-1434.

Bern

Embassy

Embassy of Israel
Alpenstrasse 32 3006 (31) 356-3500
Fax: (31) 356-3556
Email: info@emb.israel.ch

Synagogues

Synagogue & Community Center
Kapellenstrasse 2 (31) 381-4992
Fax: (31) 382-3861
Email: info@jgb.ch
Web site: www.jgb.ch

Rabbiner Dr Michael Leipziger, Tel: 41-31 381-7303.

Biel/Bienne

Synagogues

Ruschlistrasse 3 (32) 342-3670

Bremgarten / Aargau

Contact Information

Israelitische Cultusgemeinde
Werner Meyer-Moses,
Ringstrasse. 37 CH-5620 (56) 633-6626
Fax: (56) 633-6626

Synagogues

Luzernstr. 1

Davos

Hotels

Etania (81) 416-5404
Fax: (81) 416-2592
Email: etania@bluewin.ch
Supervision: Zurich Rabbinate.

Endingen

Contact Information

J. Bloch
Buckstr. 2 5304 (56) 242-1546
Can arrange visits to the old synagogues and cemetery.

Engelberg

Hotels

Hotel Marguerite
6390 Engelberg (41) 637-2522
Fax: (41) 637-2926
Supervision: Agudas Achim, Zurich.
Mikva on premises.

Fribourg

Synagogues

9 avenue de Rome (26) 322-1670

Geneva

Butchers

Boucherie Kosher
Biton 21, rue de Montchoisi (22) 736-3168

Embassy

Permanent Mission of Israel to the United Nations
9 Chemin Bonvent, Cointrin 1216

Media

Israelitsches Wochenblatt/Revue Juive
Avenue du Mail 5 1205 (22) 800-1026
Fax: (22) 800-1028
Revue Juive/Israelitisches Wochenblatt
10 rue de Beulet, 1211 1211 (22) 940-2025
Fax: (22) 940-2028

Mikvaot

(22) 346-9732
Fax: (22) 736-9632

Restaurants

Le Jardin Rose
10, rue St-Leger (22) 310-4686
Fax: (22) 317-8910
Only open for lunch but arrangements can be made so that lunches and dinners can be delivered to any hotel downtown.
Restaurant Le Neguev
Rue de la Servette 20 1201 (22) 740-4070
Supervision: Rabbi A Y Schlesinger.
Near to the town centre and 200 yards from the train station.

Meat

Heimishe Kitchen
Av Jules Crosnier 4 1206 (22) 346-1741
Fax: (22) 346-0830
Supervision: Machsike Hadas.

Synagogues

Liberal

12 Quai du Seujet (22) 732-3245

Orthodox

Beth Habad
12 rue du Lac (22) 736-3682
The Geneva Synagogue (Ashkenazi)
Place de la Synagogue
Machsike Hadass
2 place des Eaux Vives 1207 (22) 786-2589

Sephardi

Hekhal Haness
54 ter route de Malagnou (22) 736-9632

Kreuzlingen

Contact Information

Louis Hornung
Schulstr. 7 (71) 671-1630

La-Chaux-de-Fonds

Synagogues

Rue de Parc 63 2300 (039) 231-794

Lausanne

Community Organisations

Communauté Israélite de Lausanne
3 avenue Georgette 1001 (21) 341-7240
Fax: (21) 341-7241
Email: secretariat.cil@vtx.ch

Groceries

Kolbo Shalom
7 avenue Juste-Olivier (21) 312-1265

Switzerland

Mikvaot
1 avenue Juste-Olivier (21) 617-5818

Restaurants
Community Centre
3 avenue Georgette 1003 (21) 341-7242
Serves lunch only, from 12 pm to 2 pm.

Synagogues
Orthodox

1 avenue Juste-Olivier (21) 320-9911
Cnr J. Olivier and av. Florimont.

Lengnau

Contact Information
(56) 241-1203
For visits to the old synagogue and cemetery.

Lucerne

Butchers
Judische Metzgerei
Bruchstrasse 26 (41) 240-2560

Mikvaot
Bruchstrasse 51 (41) 320-4750

Synagogues
Bruchstrasse 51 (41) 240-6400

Lugano

Hotels
Hotel Dan
Via Fontana 1 6902 (91) 985-7030
Fax: (91) 985-7031
Email: danlugano@yahoo.com
Web site: pibt.de/l/dan.htm
Kashrut under the supervision of the rabbinat Lugano's Jewish Community.

Kashrut Information
via Olgiati 1 (91) 922-9955
Monday-Thursday 5.30pm-7pm

Kosher Food
Koschere Lebensmittel erhaltlich bei
Frutor SA via Bagutti 4 (91) 922-8522

Mikvaot
Via Maderno 11 (91) 923-8952

Synagogues
Via Maderno 11 (91) 923-5698
Via Maderno 11 (91) 932-6134

Solothurn

Contact Information
R. Dreyfus
Grenchenstr. 8 (32) 623-2327

St Gallen

Synagogues
Frongartenstrasse 18 (71) 223-5923

St Moritz

Hotels
Bermann's Hotel Edelweiss
(81) 836-5555
Fax: (81) 833-5556

Winterthur

Synagogues
Rosenstrasse 5 (52) 232-8136

Yverdon

Contact Information
Dr Maurice Ellkan
1400 Cheseaux-Noreaz (24) 425-1851

Zug

Restaurants
Restaurant Glashof
Baarerstr. 41 6301 (42) 221-248
Prepared kosher meals are available.

Zurich

Jews first arrived in Zurich in 1273. Over the following two centuries Jews were repeatedly expelled and allowed to return. There are five stained glass Chagall windows in the Fraumunster Church (located in Munsterhof Square) of which four are on themes from the Hebrew Bible.

Bakeries
Ruben Bollag
Brauerstrasse 110 8004 (1) 242-8700
Fax: (1) 291-4684

Ruben Bollag
Waffenplatzstrasse 5, (near Bahnhof Enge)
8002 (1) 202-3045

Booksellers
Morascha
Seestrasse 11 8002 (1) 201.11.20
Fax: (1) 201.31.20
Email: morascha@bluemail.ch
Web site: www.morascha.com
Supervision: Monday, Tuesday and Thursday 9am to 12noon and 2pm to 6.30pm, Wednesday 9am to 6.30pm and Friday 9am to 12 noon.

Butchers
Taam/Metzgerei
(1) 463-9094
Supervision: Judische Gemeinde Agudas Achim.

Zukom
8 Aemtlerst (1) 451-8384
Fax: (1) 451-8386
Supervision: Judische Gemeinde Aguda Achim and Israelitsche Religionsgellschaft..

Groceries

Jelmoli Department Store
Bahnhofstrasse
Has a kosher section.

Pick and Pay
Lavaterstrasse
Has a kosher section.

Hotels

Hotel International
(1) 311-4341
Offers kosher meals on request.

Media

Israelitisches Wochenblatt/Revue Juive
Rudigerstr 10, Postfach 8027 (1) 206-4200
Fax: (1) 206-4210
Email: redaktion@tachles.ch

Jewish City Guide of Switzerland
Spectrum Press International, Im Tannegg 1, Friesenbergstrasse 221 8055
(1) 462-6411; 462-6412
Fax: (1) 462-6462
Email: info@jewishguide.ch
Web site: www.jewishguide.ch
Published quarterly in English and German, a guide to Jewish communities throughout Switzerland.

Mikvaot

Freigutstrasse 37 (1) 201-7306
Appointment by phone between 9am & 11am.

Restaurants

Restaurant Schalom
G. van Dijk Lavaterstrasse 33-37 8002 (1) 283-2233
Fax: (1) 283-2234
Email: catering.schalom@bleuwin.ch

Dairy

Fein & Schein
Schontalstrasse 14, Corner/
Ecke Hallwylstrasse (1) 241-3040
Fax: (1) 241-2112
Supervision: IRGZ Rabbi Daniel Levy.

Meat

Club Savjon
G. van Dijk-Neufeld., Lavaterstr. 33 (1) 201-1476
Fax: (1) 201-1496
Email: catering.schalom@bluewin.ch
Supervision: Rabbi Rothschild.

Synagogues

Freigutstrasse 37 (1) 201-4998

Beth Hamidrash, Chasidei Gur
(1) 242-3899

Chabad Minjan Esra
(1) 386-8403

Israel, Religionsgesellschaft
Freigutstrasse 37 8002 (1) 201-6746

Israelitische Cultusgemeinde
Lavaterstrasse 33 8002 (1) 201-1659
Fax: (1) 202-2287
Email: info@icz.org

Judische Gemeinde Agudas Achim
Erikastrasse 8 8003 (1) 463-5798

Minjan Bels
Weststrasse 151 (1) 463-6598

Minjan Brunau
Mutschellenstrasse 11-15 (1) 202-5167

Minjan Machsikei Hadass
Anwandstrasse 60 (1) 241-3759
Rabbi Schmerler: 01-242-9046

Minjan Wollishofen
Etzelstrasse 6 8038 (1) 289-7050
Email: minjan.wollishofen@schweiz.ch
Chabad Lubavitch. Contact person Gabai H Horgenbesser.

Taiwan

Taiwan

The US Army brought the first Jews to Taiwan in the 1950s, when an American base, now closed, was set up in the country. In the 1970s, some Jewish businessmen began to work on the island, serving two- or three-year contracts with their companies. Most are Americans, although there are some Israelis and other nationalities. Services are held on the Shabbat in a hotel, and there is a Jewish community centre.

GMT + 8 hours
Country calling code (886)
Emergency Telephone (Police - 110) (Fire and Ambulance - 119)

Total Population 21,000,000
Jewish Population Under 100
Electricity voltage 110

Taipei

Organisations

Taiwan Jewish Community Centre
No 1, Lane 61, Teh Hsing East Road,
Shihlin (2) 396-0159
Fax: (2) 396-4022

Services are held on most Friday evenings at 7.30pm. Visitors to check in advance. All Holy Days and major festivals are celebrated.

Restaurants

Meat

Y.Y.'s Steakhouse
Chungshan North Road, Section 3,
cnr. The Huei St.

There are no supervised kosher restaurants in Taipei, but this steakhouse has a separate kitchen and dining room, where kosher meat meals are served on separate crockery, with separate cutlery. No milk products are available in this section.

Synagogues

Orthodox

Ritz Landis Hotel
41 Min Chuan East Road (2) 2597-1234
Fax: (2) 2596-9223
Email: ritz@theritz-taipei.com

Shabbat and festival services are held here, also, when minyan is available, Weekday Services.

Tajikistan

One of the former Soviet Republics, Tajikistan has a small Jewish population but, after the fall of the Soviet Union, many Jews emigrated to Israel. The community is a mix of forty per cent Bokharans and sixty per cent Soviet Jews from other parts of the former USSR who migrated to Tajikistan during the Second World War. The Bokharan Jews are believed to be descendants of Persian Jewish exiles. Dushanbe, the capital, and Shakhrisabz are provided with synagogues, and Dushanbe also has a Jewish library.

GMT + 5 hours
Country calling code (7)
Electricity voltage 220

Total Population 6,188,000
Jewish Population 1,200

Dushanbe

Synagogues

Ashkenazi

Proletarsky Street

Bokharan

Nazyina Khikmeta Street 26

Shakhrisabz

Synagogues

23 Bainal Minal Street

Thailand

Although the first confirmed presence of Jews in Thailand was in 1890, Thai Jewry really began with Jews who escaped from Russia and Eastern Europe in the 1920s and 1930s; but most of these emigrated after 1945.

The present community arrived in the post-War period of the 1950s and 1960s. They came from Syria and Lebanon, and also Europe, America and Israel. Jewellery is an important source of trade with Israel. Another relatively large influx came in 1979 as Jews left Iran after the fall of the Shah.

Bangkok has Ashkenazi, Sephardi and Lubavitch synagogues. The community centre is based in the Ashkenazi synagogue. The Lubavitch synagogue offers several communual activities, including Seders at Passover, which have a large attendance.

GMT + 7 hours — Total Population 61,399,000
Country calling code (66) — Jewish Population 250
Electricity voltage 220

Bangkok

Bakeries

Kosher Store and Bakery
223 Soi Sai, Nam Thip 2 (Soi 22), Sukhumvit (2) 663-8719
Hours 9 am to 5 pm.

Embassy

Embassy of Israel
'Ocean Tower II' 25th floor,
75 Sukhumvit Soi 19, Asoke Road 10110
(2) 204-9200
Fax: (2) 204-9255
Email: consul.bkk@israelfm.org

Kashrut Information

(2) 237-1697
(2) 318-1577
(2) 234-0606

Organisations

Jewish Community of Thailand
Beth Elisheva Building, 121 Soi Sai, Nam Thip 2, Sukhumvit Soi 22 (2) 663-0244
Fax: (2) 663-0245
Email: ykantor@ksc15.th.com
Web site: www.jewishthailand.com
Friday night and Shabbat services with Kiddush and Shabbat meal. Holidays services. Call to confirm.

Restaurants

Ohr Menachem - Chabad House
108/1 Ram Buttri Rd, Kaosarn Road, Banglampoo (2) 282-6388
Fax: (2) 629-1153
Supervision: Rabbi Y. Kantor.
Open 12 noon to 9 pm daily.

Synagogues

Orthodox

Beth Elisheva
121 Soi Sai Nam Thip 2, Sukhumvit Soi 22 (2) 663-0244
Fax: (2) 663-0245
Email: ykantor@ksc15.th.com
Close to Imperial Queens Park, Jade Pavilion, Rembrandt, Landmark and Sheraton Grande Hotels. Friday night service at candle lighting time followed by Shabbat meal and Shabbat services 10.00 am with Kiddush and Shabbat meal. Call to confirm.

Ohr Menachem - Chabad House
108/1 Ram Buttri Road, Kaosarn Road, Banglampoo (2) 282-6388
Fax: (2) 629-1153
Email: chabadbangkok@yahoo.com
Daily services, Friday evenings at sundown with Shabbat meal, attracts young Jewish travellers.

Even Chen
The Bossotel Inn, 55/12-14 Soi Charoenkrung, 42/1 New Road (Silom Road area) (2) 630-6120
Fax: (2) 237-3225
Daily morning service. Regular Friday evening and Shabbat morning, afternoon and evening services. Light kosher meal after Shabbat service, by advance reservation.

Tunisia

There is written proof of ancient Jewish settlement in Carthage in the year 200 CE, when the region was under Roman control. The community was successful and was left in peace. Under the Byzantine Empire, conditions for the Jews did worsen; but after the Islamic conquest the 'golden age' of Tunisian Jewry occurred. There was prosperity and many centres of learning were established. This did not continue into the Middle Ages, as successive Arab and Spanish invasions led to discrimination. Emancipation came with the French, but the community suffered under the Nazi-influenced Vichy government. After the War, many people emigrated to Israel or to France and the community is currently shrinking.

There are several synagogues in the country, together with kindergartens and schools. Tunisia is not as extreme in its attitude towards Israel as some Arab states, and there has been communication between the two countries at a high level. An Israeli Interest Bureau in Tunis acts as an unofficial embassy. The Bardo Museum in Tunis has an exhibition of Jewish ritual objects.

GMT + 1 hour — Total Population 9,586,000
Country calling code (216) — Jewish Population 2,000
Electricity voltage 220

Jerba

There are Jews in two villages on this small island off the Tunisian coast. There is also a magnificent synagogue, El Ghriba, which is many hundreds of years old, in the village of Er-Riadh (Hara Sghira). Jewish silversmiths are prominent in Hournt souk on rue Bizerte.

Sfax

Synagogues

Azriah
71 rue Habib Mazoun
Near the Town Hall.

Tunis

Kashrut Information

26 rue de Palestine — (1) 282406; 283540

Organisations

Community Offices
15 rue de Cap Vert — (1) 282469, 287153

Synagogues

Beth Yacob
3 rue Eve, Nohelle — (1) 348964

Grande
43 Av. de la Liberte

Lubavitch Yeshiva
73 rue de Palestine — (1) 791429

Turkey

There have been Jews in Turkey since at least the fourth century BCE, making Turkey one of the earliest Jewish communities. The fifteenth and sixteenth centuries were periods of major prosperity for the Jews of Turkey.

After the Expulsion of the Jews from Spain in 1492, at a time when Jews were not tolerated in most of the Christian countries of Western Europe, what was then the Ottoman (Turkish) Empire was their principal land of refuge. The Sultan was reported to have said of the Spanish King: 'By expelling the Jews, he has impoverished his country and enriched mine'.

In 1992 they celebrated the 500th anniversary of the establishment of the community. Under the national constitution, their civil rights were reconfirmed. In recent years, many Jews have emigrated to Israel, Western Europe and the United States.

GMT + 2 hours — Total Population 66,591,000
Country calling code (90) — Jewish Population 20,000
Emergency Telephone (Police - 155) (Fire - 110) (Ambulance - 112) — Electricity voltage 220

Ankara

Embassy

Embassy of Israel
Mahatma Gandhi Sok 85, Gaziosmanpasa
(312) 446-3605
Fax: (312) 446-8071

Synagogues

Birlik Sokak,
Samanpazari (312) 311-6200
This synagogue is not easy to find. Off Anafartalar Caddesi in Samanpazari, there is a stairway down at the right of the TC Ziraat Bankasi. The synagogue is several buildings along the street on the left, behind a wall. Services every morning Sabbath morning services begin at 7 or 7.30am depending on the time of year.

Balat

A coastal town about twenty miles west of Istanbul which has a 500-year-old synagogue. The synagogue is now closed and the keys are with the mosque next door.

Bursa

Synagogues

Gerush Synagogue
Kurucesme Caddesi (224) 368-636
Services on Friday evening, Shabbat morning and festivals. This Synagogue is in the old Jewish quarter. There are 180 Jews in this town.

Istanbul

Community Organisations

Buyuk Hendek
Sokak No 61, Galata (212) 293-7566
Secretary General: Lina Filiba

Embassy

Consul General of Israel
Valikonag Caddesi No 73 (212) 255-1040
Fax: (212) 225-1048
Email: isrcon@comnet.com.tr

Religious Organisations

Chief Rabbinate
Yemenici Sokak 23, Beyoglu,
Tunel 80050 (212) 293-8794/5
Fax: (212) 244-1980

Restaurants

Meat

Carne
Muallimnaci. Cad. 41/10 (212) 260-8425

Robelyu
Omerpasa Cad 38/1 (216) 385-7181
Supervision: Istanbul Rabbinate.

Synagogues

Askenazi Synagogue
Yuksekkaldinm Sok No 37,
Galata (212) 243-6909
Saturdays only.
Beth Israel
Efe Sok No 4, Sisli (212) 240-6599
Every day.
Caddesbostan Synagogue
Tasmektep Sok, Goztepe (212) 356-5922
Every day.
Etz Ahayim Synagogue
Muallim Naci Cad No 40 & 41,
Ortakoy (212) 260-1896
Every day.
Hemdat Israel Synagogue
Izettin Sok No 65, Kadikoy (212) 336-5293
Every day.
Hesed Leavraam Synagogue
Pancur Sok No 15, Buyukada (212) 382-5788
June-September including High Holy days.
Italian Synagogue
Sair Ziya Pasa Yokusu No 27,
Karakoy, Galata (212) 293-7784
Neve Shalom Buyuk Hendek Sok
No 61, Galata (212) 293-7566
Saturdays only.

Izmir

Butchers

Kosher Meat (232) 148-395
Tuesday and Thursday. Inquire at the synagogue.

Community Organisations

Jewish Community Council
Azizler Sokak 920/44, Guzelyurt (232) 123-708
Fax: (232) 421-1290

Synagogues

Beth Israel
265 Mithatpasa Street, Karatas, Kanamursil District
Shaar Ashamayan
1390 Sokak 4/2, Bikur Holim

Ukraine

Ukraine

The Ukraine has had a long and complicated history, with areas of the present country being under the rule of a number of other countries, from Austria to Romania. The history of the Jews who live in the modern-day, independent Ukraine is both long and tragic. From settlement in Kiev in the tenth century, before the concept of a Ukrainian national identity had been formed, the Jewish community grew and was joined by many Jews from Central Europe. The Chmielnicki massacre of 1648, in which up to 100,000 were killed, was the worst event to befall the Jews before the Holocaust, and much destruction occurred in the west of the country.

Throughout the nineteenth century, the Ukraine was mainly under Russian domination. After 1918, the Ukraine attempted to become independent, and many Jews were killed in the fighting. The Ukraine absorbed some of south-eastern Poland in 1939 and, after the German invasion of the Soviet Union, the Jewish community suffered terrible losses in the Holocaust.

The community today remains fairly large, and is slowly emerging from the period of atheist Soviet rule. Most Jews live in towns, and Kiev (the capital) is a major centre. There are now Jewish schools, and kosher food can be obtained. As in Belarus, there are many interesting places to visit; the graves of famous Hassidic masters and the monument to the Babi Yar massacre (near Kiev) are frequent destinations. There have been memorials erected (mainly after the fall of communism) all over the country to events which happened during the Holocaust.

GMT + 2 hours	Total Population 50,456,000
Country calling code (380)	Jewish Population 180,000
Emergency Telephone (Police - 02) (Fire - 01) Ambulance - 03)	Electricity voltage 220

Berdichev

Mikvaot

4 Dzherzhinskaya Street (4143) 23938 / 20222

Synagogues

4 Dzherzhinskaya Street (4143) 23938 / 20222

Kosher kitchen on premises.

Beregovo

Synagogues

17 Sverdlov Street

Bershad

Synagogues

25 Narodnaya Street

Chernigov

Synagogues

34 Kommunisticheskaya Street

Chernovtsy

Synagogues

24 Lukyana Kobylitsa Street 54878

Chmelnitsy

Synagogues

58 Komminnestnaya Street

Dnepropetrovsk

Synagogues

Synagogue of Dnepropetrovsk

7 Kotsubinskovo St. 320030 (562) 342-120

Fax: (562) 342-137

Email: dnepr@jewcom.dp.ua

Web site: www.jew.dp.ua

Donetsk

Synagogues

Synagogue of Donetsk

36 Oktabriskaya Street 340000 (622) 357-725

Fax: (622) 938-155

Ivano-Frankivsk

Synagogues

Synagogue of Ivano-Frankivsk

Strachenyh 7 284000 (34) 22- 23029

Fax: (34) 325-367

Rabbi Rolesnik (22-34894) is prepared to assist those doing historical or genealogical research in the Western Ukraine (Galicia).

Kharkov

Synagogues
48 Kryatkovskaya Street
Web site: www.kharkovejewish.com

Central Synagogue of Kharkov
12 Pushkinskaya St. 310057 (572) 126-526

Synagogue of Kharkov
12 Pushkinskaya Street 310057 (572) 126-526
Fax: (572) 452-140
Email: chabad@kharkov.com

Orthodox Union Project Reunite
Surnskaya 45 (572) 408-378
Fax: (572) 439-209

Kherson

Synagogues
Synagogue of Kherson
27 Gorkovo Street 325025 (552) 223-334
Fax: (552) 325-367

Kiev

Embassy
Embassy of Israel
Lesi Ukrainki 34, GPE-S 252195

Synagogues
Aish Ha-Torah Ukraine
Verhniy Val 18 (44) 417-2213

Central Synagogue of Kiev
29 Shchekovitzkaya Street (44) 417-3583

Reform
Reform Congregation
7 Nemanskaya Street (44) 296-3961
Fax: (44) 295-9604

Korosten

Synagogues
8 Shchoksa Street

Kremenchug

Synagogues
50 Sverdlov Street

Lviv

Situated on the edge of shifting imperial boundaries, this city has been under Austrian, Polish and Soviet control. It has had as many names as rulers, among them Lwów in Polish and Lemberg in German. Now called Lviv in Ukrainian. there are 6,000 Jews in the city, once a major Jewish centre in Galicia. A couple of synagogues are still functioning, and a number of monuments have been erected to commemorate the Holocaust. Many Jews on 'heritage tours' use the town as a base to explore the region, and guides (generally Yiddish-speaking) are available.

Synagogues
4 Brativ Michnovskich Street 79018 (32) 333-535
Fax: (32) 333-535
Email: bald@link.lviv.ua
Restaurant - orders must be placed in advance. Tourist information.

Nikolayev

Synagogues
Synagogue of Nikolayev
13 Karl Libknechta Street 327001 (512) 358-310
Fax: (512) 353-072

Odessa

Synagogues
Main Synagogue
Corner of ul.Evreiskaya and ul. Richlieu

Synagogue of Odessa
21 Osipovo St. 270011 (482) 218-890
Fax: (482) 247-296

Simferopol

Synagogues
Synagogue of Simferopol
24 Mironovo Street (652) 276-932

Slavuta

Synagogues
Kuzovskaya Street 2 (447) 925-452
The first edition of Tanya was printed here by the Shapira family whose tombs are in the cemetery.

Uman

Each year followers of the Breslau Chassidic sect visit the grave of Rabbi Lachman of Breslau its founder for Rosh Hashana. In 2000 there were a reported 13,000 visitors.

Zaparozhe

Synagogues
Synagogue of Zaparozhe
22 Turgeneva Street. 330063 (612) 642-961

Zhitomir

Synagogues
59 Lubarskaya Street (412) 373-468
Reb Ze'ev Wolf, disciple of Dov Baer, is buried in the Smolanka cemetery.

Synagogue of Zhitomire
7 M. Berdishevskaya St. 262001 (412) 226-608
Fax: (412) 373-428

United Kingdom

There were probably individual Jews in England in Roman and (though less likely) in Anglo-Saxon times, but the historical records of any organised settlement start after the Normal Conquest of 1066. Jewish immigrants arrived early in the reign of William the Conqueror and important settlements came to be established in London (at a site still known as Old Jewry), Lincoln and many other centres. In 1190 massacres of Jews occurred in many cities, most notably in York. This medieval settlement was ended by Edward I's expulsion of the Jews in 1290, after which date, with rare and temporary exceptions, only converts to Christianity or secret adherents of Judaism could live in the country.

After the expulsion of the Jews from Spain in 1492 a secret *Converso* community became established in London, but the present Anglo-Jewish community dates in practice from the period of the Commonwealth. In 1650 Menasseh ben Israel, of Amsterdam, began to champion the cause of Jewish readmission to England, and in 1655 he led a mission to London for this purpose. A conference was convened at Whitehall and a petition was presented to Oliver Cromwell. Though no formal decision was then recorded, in 1656 the Spanish and Portuguese Congregation in London was organised. It was followed towards the end of the seventeenth century by the establishment of an Ashkenazi community, which increased rapidly inside London as well as throwing out offshoots before long to a number of provincial centres and seaports. The London community has, however, always comprised numerically the preponderant part of British Jewry.

Although Jews in Britain had achieved a virtual economic and social emancipation by the early nineteenth century they had not yet gained 'political emancipation'. Minor Jewish disabilities were progressively removed and Jews were admitted to municipal rights and began to win distinction in the professions.

During the nineteenth century British Jews spread out from those callings which had hitherto been regarded as characteristic of the Jews.

There has always been a steady stream of immigration into Britain from Jewish communities in Europe, originally from the Iberian Peninsula and Northern Italy, later from Western and Central Europe. The community was radically transformed by the large influx of refugees which occurred between 1881 and 1914, the result of the intensified persecution of Jews in the Russian Empire. The Jewish population rose from about 25,000 in the middle of the 19th century to nearly 350,000 by 1914. It also became far more dispersed geographically.

From 1933 a new emigration of Jews commenced, this time from Nazi persecution, and again many settled in this country. Since the end of the Second World War and notably since 1956, smaller numbers of refugees have come from Iran, Arab countries and Eastern Europe.

GMT — Total Population 58,784,000
Country calling code (44) — Jewish Population 300,000
Emergency Telephone (Police, Ambulance, Fire - 999)

England

Avon

Bristol

Bristol was one of the principal Jewish centres of medieval England. Even after the Expulsion from England in 1290 there were occasional Jewish residents or visitors. A community of Coversos lived here during the Tudor period. The next Jewish settlement in Bristol was around 1754 and its original synagogue opened in 1786. The present building dates from 1871 and incorporates fittings from the earlier building.

Delicatessens

British Hebrew Congregation (0117) 970-6938
Open alternate Sundays at 10 am.

Organisations

Hillel House
45 Oakfield Road, Clifton, BS8 2BA (0117) 946-6589

Restaurants

Vegetarian

Cherries
122 St Michaels Hill, BS2 8BU (0117) 929-3675

Millwards Vegetarian Restaurant
40 Alfred Place, Kingsdown, BS2 8HD
(0117) 924-5026

Synagogues

Bristol Hebrew Congregation
9 Park Row BS1 5LP (0117) 927-3334
Email: simon770@aol.com
Kosher shop at synagogue alternate Sundays 10 am to 11.45 am. Services: Friday night at 183 Bishop Road BS7 Summer 7.45 pm, Winter 7 pm. Saturday at synagogue 9.45 am

Progressive

Bristol & West Progressive Jewish Congregation
43 Bannerman Road, Easton, BS5 0RR
(0117) 954-1937
Email: webmaster@bwpjc.org
Web site: www.bwpjc.org
Secretary: 973-8744. Chairman: 973-9312

Bedfordshire

Luton

Synagogues

PO Box 215 LU1 1HW (01582) 25032
Fri night and Sabbath morning services. Office open 9.30am to 12.30pm on Sundays.

Berkshire

Maidenhead

Synagogues

Reform

Synagogue
Grenfell Lodge, Ray Park Road, SL6 8QX
(01628) 673012
Fax: (01628) 625536
Email: mheadsyn@aol.com
Services: Friday 8.30 pm; Saturday 10.30 am

Reading

Synagogues

Goldsmid Road RG1 7YB (0118) 9571018
Email: secretary@rhc.org.uk
Web site: www.rhc.org.uk

Thames Valley Progressive Jewish Community
6 Church Street RG (0118) 781971

Buckinghamsire

Milton Keynes

Butchers

Gilbert's Kosher Foods
Kestrel House, Mount Avenue, MK1 1LJ
(01908) 646-787
Fax: (01908) 646-788
Supervision: London Board of Shechita.

Cambridgeshire

Cambridge

Community Organisations

Cambridge L'Chaim Society
33 Bridge Street CB2 1UW (01223) 366335
Fax: (01223) 366338
Email: cambridge@.chaim.org

Cambridge University Jewish Society
33 Thompson's Lane CB5 8AQ (01223) 354783
Email: soc-cujs@lists.cam.ac.uk
Web site: www.cam.ac.uk/societies.cujs

Kosher Food

Derby Stores
Derby Street (01223) 354391
Stocks a range of kosher food and wine; fresh bread products each Thursday lunchtime. Can purchase goods to order.

Kosher Meals

(01223) 352145

There is a kosher canteen during term time serving lunch most weekdays and Friday night and Shabbat meals.

Restaurants

Vegetarian

Rainbow Café
9A Kings Parade (01223) 321551
Web site: www.rainbowcafe.co.uk
Closed Sundays.

Synagogues

Orthodox

Cambridge Synagogue
Syn/Student Centre, 3 Thompsons Lane, CB5 8AQ
(01223) 354783 or 368346 answer phone
Web site: www.cam.ac.uk/societies/cujs/h_cmmnty.htm
Daily morning and evening service during term time. Friday evening and Saturday morning during vacations, other services by arrangement.

Reform

Beth Shalom Reform Synagogue
(01223) 365614

Cumbria

Grasmere

Hotels

Vegetarian

Lancrigg Vegetarian Country House Hotel
Easedale LA22 9QN (01539) 435317

Devon

Exeter

In pre-Expulsion times, Exeter was an important Jewish centre.

Synagogues

Synagogue Place, Mary Arches Street, EX4 3BA
(01392) 251529
Fax: (01392) 01363-772338
Email: fjg@exetersynagogue.org.uk
Web site: www.exetersynagogue.org.uk
The synagogue was built in 1763, while the cemetery in Magdalen Road dates from 1757. The synagogue, a Grade II* listed building, has just had a major refurbishment.

Plymouth

The congregation was founded in 1752 and a synagogue erected ten years later. This is now the oldest Ashkenazi synagogue building in England still used for its original purpose. It is a scheduled historical monument. In 1815 Plymouth was one of the most important provincial centres of Anglo-Jewry.

Libraries

Holcenberg Collection
Plymouth Central Library, Drake Circus, PL4 8AL
(01752) 305907/8
Fax: (01752) 305905
Email: ref@plymouth.gov.uk
Web site: www.plymouth.gov.uk/star/library.htm
A Jewish collection of fiction and non-fiction books, mainly lending copies.

Restaurants

Vegetarian

Plymouth Arts Centre Vegetarian Restaurant
38 Looe Street PL4 0EB (01752) 202-616
Hours: lunch, Monday to Saturday, 12 pm to 2 pm; dinner, Tuesday to Saturday, 5 pm to 8 or 8.30 pm.

Synagogues

Ashkenazi

Plymouth Hebrew Congregation
Catherine Street PL1 2AD (01752) 301955
Email: info@plymouthsynagogue.co.uk
Services: Fri., 6pm; Sat., 9:30am. The congregation offers free use of minister's modern flat as holiday accommodation in return for conducting Orthodox Friday evening and Saturday morning services.

Torquay

Synagogues

Old Town Hall, Abbey Road, TQ1 1BB (1803) 607197
Covering also Brixham and Paignton. Services first Sabbath of every month and festivals, 10.30 am.

Dorset

Bournemouth

The Bournemouth Hebrew Congregation was established in 1905, when the Jewish population numbered fewer than twenty families. Today, the town's permanent Jewish residents number 3,500 out of a total population of some 15,000. During the holiday season, however, there are many more Jews in Bournemouth, for it is an extremely popular resort, with kosher hotels, guest houses and other holiday accommodation.

Delicatessens

Louise's Butchers & Deli
164 Old Christchurch Road BH1 1NU
(01202) 295-979
Fax: (01202) 295-979

Hotels

Kosher

New Ambassador Hotel
Meyrick Road, East Cliff, BH1 3DP (01202) 555-453
Fax: (01202) 311-077
Web site: www.newamb.cjb.net

Supervision: London Beth Din.
112 rooms, all with bathroom en suite.

Normandie Hotel
Manor Road, East Cliff, BH1 3HL (01202) 552-246
Fax: (01202) 291-178

Supervision: Kedassia.
71 rooms.

Mikvaot

Orthodox

Bournemouth Hebrew Congregation
Synagogue Chambers
Wootton Gardens, BH1 1PW (01202) 557-443

Organisations

Bournemouth Jewish Representative Council
(01202) 762101

Synagogues

Orthodox

Bournemouth Hebrew Congregation
Synagogue Chambers
Wootton Gardens, BH1 1PW (01202) 557-433
Fax: (01202) 557-578
Email: bhc.1@virgin.net

Reform

Bournemouth Reform Synagogue
53 Christchurch Road BH1 3PN (01202) 557736

Essex

Basildon

Synagogues

Affiliated

Basildon Hebrew Congregation
3 Furlongs SS16 4BW (01268) 524947
Fax: (01268) 271358
Email: max.kochmann@btinternet.com

Chigwell

Synagogues

Limes Avenue, Limes Farm Estate, IG7 5NT

Harlow

Synagogues

Reform

Harlow Jewish Community
Harberts Road CM20 4DT (01279) 432503

Hornchurch

Synagogues

Affiliated

Elm Park Synagogue
Woburn Avenue Elm Park, RM12 4NG
(01708) 449305

Loughton

Synagogues

Loughton, Chigwell & District Synagogue
Borders Lane IG10 1TE (0208) 508-0303
Friday evening 8 pm; Saturday morning 9.30 am.

Redbridge

Groceries

Brownstein's
24a Woodford Avenue, Gants Hill, (020) 8550-3900
Email: deli@brownsteins.co.uk
Web site: www.brownsteins.co.uk
Under the supervision of the London Beth Din.

Butcher

N. Goldberg
12 Claybury Broadway, Redbridge (020) 8551-2828
Supervision: London Board of Shechita.

Mikvaot

Ilford Mikvah Federation of Synagogues
463 Cranbrook Road, Ilford (020) 8554-2551
(Evenings: 8554-8532).
Correspondence to 367 Cranbrook Road, Ilford.

Synagogues

Orthodox

Ilford Synagogue
22 Beehive Lane, IG1 3RT (020) 8554 5969
Fax (020) 8554 4543

Romford

Synagogues

25 Eastern Road RM1 3NH (01708) 741690
Enquiries to: Mr D. Vroobel, 2 Norton Court, Church Road, Newbury Park IG2 7ES. Tel: 0208-597 2249.

Southend-on-Sea

Jews began settling in the area in the late nineteenth century, mainly from the East End of London. The first temporary synagogue was built in 1906. The Jewish population is 4,500.

Booksellers

Dorothy Young
21 Colchester Road SS2 6HW (01702) 331218
Email: dorothy@dorothyyoung.co.uk
Web site: www.dorothyyoung.co.uk
Religious articles, Israeli giftware, etc., also stocked. Jewish software ordered. Call for appointment.

Organisations

Southend & District Representative Council
(01702) 343192

Synagogues

Southend and Westcliff Hebrew Congregation
Finchley Road SSO 8AD (01702) 344900
Fax: (01702) 391131
Email: swhc@btclick.com
Web site: www.swhc.org.uk

Southend Reform Synagogue
851 London Road, Westcliff (01702) 75809

Gloucestershire

Cheltenham

The congregation was established in 1824 and the present synagogue opened in 1839. However, after two generations, the congregation declined and the synagogue was closed in 1903. At the outbreak of the Second World War, the synagogue was re-opened following the influx of Jewish newcomers to the town.

Restaurants

Vegetarian

The Orange Tree
317 High Street GL50 3HW (01242) 234232
Fax: (01242) 234232
Email: shaipateluk@yahoo.co.uk
Strictly vegan & vegetarian cuisine. Fully licensed with selection of organic wines & beers.

Synagogues

Cheltenham Hebrew Congregation
St James Square GL50 5PU (01242) 578893
Fax: (01242) 578893
Services every Friday at 7.00 pm and High Holy Days as advised.

Hampshire

Aldershot

Contact Information

Jewish Committee for H.M. Forces
25 Enford Street W1H 2DD (020 7) 724-7778
Fax: (020 7) 706-1710
Email: jmcouncil@btinternet.com
Web site: www.jmcouncil.org
Inquiries to Senior Jewish Chaplain.

Portsmouth & Southsea

The Portsmouth community was founded in 1746. Its first synagogue was in Oyster Row, but the congregation moved to a building in White's Row which it continued to occupy for almost two centuries. A new building was erected in 1936. The cemetery is in a street which was once known as Jews' Lane.

Synagogues

Synagogue Chambers
The Thicket
Southsea, PO5 2AA (023) 9282 1494

Southampton

Libraries

Hartley Library
University of Southampton
SO17 1BJ (023) 592721
Fax: (023) 593007
Email: archives@soton.ac.uk
Houses both the Parkes Library and the Anglo-Jewish Archives.

Synagogues

Moordaunt Road
The Inner Avenue, SO2 0GP
Services Sat. morn 10am

Hertfordshire

Bushey

Synagogues

Orthodox

Bushey and District
177 Sparrows Herne
WD23 1AJ (020) 8950-7340
Fax: (020) 8421-8267
Email: mary.chambers@bushey-community.org

Hemel Hempstead

Synagogues

Morton House
Midland Road HD1 1RP (01923) 232007

St Albans

Synagogues

Oswald Road AL1 3AQ (1727) 825925

St Albans Masorti Synagogue
PO Box 23 AL1 4PH (01727) 860642
Email: sams@masorti.org.uk

Watford

Synagogues

16 Nascot Road WD17 3RE (01923) 222755
Covers also Carpenters Park, Croxley Garden, Garston, Kings Langley and Rickmansworth.

Welwyn Garden City

Synagogues

Barn Close
Handside Lane, AL8 6ST (01707) 890575
Email: floradora@hotmail.com

Humberside

Grimsby

Synagogues

Sir Moses Montefiore Synagogue
Heneage Road DN32 9DZ (01472) 351-404
Services every Friday 7:00pm and all major festivals.

Hull

In Hull, as in other English port towns, a Jewish community was formed earlier than in inland areas. The exact date is unknown, but it is thought to be the early 1700s. There were enough Jews in Hull to buy a former Roman Catholic chapel, damaged in the Gordon Riots of 1780, and turn it into a synagogue. Hull was then the principal port of entry from northern Europe, and most Jewish immigrants came through it. Both the Old Hebrew Synagogue in Osborne Street and the Central Synagogue in Cogan Street were destroyed in air raids during the Second World War.

Museums

Hull Synagogue Museum
Linnaeus Street HU3 2PD (01482) 217153
Fax: (01482) 216565
Email: jcsc@exobus.org
Correspondence to: Old Synagogue, Linnaeus Street, HU3 2PD.

Synagogues

Orthodox

Hull Hebrew Congregation
30 Pryme Street Anlaby, HU10 6SH (01482) 653242

Reform

Reform Synagogue
Great Gutter Lane West Willerby,
HU10 7JT (01482) 658312
Fax: (01482) 342836
Email: iansugarman@isa.karoo.co.uk

Kent

Canterbury

Tourist Sites

The Old Synagogue
King Street
The Old Synagogue, an Egyptian-style building of 1847, stands in King Street and is now used by the Kings School for recitals.

Margate

Synagogues

Godwin Road,
Cliftonville, CT9 2HA (01843) 223219

Ramsgate

Synagogues

Montefiore Endowment
Hereson Road

Montefiore Mausoleum & Synagogue
33 Luton Avenue, Broadstairs, (01843) 862507

Rochester

Synagogues

Magnus Memorial Synagogue
366 High Street ME1 1DJ (01634) 847665
Grade 2, listed building known as The Chatham Memorial Synagogue.

Lancashire

Blackpool

Delicatessens

The Deli
6 Station Road, Lytham St Annes (01253) 735861

Synagogues

Orthodox

United Hebrew Congregation
Synagogue Chambers
Leamington Road, FY1 4HD (01253) 28164

Reform

Reform Jewish Congregation
40 Raikes Parade FY1 4EX (01253) 23687

Lancaster

Bed & Breakfasts

Lancaster University Jewish Society
Interfaith Chaplaincy Centre
University of Lancaster,
Bailrigg Lane, LA1 4YW (01524) 594075
Jewish rooms and kosher kitchen. Contact Rev Malcolm Wiseman.

St Annes On Sea

Synagogues

Orchard Road FY8 1PJ (01253) 721831
Services 7.30 am and 8 pm

Leicestershire

Leicester

There has been a Jewish presence here since the Middle Ages, but the first record of a 'Jews' Synagogue' dates from 1861 in the *Leicester Directory*. In 2001 the Leicester City Council finally renounced the ban of Jews living in the city which was originally imposed in 1731.

Libraries

Jewish Library and Bookshop
Community Hall
Highfield Street, LE2 0NQ (0116) 212-8920

Mikvaot

Synagogue Building
Highfield Street, LE2 0NQ (0116) 270-6622

Vegetarian

The Good Earth
19 Free Lane LE1 1JX (0116) 262-6260

Synagogues

Community Centre
Highfield Street
Leicestershire LE2 0NQ (0116) 254-0477
Mikva on premises.

Progressive Jewish Congregation
24 Avenue Road (0116) 271-5584
Fax: (0116) 271-7571
Email: jeffrey@kaufmans.co.uk

Lincolnshire

Lincoln

Lincoln was one of the centres of medieval Jewry. One of England's oldest stone houses in the city is known as Aaron the Jew's House. The site of the old Jewry is remembered now at Jews' Court. In the cathedral is a recent token of ecclesiastical apology for the thirteenth-century incident of the blood libel, retold in Chaucer. Jews returned to the area in the nineteenth century. The current community is of very recent date.

Community Organisations

Lincolnshire Jewish Community
3 West End Road, Ulceby, (01469) 588951

London

Well over half the 300,000 (1991) Jews of Britain live in London. Numbering about 210,000, they are spread throughout the metropolis, with the largest concentration in north-western districts like Golders Green, Hendon, Edgware and Hampstead Garden Suburb. There are also large communities in North London (Stamford Hill) and in the East (Redbridge). Once it was in Stepney that the majority of London Jewry lived and, in spite of many changes there, Aldgate and Whitechapel should be visited, not only for the many reminders of their Jewish heyday, but also for the bustling life which is still to be seen there.

The City

There are many historically interesting sites in the City, that square mile of Central London which adjoins the East End. The Bank of England is a useful starting point.

One of the numerous streets which converge on this busy hub is Poultry, leading quickly to Cheapside. The first street on the right is Old Jewry. Here, and in the neighbourhood, the earliest community lived before England expelled all its Jews in 1290. In October 2001 a mikva was discovered which is believed to be the only remaining physical evidence of the Jewish community before the expulsion. There were synagogues in this street and in Gresham and Coleman Streets, not far from historic Guildhall, which is itself a 'must' for tourists.

Inside the Royal Exchange, situated opposite the Bank of England in Threadneedle Street, there is a series of murals including one, by Solomon J. Solomon, R.A., of 'Charles I Demanding the Five Members', and a portrait of Nathan Mayer Rothschild, who founded the London house of the famous banking firm. There was a time when the south-east corner of the Royal Exchange was known as 'Jews' Walk'.

The Rothschild headquarters is not far away, in St Swithin's Lane. To reach this handsome building (which has in its entrance-hall more Rothschild portraits, as well as a large tapestry of Moses striking the rock), cross carefully from the Royal Exchange to the Lord Mayor's Mansion House and then turn left into King William Street.

Cornhill, which stretches eastwards from the Bank, leads to Leadenhall Street and its shipping offices and, after a short walk, to Creechurch Lane and the Cunard building, on the back of which is an interesting plaque. 'Site of the First Synagogue after the Resettlement 1657–1701. Spanish and Portuguese Jews' Congregation' is the inscription. Here the post-Expulsion Jews whom Oliver Cromwell welcomed to England set up their house of prayer. In 1701 they built a synagogue in Bevis Marks (close by), modelling it on the famous Portuguese Synagogue in Amsterdam. It has been scheduled by the Royal Commission on Ancient Historical Monuments as 'a building of outstanding value', and is considered one of the most beautiful pieces of synagogue architecture extant. In it are some benches from the Creechurch Lane Synagogue.

London's chief Ashkenazi place of worship, the Great Synagogue, stood, until it was bombed during the Second World War, in Duke's Place, which adjoins Bevis Marks. The 'Duke's Place Shool' (as it was called) was the country's best-known synagogue, the scene of many great occasions and a popular choice for weddings. On the wall of International House, which has replaced it, there is a plaque informing the visitor that the synagogue stood there 'from 1690 and served the community continuously until it was destroyed in September, 1941'.

After the Second World War and until the 1970s, the Great Synagogue was in Adler Street, named after the two Chief Rabbis of that name, Rabbi Nathan Marcus Adler and his son, Rabbi Dr Hermann Adler. Duke's Place leads to Aldgate High Street where, on the opposite side, Jewry Street marks another centre of the pre-Expulsion community. At the time of Richard I's coronation many Jews, escaping from rioting mobs, moved here from Old Jewry.

The East End

Further eastwards, along Aldgate High Street, is Middlesex Street, which becomes the crowded Petticoat Lane every Sunday morning. The cheerful and cheeky language of the stall-holders has made 'The Lane' famous throughout the world. On week-days an offshoot, Wentworth Street, continues the market.

Eastwards again, to Whitechapel, which has changed almost out of all recognition since the days before the Second World War, when it had a teeming Jewish population. Just beyond Aldgate East Underground station, two familiar spots remain: Whitechapel Art Gallery and Whitechapel Library.

The library's extensive Yiddish collection has been transferred to the Taylorian Library, Oxford University's modern-language library. The next turning on the left is Osborne Street, which leads to Brick Lane. A large and sombre building in Brick Lane (at the corner of Fournier Street) represents more than anything else the changes that have taken place in the East End over the years. The Huguenots built it as a church, the Jews turned it into a synagogue (the Machzike Hadass), and now the Bengalis, who have replaced the Jews, have converted it into a mosque.

The former synagogue in Princelet Street (No. 19) is being converted into a museum by the Spitalfields Trust, which is collaborating with the Jewish Museum to develop the building to show the history of the different immigrant groups which have inhabited the Spitalfields area during the past 300 years. For further information about activities at the Princelet Street Building, contact the Jewish Museum.

In Brune Street, it is possible to see the building of the former Soup Kitchen for the Jewish Poor that was established in 1902. Its work of distributing food to the small, elderly Jewish community still resident in the area is now undertaken by Jewish Care, the largest Jewish social service organisation in Britain.

Further along Whitechapel Road, outside Whitechapel Underground station, stands a drinking fountain. It was erected in 1911 'in Loyal and Grateful Memory of Edward VII Rex et Imperator from subscriptions raised by Jewish inhabitants of East London'.

Brady Street is the site of an old cemetery, opened for the New Synagogue in 1761 and subsequently used also by the Great Synagogue. The cemetery became full in the 1790s, and it was decided to put a four-foot-thick layer of earth over part of the site, using this for further burials. This created a flat-topped mound in the centre of the cemetery. The cemetery is perhaps the only one where, because of the two layers, the headstones are placed back to back. Among those buried here are Solomon Hirschel, who was Chief Rabbi from 1802 to 1842, and Nathan Meyer Rothschild (1777-1836), the banker. To view the cemetery, contact the United Synagogue Burial Society (020-8343 3456).

In Mile End there are three more old cemeteries: two Sephardi and one Ashkenazi. Behind 253 Mile End Road, where the Sephardi Home for the Aged (Beth Holim) was located before moving to Wembley, is the first Resettlement cemetery, the oldest existing Anglo-Jewish cemetery, opened in 1657. Abraham Fernandez Carvajal, regarded as the founder of the modern Anglo-Jewish community, is buried here, and also Haham David Nieto, one of the greatest of Sephardi spiritual leaders. At 329 Mile End Road, the Nuevo Beth Chaim, opened in 1725, contains the grave of Haham Benjamin Artom. This is among the 2,000 graves remaining on the site. Some 7,500 were transferred to a site in Brentwood, Essex, during the 1970s. The earliest Ashkenazi cemetery, acquired in 1696, is in Alderney Road, and here the founders of the Duke's Place Synagogue, Moses and Aaron Hart and others, and also the 'Baal Shem of London' (the Cabbalist, Haim Samuel Falk) lie buried. In Beaumont Grove, on the south side of Mile End Road, is the Stepney B'nai B'rith Clubs and Settlement, managed in co-operation with Jewish Care, which caters primarily for the needs of the 7,500 Jews still living in the East End.

In Commercial Road, Hessel Street, another Jewish market centre, is now occupied by Bengali traders. Henriques Street is named after Sir Basil Henriques, a leading welfare worker and magistrate, and founder of the Bernhard Baron St George's Jewish Settlement, who died in 1961. On the same side, three turnings along, is Alie Street. At the Jewish Working Men's Club here in July, 1896, Theodor Herzl addressed a meeting which was effectively the launching of the Zionist movement in Britain.

West Central

Chief Rabbi Hermann Adler (1891–1911) is honoured at the Central Court of the Old Bailey (Underground station: St Paul's), where a mural over the entrance to Court No. 1, entitled 'Homage to Justice', includes the figure of Dr Adler. By the City Boundary, High Holborn is the Royal Fusiliers City of London Regiment Memorial. The names of the 38th, 39th and 40th (Jewish Battalions) are inscribed on the monument together with all other battalions which served in the First World War. At the western edge of the City, Chancery Lane Station, Holborn, is a useful centre for several points of interest. To the east, Furnival Street has the *Jewish Chronicle* office. Northward, Gray's Inn Road leads to Theobald's Road. There, at No. 22, a plaque on the wall recalls that it is the birthplace of Benjamin Disraeli. Further to the north is Great Russell Street, which runs along part of the south side of the British Museum. When visiting the Museum, one should certainly see its collection of illuminated haggadot, in particular its copy of the fifteenth-century Ashkenazi Haggadah. No. 77 Great Russell Street was the headquarters of the Zionist organisations from 1919 to 1964. Westward, in Chancery Lane, the Public Record Office has in its vast collection many documents of Jewish historical value, including the petitions to Cromwell.

Commonwealth House, 1-19 New Oxford Street, is the new centre of British Jewry's communal activities, housing the Board of Deputies and a range of other offices.

B'nai B'rith-Hillel House, the student centre, is at 1-2 Endsleigh Street, in Bloomsbury, at the heart of the University neighbourhood, and the Council of Christians and Jews in Gordon Street is close by. In the building of University College in Gower Street, the Jewish Studies Library houses the Altmann, Mishcon and Mocatta Libraries and the Margulies Yiddish Collection. The School of Oriental and African Studies in the University precinct includes Judaica and Israelitica in its library.

West End

In the Marble Arch district, in the part of Hyde Park known as 'The Dell', a Holocaust Memorial Garden was dedicated in June 1983. The garden plot was given by the British Government to the Board of Deputies, which commissioned Mr Richard Seifert to design the memorial centre-piece of rocks bearing a quotation from the Book of Lamentations. Also in the Marble Arch area, you will find an important associate of the United Synagogue (the amalgamated Western and Marble Arch Synagogues in Great Cumberland Place), the West End Great, as well as the West London (Reform) Synagogue (Upper Berkeley Street) and the magnificent Victorian New West End Synagogue in St Petersburg Place, just off Bayswater Road. The Jewish Memorial Council and Bookshop is in Enford Street.

The British Zionist Federation was inaugurated at the Trocadero Restaurant in Piccadilly Circus in January 1899. At 175 Piccadilly was the London bureau of the Zionist Organisation, set up in August 1917. Here, Dr Chaim Weizmann and other Zionist leaders worked, and here, in November 1917, the Balfour Declaration was delivered by Lord Rothschild. The Westminster Synagogue in Rutland Gardens, Knightsbridge, houses the Czech Memorial Scrolls Centre, where there is a permanent exhibition telling the story of the salvaging from Prague in 1964 of 1,564 Torah Scrolls confiscated by the Nazis during the Second World War, and of their restoration and the donation of many to communities throughout the world. The exhibition is open from 10 am to 4 pm on Tuesdays and Thursdays, and at other times by appointment.

In St John's Wood are three more interesting synagogues: the New London (Abbey Road) and the St John's Wood (Grove End Road), where the Chief Rabbi, who lives in nearby Hamilton Terrace, generally worships. The third synagogue of great interest in St John's Wood is the Liberal Jewish, opposite Lord's Cricket Ground, recently rebuilt and renovated.

Stamford Hill

Of London's many synagogues, one remarkable group is the series of Chasidic 'shtiblech' in Stamford Hill (and the yeshivot which are attached to some of them). Cazenove Road contains several of these, and it is here and in the vicinity that the long coats and wide hats of chasidim and the curled sidelocks of their children are to be seen. The Lubavitch Foundation headquarters and the Yesodey Hatorah Schools are in Stamford Hill.

AJEX House at East Bank, Stamford Hill houses an interesting Jewish military museum. In this district, also, are North African, Adeni, Indian and some Persian Jews and their synagogues.

North-East

The migration of the Jews from the East End took many of them eventually to the London borough of Redbridge where today the greatest density of London's Jews reside. To obtain a flavour of this large Jewish community one should visit the Redbridge Youth and Community Centre, Sinclair House, Woodford Bridge Road, Ilford, Essex. Sinclair House is a large modern, purpose-built Jewish community centre and it is the base for a number of organisations and the focal point of many Israeli and Zionist communal events. It also houses the Clayhall Synagogue, the Redbridge Jewish Programmes Material Project and community representative councils.

North-West

The starting point for visiting North-West London is Golders Green. Jews first settled here during the First World War, and the Golders Green Synagogue (United) in Dunstan Road, was opened in 1922. Walk down Golders Green Road from the Underground station for half a mile or so, and you will come to Broadwalk Lane on the right-hand side, where the Lincoln Institute is. This is the home of Ohel David, a congregation of Indian Jews, many of whom came to England when India was partitioned in 1947. Their forebears went to India from Baghdad.

On the opposite side of the road, at the end of a short turning called The Riding, is the Golders Green Beth Hamedrash – formerly known as 'Munk's' after its founder in the 1930s, Rabbi Dr Eli Munk. This very Orthodox congregation, mainly of German origin, adheres to the religious principles of Rabbi Samson Raphael Hirsch. There are many other strictly Orthodox congregations in Golders Green, including chasidic groups.

Any of the buses travelling along Golders Green Road away from the Underground station will take you to Bell Lane, in Hendon. A few hundred yards down on the left-hand side is Albert Road, where you will find the London School of Jewish Studies (formerly Jews' College) – established in 1855 as an Institute of Higher Education and associated with London University for many years. A group of Persian Jews holds Shabbat morning services there. Its 70,000-volume library is open to the public.

Also in Hendon in Egerton Gardens, a turning opposite Barnet Town Hall in The Burroughs, 10–15 minutes walk from Bell Lane, is Yakar, which provides a wide variety of adult educational and cultural programmes and has a lending library. Several minyanim are held here on Shabbat and festivals. Further information is available on 020-8202 5552.

Return to Golders Green Underground station from Hendon Central, either by Underground or by bus. Once there, take a bus northwards along Finchley Road for two miles or so, getting off at East End Road, which is more or less opposite the bus stop. On the right-hand side is the Sternberg

Centre, the largest Jewish community centre in Europe. The Georgian former manor house contains Leo Baeck College, with its library of 18,000 books, which trains Reform and Liberal rabbis; the offices of the Reform Synagogues of Great Britain; and the London Museum of Jewish Life, now the second centre of the Jewish Museum. In addition to permanent displays, the museum also mounts special exhibitions and runs walking tours and educational programmes. There is a Holocaust memorial, as well as a biblical garden, a bookshop and a dairy snack bar.

Bakeries

Carmelli Bakeries Ltd
126-128 Golders Green Road,
Golders Green NW11 (020) 8455-2074
Fax: (020) 8455-2789
Supervision: London Beth Din and Kedassia.

Crème de la Crème
5 Temple Fortune Parade,
Bridge Lane NW11 1QN (020) 8458-9090
Supervision: Kedassia.

Daniel's Bagel Bakery
12-13 Hallswelle Parade, Finchley Road,
Golders Green NW11 0DL (020) 8455-5826
Fax: (020) 8455-5826
Supervision: London Beth Din.

David Bagel Bakery
38 Vivian Avenue, Hendon NW4 (020) 8203-9995
Supervision: Kedassia.

Dinos Bakeries
106 Brent Street, Hendon
NW4 2HH (020) 8203-6623
Supervision: London Beth Din and Kedassia.

Dinos Bakeries
11 Edgwarebury Lane,
Edgware HA8 8LH (020) 8958-1554
Fax: (020) 8958-2554
Supervision: Kedassia.

Hendon Bagel Bakery
55-57 Church Road, Hendon NW4 (020) 8203-6919
Fax: (020) 8203-8843
Supervision: Kedassia.

Keene's Patisserie
Unit 6, Mill Hill Ind. Est., Flower Lane,
Mill Hill NW7 2HU (020) 8906-3729
Supervision: London Beth Din.

Keene's Patisserie
192 Preston Road, Wembley HA9 (020) 8904-5952
Supervision: London Beth Din.

M & D Grodzinski Hot Bread Shop
223 Golders Green Road,
Golders Green NW11 9ES (020) 8458-3654
Fax: (020) 8905-5382
Supervision: London Beth Din and Kedassia.

Mr Bagels Factory
1 Kings Yard, Carpenters Road
E15 2HD (020) 8533-7553
Supervision: Kedassia.

Parkway Patisserie Ltd.
30a North End Road,
Golders Green NW11 (020) 8455-5026
Supervision: London Beth Din and Kedassia.
Hours: Sunday, 7.30 am to 1.30 pm; Monday to Thursday, to 5.30 pm; Friday, to one hour before Shabbat.

Parkway Patisserie Ltd.
204 Preston Road, Wembley HA9 (020) 8904-7736
Supervision: London Beth Din and Kedassia.
Hours: Sunday, 7.30 am to 1.30 pm; Monday to Thursday, to 5.30 pm; Friday, to one hour before Shabbat.

Parkway Patisseries Ltd.
326-328 Regents Park Road,
Finchley N3 (020) 8346-0344
Supervision: London Beth Din and Kedassia.
Hours: Sunday, 7.30 am to 1.30 pm; Monday to Thursday, to 5.30 pm; Friday, to one hour before Shabbat.

Renbake Patisserie Ltd.
Unit a, 8-10 Timber Wharf Road,
Stamford Hill N16 6DB (020) 8800-2525
Fax: (020) 8800-2023
Supervision: London Beth Din and Kedassia.

The Cake Company
2 Sentinel Square, Hendon
NW4 2EL (020) 8202-2327
Fax: (020) 8202-8058
Email: karen@thecakecompany.co.uk
Supervision: London Beth Din & Kedassia.

Woodberry Down Bakery
47 Brent Street, Hendon NW4 (020) 8202-9962
Supervision: London Beth Din & Kedassia.

Bed & Breakfasts

Harold Godfrey Hillel House
25 Louisa Street, Stepney E1 4NF (020) 7790-9557
Summer accommodation in London. Twenty-three rooms, self-catering separate meat and milk kitchens. Very close to Stepney Green tube station with easy access to all London attractions. Please contact the warden at the above address for more information or to book a room.

Kacenberg's Guest House
1 Alba Gardens, Near Alba Court,
Golders Green NW11 9NS (020) 8455-3780
Fax: (020) 8381-4250
Shabbat meals available. "Strictly Orthodox".

Booksellers

Boreham Wood Judaice
11 Croxdale Road, Boreham Wood
WD6 4QD (020) 8381-5559

Carmel Gifts,
62 Edgware Way, Middx (020) 8958-7632
Fax: (020) 8958-6226

Hebrew Book and Gift Centre
24 Amhurst Parade, Amhurst Park
N16 5AA (020) 8802-0609
Fax: (020) 8802-0609

J. Aisenthal
11 Ashbourne Parade, Finchley Road,
Temple Fortune NW11 0AD (020) 8455-0501
Email: infor@aisenthal.co .uk
Web site: www.aisenthal.co.uk

Jerusalem the Golden
146a Golders Green Road,
Golders Green NW11 8HE (020) 8455-4960
Fax: (020) 8203-7808

Jewish Memorial Council and Bookshop
25 Enford Street W1H 2DD (020) 7724-7778
Fax: (020) 7706-1710
Email: jmcbookshop@btinternet.com
Web site: www.jmcouncil.org

Menorah Book and Gift Centre
16 Russell Parade,
Golders Green Road NW11 9NN (020) 8458-8289
Fax: (020) 8731-8403

Steimatzky Hasifria
46 Golders Green Road NW11 8LL (020) 8458-9774
Fax: (020) 8458-3449
Email: shirley@hasifria.com
Web site: www.hasifia.com

Torah Treasures
4 Sentinel Square, Brent Street,
Hendon NW4 2EL
(020) 8202-3134
Fax: (020) 8202-3161
Email: torahtreasures@btinternet.com
Seforim, Judaica and gifts.

Butchers

A. Perlmutter & Son
1-2 Onslow Parade, Hampden Square,
Southgate N14 5JN (020) 8361-5441/2
Fax: (020) 8361-5442
Supervision: London Board of Shechita.

Frohwein's
1095 Finchley Road,
Temple Fortune NW11 (020) 8455-9848
Supervision: Kedassia.
Deli and cooked food available for weekends and Shabbat.

Golders Green Kosher
132 Golders Green Road,
Golders Green NW11 8HB (020) 8381-4450
Fax: (020) 8731-6450

Greenspans
9-11 Lyttelton Road N2 0DW (020) 8455-9921
Fax: (020) 8455-3484
Supervision: London Board of Shechita.

J.D Glass & Co
100 High Road, Bushey Heath,
Bushey WD2 3JE (020) 8420-4443
Supervision: London Board of Shechita.

Jack Schlagman
112 Regents Park Road,
Finchley N3 (020) 8346-3598
Supervision: London Board of Shechita.

La Boucherie
4 Cat Hill, East Barnet EN4 8JB (020) 8449-9215
Fax: (020) 8441-1848
Supervision: London Board of Shechita.

Louis Mann
23 Edgwarebury Lane, Edgware
HA8 (020) 8958-3789
Supervision: London Board of Shechita.

M. Lipowicz
9 Royal Parade, Ealing W5 (020) 8997-1722
Fax: (020) 8997-0048
Supervision: London Board of Shechita.

Menachem's
15 Russell Parade, Golders Green Road,
Golders Green NW11 (020) 8201-8629
Fax: (020) 8201-8629
Supervision: London Board of Shechita.

R. Wolff
84 Edgware Way, Edgware
HA8 8JS (020) 8958-8454
Supervision: London Board of Shechita.

Butchers & Delicatessens

Mehadrin Meats
19 Russell Parade, Golders Green
NW11 9NN (020) 8455-9992
Fax: (020) 8455-3777/8599 0984
Supervision: Kedassia.

Mehadrin Meats
25 Belfast Road, Stamford Hill N16 (020) 8806-0000
Fax: (020) 8880-0500
Supervision: Kedassia.

Communal Organisation

Board of Deputies of British Jews
Commonwealth House, 5th Floor,
1-19 New Oxford Street
WC1A 1NU (020) 7534-5400
Fax: (020) 7534-0010
Email: info @bod.org.uk
Web site: www.bod.org.uk

Contact Information

Jewish Community Information (JCI)
Commonwealth House,
1-19 New Oxford Street WC1N 1NF
(020) 7543-5421/2
Fax: (020) 7543-0010
Email: jci@bod.org.uk
A comprehensive service of communal information. For administration please contact 020 7543 5400.

The International Jewish Vegetarianism Society
Bet Teva, 855 Finchley Road
NW11 8LX (020) 8455-0692
Fax: (020) 8455-1465
Email: ijvs@yahoo.com
Web site: www.vu.org/jvs
The International Jewish Vegetarian Society was formed 35 years ago to promote vegetarianism from a Jewish perspective.

Delicatessens

Munch Box,
41 Greville Street EC1 (020) 7242-5487
Supervision: London Beth Din.

Embassy

Embassy of Israel
2 Palace Green, Kensington W8 4QB
(020) 7957-9500
Fax: (020) 7957-9555
Email: isr-info@dircon.co.uk
Web site: www.israel-embassy.org.uk/london/

Israeli Consulate-General
15a Old Court Place, Kensington W8 4QB
(020) 7957-9500
Fax: (020) 7957-9577
Web site: www.israel-embassy.org.uk/london
Nearest tube station: High Street Kensington. Consular office hours: Monday to Thursday, 10 am to 1 pm; Friday, 10 am to 12 pm. Postal address: Consulate Section, Embassy of Israel, 2 Palace Green, London W8 4QB

Fishmongers

Leveyuson
47a Brent Street, Hendon NW4 (020) 8202-7834
Supervision: London Beth Din.

Sam Stoller
28 Temple Fortune Parade, Finchley Road,
Golders Green NW11 0QS
(020) 8455-1957; 8458-1429
Fax: (020) 8445-1957
Supervision: Sephardi Kashrut Authority.

Groceries

B Kosher
91 Bell Lane, Hendon NW4 (020) 8202-1711
Opposite Vincent Court.

Carmel Fruit Shop
40 Vivian Avenue, Hendon NW4 (020) 8202-9587
Fresh fruit and vegetables as well as a good supply of kosher products, cakes and biscuits.

Kosher King
235 Golders Green Road, Golders Green
NW11 9ES (020) 8455-1429
Fax: (020) 8201-8924
Email: kosherking@compuserve.com
Supervision: London Beth Din.

Kosher Paradise
10 Ashbourne Parade, Finchley Road,
Temple Fortune NW11 OAD (020) 8455-2454
Fax: (020) 8731-6919

Maxine's
20 Russell Parade, Golders Green Road,
Golders Green NW11 (020) 8458-3102
Fax: (020) 8455-3632
Kedassia Deli. Deliveries.

Pelter Stores
82 Edgware Way, Edgware HA8 (020) 8958-6910
Supervision: Federation Kashrus Board.

Yarden
123 Golders Green Road,
Golders Green NW11 (020) 8458-0979
Free delivery on orders over £25. Hours: Sunday, Wednesday, Thursday, 8 am to 10 pm; Monday, Tuesday, 8 am to 9 pm; Friday, 8 am.

Guest House

Sharon Guest House
7 Woodlands Close, Golders Green
(020) 8458-8531
Email: jlazenga@aol.com
Although not officially supervised it is said to be Shomer Shabbat Dati.

Hotels

Central Hotel
35 Hoop Lane, Golders Green
NW11 8BS (020) 8458-5636
Fax: (020) 8455-4792
Private bathrooms and parking.

Croft Court Hotel
44 Ravenscroft Avenue, Golders Green
NW11 8AY (020) 8458-3331
Fax: (020) 8455-9175
Twenty rooms.

King Solomon Palace Hotel
155-159 Golders Green Road
NW11 9BX (020) 8201-9000
Fax: (020) 8201-9853

Kosher Supervised

Golders Green Hotel
147-149 Golders Green Road, Golders Green
NW11 9BN (020) 8458-7127/9
Fax: (020) 8905-5143
Email: goldersgreenhotel@talk21.com
Supervision: Beth Din of the Federation of Synagogues.

Kadimah Hotel
146 Clapton Common, Stamford Hill
E5 9AG (020) 8800-5960
Fax: (020) 8800-6237
Supervision: Kedassia.

Menorah Hotel & Caterers
54-54a Clapton Common, Clapton E5
(020) 8806-4925; 6340

Kashrut Information

Federation of Synagogues Kashrus Board
65 Watford Way, Hendon
NW4 3AQ (020) 8202-2263
Fax: (020) 8203-0610
Email: info@kfkosher.org
Web site: www.kfkosher.org

Joint Kashrus Committee-Kedassia (Union of Orthodox Hebrew Congregations)
140 Stamford Hill, Stamford Hill
N16 6QT (020) 8800 6833
Fax: (020) 8809-7092

London Beth Din
735 High Road, Finchley N12 0US
(020) 8343-6255 (Kashrut hotline: 8343-6333)
Fax: (020) 8343-6254
Email: info@kosher.org.uk
Web site: www.kosher.org.uk
Publishes 'The Really Jewish Food Guide', which contains a list of all the establishments it certifies as well as guidance for the shopper in buying general consumer products.

National Council of Shechita Boards
Elscot House, Arcadia Avenue, Finchley
N3 2JU (020) 8349-9160
Fax: (020)8 346-2209
Email: shechita@freenet.co.uk

Sephardi Kashrut Authority
2 Ashworth Road, Maida Vale
W9 1JY (020) 7289-2573
Fax: (020) 7289-2709
Email: howard@sandpsyn.demon.co.uk

Libraries

British Library, Oriental & India Office Collections - Hebrew Section
96 Euston Road NW1 2DB (020) 7412-7646
Fax: (020) 7412-7641/7870
Email: oioc-enquiries@bl.uk; ilana.tahan@bl.uk
The Hebrew section contains over 70,000 printed books, 3,000 manuscripts and some 10,000 Genizah fragments. Oriental reading room open to holders of readers' passes: Monday 10 am-5 pm; Tuesday-Saturday 9.30 am-5 pm. Hebrew manuscripts on permanent display in the John Ritblat Gallery. The Golden Haggadah on the "Turning the Pages" electronic system

Institute of Contemporary History and Wiener Library
4 Devonshire Street W1W 5BH (020) 7636-7247
Fax: (020) 7436-6428
Email: lib@wl.u-net.com
Web site: www.wienerlibrary.co.uk
The world's oldest institution dedicated to the documentation of Nazi Germay and the Holocaust. The collection includes 60,000 books and pamphlets, periodicals, documents, videos and photographs as well as extensive press cuttings from 1933 onwards. Other subjects include twentieth-century Jewish history, anti-semitism, refugees, minorities, fascism, citizenship, etc.

The Jewish Studies Library
University College London Library,
Gower Street WC1E 6BT (020) 7679-2598
Fax: (020) 7679-7373
In addition to materials purchased for the College's Department of Hebrew Studies it incorporates the Mocatta Library, Altmann Library, William Margulies Yiddish Library and the Library of the Jewish Historical Society of England. Applications to use or view the collections should be made in advance in writing to the Librarian.

Media

Directories

Jewish Year Book
Vallentine Mitchell, Crown House,
47 Chase Side, Southgate N14 5BP
(020) 8920-2100
Fax: (020) 8447-8548
Email: jyb@vmbooks.com
Annual directory of all information relating to the British Jewish Community.

Internet

Brijnet
11 The Lindens, Prospect Hill,
Waltham Forest E17 3EJ (020) 8520-3531
Email: info@brijnet.org
Web site: www.brijnet.org

Listings

The Diary
32 Bell Lane NW4 2AD (020) 8922-5437
Fax: (020) 8922-8709

Newspapers

Essex Jewish News
Crown House, 47 Chase Side, Southgate
N14 5BP (020) 8920-2100
Fax: (020) 8447-8548
Quarterly publication serving East London and Essex.

Hamodia
149 Kyverdale Road N16 6PS (020) 8806 7577
Fax: (020) 8806 1222
Email: Post@Hamodia.demon.co.uk

Jewish Chronicle
25 Furnival Street EC4A 1JT (020) 7415-1500
Fax: (020) 7405-9040
Email: editorial@thejc.com
Established 1841. Weekly publication.

London Jewish News
28 St Albans Lane, Golders Green
NW11 7QE (020) 8731-8031
Fax: (020) 8381-4033

Mikvaot

Adath Yisroel Synagogue Mikvah
40a Queen Elizabeth's Walk,
cnr 28 Gazebrook Rd, Stamford Hill
N16 0HH (020) 8802-2554

Craven Walk Mikvah
72 Lingwood Road, Stamford Hill N16
(020) 8800-8555
Evening Telephone number: (020) 8809-6279.

Edgware & District Communal Mikvah
Edgware United Synagogue Grounds,
22 Warwick Avenue Drive,
Edgware HA8 (020) 8958-3233
Fax: (020) 8958-4004
Email: estrin@clara.co.uk

North West London Communal Mikvah
10a Shirehall Lane, Hendon NW4 (020) 8202-1427
(Evenings:8202-8517/5706)

Satmar Mikvah
62 Filey Avenue, Stamford Hill N16 (020) 8806-3961

South London Mikvah
42 St Georges Road, Wimbledon SW19 4ED
(020) 8944-7149
Fax: (020) 8944-7563

Stamford Hill and District Mikvah
Margaret Road, Stamford Hill N16 (020) 8806-3880
Other Telephone numbers:(020) 8809-4064 or (020) 8800-5119.

The Sternberg Centre for Judaism
80 East End Road, Finchley
N3 2SY (020) 8349-5640
Fax: (020) 8349-5699
Email: admin@reformjudaism.org.uk
Web site: www.refsyn.org.uk
Hours: 9.30 am - 5.30 pm Monday to Thursday, Friday 9.30 am - 3.30/4 pm.

Union of Orthodox Hebrew Congregations
140 Stamford Hill, Stamford Hill
N16 6QT (020) 8802-6226
Fax: (020) 8809-7097

Museums

Ben Uri Art Society & Gallery
126 Albert Street NW1 7NE (020) 7482-1234
Fax: (020) 7482-1414
Email: benuri@ort.org
The aim of the Society, which is a registered charity founded 1915, is to promote Jewish art as part of the Jewish cultural heritage. The Gallery provides a showcase for exhibitions of contemporary art as well as for the Society's own collection of over 800 works by Jewish artists, including David Bomberg, Mark Gertler, Jacob Epstein, Reuven Rubin and Leon Kossof. Open Monday-Thursday 10 am- pm, Sunday afternoons during exhibitions 2-5 pm. Closed Jewish Holy Days and Bank Holidays.

Jewish Military Museum and Memorial Room
AJEX House, East Bank, Stamford Hill N16 5RT
(020) 8800-2844; 8802-7610
Fax: (020) 8800-1117
Email: ajexuk@talk21.com
Web site: www.ajex.org.uk
Memorabilia, artefacts, medals, letters, documents, pictures and uniforms all illustrating British Jewry's contribution to the Armed Forces of the Crown from the Crimea to the present day. By appointment, Sunday to Thursday, 11 am to 4 pm.

The Holocaust Exhibition
Imperial War Museum, Lambeth Road SE1 6HZ
(020) 7416-5320
Fax: (020) 7416-5374
Email: vcook@iwm.org.uk
Web site: www.iwm.org.uk

United Kingdom / London

The Jewish Museum
Raymond Burton House, 129-131 Albert Street,
Camden NW1 7NB (020) 7284-1997
Fax: (020) 7267-9008
Email: admin@jmus.org.uk
Web site: www.jewmusm.ort.org

The Museum explores Jewish history and religious life in Britain and beyond. It has been awarded Designated status by the Museums and Galleries Commission in recognition of its outstanding collections of Jewish ceremonial art, which are amongst the finest in the world. The Museum's attractive premises include a History Gallery, Ceremonial Art Gallery and a Temporary Exhibitions Gallery offering a varied programme of changing exhibitions. Open Monday-Thursday 10 am-4 pm, Sundays 10 am-5 pm. Closed Jewish Festivals and public holidays. Group visits by prior arrangement. Admission charge.

The Jewish Museum
80 East End Road, Finchley N3 2SY
(020) 8349-1143
Fax: (020) 8343-2162
Email: admin@jmus.org.uk
Web site: www.jewmus.ort.org

Permanent exhibitions trace history of London Jewry with reconstructions of a tailoring and a furniture workshop. Holocaust education is also a major feature of the Museum's work and the Museum's displays include a moving exhibition on London-born Holocaust survivor, Leon Greenman. Hours: Monday to Thursday, 10.30 am to 5 pm; Sunday (except during August and Bank Holiday weekends), 10.30 am to 4.30 pm. Closed Friday, Saturday and Jewish festivals, public holidays and 25 December to 5 January.

Organisations

Assembly of Masorti Synagogues
1097 Finchley Road, Golders Green NW11 0PU
(020) 8201-8772
Fax: (020) 8201-8917
Email: office@masorti.org.uk
Web site: www.masorti.org.uk

Spanish & Portuguese Jews' Congregation
2 Ashworth Road, Maida Vale W9 1JY
(020) 7289-2573
Fax: (020) 7289-2709
Email: howard@sandpsyn.demon.co.uk

The Sephardi Centre
2 Ashworth Road, Maida Vale W9 1JY
(020) 7266 3682
Fax: (020) 7289 5957
Email: sephardicentre@easynet.co.uk

Union of Liberal and Progressive Synagogues
The Montagu Centre, 21 Maple Street W1T 4BE
(020) 7580-1663
Fax: (020) 7436-4184
Email: montagu@ulps.org
Web site: www.ulps.org

Union of Orthodox Hebrew Congregations
140 Stamford Hill, Stamford Hill N16 6QT
(020) 8802-6226
Fax: (020) 8809-7902

United Synagogue
Adler House, 735 High Road, Finchley N12 0US
(020) 8343-8989
Fax: (020) 8343-6262
Web site: www.unitedsynagogue.org.uk

Reform Synagogues
The Sternberg Centre for Judaism,
80 East End Road, Finchley N3 2SY
(020) 8349-5640
Fax: (020) 8343-5699
Email: admin@reformjudaism.org.uk
Web site: www.refsyn.org.uk

With more than 200 synagogues in the London area alone, not counting independent synagogues and 'shtieblach', we recommend that you contact one of the above organisations to find the synagogue of your choice nearest you, along with minyan times.

Restaurants

Dairy

Art 2 Heart
109a Golders Green Road, London NW11
(020) 8201-9991
Supervision: London Beth Din.

Café on the Green
122 Golders Green Road,
Golders Green NW11 8HB (020) 8209-0232
Supervision: London Beth Din.
Chalav Yisrael. Open Motzei Shabbat in winter.

Cassit
225 Golders Green Road,
Golders Green NW11 9PN (020) 8455-8195
Fax: (020) 8458-4837
Supervision: London Beth Din.

Croft Court
44 Ravenscroft Avenue, Golders Green NW11 8AY
(020) 8458-3331
Fax: (020) 8455-9175

Folman's Restaurant
134 Brent Street NW4 (020) 8202-5592
Supervision: London Beth Din.

Macabi King of Falafel
59 Wentworth Street E1 (020) 7247-6660
Supervision: Beth Din of the Federation of Synagogues.

Milk n' Honey
124 Golders Green Road,
Golders Green NW11 8HB (020) 8455-0664
Supervision: Kedassia.
Vegetarian/dairy restaurant/coffee shop/air-conditioned. Menus in English and Hebrew. Also take-away available.

Orli Caffe
96 Brent Street, Hendon NW4 2HH
(020) 8203-7555
Supervision: Kedassia.

Orli Caffe
108 Regents Park Road, Finchley N3 3JG
(020) 8371-9222
Supervision: Kedassia.

Taboon
17 Russell Parade, Golders Green Road NW11 9NN
(020) 8455-7451
Supervision: Sephardi Kashrut Authority.

Tasti Pizza
252 Golders Green Road, Golders Green NW11
(020) 8209-0023
Supervision: London Beth Din and Kedassia.

Tasty Pizza
23 Amhurst Parade, Amhurst Park,
Stamford Hill N16 5AA
(020) 8802-0018; 8455-0004
Supervision: London Beth Din and Kedassia.

Meat

Amor
8 Russell Parade, Golders Green NW11
(020) 8458-4221
Supervision: Kedassia.

Aviv
87 High Street, Edgware (020) 8952-2484
Fax: (020) 8952-0200
Email: info@avivrestaurant.com
Web site: www.avivrestaurant.com
Supervision: Beth Din of the Federation of Synagogues.

Blooms World-Famous Kosher Restaurant
130 Golders Green Road,
Golders Green NW11 8HB (020) 8455-1338; 3033
Fax: (020) 8455-1338
Supervision: London Beth Din.
Free delivery service, air-conditioned. Open until 1.00am Sunday to Thursday; Friday lunchtime and Saturday nights one hour after Shabbos until 4 am.

Catskills
1-4 Belmont Parade, Finchley Road,
Temple Fortune NW11 (020) 8458-1999
Fax: (020) 8209-1050
Email: catskills@hamishe.freeserve.co.uk
Web site: www.catskills.co.uk
Supervision: London Beth Din.
Kosher deli, diner, restaurant. Open Motzei Shabbat in winter.

Dizengoff
118 Golders Green Road,
Golders Green NW11 8HB
(020) 8458-7003; 8458-9958
Fax: (020) 8381-4902
Email: s.shurkin@virgin.net
Web site: www.cityscan.co.uk
Supervision: Sephardi Kashrut Authority.
Hours: Sunday to Thursday, 11 am to midnight; Friday, to 4 pm; Saturday night, winter only.

El Gaucho
239 Golders Green Road NW11 9PN
(020) 8458-0444
Fax: (020) 8455-2003
Supervision: Sephardi Kashrut.

United Kingdom / London

Kaifeng
51 Church Road, Hendon NW4 4DU
(020) 8203-7888
Fax: (020) 8203-8263
Web site: www.kaifeng.co.uk
Supervision: London Beth Din.
Luxury Chinese restaurant with take-away and delivery service. Free delivery with minimum order of £25.
Hours: Sunday to Thursday, 12.30 pm to 2.30 pm, 6 pm to 11 pm; Open Saturday evening, September to April.

Kinneret
313 Hale Lane HA8 7AX (020) 8958-4955
Supervision: Beth Din Federation of Synagogues.

Lemonade
87 Brent St. NW4 (020) 8201-5222
Supervision: Sephardi Kashrut Authority.

Marcus's
5 Hallswelle Parade, Finchley Road,
Golders Green NW11 0DL (020) 8458-4670
Supervision: London Beth Din.

Reubens
79 Baker Street W1M 1AJ (020) 7486-0035
Fax: (020) 7486-7079
Supervision: Sephardi Kashrut Authority.
Open daily except for Shabbat; open Friday until two hours before sundown.

Sami's Restaurant
157 Brent Street, Hendon NW4 4DJ
(020) 8203-8088
Fax: (020) 8203-1040
Supervision: Federation of Synagogues Kashrut Board.
Glatt kosher Middle Eastern cuisine.

Six-13
19 Wigmore Street W1 (020) 7629-6133
Supervision: London Beth Din

Solly's
148a Golders Green Road, Golders Green NW11
(020) 8455-0004
Supervision: London Beth Din.

Solly's Exclusive
146-150 Golders Green Road, Golders Green NW11
(020) 8455-2121
Supervision: London Beth Din.

The White House Restaurant
10 Bell Lane, Hendon NW4 (020) 8203-2427
Supervision: Federation of Synagogues.

Uncle Shloime's
204 Stamford Hill, Stamford Hill N16
(020) 8802-9355
Supervision: Kedassia.

Snack Bar

Sue Harris Student Centre
B'nai B'rith-Hillel Foundation,
1-2 Endsleigh Street WC1H 0DS (020) 7388-0801
Fax: (020) 7916-3973
Email: hillel@ort.org
Supervision: London Beth Din.
Hours: Monday to Thursday, Friday night Shabbat meal available if booked and paid in advance by Thursday 11 am. Please phone for details of summer months opening. Re-opens for students and all other visitors mid-September.

Tourist Information

London Line
London Tourist Board, Glen House, Stag Place,
Victoria SW1E 5LT (09068) 663344
Web site: www.londontouristboard.com
Features over thirty lines of recorded information services. Calls cost 60p per minute as at July 2001.

Travel Agencies

Goodmos Tours
Dunstan House, 14a St Cross Street EC1N 8XA
(020) 7430-2230
Fax: (020) 7405-5049

LestAir Services
80 Highfield Ave, Golders Green NW11 9TT
(020) 8455-9654
Fax: (020) 8455-9654
Email: family.schleimer@ukgateway.net
Promoting Jewish Heritage Tours to the Czech Republic, Poland, Hungary, Byelorus, Latvia and Lithuania and can be contacted for detailed information and guidance.

Longwood Travel
182 Longwood Gardens, Ilford IG5 0EW
(020) 8551-4466
Fax: (020) 8551-5588

Magic of Israel
47 Shepherds Bush Green,
Shepherds Bush W12 8PS (020) 8743-9000

Peltours
11-19 Ballards Lane, Finchley N3 1UX
(020) 8346-9144
Fax: (020) 8343-0579
Email: sales@peltours.com
Web site: www.peltours.com

Peltours
240 Station Road, Edgware HA8 7AU
(020) 8958-1144
Fax: (020) 8958-5515

Sabra Travel Ltd.
9 Edgwarebury Lane, Edgware HA8 8LH
(020) 8958-3244-7

Travelink Group Ltd.
50 Vivian Avenue NW4 3XH (020) 8931-8000
Fax: (020) 8931-8877
Email: info@travelinkuk.com
Web site: www.travelinkuk.com

Manchester

The Manchester Jewish community is the second largest in the United Kingdom, numbering about 35,000. There was no organised community until 1780. The present Great Synagogue claims to be the direct descendant of this earliest community. The leaders of Manchester Jewry in those early days came, from the neighbouring relatively important Jewish community of Liverpool. In 1871 a small Sephardi group from North Africa and the Levant drew together and formed a congregation, which extended to fill two handsome synagogues. One has now been turned into a Jewish museum.

Bakeries

Brackman's
45 Leicester Road, Salford, M7 (0161) 792-1652
Supervision: Manchester Beth Din.

State Fayre Bakeries
Unit 1, Empire Street, M3 (0161) 832-2911
Supervision: Manchester Beth Din.

Swiss Cottage Patisserie
118 Rectory Lane, Prestwich, M25 (0161) 798-0897
Fax: (0161) 798-8212
Supervision: Manchester Beth Din.

Booksellers

B. Horwitz
20 King Edwards Buildings
Bury Old Road, Prestwich, M7 4QJ (0161) 740-5897
Open 9.30 am-5.30 pm Monday to Friday; 10 am-1 pm Sunday; 9 am-2 pm Fridays during winter.

B. Horwitz Judaica World
2 Kings Road, Prestwich, M25 0LE (0161) 773-4956
Fax: (0161) 773-4956
Email: horbroom@aol.com

Hasefer Book Store
18 Merrybower Road, Salford, M7 (0161) 740-3013
Fax: (0161) 721-4649

J. Goldberg
11 Parkside Avenue, Salford, M7 0HB
(0161) 740-0732

Jewish Book Centre
25 Ashbourne Grove, Salford, M7 4DB
(0161) 792-1253
Fax: (0161) 661-5505
Hours: Sunday to Thursday, 9 am to 9 pm; Friday, 9 am-1 pm.

Butchers

Halberstadt Ltd
55 Leicester Road, Salford, M7 4AS (0161) 792-1109
Supervision: Manchester Beth Din.
Open full day Tuesday, Wednesday, and Thursday. Open half day Sunday, Monday and Friday. Only Glatt Beth Yosef Meat-Mehadrin Poultry. Electric doors/disable ramp.

Hymark Kosher Meat Ltd
39 Wilmslow Road, Cheadle, Cheshire, SK
(0161) 428-3400
Supervision: Manchester Beth Din.
Meat department only.

Hymark of Hale
The Square, Hale Barns, Cheshire (0161) 980-2836
Supervision: Manchester Beth Din.

J.A. Hyman (Titanic) Ltd
123/9 Waterloo Road M8 (0161) 792-1888
Supervision: Manchester Beth Din.
Suppliers of meat and poultry, cooked meats and delicatessen products.

Kosher Foods
49 Bury New Road, Prestwich, M25
(0161) 773-1308
Supervision: Manchester Beth Din.
Sells groceries as well.

Kosher Supreme
61 Bury Old Road, Prestwich, M25 (0161) 773-2020
Supervision: Manchester Beth Din.

Lloyd Grosberg (J. Kreger)
102 Barlow Moor Road M20 (0161) 445-4983
Supervision: Manchester Beth Din.

Park Lane Kosher Meats
142 Park Lane, Whitefield, M45 7PX
(0161) 766-5091
Supervision: Manchester Beth Din.
Hours: Sunday 8.30 am - 1 pm; Monday and Friday 8 am - 1 pm; Tuesday, Wednesday and Thursday 8 am - 6 pm.

Vidal's Kosher Meats
75 Windsor Road, Prestwich, M25 (0161) 740-3365
Supervision: Manchester Beth Din.

Delicatessens

Cottage Deli
83 Park Lane, Whitefield, (0161) 766-6216
Supervision: Manchester Beth Din.

Deli King
Kings Road, Prestwich, M25 8LQ (0161) 798-7370
Fax: (0161) 798-5654
Supervision: Manchester Beth Din.
Hours: Sunday to Friday, 8.30 am to 6 pm.

Haber's
8 Kings Road, Prestwich, M25 0LE (0161) 773-2046
Fax: (0161) 773-9101
Supervision: Manchester Beth Din.

Hyman's Delicatessen
41 Wilmstow Road, Cheadle, (0161) 491-1100
Fax: (0161) 491-1100
Supervision: Manchester Beth Din.

Groceries

Halperns Kosher Food Store
57-59 Leicester Road, Salford, M7
(0161) 792-1752 Office 792-2992
Fax: (0161) 708-8881
Email: halperns.kosherfood@virgin.net
Supervision: Manchester Beth Din.

State Fayre
77 Middleton Road (0161) 740-3435
Supervision: Manchester Beth Din.

Hotels

Fulda's Hotel
144 Old Bury Road, Salford, M7 4QY
(0161) 740-4748
Fax: (0161) 795-5920
Web site: www.here.at/fuldas
Supervision: Manchester Beth Din.
Four-star hotel open all year. Glatt kosher. Within easy access of motorways, and uniquely placed in the heart of the Manchester Jewish community in Broughton Park. Within easy walking distance of numerous synagogues and shopping facilities.

Kashrut Information

Manchester Beth Din
435 Cheetham Hill Road M8 0PF (0161) 740-9711
Fax: (0161) 721-4249
Contact them to ensure that the establishment is still certified.

Libraries

Central Library
St Peter's Square M2 5PD (0161) 234-1983; 1984
Fax: (0161) 234-1927
Email: socsci@libraries.manchester.gov.uk
Large collection of Jewish books for reference and loan, including books in Hebrew. Contact the Social Sciences Library.

Media

Newspapers

Jewish Telegraph
Telegraph House
11 Park Hill, Bury Old Road, Prestwich, M25 0HH
(0161) 740-9321
Fax: (0161) 740-9325
Email: manchester@jewishtelegraph.com
Web site: www.jewishtelegraph.com

Mikvaot

Manchester & District Mikva (Machzikei Hadass)
Sedgley Park Road, Prestwich, M25
(0161) 773-1537; 773-7403

Manchester Communal Mikvah
Broome Holme,Tetlow Lane, Salford, M7 0BU
(0161) 792-3970
During opening hours only. For appointments for Friday night and YomTov evenings: 740-4071; 740-5199. For tevilat kelim, 795-2272.

Naomi Greenberg South Manchester Mikvah
Hale Synagogue, Shay Lane, Hale Barns,
(0161) 904-8296
Use is by appointment only.

Whitefield Mikvah
Park Lane, Whitefield, M45 7PB (0161) 796-1054
Ansaphone. Evenings only: 773-7830. Use is by appointment only.

Museums

Manchester Jewish Museum
190 Cheetham Hill Road M8 8LW
(0161) 834-9879; 832-7353
Fax: (0161) 834-9801
Email: info@manchesterjewishmuseum.com
Web site: www.manchesterjewishmuseum.com
Exhibitions, Heritage trails, Demonstrations & Talks. Details of events available on request. Educational visits for schools and adult groups must be booked in advance. Open Monday-Thursday, 10.30 am to 4 pm Sundays 10.30 am to 5 pm. Admission charge. Contact Don Rainger, Administrator.

United Kingdom/ Manchester

Organisations

Machzikei Hadass
17 Northumberland Street, Salford, M7 0FE
(0161) 792-1313

Restaurants

Antonio's Pizzaria and Restaurant
JCLC, Corner Bury Old Road & Park Road
(0161) 795-8911

Supervision: Manchester Beth Din.
Open Monday-Thursday 12.3 pm-3.00 pm and 5.30 pm-11 pm; Sunday to 11 pm. In winter 1 1/2 hours after Shabbat until 2 am.

Asher's
5 Kings Road, Prestwich (0161) 773-1414
Supervision: Manchester Beth Din.

Aviv Restaurant
18 The Square, Hale Barns (0161) 980-0009
Supervision: Manchester Beth Din.

Dairy

Brackman's Bakery & Coffee Shop
45 Leicester Road (0161) 792-1652
Supervision: Manchester Beth Din.

Meat

J.S. Kosher Restaurant
7 Kings Road, Prestwich, M25 0LE (0161) 798-7776
Supervision: Manchester Beth Din.
Glatt kosher.

Synagogues

Orthodox

Adass Yeshurun
Cheltenham Crescent, Salford, M7 0FE
(0161) 792-1233

Adath Yisroel Nusach Ari
Upper Park Road, Salford, M7 0HL (0161) 740-3905

Central & North Manchester (incorporating Hightown Central and Beth Jacob)
Leicester Road, Salford, M7 4GP (0161) 740-4830

Cheetham Hebrew Congregation
Jewish Cultural Centre, Bury Old Road, M8 6FY

Congregation of Spanish and Portuguese
18 Moor Lane, Kersal, Salford, M7 0WX
(0161) 792-7406
Fax: (0161) 792-3471
Email: ahodari@antonyhodari.co.uk
Web site: www.18moorlane.freeserve.co.uk

Hale & District Hebrew Congregation
Shay Lane, Hale Barns, Cheshire, WA15 8PA
(0161) 980-8846
Fax: (0161) 980-1802

Heaton Park Hebrew Congregation
Ashdown, Middleton Road, M8 6JX (0161) 740-4766

Higher Crumpsall & Higher Broughton
Bury Old Road, Salford, M7 4PX (0161) 740-1210

Higher Prestwich
445 Bury Old Road, Prestwich, M25 1QP
(0161) 773-4800
Fax: (0161) 773-4800

Hillock Hebrew Congregation
Beverley Close, Ribble Drive, Whitefield, M45
(0161) 959-5663

Holy Law South Broughton Congregation
Bury Old Road, Prestwich, M25 0EX
(0161) 792-6349/721-4705
Fax: (0161) 720-6623
Email: office@holylaw.freeserve.co.uk

Kahal Chassidim
62 Singleton Road, Salford, M7 4LU (0161) 740-1629

Machzikei Hadass
17 Northumberland Street, Salford, M7 0FE
(0161) 792-1313

Manchester Great & New Synagogue
Stenecourt, Holden Road, Salford, M7 4LN
(0161) 792-8399
Fax: (0161) 792-1991

North Salford
2 Vine Street, Salford, M7 0NX (0161) 792-3278

Ohel Torah
132 Leicester Road, Salford, M7 0EA (0161) 740-6678

Prestwich Hebrew Congregation
Bury New Road, M25 9WN (0161) 773-1978
Fax: (0161) 773-7015

Sale & District Hebrew Congregation
14 Hesketh Road, Sale, M33 5AA (0161) 973-2172

Sedgley Park (Shomrei Hadass)
Park View Road, Prestwich, M25 5FA
(0161) 773-4828/740-1969
Email: laurencemiller@hotmail.com

South Manchester
Wilbraham Road M14 6JS (0161) 224-1366
Fax: (0161) 225-8033

United Synagogue
Meade Hill Road M8 4LR (0161) 740-9586

Whitefield Hebrew Congregation
Park Lane, Whitefield, M45 7PB (0161) 766-3732
Fax: (0161) 767-9453

Yeshurun Hebrew Congregation
Coniston Road
Gatley-Cheadle, Cheshire, SK8 4AP (0161) 428-8242
Fax: (0161) 491-5265
Email: yeshurun@btinternet.com

Reform

Cheshire Reform Congregation Menorah Synagogue
Altrincham Road M22 4RZ (0161) 428-7746
Fax: (0161) 428-0937
Email: office@menorah.org

Manchester Reform Synagogue
Jackson's Row M2 5NH (0161) 834-0415
Fax: (0161) 834-0415

Sha'arei Shalom North Manchester Reform Synagogue
Elms Street, Whitefield, M45 8GQ (0161) 796-6736
Fax: (0161) 796-6736

Travel Agencies

Goodmos Tours (Man) Ltd.
23 Leicester Road, Salford, M7 0AS (0161) 792-7333
Fax: (0161) 792-7336
Email: goodmos836@aol.com

ITS: Israel Travel Service
427/430 Royal Exchange
Old Bank Street, M2 7EP (0161) 839-1111
Fax: (0161) 839-0000
Email: all@itstravel.co.uk
Web site: www.itstravel.co.uk
Freephone 0800 0181 839

Peltours Ltd
27-29 Church Street M4 1QA (0161) 834-3721
Fax: (0161) 832-9343

Merseyside

Liverpool

There is evidence of an organised community before 1750, believed to have been composed of Sephardi Jews and to have had some connection with the West Indies and with Dublin, although some authorities believe they were mainly German Jews. The largely Ashkenazi community, who arrived later, were to some degree intending emigrants for the USA and the West Indies who changed their minds and stayed in Liverpool. By 1807 the community had a building in Seel Street, the parent of today's synagogue in Princes Road, which is one of the handsomest in the country.

Booksellers

Liverpool Jewish Bookshop
Harold House, Dunbabin Road, L15 6XL
(0151) 475-5671
Fax: (0151) 475-5671
Full range of Jewish books, artefacts and gifts.
Sundays 11 am to 1 pm.

Kashrut Information

Liverpool Kashrut Commission
(inc. Liverpool Shechita Board)
c/o Shifrin House, 433 Smithdown Road, L15 3JL
(0151) 733-2292
Fax: (0151) 734-0212

Media

Newspapers

Jewish Telegraph
Harold House, Dunbabin Road,L15 6XL
(0151) 475-6666
Fax: (0151) 475-2222
Email: liverpool@jewishtelegraph.com
Web site: www.jewishtelegraph.com

Mikvaot

Childwall Hebrew Congregation
Dunbabin Road L15 6XL (0151) 722-2079
Fax: (0151) 722-2079

Organisations

Merseyside Jewish Representative Council
433 Smithdown Road L15 3JL (0151) 733-2292
Fax: (0151) 734-0212
Email: mjrcshifrin@hotmail.com

Restaurants

JLGB Centre (0151) 475-5825; 475-5671
Open Sun, Tues., Thurs. 6.30-11.00pm. Licensed bar. Out-of-town visitors welcome. Also take-away service.

Kosher

Harold House
Dunbabin Road L15 6XL (0151) 475-5825/5671
Fax: (0151) 475-2212
Email: harold.house@ort.org
Web site: www.merseyside-jewish-community.org.uk
Supervision: Liverpool Kashrut Commission.

Vegetarian

Munchies Eating House
Myrtle Parade (0151) 709-7896

Synagogues

Orthodox

Allerton Hebrew Congregation
cnr. Mather & Booker Avenues
Allerton, L18 9TB (0151) 427-6848

Childwall Hebrew Congregation
Dunbabin Road L15 6XL (0151) 722-2079
Fax: (0151) 722-2079

Greenbank Drive Hebrew Congregation
Greenbank Drive L17 1AN (0151) 733-1417
Fax: (0151) 733-3862

Old Hebrew Congregation
Princes Road L8 1TG (0151) 709-3431
Fax: (0151) 709-4187

Grade II Listed Building. Guided talks available during the week daily. Pre-booking essential. Other times by special arrangement.

Progressive

Liverpool Progressive Synagogue
28 Church Road North L15 6TF (0151) 733-5871

Southport

Organisations

Southport Jewish Representative Council
(01704) 540704
Fax: (01704) 540704

Synagogues

Orthodox

Southport Hebrew Congregation
Arnside Road PR9 0QX (01704) 532964
Fax: (01704) 514002

Mikva on premises.

Reform

New (Reform) Synagogue
Portland Street PR8 1LR (01704) 535950
Email: snewsyn@aol.com

Middlesex

Ruislip

Synagogues

Shenley Avenue, Ruislip Manor, HA4 6BP
(01895) 632934

Staines

Synagogues

Staines & District Synagogue
Westbrook Road, South Street, TW18 4PR
(01784) 254604
Fax: (01784) 254604

Includes Slough and Windsor.

Stanmore

Delicatessens

Great Food Shop
5 Canons Corner HA8 8AE (0208) 958-9446
Fax: (0208) 905-4700
Email: srosenhead@aol.com

Supervision: London Beth Din.

Synagogues

Orthodox

Stanmore & Cannon Park
London Road HA7 4NS (020) 8954 2210
Fax: (020) 8954 4369
Email: stanmore synaogue@cwcom.net

Norfolk

Norwich

The present community was founded in 1813, Jews having been resident in Norwich during the Middle Ages, and connected with the woollen and worsted trade, for which the city was at that time famous. A resettlement of Jews is believed to have been completed by the middle of the eighteenth century.

Synagogues

3a Earlham Road NR2 3RA (01603) 503434

Progressive Jewish Community of East Anglia
c/o Frimette Carr (01603) 714162

Northamptonshire

Northampton

Synagogues

Overstone Road BB1 3JW (01604) 33345
Services on Friday night.

Nottinghamshire

Newark

Holocaust Memorial Centre

Bet Shalom
Laxton, Newark, Notts, NG22 0PA (01623) 836627
Fax: (01623) 836647

Beth Shalom Holocaust Memorial Centre was conceived as a place where some of the implications of the Holocaust can be faced. It is an education centre where Jews and non-Jews work together to forge a united front against the perils of anti-Semitism and racism in society today.

Nottingham

Jews settled in Nottingham as early as medieval times, and centres of learning and worship are known to have existed in that period. The earliest known record of an established community dates from 1822 when a grant of land for burial purposes was made by the Corporation.

Restaurants

Vegetarian

Krisha Restaurant
144 Alfreton Road, Redford, NG7 3NS
(0115) 970-8608

Maxine's Salad Table
56 Upper Parliament Street NG1 2AG
(0115) 947-3622

The Vegetarian Pot
375 Alfreton Road, Redford, NG7 5LT
(0115) 970-3333

Synagogues

Shakespeare Street NG1 4FQ (0115) 947-2004

Nottingham Progressive Jewish Congregation
Lloyd Street, Sherwood, NG5 4BP (0115) 962-4761

Oxfordshire

Oxford

There was an important medieval community here, and the present one dates back to 1842. The Oxford Synagogue and Jewish Centre, serves both the city and the university. It is available for all forms of Jewish worship.

Community Organisations

L'Chaim Society
Albion House, Little Gate, (01865) 794-462

The Synagogue and Jewish Centre
21 Richmond Road OX1 2JL (01865) 553042
Email: information@oxford-synagogue.org.uk
Regular Orthodox, Masorti and Progressive Services. Wide range of communal activities. A kosher meals service operates during term-time. Phone or email for information.

Staffordshire

Stoke On Trent

Synagogues

Birch Terrace, Hanley, ST1 3JN (01782) 616417

Surrey

Guildford

Synagogues

Guildford & District Synagogue
York Road GU1 4DR (01483) 576470
Email: gould.harry@net.ntl.com
Web site: www.geocities.com/guildfordjewishcommunity
Correspondence: Mr B. Gould, Lynwood, Hillier Road, Guildford, Surrey, GU1 2JG.

Tourist Sites

Surrey GU1
Enquiries about the recent discovery of a medieval synagogue in the town may be addressed to the Guildford Museum.

Sussex

Brighton and Hove

The first known Jewish resident of Brighton lived here in 1767. The earliest synagogue was founded in Jew Street in 1789. Henry Solomon, vice-president of the congregation, was the first chief constable of the town. His brother-in-law, Levi Emanuel Cohen, founded the *Brighton Guardian*, and was twice elected president of the Newspaper Society of Great Britain. The town's Jewish population today is about 8,000.

Community Organisations

Lubavitch Chabad House
15 The Upper Drive BN3 6GR (01273) 321-919
Fax: (01273) 821-518

Delicatessens

Cantor's of Hove
20 Richardson Road, Hove BN3 5BB (01273) 723-669

Media

Newspapers

Sussex Jewish News
PO Box 1623 (01273) 504-455

Mikvaot

Prince Regent Swimming Pool Complex.
Church Street, BN1 1YA (01273) 321-919

Organisations

Hillel House
18 Harrington Road BN1 6RE (01273) 503-450
Closed during summer vacation. Friday evening meals available.

Religious Organisations

Brighton and Hove Joint Kashrus Committee
c/o B.H.H.C.
31 New Church Road, Hove, BN3 4AD
(01273) 888855
Fax: (01273) 888810

Synagogues

Brighton & Hove Hebrew Congregation
Middle Street Synagogue
66 Middle Street, BN1 1AL (01273) 888855
Fax: (01273) 888810

Hove Hebrew Congregation
79 Holland Road, Hove, BN3 1JN (01273) 732035

West Hove Synagogue
31 New Church Road, Hove, BN3 4AD
(01273) 888855
Fax: (01273) 888810
Email: bhhc@breathemail.net

Progressive

Progressive Synagogue
6 Landsdowne Road BN3 1FF (01273) 737223
9.30am to 1pm

Reform

New (Reform)
Palmeira Avenue BN3 3GE (01273) 735343
Fax: (01273) 734-537

Eastbourne

Synagogues

22 Susans Road BN21 3TJ (01323) 640441

Hastings

Contact Information

Alfred Ross
PO Box 74, Bexhill on Sea, (01424) 848344

Tyne & Wear

Gateshead

A community with many schools, yeshivot and other training institutions.

Bakeries

Stenhouse
215 Coatsworth Road NE8 1SR (0191) 477-2001

Booksellers

J. Lehmann
28-30 Grasmere Street NE8 1TS (0191) 477-3523
Fax: (0191) 430-0555
Email: info@lehmanns.co.uk
Also has wholesale and mail order, Unit E, Viking Industrial Park, Rolling Mill Road, NE32 3DP. Tel: 0191 430-0333.

Butchers

K.L. Kosher Butcher
83 Rodsley Avenue NE8 (0191) 477-3109
Kosher.

Mikvaot

180 Bewick Road NE8 1UF (0191) 477-3552

Synagogues

138 Whitehall Road NE8 1TP (0191) 477-3012

180 Bewick Road NE8 1UF (0191) 477-0111
Mikva on premises. For appt: 477-3552

Newcastle

The community was established before 1831, when a cemetery was acquired. Jews have lived in Newcastle since 1775. There are about 1,200 Jews in the city today.

Groceries

Zelda's Delicatessen
Unit 7 Kenton Park Shopping Centre
Gosforth, NE3 4RU (0191) 213-0013
Fax: (0191) 213-0013
Email: zeldasdeli@aol.com
Supervision: Newcastle Kashrus Committee, Rabbi Yehuda Black.

Kashrut Information

Kashrus Committee
Lionel Jacobson House, Graham Park Road,
Gosforth, NE3 4BH (0191) 284-0959

Media

Newspapers

The North-East Jewish Recorder
28 Montagu Court NE3 4JL (0191) 285-4318
Email: 100410.2647@compuserve.com

Mikvaot

Graham Park Road NE3 4BH (0191) 284-0959

Organisations

Representative Council of North-East Jewry
56 Southwood Gardens NE3 3BX (0191) 285-403
Fax: (0191) 284-8941

Restaurants

Vegetarian

The Supernatural
2 Princess Square NE1 8ER (0191) 261-2730

Synagogues

Newcastle Reform Synagogue
The Croft, off Kenton Road, NE3 4RF (0191) 284-8621

Synagogues

United Hebrew Congregation
Graham Park Road NE3 4BH (0191) 284-0959
Mikva on premises.

Sunderland

Mikvaot

11 The Oaks East, Ryhope Road, SR2 8EX
(0191) 565-0224

Organisations

11 The Oaks East, Ryhope Road, SR2 8EX
(0191) 565-0224

Synagogues

Communal Rav.
11 The Oaks East, Ryhope Road, SR2 8EX
(0191) 565-0224

Sunderland Hebrew Congregation
Ryhope Road SR2 7EQ (0191) 565-8093
This building has been given Grade II listed status.

West Midlands

Birmingham

This Jewish community is one of the oldest in the provinces, dating from at least 1730. Birmingham was a centre from which Jewish pedlars covered the surrounding country week by week, returning home for Shabbat.

The first synagogue of which there is any record was in The Froggery in 1780. There was a Jewish cemetery in the same neighbourhood in 1730. The synagogue of 1780 was extended in 1791, 1809 and 1827. A new and larger synagogue, popularly known as 'Singers Hill', opened in 1856. Today's Jewish population stands at about 2,300.

Booksellers

Lubavitch Bookshop
95 Willows Road B12 9QF (0121) 440-6673
Fax: (0121) 446-4199

Contact Information

Lubavitch Centre
95 Willows Road B12 9QF (0121) 440-6673
Fax: (0121) 446-4199

Delicatessens

Gee's Butchers Ltd
75 Pershore Road B5 7NX (0121) 440-2160
Kosher butcher, baker and deli.

Information and Resource Centre

Israel Information Centre & Bookshop
Singers Hill, Blucher Street, B1 1QL (0121) 643-2688
Fax: (0121) 643-2688
Email: rjacobs@iicmids.u-net.com
Hours of opening: 10 am-4 pm Monday, Tuesdays, Thursdays or by appointment.

Kashrut Information

Shechita Board
Singers Hill, Ellis Street, B1 1HL (0121) 643-0884

Mikvaot

Birmingham Central Synagogue
133 Pershore Road B5 7PA (0121) 440-4044
Fax: (0121) 440-5405

Representative Organisations

Representative Council of Birmingham & Midland Jewry
37 Wellington Road, Edgbaston, B15 2ES
(0121) 236-1801 Evenings: 440-4142
Fax: (0121) 236-9906
Email: bjrepco@dircon.co.uk
Web site: www.brijnet.org/birmingham

Synagogues

Bimingham Hebrew Congregation
Singer's Hill, Ellis Street, B1 1HL (0121) 643-0884
Fax: (0121) 643-5950

Central Synagogue
133 Pershore Road, Edgbaston, B5 7PA
(0121) 440-4044
Fax: (0121) 440-5405

Progressive Synagogue
4 Sheepcote Street B16 8AA (0121) 643-5640
Fax: (0121) 633-8372
Email: bps@uips.org
Web site: www.bps-pro-syn.co.uk

Coventry

Synagogues

Orthodox

Coventry Hebrew Congregation
Barras Lane CV1 3BW (024) 7622-0168

Reform

Coventry Jewish Reform Community
West Midlands CV (024) 7667-2027
The Jewish presence in Coventry dates back to 1775, if not earlier.

Solihull

Synagogues

Solihull & District Hebrew Congregation
3 Monastery Drive B91 1DW (0121) 707-5199
Fax: (0121) 706-8736
Email: rabbiypink@compuserve.com
Web site: www.solihullshul.org
Services: Friday evening 6.30 pm winter, 8 pm summer; Saturday 9.45 am, Sunday 9 am.

Wolverhampton

Synagogues

Fryer Street WV1 1HT
Established over 150 years ago. Membership, fifteen families. Services Friday evening and some Shabbat mornings.

Yorkshire

Bradford

The Jewish community, although only about 140 years old, has exercised much influence on the city's staple industry: wool. Jews of German descent developed the export trade of wool yarns and fabrics.

Synagogues

Orthodox

Bradford Hebrew Congregation
Springhurst Road, Shipley, BD18 3DN
(01274) 581189
Fax: (01274) 01422-374101
Services 10am monthly on Shabbat Mevorachim, High Holy Days and certain festivals.

Reform

Bradford Synagogue
Bowland Street, Manningham Lane, BD1 3BW
(01274) 728925
Service: Saturday 11 am; Festivals, 6 pm and 11 am.

Harrogate

Synagogues

St Mary's Walk HG2 0LW
Friday 6 pm in Winter and 7 pm in Summer. Shabbat 9.30 am.

Harrogate Hebrew Congregation
St Mary's Walk (01423) 871713
Fax: (01423) 879143
Email: philip.morris@ukgateway.net
Services: Saturday 9.30 a.m. First Friday evening in month - Winter 6 pm / Summer 7 pm.

Leeds

The Leeds Jewish community is the second largest in the provinces, and numbers about 12,000. The community dates only from 1804, although a few Jews are known to have lived there in the previous half-century. The first synagogue was built in 1860.

Bakeries

Orthodox

Chalutz Bakery
378 Harrogate Road LS17 6PY (0113) 269-1350
Supervision: Leeds Kashrut Commission.
Hours: Monday to Thursday, 8 am to 6 pm; Friday, to one hour before Shabbat; Saturday, from one hour after Shabbat to 2 pm Sunday.

Butchers

The Kosherie
410 Harrogate Road LS17 6PY (0113) 268-2943
Fax: (0113) 269-6979
Supervision: Leeds Beth Din.

Community Organisations

Café Martine
Lubavitch Centre, 168 Shadwell Lane, LS17 8AD
(0113) 266-3311
Fax: (0113) 237-1130
Supervision: Leeds Kashrut Authority and Leeds Beth Din.
A community centre which provides educational activities. Restaurant on premises which is currently not open. Call to see if it has re-opened. Open Sunday 5 pm-9 pm. Thursday 6 pm-10 pm. Direct line to the Café 44-113 237 1130.

Delicatessens

Fisher's Deli
391 Harrogate Road LS17 6DJ (0113) 268-6944
Supervision: Leeds Beth Din.
Butcher and deli.

Gourmet Foods
Sandhill Parade, 584 Harrogate Road, LS17 8DP
(0113) 268-2726
Supervision: Leeds Beth Din.
Butcher and deli.

Hotels

Beegee's Guest House
18 Moor Allerton Drive,
off Street Lane, Moortown, LS17 6RZ (0113) 293-5469
Fax: (0113) 275-3300

Near all synagogues.

Libraries

Jewish Library
Porton Collection; Central Library
Municipal Buildings, LS1 3AB (0113) 247-8282
Fax: (0113) 247-8426
Web site: www.leeds.gov.uk

Media

Newspapers

Jewish Telegraph
1 Shaftesbury Avenue LS8 1DR (0113) 295-6000
Fax: (0113) 295-6006
Email: leeds@jewishtelegraph.com
Web site: www.jewishtelegraph.com

Mikvaot

411 Harrogate Road LS17 7BY
(0113) 237-1096 (answerphone)

Religious Organisations

Beth Din
Etz Chaim Synagogue LS17 6BY (0113) 269-6902
Fax: (0113) 237-0893

Information about kosher food and accommodation may be obtained here.

Representative Organisation

Leeds Jewish Representative Council
c/o Shadwell Lane Synagogue LS17 (0113) 269-7520
Fax: (0113) 237-0851

Publishes Year Book.

Restaurants

Hansa's Gujarati Restaurant
72 North Street LS2 7PN (0113) 244-4408
Web site: www.hansasrestaurant.co.uk

Indian Vegetarian restaurant.

Synagogues

Orthodox

Beth Hamedrash Hagadol
399 Street Lane LS17 6HQ (0113) 269-2181
Email: office@bhhs.freeserve.co.uk

Chassidishe
c/o Donisthorpe Hall, Shadwell Lane, LS17 6AW

Etz Chaim
411 Harrogate Road LS17 7BY (0113) 266-2214

Queenshill Synagogue
26 Queenshill Avenue LS17 6AX (0113) 2687364
Email: sabrah2936.aol.com

Shadwell Lane Synagogue (United Hebrew Congregation)
151 Shadwell Lane LS17 8DW (0113) 269-6141
Fax: (0113) 269-6165

Shomrei Hadass
368 Harrogate Road LS17 6QB (0113) 268-1461

Reform

Sinai
Roman Avenue
off Street Lane, LS8 2AN (0113) 266-5256
Fax: (0113) 266-1539
Email: synagogue@sinaileeds.freeserve.co.uk

Sheffield

Synagogues

Orthodox

Sheffield Jewish Congregation and Centre
Kingfield Synagogue
Brincliffe Crescent, S11 8UX (0114) 255-2296

There is also a mikveh in the building.

Reform

Sheffield & District Reform Jewish Congregation
PO Box 675
S11 8S (0114) 230-1054
Fax: (0114) 236-2982
Web site: www.shef-ref.co.uk

Service alternate Friday evenings.

York

Tours of Jewish Interest

Yorkwalk
3 Fairway, Clifton, Y030 5QA (01904) 622303
Fax: (01904) 656244
Email: warwick@yorkwalk.fsnet.co.uk
Web site: www.yorkwalk.netfirms.com

Introduced new walk called 'The Jewish Heritage Walk', recalling the Jewish contribution to York's history. The walk finishes at Clifford's Tower, the site of a dreadful Jewish massacre in 1190.

Channel Islands

Alderney

Memorial

Corblets Road Longy

There is a memorial to the victims of the Nazis during their occupation of the Channel Islands during the Second World War. It bears plaques in English, French, Hebrew and Russian.

Jersey

Contact Information

16 La Rocquaise
La Route des Genets
St Brelade, JE3 8HY (1534) 742-819
Fax: (1534) 747-554

Honorary secretary of the Jersey Jewish Congregation.

Synagogues

Jersey Jewish Congregation
La Petite Route des Mielles
St Brelade, JE3 8FY

Shabbat morning service, 10.30 am; Holy Days, 7 pm and 10 am.

Isle of Man

Douglas

Synagogues

Hebrew Congregation
(01624) 24214

There are more than seventy Jews on the island.

Northern Ireland

Belfast

There were Jews living in Belfast in the year 1652, but the present community was founded in 1869.

Organisations

Vegetarian & Vegans Charity
66 Ravenhill Gardens
Ulster BT6 8QG (028) 9028-1640

Restaurants

Jewish Community Centre
49 Somerton Road
Ulster BT15 3LH (028) 9077-7974

Open Sunday 6.30 pm to 9.30 pm.

Synagogues

49 Somerton Road BT15 3LH (028) 9077-7974

Services: Saturday, Sunday, Monday and Thursday; am. Friday pm.

Scotland

Aberdeen

Restaurants

Vegetarian

Jaws Wholefood Café
5 West North Street AB1 3AT (01224) 645676

10 am to 3 pm Monday-Saturday; 10 am to 9 pm Thursday and Friday.

Synagogues

74 Dee Street AB11 6DS (01224) 582135

Dundee

Synagogues

St Mary Place DD1 5RB (01382) 223557

Dunoon

Synagogues

Argyll & Bute Jewish Community
(01369) 705118

Edinburgh

The Town Council and Burgess Roll minutes of 1691 and 1717 record applications by Jews for permission to live and trade in Edinburgh.

Butchers

3 Oxgangs Road (0131) 445-3437

Regular meat deliveries from suppliers in Glasgow and Manchester. Further information from Hon. Sec. W. Simpson

Kashrut Information

Rabbi D Sedley
(0131) 667-9360

Restaurants

Vegetarian

Black Bo's
Blackfriars Street EH (0131) 557-6136

Henderson's
94 Hanover Street EH2 1DR (0131) 225-2131
Fax: (0131) 220-3542
Email: mail@hendersonsofedinburgh.co.uk
Web site: www.hendersonsofedinburgh.co.uk

Kalpna Restaurant
2/3 St Patrick Sq. EH8 9EZ (0131) 667-9890
Fax: (0131) 443-8782
Email: kalpnarestaurant@yahoo
Web site: www.kalpna.co.uk

Hours: Lunch 1100am to 2.00pm. Dinner 5.30pm to 11pm.

Synagogues

4 Salisbury Road EH16 5AB (0131) 667-3144
Email: ray.taylor@lineone.net

Glasgow

The Glasgow Jewish community dates back to 1823. The oldest synagogue building is the Garnethill Synagogue, now also the home of the Scottish Jewish Archives, which opened in 1879. The community grew rapidly from 1891 with many Jews settling in the Gorbals. In recent years the community has gradually spread southwards and is now mainly situated in the Giffnock and Newton Mearns areas.

Booksellers

J & E Levingstone
47/55 Sinclair Drive G42 9PT (0141) 649-2962
Fax: (0141) 649-2962

Religious requisites also stocked.

Well of Wisdom
Giffnock Synagogue, Giffnock G46 (0141) 577-8260
Fax: (0141) 620-0823

Delicatessens

Hello Deli
200 Fenwick Road, Giffnock G46 (0141) 638-8267
Fax: (0141) 621-2290

Marlenes Kosher Deli
2 Burnfield Road, Giffnock G46 7QB
(0141) 638-4383

Michael Morrison and Son
52 Sinclair Drive G42 9PY (0141) 632-0998
Not under official supervision. Stockist of many glatt kosher items.

Hotels

Forres Guest House
10 Forres Avenue, Giffnock G46 6LJ
(0141) 638-5554 (mobile: 07801 666-864)
Fax: (0141) 571-9301
Email: jtl@ntlworld.com
Web site: www.junedavies.com

Guest House
26 St Clair Avenue, Giffnock G46 7QE
(0141) 638-3924

Kosher, but not supervised.

Media

Newspapers

Jewish Telegraph
May Terrace, Giffnock G46 6DL (0141) 621-4422
Fax: (0141) 621-4333
Email: glasgow@jewishtelegraph.com
Web site: www.jewishtelegraph.com

Mikvaot

Giffnock & Newlands Synagogue
Maryville Avenue, Giffnock G46 7NE
(0141) 577-8250
Fax: (0141) 577-8252

Organisations

Jewish Community Centre
222 Fenwick Road, Giffnock G46 6UE
(0141) 577-8200
Fax: (0141) 577-8202
Email: glasgow@j-scot.org
Web site: www.j-scot.org/glasgow

Religious Organisations

Orthodox

Lubavitch Foundation of Scotland
8 Orchard Drive, Giffnock G46 7NR
(0141) 638-6116
Fax: (0141) 638 6478
Email: LubOfScot@aol.com
Web site: www.lubofscot.com

Restaurants

Meat

Kaye's Restaurant
Maccabi Youth Centre, May Terrace G46
(0141) 620-3233

Kosher.

Synagogues

Orthodox

Garnethill
129 Hill Street G3 6UB (0141) 322-4151
Shabbat services 10am. Yomtov services 9.45 am.

Giffnock & Newlands Hebrew Congregation
Maryville Avenue, Giffnock G46 7NE
(0141) 577-8250
Fax: (0141) 577-8252
Email: giffnock-rabbi@j-scot.org

Langside
125 Niddrie Road G42 8QA (0141) 423-4062

Netherlee & Clarkston
Clarkston Road at Randolph Drive G44
(0141) 637-8206/639-7194
Fax: (0141) 616-0743

Newton Mearns
14 Larchfield Court G77 5BH (0141) 639-4000
Fax: (0141) 639-4000

Queen's Park Hebrew Congregation
Falloch Road G42 9QX (0141) 632-1743
Fax: (0141) 636-9470

Reform

Glasgow New Synagogue
147 Ayr Road, Newton Mearns G77 6RE
(0141) 639-4083
Fax: (0141) 639-4083
Email: shul@gns.org.uk

St Andrews

Contact Information

Jewish Student's Society
c/o Sec., Students' Union
University of St Andrews, Kirkcaldy KY16 9UY

Wales

Cardiff

Mikvaot

Wales Empire Pool Building,
Wood Street CF1 1PP (029) 2038-2296

Restaurants

Vegetarian

Munchies Wholefood Co-op
60 Crwys Road, Cathays CF2 4NN (029) 2039-9677

Self-catering

Hillel House CF2 5NR (029) 2022-8845
Self catering for students.

Synagogues

Orthodox

Cardiff United Synagogue
Brandreth Road, Penylan CF
(029) 2047-3728/2048-7377
Fax: (029) 2047-3728
Email: rabbi@cardiffunited.org.uk
Web site: www.cardiffunited.org.uk

Reform

Cardiff New Synagogue
Moira Terrace CF2 1EJ (029) 2061-4915

Llandudno

Hotels

Plas Madoc Vegetarian Guesthouse
60 Church Walks, Conwy LL30 2HL
(01492) 876514
Email: plasmadoc@vegetarianguesthouse.com
Web site: www.vegetarianguesthouse.com
100% vegetarian. Synagogue 100 yards away.

Synagogues

28 Church Walks LL30 2HL (01492) 572549
No resident minister, but visiting ministers during summer months. Friday night services held throughout year, 6.15 pm (winter) and 8 pm (summer).

Newport

Synagogues

Newport Mon Hebrew Congregation
Risca Road NP9 5HH (01633) 262308
Fax: (01633) 266362
Communication: 45 St Marks Crescent, Newport, S. Wales, NP20 5HE.

Swansea

Restaurants

Vegetarian

Chris's Kitchen
The Market SA1 3PE (01792) 643455
8.30am to 5.30pm Mon.-Sat

Synagogues

Ffynone
17 Ffynone Drive SA1 6DB (01792) 473333

United States of America

The first Jews came to what is now the United States of America in 1654. The ship had come from the West Indies and included twenty-three Jews from Brazil who were attempting to escape the arrival of the Inquisition following Portugal's recapture of Brazil from the Dutch earlier that year. It is believed that they thought they were travelling to Amsterdam in the Netherlands rather than to New Amsterdam as New York was then called. Within ten years, however, the commuity was moribund. The surrender of New Amsterdam to the British in 1664 brought substantial changes to the Jewish settlement as some restrictions to both civil and religious rights were lifted. In a few colonies they were even granted the right to vote.

Following the English takeover communities were established along the eastern coast, and by 1700 there were between 200 and 300 Jews in the country. At the time of the Revolution there were between 1,500 and 2,000 Jews and they served both in the Militia (which was compulsory) and as officers and soldiers. In the decades immediately before the Civil War the Jewish population rose from 15,000 to 150,000 as a result of emigration, mainly from German areas. During that war Jews served on both sides with their respective communities.

Immigration was at its peak between 1880 and 1925 (when free emigration ended) and during this period the Jewish population grew from 280,000 to 4,500,000. Unfortunately, during the 1930s only a small number of the Jewish refugees trying to escape from Germany were able to enter the USA. America's numerical position in world Jewry has declined, with its population being in 1948 as much as ten times the population of Israel, to its current approaching parity. The largest concentration by far has always been in New York.

Each of the main religious groups has its own association of synagogues and rabbis and, unlike many other countries, there is no central religious organisation. There is therefore no central supervision of kashrut. Instead there are many hashgachot issued by both individual local communal organisations and rabbis, as well as by companies who issue such certificates on a commercial basis. Travellers may always check with a local rabbi to ascertain the appropriate supervisory body in a relevant location. **Travellers should also be aware that, following a decision in the Brooklyn (New York) District Court in July 2000, discussions are under way in several other jurisdictions to prepare for the eventuality that New York's kosher laws may be rendered unconstitutional on appeal.**

GMT -5 to 11 hours — Total Population 278,357,000
Country calling code (1) — Jewish Population 5,700,000
Emergency Telephone (Police, Fire and Ambulance - 911) — Electricity voltage 110/220

Alabama

Birmingham

Community Organisations

Birmingham Jewish Federation
3966 Montclair Road 35213 (205) 803-0416
Fax: (205) 803-1526

Contact Information

Rabbi Avraham Shmidman
3225 Montevallo Road 35223 (205) 879-1664
Fax: (205) 879-5774
Email: kicongreg@aol.com
Visitors requiring information about kashrut, temporary accommodation, etc., should contact Rabbi Shmidman.

Delicatessens

Browdy's
2607 Cahaba Road 35223 (205) 879-6411

Libraries

Hess Library
3960 Montclair Road 35213

Mikvaot

Knesseth Israel
3225 Montevallo Rd 35213 (205) 879-1464
Supervision: (O).

Synagogues

Conservative

Beth-El
2179 Highland Avenue 35205 (205) 933-2740
Fax: (205) 933-2747

Orthodox

Knesseth Israel
3225 Montevallo Road 35223 (205) 879-1464
Fax: (205) 879-5774

Reform

Emanu-El
2100 Highland Avenue 35205 (205) 933-8037

Huntsville

Synagogues

Conservative

Etz Chayim
7705 Bailey Cove Road 35802 (256) 882-2918
Fax: (256) 881-6160

Mobile

Synagogues

Reform

Spring Hill Avenue Temple
1769 Spring Hill Avenue 36607 (334) 478-0415

Montgomery

Community Organisations

Jewish Federation
PO Box 20058 36120 (334) 277-5820
Fax: (334) 277-8383

Synagogues

Conservative

Agudath Israel
3525 Cloverdale Road 36111 (334) 281-7394
Mikvah attached.

Orthodox

Etz Ahayem (Sephardi)
725 Augusta Road 36111 (334) 281-9819

Reform

Beth Or
2246 Narrow Lane 36106
Maxwell Air Force Base
Building 833, Chaplain's School

Alaska

Anchorage

Groceries

Carr's
Diamond Boulvevard

Synagogues

Orthodox

Congregation Shomrei Ohr
1210 E. 26th 99508 (907) 279-1200
Fax: (907) 279-7890
Email: lubavitchofak@gci.net
The centre offers full Shabbat meals featuring homemade dishes.

Reform

Beth Sholom
7525 E. Northern Lights Blvd 99504 (907) 338-1836
Fax: (907) 337-4013
Email: sholom@alaska.net

Denali Park Area

Groceries

PS Kosher Food Services
P.O. Box 240, Mile 248.
5 Parks Highway, Healy 99743 (907) 683-1560
Fax: (907) 683-4026
Email: psfood@juno.com
Kitchens located at Denali North Star Inn. Summer sales only.

Arizona

Phoenix

Community Organisations

Jewish Federation of Greater Phoenix
32 W. Coolidge, Suite 200 85013 (602) 274-1800
Orthodox Rabbinical Council of Greater Phoenix
515 E. Bethany Home Road 85012 (602) 277-8858
Fax: (602) 274-0713

Kashrut Information

Rabbi David Rebibo
Pheonix Vaad Hakashruth,
515 E. Bethany Home Rd 85012 (602) 277-8858
Fax: (602) 274-0713

Visitors requiring kashrut information should contact Rabbi Rebibo.

Media

Newspapers

Jewish News of Greater Phoenix
1625 E. Northern 106 85020 (602) 870-9470
Fax: (602) 870-0426
Email: jngphx@aol.com

Shalom Arizona
32 W. Coolidge, Suite 200 85013 (602) 274-1800

Synagogues

Tri-Cities Jewish Community Center
1965 E. Hermosa Temp, AZ 85282 (602) 897-0588

Conservative

Congregation Beth El
1118 W. Glendale 85021 (602) 944-3359

Temple Beth Sholom
3400 N Dobson Road,
Chandler 85224 (480) 897-3636
Fax: (480) 897-3633
Email: templebethsholom@aol.com
Web site: www.templebethsholomaz.org

Orthodox

Congregation Beth Joseph
515 E. Bethany Home Road 85012 (602) 277-8858
Fax: (602) 274-0713

Congregation Shaarei Tzedek
7608 N. 18th Avenue 85021 (602) 944-1133

Valley of the Sun Jewish Community Center
1718 W. Maryland Avenue 85015 (602) 249-1832

Young Israel of Phoenix
745 E Maryland Avenue,
Ste.120 85014 (602) 265-8888
Fax: (602) 265-8867
Email: cnsil5@home.com

Reform

Temple Beth Ami
4545 N. 36th Street,
No. 211 85018 (302) 956-0805

Temple Chai
4645 E. Marilyn Avenue 85032 (602) 971-1234

Scottsdale

Museums

Sylvia Plotkin Judaica Museum
10460 N. 56th St,
Scottsdale 85253 (480) 951-0323
Fax: (480) 951-7150
Email: museum@templebethisrael.org
Web site: www.sylviaplotkinjudaica.org

Hours: Most Sundays 12 am 3 pm, Tuesday-Friday 10 am 3 pm, Friday evenings after services. Advanced notice required for groups of ten or more.

Synagogues

Conservative

Beth Emeth of Scottsdale
5406 E. Virginia Avenue 85254 (602) 947-4604

Beth Joshua Congregation
6230 E. Shea Blvd. 85254 (602) 991-5404

Har Zion
5929 E. Lincoln Drive 85253 (602) 991-0720

Reform

Temple Kol Ami
15030 N. 64th Street 85254 (480) 951-9660
Fax: (480) 951-5231
Email: templekolami@aol.com

Temple Solel
6805 E. MacDonald Drive 85253 (480) 991-7414
Fax: (480) 451-0829
Email: mleano@templesolel.org
Web site: www.templesolel.org

Sierra Vista

Synagogues

Temple Kol Hamidbar
PO Box 908, Sierra Vista 85636
(520) 458-8637 (Ans. phone only)
Email: tkh85636@hotmail.com
Web site: www.uahcweb.org/congs/az/tkh/

Location is 228 North Canyon Drive

Sun City and West

Synagogues

Conservative

Beth Emeth of Sun City
13702 Meeker Blvd., 85373 (602) 584-1957

Reform

Beth Shalom of Sun City
12202 101st Avenue 85351 (623) 977-3240
Fax: (623) 977-3214
Email: tbsaz@goodnet.com

Tempe

Community Organisations

Tri-City Jewish Community Center
1965 E. Hermosa Drive 85282 (602) 897-0588

Synagogues

Orthodox

Chabad-Lubavitch Center
23 W. 9th Street 85281 (602) 966-5163

Reform

Temple Emanuel
5801 Rural Road 85283 (602) 838-1414

Tucson

Butchers & Delicatessens

Feig's Kosher Market & Deli
5071 E. 5th Street 85711 (520) 325-2255
Fax: (520) 325-2978

Supervision: Rabbi R. Eisen..
Fresh glatt beef, lamb and veal, full service deli, groceries. Hours: Monday to Thursday, 8 am to 5:45 pm; Friday, to 3:45 pm; Sunday, to 1:45 pm.

Community Organisations

Jewish Federation of Southern Arizona
3822 E. River Rd 85718 (520) 577-9393
Fax: (520) 577-0734
Email: stumellan@jon.cjfny.org

Synagogues

Conservative

Congregation Bet Shalom
3881 E. River Road 85718 (520) 577-1171
Fax: (520) 577-8903
Email: cbs3881@juno.com

Supervision: Rabbi Leo M Abrami.
Kosher (dairy) kitchen, operated by Sisterhood.

Orthodox

Congregation Chofetz Chayim
5150 E. 5th Street 85711 (520) 747-7780
Fax: (520) 745-6325
Email: ewbecker@flash.net

Young Israel of Tucson
2443 E 4th Street 85710 (520) 326-8362

Arkansas

El Dorado

Synagogues

Beth Israel
1130 E. Main Street

Helena

Synagogues

Temple Beth-El
406 Perry Street 72342 (501) 338-6654
Founded 1875.

Hot Springs

Synagogues

House of Israel
300 Quapaw Avenue. 71901 (501) 623-5821
Fax: (501) 622-3500
Email: houseofi@direclynx.net

Supervision: (R).
Hot Springs is known for its curative waters. The Leo Levi Memorial Hospital (for joint disorders, such as arthritis) was founded by B'nai B'rith, as was the adjacent Levi Towers, a senior citizen housing project.

Little Rock

Bakeries

Andre's
11121 Rodney Parham Rd 72212

Community Organisations

Jewish Federation of Arkansas
425 N. University Ave.,
Little Rock 72205 (501) 663-3571
Fax: (501) 663-7286
Email: jfalr@aristotle.net

Monday to Thursday 9.00am to 5.00pm. Friday 9.00am to 4.00pm.

Synagogues

Orthodox

Agudath Achim
7901 W. 5th St. 72205 (501) 225-1683
Mikvah on premises.

Reform

B'nai Israel
3700 Rodney Parham Rd 72212 (501) 225-9700
Fax: (501) 225-6058
Email: elevy@snider.net

California

As the general population of California continues to increase, the Jewish community is growing as well. Places of worship abound, from Eureka in the north to San Diego in the south, but the majority of the community lives in the Los Angeles metropolitan area.

Anaheim

Restaurants

Disneyland
Kosher meals are available at the Blue Bayou restaurant, adjacent to the Pirates of the Caribbean. Place orders at least one hour in advance.

Synagogues

Conservative

Temple Beth Emet
1770 W. Cerritos Avenue 92804 (714) 772-4720
Fax: (714) 772-4710
Email: tbe-anaheim@tea-house.com

Arcadia

Synagogues

Congregation Shaarei Torah
550 S. 2nd Avenue 91006 (818) 445-0810

Arleta

Synagogues

Reform

Temple Beth Solomon of the Deaf
13580 Osborne Street 91331 (818) 899-2202
Fax: (818) (TDD) 896-6721

Bakersfield

Synagogues

Conservative

B'nai Jacob
600 17th Street 93301 (661) 325-8017

Reform

Temple Beth El
2906 Loma Linda Drive 93305 (661) 322-7607
Fax: (661) 322-7807
Email: kernjew@aol.com

Berkeley (See also Oakland)

Mikvaot

Mikvah Taharas Israel
2520 Warring St. 94704-3111 (510) 848-7221
Fax: (510) 849-0536
Email: vaad@flash.net

Available by appointment only.
(Women 510-848-7221; Men 510-548-8729)

Museums

Judah L. Magnes Jewish Museum
2911 Russell St. 94705 (510) 549-6950
Fax: (510) 849-3673
Email: pfpr@magnesmuseum.org

Among the earliest institutions of its kind west of New York. It includes Judaica and fine arts collections, changing and permanent exhibitions, the Western Jewish History Center, & the Blumenthal Library. Open Sunday-Thursday; 10 am-4 pm.

Synagogues

Conservative

Netivot Shalom
1841 Berkeley Way 94708 (510) 549-9447
Fax: (510) 549-9448
Email: administrator@netivotshom.org
Web site: www.netivotshalom.org

Weekly Shabbat/Holy Day services at 1414 Walnut Street.

Egalitarian

Berkeley Hillel Foundation
2736 Bancroft Way 94704 (510) 845-7793
Fax: (510) 845-7753

Traditional egalitarian services on Friday evening/student programmes.

Orthodox

Chabad House
2643 College Avenue 94704

Congregation Beth Israel
1630 Bancroft Way 94703 (510) 843-5246
Fax: (510) 843-5058
Email: office@beth-israel.berkeley.ca.us
Web site: www.beth-israel.berkeley.ca.us

Reform

Congregation Beth El
2301 Vine Street 94708 (510) 848-3988
Fax: (510) 848-9434
Email: frontoffice@bethelberkeley.org

Burlingame

Synagogues

Peninsula Temple Sholom
1655 Sebastian Drive 94010 (415) 697-2266
Fax: (415) 697-2544

Carmel

Synagogues

Congregation Beth Israel
5716 Carmel Valley Road 93923 (831) 624-2015
Fax: (831) 624-4786
Email: shalomcbi@aol.com
Services: Friday night 8.00 pm and Saturday 11 am.

Castro Valley

Synagogues

Shir Ami
4529 Malabar Avenue 94546 (415) 537-1787

Costa Mesa

Gift Shop

The Golden Dreidle
1835 Newport Blvd. #A111 92627 (949) 645-3878
Fax: (949) 646-5081

Organisations

Jewish Federation of Orange County
250 E. Baker Street 92626 (714) 755-5555 ext 241
Fax: (714) 755-0307
Email: alison@jfoc.org

Daly City

Synagogues

Conservative

B'nai Israel
1575 Annie Street 94015 (415) 756-5430

Davis

Synagogues

Reform

Davis Jewish Fellowship
1821 Oak Avenue 95616 (916) 758-0842

Eureka

Synagogues

Beth El
Hodgson & T Streets, PO Box 442 95502
(707) 444-2846

Fresno

Community Organisations

Jewish Federations Office
1340 W. Herndon, Suite 103 93711

Synagogues

Conservative

Beth Jacob
406 W. Shields Avenue 93705 (209) 222-0664

Orthodox

Chabad House
6735 N. ILA 93711 (209) 432-2770

Reform

Temple Beth Israel
6622 N. Maroa Avenue 93704 (209) 432-3600
This temple has its own etrog tree, planted from a sprig brought to the USA from Israel.

Gardena

Synagogues

Conservative

Southwest Temple Beth Torah
14725 S. Gramercy Place 90249 (310) 327-8734

Greater Los Angeles

Los Angeles is America's, and the world's, second largest Jewish metropolis, with a Jewish population of around 600,000. Fairfax Avenue and Beverly Blvd together form the crossroads of traditional Jewish life while a growing Orthodox enclave is centred around Pico and Robertson Blvds.

Important note: Area telephone codes have recently been split in to 310 and 213 for central Los Angeles. We have endeavored in all cases to correct our information, but cannot guarantee the accuracy of those entries where updates have not been submitted

Bakeries

Fairfax Kosher Market & Bakery
11196-98 Los Alamitos Blvd 90720 (714) 828-4492

Noah's New York Bagels
1737 Santa Rita Road #400,
Pleasanton 94566 (510) 485-1921
Email: noah@noahs.com
Supervision: California Rabbinical Council.
All stores in Southern California are under RCC supervision; for the location of a store near you, call the above number.

Schwartz Bakery
8616 W. Pico Blvd (310) 854-0592
Fax: (310) 653-6142
Supervision: RCC.

Schwartz Bakery
441 N. Fairfax Ave. 90036 (213) 653-1683
Fax: (213) 653-6142
Supervision: RCC.

Booksellers

House of David
9020 W. Olympic Blvd,
Beverly Hills 90211 (310) 276-9414
Probably the most complete selection of books of Jewish interest can be found here.

Steimatzky
19566 Ventura Blvd, Tarzana (818) 708-2347
Fax: (818) 708-2319
Email: stmla@earthlink.net

Community Organisations

Jewish Federation of Greater Long Beach & W. Orange County
3801 E. Willow St. 90815 (310) 426-7601

Jewish Federation of Greater Los Angeles
6505 Wilshire Blvd 90048 (323) 761-8000
Fax: (323) 761-8123
Web site: www.jewishla.org

Los Angeles West Side Community Center
5870 W. Olympic Blvd 90036 (323) 938-2531
Fax: (323) 954-9175
Email: westsidejcc@jcc-gla.org

Delicatessens

Pico Kosher Deli
8826 W. Pico Blvd 90035 (310) 273-9381
Fax: (310) 273-8476
Supervision: RCC.
Hours: Sunday to Thursday, 10 am to 9 pm; Friday, 9 am to 3 pm. Glatt.

Embassy

Consul General of Israel
Suite 1700, 6380
Wilshire Blvd 90048 (213) 852-5523
Fax: (213) 852-5555
Email: israinfo@primenet.com
Web site: www.israelemb.org/la

Groceries

PS Kosher Food Services
9760 W. Pico Blvd 90035 (310) 553-8804
Fax: (310) 385-1399
Email: psfood@juno.com
Web site: www.pskosherfood.com
Kitchens located at Yeshiva University.

Hospital

Cedars Sinai Hospital
8700 Beverly Blvd (310) 855-4797
Supervision: RCC.

Kashrut Information

Board of Rabbis of Southern California
6505 Wilshire Blvd, Suite 415 90036 (323) 761-8600
Fax: (323) 761-8603

Kosher Information Bureau
15365 Magnolia Blvd,
Sherman Oaks 91403 (818) 762-3197 & 262-5351
Fax: (818) 766-8537
Email: eeidlitz@kosherquest.org
Web site: www.kosherquest.org

Rabbi Bukspan
6407 Orange Street 90048 (310) 653-5083

Rabbinical Council of California
1122 S. Robertson Blvd 90035 (310) 271-4160
Fax: (310) 271-714

Media

Newspapers

Heritage Southwest Jewish Press
Weekly publication, coming out on Fridays.

Jewish Community Chronicle
3801 E. Willow St. 90815 1791

Jewish Journal
Weekly publication, coming out on Fridays.

Jewish News

Yisrael Shelanu

Mikvaot

3847 Atlantic Avenue 90807

Los Angeles Mikva
9548 W. Pico Blvd.90035

Museums

Museum of Tolerance (Beit Hashoah)
9786 West Pico Blvd 90035 (310) 553-8403
Fax: (310) 553-4521
Email: information@wiesenthal.net
Web site: www.museumoftolerance.com
High-tech, hands-on museum that focuses on two themes through interactive exhibits: the dynamics of racism and prejudice, and the history of the Holocaust – the ultimate example of man's inhumanity to man.

Organisations

Jewish Social Action Organisation
Simon Wiesenthal Center,
1399 South Roxbury Dr. 90035 (310) 553-9036
Fax: (310) 553-4521
Email: information@wiesenthal.net
Web site: www.wiesenthal.com

National Council of Young Israel
West Coast Regional Office
1050 Indiana Avenue 90291 (310) 396-3935
Fax: (310) 581-0904
Email: ncyi.west@youngisrael.org

Restaurants

Dairy

Fish Grill
7226 Beverly Blvd. (323) 937-7162

Fish Place Restaurant
9340 W. Pico Blvd (310) 858-8737
Supervision: Kehila Kosher.

Milk & Honey
8837 W. Pico Blvd (310) 858-8850

Pizza Delight
435 N. Fairfax Avenue (323) 655-7800

Pizza World
365 S. Fairfax Avenue (323) 653-2896

Meat

Chick 'N Chow
9301 W. Pico Blvd (310) 274-5595

Cohen Restaurant
316 E. Pico Blvd 90015 (213) 742-8888
Fax: (213) 742-0066
Supervision: RCC.

Glatt Hut
9303 W. Pico Blvd (310) 246-1900

Grill at the Beverly Carlton
9400 W. Olympic (310) 282-0945

Magic Carpet
8566 W. Pico Blvd 90035 (310) 652-8507
Fax: (310) 652-3568
Supervision: Kehillah of Los Angeles.

Shimon's LA Glatt
446 N. Fairfax Avenue (323) 658-7730

Pizzerias

Pizza Delight
435 N. Fairfax Avenue 90036 (323) 655-7800
Fax: (323) 655-1142
Supervision: Kehillah of Los Angeles.
Chalav Yisrael.

Shalom Pizza
8715 W. Pico Blvd (310) 271-2255
Email: shalompizza@la.com
Supervision: RCC.

Synagogues

Jewish Pacific Center
505 Ocean Front Walk & 720 Rosa Avenue 90291
(310) 392-8749
Email: office@pjcenter.com
Web site: www.pjcenter.com

Mikva and an elementary day school with summer camp facilities for visitors. It also offers a full range of kosher food, bakery products and meat, as well as accommodation.

Conservative

Adat Shalom
3030 Westwood Blvd 90034 (310) 475-4985

Beth Shalom
3635 Elm Avenue 90807

Congregation Shalom of Leisure World
1661 Golden Rain Road,
Northwood Clubhouse No. 3, Seal Beach 90740

Sinai Temple
10400 Wilshire Blvd 90024 (310) 474-1518

Temple Beth Am
1039 S. La Cienega Blvd 90035 (310) 652-7353
Fax: (310) 652-2384
Email: betham@tbala.org
Web site: www.tbala.org

Orthodox

Beth Jacob
9030 Olympic Blvd 90211

B'nai David Congregation
8906 W. Pico Blvd 90035

Breed St. Shule
247 N. Breed St. 90033
This synagogue is of historial interest.

Chabad House
741 Gayley Avenue, West Los Angeles 90025

Congregation Lubavitch
3981 Atlantic Avenue 90807 (562) 596-1681

Etz Jacob Congregation
7659 Beverly Blvd 90036 (323) 938-2619
Fax: (323) 930-2373
Email: lgbkg@earthlink.net

Ohel David
7967 Beverly Blvd

Ohev Shalom
525 S. Fairfax Avenue 90036 (310) 653-7190

Young Israel of Beverly Hills
8701 Pico Blvd 90035 (310) 275-3020

Young Israel of Century City
9317 West Pico Blvd,
Century City 90035 (310) 273-6954
Fax: (310) 273-7103
Email: shuloffice@yicc.org
Web site: www.yicc.org

Young Israel of Hancock Park
225 South La Brea (323) 931-4030
Fax: (323) 935-3819

Young Israel of Long Beach
PO Box 7041 90807-0041 (310) 527-3163

Young Israel of Los Angeles
660 N. Spaulding Avenue 90036 (323) 655-0300
Fax: (323) 655-0322

Young Israel of North Beverly Hills
9350 Civic Center Drive,
North Beverly Hills 90210 (310) 203-0170

Orthodox Sephardi

Kahal Joseph
10505 Santa Monica Blvd 90025 (310) 474-0559

Magen David
322 N. Foothill 90210 (310) 285-9957

Temple Tifereth Israel
10500 Wilshire Blvd, 90024 (310) 475 7311

Reconstructionist

Kehillat Israel
16019 Sunset Blvd,
Pacific Palisades 90272 (310) 459-2328
Fax: (310) 573-2098
Email: kihome@aol.com

Kehillat Israel has a modern sanctuary in the round. It is the largest reconstructionist synagogue in the United States.

Reform

Beth Chayim Chadishim
6000 W. Pico Blvd 90035 (213) 931-7023

Leo Baeck Temple
1300 N. Sepulveda Blvd 90049 (310) 476-2861

Stephen S. Wise Temple
15500 Stephen S. Wise Drive, Bel Air 90024
(310) 476-8561

Temple Akiba
5249 S. Sepulveda Blvd, Culver City 90230
(310) 398-5783

Temple Emanuel
8844 Burton Way 90211 (310) 274-6388
Fax: (310) 271-7976

Temple Isaiah
10345 W. Pico Blvd 90064

University Synagogue
11960 Sunset Blvd. 90049 (310) 472-1255
Fax: (310) 476-3237

Wilshire Blvd. Temple
3663 Wilshire Blvd, 90010 (213) 388-2401
Fax: (213) 388-2595

La Jolla

Synagogues

Orthodox

Congregation Adat Yeshurun
8625 La Jolla Scenic Dr., N. 92037 (858) 535-1196
Fax: (858) 535-0037
Web site: www.adatyeshurun.org

Laguna Hills

Delicatessens

The Kosher Bite
23595 Moulton Parkway 92653 (949) 770-1818
Fax: (949) 770-5321
Email: kosherbite.com

Supervision: Rabinical Council of Orange County.
Monday, Tuesday, Thursday 9am to 5pm. Wednesday 9 am to 7 pm. Friday 9 am-3 pm.

Lakewood

Synagogues

Conservative

Temple Beth Zion Sinai
6440 Del Amo Blvd 90713 (562) 429-0715
Fax: (562) 429-0715
Email: tbzs@jps.net

Northridge

Synagogues

Orthodox

Young Israel of Northridge
17511 Devonshire Street 91325 (818) 368-2221
Fax: (818) 360-5754
Email: rebbe@idt.net

Oakland

Delicatessens

Oakland Kosher Foods
677 Rand Avenue 94610 (510) 272-0535
Glatt kosher.

Mikvaot

Beth Jacob Synagogue
3778 Park Blvd 94610 (510) 482-1147
Fax: (510) 482-2374
Email: bjc-office@eb.jfed.org

Organisations

Jewish Federation of the Greater East Bay
401 Grand Avenue #500 94610

Synagogues

Reform

Temple Beth Torah
42000 Paseo Padre Pkwy 94539 (415) 656-7141

Temple Israel
3183 Mecartney Road 94501

Orthodox

Beth Jacob Synagogue
3778 Park Blvd 94610 (510) 482-1147
Fax: (510) 482-2374
Email: bjc-office@eb.jfed.org

Palm Springs

Community Organisations

Jewish Federation of Palm Springs Desert Area
611 S. Palm Canyon Drive 92264 (760) 325-7281

Synagogues

Conservative

Temple Isaiah
332 W. Alejo Road 92262 (760) 325-2281
Fax: (760) 325-3235
Jewish community centre at this location.

Orthodox

Chabad of Palm Springs
425 Avenue, Ortega (619) 325-0774
Daily Services

Desert Synagogue
1068 N. Palm Canyon Drive 92262
(760) 327-4848
Daily minyan: January through Purim (call shul to confirm).

Palo Alto

Community Organisations

Albert L. Schultz Community Center
655 Arastradero Road 94306 (650) 493-9400

Groceries

Garden Fresh
1245 W. El Camino Road, Mount View 94040
(650) 961-7795

Synagogues

Orthodox

Chabad of Greater South Bay
3070 Louis Road 94303 (650) 424-9800
Fax: (650) 493-0146
Email: chabad@jewish.org

Palo Alto Orthodox Minyan
260 Sheridan Avenue 94306 (650) 948-7498

Pasadena

Synagogues

Conservative

Pasadena Jewish Temple and Center
1434 North Altadena Drive 91107 (626) 798-1161

Poway

Synagogues

Orthodox

Chabad of Poway
16934 Chabad Way 92064 (858) 451-0455
Fax: (858) 673-0299

Sacramento

Community Organisations

Jewish Federation of Sacramento
2351 Wyda Way 95825 (916) 486-0906
Fax: (916) 486-0816
Email: jfed@juno.com
Web site: www.jewishsac.org

Groceries

Bob Butcher Block & Deli
6426 Fair Oaks Blvd, Carmichael 95608

Restaurants

Meat

Bob's Butcher Block
6436 Fair Oaks Blvd.,
Carmichael Oaks Shopping Ctr (916) 482-6884

Synagogues

Conservative

Mosaic Law
2300 Sierra Blvd. 95825 (916) 488-1122
Fax: (916) 488-1165
Web site: www.mosaiclaw.org

Orthodox

Kenesset Israel Torah Center
1165 Morse Avenue 95864 (916) 481-1159
Email: ravshlomo@softcom.net

Reform

B'nai Israel
3600 Riverside Blvd. 95818 (916) 446-4861
Beth Shalom
4746 El Camino Avenue 95608 (916) 485-4478

San Bernardino

Synagogues

Emanu El
3512 N. E Street 92405 (909) 886-4818
Fax: (909) 883-5892
Email: cee@emanuelsb.org

This congregation is the oldest in southern California. The 'Home of Eternity' cemetery, 8th St. & Sierra Way, presented by the Mormons, is one of the oldest Jewish cemeteries in western USA.

San Carlos

Accommodation Information

Jewish Travel Network
PO Box 283 94070 (650) 368-0880
Fax: (650) 599-9066
Email: info@jewishtravelnetwork.com
Web site: www.jewishtravelnetwork.com/

International hospitality exchange. Bed and breakfast and home exchanges.

San Diego

The largest public park in San Diego includes the house of Pacific Relations, which comprises thirty cottages for various ethnic groups. These include the cottage of Israel, which mounts exhibitions throughout the year, portraying the history and traditions of the Jewish people, biblical and modern Israel. Open Sunday 1:30-4:30 pm, except on Holy Days and major festivals.

Bakeries

Sheila's Café & Bakery
4577 Clairemont Drive 92117 (858) 270-0251
Fax: (858) 274-5797
Email: SheilasSanDiego@hotmail.com
Web site: www.sheilascafe.com

Full time Shomer Shabbos Mashgiach on the premises

Restaurants

Dairy

Sababa, Kosher Restaurant
7520 El Cajon Blvd (619) 337-1880
Fax: (619) 523-9963

Meat

Sheila's Café & Bakery
4577 Clairemont Dr. 92117 (858) 270-0251
Fax: (858) 274-5797
Email: SheilasSanDiego@hotmail.com
Web site: www.sheilascafe.com

Synagogues

Orthodox

Ohr Shalom
1260 Morena Blvd, Suite 100 92100
(619) 275-9299
Fax: (619) 275-2078

San Diego Area

Community Organisations

United Jewish Federation of San Diego County
4950 Murphy Canyon 92123-4325
(858) 571-3444
Fax: (858) 571-0701
Email: outreach@ujfsd.org
Web site: www.jewishinsandiego.org

Hours of opening: 8.30 am.

Delicatessens

Eva's Fresh & Natural
6717 El Cajon Blvd 92115 (619) 462-5018
Fax: (619) 453-5659

Supervision: Vaad of San Diego.
Dairy and vegetarian food. Meat dinners are available to go only upon request in advance.

Media

Newspapers

San Diego Jewish Press Heritage
3443 Camino Del Rio S.,
Suite 315 92108 (619) 282-7177
Fax: (619) 282 1774

San Diego Jewish Times
4731 Palm Avenue, La Mesa 91941 (619) 463-5515
Email: jewishtimes@msn.com

Mikvaot

(858) 546-1563
Call to arrange an appointment.

Restaurants

Dairy

Aarons Glatt Kosher Market
4488 Convoy Street 92111 (858) 636-7979
Fax: (858) 636-7980
Web site: www.kosherfooddelivery.com

Lang's
6165 El Cajon Blvd 92115
(619) 287-7306; 800-60-LANGS
Fax: (619) 582-1545
Email: sales@kosherbread.com
Web site: www.kosherbread.com
Supervision: Vaad HaRabbanim of San Diego.
Kosher pareve bakery, dairy deli and foods.

Shmoozers Vegetarian & Pizzeria
6366 El Cajon Blvd 92115 (619) 583-1636
Fax: (619) 583 1635
Email: shmoozers1@aol.com
Supervision: Vaad HaRabbanim of San Diego.
Hours: Sunday to Thursday, 11.30 am to 9 pm; Friday, to 2 pm; Saturday, Motzei Shabbat to 11 pm.

Meat

Western Glatt Kosher & N.Y. Deli
7739 Fay Avenue, La Jolla 92037 (619) 454-6328

Synagogues

Conservative

Congregation Beth Am
5050 Black Mtn. Road 92130 (858) 481-8454
Fax: (858) 481-6068
Email: betham@betham.com

Congregation Beth El
8660 Gilman Drive, La Jolla 92037 (858) 452-1734
Fax: (858) 452 5578
Email: congregationbethel.com

Ner Tamid
16770 West Bernardo Drive,
Suite A 92127 (858) 592-9141
Fax: (858) 592-4889
Email: nertamid@altavista.com

Temple Beth Sholom
208 Madrona Street,
Chula Vista 91910 (619) 420-6040

Tifereth Israel Synagogue
6660 Cowles Mountain Blvd 92119 (619) 697-6001
Fax: (619) 697 1102
Email: tiferethisrael.com

Orthodox

Beth Eliyahu Torah Center
5012 Central Avenue, Bonita 91902
(619) 472-2144
Fax: (619) 472 0718

Beth Jacob Synagogue
4855 College Avenue 92115 (619) 287-9890
Fax: (619) 287-0578

Chabad at La Costa
1980 La Costa Avenue,
Carlsbad 92009 (760) 943-8891
Fax: (760) 943-8892
Email: chabad@inetworld.net

Chabad House
6115 Montezuma Road 92115 (619) 265-7700
Fax: (619) 265 0346

Chabad of La Jolla
3813 Governor Drive,
Suite N 92122 (619) 455-1670
Fax: (619) 451 1443

Congregation Adat Yeshurun
8950 Villa La Jolla Drive,
Suite 1224, La Jolla 92037 (858) 535-1196
Fax: (858) 535-0037
Email: adatyeshurun.org

Young Israel of San Diego
7920 Navajo Road,
Suite 102 92119 (619) 589-1447

Reconstructionist

Congregation Dor Hadash
4858 Ronson Court, Suite A 92111 (858) 268-3674
Fax: (858) 794 4087

Reform

Congregation Beth Israel
2512 3rd Avenue 92103 (619) 239-0149
Fax: (619) 239 2134

Etz Chaim
PO Box 1138, Ramona 92065 (760) 789-7393

Temple Adat Shalom
15905 Pomerado Road,
Poway 92064 (858) 451-1200
Fax: (858) 451 2409

Temple Emanu-El
6299 Capri Drive 92120 (619) 286-2555
Fax: (619) 286 3176

Temple Solel
552 S.Camino Real,
Encinitas 92024 (760) 436-0654
Fax: (760) 436-2748
Email: solel@sciti.com

San Fernando Valley

Bakeries

Continental Kosher Bakery
12419 Burbank Blvd (818) 762-5005

Caterer

Hadar Restaurant and Catering
12514 Burbank Blvd 91607 (818) 762-1155
Supervision: RCC.

Community Organisations

North Valley Center
16601 Rinaldi Street, Granada Hills 91344
Valley Cities Center
13164 Burbank Blvd., Van Nuys 91401
West Valley Center
22622 Vanowen Street, West Hills 91307

Ice Cream Parlor

Carvel's Ice Cream
25948 McBean Parkway, Valencia (805) 259-1450
Supervision: Kof-K.

Kashrut Information

The Kashrus Information Bureau
12753 Chandler Blvd,
N. Hollywood 91607 (818) 762-3197 & 262-5351
Fax: (818) 766-8537
Email: eeidlitz@kosherquest.org
Web site: www.kosherquest.org

Mikvaot

Teichman Mikvah Society
12800 Chandler Blvd,
N. Hollywood 91607 (818) 506-0996

Restaurants

Apropo Falafel
6800 Reseda Blvd (818) 881-6608

Dairy

Orly Dairy Restaurant & Pizza
12454 Magnolia Blvd (818) 508-5570

Meat

Drexler's Kosher Restaurant
12519 Burbank Blvd, N. Hollywood (818) 984-1160
Falafel Express
5577 Reseda Bl (818) 345-5660
Flora Falafel
12450 Burbank Blvd, N. Hollywood (818) 766-6567
Supervision: RCC.
Sportsman Lodge
Sherman Oaks (818) 984-0202

Pizzerias

La Pizza
12515 Burbank Blvd (818) 760-8198
Pacific Kosher Pizza
12460 Oxnard (818) 760-0087

Synagogues

Conservative

Beth Meier Congregation
11725 Moorpark, Studio City (818) 769-0515
Shomrei Torah
7353 Valley Circle, West Hills (818) 346-0811
Temple B'nai Hayim
4302 Van Nuys Blvd, Sherman Oaks (818) 788-4664
Temple Emanu-El
1302 N. Glenoaks Avenue, Burbank 91504
(818) 845-1734
Temple Ramat Zion
17655 Devonshire Avenue, Northridge
(818) 360-1881
Valley Beth Shalom
15739 Ventura Blvd, Encino 91316 (818) 788-6000

Orthodox

Adat Ari El Synagogue
5540 Laurel Canyon Blvd, N. Hollywood 91607
There are eleven beautiful stained-glass windows, designed by Mischa Kallis, depicting significant dates in the religious calendar.
Chabad House
4915 Hayvenhurst, Encino 91346
Shaarey Zedek
12800 Chandler Blvd,
N. Hollywood 91607 (818) 763-0560
Fax: (818) 763-8215

Reform

Beth Emet
320 E. Magnolia Blvd, Burbank 91502
Shir Chadash,
17000 Ventura Blvd, Encino
Temple Ahavat Shalom
11261 Chimineas Avenue, Northridge
Temple Judea
5429 Lindley Avenue, Tarzana

San Francisco

Embassy

Consul General of Israel
Suite 2100, 456 Montgomery Street 94104

Groceries

Gourmet Kosher Meals
Cong. Adath Israel, 1851 Noriega St., 94122
Supervision: Orthodox Rabbinical Council.
Grill Middle Eastern Cuisine
430 Geary Street (415) 749-0201

Jacob's Kosher Meats
2435 Noriega Street 94122 (415) 564-7482
Jerusalem
420 Geary (at Mason) 94108 (415) 776-2683
Supervision: Cong. Thilim.
Kosher Meats Israel & Cohen Kosher Meats
5621 Geary Blvd 94121 (415) 752-3064
Kosher Nutrition Kitchen
Montefiore Senior Center, 3200 California Av.,
Supervision: Orthodox Rabbinical Council.
Tel Aviv Strictly Kosher Meats
2495 Irving Street 94122 (415) 661-7588
Fax: (415) 661-8258
Supervision: Orthodox Rabbinical Council.

Libraries

Holocaust Library & Research Center
601 14th Avenue 94118 (415) 751-6040

Mikvaot

Mikva,
3355 Sacramento Street 94118 (415) 921-4070

Museums

The Jewish Museum San Francisco
121 Steuart St 94105 (415) 543-8880
Fax: (415) 788-9050
Email: info@jewishmuseumsf.org
Web site: www.jewishmuseumsf.org
Administrative offices 166 Geary St. Suite 1500, San Fransisco, CA 94108. Tel: 415-788-9990. Contact: Victoria Shelton.

Organisations

Jewish Com. Fed. of San Francisco, the Peninsula, Marin & Sonoma Counties
121 Steuart St. 94105 (415) 777-4545
Fax: (415) 495-6635
Email: JewishNfo@aol.com
Publishes 'Resource guide to the Bay Area' and 'Resource guide to Jewish life in Northern California'.

Restaurants

Meat

Red Ox
1271 South Carolina Blvd, Walnut Creek
(925) 256-6500
Supervision: Glatt kosher.

Sabra
419 Grant Avenue, Chinatown (415) 982-3656
Fax: (415) 982-3650
Supervision: Vaad Hakashrus of Northern CA.
Bishul Yisrael, Pat Yisrael and Mashgiach Temidi. Israeli mediterranean cuisine. Catering available.

This Is It
430 Geary Street 94210 (415) 749-0201
Middle Eastern cuisine.

Synagogues

Conservative

B'nai Emunah
3595 Taraval Street 94116 (415) 664-7373
Fax: (415) 664-4209
Email: emuna@jps.net
Web site: www.uscj.org/ncalif/sanfranbe

Beth Israel-Judea
625 Brotherhood Way 94132 (415) 586-8833

Beth Sholom
14th Avenue & Clement Street 94118
(415) 221-8736
Fax: (415) 221-3944
Email: cbsholom@aol.com

Ner Tamid
1250 Quintara Street 94116 (415) 661-3383

Orthodox

Adath Israel
1851 Noriega Street 94122 (415) 564-5565

Anshey Sfard
1500 Clement Street 94118 (415) 752-4979

Chabad House
11 Tillman Place 94108 (415) 956-8644

Chevra Thilim
751 25th Avenue 94121 (415) 752-2866

Keneseth Israel
873 Sutter Street 94109 (415) 771-3420
A downtown synagogue offering meals over Shabbat.

Torat Emeth
768 27th Avenue 94121 (415) 386-1830

Young Israel of San Francisco
1806 A Noriega Street 94122 (415) 387-1774

Reform

Emanu-El
Arguello Blvd & Lake Street 94118 (415) 751-2535
Fax: (415) 751-2511
Email: mail@emanuelsf.org

Sha'ar Zahav
290 Dolores Street 94103 (415) 861-6932
Fax: (415) 841-6081
Email: office@shaarzahav.org

Sherith Israel
2266 California Street 94115 (415) 346-1720
Fax: (415) 673-9439
Email: ed@sherithisrael.org

Sephardi

Magain David
351 4th Avenue 94118 (415) 752-9095

Tourist Information

Jewish Community Information & Referral
121 Steuart St 94105 (415) 777-4545
Fax: (415) 495-6635
Email: judym@sfjcf.org
Web site: www.sfjcf.org
Local toll free within the Bay Area 877/777-JCIR (5247).

San Jose

Booksellers

Alef Bet Judaica
14103-0 Winchester Blvd,
Los Gatos 95032 (408) 370-1818
Fax: (408) 725-8269
Email: nurit@best.com

Community Organisations

Jewish Federation of Greater San Jose
14855 Oka Road, Los Gatos 95030 (408) 358-3033
Fax: (408) 356-0733

Delicatessens

Willow Glen Kosher Deli
1185 Lincoln Avenue 95125 (408) 297-6604
Fax: (408) 297-0122
Email: kosher@visto.com
Under Orthodox Rabbinical supervision. Glatt kosher. Catering & meals for travellers available.

Restaurants

Meat

Willow Glen Kosher Market
1185 Lincoln Avenue 95125 (408) 297-6604
Supervision: Va'ad Hakashrus San Jose.
Will deliver to local hotels.

Synagogues

Conservative

Congregation Beth David
19700 Prospect Road,
Saratoga 95070 (408) 257-3333
Fax: (408) 257-3338
Email: admin@beth-david.org

Congregation Emeth
PO Box 1430, Gilroy 95021 (408) 847-4111

Orthodox

Ahavas Torah
1537-A Meridian Avenue 95125 (408) 266-2342
Fax: (408) 264-3139
Web site: www.ahava.org

Almaden Valley Torah Center
1281 Juli Lynn Drive 95120 (408) 997-9117

Am Echad Community
1504 Meridian Avenue 95125 (408) 236-2081
Email: info@amechad.org
Web site: www.amechad.org

Orthodox community offering Shabbos hospitality, shiurium and daily minyonim.

Reform

Congregation Shir Hadash
16555 Shannon Road, Los Gatos 95032
(408) 358-1751
Fax: (408) 358-1753
Web site: www.shirhadash.org

Temple Beth Sholom
2270 Unit D, Canoas Garden Avenue 95153
(408) 978-5566

Temple Emanu-El
1010 University Avenue 95126 (408) 292-0939

Traditional

Congregation Sinai
1532 Willowbrae Avenue 95125-4450
(408) 264-8542
Fax: (408) 264-4316
Email: eitanj@cs.com

San Rafael (Marin County)

Synagogues

Reform

Rodef Sholom
170 N. San Pedro Rd 94903

Santa Barbara

Synagogues

Orthodox

Chabad of S. Barbara
6047 Stow Canyon, Fairview 93117 (805) 683-1544
Fax: (805) 683-1545
Email: rabbi@sbchabad.org

Young Israel of Santa Barbara
1826 C Cliff Drive 93109 (805) 966-4565

Reform

Congregation B'nai B'rith
1000 San Antonio Creek Road 93111
(805) 964-7869
Fax: (805) 683-6473
Email: cbbrav@aol.com

Santa Monica

Synagogues

Orthodox

Chabad House
1428 17th Street 90404

Young Israel of Santa Monica
21 Hampton Avenue (213) 399-8514
Mailing address is: PO Box 5725, 90405.

Reform

Beth Sholom
1827 California Avenue 90403 (310) 453-3361

Santa Rosa

Synagogues

Conservative

Beth Ami
4676 Mayette Avenue 95405 (707) 545-4334
Dairy kitchen on premises.

Reform

Congregation Shomrei Torah
1717 Yulupa Avenue 95405 (707) 578-5519
Fax: (707) 578-3967
Email: shomrei@pacbell.net

Sherman Oaks

Restaurants

Dairy

Fish Grill
13628 Ventura Blvd (818) 788-9896

Stockton

Stockton is one of the oldest communities west of the Mississippi River, founded in the days of the California Gold Rush. Temple Israel was founded as Congregation Ryhim Ahoovim in 1850 and erected its first building in 1855.

Synagogues

Reform

Temple Israel
5105 N. El Dorado St. 95207 (209) 477-9306

Thousand Oaks

Synagogues

Conservative

Temple Etz Chaim
1080 E. Janss Rd 91360 (805) 497-6891
Fax: (805) 497-0086
Kosher catering. Synagogue contains unique artistic Aron Kodesh and Holocaust memorial.

Tiburon

Synagogues

Congregation Kol Shafar
215 Blackfield Dr. 94920 (415) 388-1818

Tustin

Synagogues

Congregation B'nai Israel
655 S. "B" St. 92680 (714) 259-0655

Vallejo

Synagogues

Unaffiliated

Congregation B'nai Israel
1256 Nebraska St. 94590 (707) 642-6526

Ventura

Community Organisations

Jewish Community Centre
259 Callens Road (805) 658-7441

Synagogues

Reform

Temple Beth Torah
7620 Foothill Road 93004 (805) 647-4181

Walnut Creek

Synagogues

Conservative

Congregation B'nai Shalom
74 Eckley Lane 94595 (925) 934-9446
Fax: (925) 934-9450

Contra Costa Jewish Community Center
2071 Tice Valley Blvd 94595

Reform

Congregation B'nai Tikvah
25 Hillcroft Way 94595 (925) 933-5397

Whittier

Synagogues

Conservative

Beth Shalom Synagogues Center
14564 E. Hawes Street 90604 (310) 914-8744

Colorado

Boulder

Organisations

Lubavitch of Boulder County
4900 Sioux Drive 80303 (303) 494-1638
Fax: (303) 938-8350
Email: lubavbldr@cs.com
Web site: www.lubavitchofboulder.org
Offering home hospitality.

Restaurants

JCC
3800 Kalmia Avenue 80304

Synagogues

Hillel Foundation
2795 Colorado Avenue,
University of Colorado (303) 442-6571

Conservative

Congregation Bonai Shalom
1527 Cherryvale Rd, 80303 (303) 442-6605
Fax: (303) 442-7545
Email: bonaishalom@aol.com
Web site: www.bonaishalom.org
Offering home hospitality.

Reform

Congregation Har Hashem
3950 Baseline Road 80303 (303) 499-7077

Jewish Renewal Community of Boulder
5001 Pennsylvania 80303 (303) 271-3541
Meets third Friday of each month.

Colorado Springs

Synagogues

Conservative & Reform

Temple Shalom
1523 E. Monument Street 80909 (719) 634-5311
Reform services are held on Friday evening & Conservative services on Saturday morning.

Orthodox

Chabad House
3465 Nonchalant Circle 80909 (719) 596-7330

Denver

Bakeries

New York Bagel Boys
6449 E Hampden Avenue 80231 (303) 759-2212
Supervision: Vaad Hakashrus of Denver.

The Bagel Store
942 South Monaco 80224 (303) 388-2648
Supervision: Vaad Hakashrus of Denver.

Groceries

Cub Foods
1985 Sheridan Blvd, Edgewater (303) 232-8972
With kosher section.

King Soopers
890 S.Monaco Parway (303) 333-1535
With kosher section.

King Soopers
6470 East Hampden Avenue (303) 758-1210
With kosher section.

Safeway
7150 Leetsdale Drive (& Quebec) (303) 377-6939
With kosher section.

Safeway
6460 E. Yale (& Monaco) (303) 691-8870
With kosher section.

Kashrut Information

Rabbi Mordecai Twerski
295 South Locust Avenue 80224 (303) 377-1200
Fax: (303) 355-6010
Email: ravtwerski@aol.com

Scoll K Vaad Hakashrus of Denver
1350 Vrain 80204 (303) 595-9349
Fax: (303) 629-5159

Media

Newspapers

Intermountain Jewish News
1275 Sherman Avenue, Suite 214 80203
(303) 861-2234
Weekly American Jewish newspaper of the intermountain region

Mikvaot

Mikvah of Denver
1404 Quitman 80204 (303) 893-5315
Fax: (303) 825-5810

Organisations

Allied Jewish Federation of Colorado - Israel Center
300 S. Dahlia Street 80246 (303) 321-3399
Fax: (303) 322-8328
Email: mgardenswartz@ajfcolorado.org
Web site: www.jewishfamilyservice.org

Com. Center
4800 E. Alameda Avenue 80222

Jewish Family & Children's Service
1355 S. Colorado Blvd 80222 (303) 759-4890
Fax: (303) 759-5998
Email: jfs@jewishfamilyservice.org
Web site: www.jewishfamilyservice.org

Rocky Mountain Rabinnic Council
6445 East Ohio Avenue 80224 (303) 388-4441

Synagogue Council of Greater Denver
PO Box 102732 80250 (303) 759-8484

Pizzeria

Pete's Pizza
5600 Cedar Avenue (303) 355-5777

Restaurants

Dairy

Mediterranean Health Cafe
2817 East 3rd Avenue 80206 (303) 399-2940
Supervision: Vaad Hakashrus of Denver.
Kosher/dairy/vegetarian food. Chalav Yisrael and Pat Yisrael available. Hours: Sunday, 12 pm to 8 pm; Monday to Thursday, 11 am to 8 pm; Friday, to 2 pm.

Meat

East Side Kosher Deli
5475 Leetsdale Drive 80246 (303) 322-9862
Fax: (303) 331-3290
Email: eskd1@aol.com
Supervision: Vaad Hakashrus of Denver.
Glatt kosher. Deli, restaurant, grocer, butcher shop and caterer. Closed on Saturday and Friday afternoon.

Jeff's Diner
731 Quebec Street 80220 (303) 333-4837

Synagogues

Beth Shalom
2280 East Noble Place,
Littleton 80121 (303) 794-6643
A congregation serving the southern metropolitan area. Provides religious services religious school (weekend and afternoon) social and educational activities, and rabbinic services.

Conservative

Hebrew Educational Alliance (HEA)
3600 South Ivanhoe St. 80237 (303) 758-9400
Fax: (303) 758-9500
Email: info@headenver.org

Rodef Shalom
450 S. Kearney 80224 (303) 399-0035
Fax: (303) 399-7623
Email: crsoffice@aol.com

Orthodox

A havas Yisroel; A center for Jewish learning
9550 E Belleview Ave,
Greenwood Village 80111 (303) 220-7200
Fax: (303) 290-9191
Email: ymeyer@aish.com

Bais Medrash Kehillas Yaakov
295 S. Locust Street 80222 (303) 377-1200
Fax: (303) 355-6010
Email: tai@jewishpeople.com

Congregation Zera Abraham
1560 Winona Court 80204 (303) 825-7517
100 + year old Orthodox Congregation. Two morning Minyanim, Mincha and Maariv every day. Call for Davening times. Mikvah, Eruv, nationally recognized Vaad HaKashrus. "We are a very warm, welcoming community that looks foreward to every opportunity to welcome guests and assist visitors."

Reconstructionist

B'Nai Havurah
6445 East Ohio Avenue 80224 (303) 388-4441

Reform

Congregation Emanuel
51 Grape Street 80231 (303) 388-4013
Fax: (303) 388-6328
Email: bronitsky@congregationemanuel.com
Web site: www.congregationemanuel.com

Temple Micah
2600 Leyden Street 80207 (303) 388-4239
Fax: (303) 773-0321
Email: office@micahdenver.org
Web site: www.micahdenver.org
A small but long-established Reform Jewish congregation, style is warm and traditional though progressive. Encourages members participation welcomes visitors.

Temple Sinai
3509 South Glencoe Street 80237 (303) 759-1827
Fax: (303) 759-2519
Email: mail@sinaidenver.org
Web site: www.sinaidenver.org

Traditional

B.M.H.-BJ Congregation
560 S. Monaco Pkwy. 80224 (303) 388-4203
Fax: (303) 388-4210

Evergreen

Synagogues

Liberal

Congregation Beth Evergreen
2931 Evergreen Parkway 80439 (303) 670-4294
Fax: (303) 836-6470
Email: cyberrebbe@aol.com

Littleton

Synagogues

Reform

Beth Shalom
2280 E. Noble Place 80121 (303) 794-6643

Pueblo

Synagogues

Conservative

United Hebrew Congregation
106 W. 15th Street 81003 (719) 544-6448

Reform

Temple Emanuel
1325 Grand Avenue 81003

Connecticut

Bridgeport

Media

Radio

WVOF Radio
c/o Fairfield University, Fairfield 06430
(203) 254-4111
Jewish public affairs show on Sundays at 7pm on 88.5FM

Mikvaot

Mikveh Israel
1326 Stratfield Road, Fairfield 06432

Organisations

Jewish Center for Community Services of Eastern Fairfield County
4200 Park Avenue 06604 (203) 372-6567
Fax: (203) 374-0770
Email: info@jccs.org
Serving Bridgeport, Easton, Fairfield, Monroe, Shelton, Stratford, Trumbull and Westport.

Religious Organisations

Va'ad of Fairfield County
1571 Stratfield Road, Fairfield 06432
(203) 372-6529
Fax: (203) 373-0467
Email: rbaun64732@aol.com

Restaurants

Cafe Shalom
c/o Abel, Community Center (203) 372-6567

Synagogues

Conservative

B'nai Torah
5700 Main St., Trumbull 06611

Rodeph Sholom
2385 Park Avenue 06604 (203) 334-0159
Fax: (203) 334-1411
Email: cong.rodeph.sholom@suet.net
Web site: www.rodephsholom.com

Orthodox

Agudas Achim
85 Arlington Street 06606

Bikur Cholim
Park & Capitol Avenues 06604 (203) 336-2272
Email: jbm@ou.org
Web site: www.ou.org

Shaare Torah Adath Israel
3050 Main Street 06606

Reconstructionist

Congregation Shirei Shalom
PO Box 372, Monroe 06468

Reform

Temple B'nai Israel
2710 Park Avenue 06604 (203) 336-1858
Fax: (203) 367-7889
Email: welcome@congregationbnaiisrael.org

Danbury

Organisations

Jewish Federation
105 Newtown Road 06810 (203) 792-6353
Fax: (203) 748-5099

Issuing monthly publication.

Synagogues

Conservative

Congregation B'nai Israel
193 Clapboard Ridge Road 06811 (203) 792-6161
Fax: (203) 792-8315
Email: cbi193clab@juno.com

Reform

United Jewish Center
141 Deer Hill Avenue 06810 (203) 748-3355

Fairfield

Bakeries

Carvel Ice Cream Bakery
1838 Black Rock Turnpike (203) 384-2253
Supervision: Vaad Hakashrus of Fairfield County.
Ice cream, cakes & novelties. All products in the store are under supervision, except for those Snapple drinks not marked with an "OK".

Synagogues

Conservative

Congregation Beth El
1200 Fairfield Woods Rd, Fairfield 06432
(203) 374-5544
Fax: (203) 374-4962
Email: congbethel@aol.com
Web site: www.uscj.org/ctvalley/fairfield

Kosher facility.

Orthodox

Congregation Ahavath Achim
1571 Stratfield Road, Fairfield 06432
(203) 372-6529
Fax: (203) 373-0647
Email: rbaum64732@aol.com
Web site: 222.ahavathachim.org

Home hospitality, mikva, youth programs, adult education.

Hartford

Kashrut Information

Kashrut Commission
162 Brewster Road 06117 (860) 563-4017

Media

Guides

All Things Jewish
333 Bloomfield Avenue 06117 (860) 232-4483

Mikvaot

Mikva
61 Main Street 06119

Organisations

Jewish Federation of Hartford
333 Bloomfield Avenue 06117 (860) 232-4483
Publishes "All Things Jewish".

Synagogues

Conservative

Beth El
2626 Albany Avenue, West Hartford 06117
Beth Tefilah
465 Oak St., East Hartford 06118
Congregation B'nai Sholom
26 Church St., Newington 06111 (860) 667-0826
Fax: (860) 667-0827
Email: cbsnewington@aol.com

Emanuel Synagogue
160 Mohegan Dr., West Hartford 06117
(860) 236-1275
Fax: (860) 231-8890
Email: emansyn@ziplink.net

Orthodox

1137 Troutbrook Drive 06119 (860) 523-7804
Agudas Achim
1244 N. Main St., West Hartford 06117
Beth David Synagogue
20 Dover Road, West Hartford 06119
(860) 236-1241
Fax: (860) 232-8272
Email: rabbi@bethdavidwh.org
Chabad House of Greater Hartford
798 Farmington Avenue 06119
Contact for kosher meal & Shabbat arrangements.
Teferes Israel
27 Brown St, Bloomfield 06002
United Synagogue of Greater Hartford
840 N. Main St., West Hartfordv 06117

Reform

Beth Israel
701 Farmington Avenue, West Hartford 06119
(860) 233-8215
Fax: (860) 523-0223

Temple Sinai
41 W. Hartford Road, Newington 06011

Manchester

Synagogues

Conservative

Temple Beth Sholom
400 Middle Turnpike E 06040 (860) 643-9563
Fax: (860) 643-9565
Email: riplavin@prodigy.net
Web site: www.uscj.org/ctvalley/manchestertbs
Services seven days a week. Call for times.

Meriden

Synagogues

B'nai Abraham
127 E. Main St. 06450 (203) 235-2581

Middletown

Synagogues

Adath Israel
48 Church St. 06457 (860) 346-4709

New Britain

Synagogues

Conservative

B'nai Israel
265 W. Main St. 06051 (860) 224 0479

Orthodox

Tephereth Israel
76 Winter Street 06051

New Haven

Contact Information

Young Israel House at Yale University
Web site: www.yale.edu/hillel/orgs/yihy.html

Delicatessens

The Westville
1460 Whalley Avenue 06515 (203) 397-0839
Fax: (203) 387-4129
Email: pweinb@aol.com

Zackey's
1304 Whalley Avenue 06515 (203) 387-2454

Groceries

Westville Kosher Meat Market
95 Amity Road 06525 (203) 389-1723

Mikvaot

86 Hubinger Street 06511 (203) 387-2184

Organisations

Jewish Federation of Greater New Haven
360 Amity Road, Woodbridge Ct, 06525
(203) 387-2424

Restaurants

Vegetarian

Claire's Gourmet Vegetarian Restaurant & Caterer
1000 Chapel Street 06510 (203) 562-3888
Supervision: Young Israel of New Haven.

Synagogues

Conservative

Beth-El Keser Israel
85 Harrison Street 06515 (203) 389-2108

Orthodox

Beth Hamedrosh Westville
74 West Prospect Street 06515 (203) 389-9513

Congregation Bikur Cholim Sheveth Achim
112 Marvel Road 06515 (203) 387-4699

Yeshiva of New Haven
765 Elm Street, New Haven 06511 (203) 777-7199
Fax: (203) 777-7198

New London

Organisations

Jewish Federation of Eastern Connecticut
28 Channing Street 06320 (203) 442-8062

Norwalk

Organisations

Jewish Federation of Greater Norwalk
Shorehaven Road 06855 (203) 853-3440

Norwich

Synagogues

Orthodox

Brothers of Joseph
Broad & Washington Avs, 06360 (203) 887-3777
Mikva attached.

Stamford

Delicatessens

Delicate-Essen at the JCC
1035 Newfield Avenue 06902 (203) 322-0944
Fax: (203) 322-5160
Supervision: Vaad Hakashrus of Fairfield County.
Glatt kosher sit down café serving hot and cold sandwiches, soups and grilled items.

Nosherye
JCC Building, 1035 Newfield Av., 06905
(203) 321-1373

Kosher Food

Delicate-Essen
111 High Ridge Road 06905 (203) 316-5570
Fax: (203) 316-5573
Email: bhert2b111@aol.com
Supervision: Vaad Hakashrus of Fairfield County.
Full selection of grocery items. Glatt kosher butcher and take-out products available. Open six days a week.

Organisations

United Jewish Federation
1035 Newfield Avenue 06905 (203) 321-1373

Synagogues

Orthodox

Young Israel of Stamford
69 Oak Lawn Avenue 06905 (203) 348-3955

Waterbury

Organisations

Jewish Federation of Greater Waterbury
73 Main Street, South Woodbury 06798
(203) 263-5121

West Hartford

Booksellers

The Judaica Store
31 Crossroads Plaza 06117 (860) 236-9956

Synagogues

Orthodox

Young Israel of West Hartford
2240 Albany Avenue 06117 (860) 233-3084
Fax: (860) 232-6417
Email: yiwhrdc@aol.com

Westport

Synagogues

215 Post Road West 06880 (203) 226-6901

Woodbridge

Libraries

Center Cafe & Jewish Library
360 Amity Road 06525 (203) 387-2424

Department of Jewish Education Library
360 Amity Road 06525 (203) 287-2424 ext. 330
Fax: (203) 387-1818
Email: library@jewishnewhaven.org
Judaic library and media center serving adults and children of all ages. Open to all.

Delaware

Dover

Synagogues

Conservative

Congregation Beth Sholom of Dover
PO Box 223 19903 (362) 734-5578

Newark

Synagogues

Reconstructionist

Temple Beth El
101 Possum Park Rd 19711 (302) 366-8330

Wilmington

Community Organisations

Jewish Community Center
101 Garden of Eden Road 19803 (302) 478-5660
Fax: (302) 478-6068
Email: jccinfo@jccdelaware.org

Synagogues

Conservative

Beth Shalom
18th St. and Baynard Blvd 19802

Orthodox

Adas Kodesh Shel Emeth
Washington Blvd & Torah Drive 19802
(302) 762-2705
Fax: (302) 762-3236

Reform

Beth Emeth
300 W. Lea Blvd 19802 (302) 764-2393
Fax: (302) 764-2395

District of Columbia

Washington

Delicatessens

Hunan Deli
"H" Street (202) 833-1018

Posins Bakery & Deli
5756 Georgia Avenue (202) 726-4424
Bakery is under Conservative hashgacha.

Embassy

Embassy of Israel
3514 International Drive 20008 (202) 364-5500
Fax: (202) 364-5423

Eruv Information

Eruv in Georgetown
(202) 338-ERUV

Galleries

The National Portrait Gallery
"F" Street between 7th & 8th Sts,
Houses more than 100,000 portraits including Albert Einstein, Golda Meir and George Gershwin.

Kashrut Information

Rabbinical Council of Greater Washington
7826 Eastern Avenue 20012 (202) 291-6052
Fax: (202) 291-5377
Web site: www.capitolk.org

Libraries

National Museum of American Jewish Military History
1811 R. Street N.W. 20009 (202) 265-6280
Fax: (202) 462-3192
Email: mnmajmh@nmajmh.org
Web site: www.nmajmh.org

The National Museum of American Jewish Military History, under the auspices of the Jewish War Veterans of the USA, documents and preserves the contributions of Jewish Americans to the peace and freedom of the United States, educates the public concerning the courage, heroism and sacrifices made by Jewish Americans who served in the armed forces, and works to combat anti-Semitism. The Museum includes exhibitions, a library, a chapel and a Study Center. Hours: 9 am to 5 pm Monday to Friday and 1 pm to 5 pm on Sundays.

Groceries

Shaul & Hershel Meat Market (301) 949-8477

Media

Directories

Jewish Com. Council of Greater Washington
American Israel Public Affairs Com.,
500 N. Capitol St., N.W., Suite 412 20001.

Newspapers

The Jewish Week
1910 "K" Street 20006

Museums

B'nai B'rith Klutznick National Jewish Museum
1640 Rhode Island Av. 20036 (202) 857-6583
Fax: (202) 857-1099
Email: eberman@bnaibrith.org
Web site: www.BBInet.org
Hours 10 am to 5 pm, Sunday through Friday and early close on Fridays in winter.

John F. Kennedy Center
2700 "F" Street
Israeli lounge donated by the people of Israel

Lillian & Albert Small Museum
3rd & "G" Sts N.W. 20008
Housed in Washington's oldest synagogue building, Adas Israel, built in 1876

Smithsonian Institute
The Natural History Building,
10th & Constitution Avs. N.W. 20001
Contains a collection of Jewish ritual articles.

The Isaac Polack Building
2109 Pennsylvania Av. N.W.
Built in 1796, The Isaac Polack Building was the home of the first Jew to settle in Washington.

United States Holocaust Memorial Museum
100 Raoul Wallenberg Place S.W. 20024-2150
(202) 488-0400
Fax: (202) 488-2606
Email: group_visit@ushmm.org
Web site: www.ushmm.org
Hours: 10 am to 5.30 pm. The Museum is accessible to people with disabilities. The permanent exhibition recommended for visitors eleven years; and older presents a comprehensive history of the Holocaust through artefacts photographs films and eyewitness testimonies. There are other changing special exhibitions and an exhibition designed for children eight years and older.

Jewish Historical Society of Greater Washington
701 3rd Street N. W. 20001-2624 (202) 789-0900
Fax: (202) 789-0485
Email: info@jhsgw.org
Also the Lillian & Albert Small Jewish Museum. Hours: Sunday-Thursday 12 am-4 pm.

Restaurants

Jewish Community Centre
16th Street at Q
Supervision: Va'ad Hakashrut of Washington.
Kosher restaurant on site (dairy and fish) with Hechser.

Meat

Letoile
1310 New Hampshire Avenue NW (202) 835-3030
Fax: (202) 466-1988

Pizzerias

Nuthouse Pizza (301) 942-5900

Synagogues

Orthodox

Kesher Israel
208 N. Street NW (202) 333-2337

Conservative

Tifereth Israel
7701 16th Street NW (202) 882-1605

Reform

Tempke Micah
2829 Wisconsin Avenue NW (202) 342-9175

Florida

Boca Raton

Mikvaot

Boca Raton Synagogue
7900 Montoya Circle 33433 (561) 394-5854

Organisations

Jewish Federation of South Palm Beach County
9901 Donna Klein Blvd 33428-1788 (407) 852-3100

Restaurants

Dairy

Campus Café
Cultural Arts Building,
9801 Donna Klein Blvd 33428-1788
(561) 852-3200 ext. 4103
Fax: (561) 852-3282
Breakfast - dairy; Lunch - meat. Jewish Federation of South Palm Beach County on the Richard and Carole Siemens Campus.

Eilat Café
6853 SW 18th Street,
Wharfside Shopping Center 33428-1788
(561) 368-6880

Jon's Place
22191 Powerline Road, (southwest corner Palmetto & Powerline) (561) 338-0008

Meat

City Grill
Delmar Shopping Village, 7158 N. Beracasa Way
33434 (561) 417-8936

Orchids Garden
9045 La Fontana Blvd,
Boca Raton 33434 (561) 482-3831
Fax: (561) 482-5951
Supervision: So Palm Beach County. Vaad Hakasrut.
Hours: Monday to Thursday, 11.30 am to 9 pm; Sunday, 3 pm to 9 pm.

Synagogues

Conservative

Beth Ami Congregation
1401 N.W. 4th Avenue 33432 (561) 347-0031

Orthodox

Boca Raton Synagogue
7900 Montoya Circle 33433 (561) 394-5732

Young Israel of Boca Raton
7200 Palmetto Circle Blvd 33433 (561) 391-3235
Fax: (561) 391-5509
Email: yiboca@bellsouth.net

Reform

Congregation B'nai Israel
2200 Yamato Road 33431 (561) 241-8118
Fax: (561) 241-8118

Clearwater

Organisations

Jewish Federation of Pinellas County
13191 Starkey Road,
Suite 8, Largo 33773-1438 (727) 530-3223
Fax: (727) 531-0221
Email: pinellas@jfedpinellas.org

Synagogues

Conservative

Beth Shalom
1325 S. Belcher Road 33764 (727) 531-1418
Fax: (727) 531-0798

Orthodox

Young Israel of Clearwater
2385 Tampa Road, Suite 1
Palm Harbor 34684 (727) 789-0408

Reform

B'nai Israel
1685 S. Belcher Road 34624 (727) 531-5829
Temple Ahavat Shalom
1575 Curlew Road, Palm Harbor 34683
(727) 785-8811
Fax: (727) 785-8822
Email: rabgar@tampabay.rr.com

Daytona Beach

Organisations

Jewish Federation of Volusia & Flagler Counties
733 S. Nova Road,
Ormond Beach 32174 (904) 672-0294
Fax: (904) 673-1316

Synagogues

Conservative

Temple Israel
1400 S. Peninsula Drive 32118 (904) 252-3097

Deerfield Beach

Synagogues

Orthodox

Young Israel of Deerfield Beach
1880 H West Hillsboro Blvd 33442 (954) 421-1367
Fax: (954) 426-9127

Delray Beach

Groceries

Meat Market
Oriole Kosher Market,
7345 West Atlantic Ave., 33446

Synagogues

Conservative

Temple Anshei Shalom of West Delray
Oriole Jewish Center,
7099 W. Atlantic Avenue 33446 (561) 495-1300
Temple Emeth
5780 W. Atlantic Avenue 33446 (561) 498-3536

Orthodox

Anshei Emuna
16189 Carter Road 33445 (561) 499-9229

Reform

Temple Sinai
2475 W. Atlantic Avenue 33445 (561) 276-6161
Fax: (561) 276-3485
Email: sinai1@juno.com

Fort Lauderdale

Delicatessens

East Side Kosher Restaurant & Deli
6846 W. Atlantic Blvd, Margate 33063

Organisations

Jewish Federation of Greater Fort Lauderdale
8358 W. Oakland Park Blvd 33321 (305) 748-8400
Fax: (305) 748-6332

Restaurants

Meat

Amore' Ristorante
8067 West Oakland Park Blvd, Sunrise
(954) 749-6888
Supervision: Glatt kosher.
Galt Kosher Market
3515 Galt Ocean Drive 33308 (954) 563-2026

Fort Meyers

Synagogues

Reform

Temple Beth El
16225 Winkler Road Ext 33908 (941) 433-0018

Fort Pierce

Synagogues

Temple Beth-El Israel
4600 Oleander Drive 34982 (407) 461-7428

Hollywood & Vicinity

Media

Newspapers

The Jewish Community Advocate of South Broward
2719 Hollywood Blvd 33020 (305) 922-8603

Mikvaot

Mikveh/Young Israel of Hollywood - Ft. Lauderdale
3291 Stirling Road,
Fort Lauderdale 33312 (954) 963-3952
Fax: (954) 962-5566

Organisations

Jewish Federation of South Broward
2719 Hollywood Blvd 33020 (305) 921-8810

Restaurants

Meat

Pita Plus
5650 Stirling Road 33021 (305) 985-8028

Pizzerias

Jerusalem Pizza II
5650 Stirling Road 33021 (954) 964-6811
Fax: (954) 964-2911

Synagogues

Conservative

B'nai Aviv
200 Bonaventure Blvd, Weston

Century Pines Jewish Center
13400 S.W. 10 St., Pembroke Pines

Hallandale Jewish Center
416 N.E. 8 Av., Hallandale

Temple Beth Ahm Israel
9730 Stirling Rd (954) 431-5100

Temple Beth Shalom
1400 N. 46 Avenue, Hollywood (954) 987-0026

Temple Judea of Carriage Hills
6734 Stirling Rd, Hollywood

Temple Sinai
1201 Johnson St., Hollywood (954) 987-0026

Orthodox

Chabad Ocean Synagogue
4000 S. Ocean Drive, Hallandale (954) 458-7999

Chabad of Southwest Broward
11251 Taft St., Pembroke Pines

Congregation Ahavat Shalom
315 Madison St., Hollywood (954) 922-4544

Congregation Levi Yitzchok-Lubavitch
1295 E. Hallandale Beach Blvd,
Hallandale 33009 (954) 458-1877
Fax: (954) 458-1651
Email: chai@dialisdn.com

Young Israel of Hollywood/Ft. Lauderdale
3291 Stirling Road,
Ft Lauderdale 33312 (954) 966-7877
Fax: (954) 962-5566
Email: rred@gate.net

Young Israel of Pembroke Pines
13400 S.W. 10 St., Pembroke Pines

Reform

Temple Beth El
1351 S. 14 Av, Hollywood

Temple Beth Emet
4807 South Flamingo Road,
Cooper City, Pembroke Pines (954) 680-1882
Email: bethemet@aol.com

Temple Solel
5100 Sheridan St., Hollywood (954) 989-0205

Sephardi

B'nai Sephardim
3670 Stirling Rd, Ft Lauderdale

Jacksonville

Mikvaot

Etz Chaim
10167 San Jose Blvd 32257 (904) 262-3565

Organisations

Jacksonville Jewish Federation
8505 San Jose Blvd 32217 (904) 448-5000

Kosher Nutrition Center
5846 Mt Carmel Terrace. 32216 (904) 737-9075

Kendall

Synagogues

Orthodox

Young Israel of Kendall
7880 SW 112th Street 33156 (305) 232-6833
Email: yikendall@aol.com

Key West

Synagogues

Conservative

B'nai Zion
750 United Street 33040-3251 (305) 294-3437

Lakeland

Synagogues

Temple Emanuel
600 Lake Hollingsworth Drive 33803
(813) 682-8616

Melbourne

Groceries

Brevard Kosher Zone
416N Harbor City Blvd,
1/4 mile south of Eau Gallie (321) 752-8000
Fax: (321) 752-8000
Email: bkz1@mindspring.com

Miami/Miami Beach

Booksellers

Jerusalem Judaica
459 41st Street 33140 (305) 535-8888

Embassy

Consul General of Israel
Suite 1800, 100N Biscayne Blvd 33132

Groceries

Kosher World-Fine Food Market
514 W. 41st Street 33140 (305) 532-2210
Fax: (305) 532-8816
Supervision: Delivers to all hotels in the Miami Beach area..

Hotels

The Saxony
3201 Collins Avenue,
Miami Beach 33140 (305) 538-6811
Fax: (305) 672-3721
Supervision: National Kashruth.

Media

Directories

Jewish Life in Dade County
4200 Biscayne Blvd 33137 (305) 576-4000
Fax: (305) 573-8115
Web site: www.jewishmiami.org

Mikvaot

B'nai Israel & Greater Miami Youth Synagogue Mikveh
16260 S.W. 288th Street, Naranja 33033
(305) 264-6488
Congregation and Mikvah Adas Dej
225 37th Street 33140 (305) 538-0070
Daughters of Israel
2530 Pinetree Drive 33140 (305) 672-3500
Mikveh Blima of North Dade, Inc.,
1054 N.E. Miami Gardens Drive 33179
(305) 949-9650
Rabbi Meisel's Mikveh
Washington Av. & 2nd Street 33139 (305) 673-4641
For men only.
Shul of Bal Harbour Mikvah
9540 Collins Avenue, Surfside 33154
(305) 868-1411
Email: info@theshul.org

Museums

Jewish Museum of Florida
301 Washington Avenue, Miami Beach 33139-6965
(305) 672-5044
Fax: (305) 672-5933
Email: mzerivitz@aol.com
Web site: www.jewishmuseum.com
Open Tuesday to Sunday 10.00am to 5.00pm. Closed Mondays and Jewish holidays.

Organisations

Orthodox

National Council of Young Israel
Southern Regional Office
1035 NE 170th Terrace 33162 (305) 770-3993
Email: ncyi.south@youngisrael.org

Religious Organisations

Young Israel Southern Regional Office
173575 NE 7th Avenue 33162 (305) 770-3993
Fax: (305) 770-3993
Email: ncyi.south@youngisrael.org

Restaurants

Aviva's Kitchen
16355 W. Dixie Hwy., 33160 (305) 944-7313
Pinati Restaurant
2520 Miami Gardens Drive 33180 (305) 931-8086
Shalom Haifa
1330 N.E. 163 Street 33162 (305) 945-2884

Dairy

Bagel Time
3915 Alton Road 33140 (305) 538-0300
Supervision: Star-K.
Eat in or take-out. Hours: Sunday to Friday, 6.30 am to 4 pm.
Gitty's Hungarian Kitchen
6565 Collins Avenue, Sherry Frontenac Hotel 33141
(305) 865-4893
Milky Way
530 41st Street (305) 534-4144
Ocean Terrace Restaurant & Grille
4041 Collins Avenue 33140 (305) 531-5771

Shemtov's Pizza
514 41st Street 33140 (305) 538-2123
Fax: (305) 534-4213
Supervision: Star-K.
Cholov Yisroel. Sun-Thurs 11am-10pm, Fri 11am-3pm, Sat - Motzei Shabbos - 1am
The Noshery (Seasonal dairy)
Saxony Hotel, 3201 Collins Ave., 33140
(305) 538-6811

Meat

China Kikar Tel Aviv
5005 Collins Avenue 33140 (305) 866-3316
Embassy Peking Tower Suite
4101 Pine tree Drive,
Tower 41 33140 (305) 538-7550
Fax: (305) 538-7570
Supervision: NK.
Giuliani's Café
3439 NE 163rd Street,
North Miami Beach (305) 940-8141

Harissa Café
19201 Collins Avenue, in Ramada Plaza
(305) 932-2233
Kosher World
514 - 41st. (305) 532-2263
Mexico Bravo
16850 Collins Avenue, Sunny Isles Beach
(305) 945-1999
Pita Plus
20103 Biscayne Blvd 33180 (305) 935-0761
Tani Guchi's Place
2224 N.E. 123rd St, North Miami (305) 892-6744
Fax: (305) 892-1035
Supervision: Glatt Kosher.
Wing Wan II
1640 N.E. 164 Street 33162 (305) 945-3585

Pizzerias

Jerusalem Pizza
761 N.E. 167th Street 33162 (305) 653-6662
Sarah's Kosher Pizza
2214 N.E. 123 Street 33181 (305) 891-3312
Sarah's Kosher Pizza
1127 N. E. 163 Street 33162 (305) 948-7777
Yonnie's Kosher Pizza
19802 W. Dixie Hwy. 33180 (305) 932-1961

Synagogues

Conservative

Beth Raphael
1545 Jefferson Avenue 33139 (305) 538-4112
This synagogue is dedicated to the six million martyrs of the Holocaust. On an outside marble wall, a large six-light menorah burns every night in their memory. Six hundred names, representing each city, have been inscribed on the marble. There is also a notable Holocaust Memorial at Dade Av., and Meridian Av.;

Orthodox

Young Israel of Greater Miami
990 NE 171st Street,
North Miami Beach 33162 (305) 651-3591
Young Israel of Miami Beach
4221 Pine Tree Drive 33140 (305) 538-9462
Young Israel of Sky Lake
1850 NE 183rd Street,
North Miami Beach 33179 (305) 945-8712/8715

Orlando

Delicatessens

Market Place Deli, Hyatt Orlando
6375 W. Irlo Bronson Highway (407) 396-1234
Has frozen kosher food only.

Groceries

Amira's Catering and Specialty
1351 E. Altamonte,
Altamonte Springs (407) 767-7577
Cold cuts, side dishes, frozen meals, groceries.
Kosher Korner
8464 Palm Parkway,
Vista Center 32836 (407) 238-9968
Fax: (407) 238-2008
Supervision: Florida Kosher Services.
Complete kosher grocery and take-out. Packaged frozen glatt meat. Will deliver to hotels. Two minutes from downtown Disney.

Hotels

Quality Inn Kosher Hotel
4944 W. 192 Orlando-Kissimmee 34746
(407) 787-3400
Fax: (407) 397-1116
Web site: www.kosher-korner.com
The Lower East Side Restaurant
8548 Palm Parkway 32836 (407) 465-0565
Fax: (407) 238-6427
Supervision: Florida Kosher Services.
There is a shul next door to the restaurant.

Mikvaot

Mikvah Yisrael
8 Lake Howell Road 32751 (407) 644-2362

Organisations

Jewish Federation of Greater Orlando
851 N. Maitland Avenue,
Maitland 32751 (407) 645 5933
Fax: (407) 645 1172
Email: postmaster@orlandojewishfed.org

Restaurants

Kinneret Kitchens
517 South Delany (407) 422-7205
Senior Citizens dining room. Meals: d, Mon.-Fri at 5 pm. Call at least twenty-four hours in advance to reserve a meal.

Meat

Kosher Korner
Vista Center, 8464 Palm Pkwy. 32836
(407) 238-9968
Fax: (407) 238-2008
Glatt kosher. Dine in take-out and delivery.

Synagogues

Conservative

Congregation Beth Shalom
13th & Center Streets,
Leesburg 32748 (407) 742-0238

Congregation Ohev Shalom
5015 Goddard Avenue 32804 (407) 298-4650

Congregation Shalom (Williamsburg)
c/o Sydney Ansell, 11821 Soccer Lane 32821-7952

Congregation Shalom Aleichem
PO Box 424211, Kissimmee 34742-4211

Southwest Orlando Jewish Congregation
11200 S. Apopka-Vineland Road 32836
Web site: www.sojc-orlando.org
The closest Synagogue to Walt Disney world (one mile away).

Temple Israel
4917 Eli Street 32804 (407) 647-3055

Orthodox

Cong. Ahavas Yisrael/Chabad
708 Lake Howell Road, Maitland 32751
(407) 644-2500
Fax: (407) 644-7763
Email: rabbidubov@aol.com

Reform

Congregation of Liberal Judaism
928 Malone Drive 32810 (407) 645-0444

Ormond Beach

Synagogues

Temple Beth El
579 N. Nova Road, Ormond Beach 32174
(904) 677-2484

Palm Beach

Synagogues

Conservative

Temple Emanu-el
190 N. County Road 33480 (561) 832-0804

Orthodox

Palm Beach Orthodox Synagogue
120 North County Road, PO Box 3225 33480
(561) 838-9002
Fax: (561) 838-5356
Web site: www.pbos.org

Palm City

Synagogues

Conservative

Treasure Coast Jewish Center-Congregation Beth Abraham
3998 S.W. Leighton Farms Avenue 34990
(407) 287-8833

Palm Coast

Synagogues

Temple Beth Shalom
40 Wellington Drive
POB 350557 32135-0557 (904) 445-3006

Pembroke Pines

Synagogues

Orthodox

Young Israel of Pembroke Pines
13400 SW 10th Street 33027 (954) 433-8666

Pensacola

Synagogues

Conservative

B'nai Israel
1829 N. 9th Avenue,
PO Box 9002 32513 (805) 433-7311
Fax: (805) 435-9597

Reform

Beth El
800 N. Palafox Street 32501 (805) 438-3321

Rockledge

Organisations

Jewish Federation of Brevard
108A Barton Avenue (321) 636-1824
Fax: (321) 636-0614
Email: jfbrevard@aol.com

Sarasota

Organisations

Sarasota-Manatee Jewish Federation
580 S. McIntosh Road 34232-1959 (941) 371-4546
Fax: (941) 378-2947
Email: smjf@jon.cjfny.org

Sky Lake

Synagogues

Orthodox

Young Israel of Sky Lake
1850 NE 183rd Street, North Miami Beach 33179
(305) 945-8712/8715

St Augustine

Synagogues

The First Congregation Sons Of Israel
161 Cordova Street 43084

St Petersburg

Groceries

Jo-El's Specialty Foods
2619 23rd Avenue N. 33713 (727) 321-3847
Fax: (727) 327-0682
Also has delicatessen and butcher shop. Hours: Tuesday to Thursday, 9 am to 5 pm; Friday, to 4 pm; Sunday, to 1 pm.

Synagogues

Conservative

B'nai Israel
300 58th Street North 33710 (813) 381-4900
Fax: (813) 344-1307
Email: rabbissec@cbistpete.org

Beth Shalom
1844 54th Street S. 33707 (813) 321-3380

Reform

Beth-El
400 Pasadena Avenue S. 33707 (813) 347-6136

Sunny Isles

Synagogues

Orthodox

Young Israel of Sunny Isles
17395 North Bay Road,
North Miami Beach 33160 (305) 935-9095

Surfside

Synagogues

The Shul of Bal Harbor, Bay Harbor & Surfside
9540 Collins Avenue 33154 (305) 868-1411
Email: info@theshul.org

Tamarac

Synagogues

Young Israel of Taramac
8565 W McNab Road 33321 (954) 726-3586

Tampa

Delicatessens

Jo-El's
11727 N Dale Mabry 33618 (813) 964-9299
Also has bakery and groceries. Hours Monday to Thursday 10 am to 7.30 pm; Friday 10 am to 3.30 pm and Sunday 9 am to 2.30 pm.

Mikvaot

Bais Tefilah
14908 Pennington Road 33624 (813) 963-2317
Mikva, Orthodox pre-school on premises.

Organisations

Tampa Jewish Federation
13009 Community Campus Drive 33625-4000
(813) 264-9000
Fax: (813) 265-8450
Email: tjfjcc@aol.com

Synagogues

Conservative

Kol Ami
3919 Moran Road 33618 (813) 962-6338
Rodeph Shalom
2713 Bayshore Blvd 33629 (813) 837-1911
Temple David
2001 Swann Avenue 33606 (813) 254-1771

Orthodox

Hebrew Academy
14908 Penington Road 33624 (813) 963-0706
Young Israel of Tampa
3721W Tacon Street 33629 (813) 832-3018

Reform

Schaarai Zedek
3303 Swann Avenue 33609 (813) 876-2377

Vero Beach

Synagogues

Temple Beth Shalom
365 43rd Avenue (561) 569-4700
Fax: (561) 569-4701
Email: tbsoff@aol.com

West Palm Beach

Community Organisations

Chabad House
4800 23rd St. N 33407 (561) 640-8111

Delicatessens

Mr Glatt Mart
4869 Okeechobee Blvd 33417 (561) 689-6267
Fax: (561) 689-2595
Email: rav613@hotmail.com

Organisations

Jewish Federation of Palm Beach County
4601 Community Drive 33417 (561) 478-0700
Fax: (561) 478-9696

Georgia

Athens

Synagogues

Reform

Congregation Children Of Israel
Dudley Drive 30606 (404) 549-4192

Atlanta

Bed & Breakfasts

Bed & Breakfast Atlanta
1608 Briarcliff Road, Suite 5 30306 (404) 875-0525
Fax: (404) 875-8198
Web site: www.bedandbreakfast.com
Kosher and Shomer Shabbat accommodation.

Community Organisations

Jewish Federation
1753 Peachtree Road, NE 30309 (404) 873-1661
Fax: (404) 874-7043
Publishes an annual community guide.

Delicatessens

Chai Peking
2205 La Vista Road, N.E. 30329 (404) 327-7810
Fax: (404) 327-7811
Web site: www.chaipeking.com
Supervision: Atlanta Kashruth Commission.
Inside Kroger Supermarket. Authentic Glatt kosher Chinese cuisine.

Quality Kosher
2153 Briarcliff Road 30329
(404) 636-1114 or 1-800-305-6328
Fax: (404) 636-8675
Supervision: Atlanta Kashrut Commission.
Glatt and take-out foods butcher, deli and grocery.
Open 7.30 am-6 pm Monday to Thursday. 7.30 am-3 pm Friday and Sunday.

Embassy

Consul General of Israel
Suite 440, 1100 Spring Street, NW 30309-2823

Kashrut Information

Atlanta Kashrut Commission
1855 La Vista Road, N.E. 30329 (404) 634-4063
Fax: (404) 634-4254
Email: akc613@usa.com
A non-profit organisation dedicated to promoting kashrut through education, research and supervision. Publishes a monthly kashrut newsletter.

Restaurants

Dairy

Broadway Café
2166 Briarcliff Road 30329 (404) 329-0888
Fax: (404) 329-9888
Supervision: Atlanta Kashrut Commission.
Seafood, vegetarian, and vegan foods.

CJ's Café
5825 Glenridge Drive, Bldg 2,
Suite 115 30342 (404) 705-9100

Wall Street Pizza
2470 Briarcliff Road, 30329 (404) 633-2111
Supervision: Atlanta Kashrut Commission.
Delivery available.

Meat

Quality Kosher
2153 Briarcliff Road 30329 (404) 636-1114
Fax: (404) 636-8675
Supervision: Atlanta Kashrut Commission.

Synagogues

Conservative

Ahavath Achim
(404) 355-5222

Orthodox

Anshi S'Fard
1324 North Highland Avenue,
N.E. 30306 (404) 874-4513
Email: greggbrenner@aol.com

Congregation Beth Jacob
1855 La Vista Road NE 30329 (404) 633-0551
Fax: (404) 320-7912
Email: cbj@mindspring.com
Web site: www.toll-free.com/bethjacob
Mikva on premises.

Young Israel of Toco Hills
2074 La Vista Road,
Toco Hills 30329 (404) 315-1417
Fax: (404) 315-1417
Email: youngisrael@toll-free.com

Reform

Temple Sinai
5645 Dupree Drive, N.W. 30327 (404) 252-3073

The Temple
1589 Peachtree Road (404) 873-1731

Sephardic

Ner Hamizrach
1858 La Vista Road, N.E. 30329 (404) 315-9020

Augusta

Bakeries

Sunshine Bakery
1209 Broad Street 30902

Delicatessens

Parti-Pal
Daniel Village 30904

Strauss
965 Broad Street 30902

Synagogues

Orthodox

Adas Yeshuron
935 Johns Road,
Walton Way 30904 (706) 733-9491

Columbus

Synagogues

Conservative

Shearith Israel
2550 Wynnton Road 31906 (706) 323-1443

Reform

Temple Israel
1617 Wildwood Avenue 31906 (706) 323-1617

Decatur

Restaurants

Meat

Twelve Oaks Barbecue
1451 Scot Blvd (404) 377-0120

Tours

Kosher Expeditions
2932 Westbury Drive, Suite 100 (770) 441-2545
Fax: (770) 234-5170
Email: dl@kosherexpeditions.com
Web site: www.kosherexpeditions.com
World wide kosher travel organisers.

Macon

Synagogues

Conservative

Sha'arey Israel
611 First Street 31201 (478) 745-4571
Fax: (478) 745-5892
Web site: www.csimacon.org

Reform

Beth Israel
892 Cherry Street 31201 (912) 745-6727

Savannah

Community Centre

Savannah Jewish Federation
5111 Abercorn Street 31405 (912) 355-8111
Fax: (912) 355-8116
Email: sharon@sauj.org

Contact Information

Rabbi Avigdor Slatus
5444 Abercorn Street 31405 (912) 354-2359
Fax: (912) 354-5272
Visitors requiring information about kashrut, temporary accommodation, etc., should contact Rabbi Slatus.

Guest Apartments

Buckingham South
5450 Abercorn Street 31405 (912) 355-5550
Fax: (912) 353-9393
Email: information@buckinghamsouth.com
Supervision: Rabbi Avigdor Slatus.
Glatt kosher meals available on request. Next door to Orthodox snagogue, minyan available.

Synagogues

Mickve Israel
Bull & Gordon Sts. 31401 (912) 233-1547
The oldest synagogue in Georgia, having been founded before 1790.

Conservative

Agudath Achim
9 Lee Blvd 31405 (912) 352-4737

Orthodox

B'nai B'rith Jacob
5444 Abercorn Street 31405 (912) 354-7721
Fax: (912) 354-9923

Hawaii

Hilo

Synagogues

Unaffiliated

Temple Beth Aloha
PO Box 96720 (808) 969-4153

Honolulu

Bed & Breakfasts

Bed & Breakfast Honolulu (Statewide)
3242 Kaohinani Drive 96817
(808) 595-7533; 800-288-4666
Fax: (808) 595-2030
Email: rainbow@hawaiibnb.com
Web site: www.hawaiibnb.com
Not specifically kosher, but within walking distance of Orthodox services for the High Holy Days.

Groceries

Down To Earth
King's Street, Near University Av.,
Foodland Supermarket Beretania
1460 S. Beretania St.

Organisations

Jewish Federation of Hawaii
44 Hora Lane 96813 (808) 941-2424

Synagogues

Conservative

Congregation Sof Ma'arav
2500 Pali Highway 96817 (808) 595-3678

Orthodox

Chabad of Hawaii
2nd floor conference room,
1777 Ala Moana Blvd, 96822 (808) 735-8161
Fax: (808) 735-4130

Temple Emanu-El
2550 Pali Highway 96817 (808) 595-7521
Temple Emanu-El is the oldest congregation in Hawaii, the only one in its own building and the only congregation with its own full-time rabbi.

Kihei

Synagogues

Jewish Congregation of Maui
PO Box 6101, Maui 96732 (808) 243-2499

Reform

Congregation Gan Eden
PO Box 555, Kihei Road 96753 (808) 879-9221
Fax: (808) 874-8570

Kona

Synagogues

Kona Beth Shalom Kailua-Kona
(808) 322-4192 or 322-6004

Waikiki

Synagogues

Orthodox

Chabad
Alana Hotel, Park Plaza, 1956 Ala Moana Blvd
(808) 735-8161

Idaho

Boise

Synagogues

Conservative

Ahavath-Beth Israel
1102 State Street 83702 (208) 343-6601
The oldest continually functioning synagogue in the western USA.

Illinois

Champaign-Urbana

Community Organisations

Champaign-Urbana Jewish Federation
503 E. John St 61820 (217) 367-9872
Fax: (217) 344-1540
Email: cujf@shalomcu.org
Web site: www.shalomcu.org

Synagogues

Reform

Sinai Temple
3104 Windsor Road 61821 (217) 352-8140

Chicago

Chicagoland (Greater Chicago) consists of the City of Chicago and the surrounding collar counties of Cook, Dupage, Kane, Lake and McHenry Counties. The Jewish community is spread throughout Chicagoland, with the main concentrations being in West Rogers Park (City of Chicago), Skokie (Cook County), Buffalo Grove and Highland Park (Lake County).

Greater Chicago has a Jewish population of about 260,000. For a history of the Jews of Chicago see: I. Cutter, "The Jews of Chicago: from Shtetl to Suburbs".

There are three basic divisions in Chicagoland:
a. City of Chicago (telephone area code 312 and 773) includes West Rogers Park and the California/Dempster Avenue areas.
b. North and Northwest Suburbs (includes Cook, Lake and McHenry counties; telephone area codes 773, 815 and 847) includes Buffalo Grove, Deerfield, Evanston, Highland Park, Northbrook, and Skokie.
c. South and West Suburbs (includes DuPage and Kane counties' telephone area codes 630 or 708) includes Flossmoor and Olympia Fields.

Chicago below covers area a. The areas b and c are listed under the respective town name where appropriate.

For more information see the Jewish Chicago website at www.jewishchicago.com

Booksellers

Chicago Hebrew Book Store
2942 W. Devon City of Chicago 60659
(733) 973-6636
Fax: (733) 973-6465

Rosenblum's World of Judaica, Inc.
2906 W. Devon Ave City of Chicago 60659
(773) 262-1700
Fax: (773) 262-1930
Email: afox@rosenblums.com
Web site: www.rosenblums.com

The Barriff Shop at the Spertus Museum
618 S. Michigan Avenue City of Chicago 60605
(312) 322-1740
Fax: (312) 922-6406
Email: bariff_shop@spertus.edu
Web site: www.bariff.org
Hours: Sunday to Wednesday 10 am to 5 pm. Thursday 10 am to 8 pm. Friday 10 am to 3 pm. Closed Saturday. Toll free (888) 322-1740.

Butchers

Jacob Miller & Sons
2727 W. Devon City of Chicago 60659
(773) 761-4200
Supervision: Chicago Rabbinical Council.

Delicatessens

Kosher Karry
2828 W. Devon City of Chicago 60659
(773) 973-4355
Fax: (773) 973-7913
Supervision: Chicago Rabbinical Council.
Sells groceries as well. Prepared goods and take-away.

Romanian Kosher Sausage
7200 N. Clark City of Chicago 60625
(773) 761-4141
Supervision: Orthodox Union.

Embassy

Consul General of Israel
Suite 1308
111 East Wacker Drive, City of Chicago 60601

Museums

Spertus Museum
Spertus Institute of Jewish Studies
618 S. Michigan Avenue,
City of Chicago 60605
(312) 322-1747
Fax: (312) 922-3934
Email: musm@spertus.edu
Web site: www.spertus.edu
Hours: 10 am-5 pm Sunday to Wednesday. 10 am-8 pm Thursday. 10 am-3 pm Friday. Closed Saturday.

Restaurants

Dairy

Jerusalem Kosher Restaurant
3014 W. Devon
City of Chicago 60659
(773) 262-0515
Supervision: OK.

Meat

Great Chicago Food & Beverage Co.
3149 W. Devon
City of Chicago 60659
(773) 465-9030
Fax: (773) 465-9011
Email: gcfbken@aoi.com
Supervision: Chicago Rabbinical Council.

Mi Tsu Yun Kosher Chinese Rest.
3010 W. Devon
City of Chicago 60659
(773) 262-4630
Fax: (773) 262-4835
Supervision: Chicago Rabbinical Council.
Sunday-Thursday 12 pm-9 pm.

Shallots
2324 N. Clark St.
City of Chicago 60614
(773) 755-5205
Web site: www.shallots-chicago.com

Synagogues

Orthodox

K.I.N.S of West Rogers Park
2800 W. North Shore Avenue
City of Chicago 60645
(773) 761-4000
Fax: (773) 761-4959
Email: congkins@cs.com

Lake Shore Drive Synagogue
70 E. Elm street (312) 337-6811
City of Chicago 60611

Loop synagogue
16 S Clark street (312) 346 7370
City of Chicago 60603

Young Israel of Chicago
4931 North Kimball Street (773) 338-6380
City of Chicago 60625

Young Israel of West Rogers Park
2716 West Touhy Avenue
City of Chicago 60645 (773) 743-9400

Evanston

Bakeries

King David's Bakery
1731 W. Howard St.
North and Northwest 60202 (847) 475-0270
Supervision: Chicago Rabbinical Council.

Glenview

Bakeries

The Glenview Breadsmith
2771 Pfingsten
North and Northwest 60025 (847) 509-9955
Supervision: Chicago Rabbinical Council.

Highland Park

Delicatessens

Best's Kosher Outlet Store
1630 Deerfield Rd.
North and Northwest 60035 (847) 831-9435
Fax: (847) 831-9440

Now we're cooking grill
710 Central
North and Northwest 60035 (847) 432-7310
Fax: (847) 432-8352
Supervision: Chicago Kashrut Association Inc.
Eat in and take-out.

Synagogues

Conservative

North Surburban Synagogue Beth El
1175 Sheriden Road
North and Northwest 60035 (847) 432-8900

Lincolnwood

Delicatessens

Dairy

Wally's Milk Pail
3320 W. Devon
City of Chicago 60645 (773) 673-3459
Supervision: Chicago Rabbinical Council.
Sells groceries as well.

Northbrook

Synagogues

Orthodox

Young Israel of Northbrook
3545 West Walters Road
North and Northwest Suburbs 60062 (708) 480-9462

Peoria

Community Organisations

Jewish Federation
Town Hall Building,
5901 N. Prospect Road 61604 (309) 689-0063

Synagogues

Orthodox

Agudas Achim
5614 N. University 61614 (309) 692-4848
Fax: (309) 692-7255

Reform

Anshai Emeth (309) 691-3323

Rock Island

Community Organisations

Jewish Federation of the Quad Cities
209 18th Street 61201 (309) 793-1300
Fax: (309) 793-1345

Rockford

Community Organisations

Jewish Federation of Greater Rockford
1500 Parkview Avenue 61107 (815) 399-5497
Fax: (815) 399-9835
Email: rockfordfederation@juno.com

Synagogues

Conservative

Ohave Sholom
3730 Guildford Road 61107

Reform

Temple Beth El
1203 Comanche Drive 61107 (815) 398-5020

Skokie

Judaica

Hamakor Gallery Ltd.
4150 Dempster
North and Northwest 60076 (847) 677-4150
Fax: (847) 677-4160
Email: gallery@jewishsource.com
Web site: www.jewishsource.com

Media

Newspapers

Chicago Jewish Star
PO Box 268
North and Northwest 60076 (847) 674-7827
Fax: (847) 674-0014
Email: chicago-jewish-star@mcimail.com

Restaurants

Dairy

Bagel Country
9306 Skokie Blvd
Skokie, IL, North and Northwest 60077
(847) 673-3030
Fax: (847) 673-4040
Supervision: Chicago Rabbinical Council.

Da'Nali's
4032 W. Oakton
North and Northwest 60076 (847) 677-2782
Supervision: Chicago Rabbinical Council.

Slice of Life
4120 W. Dempster
North and Northwest 60076 (847) 674-2021
Supervision: Chicago Rabbinical Council.

Meat

Bugsy's Charhouse
3355 W. Dempster
North and Northwest 60076 (847) 679-4030
Fax: (847) 835-3354
Email: gcfbken@aol.com
Supervision: Chicago Rabbinical Council.

Hy Life, 4120 W. Dempster, Skokie 60076
(847) 674-2021
Supervision: Chicago Rabbinical Council.

Ken's Diner
3353 W. Dempster
North and Northwest 60076 (847) 679-4030
Fax: (847) 835-3354; 3835- Deli
Email: gcfbken@aoi.com
Supervision: Chicago Rabbinical Council.

Vegetarian

Mysore Woodlands
2548 Devon Avenue
North and Northwest 60659 (773) 338-8160
Fax: (773) 338-8162
Supervision: CKA.

Synagogues

Orthodox

Young Israel of Skokie
P O Box 3572
3740 W Dempster, North and Northwest Suburbs
60076 (847) 329-0990
Shul is located in the Timber Ridge School, Samoset and Davis

Indiana

Bloomington

Synagogues

Orthodox

Chabad House
516 E. 17th Street 47408 (812) 332-6784

Reform

Congregation Beth Shalom
3750 E. Third 47401 (812) 334-2440

East Chicago

Synagogues

Orthodox

B'nai Israel
3517 Hemlock Street 46312

Evansville

Synagogues

Conservative

Temple Adath B'nai Israel
3600 E. Washington Avenue 47715 (812) 477-1577
Fax: (812) 477-1577
Email: tabi@evansville.net

Reform

Tempe
Washington Avenue Temple,
100 Washington Avenue 47714

Fort Wayne

Synagogues

Conservative

B'nai Jacob
7227 Bittersweet Moors Drive 46814
(219) 672-8459
Fax: (219) 672-8928

Reform

Achduth Vesholom
5200 Old Mill Road 46807 (219) 744-4245

Gary

Synagogues

Temple Israel
601 N. Montgomery Street 46403 (219) 938-5232

Hammond

Synagogues

Conservative

Beth Israel
7105 Hohman Avenue 46324 (219) 931-1312

Reform

Temple Beth-El
6947 Hohman Avenue 46324 (219) 932-3754

Highland

Organisations

Jewish Federation of North West Indiana
2939 Jewett Street, Highland 46322
(219) 972-2251
Fax: (219) 972-4779
Serving Lake Porter and LaPorte Counties.

Indianapolis

Organisations

Bureau of Jewish Education
6711 Hoover Road 46260 (317) 255-3124
Anglo-Jewish visitors are invited to get in touch with the Executive Vice President.

Jewish Federation of Greater Indianapolis
6705 Hoover Road 46260 (317) 726-5450
Fax: (317) 205-0307
Email: hnadler@jewishinindy.org

Synagogues

Conservative

Shaarey Tefilla Congregation
5879 Central Avenue 46220-2509 (317) 253-4591
Fax: (317) 253-8529
Email: execdir@shaareytefilla.org
Web site: www.shaareytefilla.org

Conservative/Reconstructionist

Beth-El Zedeck
600 W. 70th Street 46260 (317) 253-3441
Fax: (317) 259-6849
Email: bez613@bez613.com

Orthodox

B'nai Torah
6510 Hoover Road 46260 (317) 253-5253
Fax: (317) 253-5459
Email: scrandall@iguest.net

Etz Chaim Sephardic Congregation
826 West 64 Street 46260 (317) 251-6220

Reform

Indianapolis Hebrew Congregation
6501 N. Meridian Street 46260 (317) 255-6647

Lafayette

Synagogues

Orthodox

Sons of Abraham
661 N. 7th Street 47906 (765) 742-2113
Email: retrovir@bragg.bio.purdue.edu

Reform

Temple Israel
620 Cumberland Street 47901 (765) 463-3455
Fax: (765) 463-9309
Email: rsw@nlci.com

Michigan City

Synagogues

Sinai Temple
2800 S. Franklin Street 46360 (219) 874-4477

Muncie

Synagogues

Temple Beth El
525 W. Jackson Street,
cnr. Council Street 47305 (317) 288-4662

South Bend

Contact Information

Rabbi Y. Gettinger
Hebrew Orthodox Congregation,
3207 S. High Street 46614 (219) 291-4239
Fax: (219) 291-9490
Visitors requiring information about kashrut, temporary accommodation, etc., should contact Rabbi Gettinger. Or contact Michael Lerman, 1-800-348-2529. Ext.137.

Kashrut Information

Hebrew Orthodox Congregation
3207 S. High Street 46614 (219) 291-4239
Fax: (219) 291-9490

Mikvaot

(219) 291-6240

Organisations

Jewish Federation of St Joseph Valley
3202 Shalom Drive, South Bend 46615
(219) 233-1164
Fax: (219) 288-4103
Email: mgardner@jon.cjfny.org

Synagogues

Conservative

Sinai
1102 E. Laselle Street 46617 (219) 234-8584
Fax: (219) 234-6856
Email: sinai@michiana.org
Web site: www.uscj.org/midwest/southbend

Orthodox

Hebrew Orthodox Congregation
3207 S. High Street 46614 (219) 291-4239
Fax: (219) 291-9490

Reform

Beth-El
305 W. Madison Street 46601 (219) 234-4402

Terre Haute

Delicatessens

Kosher Meat & Sandwiches
410 W. Western Avenue 47807

Valparaiso

Synagogues

Conservative

Temple Israel
PO Box 2051 46383

Whiting

Synagogues

Orthodox

B'nai Judah
116th Street & Davis Avenue 46394 (219) 659-0797

Iowa

Cedar Rapids

Synagogues

Reform

Temple Judah
3221 Lindsay Lane S.E. 52403 (319) 362-1261

Davenport

Synagogues

Temple Emanuel
12th Street & Mississippi Avenue 52803
Davenport is part of the Rock Island, Illinois area, which is divided by the Mississippi River. See the Rock Island entry.

Des Moines

Delicatessens

The Nosh
800 First Street 50265

Organisations

Jewish Federation of Greater Des Moines
910 Polk Blvd 50312 (515) 277-6321

Synagogues

Conservative

Tifereth Israel
924 Polk Blvd 50312 (515) 255-1137

Orthodox

Beth El Jacob
954 Cummins Parkway 50312 (515) 274-1551
Fax: (515) 274-1552
Email: rav613@hotmail.com
Web site: www.cyberconnect.com/bej
Vaad Hakashrut of Des Moines offer information on kosher establishments & home hospitality. Contact rabbi. Mikva available by appointment.

Reform

Temple B'nai Jeshurun
5101 Grand Avenue 50312 (515) 274-4679
Fax: (515) 274-2072
Email: arptbj@aol.com
Web site: www.shamash.org/reform/uahc/congs/ia/ia001

Dubuque

Synagogues

Beth El
475 W. Locust Street 52001 (563) 583-3483

Fort Dodge

Synagogues

Conservative

Beth El
501 N. 12th Street 50501 (515) 572-8925

Iowa City

Synagogues

Conservative & Reform

Agudas Achim
602 E. Washington Street 52240 (319) 337-3813
Fax: (319) 337-6764
Email: agudasachim@aol.com

Postville

Contact Information

Aaron Koschitsky
P.O. Box 126 (319) 864 7140
Postville 52162 Fax: (319) 864 7890

Synagogue

Orthodox
440 South Lawlor Street (319) 863-3013

Sioux City

Groceries

Sam's Food Market
1911 Grandview 51104

Organisations

Jewish Federation
525 14th Street 51105 (712) 258-0618

Synagogues

Conservative

Congregation Beth Shalom
815 38th Street 51104 (712) 255-1990
Fax: (712) 258-0619
Email: drosen4005@aol.com

Orthodox

United Orthodox
14th & Nebraska Streets 51105 (712) 258 4455

Kansas

Lawrence

Synagogues

Lawrence Jewish Community Center
917 Highland Drive 66046 (785) 841-7636
Email: ljcc@grapevine.net
Web site: www.grapevine.net/~ljcc

Overland Park

Synagogues

Orthodox

Congregation Beth Israel Abraham & Voliner
9900 Antioch 66212 (913) 341-2444
Fax: (913) 341-2467

Kehilath Israel Synagogue
10501 Conser 66212 (913) 642-1880
Fax: (913) 642-7332

Reform

Congregation Beth Torah
6100 W 127th Street 66209 (913) 498-2212
Fax: (913) 498-1071

Prairie Village

Butchers

Jacobsons Strictly Kosher Foods
5200 W95th Street 66207

Synagogues

Conservative

Ohev Sholom
5311 W. 75th Street 66208 (913) 642-6460
Fax: (913) 642-6461
Email: rabbidanny@aol.com

Conservative Egalitarian.

Topeka

Organisations

Topeka Lawrence Jewish Federation
4200 Munson Street 66604

Synagogues

Reform

Beth Sholom
4200 SW Munson Avenue 66604-1818
(785) 272-6040

Wichita

Groceries

Dillon's
21st Street & Rock Road 67208
Dillon's
13th Street & Woodlawn Street 67208
Dillon's
Foodbarn Woodlawn & Central Sts, 67208
The Bread Lady
20205 Rock Road, #80 2607

Synagogues

Orthodox

Hebrew Congregation
1850 N. Woodlawn 67208 (316) 685-1139

Reform

Congregation Emanu-El
7011 E. Central Street 67206 (316) 685-5148

Kentucky

Lexington

Organisations

Central Kentucky Jewish Federation
340 Romany Road 40502 (606) 268-0672
Fax: (606) 268-0775
Email: ckjf@jewishlexington.org

Synagogues

Conservative

Lexington Havurah
PO Box 54958 40551

Ohavay Zion
2048 Edgewater Ct. 40502 (859) 266-8050
Fax: (859) 268-3357
Email: ozslex@gte.net
Web site: www.ozs.org

Reform

Adath Israel
124 N. Ashland Avenue 40502 (859) 269-2979
Fax: (859) 269-7347

Louisville

Organisations

Jewish Community Federation
3630 Dutchman's Lane 40205 (502) 451-8840
Fax: (502) 458-0702
Email: jfed@iglou.com

Synagogues

Conservative

Adath Jeshurun
2401 Woodbourne Avenue 40205 (502) 458-5359

Knesseth Israel
2531 Taylorsville Road 40205 (502) 459-2780

Orthodox

Anshei Sfard
3700 Dutchman's Lane 40205 (502) 451-3122
Mikva attached.

Reform

Temple Shalom
4615 Lowe Road 40220 (502) 458-4739
Fax: (502) 451-9750
Email: rsmiles@pipeline.com

The Temple
5101 Brownsboro Road 40241 (502) 423-1818

Paducah

Synagogues

Temple Israel
330 Joe Clifton Drive 42001

Louisiana

Alexandria

Contact Information

Jewish Welfare Federation
(318) 445-4785

Groceries

Dr & Mrs B Kaplan
100 Park Place 71301 (318) 445-9367
Fax: (318) 445-9369

Kosher food by arrangement.

Libraries

Meyer Kaplan Memorial Library (Judiaca)
c/o B'nai Israel, 1908 Vance Street 71301

Synagogues

Conservative

B'nai Israel
1907 Vance Street 71301 (318) 455-9367

Reform

Gemiluth Chassodim
2021 Turner Street 71301 (318) 455-3655

Baton Rouge

Organisations

Jewish Federation of Greater Baton Rouge
PO Box 80827 70898 (504) 291-5895

Synagogues

Reform

B'nai Israel
3354 Kleinert Avenue 70806 (504) 343-0111

Beth Shalom
9111 Jefferson Highway 70809 (504) 924-6773

Lafayette

Synagogues

Temple Sholom
603 Lee Avenue,
PO Box 53711 70505 (318) 234-3760
There is a fine Judaica library at the University of Southwestern Louisiana.

New Orleans

Delicatessens

Kosher Cajun
3519 Severn Avenue, Metairie (504) 888-2010
Fax: (504) 888-2014

Kosher Cajun Deli & Grocery
3250 N. Hullen Street,
Metairie 70002 (504) 888-2010
Fax: (504) 888-2014
Glatt N.Y. Deli - Dine in or take-out. Challah, wine, large selection of kosher grocery items - refrigerated/frozen/dry. Under strict rabbinical supervision. Hours: Monday to Thursday, 10 am to 7 pm; Friday and Sunday, 10am to 3 pm. We also deliver to hotels.

Groceries

Casablanca
3030 Seven Avenue, Metrairie 70002-4826
(504) 888-2209

Touro Infirmary
1401 Foucher Street 70115 (504) 897-8246
Glatt kosher meals available.

Media

Newspapers

The Jewish News
3500 N. Causeway Blvd, #1240, Metairie 70002
(504) 828-2125
Fax: (504) 828-2827
Email: jewishnews@jewishnola.com

Mikvaot

Beth Israel
7000 Canal Blvd 70124 (504) 283-4366

Organisations

Jewish Federation of Greater New Orleans
3500 N. Causeway Blvd, #1240, Metairie 70002
(504) 828-2125
Fax: (504) 828-2827

Restaurants

Meat

Casablanca
3030 Severn Avenue, Metair (504) 888-2209
Fax: (504) 888-5605
Supervision: Lubavitch Shechita & Chabad.

Synagogues

Orthodox

Anshe Sfard
2230 Carondelet Street 70130 (504) 422-4714

Shreveport

Community Organisations

Jewish Federation
2032 Line Avenue 71104 (318) 221-4129

Synagogues

Conservative

Agudath Achim
9401 Village Green Drive 71115 (318) 797-6401
Fax: (318) 797-6402

Reform

B'nai Zion
245 Southfield Road 71105 (318) 861-2122

Maine

Auburn

Community Organisations

Lewiston-Auburn Jewish Federation
74 Bradman Street 04210 (207) 786-4201
Fax: (207) 786-4202
Email: temple6359@aol.com

Synagogues

Conservative

Congregation Beth Abraham
Main Street & Laurel Avenue 04210 (207) 783-1302

Temple Shalom
74 Bradman Street 04210 (207) 786-4201
Fax: (207) 786-4202
Email: temple6359@aol.com

Bangor

Restaurants

Bagel Central
33 Central Street 04401 (207) 947-1654
Supervision: Beth Abraham Rabbi Fred Neble.

Synagogues

Conservative

Congregation Beth Israel
144 York Street 04401 (207) 945-3433
Fax: (207) 945-3840

Orthodox

Beth Abraham
145 York Street 04401 (207) 947-0876

Old Orchard Beach

Kashrut Information

Eber Weinstein
187 E. Grand Avenue 04064 (207) 934-7522
Eddie Hakim (207) 934-7223
Harold Goodkovski
(207) 934-4210

Synagogues

Orthodox

Beth Israel
49 E. Grand Avenue 04064 (207) 934-2973
Fax: (207) 934-5800
Daily minyan, May 28 to Yom Kippur, Shabbat & Yom Tov. Minyan all year round.

Portland

Butchers

Penny Wise Super Market
182 Ocean Avenue 04130
Take-out counter at a local supermarket.

Mikvaot

Shaarey Tphiloh
76 Noyes Street 04103 (207) 773-0693

Organisations

Jewish Fed.-Com. Council of Southern Maine
57 Ashmont Street 04103 (207) 773-7254

Synagogues

Conservative

Temple Beth El
400 Deering Avenue 04103 (207) 774-2649
Fax: (207) 774-7518
Email: office@templebethel-maine.org

Orthodox

Etz Chaim
267 Congress Street 04101 (207) 773-2339
Shaarey Tphiloh
76 Noyes Street 04103 (207) 773-0693
Mikva & Hebrew Day School on premises.

Rockland

Synagogues

Adas Yoshuron
Willow Street (207) 594-4523

Maryland

Bethesda, Bowie, Chevy Chase, Gaithersburg, Greenbelt, Hyattsville, Kensington, Laurel, Lexington Park, Olney, Potomac, Rockville, Silver Spring and Wheaton and Temple Hills are all part of Greater Washington, DC.

Annapolis

Synagogues

Conservative

Congregation Kol Ami
1909 Hidden Meadow Lane 21401 (410) 266-6006
Email: kolami2@toadmail.toad.net

Reform

Temple Beth Shalom
1461 Baltimore-Anaapolis Blvd., 21012

Baltimore

There are more than fifty synagogues in the Baltimore metropolitan area. Visitors are advised to contact one of the community organisations in the area to find the synagogue nearest to them.

Bakeries

Dunkin Donuts
7000 Reisterstown Road 21215 (410) 764-6846
Supervision: Rabbi Salfer.
Dunkin Donuts
1508 Reisterstown Road 21208 (410) 653-8182
Supervision: Rabbi Salfer.
Goldman's Kosher Bakery
6848 Reistertown Road,
Farstaff Shopping Center 21215 (410) 358-9625
Fax: (410) 358-5859
Email: mcohn@home.com
Web site: www.goldmanskosherbakery.com
Star-K Certified.
Pariser's Kosher Bakery
6711 Reistertown Road 21215 (410) 764-1700
Schmell & Azman Kosher Bakery
(410) 484-7343
Schmell-Azman
7006 Reisterstown Road 21215 (410) 484-7373
Supervision: Star K.

Butchers

Shlomo Meat & Fish Market
4135 Amos Ave., (Menlo Industrial Park) 21215
(410) 358-9633

Wasserman & Lemberger
7006-D Reisterstown Road 20208 (410) 486-4191

Communal Information

Jewish Information and Referral Service
5750 Park Heights Avenue 21215 (410) 466-4636
Fax: (410) 664-0551
Email: jfs@jfs.org

Open daily from 9am to 3.0pm for help on almost anything.

Community Organisations

Associated Jewish Community Federation of Baltimore
101 W. Mount Royal Avenue 21201 (410) 727-4828

Delicatessens

Knish Shop
508 Reisterstown Road 21208 (410) 484-5850
Conservative supervision

Liebes Kosher Deli Carry Out
607 Reistertown Road 21208 (410) 653-1977
Only glatt kosher meats. Hours: Sunday to Wednesday, 8.30 am to 6 pm; Thursday, late night Friday, to one hour before sundown. Specialising in party trays.

Groceries

Shlomo Meat & Fish
506 Reisterstown Road 21215 (410) 358-9633

Wasserman & Lemberger
7006-D Reistertown Road 21208 (410) 486-4191

Kashrut Information

Star-K Kosher Certification
11 Warren Road 21208 (410) 484-4110
Fax: (410) 653-9294
Email: star-k@star-k.org
Web site: www.star-k.org

Also issues Worldwide Kashrut Certification.

Mikvaot

Mikva of Baltimore Inc.,
3207 Clarks Lane 21215 (410) 764-1448
Fax: (410) 578-0018

Museums

The Jewish Museum of Maryland
15 Lloyd Street 21202 (410) 732-6400
Fax: (410) 732-6451
Email: info@jewishmuseummd.org

This newly enlarged complex of museum buildings is unlike anything else in the United States, comprising two historic synagogues (Lloyd Street Synagogue, built in 1845, and B'nai Israel, built in 1876) and an adjoining research center and museum featuring changing exhibits and regional Judaica.Opening hours: Tuesday, Wednesday, Thursday and Sunday 12 pm-4 pm.

Organisations

The Baltimore Jewish Council
Gay & Water Sts,

Restaurants

Caramel's Pizza & Ice Cream
700 Reisterstown Road (410) 486-2365
Supervision: Star-K.

Goldberg's Bagels
708 Reisterstown Road (410) 415-7001
Supervision: Star-K

Krispy Kremes
10021 Reisterstown Road (nr. Painters Mill Rd).
(410) 356-2655
Supervision: Star-K.

Mama Leah's Pizza
604 Reisterstown Road (410) 653-7600
Supervision: Star-K

Dairy

Carmel
700 Reistertown Road (410) 488-2385

I Can't Believe It's Yogurt
1430 Reisterstown Road (410) 484-4411
Supervision: Rabbi Salfer.

Milk and Honey Bistro
Commercecentre, 1777 Reisterstown Road
(410) 484-3544
Supervision: Star-K.

Meat

Kosher Bite
6309 Reistertown Road 21215 (410) 358-6349
Supervision: Star-K.

Royal Restaurant
7006 Reistertown Road 21208 (410) 484-3544
Supervision: Star-K.

The Brasserie
Pomona Square Shopping Center,
1700 Reistertown Rd, 21208 (410) 484-0476
Supervision: Star-K.

Supermarket

Seven Mile Market
4000 Seven Mile Lane 21208
(410) 653-2000; 2002
Supervision: Star K.
Items sold in the Fresh Meat, Fresh Fish, Fresh Bakery, Fresh Deli, Fresh Dairy, Hot Prepared Foods & Salad Departments are approved by the Vaad Hakashrus of Baltimore, when so stated on sign or label.

Tours of Jewish Interest

Holocaust Memorial
Gay & Lombard Sts (410) 542-4850
Fax: (410) 542-4834
Email: mtishler@aea-bal.tjc.org

College Park

Libraries

The National Archives
8601 Adelphi Road 20740
Containing historical Jewish documentation.

Cumberland

Synagogues

Conservative

Beth Jacob
1 Columbia Street 21502 (301) 777-3717

Reform

B'Er Chayim
107 Union Street 21502 (301) 722-5688

Hagerstown

Delicatessens

Celebrity Deli
6700 Adelphi Road 20782 (301) 927-5525

Synagogues

Reform

B'nai Abraham
53 E. Baltimore Street 21740 (301) 733-5039

Pocomoke

Synagogues

Conservative

Temple Israel
3rd Street 21851

Salisbury

Synagogues

Beth Israel
Camden Avenue & Wicomico Street 21801
(410) 742-2564

Massachusetts

Acton

Synagogues

Independent

Beth Elohim
10 Hennessy Drive 07120 (978) 263-8610

Amherst

Synagogues

Jewish Community
742 Main Street 01002 (413) 256-0160
Fax: (413) 256-1588
Web site: www.j-c-a.org

Andover

Synagogues

Reform

Temple Emanuel
7 Haggett's Pond Road 01810 (978) 470-1356
Fax: (978) 470-1783

Athol

Synagogues

Conservative

Temple Israel
107 Walnut Street 01331 (978) 249-9481

Have you any information for us?

Any comments you may have on this guide are always welcomed. Please do get in touch if you have any relevant information which you may feel will be of use to other travellers. Details on how to do this are on page iv.

Also forms are available at the back of the book.

Attleboro

Synagogues

Reconstructionist

Agudas Achim Congregation
901 N. Main Street 02703 (508) 222-2243
Email: agudasachim@netzero.net
Web site: www.shamash.org/jrf/agudasma

Ayer

Synagogues

Independent

Congregation Anshey Sholom
Cambridge Street 01432 (508) 772-0896

Belmont

Synagogues

Reform

Beth El Temple Center
2 Concord Avenue 02478 (617) 484-6668
Fax: (617) 484-6020
Web site: www.uahc.org/ma/betc

Beverly

Synagogues

Conservative

B'nai Abraham
200 E. Lothrop Street 01915 (978) 927-3211
Fax: (978) 922-5281
Email: TBA200East@cs.com

Boston (Greater Boston)

Embassy

Consul General of Israel
1020 Statler Office Blvd 02116

Kashrut Information

Synagogue Council of Massachusetts
1320 Centre Street, Newton Centre 02459-2400
(617) 244-6506
Fax: (617) 964-7055
Email: syncouncil@aol.com.

The Kashruth Commission
177 Tremont Street 02111 (617) 426-2139
Fax: (617) 426-6268
Email: kvh613@aol.com

Vaad Harabonim of Massachusetts
177 Tremont Street 02111 (617) 426-2139
Fax: (617) 426-6268

Media

Guides

Jewish Guide to Boston and New England
15 School Street 02108 (617) 267-9100
Fax: (617) 267-9310

Newspapers

Boston Jewish Times
15 School Street 02108 (617) 267-9100
Fax: (617) 367-9310

The Jewish Advocate
15 School Street 02108 (617) 367-9100
Fax: (617) 367-9310
Email: thejewadv@aol.com
Web site: www.thejewishadvocate.com

Mikvaot

Daughters of Israel
101 Washington Street, Brighton 02135
(617) 782-9433

Organisations

Jewish Community Relations Council of Greater Boston
1 Lincoln Plaza, Suite 308 02111 (617) 330-9600
Represents thirty-four community organisations in the area.

Religious Organisations

Rabbinical Council of New England
177 Tremont Street 02111 (617) 426-2139
Fax: (617) 426-6268

Rabbinical Court
177 Tremont Street 02111 (617) 426-2139
Fax: (617) 426-6268

Restaurants

Dairy

Milk Street Cafe
50 Milk Street (617) 542-FOOD
Fax: (617) 451-5FAX
Supervision: Orthodox Rabbinic Council of Greater Boston.
Hours: Monday to Friday, 7 am to 3 pm.

Meat

Rubin's Kosher Deli and Restaurant
500 Harvard Street, Brookline 02146 (617) 731-8787

Synagogues

Conservative

Hillel B'nai Torah
120 Corey St, W. Roxbury 02132 (617) 323-0486

Temple B'nai Moshe
1845 Commonwealth Avenue,
Brighton 02135 (617) 254-3620
Fax: (617) 254-3620
Email: templebnaimoshe.org

Orthodox

Chabad House
491 Commonwealth Avenue 02215 (617) 424-1190
Fax: (617) 266-5997
Email: chabad@peoplepc.com

Congregation Kadimah-Toras Moshe
113 Washington Street, Brighton 02135
(617) 254-1333

Lubavitch Shul of Brighton
239 Chestnut Hill Avenue, Brighton 02135
(617) 782-8340

The Boston Synagogue (at Charles River Park), 55 Martha Road 02114 (617) 523-0453
Fax: (617) 723-2863

Administrator: Rebecca Sussman. Services: Friday evening, Saturday, 9.15 am.

Zvhil-Mezbuz Beis Medrash
15 School Street 02108 (617) 227-8200
Fax: (617) 227-8420
Web site: www.rebbe.org

Reform

Temple Israel
Longwood Ave & Plymouth Street 02215
(617) 566-3960
Fax: (617) 731-3711
Web site: www.tisrael.org

Braintree

Synagogues

Conservative

Temple Bnai Shalom
41 Storrs Avenue 02184 (781) 843-3687

Brighton

Synagogues

Orthodox

Chai Odom
77 Englewood Av 02135 (617) 734-5359
Web site: www.netcom/~coriat/chaidom

Talner Congregation Beth David
64 Corey Road 02135 (617) 232-2349

Brockton

Synagogues

Conservative

Temple
479 Torres Street 02401 (508) 583-5810

Orthodox

Agudath Achim
144 Belmont Avenue 02401 (508) 583-0717

Reform

Temple Israel
184 W. Elm Street 02401 (508) 587-4130

Brookline

Bakeries

Catering by Andrew
402 Harvard Street 02446 (617) 731-6585
Fax: (617) 232-3788
Email: cbandrew@aol.com

Supervision: Vaad Harabonim of Massachusetts. Shomer Shabbat.

Kashrut Information

Jewish Commercial Center
Harvard Street
Harvard Street is the Jewish commercial center, with art & bookshops, as well as many kosher butchers' shops and bakeries.

Restaurants

Dairy

Zaatar's Oven
242 Harvard Street (617) 731-6836

Meat

Cafe Shiraz
1030 Commonwealth Avenue 02215
(617) 566-8888

New private function rooms for group parties. Glatt kosher Persian and Middle Eastern cuisine. Wheelchair accessible. Hours: Monday to Thursday, 5 pm to 10 pm; Saturday, forty-five minutes after sundown to midnight; Sunday, 4 pm to 10 pm.

Ruth's Kitchen
401 Harvard Street (617) 734-9810

Shalom Hunan
92 Harvard Street 02445-46 (617) 731-9778
Fax: (617) 731-9760

Pizzerias

Victor's Pizza
1364 Beacon Street 02146 (617) 730-9903

Synagogues

Conservative

Kehillath Israel
384 Harvard St 02146 (617) 277-9155

Orthodox

Beth Pinchas (Bostoner Rebbe)
1710 Beacon Street 02146 (617) 734-5100
Fax: (617) 739-0163
Email: rofeh@world.std.com

Congregation Lubavitch
100 Woodcliff Road 02167 (617) 469-0088
Fax: (617) 469-0089

Young Israel of Brookline
62 Green Street 02446 (617) 734-0276
Fax: (617) 734-8475
Email: yibrookline@yahoo.com
Web site: www.yibrookline.org

Reform

Ohabei Shalom
1187 Beacon St. 02446 (617) 277-6610
Email: dberman@ohabei.org
Web site: www.ohabei.org

Temple Sinai
50 Sewall Av, Coolidge Corner 02146
(617) 277-5888

Sephardic

Sephardic Congregation
1566 Beacon St. 02146 (617) 566-8171

Burlington

Synagogues

Reform

Temple Shalom Emeth
14-16 Lexington Street 01803 (781) 272-2351

Cambridge

Kashrut Information

Harvard Hillel
Harvard University, 52 Mt. Auburn St. 02138
(617) 495-4696
Fax: (617) 864-1637
Email: linda@hillel.harvard.edu

Kosher meals are obtainable during the school year (September - May). Reservations are required for Shabbat meals and can be made by calling Linda at extension 221.

Restaurants

Meat

M.I.T. Hillel
40 Massachusetts Avenue 02139 (617) 253-2982
Fax: (617) 253-3260
Email: hillel@mit.edu

Supervision: Vaad Harabonim of Massachusetts.

Synagogues

Hillel House
Harvard University (617) 495-4696

Conservative

Temple Beth Shalom of Cambridge
8 Tremont Street 02139 (617) 864-6388
Fax: (617) 864-0507
Email: office@tremontstreetshul.org

Canton

Synagogues

Beth Abraham
1301 Washington Street 02021 (781) 828-5250

Reform

Temple Beth David of the South Shore
1060 Randolph Street 02021 (781) 828-2275
Fax: (781) 821-3997
Email: info@templebethdavid.com
Web site: www.templebethdavid.com

Cape Cod

Synagogues

Orthodox

Beth Israel
cnr. of Onset Avenue & Locust Street,
PO Box 24, Onset 02558 (508) 295-9185
Email: capeshul@att.net
Web site: www.home.att.net/capeshul

Services three times daily from last Saturday in June to Labour Day. Services are also held on the Holy Days. Apartments available near synagogue. Further information from Burt Parker.

Chelmsford

Synagogues

Reform

Congregation Shalom
Richardson Road 01824 (978) 251-8090

Clinton

Synagogues

Independent

Shaarei Zedeck
Water Street 01510 (978) 365-3320

East Falmouth

Synagogues

Reform

Falmouth Jewish Congregation
7 Hatchville Road 02536 (508) 540-0602
Fax: (508) 540-8094
Web site: www.falmouthjewish.org

Easton

Synagogues

Traditional

Temple Chayai Shalom
238 Depot Street 02334 (508) 238-6385
Mail address: PO Box 404, N. Easton 02356

Everett

Synagogues

Tifereth Israel
34 Malden Street 02149 (617) 387-0200

Fall River

Organisations

Fall River Jewish Community Council
Room 327, 56 N. Main St., 02720 (508) 673-7791
Fax: (508) 673-7791

Synagogues

Conservative

Beth El
385 High Street 02720 (508) 674-9761

Orthodox

Adas Israel
1647 Robeson Street 02720 (508) 674-9761
Fax: (508) 678-3195

Fitchburg

Synagogues

Independent

Agudas Achim
40 Boutelle Street 01420 (978) 342-7704

Framingham

Synagogues

Conservative

Beth Sholom
50 Pamela Road 01701 (508) 877-2540
Fax: (508) 877-8278

Orthodox

Chabad House
74 Joseph Road 01701 (508) 877-5313
Fax: (508) 877 5313

Reform

Beth Am
300 Pleasant Street 01701 (508) 872-8300
Fax: (508) 872-9773
Email: tempbetham@aol.com

Gloucester

Synagogues

Conservative

Ahavat Achim
86 Middle Street 01930 (978) 281-0739
Fax: (978) 281-0739

Greenfield

Synagogues

Temple Israel
27 Pierce Street 01301 (413) 773-5884

Haverhill

Synagogues

Orthodox

Anshe Sholom
427 Main Street 01830 (508) 372-2276

Reform

Temple Emanu-El
514 Main Street 01830 (508) 373-3861

Hingham

Synagogues

Congregation Sha'aray Shalom
1112 Main Street 02043 (781) 749-8103
Fax: (781) 740-1480
Email: cssadm@aol.com

Holbrook

Synagogues

Conservative

Temple Beth Shalom
95 Plymouth Street 02343 (617) 767-4922

Holliston

Synagogues

Temple Beth Torah
2162 Washington Street 01746 (508) 429-6268

Holyoke

Synagogues

Sons of Zion
378 Maple Street 01040 (413) 534-3369

Orthodox

Rodphey Sholom
1800 Northampton Street 01040 (413) 534-5262

Hull

Synagogues

Conservative

Temple Beth Sholom
600 Nantasket Avenue 02045 (781) 925-0091
Fax: (781) 925-9053

Temple Israel of Nantasket
9 Hadassah Way 02045 (617) 925-0289
Summer only.

Hyannis

Synagogues

Reform

Cape Cod Synagogue
145 Winter Street 02601 (508) 775-2988

Hyde Park

Synagogues

Conservative

Temple Adas Hadrath Israel
28 Arlington Street 02136 (617) 364-2661

Lawrence

Organisations

Jewish Com. Council of Greater Lawrence
580 Haverhill Street 01841 (617) 686-4157

Synagogues

Orthodox

Anshai Sholum
411 Hampshire Street 01843 (508) 683-4544

Leominster

Synagogues

Conservative

Congregation Agudat Achim
268 Washington Street 01453 (508) 534-6121

Lexington

Synagogues

Temple Emunah
9 Piper Road 02421 (781) 861-0300
Fax: (781) 861-7141
Email: rholmes@emunahlex.org
Web site: www.templeemunah.org

Orthodox

Chabad Center
9 Burlington Street 02173 (781) 863-8656

Reform

Temple Isaiah
55 Lincoln Street 02173 (781) 862-7160

Lowell

Mikvaot

Mikvah
48 Academy Drive (508) 970-2008

Synagogues

Conservative

Temple Beth El
105 Princeton Blvd 01851 (508) 453-7744

Orthodox

Montefiore Synagogue
460 Westford Street 01851 (978) 459-9400

Reform

Temple Emanuel of Merrimack Valley
101 W. Forest Street 01851 (508) 454-1372

Lynn

Synagogues

Orthodox

Ahabat Sholom
151 Ocean Street 01902 (617) 593-9255
Email: ahabat@juno.com
Web site: www.ahabatsholom.org
Houses the Eliot Feuerstein Library.

Anshai Sfard
150 S. Common Street 01905 (617) 599-7131

Chevra Tehilim
12 Breed Street 01902 (617) 598-2964

Malden

Synagogues

Conservative

Ezrath Israel
245 Bryant Street 02148 (617) 322-7205

Orthodox

Congregation Beth Israel
10 Dexter Street 02148 (781) 322-5686
Fax: (781) 322-6678
Email: congbi@aol.com

Young Israel of Malden
45 Holyoke Street 02148 (617) 961-9817

Reform

Tifereth Israel
539 Salem Street 02148 (617) 322-2794

Traditional

Agudas Achim
160 Harvard Street 02148 (781) 322-9380

Marblehead

Synagogues

Conservative/Masorti

Temple Sinai
1 Community Road 01945 (781) 631-2763
Fax: (781) 631-2244
Email: Tmpsinai@gis.net

Orthodox

Orthodox Congregation of the North Shore
4 Community Road 01945 (617) 598-1810

Reform

Temple Emanu-El
393 Atlantic Avenue 01945 (617) 631-9300

Marlboro

Synagogues

Conservative

Temple Emanuel
150 Berlin Road 01752
(508) 485-7565; 508-562-5105

Medford

Synagogues

Temple Shalom
475 Winthrop Street 02155 (781) 396-3262

Melrose

Synagogues

Reform

Temple Beth Shalom
21 E. Foster Street 02176 (617) 665-4520

Milford

Synagogues

Conservative

Temple Beth Shalom
55 Pine Street 01757 (508) 473-1590
Web site: www.templebethshalom.com

Millis

Synagogues

Ael Chunon
334 Village Street 02054 (508) 376-5984
Fax: (508) 533-3802
Email: TNULB@mediaone.net

Milton

Synagogues

Temple Shalom
180 Blue Hill Avenue 02186 (617) 698-3394

Orthodox

B'nai Jacob
100 Blue Hill Parkway 02187 (617) 698-0698

Natick

Synagogues

Conservative

Temple Israel
145 Hartford Street 01760 (508) 650-3521
Fax: (508) 655-3440
Email: tiofnatick@aol.com

Orthodox

Chabad Lubavitch Center
2 East Mill Street 01760 (508) 650-1499

Needham

Synagogues

Conservative

Temple Aliyah
1664 Central Avenue 02492 (781) 444-8522
Fax: (781) 449-7066

Reform

Temple Beth Shalom
670 Highland Avenue 02494 (781) 444-0077
Fax: (781) 449-3274
Email: tbshalom@fcl-us.net

New Bedford

Organisations

Jewish Federation of Greater New Bedford
467 Hawthorn Street, N. Dartmouth 02747
(508) 997-7471

Synagogues

Conservative

Tifereth Israel
145 Brownell Avenue 02740 (508) 997-3171
Fax: (508) 997-3173

Orthodox

Ahavath Achim
385 County Street 02740 (508) 994-1760
Fax: (508) 994-8186
Email: rabbibarry@aol.com
Web site: www.members.aol.com/rabbibarry

Newburyport

Synagogues

Congregation Ahavas Achim
Washington & Olive Streets 09150 (508) 462-2461

Newton

Cafeteria

Orthodox Rabbinical Council of Massachusetts
(617) 558-6475

Provides snack bar for Jewish Community Center of Greater Boston.

Organisations

Jewish Community Center of Greater Boston
333 Nahanton Street 02159 (617) 558-6522
Kosher snack bar provided. See below.

Synagogues

Orthodox

Congregation B'nai Jacob (Zvhil-Mezbuz Rebbe)
955 Beacon Street (617) 227-8200
Fax: (617) 227-8420
Web site: www.rebbe.org

North Adams

Synagogues

Conservative

Congregation Beth Israel
265 Church Street 01247 (413) 663-5830
Fax: (413) 663-5830
Email: cbi@bcn.net

Northampton

Synagogues

B'nai Israel
253 Prospect Road 01060 (413) 584-3593

Norwood

Synagogues

Temple Shaare Tefilah
556 Nichols Street 02062 (781) 762-8670
Fax: (781) 762-8670
Web site: www.uscj.org/neweng/norwood

Onset

Hotels

Bridge View Hotel
12 S. Water Street 02558 (508) 295-9820
Welcomes Jewish guests. Self-catering flatlets available. Kosher meat and other products available.

Peabody

Synagogues

Conservative

Temple Ner Tamid
368 Lowell Street 01960 (978) 532-1293
Fax: (978) 532-0101

Independent

Congregation Tifereth Israel
Pierpont Street 01960 (508) 531-8135

Reform

Beth Shalom
489 Lowell Street 01960 (978) 535-2100
Fax: (978) 536-3115

Traditional

Congregation Sons of Israel
Park & Spring Streets 01960 (508) 531-7576

Pittsfield (Berkshires)

Organisations

Jewish Federation of the Berkshires
235 East Street 01201 (413) 442-4360

Plymouth

Synagogues

Reform

Congregation Beth Jacob
Synagogue on Pleasant Street,
Community Center on Court Street,
PO Box 3284 02361 (508) 746-1575
Email: cbethjacob@juno.com

Quincy

Synagogues

Conservative

Adas Shalom
435 Adams Street 02169 (617) 471-1818
Email: adasshalom@aol.com

Temple Beth El
1001 Hancock Street 02169 (617) 479-4309

Orthodox

Beth Israel
33 Grafton Street,
PO Box 690388 02269-0388 (617) 472-6796

Randolph

Booksellers

Davidson's Hebrew Book Store
1106 Main Street 02368 (781) 961-4929

Synagogues

Conservative

Temple Beth Am
871 N. Main Street 02368 (617) 963-0440

Orthodox

Young Israel - Kehillath Jacob of Mattapan & Randolph
374 N. Main Street
PO Box 880 02368 (781) 986-6461
Email: Youngisrael@Juno.com

Revere

Delicatessens

Myer's Kosher Kitchen
168 Shirley Avenue 02151

Synagogues

Independent

Temple B'nai Israel
1 Wave Avenue 02151 (781) 284-8388

Orthodox

Ahavas Achim Anshei Sfard
89 Walnut Way 02151 (617) 289-1026

Tifereth Israel
43 Nahant Avenue 02151 (617) 284-9255

Salem

Community Organisations

Jewish Federation of the North Shore
21 Front Street 01970 (978) 745-4222
Fax: (978) 741-7507
Email: mail@jfns.org

Synagogues

Conservative

Temple Shalom
287 Lafayette Street 01970 (508) 741-4880
Fax: (508) 741-4882

Sharon

Bed & Breakfasts

Sharon Woods Inn
80 Brook Road 02067 (781) 784-9401
Fax: (781) 784-5162
Email: kctova@yahoo.com

Mikvaot

Chevrat Nashim
9 Dunbar Street 02067 (781) 784-7444
Operated by the Mikvah Organisation of the South Shore, Chevrat Nashim Mikvah

Religious Organisations

Eruv Society (614) 784-6112
Eruv maintained by Sharon County Eruv Society.

Synagogues

Conservative

Adath Sharon
18 Harding Street 02067 (617) 784-2517

Temple Israel
125 Pond Street 02067 (781) 784-3986
Fax: (781) 784-0719

Orthodox

Chabad Center
101 Worcester Road 02067 (617) 784-8167

Young Israel of Sharon
100 Ames Street 02067 (781) 784-6112
Fax: (781) 784-7758
Web site: www.yisharon.org

Reform

Temple Sinai
25 Canton Street 02067 (617) 784-6081
Fax: (617) 784-2616
Email: office@temple-sinai.com

Somerville

Synagogues

Independent

B'nai B'rith of Somerville
201 Central Street 02145 (617) 625-0333
Email: tbb@templebnaibrith.org

Springfield & Longmeadow

Groceries

Waldbaum's Food Mart
355 Belmont Avenue 01108 (413) 732-3866

Mikvaot

Mikveh Association
1104 Converse, Long. MA 01106 (413) 567-1607

Organisations

Jewish Community Center
1160 Dickinson Street 01108 (413) 739-4715
Fax: (413) 739-4747

Restaurant

Kosher Coffee Corner
Jewish Federation of Greater Springfield
1160 Dickinson Street 01108 (413) 737-4313

Synagogues

Conservative

B'nai Jacob
2 Eunice Dr 01106 (413) 567-3163

Orthodox

Beth Israel
1280 Williams St 01106 (413) 567-3210

Congregation Kodimoh
124 Sumner Avenue, Springfield 01108
(413) 781-0171
Fax: (413) 737-8002
Email: kodimoh@TheSpa.com
The largest Orthodox congregation in New England.

Kesser Israel
19 Oakland Street 01108 (413) 732-8492

Lubavitcher Yeshiva Synagogue
1148 Converse St 01106 (413) 567-8665

Reform

Temple Sinai
1100 Dickinson Street 01108 (413) 736-3619

Stoughton

Bakeries

Ruth's Bake Shop
987 Central Street 02072 (781) 344-8993
Supervision: Vaad Harabonim of Massachusetts.

Synagogues

Conservative

Adhavath Torah Congregation
1179 Central Street 02072 (781) 344-8733
Fax: (781) 344-4315

Sudbury

Synagogues

Independent

Congregation B'nai Torah
Woodside Road 01776 (508) 443-2082

Reform

Congregation Beth El
105 Hudson Road 01776 (978) 443-9622
Fax: (978) 443-9629
Email: secretary@bethelsudbury.org
Web site: www.bethelsudbury.org

Swampscott

Synagogues

Conservative

Beth El
55 Atlantic Avenue 01907 (617) 599-8005
Fax: (617) 599-1860

Temple Israel
837 Humphrey Street 01907 (781) 595-6635
Fax: (781) 595-0033
Web site: www.templeisraelswampscott.org

Vineyard Haven

Synagogues

Martha's Vineyard Hebrew Center
Center Street 02568 (508) 693-0745

Wakefield

Synagogues

Conservative

Temple Emmanuel
120 Chestnut Street 01880 (781) 245-1886
Web site: www.geocities.com/temple_emanuel

Waltham

Synagogues

American Jewish Historical Society (Brandeis University campus)
2 Thornton Road 02154 (617) 891-8110
Fax: (617) 899-9208

Conservative

Beth Israel
25 Harvard Street 02154 (617) 894-5146

Wayland

Synagogues

Reform

Templr Shir Tikva
141 Boston Post Road 01778 (508) 358-5312

Wellesley Hills

Synagogues

Beth Elohim
10 Bethel Road 02181 (617) 235-8419

Westboro

Synagogues

B'nai Shalom
117 E. Main Street,
PO Box 1019 01581-6019 (508) 366-7191

Westwood

Synagogues

Beth David
40 Pond Street 02090 (617) 769-5270

Winchester

Synagogues

Temple Shir Tikvah
PO Box 373 01890 (617) 792-1188

Winthrop

Synagogues

Orthodox

Tifereth Abraham
283 Shirley Street 02152 (617) 846-5063
Tifereth Israel
93 Veteran's Road 02152 (617) 846-1390

Worcester

Contact Information

Agudath Israel of America Hachnosas Orchim Committee
69 S. Flagg Street 01602 (508) 754-3681
Contact Rabbi Reuven Fischer.
Rabbi Hershel Fogelman
22 Newton Avenue (617) 752-5791
Visitors requiring information about kashrut, temporary accommodation, etc., should contact Rabbi Fogelman.

Mikvaot

Mikva
Huntley Street 01602 (508) 755-1257

Organisations

Jewish Federation
633 Salisbury Street 01609 (508) 756-1543
Fax: (508) 798-0962
Email: bluks@jfcm.org
Web site: www.jfcm.org

Synagogues

Orthodox

Young Israel of Worcester
889 Pleasant Street 01602 (508) 754-3681

Michigan

Ann Arbor

Mikvaot

Chabad House
715 Hill 48104 (734) 995-3276
Email: chabad@jewmich.com

Organisations

Jewish Federation/UJA
2939 Birch Hollow Drive 48108 (734) 679-0100
Fax: (734) 679-0109
Email: jccfed@aol.com

Synagogues

Orthodox

Ann Arbor Orthodox Minyan
1429 Hill Street 48104 (734) 994-5822

Benton Harbour (St Joseph)

Synagogues

Conservative

Temple B'nai Shalom
2050 Broadway 49022

Detroit

With tens of synagogues in the Bloomfield, Oak Park and Southfield areas, visitors are recommmended to contact one of the local religious organisations listed for the nearest synagogue.

Delicatessens

Sarah's Glatt Kosher Deli
15600 W. Ten Mile Road,
Southfield 48075 (313) 443-2425

Groceries

Sperber's Kosher Karry-Out
25250 W. Ten Mile Road,
Oak Park 48237 (313) 443-2425

Kashrut Information

Council of Orthodox Rabbis of Greater Detroit
16947 W. Ten Mile Road,
Southfield 48075 (248) 559-5005/6
Fax: (248) 559-5202
Email: cordetroit@hotmail.com

Media

Newspapers

Jewish News
Franklin Road, Southfield 48034

Mikvaot

Mikveh Israel
10 Mile Road, Oak Park 48237 (313) 967-0289

Organisations

B'nai B'rith Hillel Foundations
Wayne State University, 667 Charles Grosberg Religious Ctr. 48202
Hot lunch, sandwiches, salads, soups served during academic year (September-April).

Council of Orthodox Rabbis of Detroit (Vaad Harabonim)
16947 W. Ten Mile Road,
Southfield 48075 (248) 559-5005/06
Fax: (248) 559-5202

Jewish Community Center of Metr. Detroit
6600 W. Maple Road,
W. Bloomfield 48322 (810) 661-1000
Fax: (810) 661-3680

Jewish Federation of Metr. Detroit
Telegraph Road, Bloomfield Hills 48303

Machon L'Torah (The Jewish Network of Michigan)
W. 10 Mile Road 48237

Restaurants

Dairy

Jerusalem Pizza
26025 Greenfield, Southfield (313) 552-0088

La Difference
7295 Orchard Lake Road (248) 932-8934
Fax: (248) 932-8942
Supervision: Orthodox Rabbis of Greater Detroit.

Meat

Unique Kosher
25270 Greenfield, Southfield (313) 967-1161

East Lansing

Organisations

B'nai B'rith Hillel Foundation
Michigan State University, 112 Olds Hall
(517) 332-1916
Fax: (517) 332-4142
Kosher meals available during academic year.

Synagogues

Conservative & Reform

Shaarey Zedek
1924 Coolidge Road 48823

Flint

Organisations

Flint Jewish Federation
619 Wallenberg Street 48502 (810) 767-5922
Fax: (810) 767-9024
Email: fjf@tm.net

Synagogues

Conservative

Congregation Beth Israel
5240 Calkins Road 48532 (810) 732-6310
Fax: (810) 732-6314
Email: cbiflint@tir.com
Web site: www.uscj.org/michigan/flint/

Orthodox

Chabad House
5385 Calkins 48532 (810) 230-0770

Reform

Temple Beth El
501 S. Ballenger Highway 48532 (810) 232-3138

Grand Rapids

Synagogues

Conservative

Congregation Ahavas Israel
2727 Michigan Street N.E. 49506 (616) 949-2840
Fax: (616) 949-6929
Email: davkrishef@aol.com

Orthodox

Chabad House of Western Michigan
2615 Michigan Street N.E. 49506

Reform

Temple Emanuel
1715 E. Fulton Street 49503

Jackson

Synagogues

Temple Beth Israel
801 W. Michigan Avenue 49202

Kalamazoo

Synagogues

Conservative

Sons of Moses
2501 Stadium Drive 49008 (616) 342-5463

Lansing

Synagogues

Reconstructionist

Kehillat Israel
2014 Forest Road 48910 (517) 882-0049
Fax: (517) 882-9270
Email: kilori@msu.edu

Saginaw

Synagogues

Conservative

Temple B'nai Israel
1424 S. Washington Avenue 48601 (517) 753-5230

Reform

Congregation Beth El
100 S. Washington Avenue 48607 (517) 754-5171

South Haven

Synagogues

Orthodox

First Hebrew Congregation
249 Broadway 49090 (616) 637-1603

Southfield

Synagogues

Young Israel of Southfield
27705 Lahser Road 48034 (248) 358-0154
Fax: (248) 358-0154
Email: rabg@aol.com

West Bloomfield

Museums

Holocaust Memorial Center
6602 W. Maple Road 48322-3005 (248) 661-0840
Fax: (248) 661-4204
Email: info@holocaustcenter.org
Web site: www.holocaustcenter.org

First free-standing holocaust museum in USA. Consists of museum, library-archive, garden. Services include tours, lectures, oral history program, exhibits, speakers' bureau. No admission fee.

Synagogues

Orthodox

Young Israel of West Bloomfield
6111 West Maple Road 48322
(810) 661-4183/855-8722/626-7651

Minnesota

Duluth

Organisations

Jewish Federation & Com. Council
1602 E. 2nd Street 55812 (218) 724-8857

Synagogues

Conservative & Reform

Temple Israel
1602 E. 2nd Street 55812 (218) 724-8857

Orthodox

Adas Israel
302 E. Third Street 55802 (218) 722-6459

Minneapolis

Butchers

Fishman's Kosher Market
4100 Minnetonka Blvd,
St Louis Park 55416 (952) 926-5611
Glatt butcher, deli, bakery and eat-in/ take-out certified by the local Orthodox Vaad.

Mikvaot

Knesseth Israel
4330 W. 28th Street,
St Louis Park 55416 (612) 926-3829
Fax: (612) 920-2184
Email: office@kenessethisrael.org

Organisations

Jewish Com. Center of Greater Minneapolis
4330 Cedar Lake Rd S., 55416

Restaurants

Dairy

Calypso Coffee Co.
3238 W. Lake St. 55416 (612) 929-6245
Restaurant, coffee, and ice cream certified by the local Orthodox Vaad. (Chalav Yisrael)

Synagogues

Orthodox

Congregation Bais Yisroel
4221 Sunset Blvd 55416 (952) 926-7867
Kenesseth Israel
4330 W. 28th Street,
St Louis Park 55416 (952) 920-2183
Fax: (952) 920-2184
Email: rabbi@kenessethisrael.org
Web site: www.kenessethisrael.org

Rochester

Home Hospitality

Lubavitch Bais Chaya Moussia Hospitality Center
730 2nd Street S.W. 55907 (507) 288-7500
Fax: (507) 286-9329
Email: rstrav@rconnect.com
Also provides Shabbat dinners and hospital visitations. Mikva on premises.

Synagogues

B'nai Israel
621 SW 2nd Street 55902 (507) 288-5825
Email: bnaisrael@aol.com

St Paul

Groceries

L'chaim
655 Snelling Avenue 55116

Restaurants

Dairy

Old City Cafe
1571 Grand Avenue (612) 699-5347
Supervision: Upper Midwest Kashrus.
Dairy/vegetarian. Hours: Sunday, 10 am to 9 pm; Monday to Thursday, 11 am to 9 pm; Friday, to 2 pm. Corner of Grand and Snelling Avenues, both of which are buslines.

Mississippi

Greenville

Synagogues

Reform

Hebrew Union Congregation
504 Main Street 38701 (662) 332-4153

Greenwood

Synagogues

Orthodox

Ahavath Rayim
Market & George Streets,
PO Box 1235 38935-1235 (662) 453-7537
Only services on the first Friday of each month.

Natchez

Synagogues

Reform

B'nai Israel
Washington & S. Commerce Streets,
PO Box 2081 39120
Oldest synagogue in Mississippi.

Tupelo

Synagogues

Conservative

B'nai Israel
Marshall & Hamlin Streets 38801 (601) 842-9169

Missouri

Fort Leavenworth

Synagogues

Reform

Ft Leavenworth Jewish congregation
Main Post Chapel,
Pope Avenue 64114 (816) 523-5757

Kansas City

Media

Newspapers

Kansas City Jewish Chroncicle
7375 W. 107th Street, Overland Park 66204

Organisations

Jewish Federation of Greater Kansas City
5801 W. 115th Street, Suite 201,
Overland Park 66211 (913) 327-8100
Fax: (913) 327-8110
Email: www.jewishkc.org

Restaurants

Sensations
1148 W. 103 Street 64114

Synagogues

Conservative

Congregation Beth Shalom
9400 Wornall road 64114 361-2990
Fax: 361-4495

Reform

Temple B'nai Jehudah
712 E. 69th Street 64131 (816) 363-1050
Fax: (816) 363-8610

The New Reform Temple
7100 Main 64114 (816) 523-7809
Fax: (816) 523-2454
Email: nrt7100@aol.com

St Joseph

Synagogues

Conservative

Temple B'Nai Sholem
615 S. 10th Street 64501 (816) 279-2378
Fax: (816) 361-4495

St Louis

Bakeries

Schnuck's Nancy Ann Bakery
Olive & Mason (314) 434-7323

Butchers

Diamant's Kosher Meat Market
618 North & South Road (314) 721-9624

S. Kohn's
10405 Old Olive St. Road 63141 (314) 569-0727
Fax: (314) 569-1723

Sol's
8627 Olive (314) 993-9977

Groceries

Lazy Suzan Imaginative Catering
110 Millwell Drive (314) 291-6050

Simon Kohn's Kosher Meat & Deli
10405 Old Olive Street (314) 569-0727
Fax: (314) 569-1723
Complete kosher deli & meat market. Seating available. Fresh cold & hot selections available daily. Pizza available for carry-out.

Libraries

The Brodsky Jewish Community Library
12 Millstone Campus Drive 63146

Mikvaot

Mikva
4 Millstone Campus 63146 (314) 569-2770

Museums

Holocaust Museum and Learning Center
12 Millstone Campus Drive (314) 432-0020

Organisations

Jewish Federation of St Louis
12 Millstone Campus Drive 63146 (314) 432-0020
Fax: (314) 432-1277
Email: stljf@jon.cjfny.org

The Vaad Hoeir
(United Orthodox Jewish Community of St Louis)
4 Millstone Campus 63146 (314) 569-2770
Fax: (314) 569-2774
Recognised Orthodox religious authority for the city.

Restaurants

Meat

Diamant's
618 North & South Rd. (314) 712-9624

Simon Kohn's
10405 Old Olive Street (314) 569-0727

The Empire Steak Building
8600 Olive Blvd., just off Mc Knight (314) 993-9977
Fax: (314) 993-6647
Web site: www.chef2-go.com

Synagogues

Orthodox

Young Israel of St Louis
8101 Delmar Blvd 63130 (314) 727-1880
Fax: (314) 727-2177
Email: yi-stl@juno.com

Tours of Jewish Interest
Jewish Tercentenary
Forest Park
The Jewish Federation of St Louis can provide information on tours of Jewish interest in the city. For more information visit their web site: www.jewishinstlouis.org.

Montana

Billings

Synagogues

Reform

Congregation Beth Aaron
1148 N. Broadway 59101 (406) 248-6412

Great Falls

Congregation
Aitz Chaim
PO Box 6192 59406-6192 (406) 468-2073
Email: aaron@weissman.com

Missoula

Synagogues
Har Shalom
PO Box 7581 59807 (406) 523-5671

Nebraska

Lincoln

Synagogues

Conservative

Tifereth Israel
3219 Sheridan Blvd 68502 (402) 423-8569

Reform

South Street Temple B'nai Jeshurun
20th & South Streets 68502 (402) 435-8004

Omaha

Mikvaot
Com. Mikva
323 S. 132nd Street 68154 (402) 334-8200

Organisations
Jewish Federation of Omaha
333 S. 132nd Street (402) 334-8200
Fax: (402) 334-1330
Email: pmonsk@top.net
Web site: www.jewishomaha.org

Synagogues
B'nai Israel
PO Box 24161 68124

Conservative

Beth El
14506 California Street 68154 (402) 492-8550

Orthodox

Beth Israel
1502 N. 52nd Street 68104 (402) 556-6288

Reform

Temple Israel
7023 Cass Street 68132 (402) 556-6536

Nevada

Las Vegas

Delicatessens
Casba Glatt Kosher
2845 Las Vegas Blvd (702) 791-3344
Jerusalem Kosher Restaurant & Deli
1305 Vegas Valley 89109 (702) 791-3668
Rafi's Place
6135 West Sahara 89102 (702) 253-0033
Sara's Place
4972 S. Maryland

Kashrut Information
Community Relations
(702) 732-0556

Restaurants

Meat

Haifa Restaurant
855 E. Twain (702) 791-1956
Fax: (702) 791-2966

Jerusalem Glatt Kosher Restaurant
1305 Vegas Valley Dr., 89109 (702) 696-1644
Fax: (702) 696-0919

Las Vegas Kosher Deli
3317 L.V. Blvd S. (702) 892-9080
Shalom Hunan
4850 W Flamingo Road (702) 871-3262
Fax: (702) 871-3083
Supervision: Chabad of Southern Nevada.

Synagogues

Conservative

Midbar Kodesh Temple
33 Cactus Garden, Henderson (702) 454-4848
Fax: (702) 454-4847
Shabbat Services: weekly, Friday 7.30 pm, Saturday 9 am and all holidays. Special services.

Temple Beth Shalom
1600 E. Oakley Blvd (702) 384-5070
Fax: (702) 383-3246
Shabbat Service: Friday 7.30 pm (at the Hebrew Academy); Saturday 9.30 am; Daily minyon Monday-Friday 7.30 am; Saturday, Sunday & holidays 9 am (at the synagogue).

Temple Emanu-El
(702) (Wally Klein) 248-6515 or (Mae Futterman) 255-1666.
Shabbat service: Friday 7.30pm. Organizations: Sisterhood, Chavurah.

Orthodox

Congregation Or-Bamidbar
2959 Emerson Ave. (702) 369-1175
Shabbat service: Monday-Frida 7 am; Saturday 8.30 am; Sunda 9 am; Mincha & Ma'ariv daily at sunset. Education: Hebrew School, Sunda 12 am-2 pm; Judaism Class, Wednesda 8 pm.

Young Israel of Las Vegas
9510 West Sahara 89117 (702) 360-8909
Shabbat service: Saturday 9 am, Sunday 9 am. Beginners minyon for ages 10-15. Radio-talk show: 1230AM, Tuesday at 8 pm.

Reconstructionist

Valley Outreach Synagogue
Luthern Church, 2 S. Pecos Rd., Henderson
(702) 436-4900
Fax: (702) 436-4901
Shabbat service: 1st Friday of month 8 pm.

Reform

Adat Ari El
3310 S. Jones Blvd (702) 221-1230
Fax: (702) 221-1385
Email: info@adatariel.com
AAE Event Hotline: (702) 390-8142. Shabbat service: Friday 7.30 pm.

Bet Knesset Bamidbar
Desert Vista Community Center, 10360 Sun City Blvd, Sun City (702) 391-2750
Shabbat Service: 2nd & 4th Friday 7.30 pm.

Congregation Ner Tamid
2761 Emerson Ave. (702) 733-6292
Fax: (702) 733-8553
CNT Event Hotline: (702) 263-5960. Shabbat service: Friday 7.30 pm.

Temple Adat Chavarim
Bonner School, 765 Crestdale Lane
(702) 647-7254
Shabbat service: Friday 7.30 pm.

Temple Bet Emet
Presbyterian Church,
8601 Del Webb Blvd, Sun City (702) 255-2348
Shabbat service: 1st & 3rd Friday 7.30 pm.

Temple Beth Am
9001 Hillpointe Road (702) 254-5110
Fax: (702) 254-0997
Shabbat service: Friday 7.30 pm; Saturday 10.30 am; Saturday Torah Study 9.30 am.

Traditional

Chabad of Southern Nevada
1261 So. Arville (702) 259-0770 extension 8
Fax: (702) 877-4700
Email: chabadlv@aol.com
Web site: www.chabadlv.org
Daily services. Mikva on premises (call (702) 224-0184).

Chabad of Summerlin
2620 Regatta Dr. #117 (702) 259-0770
Shabbat service: Friday 6 pm; Saturday 10 am. Special children's service, 11 am; Sunday 8.30 am is the B-L-T service (Bagels, Lox, Tefillah).

Reno

Synagogues

Reform

Temple Sinai
3405 Gulling Road 89503 (775) 747-5508
Fax: (775) 747-1911
Email: temple.sinai@juno.com

New Hampshire

Bethlehem

Hotels

Arlington Hotel
(603) 869-3353
The hotel which is only open in the summer has a mikvah and synagogue. For information during other periods phone 718-486-6367.

Mikvaot

Orthodox

Machzikei Hadas
Lewis Hill Road 03574 (603) 869-3336

Synagogues

Conservative

Bethlehem Hebrew Congregation
Strawberry Hill 03574 (603) 869-5465

Temple Israel
66 Salmon Street 03104 (603) 622-6171

Orthodox

Machzikei Hadas
Lewis Hill Road 03574 (603) 869-3336

Manchester

Media

Newspapers

The Reporter
698 Beech Street 03104 (603) 627-7679
Fax: (603) 627-7963

Lists further communities in Amherst, Concord, Derry, Dover, Durham, Hanover, Keene, Laconia and Nashua.

Organisations

Jewish Federation of Greater Manchester
698 Beech Street 03104 (603) 627-7679
Fax: (603) 627-7963

Synagogues

Orthodox

Lubavitch
7 Camelot Drive 03104 (603) 647-0204

Reform

Adath Yeshurun
152 Prospect Street 03104 (603) 669-5650

Portsmouth

Synagogues

Conservative

Temple Israel
200 State Street 03801 (603) 436-5301

New Jersey

Aberdeen

Synagogues

Orthodox

Bet Tefilah
479 Lloyd Road 07747 (908) 583-6262

Atlantic City

Restaurants

Meat

Jerusalem
6410 Ventnor Ave, Ventnor 08406 (609) 822-2266
Supervision: Rabbi Abraham Spacirer.

Synagogues

Conservative

Beth El
500 N. Jerome Ave, Margate 08402
Fax: (609) 823-1810

Beth Judah
700 N Swarthmore Avenue,
Ventnor 08406 (609) 822-7116
Fax: (609) 822-4654
Email: congbethjudah@aol.com

Chelsea Hebrew Congregation
4001 Atlantic Av 08401 (609) 345-0825

Community Synagogue
Maryland & Pacific Avs 08401 (609) 345-3282

Orthodox

Rodef Shalom
3833 Atlantic Av 08401 (609) 345-4580

Reform

Beth Israel
2501 Shore Rd, Northfield 08225 (609) 641-3600

Temple Emeth Synagogue
8501 Ventnor Av, Margate 08402 (609) 822-4343

Bayonne

Community Organisations

Jewish Community Centre
1050 Kennedy Blvd 07002 (201) 436-6900

Synagogues

Conservative

Temple Emanuel
735 Kennedy Blvd 07002 (201) 436-4499

Orthodox

Ohab Sholom
1016-1022 Ave. C 07002

Ohav Zedek
912 Ave. C 07002 (201) 437-1488

Uptown Synagogue
49th St. & Ave. C 07002

Reform

Temple Beth Am
111 Av. B 07002 (201) 858-9052

Belmar

Synagogues

Orthodox

Sons of Israel Congregation
PO Box 298 07719 (973) 681-3200

Bergenfield

Butchers

Glatt World
89 Newbridge Road (201) 439-9675
Fax: (201) 439-0342

Supervision: RCBC.

Delicatessens

Meat

Foster Village Kosher Delicatessen & Catering
469 S. Washington Avenue 07621 (201) 384-7100
Fax: (201) 384-0303
Supervision: Quality Kashrut Supervisory Service.

Synagogues

Conservative

Congregation Beth Israel of Northern Valley
169 N. Washington Avenue 07621 (201) 384-3911
Fax: (201) 384-3738
Email: cbitemple@juno.com
Web site: www.uscj.org/njersey/bergenfield

Bradley Beach

Synagogues

Orthodox

Congregation Agudath Achim
301 McCabe Avenue 07720 (973) 774-2495

Bridgeton

Organisations

Jewish Federation of Cumberland County

Synagogues

Conservative

Congregation Beth Abraham
330 Fayette Street 08302

Burlington

Synagogues

B'nai Israel
212 High Street 08332 (609) 386-0406

Cherry Hill

Bakeries

Pastry Palace Kosher Bakery
State Highway 70 08034 (609) 429-3606

Butchers

Cherry Hill Kosher Market
907 W. Marlton Pike 08002 (609) 428-6663
Fax: (609) 216-0752

Delicatessens

Leo's Deli
J.C.C. 1301 Springdale Road (856) 424-4444 Ext 158
Supervision: Tri-County Vaad.

Media

Newspapers

The Jewish Community Voice
2393 W. Marlton Pike 08002

Mikvaot

Sons of Israel
720 Cooper Landing Road 08002 (856) 667-3515

Organisations

Jewish Federation of Southern New Jersey
2393 W. Marlton Pike 08002 (609) 665-6100

Restaurants

Maxim's Restaurant
404 Route 70 (856) 428-5045

Synagogues

Conservative

Beth El
2901 W. Chapel Avenue 08002 (609) 667-1300

Beth Shalom
1901 Kresson Road 08003 (609) 751-6663

Congregation Beth Tikva
115 Evesboro-Medford Road, Marlton

Orthodox

Congregation Sons of Israel
720 Cooper Landing Road 08002 (856) 667-9700
Fax: (856) 667-9765
Email: congsonsisrael@netzero.net

Daily minyan.

Reform

Congregation M'kor Shalom
850 Evesham Road (609) 424-4220
Fax: (609) 424-2890

Temple Emmanuel
1101 Springdale Road

Cinnaminson

Synagogues

Conservative

Temple Sinai
2101 New Albany Road 08077 (609) 829-0658
Fax: (609) 829-0310
Email: tsoffice@snip.net
Web site: www.uscj.org/njersey/cinnaminson

Clark

Synagogues

Temple Beth O'r
111 Valley Road 07066 (609) 381-8403

Clifton

Media

Newspapers

Jewish Community News
199 Scoles Avenue 07012

Organisations

Jewish Federation of Greater Clifton-Passaic
199 Scoles Avenue 07012 (973) 777-7031
Fax: (973) 777-6701
Email: yymuskin@jon.cjfny.org

Restaurants

Jerusalem II Pizza
224 Brook Avenue 07055 (201) 778-0960

Kosher Konnection
200 Main Avenue 07055 (201) 777-1120

Synagogues

Conservative

Clifton Jewish Center
18 Delaware Street 07011 (973) 772-3131

Reform

Beth Shalom
733 Passaic Avenue 07012 (973) 773-0355

Colonia

Synagogues

Conservative

Ohev Shalom
220 Temple Way 07067 (908) 388-7222

Cranbury

Synagogues

Jewish Congregation of Concordia
c/o Club House 08512 (609) 655-8136

Cranford

Contact Information

Rabbi Hoffberg
(201) 276-9231

Contact for kosher hospitality.

Synagogues

Conservative

Temple Beth El Mekor Chayim
338 Walnut Avenue 07016 (908) 276-9231
Fax: (908) 276-6570
Web site: www.uscj.org/njersey/cranfotb

Deal

Restaurants

Pizzerias

Jerusalem II Pizza
106 Norwood Avenue 07723 (908) 531-7936

Synagogues

Orthodox

128 Norwood Avenue 07723 (908) 531-3200

Ohel Yaacob Congregation
6 Ocean Avenue, PO Box 225 07723
(732) 531-0217/531-2405

East Brunswick

Butchers

East Brunswick Kosher Meats
1020 State Highway 18 08816 (908) 257-0007

Synagogues

Conservative

E. Brunswick Jewish Center
511 Ryders Lane 08816 (908) 257-7070

Reform

Temple B'nai Shalom
Old Stage Road & Fern Road 08816 (908) 251-4300

Edison

Butchers

Edison Kosher Meats
State Highway 27, and Evergreen Rd (201) 549-3707

Community Organisations

Jewish Community Center of Middlesex County
1775 Oak Tree Road 08820 (732) 494-3232
Fax: (732) 548-2850

Synagogues

Conservative

Beth El
91 Jefferson Blvd 08817 (732) 985-7272

Elizabeth

Groceries

Kosher Express
155 Elmora Avenue 07202

Mikvaot

Mikvah Tomor Deborah
35 North Avenue 07208 (908) 352-5048
Fax: (908) 289-5245

Restaurants

Dairy

Dunkin' Donuts
186 Elmora Avenue 07202

Meat

New Kosher Special
163 Elmora Avenue 07202 (908) 353-1818

Pizzerias

Jerusalem Restaurant
150 Elmora Avenue 07202 (908) 289-4810

Synagogues

Orthodox

Adath Israel
1391 North Avenue 07208 (908) 355-4850

Bais Yitzchak
153 Bellevue Street 07202 (908) 354-4789

Elmwood Park

Organisations

Elmwood Park Jewish Center
100 Gilbert Ave., (201) 797-7320/797-9749

Englewood

Delicatessens

Meat

Sol & Sol
54 E Palisade Avenue 07631 (201) 541-6880
Fax: (201) 541-6883
Supervision: Kashrut Committee of Bergen County.

Groceries and meats

Kosher By the Case & Less
255 Van Nostrand Avenue 07631 (201) 568-2281
Fax: (201) 568-5681
Supervision: RCBC.

Mikvaot

Mikva
89 Huguenot Avenue (201) 567-1143

Restaurants

Dairy

The Fish Grill
16 W. Palisade Avenue (201) 227-6182
Supervision: RCBC.

Synagogues

Conservative

Temple Emanu-El
147 Tenafly Road 07631 (201) 567-1300
Fax: (201) 569-7580

Orthodox

Ahavath Torah
240 Broad Avenue 07631 (201) 568-1315
Fax: (201) 568-2991
Web site: www.ahavathtorah.org

Shomrei Emunah
89 Huguenot Avenue 07631 (201) 567-9420
Daily morning services, and mikva.

Fair Lawn

Bakeries

New Royal Bakery
19-09 Fair Lawn Avenue 07410 (201) 796-6565
Fax: (201) 796-8501
Supervision: RCBC.
Pat Yisrael.

Butchers

Food Showcase
24-28 Fair Lawn Avenue 07410 (201) 475-0077
Fax: (201) 794-6728

Supervision: RCBC.
Sells food provisions as well.

Restaurants

Dairy

J.C. Pizza of Fairlawn
14-20 Plaza Road 07410 (201) 703-0801
Supervision: RCBC.

Synagogues

Bris Arushon
2204 Fairlawn Ave., (201) 791-7200

Fort Lee

Butchers

Blue Ribbon Self-Service Kosher Meat Market
1363 Inwood Terr. 07024 (201) 224-3220
Fax: (201) 224-7281
Email: koshercomida@msn.com

Delicatessens

Meat

Al's Kosher Deli
209 Main Street 07024 (201) 461-3044
Fax: (201) 461-7188
Supervision: Quality Kashrut Supervisory Service.

Synagogues

Conservative

Jewish Community Center of Fort Lee
1449 Anderson Avenue 07024 (201) 947-1735
Fax: (201) 947-1530
Email: aschafer@jcc.org

Orthodox

Young Israel of Fort Lee
1610 Parker Avenue 07024 (201) 592-1518
Fax: (201) 592-8414

Freehold

Restaurants

Fred and Murry's
Pond Road Shopping Center,
Route 9 07728 (732) 462-3343
Web site: www.fredandmurrys.com
Not glatt kosher or shomer Shabbat, but has Conservative supervision.

Synagogues

Orthodox

Agudath Achim/Freehold Jewish Center
Broad & Stokes Streets 07728 (732) 462-0254
Fax: (732) 462-0217
Traditional congregation with daily minyans.

Hackensack

Organisations

Jewish Federation of Community Services of Bergen County
170 State Street 07601

Synagogues

Conservative

Temple Beth El
280 Summit Avenue 07601 (201) 342-2045

Haddonfield

Butchers

Sarah's Kosher Kitchen
63 Ellis Road

Hasbrouck Heights

Synagogues

Reform

Temple Beth Elohim
Bourlevard & Charlton Aves., (201) 393-7707

Highland Park

Groceries

Berkley Bakery
405 Raritan Avenue 08904
Dan's Deli & Meat Market
515 Raritan Avenue 08904
Kosher Catch
239 Raritan Avenue (908) 572-9052

Mikvaot

Park Mikva
112 S. 1st Avenue 08904 (732) 249-2411

Synagogues

Conservative

Highland Park Conservative Temple & Center
201 S. 3rd Ave. 08904 (732) 545-6482
Fax: (732) 246-3100

Orthodox

Congregation Ahavas Achim
(732) 247-0532
Fax: (732) 247-6739
Email: aa613@juno.com

Congregation Etz Ahaim (Sephardi)
230 Denison St 08904 (732) 247-3839
Fax: (732) 545-3191
Email: etzahaim@earthlink.net
Web site: www.home.earthlink.net/netzahaim

Congregation Ohav Emeth
415 Raritan Avenue 08904 (732) 247-3038
Fax: (732) 247-1438
Email: office@ohavemeth.org

Hillside

Synagogues

Conservative

Shomrei Torah Ohel Yosef Yitzchok
910 Salem Avenue 07205 (908) 289-0770

Orthodox

Congregation Sinai Torath Chaim
1531 Maple Avenue 07205 (908) 923-9500

Hoboken

Synagogues

Conservative

United Synagogue of Hoboken
830 Hudson Street & 115 Park Avenue 07030
(201) 659-2614
Fax: (201) 659-7944

Jamesburg

Synagogues

Rossmoor Jewish Congregation Meeting Room
(609) 655-0439

Jersey City

Synagogues

Orthodox

Congregation Mount Sinai
128 Sherman Avenue 07307 (201) 659 4267
Offers shabbat hospitality for travellers.

Lakewood

Bakeries

Gelbsteins Bakery
415 Clifton Avenue 08701 (732) 363-3636
Supervision: Orthodox supervision.

Lakewood Heimishe Bakeshop
225-2nd St. 08701 (732) 905-9057
Supervision: Orthodox supervision.

Booksellers

Torah Treasures
254-2nd St 08701 (732) 901-1911
Fax: (732) 905-6482

Butchers

Shloimy's Kosher World
23 E. County Line Road 08701 (732) 363-3066

Kashrut Information

Orthodox

KCC - Cashrus Council of Lakewood
(732) 901-1888

Mikvaot

Mikvah Tahara
1101 Madison Avenue 08701 (732) 370-1666
Call to schedule appointment.

Organisations

Ocean County Jewish Federation
301 Madison Avenue 08701 (201) 363-0530

Restaurants

Pizza Plus
241-4th St 08701 (732) 367-0711
Supervision: Orthodox supervision.

Dairy

Bagel Nosh
380 Clifton Avenue 08701 (732) 363-1115

Meat

Kosher Experience
Kennedy Blvd., 08701
Supervision: Rabbi Chumsky.

R. & S. Kosher Restaurant and Deli
416 Clifton Avenue 08701 (732) 363-6688
Glatt kosher meat only. Hours: Sunday to Thursday, 12.30 pm to 9 pm; Friday, 8 am to 2.30 pm. On Friday, take-out only.

Yum Mee Glatt
116 Clifton Avenue 08701 (732) 886-9688
Chinese and American.

Synagogues

Conservative

Ahavat Shalom
Forest Avenue & 11th Street 08701 (732) 363-5190
Fax: (732) 363-5225
Email: ahavat_shalom_nj@netzero.com
Web site: www.uscj.org/njersey/lakewood

Orthodox

Kol Shimshon
323 Squamkum Road 08701 (732) 901-6680

Lakewood Yeshiva
Private Way & 6th Street 08701 (732) 367-1060

Sons of Israel
Madison Avenue & 6th Street 08701 (732) 364-2230

Reform

Beth Am
Madison Avenue & Carey Street 08701
(732) 363-2800

Lawrenceville

Synagogues

Orthodox

Young Israel of Lawrenceville
2556 Princeton Pike 08648 (609) 883-8833
Web site: www.yiol.com

Linden

Synagogues

Conservative

Mekor Chayim Suburban Jewish Center
Deerfield Road & Academy Terrace 07036
(908) 925-2283

Orthodox

Congregation Anshe Chesed
100 Orchard Terrace at St George Ave. 07036
(908) 486-8616

Livingston

Restaurants

Moshavi
515 S. Livingston Avenue 07039 (973) 740-8777
Supervision: Vaad Hakashrus of the Council of Orthodox Rabbis Metrowest.

Dairy

Jerusalem Restaurant
99-101 West Mt Pleasant Avenue 07039
(973) 533-1424
Fax: (973) 533-9275
Supervision: Vaad Hakashrus of the Council of Orthodox Rabbis Metrowest.

Synagogues

Conservative

Temple Beth Shalom
193 E. Mt. Pleasant Ave. 07039 (973) 992-3600

Independent

Temple B'Nai Abraham
300 E. Northfield Rd 07039 (973) 994-2290
Fax: (973) 994-1838
Email: lwold@templebnaiabraham.org
Web site: www.templebnaiabraham.org

Orthodox

Etz Chaim Synagogue
304 Mt Pleasant Avenue 07039 (973) 597 1655

Synagogue of the Suburban Torah Center
85 W. Mount Pleasant Avenue 07039
(973) 994-0122; 994-2620
Fax: (973) 535-3898

Reform

Temple Emanu-el of West Essex
264 W. Northfield Rd 07039 (973) 992-5560

Mahwah

Synagogues

Temple Beth Haverim
280 Remjo Valley Road (201) 512-1983

Maplewood

Booksellers

Rabbi L. Sky Hebrew Book Store
1923 Springfield Avenue, Maplewood 07040
(973) 763-4244/5
Fax: (973) 763-1412

Metuchen

Synagogues

Conservative

Neve Shalom
250 Grove Avenue 08840 (732) 548-2238
Fax: (732) 603-7976
Email: neveshal@webspan.net

Millville

Synagogues

Beth Hillel
3rd Avenue & Oak Street 08332 (609) 825-8672

Morris Plains

Restaurants

Kosher Delicatessen

Jonathan's Deli Restaurant
2900 Route 10 West 07950 (973) 539-6010
Fax: (973) 539-6011

Morristown

Kashrut Information

Congregation of Ahavath Yisrael
9 Cutler Street 07960 (973) 267-4184
Fax: (973) 898-1711
Email: sofernj@aol.com

This synagogue operates a kosher food buying service for the community, dealing only in strictly kosher products.

Rabbinical College of America
226 Sussex Avenue 07960 (973) 267-9404
Fax: (973) 267-5208
Email: rca226@aol.com

Mikvaot

Mikvah Bais Chana, Sarah Esther Rosenhaus Mikvah Institutue
93 Lake Road 07960 (973) 292-3932

Synagogues

Conservative

Morristown Jewish Center
177 Speedwell Avenue 07960 (973) 538-9292

Orthodox

Congregation Levi Yitzchak
226 Sussex Avenue 07960 (973) 984-6326

New Brunswick

Synagogues

Orthodox

Chabad House Friends of Lubavitch
8 Sicard St 08901 (908) 828-9191

Reform

Anshe Emeth Memorial Temple
222 Livingston Ave. 08901 (732) 545-6484
Fax: (732) 745-7448
Email: anshe.emeth@rcn.com
Web site: www.uahc.org/hj/aemt

Unaffiliated

Congregation Poile Zedek
145 Neilson St. 08901 (908) 545-6123

North Brunswick

Synagogues

Conservative

Congregation B'nai tikvah
1001 Finnegans Lane 08902 (732) 297-0696
Fax: (732) 297-2673
Email: administrator@bnaitikvah.org
Web site: www.bnaitikvah.org

Paramus

Butchers

Harold's Self Service Kosher Meat
67-A E. Ridgewood Avenue 07652 (201) 262-0030

Organisations

Jewish Center of Paramus
304 Midland Ave. (201) 262-7691

Synagogues

Conservative

Jewish Community Center of Paramus
E-304 Midland Ave., 07652 (201) 262-7691
Fax: (201) 262-6516
Email: jccparam@mail.idt.net
Web site: www.uscj.org/njersey/paramus

Parlin

Synagogues

Ohav Shalom
3018 Bordertown Avenue 08859 (201) 727-4334

Parsipanny

Delicatessens

Arlington Kosher Deli, Restaurant & Caterers
Arlington Shopping Center,
744 Route 46W 07054 (973) 335-9400

Passaic

Delicatessens

B&Y Kosher Korner Inc.
200 Main Avenue 07055 (201) 777-1120

Restaurants

Meat

Main-Ly Chow
227 Main Avenue 07055 (201) 777-4900

Synagogues

Orthodox

Young Israel of Passaic-Clifton
200 Brook Avenue 07055 (201) 778-7117

Paterson

Synagogues

Conservative

Temple Emanuel
151 E. 33rd Street 07514 (973) 684-5565

Perth Amboy

Synagogues

Beth Mordechai
224 High Street 08861 (732) 442-2431

Orthodox

Shaarey Teflioh
15 Market Street 08861 (732) 826-2977

Piscataway

Synagogues

Reform

B'nai Shalom
25 Netherwood Avenue 08854 (908) 885-9444

Plainfield

Synagogues

Orthodox

United Orthodox Synagogue
526 W. 7th Street 07060 (908) 755-0043

Reform

Temple Sholom
815 W. 7th Street 07063 (201) 756-6447

Princeton

Synagogues

Traditional

Jewish Center
435 Nassau Street 08540 (609) 921-0100
Fax: (609) 921-7531
Email: JCenter@thejewishcenter.org

Rahway

Synagogues

Conservative

Temple Beth Torah
1389 Bryant Street 07065 (609) 576-8432

Ridgewood

Synagogues

Temple Israel
475 Grove Street (201) 444-9320

River Edge

Synagogues

Reform

Temple Sholom
385 Howland Avenue 07661 (201) 489-2463
Fax: (201) 489-0775
Web site: www.uahcweb.org/nj/tsholomre/

Roselle

Media

Guides

Shalom Book
843 St Georges Avenue 07203 (908) 298-8200
Fax: (908) 298-8220

Organisations

Jewish Federation of Central New Jersey
843 St Georges Avenue 07203 (908) 298-8200
Fax: (908) 298-8220

Rumson

Synagogues

Conservative

Congregation B'nai Israel
Hance & Ridge Roads 07760 (908) 842-1800

Scotch Plains

Organisations

Jewish Community Center of Central New Jersey
1391 Martine Avenue 07076 (908) 889-1830

Synagogues

Conservative

Congregation Beth Israel
1920 Cliffwood Street 07076 (908) 889-1830
Fax: (908) 889-5523

Short Hills

Synagogues

Reform

B'Nai Jeshurun
1025 South Orange Ave. 07078 (973) 379-1555
Fax: (973) 379-4345
Email: info@tbj.org

Somerset

Synagogues

Conservative

Temple Beth El
1945 Amwell Road 08873 (201) 873-2325

South Orange

Groceries

Zayda's Super Value Meat Market & Deli
309 Irvington Avenue 07079 (973) 762-1812

Synagogues

Conservative

Oheb Shalom Congregation
170 Scotland Rd 07079 (973) 762-7067

Reform

Temple Sharey Tefilo-Israel
432 Scotland Rd 07079 (973) 763-4116

South River

Synagogues

Traditional

Congregation Anshe Emeth of South River
88 Main Street 08882 (732) 257-4190
Fax: (732) 254-8819
Web site: www.members.home.net/ebweiss

See also Edison.

Community Organisations

Jewish Federation of Greater Middlesex County
230 Old Bridge Turnpike
South River, Middlesex County, 08882
(732) 432-7711
Fax: (732) 432-0292
Email: middlesexfed@aol.com

Spotswood

Synagogues

Reform

Monroe Township Jewish Center
11 Cornell Avenue 08884 (201) 251-1119

Teaneck

Bakeries

Butterflake Bake Shop
448 Cedar Lane 07666 (201) 836-3516
Fax: (201) 836-3056

Supervision: RCBC.
Pat Yisrael.

Sammy's Bagels
1443 Queen Anne Road 07666 (201) 837-0515
Fax: (201) 837-9733

Supervision: Kof-K.
Pat Yisrael.

Booksellers

Zoldan's Judaica Center
406 Cedar Lane 07666 (201) 907-0034

Butchers

Glatt Express
1400 Queen Anne Road 07666 (201) 837-8110
Fax: (201) 837-0084

Supervision: RCBC.
Sells food provisions as well.

Delicatessens

Chopstix
172 West Englewood Avenue 07666
(201) 833-0200
Fax: (201) 833-8326

Supervision: RCBC.
Glatt kosher Chinese take-out. Hours: Sunday to Thursday, 11.30 am to 10 pm; Friday, closing times vary – please call.

Mikvaot

Mikveh
1726 Windsor Road 07666 (201) 837-8220

Restaurants

Dairy

Jerusalem Pizza
496 Cedar Lane 07666 (201) 836-2120
Fax: (201) 836-2261

Supervision: RCBC.

Plaza Pizza & Restaurant
1431 Queen Anne Road 07666 (201) 837-9500
Fax: (201) 836-2261

Supervision: RCBC.

Shelly's
482 Cedar Lane 07666 (201) 692-0001
Fax: (201) 692-1890
Email: shellys@noahsark.net

Supervision: RCBC.
Cholov Yisrael. Hours: Monday to Thursday, 10.30 am to 9.30 pm; Sunday, 10 am to 9 pm. Ten minutes from the George Washington Bridge.

Meat

Grill Street
184 West Englewood Avenue 07666 (201) 833-0001
Fax: (201) 833-8030

Supervision: RCBC.

Hunan Teaneck
515 Cedar Lane 07666 (201) 692-0099
Fax: (201) 692-1907
Supervision: RCBC.
Glatt kosher Chinese and American cuisine. Eat in or take-out. Mashgiach temidi. Hours: Sunday to Thursday, 11.30 am to 9.45 pm; Friday, to 3 pm; Saturday night, after Shabbat until midnight.

Noah's Ark
493 Cedar Lane 07666 (201) 692-1200
Fax: (201) 692-1890
Email: info@noahsark.net
Supervision: RCBC.
Chassidishe shechita meats. Hours: Monday to Thursday, 10.30 am to 10.30 pm; Friday, 8 am to 4 pm; Sunday, 9:30 am to 10.30 pm; Saturday during winter, after Shabbat to midnight. Ten minutes from the George Washington Bridge.

Synagogues

Conservative

Congregation Beth Sholom
354 Maitland Avenue 07666 (201) 833-2620
Fax: (201) 833-2323
Email: bsteaneck@aol.com
Web site: www.uscj.org/njersey/teaneckcbs

Jewish Center of Teaneck
70 Sterling Place 07666 (201) 833-0515
Fax: (201) 833-0511
Email: execdir@aol.com

Orthodox

Congregation Beth Aaron
950 Queen Anne Rd 07666 (201) 836-6210
Fax: (201) 836-0005
Email: mail@bethaaron.org
Web site: www.bethaaron.org

Congregation Bnai Yeshurun
641 W. Englewood Avenue 07666 (201) 836-8916
Fax: (201) 836-1888

Rinat Yisrael
389 W. Englewood Av 07666 (201) 837-2795
Fax: (201) 837-2091
Email: office@rinat.org

Roemer Synagogue
Whittier School, W. Englewood Ave., 07666

Reform

Congregation Beth Am
510 Claremont Av 07666 (201) 836-5752
Fax: (201) 836-5760

Temple Emeth
1666 Windsor Rd 07666 (201) 833-1322
Fax: (201) 833-4831
Email: temple@emeth.org
Web site: www.emeth.org

Tenafly

Synagogues

Temple Sinai of Bergen County
1 Engle Street 07670 (201) 568-3035
Fax: (201) 568-6095
Email: temsinai@idt.net
Web site: www.uahc.org/congs.nj/nj009

Trenton

Organisations

Jewish Federation of Mercer & Bucks Counties
999 Lower Ferry Road 08628 (609) 883-5000

Union

Organisations

Jewish Federation of Central New Jersey
Green Lane 07083 (201) 351-5060

Synagogues

Conservative

Beth Shalom
2046 Vauxhall Road 07083 (908) 686-6773

Temple Israel
2372 Morris Avenue 07083 (201) 686-2120

Vineland

Organisations

Jewish Federation of Cumberland County
1063 East Landis Avenue,
Suite B 08360-3785 (856) 696-4445
Fax: (856) 696-3428
Email: jfedcc@aol.com
Also serves the Bridgeton & Cumberland County areas.

Synagogues

Conservative

Beth Israel
1015 E. Park Avenue 08630 (609) 691-0852

Orthodox

Ahavas Achim
618 Plum Street 08360 (609) 691-2218

Sons of Jacob Congregation
321 Grape Street 08360 (609) 692-4232
Fax: (609) 691-4985
Monday to Friday 6.45 am. Saturday 9 am. Sunday 7.30 am. For evening service, please call synagogue.

Warren

Organisations

Jewish Federation of Central New Jersey
Suburban Services Office,
150 Mt. Bethel Rd, 07059 (908) 647-0232
Fax: (908) 647-3115

Synagogues

Reform

Mountain Jewish Community Center
104 Mount Horeb Road 07060 (908) 356-8777

Washington Township

Synagogues

Temple Beth Or
56 Ridgewood Rd, (201) 664-7422

Wayne

Organisations

Jewish Federation of New Jersey
1 Pike Drive 07470 (973) 595-0555

Synagogues

Conservative

Shomrei Torah
30 Hinchman Avenue 07470 (973) 694-6274

Reform

Temple Beth Tikvah
950 Preakness Avenue 07470 (973) 595-6565
Fax: (973) 595-8192

West Caldwell

Delicatessens

David's Deco-Tessen
555 Passaic Avenue 07006 (973) 808-3354
Fax: (973) 808-5806
Supervision: Rabbi Herman Savitz (Conservative).
Open 7 days, 8 am to 7 pm and Mondays 9 am to 3 pm.

West New York

Synagogues

Orthodox

Congregation Shaare Zedek
5308 Palisade Avenue 07093 (201) 867-6859

West Orange

Groceries

Gourmet Galaxy
659 Eagle Rock Avenue 07052 (973) 736-0060
Supervision: Vaad Hakashrus of the Council of Orthodox Rabbis Metrowest.
Dairy and meat available.

Judaica

Lubavitch Center of Essex County
456 Pleasant Valley Way 07052 (973) 731-0770
Fax: (973) 731-6821
Books, gifts, Judaica and all Chabad Outreach activities.

Restaurants

Meat

Eden Wok
478 Pleasant Valley Way 07052 (973) 243-0115
Fax: (973) 243-1332
Supervision: Vaad Hakashrus of the Council of Orthodox Rabbis Metrowest.
Chinese food, also a sushi bar.

Pleasantdale Kosher Meat
470 Pleasant Valley Way 07052 (973) 731-3216

Synagogues

Conservative

B'Nai Shalom
300 Pleasant Valley Way 07052 (973) 731-0160

Orthodox

Congregation Ahawas Achim B'nai Jacob and David
700 Pleasant Valley Way 07052 (973) 736-1407
Fax: (973) 669-0079
Email: aabjd@aol.com

Westfield

Synagogues

Reform

Temple Emanu-El
756 E. Broad Street 07090 (908) 232-6770
Fax: (908) 233-3959
Email: shantee@aol.com

Whippany

Media

Newspapers

The New Jersey Jewish News
901 Route 10 07981 (973) 887-3900
Weekly publication owned by United Jewish Fed. of Metrowest; also publishes a weekly edition in arrangement with the Jewish Federation of Central New Jersey.

Organisations

United Jewish Federation of Metrowest
901 Route 10 07981 (973) 884-4800
Fax: (973) 884-7361

Willingboro

Synagogues

Reform

Adath Emanu-El
299 John F. Kennedy Way 08046 (609) 871-1736

Woodbridge

Synagogues

Conservative

Adath Israel
424 Amboy Avenue 07095 (732) 634-9601
Fax: (732) 634-1593

Wykoff

Synagogues

Reform

Temple Beth Rishon
585 Russell Ave. (201) 891-4466

New Mexico

Alberquerque

Kashrut Information

JFGA (505) 821-3214

Media

Newspapers

The Link
5520 Wyoming Blvd 87109 (505) 821-3214
Fax: (505) 821-3351

Organisations

Jewish Federation of Greater Alberquerque
5520 Wyoming Blvd N.E. 87109 (505) 821-3214
Fax: (505) 821-3351
Email: andrewl@jon.cjfny.org

Synagogues

Conservative

Conservative B'nai Israel
4401 Indian School Road 87110 (505) 266-0155

Orthodox

Chabad of New Mexico
4000 San Pedro 87110 (505) 880-1181

Las Cruces

Synagogues

Reform

Temple Beth El
702 Parker Road, at Melendres 88004
(505) 524-3380
Fax: (505) 521-3737
Email: rabbikane@cs.nmsu.edu
Web site: www.uahc.org/nm/nm002/

Los Alamos

Synagogues

Los Alamos Jewish Center
2400 Canyon Road 87544 (505) 662-2440

Rio Rancho

Synagogues

Reform

Rio Rancho Jewish Center
2009 Grande Blvd 87124 (505) 892-8511

Santa Fe

Contact Information

(505) 986-2091
For information about home hospitality, Shabbat and mikva.

Synagogues

Chabad Jewish Center
242 West S. Mateo (corner Galisteo) (505) 983-2000
Fax: (505) 983-2055
Email: ChabadSantaFe@aol.com
Web site: www.chabadsf.com
Friday night and Shabbat services. Call for reservation to a community Shabbat dinner. Thursday morning minyans at 8 am. Kadish minyans. Kosher catering and take-out.

Orthodox

Pardes Yisroel
1307 Don Diego Avenue 87505 (505) 986-1603
Email: shammes@pardes-yisroel.org
Web site: www.pardes-yisroel.org/py/
Mailing address: 1307 Don Diego Ave., Santa Fe, NM. 87505, USA. Shabbat home hospitality. Kosher meals.

Reform

Congregation Beit Tikvah
PO Box 2112 87504 (505) 820-2991
Fax: (505) 820-2991
Email: rap1818@aol.com
Web site: www.beittikva.org

Temple Beth Shalom
205 E. Barcelona Road 87501 (505) 982-1376
Also Conservative service Shabbat morning. Religious pre-school on premises.

New York

New York City encompasses so much territory and so much activity that it can sometimes be easy to forget that there is also a whole state named New York. The Empire State stretches from New York City in the south to the Canadian border at Quebec and Ontario provinces in the north; from the New England border with Connecticut, Massachusetts and Vermont in the east to Pennsylvania and the Great Lakes of Erie and Ontario in the southwest and west.

Within this 50,000 square mile expanse lie metropolis, suburb, small town, large city, village, vast state parks and preserves, seashores, islands, high mountains and rolling foothills, and abundant natural wilderness.

To New York City residents, anything outside the five boroughs (Manhattan, Queens, Brooklyn, the Bronx, and Staten Island) is either upstate or Long Island. But within those areas are numerous large and thriving Jewish communities. The cities of Buffalo, Rochester, Binghamton, Syracuse, and Schenectady, the suburban counties of Westchester and Rockland, and the Long Island counties of Nassau and Suffolk count hundreds of thousands of Jews among their residents.

Jewish settlement began in New York in early September 1654 when twenty-three Sephardic and Ashkenazi Jews disembarked at the harbour of New Amsterdam from the French ship St Catherine. They had escaped the Spanish Inquisition in Recife, Brazil to settle in the Dutch colony. Though Governor Peter Stuyvesant forbade their admission to his jurisdiction, the travellers' protests to his bosses at the Dutch West India Company were accepted and the Jews were allowed to settle. Ten years later, in 1664, four British men-of-war appropriated New Amsterdam in the name of King Charles II of England, who, in turn, made a gift of it to his brother, James, Duke of York. Hence the name, New York.

Jewish immigration was sparse for the next 150 years, but it increased dramatically, especially in New York City between 1880 and 1924, as more than two million Jews made their way to 'der goldene medinah' (the golden door) from eastern and central Europe.

From that original group of twenty-three Jews in 1654, some made their way up the Hudson River as far as Albany (now the state capital). Two of them, Asser Levy and Jacob de Lucena, became Hudson River traders and also dealt in real estate in the Albany and Kingston areas. South of Albany, in nearby Newburgh, Jewish merchants established a trading post in 1777, but no Jewish community existed there until 1848.

New York's first Jewish community outside of New York City was the town of Sholom in the Catskill mountains in Ulster county. Founded by twelve families, it no longer exists. The oldest existing community is Congregation Beth El, founded in 1838 in Albany and later merged with Congregation Beth Emeth.

Westchester (just north of New York City) county's present Jewish population of close to 150,000 dates from 1860.

Rockland

Southeast of the Catskills, in Rockland county just north of New York City, are a number of communities with large Hasidic and Orthodox populations. New Square, a corruption of the name Skvir, was founded by the Skvirer Hasidim and is incorporated as a separate village within the town of Ramapo. With such an administrative and legal designation, New Square has its own zoning rules, its own village council, its own mayor, etc., and is run on strictly orthodox precepts. Monroe, Monsey and Spring Valley have very large Orthodox and Hasidic communities. Though observant Jews are predominant, these communities are also home to non-Jews and less-observant Jews. There are a number of villages in the area which have been incorporated with the express purpose of keeping Orthodox and Hasidim out, through regulations such as zoning to prevent synagogues from being built too close to residences and through the prohibition of having a synagogue in one's house.

Albany

Groceries

Price Chopper Market
1892 Central Avenue 12205 (518) 456-2970
Supervision: Vaad Hakashruth.
Full service kosher department.

Jewish Student Centre

Shabbos House
State University of New York, 316 Fuller Road
(518) 438-4227
Email: shabbos@albany.net
Web site: www.shabboshouse.com
Is also a synagogue.

Mikvaot

340 Whitehall Road (518) 437-1303

Restaurants

Meat

Goldberg's Café
Located at Howard Johnson Hotel (518) 465-1335
Supervision: Vaad Hakashruth of the Capital District.

Synagogues

Conservative

Ohav Shalom
New Krumkill Rd 12208 (518) 489-4706

Temple Israel
600 New Scotland Ave. 12208 (518) 438-7858

Orthodox

Beth Abraham-Jacob
380 Whitehall Rd 12208
(518) 489-5819; 489-5179
Fax: (518) 489-5179
Email: mbomzer@aol.com

Chabad-Lubavitch Center of the Capital District
122 S. Main Av 12208 (518) 482-5781
Fax: (518) 482-3684
Email: albanychabad@knick.net
Web site: www.chabadonline.com/albany

Shomray Torah
463 New Scotland Av 12208 (518) 438-8981

Reform

B'nai Sholom
420 Whitehall Rd 12208 (518) 482-5283

Beth Emeth
100 Academy Rd 12208 (518) 436-9761
At this 160-year-old congregation, Rabbi Isaac Mayer Wise, founder of American Reform Judaism, served when he first arrived in the United States.

Daughters of Sarah Senior Community
180 Washington Avenue Extension 12203
(518) 456-7831
Fax: (518) 456-1563
Email: info@daughtersofsarah.org
Web site: www.daughtersofsarah.org
Traditional service, Saturday 9.15 am. Reform service, Friday 3 pm. Traveller's advisory and kosher facility.

Amherst

Synagogues

Reconstructionist

Temple Sinai
50 Alberta Dr. 14226 (716) 834-0708
Fax: (716) 838-2597
Email: templesinai@juno.com

Amsterdam

Synagogues

Conservative

Congregation of Sons of Israel
355 Guy Park Avenue 12010 (518) 842-8691

Beacon

Synagogues

Hebrew Alliance
55 Fishkill Avenue 12508 (914) 831-2012

Binghamton

Mikvaot

Beth David Synagogue
39 Riverside Drive 13905 (607) 722-1793
Fax: (607) 722-7121
Email: bethdavidrabbi@aol.com

Synagogues

Community Center
500 Clubhouse Road 13903 (607) 724-2417
Fax: (607) 824-2311
Email: JCC13850@AOL.com

Conservative

Temple Israel
Deerfield Place, Vestal 13850 (607) 723-7461

Reform

Temple Concord
9 Riverside Drive 13905 (607) 723-7355

Buffalo

Delicatessens

Tops Kosher Deli
Cnr of North Bailey and Maple Road (716) 615-0076

Media

Guides

Shalom Buffalo
787 Delaware Ave. 14209 (716) 886-7750
Fax: (716) 886-1367

Newspapers

Buffalo Jewish Review
15 Mohawk Street 14203 (716) 854-2192

Mikvaot

Mikva
1248 Kenmore Avenue 14216 (716) 875-8451

Organisations

Jewish Federation of Greater Buffalo
787 Delaware Avenue 14209 (716) 886-7750
Fax: (716) 886-1367

Synagogues

Conservative

Beth El
2360 Eggert Road, Tonawanda 14223
(716) 836-3762

Hillel of Buffalo
Campus Center for Jewish Life,
520 Lee Entrance, The Commons/Suite #204,
Amherst, NY 14228
(716) 639-8361
Fax: (716) 639-7817

Shaarey Zedek
621 Getzville Rd 14226 (716) 838-3232

Orthodox

B'nai Shalom
1675 N. Forest Rd 14221 (716) 689-8203

Beth Abraham
1073 Elmwood Ave. 14222 (716) 874-4786

Chabad House
3292 Main St., & N. Forest Rd
14214 &14068 (716) 688-1642

Saranac Synagogue
85 Saranac Avenue 14216 (716) 876-1284
Fax: (716) 833-7178

Daily Minyan.

Young Israel of Greater Buffalo
105 Maple Rd, Williamsville 14221 (716) 634-0212

Reform

Beth Am
4660 Sheridan Dr 14221 (716) 633-8877
Fax: (716) 633-8952
Email: rabbif@aol.com

Beth Shalom
Union & Center Sts, Hamburg

Cofeld Judaic Museum of Temple Beth Zion
805 Delaware Avenue 14209 (716) 836-6565
Fax: (716) 831-1126
Email: zbt@webt.com
Web site: www.tbz.org

Congregation Havurah
6320 Main St. 14221 (716) 874-3517

Traditional

Kehilat Shalom
700 Sweet Home Rd 14226 (716) 885-6650

Catskills

Ellenville

Mikvaot

Congregation Ezrath Israel
Rabbi Herman Eisner Square 12428
(845) 647-4450/72
Fax: (845) 647-4472
Email: ezrathisrael@cs.com

Mikvah - call for hours.

Fleischmanns

Hotels

Kosher

Oppenheimer's Regis
PO Box 700, Fleischmanns 12430 (845) 254-5080
Fax: (845) 254-4399
Email: kurtopp@aol.com

Supervision: Rabbinate of K'hal Adas Jeshurun, NYC. Open from Pesach to Succoth. Off-season: fax 1-732-367-5417

Loch Sheldrake

Synagogues

Orthodox

Young Israel of Vacation Village
PO Box 650 12759 (914) 436-8359

Monticello

Hotels

Kutsher's Country Club
(845) 794-6000
Fax: (845) 794-0157
Email: kutshers@warwick.net
Daily services.

Mikvaot

Mikva
16 North Street 12701 (914) 794-6757
Summer: opens at sunset for two hours. Winter: by appointment only.

Synagogues

Orthodox

Landfield Avenue Synagogue
18 Landfield Avenue 12701 (845) 794-8470
Fax: (845) 794-8478
Daily services.

Reform

Temple Sholom
Port Jervis & Dillon Roads 12701 (914) 794-8731
Daily services.

Sharon Springs

Hotels

Yarkony's Adler Spa Hotel
PO Box 328 13459
(518) 284-2285 or 1 800 448-4314
Fax: (518) 284-2215
Supervision: OU.

Woodbourne

Hotels

Chalet Vim (914) 434-5124
Glatt kosher.

Woodridge

Hotels

The Lake House Hotel
(914) 434-7800
Glatt kosher. Chalav Yisrael products only. Open Pesach to Succoth.

Clifton Park

Synagogues

Conservative

Beth Shalom
Clifton Park, Center Road 12065 (716) 371-0608

Delmar

Synagogues

Orthodox

Delmar Chabad Center
109 Elsmere Avenue 12054 (518) 439-8280

Reconstructionist

Reconstructionist Havurah of the Capital District
98 Meadowland Street 12054 (716) 439-5870

Elmira

Synagogues

Orthodox

Shomray Hadath
Cobbles Park 14905 (607) 732-7410

Reform

B'nai Israel
Water & Guinnip Streets 14905 (607) 734-7735

Geneva

Synagogues

Temple Beth El
755 South Main Street 14456 (315) 789-9710
Email: rosenfield@hws.edu

Glens Falls

Synagogues

Conservative

Shaaray Tefila
68 Bay Street 12801 (518) 792-4945
Fax: (518) 792-4945

Reform

Temple Beth El
3 Marion Avenue 12801 (518) 792-4364

Gloversville

Synagogues

Community Center
28 E. Fulton Street 12078

Conservative

Knesseth Israel
34 E. Fulton Street 12078 (518) 725-0649

Harrison

Synagogues

Orthodox

Young Israel of Harrison
207 Union Avenue 10528 (914) 777-1236

Haverstraw

Synagogues

Congregation Sons of Jacob
37 Clove Avenue 10927

Hudson

Synagogues

Conservative

Anshe Emeth
240 Jolsen Blvd 12534 (518) 828-9040

Ithaca

Synagogues

Temple Beth El
402 N. Tioga Street 14850 (607) 273-5775
Email: tbe18@aol.com

Orthodox

Young Israel of Cornell
106 West Avenue 14850 (607) 272-5810

Lake Placid

Synagogues

Traditional

30 Saranac Avenue,
PO Box 521 12946-0521 (518) 523-3876
Fax: (518) 891-2629

Long Island

Jews had settled on Long Island by 1760, which has a present-day Jewish population is around 500,000 and some 150 synagogues. Though two of New York City's five boroughs, Brooklyn and Queens, are geographically part of Long Island, when New Yorkers say 'Long Island' they mean the counties of Nassau and Suffolk. There are large concentrations of Jews in the communities of West Hempstead, Plainview, Great Neck, Long Beach, Cedarhurst, Lawrence, Hewlett and Woodmere. The latter four are part of what is known as the Five Towns.

Kashrut Information

Long Island Commission of Rabbis
1300 Jericho Turnpike
Nassau County 11040 (718) 343-5993

Nassau County

Baldwin

Restaurants

Ben's Kosher Delicatessen
933 Atlantic Avenue (516) 868-2072
Fax: (516) 868-2062
Email: info@bensdeli.net
Web site: www.bensdeli.net
Supervision: Supervised.

Five Towns

Incorporates the towns of Cedarhurst, Hewlett, Inwood, Lawrence and Woodmere.

Bakeries

Tasty Heimish Bakery
343 Central Avenue, Lawrence
(516) 569-5551/5552

Zomick's Bake Shop
444 Central Avenue, Cedarhurst (516) 569-5520
Supervision: Vaad HaKashrus of the Five Towns.

Kashrut Information

Vaad HaKashrus of the Five Towns
859 Peninsula Blvd, Woodmere 11598
(516) 569-4536
Fax: (516) 295 4212

Restaurants

Dairy

Dairy Review
143 Washington Avenue, Lawrence (516) 295-7417
Supervision: Vaad HaKashrus of the Five Towns.

Primavera
357 Central Avenue, Lawrence, (516) 374-5504
Fax: (516) 374-5589
Supervision: Supervised.

Ruthie's Kosher Dessert and Dairy Café
560A Central Avenue, Cedarhurst (516) 569-1818
Supervision: Vaad HaKashrus of the Five Towns.

Meat

Burger Express
140 Washington Avenue, Lawrence (516) 374-1714
Supervision: Vaad HaKashrus of the Five Towns.

Cho-Sen Island
367 Central Avenue, Lawrence11559
(516) 374-1199
Fax: (516) 374-1459
Supervision: Vaad HaKashrus of the Five Towns.

K.D.'s El Passo BBQ
546 Central Avenue, Cedarhurst (516) 569-2920
Supervision: Supervised.

K Roasters
72 Columbia Avenue, Cedarhurst (516) 791-5100
Supervision: Vaad HaKashrus of the Five Towns.

King David Delicatessen
550 Central Avenue, Cedarhurst (516) 569-2920
Supervision: Vaad HaKashrus of the Five Towns.
Glatt kosher, Shomer Shabbat. Ten minutes from JFK International Airport.

Off the Grill
600 Central Avenue, Cedarhurst
Supervision: Vaad HaKashrus of the Five Towns.

Wok Tov
594 Central Avenue, Cedarhurst (516) 295-3843
Fax: (516) 295-3865
Supervision: Vaad HaKashrus of the Five Towns.

Synagogues

Orthodox

Young Israel of North Woodmere
634 Hungry Harbor Road, North Woodmere 11581
(516) 791-5099
Email: info@yinw.org

Great Neck

Butchers

Butcher and Delicatessen

Great Neck Glatt
501 Middle Neck Road 11023 (516) 773-6328
Fax: (516) 773-4694
Supervision: Vaad Harabonim of Queens.

Media

Newspapers

Long Island Jewish Week
98 Cutter Mill Road 11020 (516) 773-3679

Long Island Jewish World
115 Middle Neck Road 11021 (516) 829-4000

Mikvaot

26 Old Mill Road
Nassau County 11023 (516) 487-2726

Restaurants

Meat

Ben's Kosher Delicatessen
140 Wheatley Plaza (516) 621-3340
Fax: (516) 621-2178
Email: info@bensdeli.net
Web site: www.bensdeli.net
Supervision: Supervised.

Colbeh
75 N. Station Plaza, Greatneck (516) 466-8181
Supervision: Kof-K.

Hunan
507 Middle Neck Road, Greatneck (516) 482-7912
Supervision: Vaad Rab. of Queens.

Soprano's
113 Middle Neck Road (516) 482-0000

Jericho

Delicattessen

Ben's Kosher Delicatessen
437 No. Broadway (516) 939-2367
Fax: (516) 939-2294
Email: info@bensdeli.net
Web site: www.bensdeli.net
Supervision: Supervised.

Long Beach

Mikvaot

Sharf Manor 274 W. Broadway 11561 (516) 431-7758

Synagogues

Conservative

Beth Shalom of Long Beach and Lido
700 E. Park Ave., 11561 (516) 432-7464

Orthodox

Temple Bet El
570 W. Walnut St 11561 (516) 432-1678

Merrick

Restaurants

Meat

Kosher Food Emporium
1984 Merrick Road (516) 378-6463
Fax: (516) 377-1456
Supervision: Rabbi Gershon Kreuser.

Syosset

Representative Organisations

Conference of Jewish Organisations of Nassau County
North Shore Atrium, 6900 Jericho Turnpike 11791
(516) 364-4477
Fax: (516) 921-5092

Wantagh

Bakeries

B & B Bakery Bagels
2845 Jerusalem Avenue 11793
Supervision: Kof-K.
Pat Yisrael.

Mikvaot

775 Hempstead Avenue 11552 (516) 489-9358

Woodbury

Restaurants

Ben's Kosher Delicatessen
7971 Jericho Turnpike (516) 496-4236
Fax: (516) 496-4354
Email: info@bensdeli.net
Web site: www.bensdeli.net
Supervision: Supervised.

Suffolk County

Commack

Community Organisations

Suffolk Jewish Communal Planning Council
74 Hauppauge Road 11725 (631) 462-5826
Email: sjcpc@att.net
Web site: www.lijewishlinks.org
Publishes "Suffolk Jewish Directory".

Restaurants

Meat

Pastrami 'N Friends
110a Commack Road 11725 (516) 499-9537

Dix Hills

Tourist Information

Jewish Genealogy Society of Long Island
37 Westcliff Drive 11746-5627 (631) 549-9532
Email: jgsli@suffolk.lib.ny.us
Web site: www.jewishgen.org/jgsli
Offers assistance to Jewish travellers on their New York or US roots.

Monroe

Synagogues

Conservative

Congregation Eitz Chaim
County Route 105 10950 (914) 783-7424

Reform

Monroe Temple of Liberal Judaism
314 N. Main Street 10950

Monsey

Bakeries

Bubba's Bagels
Wesley Hills Plaza, Wesley Hills 10952
(914) 362-1019
Fax: (914) 362-0549
Supervision: Va'ad Harabonim of Greater Monsey.

Delicatessens

Sammy's Bagels
421 Route 59 10952

Restaurants

Dairy

Al di La
455 Route 306, Wesley Hills 10952
(914) 354-2672
Supervision: Va'ad Harabonim of Greater Monsey.
Italian/Dairy. Cholov Yisrael.

Chai Pizza
94 Route 59 10952 (914) 356-2135

Jerusalem Pizza & Restaurant
190 Route 59 10952 (914) 426-1500

New York Café
Cot Route 59 & 306 10952 (914) 352-0710

Meat

Fleigals Restaurant
43 Route 59 10952 (914) 352-4200
Glatt kosher.

Pulkies
455 Route 306, Wesley Hills 10952 (914) 362-7855
Glatt kosher.

Synagogues

Orthodox

Young Israel of Monsey and Wesley Hills Inc
58 Parker Blvd 10952 (914) 362-1838

Mount Vernon

Synagogues

Brothers of Israel
116 Crary Avenue 10550 (914) 667-1302
Fax: (914) 667-0278

Fleetwood
11 E. Broad Street 10552

New City

Delicatessens

Steve's Deli-Bake
179 South Main Street 10956 (914) 634-8749

Groceries

M&S Kosher Meats
191a South Main Street 10956 (914) 638-9494

Synagogues

Conservative

New City Jewish Center
47 Old Schoolhouse Road 10956 (845) 634-3619
Fax: (845) 634-3481
Email: ncjc@j51.com
Web site: www.uscj.org/metny/newcity/index.html

Reform

Temple Beth Sholom
228 New Hempstead Road 10956 (845) 638-0770
Fax: (845) 638-1696
Web site: www.tbs-nc.org

New Rochelle

Restaurants

Eden Wok
1327 North Avenue 10804 (914) 637-9363
Fax: (914) 637-9371

Supervision: Vaad of Westchester.

Synagogues

Conservative

Bethel
Northfield Road

Orthodox

Cong. Anshe Sholom
50 North Avenue, New Rochelle, NY 10805
(914) 632-9220
Fax: (914) 632-8182
Email: ashewroch@aol.com

Young Israel of New Rochelle
1228 North Avenue 10804 (914) 777-1236
Contact Rabbi on 835-5581

Reform

Temple Israel
1000 Pine Brook Blvd. 10804

New York City

Nowhere in the United States is there a city richer in Jewish heritage than New York. From the city's beginnings as a Dutch trading post in the seventeenth century up to the present day, Jews have flocked to New York, made it their home, and left an indelible mark on the city's heritage, language, culture, physical structure, and day to day life. There are more Jews in the New York metropolitan area than in any other city in the world, and more than in any country except Israel. So, without a great deal of effort, just being in this largest urban Jewish community in history affords you the opportunity to be a tourist without concern about the ease of observing kashrut and Shabbat.

The estimated Jewish population of New York City proper is just over one million. Another million or so live in the immediate suburbs which include not only New York, but also New Jersey and Connecticut. Roughly one-third of American Jews live in and around New York City and virtually every national Jewish organisation has its headquarters here.

New York City neighbourhoods with large Jewish populations are the upper west and upper east sides of Manhattan (modern Orthodox and secular Jewish), Borough Park, Williamsburg (Orthodox and Hasidic) and Brighton Beach (Russian) in Brooklyn, Forest Hills (Israelis and Russians), Kew Gardens, Kew Garden Hills (Orthodox) in Queens, Riverdale in the Bronx, and Staten Island.

In this largest urban Jewish community in history, the Jewish traveller is overwhelmed with choices of where to eat, where to find a minyan, what to see of Jewish interest and so on. And the variety of kosher restaurants makes choosing a pleasure: Chinese, Moroccan, Italian (both meat and dairy), traditional European, Indian, Japanese and seafood.

Though Jews from numerous countries of origin live together throughout New York's Jewish communities, many groups tend to congregate in their own neighbourhoods or sections of neighbourhoods.

Ever since the fateful year of 1654 Jews have been coming to New York City. Sometimes a few, sometimes more, and sometimes by the boatload, as was the case between 1880 and 1924 when some two million Jews entered the United States. And though one might argue cause and effect, New York City is still the commercial, intellectual and financial centre of the country.

Synagogues

Hundreds if not thousands of synagogues, chavurot and shtiblech lie within the city, representing the myriad expressions of Judaism: Orthodox, Hasidic, Conservative, Reform and Reconstructionist.

Complete lists of synagogues in all five boroughs can be obtained from the various umbrella organisations listed in the beginning of the section on the USA .

The 1,300-seat, Moorish-style Central Synagogue (Reform) at 652 Lexington Avenue in Manhattan reopened its doors in October 2001, three years after a devastating fire. It is the city's oldest synagogue on an original site and is an official New York City landmark; the oldest Ashkenazi congregation, founded in 1825, is B'nai Jeshrun (Conservative) at 270 West 89th Street; Shearith Israel, the Spanish and Portuguese synagogue on Central Park West at 70th Street, is one of the oldest congregations in the United States and originated with those twenty-three refugees from the Spanish Inquisition in Brazil in 1654. The present building still has religious items from the earliest days of the congregation and its small chapel is representative of the American colonial period; Temple Emanu-El (Reform) at Fifth Avenue and 65th Street is not only the city's largest, but the world's largest synagogue. The congregation was founded in 1848 and the building, built in 1929, can seat over 2,000 people; the Fifth Avenue synagogue at 5 East 62nd Street was, until early 1967, presided over by the then Rabbi Dr Immanuel Jakobovits, who later became the Chief Rabbi of Great Britain and the Commonwealth; the Park East synagogue at 163 East 67th Street on the very fashionable Upper East Side was founded in 1890 and is an historic landmark. Kehilath Jeshurun (Orthodox), 125 E. 85th Street, is a popular option if you are on the Upper East Side. On the Upper West Side, Lincoln Square Synagogue (Orthodox), 200 Amsterdam Avenue at 69th Street, and Ohab Zedek (Orthodox), 118 West 95th Street, are both very popular options.

Visitors may be interested in a late 9 am minyan on the Upper West Side at 303 W.91st East between West End Avenue and Riversdale Drive.

Libraries, Museums, and Institutes of Learning

New York's newest educational research centre and one of the country's most important resources for Jewish scholarship opened in October 2000 and is located at 15 West 16th Street. The centre is a partnership of five major institutions of Jewish scholarship. American Jewish Historical Society, American Sephardi Federation, Leo Baeck Institute, Yeshiva University Museum and YIVO Institute for Jewish Research. The combined collections and the professional staff of these five institutions create an opportunity for an unparalleled comprehensive study of modern Jewish history.

The Jewish Museum (Fifth Avenue and 92nd Street, 212-423-3200) has been in existence since 1904. Under the auspices of the Conservative Jewish Theological Seminary, the museum has permanent and changing exhibits and programmes and an excellent collection of Jewish ritual and ceremonial objects.

The library at the Jewish Theological Seminary (3080 Broadway at 122nd Street, 212-678-8000), houses one of the greatest collections of Judaica and Hebraica in the world. Its holdings include a rare manuscript by Maimonides (the Rambam).

Other libraries with large Judaica collections are at Yeshiva University (212-960-5400), the Judaica Collection at the New York Public Library (212-340-0849), New York University (212-998-1212), Columbia University (212-854-1754), the House of Living Judaism at Temple Emanu-El (212-744-1400) and the Leo Baeck Institute (212-744-6400). Inquire at each one individually as to availability of the collections.

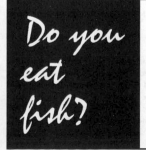

One of New York's living museums is the Eldridge Street Synagogue (14 Eldridge Street, 212-219-0888). At over 100 years old, the Eldridge Street synagogue is a ghost of its former splendour. But, in its heyday at the turn of the century, it was among the busiest synagogues on the Lower East Side, and the first built for that purpose by New York's eastern European Jews. An official New York City landmark, and listed on the National Register of Historic Places, the synagogue is an ongoing restoration project. The synagogue functions as a museum and has a whole host of programmes.

In the same neighbourhood and sociologically related is the Lower East Side Tenement Museum (97 Orchard Street, 212-431-0233). Contrary to popular opinion, the word tenement does not mean slum housing, but a particular building design devised to house the masses of immigrants who came to New York in the latter part of the nineteenth century. Tenements are five- or six-storey walk-up buildings distinguished by narrow entry halls and a central air shaft. Each floor contained four apartments. Toilet facilities, located in the hallway, were shared by all the residents. Baths were taken at numerous local public bath houses. The museum, located in a restored tenement built in 1863, shows visitors what tenement life was like via a model apartment. In addition, actors in period dress present ninety-minute shows in a small theatre. This is how the vast majority of Jews lived when they first came to New York City.

Ellis Island National Monument (212-269-5755) was once the point of entry for Jews and other immigrants. Some five million Jews came to the United States between 1850 and 1948 and most were processed through immigration at Castle Garden (the present ferry ticket office) or, after 1890, Ellis Island.

Neighbourhoods and areas of historical interest

Manhattan

The Lower East Side has physically changed very little in over a century. Cramped tenements and crowded, dirty streets have always characterised the area. But for the absence of vendors calling out 'I cash clothes' one can get a pretty good idea of what life looked like for Jews newly arrived in New York City from Eastern European countries, although it is difficult to imagine the strangeness of a new language or being away from home for the first time.

Although the Lower East Side is not as Jewish as it once was and many Jewish shops have closed, it is appropriate that historical jaunts in New York begin in its tangle of streets and alleys. For the ancestors of some eighty per cent of American Jews, this was the first piece of America they saw. Now other immigrant groups call the Lower East Side home. Settlement houses such as the Henry Street Settlement and the Educational Alliance on East Broadway once served the Jewish immigrant population in their need to learn English and become Americanised. Still in existence, they provide services to current residents, Jewish and non-Jewish alike.

Many Jews still do business in the neighbourhood and the area is full of historic buildings, Jewish shops, foodstores and stores selling all manner of ritual items (kipot, taliltot, tefilin, siddurim, etc.). Look along Essex, Orchard, Grand, Rivington, Hester and Canal streets.

One of the best guidebooks for this area (as well as the rest of New York City) is the "AIA [American Institute of Architects] Guide to New York City" by Elliot Willensky and Norval White. An organisation called Big Onion Walking Tours gives Lower East Side tours and they are worth a telephone call (212-439-1090).

You may notice that a number of churches on the Lower East Side used to be synagogues. They were re-consecrated as churches when the Jewish community dwindled. But in many cases you still can tell which were synagogues. Look for things like Stars of David on building cornerstones, darkened mezuzah shaped areas on doorposts, and shadows of Stars of David on building façades. They are quite evident if you look.

Synagogues of note in the area are the Bialystoker synagogue (7 Wilet Street); Beth Midrash HaGadol (60 Norfolk Street); First Roumanian American Congregation (89 Rivington Street); and the Eldridge Street Synagogue (14 Eldridge Street).

The only kosher winery in Manhattan is Schapiro's Kosher Winery (126 Rivington Street, 674-4404), founded in 1899. Call for tour information.

Along Second Avenue below 14th Street you can still see the remnants of the scores of Yiddish theatres that once lined the street. Note particularly the movie theatre on Second Avenue at 12th Street, currently the City Cinemas Village East. In the upper level auditorium you can get an idea of what the place looked like when stars like Molly Picon and Boris Tomeshevsky held forth on the stage.

Forty-seventh Street between Fifth Avenue and Avenue of the Americas is the diamond centre. Some seventy-five per cent of all the diamonds which enter the United States pass through here. As this is overwhelmingly a Jewish and Hasidic business, the street is bustling with diamond dealers concluding deals in the open market atmosphere that is pervasive. Most deals are made with a handshake. There are a number of kosher restaurants up and down the block and on the mezzanines of office buildings.

Historical Cemeteries

Manhattan

Shearith Israel Cemeteries

Vestiges of early Jewish settlement in New York can be gleaned from the remnants of the community's first cemeteries. The following three are owned by New York's oldest congregation, Shearith Israel, the Spanish Portuguese Synagogue.

First: Shearith Israel Graveyard: 55 St James Place (between Oliver and James St.), the first Jewish cemetery in New Amsterdam, was consecrated in 1656 and was located near the present Chatham Square. Its remains were moved to this location. It contains the remains of Sephardic Jews who emigrated from Brazil.

Second: Cemetery of the Spanish and Portuguese Synagogue (1805–1829): 72-76 West 11th Street, just east of Sixth Avenue on the south side of the street.

Third: Cemetery of the Spanish and Portuguese Synagogue (1829-1851): 98-110 West 21st Street, just west of Sixth Avenue on the south side of the street.

Brooklyn

Green-Wood Cemetery (Fifth Avenue and Fort Hamilton Parkway, Brooklyn) contains the graves of many prominent Jewish figures.

Queens

Fourth Cemetery of the Spanish and Portuguese Synagogue: Cypress Hills Street and Cypress Avenue, Queens. The beautiful chapel and gate were built in 1885.

Arts and Entertainment

As American entertainment is largely a secular Jewish enterprise, one need not look very far for Jewish references in plays and musicals. However, there are some dedicated Jewish theatrical companies and venues: the Jewish Repertory Company (212-831-2000); the American Jewish Theater (212-633-1588); the YM & YWHA (212-427-6000) has several outstanding lecture series, some with specific Jewish themes. For other events of Jewish interest consult one of the weekly listings magazines such as Time Out New York or New York Magazine, or the Sunday Arts & Leisure section of the New York Times. Jewish newspapers with events listings are Jewish Week, Forward, and Jewish Press, all available at most newsstands.

Jewish Neighbourhoods of Interest outside Manhattan

Brooklyn

Williamsburg was for many years the centre of Hasidic life in New York City. But in the last decade many rebbes and their followers have moved to the suburbs, particularly Rockland county. However, a trip to Williamsburg is still worthwhile.

Boro Park is almost completely Orthodox and is a world apart from the rest of the city.

Crown Heights is populated by Hasidim of many sects, but particularly the Lubavitch, whose world headquarters is at 770 Eastern Parkway. The neighbourhood is not totally Jewish and there are often clashes (sometimes violent) between the Caribbean residents and Jewish residents.

New Jersey

Many towns in northern and central New Jersey are less than forty minutes travel time by either car or public transport from Manhattan, and as such are part of metropolitan New York. They are: Bayonne, Clifton, Elizabeth, Englewood, Fairlawn, Hackensack, Hoboken, Jersey City, Newark, Passaic, Teaneck, Union and West New York.

Restaurants

By law in New York State, the selling of non-kosher food as kosher is a punishable fraud. Administered by the Kosher Law Enforcement Section of the New York State Department of Agriculture, heavy penalties are imposed on violators. An Orthodox rabbi oversees the operation. Businesses selling kosher food must display proper signage, indicating under whose hashgacha they operate, and establishments which sell both kosher and non-kosher food must display that as well, with a sign in block letters no smaller than four inches high.

In August 2000 a Federal Judge ruled that this law violated the First Amendment. Later in October 2000 there was a stay of this ruling pending appeal.

"The Kosher Directory",s issued by the Union of Orthodox Jewish Congregations, lists foods and services which bear the symbol. It is available for a charge by calling 212-563-4000. Other reliable kashruth insignias also exist.

Note that kosher packaged foods, including bread, meat, fish, cake, biscuits and virtually anything you can think of, are widely available in supermarkets throughout the New York metropolitan area. Many foodstores, especially on the Upper West Side of Manhattan and in Jewish neighbourhoods in Brooklyn and Queens, sell fresh kosher prepared meals as well.

Bronx

Restaurants

Riverdelight
3534 Johnson Avenue, Riverdale 10463
(718) 543-4270
Fax: (718) 543-7545
Supervision: Vaad Harabonim of Riverdale.
Glatt Kosher. Grill, deli and Middle-Eastern cuisine.
Take-out and catering.

Second Helping
3532 Johnson Avenue 10463 (718) 548-1818
Supervision: Vaad Harabonim of Riverdale.
Take-out food only; Glatt kosher.

Yeshiva University: Bronx Center
Eastchester Rd & Morris Park Avenue 10461
(718) 430-2131

Dairy

Main Event
3708 Riverdale Avenue, Riverdale 10463
(718) 601-6246
Fax: (718) 601-0008
Email: maineventc@aol.com
Supervision: Rabbi Jonathan Rosenblatt, Riverdale Jewish Center.

Brooklyn

Hotels

Avenue Plaza Hotel
4624 13th Avenue 11219 (718) 552-3200
Fax: (718) 552-3276
Email: info@theavenueplaza.com
Web site: www.theavenueplaza.com

Midwood Suites
1078 East 15 St. 11230 (718) 253-9535
Fax: (718) 253-3269
Email: shalom@midwoodsuites.com

Scharf's Ateret of Midwood
1410 East 10th Street 11230 (718) 998-5400
Fax: (718) 645-8600
Daily Minyon. Under strict Hashgocha. Cholov Yisroel/Glatt kosher.

The Crown Palace Hotel
570-600 Crown Street (718) 604-1777
Glatt kosher.

The Park House Hotel
1206 48th Street 11219 (718) 871-8100

Libraries

Levi Yitzhak Library
305 Kingston Avenue 11213

Museums

The Chasidic Art Institute
375 Kingston Avenue

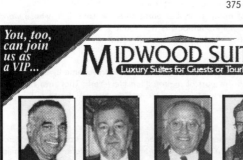

Organisations

Orthodox

Lubavitch Movement
770 Eastern Parkway 11213 (718) 221-0500
Fax: (718) 221-0985

Restaurants

Dairy

Bernies Place
1287 Ave. J. (718) 677-1515
Supervision: Rabbi Gornish.

Chapp-u-Ccino
4815 12th Avenue (718) 633-4377
Supervision: Rabbi Amrom Roth.

Fontana Bella
2086 Coney Island Avenue (718) 627-3904
Supervision: Rabbi Gornish.

Il Cup Caffe
1320 East 19th Street, off Avenue M in Midwood

Milk 'N Honey
5013 - 10 Ave. (718) 871-4319
Fax: (718) 871-4297
Supervision: Rabbi Friedlander.

Sunflower Café
1223 Kings Highway, cor. E. 13th St.
(718) 336-1340
Supervision: Rabbi Gornish.

Tea For Two Café
547 Kings Highway (718) 998-0020/0990
Supervision: Rabbi Gornish.

Wendy's Plate
434 Ave. (718) 376-3125
Fax: (718) 871-4297
Supervision: Rabbi Friedlander.

Meat

47th St. Kosher Restaurant
(718) 492-2000

Bamboo Garden
904 Kings Highway (718) 375-8501
Supervision: Rabbi Yisroel P. Gornish.

Cancun
448 Avenue P. (718) 375-4916
Supervision: Vaad Harabonim of Flatbush.

Chap-A-Nosh Plus
1424 Elm Avenue 11230 (718) 627-0072
Fax: (718) 645-6336

Dougies
4310 18th Ave., Bet. McDonald Ave. & E. 2nd St.,
Off Ocean Parkway (718) 686-8080
Supervision: Udvar Kashruth of America.

Essex on Coney
1359 Coney Island Ave. (718) 253-1002
Supervision: Vaad Harabonim of Flatbush.

Fuji Hana
512 Av. U. (718) 336-3888
Supervision: Vaad Harabonim of Flatbush.

Glatt Kosher Family
4305 18th Ave., Bet. McDonald & E. 2nd St.
(718) 972-8085/6
Supervision: Vaad of Flatbush.

Glatt-a-la-Carte
5502 18th Ave. (718) 621-3697
Supervision: R'Yechiel Babad.

Kineret Steak House
521 Kings Highway, Bet. E. 2nd - E. 3rd Sts
(718) 336-8888
Supervision: Kehilah Kashruth.

Kosher Delight Glatt Kosher
1223 Avenue J (E. 13th Street),
Flatbush 11230 (718) 377-6873
Fax: (718) 677-0831
Supervision: Rav S.D. Beck and Vaad Rabonim of Flatbush.

Mama's Restaurant
906 Kings Highway 11223 (718) 382-7200
Supervision: Rabbi Gornish.

McFleishig's
5508 16th Avenue (718) 435-2779
Supervision: Rabbi Babad, Tartikover.

Nathan's Famous
825 Kings Highway, cor. E. 9 (718) 627-5252
Supervision: Kehilah Kashrus.

Olympic Pita
1419 Coney Island Avenue, Bet. J & K
(718) 258-6222
Supervision: Kehilah Kashrus.

Shalom Hunan
1619 Avenue M (718) 382-6000

Tokyo of Brooklyn
2954 Ave. U. off Nostrand Ave. (718) 891-6221
Supervision: Kehilah Kashrus.

Yun-Kee Glatt Kosher
1424 Elm Avenue, cnr. E.15th Street & Avenue M
(718) 627-0072
Supervision: ARK.

Manhatten

There are of course a large number of synagogues of all kinds in New York.

The major synagogues in Manhattan, and of possible interest to visitors are the following:

Orthodox

Fifth Avenue Synagogue
5 East 62nd Street, NY, 1002 838 2122

Kehilath Jeshurun
125 East 85th Street, NY, 10028 427 1000

Lincoln Square
220 Amsterdam Avenue at 69th Street
NY 10023 874 6100
Ohab Zedeck
118 West 95th Street, NY 10025 749 5150
Park East
163 East 67th Street, NY 10021 737 6900
Fax: 570 648

Sephardi

Shearith Israel
2 West 70th Street, NY 10023

Reform

Central Synagogue
652 Lexington Avenue, NY 10022 838 5122
Temple Emanuel-El
1 East 65th Street, NY 10023 744 1400

Conservative

B'nai Jeshrun
270 West 89th Street, NY 10010 787 7600
Park Avenue Synagogue
50 East 87th Street, NY 10128 369 2600
Fax: 410 7879

Visitors wishing to ascertain details of other synagogues in Manhattan or of synagogues in outlying areas should contact the appropriate central authority as detailed below.

Orthodox

Agudat Israel World Organization
84 William Street, NY 10038 (212) 797 9600
Fax: (212) 269 2843
Lubavitch Movement
770 Eastern Parkway,Brooklyn, NY 11213
(718) 221 0500
Fax: (718) 221 0985
National Council of Young Israel National Office
3 West 16th Street, NY 10011 (212) 929 1525
Fax: (212) 727 9526
Email: nyci@youngisrael.org
www.youngisrael.org
Union of Orthodox Jewish Congregations of America
333 Seventh Avenue, NY 10001 (212) 563 4000
Fax: (212) 613 8333

Conservative

United Synagogue of America
155 Fifth Avenue, NY 10010 (212) 533 7800
World Council of Synagogues can be found at the same location.

Progessive

World Union for Progressive Judaism
838 Fifth Avenue, NY 10021 (212) 650 4090
Fax: (212) 650 4090
Email: 5448032@mcimail.com

Reform

Union of America Hebrew Congregations
838 Fifth Avenue, NY 10021 (212) 650 4085
Fax: (212) 650 4169

Sephardi

Union of Sephardi Congregations
8 West 70th Street, NY 10023 (212) 873 0300

Bakeries

H & H / The Excellent Bagel
2239 Broadway 10024 (212) 595-8000
Supervision: Kof-K.

Delicatessens

Second Avenue Delicatessan-Restaurant
156 2nd Avenue, cnr. 10th Street (212) 677-0606
Fax: (212) 477-5327
Email: 2ndavedeli@quicklink.com
Hours - Sunday-Thursday 7.30 am-12 am. Friday & Saturday 7.30 am-3 am.

Embassy

Consul General of Israel
800 Second Avenue 10017 (212) 499-5400
Fax: (212) 499-5555

Libraries

Butler Library of Colombia University
Broadway at 116th Street 10027
Has some 6,000 Hebrew books and pamphlets, plus 1,000 manuscripts and a Hebrew psalter printed at Cambridge University in 1685 and used by Samuel Johnson at the graduation of the first candidates for bachelor's degrees.
New York University of Judaica and Hebraica
Houses a stunning collection of priceless items.
The Jewish Division of the New York Public Library
Fifth Avenue at 42nd Street 10018 (212) 930-0601
Fax: (212) 642-0141
Has 125,000 volumes of Judaica and Hebraica, along with extensive microfilm and bound files of Jewish publications, one of the finest collections in existence.

Museums

Centre for Jewish History
15 West 16th Street 10011 (212) 294-8301
Fax: (212) 294-8302
Web site: www.centerforjewishhistory.org
The Center has brought together the following five institutes to create the largest single repository for Jewish history in the Diaspora: American Jewish Historical Society, American Sephardi Federation, Leo Baeck Institute, Yeshiva University Museum and YIVO Institute for Jewish Research. It has over 500,000 volumes and over 100 million documents. A wide variety of exhibitions illustrate the diversity of Jewish art, textiles sculpture architecture, religious objects and folklore. Tours are available and there is a kosher café open 11 am to 4.30 pm.

Jewish Museum
1109 Fifth Avenue 10028
This is one of the outstanding museums in the city and a 'must' not just for Jewish visitors but for all interested in art. The permanent display consists of one of the finest collection of Jewish ritual and ceremonial art in the world, along with notable paintings and sculptures.

Jewish Theological Seminary of America
3080 Broadway at 122nd Street 10027
(212) 678-8975
Email: shmintz@jtsa.edu
The Library of the Jewish Theological Seminary is one of the world's premier research libraries of Judaica and Hebraica. More than a thousand years of written history are to be found within the library's 375,000 rare books, 40,000 Genizah fragments and thousands of rare documents and prints. The remarkable treasures represent scholarship in the areas of Bible, liturgy, rabbinics, kabbala, philosophy, philology and history. Throughout the year, exhibitions featuring selected pieces from the collection, showcase the library's treasures. Sundays, 10 am to 5 pm; Monday through Thursday, 9 am to 6 pm; Fridays, 9 am to 2 pm; closed Saturday.

Lower East Side Tenement Museum
90 Orchard Street 10002 (212) 431-0233
Fax: (212) 431-0402
Web site: www.tenement.org
Housed in a 1863 structure, the Museum presents and interprets the variety of immigrant experience on Manhattan's Lower East side, "A gateway to America".

The House of Living Judaism
5th Avenue and 65th Street
Frequently shows paintings and ritual objects. Twelve marble pillars symbolise the Twelve Tribes.

The Museum of Jewish Heritage
18 First Place, Battery Park City 10004
(212) 509-6130
Web site: www.mjhnyc.org
The Museum's core exhibition combines archival material with modern media as a living memorial to the Holocaust.

Theological Seminary of America
Fifth Avenue & 92nd Street 10028
An outstanding museum, with permanent displays of Jewish ritual and ceremonial art, along with notable paintings and sculptures.

Organisations

UJA-Federation Resource Line
130 E. 59th Street 10022 (212) 753-2288
Fax: (212) 888-7538
Email: resourceline@ujafedny.org
Web site: www.ujafedny.org

Conservative

United Synagogue of Conservative Judaism
155 Fifth Avenue 10010 (212) 533-7800
Fax: (212) 353-9439
Email: info@uscj.org
Web site: www.uscj.org

Orthodox

Agudat Israel World Organization
42 Broadway, 14th Floor 10004 (212) 797-9000
Fax: (212) 646-254-1600

Union of Orthodox Jewish Congregations of America
11 Broadway 10004 (212) 564-9058
Fax: (212) 613-8333
Email: info@ou.org
Web site: www.ou.org
The Orthodox Union provides the "OU" kosher symbol. Kashrut enquiries should be directed to: Tel, 1-212-613-8241.

Young Israel National Office
3 West 16th Street 10011 (212) 929-1525
Fax: (212) 727-9526
Email: ncyi@youngisrael.org
Web site: www.youngisrael.org
Contact the Department of Synagogue Services at this number for information regarding the Young Israel shul nearest you.

Progressive

World Union for Progressive Judaism
838 Fifth Avenue 10021 (212) 249-0100 ext. 502
Fax: (212) 517-3940

Reform

Union of American Hebrew Congregations
633 Third Avenue 10017-6778 (212) 650-4000
Email: uahc@uahc.org

Sephardic

Union of Sephardic Congregations
8 West 70th Street 10023 (212) 873-0300
Web site: www.shearith-israel.org

Restaurants

Ben's Kosher Delicatessen
209 West 38th Street (212) 398-2367
Fax: (212) 398-3354
Email: info@bensdeli.net
Web site: www.bensdeli.net
Supervision: Supervised.
Hours: 11am to 9.30 pm.

Deniz
400 East 57th 10022 (212) 486-2255

Eden Wok
127 W. 72 Street 10023 (212) 787-8700
Fax: (212) 787-9801
Supervision: OU.

Yeshiva University: Main Center
500 W. 185th Street 10033-3201 (212) 960-5248
Fax: (212) 960-0070

Dairy

Bagels & Co.
1428 York Ave., cnr. E. 76th St. (212) 717-0505
Supervision: New York Kosher.

Broadway's Jerusalem 2
1375 Broadway, at 38th Street 10018
(212) 398-1475
Fax: (212) 212-398-6797
Email: n.y.pies@.com
Supervision: OU.
Chalav Yisrael, Prs Yisruel. Home of the N.Y. Flying Pizza Pies. Visit the 'Jewish Wall of Fame', 7 am to 12 pm. Saturday nights to 2.00am.

Café 18
8 East 18th Street, Bet. 5th and Broadway
(212) 620-4182

Cafe I23
2 Park Avenue (212) 685-7117

Cafe Roma Pizzeria
175 W. 90th Street (212) 875-8972

Diamond Dairy Kosher Lunchonette
4 W. 47th Street 10036 (212) 719-2694
On the gallery overlooking the diamond & jewelry exchange. Hours: Monday to Thursday, 7.30 am to 5 pm; Friday, to 2 pm.

Great American Health Bar
35 W. 57th Street (212) 355-5177

Gusto va Mare
237 E. 53rd Street (212) 583-9300
Supervision: Organised Kashrut.

Mom's Bagels of NY
15 West 45th Street 10036 (212) 764-1566
Fax: (212) 764-1566
Email: info@momsnyc.com
Supervision: Kof-K.
Chulov Yisruel

My Most Favorite Desert
120 West 45th Street (212) 997-5130
Fax: (212) 997 5046
Supervision: OU.
Chalav Yisrael.

Provi, Provi
228 W, 72nd St., Bet. B'way and West End Ave.
(212) 875-9020
Supervision: Organised Kashrut.

Va Bene
1589 Second Avenue 10028
(212) 517-4448
Fax: (212) 517-2258
Supervision: OU.
Chalav Yisrael Italian restaurant.

Vegetable Garden
48 East 41st St., (Bet. Mad & Park) (212) 883-7668

Village Crown Italian
94 Third Avenue @ 12th Street 10003
(212) 777-8816
Fax: (212) 388-9639
Email: info@villagecrown.com
Web site: www.villagecrown.com
Supervision: Kof-K/Cholev Israel.

Meat

Abigael's Grill and Caterers
9 East 37th Street 10016 (212) 725-0130
Fax: (212) 725-3577
Supervision: Kof-K.
Glatt kosher.

Abigael's on Broadway
1407 Broadway, at 39th Street 10016
(212) 575-1407
Fax: (212) 866-0666
Supervision: Kof-K.
Glatt kosher. Lunch Monday-Friday 12 pm-3 pm. Dinner Sunday-Thursday 5 pm-10 pm.

Cafe Classico
35 West 57th Street (212) 355-5411
Glatt kosher.

Colbeh
43 West 39 St, (Mid Town) (212) 354-8181

Deli Glatt
150 Fulton Street (212) 349-3622

Deli Kasbah
2553 Amsterdam Avenue
(212) 568-4600

Domani Ristorante
1590 First Ave., Bet. 82nd-83rd St.
(212) 717-7575/7557
Supervision: Organised Kashrut.

Estihana
221 W. 79 St. (212) 501-0393
Fax: (212) 501-0458
Web site: www.estihana.com
Japanese cuisine, Glatt kosher

Glatt Dynasty
1049 Second Avenue,
East 55th & East 56th Street 10022
(212) 888-9119
Fax: (212) 888-9163
Supervision: Kof-K.
Glatt kosher.

Haikara
1016 2nd Avenue 10022 (212) 355-7000
Supervision: OU.

Hapisgah Steakhouse
147-25 Union Turnpike,
Kew Gardens Hills (212) 380-4449

Il Patrizio
206 East 63rd St., Bet. 2nd and 3rd Aves
(212) 980-4007
Supervision: OU.

Jasmine
11 East 30 Street, between Madison and 5th Avenues
(212) 251-8884
Supervision: Vaad l'Kashrut Badatz Sepharadic.
Glatt kosher Persian and Middle Eastern cuisine. Open Sunday to Friday, for lunch and dinner.

Jerusalem Pita
212 E. 45th Street (212) 922-0009
Fax: (212) 922-0018
Under Rabbinical Supervision

Jewish Theological Seminary Dining Hall
3080 Broadway at 122nd Street 10027
(212) 678-8822
Open September through to July (closed August) for breakfast and lunch: 7.30am to 10.00am; 11.00am to 2.00pm. Strictly kosher, Shomer Shabbat.

Kasbah Restaurant
251 W. 85th Street (212) 496-1500
Fax: (212) 496-2273
Supervision: Circle K.
Hours: Sunday to Thursday, 12 pm to 11 pm. American and Mediterranean food.

Kosher Delight
1359 Broadway (37th Street) (212) 563-3366

Kosher Deluxe
10 W. 46th St, (Off 5th Avenue) (212) 869-6699

Le Marais
150 W. 46th Street 10036 (212) 869-0900
Fax: (212) 869-1016
Supervision: Circle K.
Glatt kosher. Hours: Sunday to Thursday, 12 pm to 12 am; Friday, to 3 pm; Saturday, October to May, one hour after sundown to 1 am.

Le Marais 2
15 John St @ B'way (212) 285-8585
Fax: (212) 791--3280
Supervision: Organised Kashrut.

Levana
141 West 69th Street 10023 (212) 877-8457
Fax: (212) 595-7522
Email: info@levana.com
Web site: www.levana.com
Supervision: Orthodox Union.
Glatt kosher.

Mendy's
Rockfeller Center, 30 Rockfeller Plaza
(212) 262-9600

Mendy's West
208 West 70th Street 10023 (212) 877-6787
Supervision: OU.

Mr Broadway
1372 Broadway, (Bet. 37 & 38 St) (212) 921-2152

Penguin
258 W. 15th St., Bet. 7-8 Ave. (212) 255-3601
Supervision: Vaad Hakashrus.

Pita Express
1470 2nd Avenue (77th Street) (212) 249-1300
Glatt kosher.

Shallots
550 Madison Avenue, New York 10022
(212) 833-7800
Email: shallotsny.com
In the Sony Plaza Atrium. Between 55th and 56th Sts.

Tuscan Grill
228 West 72nd Street, (Bet. Bway & West End)
(212) 875-9020

Wolf & Lamb Steakhouse
10 E. 48th St., Nr Rockerfeller Ctr.,
Between 5th & Madison 10017 (212) 317-1950
Fax: (212) 317-0159
Supervision: Organised kashrut.

Organic

Caravan of Dreams
405 East 6th Street, Bet. 1st Ave. & Ave. A
(212) 254-1613
Email: angel@caravanofdreams.net
Supervision: Orthodox Rabbinical Supervision.

Vegetarian

Maharani Restaurant
156 W. 29 St, (Bet. 6 & 7 Ave.)
(212) 868-0707/2211

Saffron (Indian Vegetarian Cuisine)
81 Lexington Avenue 10016 (212) 696-5130
Fax: (212) 696-5146

Theatre

Dramatics

Jewish Repertory Theatre
c/o Midtown YMHA, 344 E. 14th Street (212) 505-2667; 674-7200

Vineyard

Shapiro's Wine Company
124 Rivington Street (212) 475-7383
In business since 1899. Providing free tours on telephone call.

Queens

Butchers

Herskowitz Glatt Meat Market
164-08 69th Avenue, Hillcrest 11365
(718) 591-0750
Fax: (718) 591-0750
Supervision: Vaad Harabonim of Queens.

Delicatessens

Berso Foods
64-20 108th Street, Forest Hills 11375
(718) 275-9793
Supervision: Vaad Harabonim of Queens.
Take out only.

Meal Mart
72-10 Main Street, Flushing 11367 (718) 261-3300
Fax: (718) 261-3435
Supervision: Vaad Harabonim of Queens.
Catering and take-out.

Restaurants

Ben's Best Deli Restaurant
96-40 Queens Blvd, Rego Park 11374
(718) 897-1700
Fax: (718) 997-6503
Email: bensbest@worldnet.att.net

Knish-Knosh
101-2 Queens Blvd, Forest Hills 11375
(718) 897-5554

Dairy

Habustan Mediterranean Cuisine
188-2 Union Turnpike, Jamaica Estate

Meat

Cho-Sen Garden
64-43 108th Street, Forest Hills 11375
(718) 275-1300
Supervision: Vaad Harabonim of Queens.
Chinese food.

Colbeh
68-34 Main Street, Flushing (718) 268-8181
Supervision: Kof-K.

Dougie's
73-27 Main Street, Kew Gardens Hills
(718) 793-4600
Fax: (718) 793-9003
Supervision: Vaad Harabonim of Queens.

Glatt Kosher International Restaurant
JFK Airport, Terminal 4, 3rd floor (718) 751-4787
Email: erwin7@nyc.rr.com
Supervision: Vaad Harabanim of Queens.

Glatt Wok Express
190-11 Union Turnpike, Flushing 11366
(718) 740-1675
Supervision: Vaad Harabonim of Queens.
Chinese food. Take-away service available.

Pita House
98-102 Queens Blvd, Bet. 66-67th Ave.
(718) 897-4829
Supervision: Rabbi David Katz.

Pizzerias

Dan Carmel Ice Cream and Pizza
98 Queens Blvd, Forest Hills 11375 (718) 544-8530
Supervision: Vaad Harabonim of Queens.

Vegetarian

Budda Bodai
42-96 Main Street, Flushing (718) 939-1188
Supervision: Rabbi Mayer Steinberg.

Staten Island

Kashrut Information

Directories

Organised Kashrus Laboratories
PO Box 218, Brooklyn (718) 851-6428
Including the Circle K trademark.

"The Dining Guide of the Jewish Press"
(718) 330-1100
Providing information on where to get kosher Won-Ton soup, couscous, hot pastrami and corned (salt) beef sandwiches, gefilte fish, hummus, tehina etc.

UOJC
333 7th Avenue 10001 (212) 563-4000

Restaurants

Dairy

Joseph's Cafe
50 West 72 St (212) 721-1943

Newburgh

Kashrut Information

Agudas Israel
290 North Street 12550 (845) 562-5604
Fax: (845) 562-5622
Email: agudasisrael@aol.com

Museums

Gomez Mill House
Millhouse Road, Marlboro 12542 (845) 236-3126
Fax: (845) 236-3365
Email: gomezmillhouse@juno.com
Web site: www.gomez.org
Oldest Jewish residence now maintained as a museum.

Niagara Falls

Organisations

Jewish Federation of Niagara Falls
c/o of Beth Israel (716) 284-4575

Synagogues

Conservative

Beth Israel
College & Madison Avenues 14305 (716) 285-9894

Reform

Beth El
720 Ashland Avenue 14301 (716) 282-2717
Call for time of services.

Orangeburg

Synagogues

Conservative

Orangetown Jewish Center
Independence Avenue 10962

Peekskill

Synagogues

First Hebrew Congregation
1821 E. Main Street 10566 (914) 739-0500
Fax: (914) 739-0684

Port Chester

Restaurants

Vegetarian

Green Symphony
427 Boston Post Road 10573 (914) 937-6537

Synagogues

Conservative

Kneses Tifereth Israel
575 King Street 10573 (914) 939-1004
Fax: (914) 939-1086

Poughkeepsie

Organisations

Jewish Community Center of Dutchess County
110 Grand Avenue 12603 (914) 471-0430

Synagogues

Conservative

Temple Beth El
118 Grand Avenue 12603 (914) 454-0570
Fax: (914) 454-7257
Web site: www.uscj.org/empire/poughktb

Orthodox

Shomre Israel
18 Park Avenue 12603 (914) 454-2890

Reform

Vassar Temple
140 Hooker Avenue 12601 (914) 454-2570

Rochester

Bakeries

Brighton Donuts
Monroe Avenue (716) 271-6940

Delicatessens

Brownstein's Deli and Bakery
1862 Monroe Avenue 14618

Fox's Kosher Restaurant and Deli
3450 Winton Place 14623

Media

Newspapers

Jewish Ledger
2525 Brighton-Henrietta Town Line R 14623

Organisations

Jewish Community Federation
441 E. Avenue 14607 (716) 461-0490

Restaurants

Meat

Jewish Home of Rochester Cafeteria
2021 S. Winton Road 14618

Saratoga Springs

Synagogues

Conservative

Shaare Tfille
260 Broadway 12866 (518) 584-2370

Orthodox

Congregation Mikveh Israel
26 Lafayette Street 12866 (518) 584-6338
Services in July & August. Kosher food available.

Orthodox Minyan
510 1/2 Broadway 12866 (518) 437-1738; 584-3091

Reform

Temple Sinai
509 Broadway 12866 (518) 584-8730

Scarsdale

Synagogues

Magen David Sephardie Congregation
1225 Weaver Street, PO Box 129H 10583
(914) 633-3728
Fax: (914) 636-0608
Email: mitchser@aol.com

Orthodox

Young Israel of Scarsdale
1313 Weaver Street 10583 (914) 636-8686
Fax: (914) 636-1209

Schenectady

Synagogues

Conservative

Agudat Achim
2117 Union Street 12309 (518) 393-9211

Orthodox

Beth Israel
2195 Eastern Parkway 12309 (518) 377-3700

Reform

Gates of Heaven
852 Ashmore Avenue 12309 (518) 374-8173

Spring Valley

Delicatessens

GPG Deli
Main Street 10977

Home Hospitality

Mendel & Margalit Zuber
32 Blauvelt Road, Monsey 10952
(845) 425-6213
The Zuber's write "Anyone wishing to spend a Shabbat or Yom Tov with us is more than welcome. We are Lubavitch Chasidim, Glatt kosher."

Restaurants

Eli's Bagel Shop
58 N. Myrtle Avenue 10977 (845) 425-6166
Hours: Sunday - Thursday 6.30 am-5 pm. Friday 6.30 am-2 pm. Open Motzei Shabbos from after Succos until Pesach. Catering and Platters for all occasions. Under the Hashgocha of Rabbi B. Gruber/ Yoshen.

Mehadrin Restaurant
82 Route 59, Monsey 10952

Dairy

Sheli's Café and Pizza
126 Maple Avenue 10977 (914) 426-0105
Fax: (914) 362-5004
Email: shely@ucs.net
Supervision: Rabbi Breslaver.

Synagogues

Orthodox

Young Israel of Spring Valley
23 Union Road 10977 (914) 356-3363

Suffern

Synagogues

Bais Torah
89 West Carlton Road 10901 (914) 352-1343
Fax: (914) 352-0841
Email: yhaber@ou.org

Syracuse

Synagogues

Young Israel Shaarei Torah of Syracuse
4313 E. Genesee Street 13214 (315) 446-6194
Fax: (315) 446-7936

Troy

Mikvaot

Troy Chabad Center
2306 15th Street 12180 (518) 274-5572

Synagogues

Conservative

Temple Beth El
411 Hoosick Street 12180 (518) 272-6113

Reform

Congregation Berith Shalom
167 3rd Street 12180 (518) 272-8872
Fax: (518) 272-8984

Utica

Organisations

Jewish Community Federation of the Mohawk Valley
2310 Oneida Street, Utica, NY 13501
(315) 733-2343
Fax: (315) 733-2346
Email: jcci@borg.com

The Federation supports the Jewish Community Center.

Synagogues

Conservative

Temple Beth El
1607 Genesee Street 13501 (315) 724-4751

Orthodox

Congregation Zvi Jacob
112 Memorial Parkway 13501 (315) 724-8357

Reform

Temple Emanu-El
2710 Genesee Street 13502 (315) 724-4177

Vestal

Media

Newspapers

The Reporter
500 Clubhouse Road 13850 (607) 724-2360
Fax: (607) 724-2311
Email: treporter@aol.com

Organisations

Jewish Federation of Broome County
500 Clubhouse Road 13850 (607) 724-2332
Fax: (607) 724-2311

West Point

Synagogues

United States Military Academy Jewish Chapel
Building 750 10096 (914) 938-2766
Fax: (914) 446-7706

With a local community of over 200 the Chapel was designed by the firm responsible for the United Nations building and the Lincoln Center.

White Plains

Synagogues

Conservative

Temple Israel Center
280 Old Mamaroneck Road,
at Miles Avenue 10605 (914) 948-2800
Fax: (914) 948-4755

Orthodox

Hebrew Institute of White Plains
20 Greenridge Avenue 10605 (914) 948-3095
Fax: (914) 949-4676
Email: hebinst@idt.com

Young Israel of White Plains
135 Old Mamaroneck Road, NY 10605
(914) 683-YIWP
Email: yiwp.org
Web site: www.yiwp.org

Reconstructionist

Bet Am Shalom
295 Soundview Avenue 10606 (914) 946-8851

Reform

Jewish Community Center
252 Soundview Avenue 10606

Yonkers

Synagogues

Conservative

Agudas Achim
21 Hudson Street 10701

Lincoln Park Center
323 Central Park Avenue 10704 (914) 965-7119

Orthodox

Rosh Pinah
Riverdale Avenue 10705

Reform

Temple Emanu-El
306 Rumsey Road 10705 (914) 963-0575

North Carolina

Asheville

Synagogues

Conservative

Congregation Beth Israel
229 Murdock Avenue 28804 (828) 252-8431
Fax: (828) 252-3882
Email: bethisrael@buncombe.main.nc.us

Reform

Beth Ha-Tephila
43 N. Liberty Street 28801

Charlotte

Delicatessens

The Kosher Mart & Delicatessen
Amity Gardens Shopping Center,
3840 E. Independence Blvd 28205
(704) 563-8288
Fax: (704) 532-9111
Email: koshermartusa@mindspring.com
Web site: www.koshermartusa.com

Sandwiches and deli department are glatt kosher. Groceries also sold here. Hours: Monday to Wednesday, 10 am to 6 pm; Thursday, to 7 pm; Friday to 3 pm; Sunday, to 3.30 pm; Shabbat, closed.

Libraries

Speizman Jewish Library
5007 Providence Road 28226

Media

Newspapers

Charlotte Jewish News
(704) 366-5007

Mikvaot

Chabad House
6619 Sardis Road 28270 (704) 366-3984
Fax: (704) 362-1423

Organisations

Jewish Federation
5007 Providence Road 28226 (704) 366-5007

The Hebrew Academy & Social Services
5007 Providence Rd 28226

Synagogues

Conservative

Temple Israel
4901 Providence Road (704) 362-2796
Fax: (704) 362-1098
Email: templeisraelnc.org

Orthodox

Chabad House
6619 Sardis Road 28270 (704) 366-3984
Fax: (704) 362-1423
Email: sardis@earthlink.net

Reform

Temple Beth El
5101 Providence Road 28207 (704) 366-1948

Durham

Kashrut Information

Leon Dworsky
1100 Leon Street, Apt. 28 27705

Organisations

Durham-Chapel Hill Jewish Federation and Community Council
205 Mt. Bolus Road, Chapel Hill 27514
(919) 967-6916

Synagogues

Conservative

Beth El
1004 Watts Street 27701 (919) 682-1238

Reform

Judea Reform Congregation
1955 Cornwallis Road 27705 (919) 489-7062
Fax: (919) 489-0611
Email: infobox@judeareform.org

Fayetteville

Synagogues

Conservative

Beth Israel Congregation
2204 Morganton Road 28303 (910) 484-6462

Greensboro

Organisations

Greensboro Jewish Federation
5509 C West Friendly Avenue 27410-4211
(336) 852-5433
Fax: (336) 852-4346
Email: mfcgsonc@jon.cjfny.org

Synagogues

Conservative

Beth David
804 Winview Drive 27410 (336) 294-0006

Hendersonville

Synagogues

Agudas Israel Congregation
328 N. King Street, PO Box 668 28793

Raleigh

Groceries

Congregation of Sha'arei Israel
7400 Falls of the Neuse Road 27615 (919) 847-8986

Mikvaot

Congregation of Sha'arei Israel
7400 Falls of the Neuse Road 27615 (919) 847-8986

Organisations

Wake County Jewish Federation
3900 Merton Drive 27609 (919) 751-5459

Synagogues

Conservative

Beth Meyer
504 Newton Road 27615 (919) 848-1420

Orthodox

Congregation of Sha'arei Israel - Lubavitch
7400 Falls of the Neuse Road 27615 (919) 847-8986
Fax: (919) 847-3142

Reform

Temple Beth Or
5315 Creedmoor Road 27612 (919) 781-4895
Pre-school.

Wilmington

Synagogues

Conservative

Beth Jacob
1833 Academy Street 27101

Reform

Temple Emanuel
201 Oakwood Drive 27103 (919) 722-6640

North Dakota

Fargo

Synagogues

Orthodox

Fargo Hebrew Congregation
901 S. 9th Street 58103 (701) 237-5629

Reform

Temple Beth El
809 11th Avenue S. 58103 (701) 232-0441

Ohio

Akron

Mikvaot

(330) 867-6798

Organisations

Jewish Community Board of Akron
750 White Pond Drive 44320 (330) 869-2424
Fax: (330) 867-8498
Web site: www.jewishakron.org

Synagogues

Conservative

Beth El
464 S. Hawkins Avenue 44320 (330) 864-2105

Orthodox

Anshe Sfard Synagogue
646 N.Revere Road 44333 (330) 867-7292
Fax: (330) 867-7719

Reform

Temple Israel
133 Merriman Road 44303 (330) 762-8617
Fax: (330) 762-8619
Email: rabbi@neo.rr.com

Beachwood

Synagogues

Orthodox

Young Israel of Beachwood
2463 South Green Road 44122 (216) 691-9007

Blue Ash

Restaurants

Bakeries

Breadsmith
9708 Kenwood Road 45242 (513) 791-8817

Dairy

Marx Hot Bagels
9701 Kenwood Road 45242 (513) 891-5542
Fax: (513) 891-1063

Canton

Organisations

Jewish Community Federation
2631 Harvard Avenue 44709 (216) 452-6444

Synagogues

Conservative

Shaaray Torah
423 30th Street N.W. 44709 (216) 492-0310

Orthodox

Agudas Achim
2508 Market Street N. 44704 (216) 456-8781

Reform

Temple Israel
333 25th Street N.W. 44709 (216) 455-5197

Cincinnati

Bakeries

Just Desserts
6964 Plainfield Road 45236 (513) 793-6627

Delicatessens

Bilkers
7648 Reading Road 45237

Groceries

Pilder's Kosher Foods
7601 Reading Road 45237

Libraries

The Hebrew Union College-Jewish Institute of Religion
3101 Clifton Avenue 45220 (513) 221-1875
Fax: (513) 221-0519
Email: klau@cn.huc.edu

One of the largest Jewish libraries in the world. It is also has an art gallery of artefacts, and houses a collection Jewish 'objets d'art' and religious and ceremonial appurtenances as well as rare books and manuscripts.

Media

Newspapers

American Israelite
906 Main Street 45202
Oldest Anglo-Jewish weekly in the US.

Mikvaot

Kehelath B'nai Israel
1546 Beaverton Avenue 45237 (513) 761-5260

Organisations

Community Center
1580 Summit Road 45237 (513) 761-7500
Fax: (513) 761-0084

Jewish Federation
1811 Losantiville, Suite 320 45237 (513) 351-3800

Restaurants

Dairy

Dunkin' Donuts
9385 Colerain Avenue 45231 (513) 385-0930

Meat

Pilder's Deli
4070 East Galbraith Road 45236 (513) 792-9961
Fax: (513) 792-9605

Synagogues

Conservative

Northern Hills Synagogue - Congregation B'nai Avraham
715 Fleming Road 45231 (513) 931-6038
Fax: (513) 931-6147
Email: berniceu@fuse.net
Web site: www.uscj.org/ohio/glr/cincincb/index.htm

Orthodox

Downtown Synagogue
Bartlett Building, 36 E. Fourth, 7th Floor 45202
(513) 241-3576

Golf Manor Synagogue
6442 Stover Avenue 45237 (513) 531-6654

Sephardic Beth Shalom
Manss Avenue, PO Box 37431 45222
(513) 793-6936

Reform

Isaac M. Wise Temple
8329 Ridge Road 45236 (513) 793-2556

Cleveland

Butcher

Tibor's Glatt Meat Market
2185 S. Green Road, S. Euclid 44121
(216) 381-7615
Fax: (216) 381-5215

Delicatessen

Unger's Kosher Market and Bakery
1831 S. Taylor Road, Cleveland Heights 44118
(216) 321-7176
Fax: (216) 321-0777

Libraries

The Temple Museum of Religious Art Library.
University Circle, Silver Park 44106
Houses the Abba Hillel Silver Archives. (Jewish art objects, religious & ceremonial treasures, rare books and manuscripts.)

Media

Newspapers

Cleveland Jewish News
3645 Warrensville Center Road, Suite 230 44122

Mikvaot

Cleveland Heights (216) 387-1040

Charlotte Goldberg Community Mkvah of the Park Synagogue
3300 Mayfield Road, Cleveland Heights 44118
(216) 371-2244 ext 198
Fax: (216) 321-0639

K'hal Yereim Synagogue
1771 S. Taylor Road, Cleveland Heights 44118
(216) 321-5855

Museums

Park Synagogue
3300 Mayfield Road 44118
Holding a collection of Jewish art and sculpture.

Organisations

Jewish Community Federation of Cleveland
1750 Euclid Avenue 44115 (216) 566-9200
Fax: (216) 861-1230
Email: info@jcfcleve.org
Web site: www.jewishcleveland.org

With literally dozens of synagogues of each demonination, it is advisable to contact the local religious organisation for specific details.

Restaurants

Dairy

Issi's Place
14100 Cedar Road, Waterstone Medical Bldg., University Heights 44121 (216) 291-4251

Meat

Abba's Market and Grille
13937 Cedar Road, S. Euclid 44121
(216) 321-5660
Fax: (216) 321-4135

Contempo Cuisine
13898 Cedar Road, University Heights 44118
(216) 397-3520
Fax: (216) 397-3523

Empire Kosher Kitchen
2234 Warrensville Center Road (216) 691-0006

Ruchama's Singapore
2172 Warrensville Center Road
University Heights 44118 (216) 321-1100
Fax: (216) 321-1485

Synagogues

Orthodox

K'hai Yereim
1771 S. Taylor Road, Cleveland Heights 44118
(216) 321-6855

Shomrei Shaabboth
1801 S. Taylor Road, Cleveland Heights 44118
(216) 832-2109

Columbus

Restaurants

Dairy

Sammy's New York Bagels
40 N. James Road 43213 (614) 237-2444
Fax: (614) 235-4177
Supervision: Vaad Ho-ir of Columbus.
Deli as well.

Synagogues

Orthodox

Agudas Achim Synagogue
2767 E. Broad Street 43209 (614) 237-2747

Congregation Ahavas Sholom
2568 E. Broad Street 43209 (614) 252-4815
Fax: (614) 252-1316
Email: ahavas@beol.net
Web site: www.ahavas-sholom.org
Nusach sefard; daily and Shabbat minyan.

Dayton

Accommodation Information

Home Hospitality

Shomrei Emunah
1706 Salem Avenue 45406 (937) 274-6941
Fax: (937) 274-7511
Email: shomrei@earthlink.net
Please contact to arrange for accommodations.

Bakeries

Rinaldo's Bakery
910 West Fairview Avenue 45406
(513) 274-1311
Supervision:Rabbi Hillel Fox, Beth Jacob Congregation.
Certain products only, please ask for certificate.

Media

Newspapers

Dayton Jewish Observer
4501 Denlinger Road 45426 (937) 854-4150
Fax: (937) 854-2850
Email: dayjobs@aol.com

The Dayton Jewish Advocate
(937) 854-4150 ext. 118
Published by the Jewish Federation of Greater Dayton by Marshall Weiss, editor.

Mikvaot

556 Kenwood Avenue 45406

Organisations

Jewish Federation of Greater Dayton
4501 Denlinger Road 45426 (937) 854-4150

Kollel

Dayton Community Kollel
1706 Salem Avenue 45406 (937) 274-6941
Email: KollelDayton@Juno.com
The Kollel offers classes in a variety of Judaic topics in addition to schedule of Torah study. Visitors are warmly welcomed. Please call for details. There are no kosher restaurants, hotels or butchers in Dayton or in the area. However, the Kollel families will offer kosher hospitality.

Synagogues

Orthodox

7020 North Main Street 45415 (937) 274-2149
Fax: (937) 274-9556
Email: bethjacob1@aol.com
Web site: www.bethjacobcong.org
Supervision: Rabbi Hillel Fox, Beth Jacob Congregation.
Shomrei Emunah/Young Israel of Dayton
1706 Salem Avenue 45406 (937) 274-6941
Fax: (937) 274-6941
Rabbi's study: (937)-277-4626. Shachris daily: 6.45 am. Sundays and National holidays 8.30 am. Shabbos and Yom Tov 9.15 am. Mincha and Maariv at sunset, call for details.

Traditional

Beth Jacob Synagogue
Supervision:Rabbi Hillel Fox, Beth Jacob Congregation.. Runs a kosher restaurant approximately every sixth Sunday.

Lorain

Synagogues

Conservative

Agudath B'nai Israel
1715 Meister Road 44053 (216) 282-3307

Toledo

Synagogues

B'nai Israel
2727 Kenwood Blvd. 43606 (419) 531-1677

Orthodox

Congregation Etz Chayim
3852 Woodley Road 43606 (419) 473-2401

Reform

The Temple-Congregation Shomer Emunium
6453 Sylvania Avenue 43560 (419) 883-3341

Youngstown

Mikvaot

Children of Israel
3970 1/2 Logan Way 44505 (330) 759-2167

Organisations

Youngstown Area Jewish Federation
505 Gypsy Lane 44501 (216) 746-3251

Synagogues

Conservative

Beth Israel Temple Center
2138 E. Market Street, Warren 44483-6104
(330) 395-3877
Fax: (330) 394-5918
Email: bethisrael1@juno.com
Ohev Tzedek-Shaarei Torah
5245 Glenwood Avenue 44512 (216) 758-2321
Temple El Emeth
3970 Logan Way 44505 (216) 759-1429

Reform

Rodef Sholom
Elm Street & Woodbine Avenue 44505

Oklahoma

Oklahoma City

Bakeries

Ingrid's Kitchen
2309 N.W. 36th Street 73112

Kashrut Information

Chabad House
6401 Lenox Avenue 73116 (405) 810-1770
Fax: (405) 810-1772

Organisations

Jewish Federation of Greater Oklahoma City
3022 N.W. Expressway, Suite 116 73112
(405) 949-0111

Synagogues

Conservative

Emanuel Synagogue
900 N.W. 47th Street 73106 (405) 528-2113

Reform

Temple B'nai Israel
4901 N. Pennsylvania Avenue 73112 (405) 848-0965

Tulsa

Kashrut Information

Chabad House
6622 S. Utica Avenue 74136
(918) 492-4499; 493-7006
Fax: (918) 492-4499
Hospitality for travellers. Services: Shabbat and Sunday 9:00 am and by arrangement (Kaddish, Yarziet, etc.).

Media

Newspapers

Tulsa Jewish Review
2021 E. 71st Street 74136 (918) 495-1100

Mikvaot

Congregation B'nai Emunah
1719 S. Owasso 74120 (916) 583-7121
Fax: (916) 747-9696
Email: thesynagogue@bnaiemunah.com
Open 8 am to 6 pm daily.

Mikva Shoshana - Chabad
6622 So. Utica Avenue 74136 (918) 493-7006
Ask for Etel Weg

Museums

The Gershon & Rebecca Fenster Museum of Jewish Art
Box 52188 74152 (918) 294-1366
Email: fenstermuseum@ibm.net
Only Jewish museum in the South-West.

Organisations

Jewish Federation
2021 E. 71st Street 74136 (918) 495-1100
Fax: (918) 495-1220
Email: federation@jewishtulsa.org

Restaurants

Congregation B'nai Emunah
1719 S. Owasso 74120 (916) 583-7121
Fax: (916) 747-9696
Email: thesynagogue@bnaiemunah.com
Open 8 am to 6 pm daily.

Synagogues

Chabad House
6622 S Utica Avenue 74136
(918) 492-4499; 493-7006
Fax: (918) 492-4499
Services: Shabbat and Sunday 9 am and by arrangement (Kaddish, Yarziet, etc).

Conservative

Congregation B'nai Emunah
1719 S. Owasso 74120 (918) 583-7121
Fax: (918) 747-9696
Email: thesynagogue@bnaiemunah.com

Orthodox

Beth Torah - Chabad
6622 So. Utica Avenue 74136 (918) 496-4555

Reform

Temple Israel
2004 E. 22nd Place 74114 (918) 747-1309
Fax: (918) 747-3564
Email: templeis@ionet.net

Oregon

Ashland

Synagogues

Temple Emek Shalom-Rogue Valley Jewish Community
1081 East Main St (541) 488-2909
Fax: (541) 488-2814
Email: teshalom@mind.net
Web site: www.mind.net/TESweb
Office hours 10 am-3 pm Tuesday-Friday Mailing address: PO Box 1107, Ashland, Oregon 97520. Call for schedule of services.

Eugene

Synagogues

Conservative

Temple Beth Israel
42 W. 25th Avenue 97405 (541) 485-7218

Portland

Groceries

Albertson's
5415 SW Beaverton Hillsdale Highway 97221
(503) 246-1713

Mikvaot

Ritualarium
1425 S.W. Harrison Street 97219 (503) 224-3409

Organisations

Jewish Federation of Portland
6680 S.W. Capitol Highway 97219 (503) 245-6219
Fax: (503) 245-6603
Email: federation@jewishportland.org
Web site: www.jewishportland.org

Restaurants

Mittleman Jewish Community Center (Kosher restaurant)
6651 S. W. Capitol Highway 97219 (503) 244-0111

Synagogues

Orthodox

Ahavath Achim
3225 S.W. Barbur Blvd 97201 (503) 775-5895

Kesser Israel
136 S.W. Meade Street 97201 (503) 222-1239

Shaare Torah
920 N.W. 25th Avenue 97209 (503) 226-6131

Reform

Neveh Shalom Synagogue
2900 SW Peaceful Lane 97201 (503) 246-8831
Fax: (503) 246-7553
Web site: www.nevehshalom.org

Temple Beth Israel
1972 NW Flanders 97209 (503) 222-1069

Salem

Synagogues

Reconstructionist

Beth Shalom
1795 Broadway NE 97303 (503) 362-5004

Pennsylvania

Allentown

Mikvaot

1834 Whitehall Street 18104 (610) 776-7948

Organisations

Jewish Federation
702 22nd Street 18104 (610) 821-5500

Restaurants

Meat

Glatt Kosher Community Center
702 N. 22nd Street 18104 (610) 435-3571
Since opening hours vary according to season, it is advisable to call before visiting.

Synagogues

Conservative

Temple Beth El
1702 Hamilton St 18104 (610) 435-3521

Orthodox

Congregation Sons of Israel
2715 Tilghman St 18104 (610) 433-6089

Bala Cynwyd

Synagogues

Orthodox

Young Israel of the Main Line
PO Box 117 19004 (215) 667-3255

Bethlehem

Synagogues

Conservative

Congregation Brith Sholom
Macada & Jacksonville Roads 18017 (215) 866-8009

Orthodox

Agudath Achim
1555 Linwood Street 18017 (610) 866-8891
Contact person: Gerald Wekberger. 1-610-838-0767.

Blue Bell

Synagogues

Conservative

Tiferet Bet Israel
1920 Skippack Pike 19422 (610) 275-8797

Easton

Synagogues

B'nai Abraham
16th & Bushkill Streets 18042 (610) 258-5343
Established 1888.

Reform

Temple Covenant of Peace
1451 Northampton Street 18042 (610) 253-2031
Fax: (610) 253-7973
Email: tcp@ fast.net

Established 1839.

Elkins Park

Synagogues

Orthodox

Young Israel of Elkins Park
7715 Montgomery Avenue 19027 (215) 635-3152
Web site: www.philly-direct.com/frum/brisman.html

Erie

Organisations

Jewish Community Council
Suite 405, Professional Building,
161 Peach St., 16501 (814) 455-4474
Fax: (814) 455-4475

Synagogues

Conservative

Brith Sholom Jewish Center
3207 State Street 16508 (814) 454-2431
Fax: (814) 452-0790

Reform

Temple Anshe Hesed
930 Liberty Street 16502 (814) 454-2426
Fax: (814) 454-2427
Email: anshhsd@velocity.net

Harrisburg

Caterer

Norman Gras Catering
3000 Green Street 17110-1234 (717) 234-2196
Fax: (717) 234-3943
Email: normangras@aol.com

Glatt kosher. Offers catering for groups. Stocks kosher vending machines at the JCC, 3301 N Front St. Tel: 717-236-9555 ext. 3105.

Groceries

Bakeries Giant Food Store and Weis Market
Linglestown Road

Quality Kosher
7th Division Street 17110

Organisations

United Jewish Community of Greater Harrisburg
100 Vaughn Street 17110 (717) 236-9555

Synagogues

Conservative

Beth El
2637 N. Front Street 17110 (717) 232-0556
Fax: (717) 232-6240

Chisuk Emuna
5th & Division Streets 17110 (717) 232-4851
Fax: (717) 232-7950
Email: muroff@juno.com

Orthodox

Kesher Israel
2945 N. Front Street 17110 (717) 238-0763

Reform

Ohev Sholom
2345 N. Front Street 17110 (717) 233-6459
Fax: (717) 236-7844

Hazleton

Synagogues

Conservative

Agudas Israel
77 N. Pine Street 18201 (717) 455-2851

Reform

Beth Israel
98 N. Church Street 18201 (717) 455-3971

Hershey

Snack Bar

Meat

Central PA's Kosher Mart
Hershey Park (717) 534-3119

Johnstown

Organisations

United Jewish Federation of Johnstown
700 Indiana Street 15905 (814) 536-0647

Synagogues

Conservative

Beth Sholom Congregation
700 Indiana Street 15905 (814) 536-0647

Lancaster

Organisations

Jewish Federation
2120 Oregon Pike 17601 (717) 597-7354

Synagogues

Jewish Community Center
2120 Oregon Pike 17601

Conservative

Beth El
25 N. Lime Street 17602 (717) 392-1379

Orthodox

Degel Israel
1120 Columbia Avenue 17603 (717) 397-0183
Fax: (717) 509-6188

Reform

Temple Shaarei Shomayim
N. Duke & James Streets 17602 (717) 397-5575

Levittown

Synagogues

Conservative

Congregation Beth El
21 Penn Valley Road, Fallsington 19054
(215) 945-9500

Reform

Temple Shalom
Edgley Road, off Mill Creek Pkwy. 19057
(215) 945-4154

McKeesport

Synagogues

Conservative

Tree of Life-Sfard
Cypress Avenue 15131 (412) 673-0938

Orthodox

Gemilas Chesed
1400 Summit Street, White Oak 15131
(412) 678-9859

Reform

B'nai Israel
536 Shaw Avenue 15132 (412) 678-6181
Fax: (412) 678-6908
Email: tbi536@juno.com or tbi536@aol.com

Melrose Park

Libraries

Tuttleman Library
Gratz College, Mandell Education Campus
7605 Old York Road 19027
(215) 635-7300 ext. 169
Fax: (215) 635-7320
Email: libraryinfo@gratz.edu
Specialised library of Judaic and Hebraic studies. Multilingual collection of approximately 100,000 books, periodicals, music and audio-visual materials. Special collections include a rare book room, a music library, and a Holocaust oral history archive. Open to the public.

Philadelphia

Bakeries

Arthur's Bakery
Academy Plaza,
Red Lion and Academy Roads 19114
(215) 637-9146
Supervision: Rabbinical Assembly.

Best Cake Bakery
7594 Haverford Avenue 19151 (215) 878-1127
Email: rugalah@aol.com
Supervision: Orthodox Vaad of Philadelphia.
Closed Shabbat and holidays. Intersection Route 1 and Haverford Avenue (close to Route 3).

Buy the Dozen
219 Haverford Avenue, Narberth 19072
(610) 667-9440
Supervision: Orthodox Vaad of Philadelphia.
Wholesale croissant bakery open to the public.

Dante's Bakery
Richboro Centre, Bustleton and Second Street Pikes, Richboro 18954 (215) 357-9599
Supervision: Rabbinical Assembly.

Hesh's Eclair Bake Shoppe
7721 Castor Avenue 19152 (215) 742-8575
Supervision: Vaad Hakashruth.
Closed on Shabbat.

Hutchinson's Classic Bakery
13023 Bustleton Pike 19116 (215) 676-8612
Supervision: Rabbinical Assembly.

Kaplan's New Model Bakery
901 North 3rd Street 19123 (215) 627-5288
Supervision: Rabbi Solomon Isaacson.

Lipkin and Sons Bakery
8013 Castor Avenue 19152 (215) 342-3005
Supervision: Rabbi Abraham Novitsky.

Michael's
6635 Castor Avenue 19149 (215) 745-1423
Supervision: Rabbi Dov Brisman.

Moish's Addison Bakery
10865 Bustleton Avenue 19116 (215) 469-8054
Supervision: Rabbinical Assembly.

Rilling's Bakery
2990 Southampton Road 19154 (215) 698-6171
Supervision: Rabbinical Assembly.

The Village Baker
2801 South Eagle Road
Newton 18940 (215) 579-1235
Supervision: Rabbinical Assembly.

Viking Bakery
39 Cricket Avenue, Ardmore 19003 (215) 642-9227
Supervision: Rabbi Joshua Toledano.

Weiss Bakery
6635 Castor Avenue 19149 (215) 722-4506
Supervision: Rabbi Dov Brisman.
Closed on Shabbat.

Zach's Bakery
6419 Rising Sun Avenue 19111 (215) 722-1688
Supervision: Rabbinical Assembly.

Booksellers

Gratz College
Old York Road and Melrose Avenue,
Melrose Park 19027 (215) 635-7300
Fax: (215) 635-7320
Email: gratzinfo@aol.com

Jerusalem Israeli Gift Shop
7818 Castor Avenue 19152 (215) 342-1452

Rosenberg Hebrew Book Store
6408 Castor Avenue 19149

Rosenberg Hebrew Book Store
409 Old York Road, Jenkintown 19046
(215) 884-1728; 800-301-8608
Fax: (215) 884-6648

Butchers

Aries Kosher Meats
6530 Castor Avenue 19149 (215) 533-3222
Supervision: Vaad Hakashruth.

Best Value Kosher Meat Center
8564 Bustleton Avenue 19152 (215) 342-1902
Fax: (215) 342-5775
Supervision: Rabbi Dov Brisman.

Bustleton Kosher Meat Market
6834 Bustlton Avenue 19149 (215) 332-0100
Supervision: Rabbi Shalom Novoseller.

Glendale Meats
7730 Bustleton Avenue 19152 (215) 725-4100
Supervision: Vaad Hakashruth.

Main Line Kosher Meats
75621 Haverford Avenue 19151 (215) 877-3222
Supervision: Vaad Hakashruth.

Simons Kosher Meats and Poultry
6926 Bustleton Avenue 19149 (215) 624-5695
Supervision: Vaad Hakashruth.

Wallace's Krewstown Kosher Meat Market
8919 Krewstown Road 19115 (215) 464-7800
Supervision: Vaad Hakashruth.

Contact Information

Jewish Information and Referral Service
2100 Arch Street, 7th Floor 19103 (215) 832-0821
Fax: (215) 832-0833
Email: lyouman@philafederation.org
A free confidential service that provides answers to questions about Jewish organisations, institutions, community services and various subjects of Jewish interest in the five-county Greater Philadelphia area. JIRS is the connection to the Jewish community. It is open to callers during regular working hours.

Embassy

Consul General of Israel
230 South 15th Street 19102 (215) 546-5556
Fax: (215) 545-3986
Email: info.ph@israelfm.org
Web site: www.israelemb.org/pa

Groceries

Best Value Losher Meat Center
8564 Bustleton Avenue 19152 (215) 342-1902
Supervision: Rabbi Dov Brisman.

Milk and Honey
7618 Castor Avenue 19152 (215) 342-3224
Supervision: Vaad Hakashruth.

Judaica

Bala Judaica Center
222 Bala Avenue, Bala Cynwyd 19004
(610) 664-1303
Fax: (610) 664-4319
Email: jewishwedding@erols.com

Kashrut Information

Board of Rabbis of Greater Philadelphia
2100 Arch Street - 3rd Floor 19103 (215) 832-0675
Fax: (215) 832-0689
Email: info@brdavphila.com

Ko Kosher Service
5871 Drexel Road 19131 (610) 696 0408
Fax: (610) 696-9249
Email: ko_kosher_service@msm.com
Web site: www.ko-kosher-service.org

Orthodox Vaad of Philadelphia
7505 Brookhaven Road 19151 (215) 473-0951
Fax: (215) 473-6220
Rabbi Shlomo Caplan (610) 658-1967 Rabbi Aaron Felder (215) 745-2968 Rabbi Yehoshua Kaganoff (215) 742-8421

Rabbinical Assembly
United Synagogue of Conservative, Judaism,
1510 Chestnut Street 19102 (215) 563-8814

Rabbinical Council of Greater Philadelphia
44 North 4th Street, Philadelphia 19106
(215) 922-5446
Fax: (215) 922-1550
Supervision: (O).

Vaad Hakashruth and Beth Din of Philadelphia
1147 Gilham Street, Philadelphia 19111
(215) 725-5181
Fax: (215) 725-5182
Supervision: (O).

Landmarks

Beth Sholom Congregation
8231 Old York Road, Elkins Park 19027
(215) 887-1342
Fax: (215) 887-6605
Web site: www.bethsholomcongregation.org
Conservative synagogue whose building is the only synagogue ever designed by renowned architect Frank Lloyd Wright.

Congregation Beth T'fillah of Overbrook Park
7630 Woodbine Avenue 19151 (215) 477-2415
Fax: (215) 477-2417
Conservative synagogue with a ten-foot high replica of the Western Wall in its lobby.

Mikveh Israel Cemetery
8th and Spruce Streets 19107 (215) 922-5446
One of the oldest Jewish cemeteries in the United States, with graves dating from 1740. Interred here are Haym Solomon, Rebecca Gratz, and twenty-one veterans of the American Revolution.

Monument to the Six Million Jewish Martyrs
16th Street and the Benjamin, Franklin Parkway 19103
This memorial sculpture was the first public Holocaust monument in the United States.

The Frank Synagogue
Albert Einstein Medical Center,
Old York and Tabor Roads 19141 (215) 456-7890
Modelled after first- and second-century synagogues discovered in the Galilee region of north central Israel, this small, historically certified synagogue was originally dedicated in 1901

Libraries

Philadelphia Jewish Archives Center
Balch Institute for Ethnic Studies,
18 South 7th Street 19106 (215) 925-8090
Jewish community archives containing records of agencies synagogues and community organisations personal and family papers autobiographies and memoirs and a photograph collection Open to the public.

Reconstructionist Rabbinical College Library
Church Road and Greenwood Avenue,
Wyncote 19095 (215) 576-0800
The Kaplan Library serves rabbinical students and the general public 33,000 books and periodicals in English, Hebrew, and other languages The Kaplan Archives house documents of the Reconstructionist movement.

Talmudical Yeshivah Library
6063 Dexel Road 19131 (215) 477-1000
Library of Sefarim (Hebrew books on the Bible the Talmud Responsa etc.) among the finest of its kind in the city. Open for in-library work to the general public by appointment.

Temple University
Paley Library, 13th Street and Berks Mall 19122
(215) 787-8231
Large collection of Judaica Hebraica and Talmudic studies and literature in Hebrew and in translation. Main stacks are open Borrowing can be arranged through inter-library loan

The Free Library of Philadelphia
Central Library, Logan Square 19103 (215) 686-5392
Fax: (215) 563-3628
Web site: www.library.phila.gov
3,000-volume Moses Marx Collection of Judaica and Hebraica in the Central Library, covers history liturgy, printing and bibliography with some books on philosophy, religion, the Bible, the Talmud, and Passover haggadahs. Open to the public. Russian-language collection available at the Northeast Regional Library.

University of Pennsylvania
Van Pelt Library, 3420 Walnut Street 19104
(215) 898-7556
Large collection of biblical studies rabbinics Jewish history and medieval and modern Hebrew language and literature. Stacks and seminar rooms open to the public.

Media

Magazines

Inside Magazine
Jewish Publishing Group, 2100 Arch Street 19103
(215) 893-5797
Fax: (215) 546-3957
Email: rleiter@jewishexponent.com
Quarterly magazine of Jewish life and style. Sold at news-stands and sent to all "Jewish Exponent and Jewish Times" subscribers.

Jewish Quarterly Review
420 Walnut Street 19106 (215) 238-1290
Email: jqroffice@sas.upenn.edu
Scholarly journal of the Annenberg Research Institute published four times a year.

Shofar Magazine
PO Box 51591 19115 (215) 676-8304
Russian-language monthly magazine.

Newspapers

Jewish Exponent
Jewish Publishing Group, 2100 Arch Street, Philadelphia 19103 (215) 832-0700
Fax: (215) 832-0786
Email: dalpher@jewishexponent.com
Weekly newspaper covering world news of Jewish interest and detailed information on local activities including Jewish Federation of Greater Philadelphia meetings and events. Special sections include community and health calendars singles and campus activities a Russian-language column and synagogue activities.

Jewish Post
PO Box 442, Yardley 19067 (215) 321-3443
Monthly newspaper serving Bucks County Pa and Mercer County N.J.

Jewish Times
Jewish Publishing Group, 103A Tomlinson Road, Huntingdon Valley 19006 (215) 938-1177
Weekly newspaper covering issues and programmes of interest to area Jewish residents of the greater Northeast and Bucks County including Jewish Federation of Greater Philadelphia meetings and events. Special sections include synagogue senior adult singles and campus activities.

Mir
PO Box 6162, Philadelphia 19115 (215) 934-5512
Local weekly Russian-language newspaper.

Radio

Meridian (609) 962-8000
Russian-language program Saturdays 10 to 10.30 am

Radio & TV

Barry Reisman Show
(609) 365-5600
WSSJ (1310AM) Jewish music in Yiddish and Hebrew, and English and Jewish news. Mondays through Fridays 3.30 to 5.30 pm Sundays 9.30 am to 1 pm.

Bucks County Jewish Life
(215) 949-1490
WBCB (1490AM) Rabbi Allan Tuffs hosts this weekly Sunday morning radio program at 10 am

Comcast Cablevision of Philadelphia
4400 Wayne Avenue 19140 (215) 673-6600
Channel 66 (Cable Television) Half-hour programme on Jewish culture shown twice a week in the evening usually midweek and Sundays. See local listings for exact time.

Dialogue (215) 878-9700
WPVI - TV (channel 6) Discussion Program on religious issues sponsored by Delaware Valley Media Ministry. Sundays 6.30 to 7.30 am.

Keneseth Israel Sabbath Services
(215) 581-2100
Hour of Jewish worship for shut-ins the elderly and people unable to attend Sabbath services Saturdays 11am to noon.

Pulse
WSSJ, Camden (609) 365-5600
WSSJ (1310AM) Russian-language news and music program Sundays 9.30 to 10.30 am.

Mikvaot

Mikveh Association of Philadelphia (Ardmore)
Torah Academy, Wynnewood and Argyle Roads, Ardmore 19003 (610) 642-8679

Mikveh association of Philadelphia (Northern)
7525 Loretto Avenue, Philadelphia 19111
(215) 745-3334

Museums

Balch Institute for Ethnic Studies
18 South 7th Street 19106 (215) 925-8090
Documents and interprets American multi-culturalism Research library has a Yiddish collection. Houses the Jewish Archives Center.

Borowsky Gallery
Jewish Community Centers of Greater, Philadelphia, 401 South Broad Street 19147 (215) 545-4400
Continuing exhibits of special interest to the Jewish community.

Fred Wolf Jr Gallery
Jewish Community Centers of Greater, Philadelphia, 10100 Jamison Avenue 19116 (215) 698-7300
Continuing exhibits of special interest to the Jewish community.

Holocaust Awareness Museum
Gratz College, Mandell Education Campus, 7601 Old York Road, Melrose Park 19027
(215) 635-6480
Previously known as the Jewish Identity Center the Holocaust Awareness Museum contains donations form Holocaust survivors and concentration camp liberators. The collection documents and teaches the facts of genocide and dangers of ethnic hatred and bigotry.

National Museum of American Jewish History
55 North 5th Street, Independence Mall East 19106-2197 (215) 923-3811
Fax: (215) 923-0763
Email: nmajh@nmajh.org
Web site: www.nmajh.org
Presents programmes and experiences that preserve, explore and celebrate the history of Jews in America. Award-winning gift shop.

Philadelphia Congregation Rodeph Shalom
615 North Broad Street 19123 (215) 627-6747
Nationally recognised for exhibits of contemporary Jewish art and history. Permanent collection of twentieth-century Jewish art and photographs.

Rosenbach Museum & Library
2010 Delancey Place 19103 (215) 732-1600
Fax: (215) 545-7529
Email: info@rosenbach.org
The collection includes the first Haggadah printed in America and letters, portraits and furniture of the Gratz family of Philadelphia. Access to books is by appointment only. Also home to the earliest printing of the Pentateuch in Hebrew of which complete copies are known.

Temple Judea Museum of Keneseth Israel
8339 Old York Road, Elkins Park, PA 19027
(215) 887-2027; 887-8700
Fax: (215) 887-1070
Email: tjmuseum@aol.com
This synagogue museum has four changing exhibitions of Judaica and Jewish art each year.

Organisations

Annenberg Research Institute
420 Walnut Street 19106 (215) 238-1290
Approximately 180,000 books and thousands of periodicals with emphasis on Judaic and Near Eastern studies. Rare book collection archives of American Judaica particularly that of Philadelphia.

Restaurants

Holyland Pizza
8010 Castor Avenue (215) 725-7444

Irv's Place
(Kosher Dining at Univ. of Pennsylvania),
4051 Irving Street 19104 (215) 573-7596
Hours of operation are for lunch and dinner during the school year.

Dairy

Cherry Street Chinese vegetarian
1010 Cherry Street 19107 (215) 923-3663
Supervision: Rabbinical Assembly.

Shalom Pizza
7598a Haverford Avenue (215) 878-1500
Email: shalom2u@rcn.com
Supervision: Orthodox Vaad of Philadelphia.
Vegetarian, Middle-Eastern. Open 11 am to 9 pm daily. Friday closed at 4 pm (winter at 2 pm). Closed Shabbat. Cholov Israel and Pas Israel.

Meat

Sim's Place
300 Levering Mill Road, Bela Cynwyd (215) 949-9420

Synagogues

With dozens of synagogues of the various demoninations in the area, travellers are advised to contact a local religious organisation for specific details.

Congregation Mikveh Israel
44 North 4th Street 19106 (215) 922-5446
Fax: (215) 922-1550
Web site: www.mikvehisrael.org
Spanish-Portuguese synagogue founded in 1740. Located on Independence Mall. Entrance is shared with the National Museum of American Jewish History. All Shabbat and holiday and Monday and Thursday services are still conducted using historic artifacts and tradition.

Orthodox

Congregation Rodeph
615 North Broad Street (215) 627-6747
The congregation is the oldest Ashkenazi one in the United States having been founded in 1795.

Young Israel of Oxford Circle
6427 Large Street 19149 (215) 725-7087

Theatre

Theatre Ariel/Habima Ariel
PO Box 0334, Merion Station 19066 (215) 567-0670
Theatre productions, readings workshops mini-performances and speakers all dedicated to exploring the Jewish theatrical experience.

Tours of Jewish Interest

American Jewish Committee Historic Tour
117 South Seventeenth Street, Suite 1010
(215) 665-2300
Fax: (215) 665-8737
Tours, run by Simmi Hurwitz, may be arranged to suit personal or group interests or needs.

Pittsburgh

Bakeries

Pastries Unlimited
4743 Liberty Avenue

Pastries Unlimited
2119 Murray Avenue 15217 (412) 521-6323

Books and Judaica

Pinskers Judaica Center
2028 Murray Avenue 15217
(412) 421-3033;1- 800-JUDAISM (1-800-583-2476)
Fax: (412) 421-6103
Email: info@judaism.com
Web site: www.judaism.com

Groceries

Brauner's Emporium
2023 Murray Avenue 15217

Koshermart
2121 Murray Avenue 15217

Media

Newspapers

Pittsburgh Jewish Chronicle
5600 Baum Blvd (412) 687-1000
Fax: (412) 687-5119
Email: pittjewchr@aol.com

Mikvaot

2326 Shady Avenue 15217 (412) 422-8010

Museums

Holocaust Center of the United Jewish Federation of Greater Pittsburgh
5738 Darlington Road 15217 (412) 421-1500
Fax: (412) 422-1996
Email: lhurwitz@ujf.net
Web site: www.ujfhc.net

Serves as a living memorial by providing educational resources, sponsoring community activities, housing archives and cultural materials related to the Holocaust.

Organisations

United Jewish Federation of Greater Pittsburgh
234 McKee Place 15213 (412) 681-8000
Fax: (412) 681-3980
Email: enaveh@ujf.net
Web site: www.ujf.net

Houses all administrative offices of the Federation and commission on Public Affairs.

Restaurants

Dairy

Yaacov's
2109 Murray Ave., 15217 (412) 421-7208

Meat

Greenberg's Kosher Poultry
2223 Murray Avenue 15217

King David's
2020 Murray Avenue 15217 (412) 422-3370

Prime Kosher
1916 Murray Avenue 15217 (412) 421-1015

Synagogues

Conservative

Ahavath Achim
500 Chestnut St., Carnegie 15106 (412) 279-1566

Beth El of South Hills
1900 Cochran Rd 15220 (412) 561-1168

Beth Shalom
Beacon & Shady Avs 15217 (412) 421-2288
Fax: (412) 421-5923
Web site: www.bethshalom-pgh-org

New Light
1700 Beechwood Blvd. 15217 (412) 421-1017

Parkway Jewish Center
300 Princeton Dr. 15235 (412) 823-4338
Fax: (412) 823-4338

Tree of Life
Wilkins & Shady Avs 15217 (412) 521-6788

Orthodox

B'nai Emunoh Congregation
4315 Murray Av. 15217 (412) 521-1477
Fax: (412) 521-1762
Email: drmaimon@netzero.net

B'nai Zion
6404 Forbes Av. 15217 (412) 521-1440

Beth Hamedrash Hagodol
1230 Colwell St. 15219 (412) 471-4443
Fax: (412) 281-1965

Bohnei Yisroel
6401 Forbes Av. 15217 (412) 521-6407

Kether Torah
5706 Bartlett St. 15217 (412) 521-9992

Poale Zedeck
6318 Phillips Avenue 15217 (412) 421-9786
Fax: (412) 421-3383
Email: mil313@aol.com
Web site: www.pzonline.com

Shaare Tefillah
5741 Bartlett St. 15217 (412) 521-9911

Shaare Torah
2319 Murray Ave. 15217 (412) 421-8855

Shaare Zedeck
5751 Bartlett St. 15217

Torath Chaim
728 N. Negley Ave. 15206
(412) 362-7736; 362-0036
Email: joeberger1@juno.com

Contact person is Arnie Schwartz at 362-0036.

Young Israel of Greater Pittsburgh
5831 Bartlett Street 15217-1636 (412) 421-7224

Reconstructionist

Dor Hadash
6401 Forbes Ave. 15217

Reform

Rodef Shalom
4905 5th Ave. 15213 (412) 621-6566
Fax: (412) 621-5475
Email: rshalom@pgh.net

Temple David
4415 Northern Pike, Monroeville 15146

Temple Emanuel of South Hills
1250 Bower Hill Rd 15243 (412) 279-2600
Fax: (412) 279-7628
Hours: Monday-Thursday 9 am to 5 pm. Friday 9 am to 4 pm.

Temple Sinai
5505 Forbes Ave. 15217 (412) 421-9715

Pottstown

Synagogues

Conservative

Congregation Mercy & Truth
575 N. Keim Street 19464 (610) 326-1717

Reading

Organisations

Jewish Federation
1700 City Line St. 19604 (610) 921-2766
Fax: (610) 921-2766
Email: sramati@epix.net

Synagogues

Conservative

Kesher Zion
Eckert & Perkiomen Streets 19602 374-1763

Orthodox

Shomrei Habrith
2320 Hampden Blvd 19604 (610) 921-0881

Reform

Reform Congregation Oheb Sholom
555 Warwick Drive,
Wyomissing Hill 19610 (610) 375-6034
Fax: (610) 375-6036
Email: office@ohebsholom.org
Web site: www.ohebsholom.org

Scranton

Butchers

Blatt's Butcher Block
420 Prescott Avenue 18510 (570) 342-3886
Fax: (570) 342-9711
Supervision: Rabbi Fine and Rabbi Herman of Scranton Rabbinate.
Glatt kosher meat, poultry, delicatessen and groceries. Also meat restaurant.

Museums

Houdini Museum Tour and Magic Show
1433 N. Main 18508 (570) 342-5555
Email: magicusa@microserve.net
Web site: www.houdini.org
The only museum totally devoted to Harry Houdini (Eric Weiss born in Budapest, the son of Rabbi Mayer Samuel Weiss).

Organisations

Jewish Federation of Northeastern Pennsylvania
601 Jefferson Avenue 18510 (570) 961-2300
Fax: (570) 346-6147
Email: jfednepa@epix.net

Synagogues

Conservative

Temple Israel
Gibson Street & Monroe Avenue 18510
(570) 342-0350
Fax: (570) 342-7250
Email: tiscron@epix.net
Web site: www.ncx.com.wwi/tis

Orthodox

Beth Shalom
Clay Avenue at Vine Street 18510 (570) 346-0502
Fax: (570) 346-8800
Daily service. Close to motels & hotels.

Congregation Machzikeh Hadas
cnr. Monroe & Olive 18510 (570) 342-6271

Ohev Zedek
1432 Mulberry Street 18510 (717) 343-2717

Reform

Temple Hesed
Lake Scranton 18505 (717) 344-7201

Sharon

Synagogues

Reform

Temple Beth Israel
840 Highland Road, Sharon 16146 (724) 346-4754
Fax: (724) 981-4424
Supervision: Reform and Orthodox.

Wallingford

Synagogues

Conservative

Ohev Shalom
2 Chester Road 19086 (610) 874-1465
Web site: www.uscj.org/delvlly/wallingford

The synagogue vestibule contains twelve stained-glass panes (designed and executed by Rose Isaacson), each depicting a Jewish holiday. In the main lobby is an additional stained-glass panel erected as an Holocaust memorial.

Wilkes-Barre

Organisations

Jewish Federation of Greater Wilkes-Barre & Community Center
60 S. River Street (570) 822-4146
Fax: (570) 824-5966

Synagogues

Conservative

Temple Israel
236 S. River Street 18702 (570) 824-8927

Orthodox

Ohav Zedek
242 S. Franklin Street 18701 (570) 825-6619
Fax: (570) 825-6634
Email: info@ohavzedek.org

Reform

B'nai B'rith
408 Wyoming Street, Kingston 18704

Williamsport

Synagogues

Conservative

Ohev Sholom
Cherry & Belmont Streets 17701 (717) 322-4209

Reform

Beth Ha-Sholom
425 Center Street 17701 (717) 323-7751

Rhode Island

Barrington

Synagogues

Temple Habonim
165 New Meadow Road 02806 (401) 245-6536

Bristol

Synagogues

Conservative

United Brothers
215 High Street 02809 (401) 253-3460

Cranston

Synagogues

Temple Torat Yisrael
330 Park Avenue 02905 (401) 785-1800

Reform

Temple Sinai
30 Hagan Avenue 02920 (401) 942-8350

Middletown

Synagogues

Conservative

Temple Shalom
223 Valley Road 02842 (401) 846-9002
Fax: (401) 682-2417

Narragansett

Synagogues

Congregation Beth David
Kingstown Road 02882 (401) 846-9002

Newport

Bed and Breakfast

Admiral Weaver Inn (401) 849-0061

Tours of Jewish Interest

Touro Synagogue
85 Touro Street 02840 (401) 847-4794
Fax: (401) 847-8121

The synagogue, designed by Peter Harrison and dedicated in 1763, is one of the finest examples of eighteenth-century Colonial architecture. It has been declared a national site by the US government. The Jewish cemetery, the second oldest in the US, dates back to 1677 and was immortalised in Longfellow's poem "The Jewish Cemetery of Newport". Judah Touro is buried here.

Pawtucket

Synagogues

Orthodox

Ohawe Sholam/Young Israel of Pawtucket
671 East Avenue 02860 (401) 722-3146
Email: rijewish@aol.com
Web site: www.members.tripod.com/~ohave
Mailing address: 77 Blodgett St.

Providence

Documentation Centre

Rhode Island Jewish Historical Association
(401) 863-2805
Has a vast amount of material regarding Colonial Jewry.

Kashrut Information

Brown University-RISD Hillel
80 Brown Street 02906 (401) 863-2805
Fax: (401) 863-1591
Email: spf@brown.edu

Vaad Hakashrut
(401) 621-9393
Fax: (401) 331-9393
Email: bethshalom1@juno.com

Media

Magazines

L'Chaim
130 Sessions Street 02906 (401) 421-4111

Mikvaot

401 Elmgrove Avenue 02906

Museums

Rhode Island Holocaust Memorial Museum
401 Elmgrove Avenue 02906 (401) 861-8800
The state memorial to the victims of the Holocaust. Many survivors now living in Rhode Island have donated memorabilia and personal mementoes. There is also a garden of remembrance.

Organisations

Jewish Federation of Rhode Island
130 Sessions Street 02906 (401) 421-4111

Synagogues

Conservative

Temple Emanu-El
99 Taft Avenue 02906 (401) 331-1616

Orthodox

Beth Shalom
275 Camp Avenue 02906 (401) 621-9393
Fax: (401) 331-9393
Email: bethshalom1@juno.com

Congregation Sons of Jacob
24 Douglas Avenue 02908 (401) 274-5260

Mishkon Tfiloh
203 Summit Avenue 02906 (401) 521-1616

Shaare Zedek
688 Broad Street 02907 (401) 751-4936

Reform

Beth El
70 Orchard Avenue 02906 (401) 331-6070

Warwick

Synagogues

Conservative

Temple Am David
40 Gardiner Street 02888 (401) 463-7944

Westerly

Synagogues

Orthodox

Congregation Shaare Zedek
Union Street 02891 (401) 596-4621

Woonsocket

Synagogues

Conservative

Congregation B'nai Israel
224 Prospect Street 02895 (401) 762-3651
Fax: (401) 767-5243
Email: cbi_synagogue@yahoo.com

South Carolina

Charleston

Bakeries

Ashley Bakery
1662 Savannah Highway 29407 (803) 763-4125

Great Harvest Bread Company
975 Savannah Highway 29407 (803) 763-2055

Delicatessens

Nathan's Deli
1836 Ashley River Road 29407 (803) 556-3354

West Side Market and Deli
1300 Savannah Highway 29407 (803) 763-9988
Fax: (803) 763-4476
Kosher market, restaurant and catering. Open Sunday to Friday.

Organisations

Jewish Federation and Community Center
1645 Raoul Wallenberg Blvd,
PO Box 31298 29416 (803) 571-6565
Fax: (803) 556-6206

Synagogues

Orthodox

Brith Shalom Beth Israel
182 Rutledge Avenue (803) 677-8599

Reform

Beth Elohim
86 Hasell Street 29401 (843) 723-1090
Fax: (843) 723-0537
Email: office@kkbe.org
Web site: www.kkbe.org

Tours of Jewish Interest

Beth Elohim
86 Hasell Street 29401 (843) 723-1090
Fax: (843) 723-0537
Email: office@kkbe.org

Dating from 1749, it is the birthplace of Reform Judaism in the United States, the Second oldest synagogue building in the country, and the oldest surviving Reform Synagogue in the world. It has been designated as a national historic landmark. A museum is housed in the administration building next door.

Columbia

Delicatessens

Groucho's
Five Points 29205

Organisations

Columbia Jewish Federation
4540 Trenholm Road, Cola 29206 (803) 787-2023

Synagogues

Conservative

Beth Shalom
5827 N. Trenholm Road 29206 (803) 782-2500

Reform

Tree of Life
6719 Trenholm Road 29206 (803) 787-2182
Fax: (803) 787-0309

Georgetown

Cemeteries

Although there are now very few Jews in Georgetown, and there is no synagogue, there is a very old Jewish cemetery, which is maintained by the city.

Myrtle Beach

Synagogues

Orthodox

Beth El
401 Highway 17 N., 56th Avenue 29577
(803) 449-3140

Chabad Lubavitch
2803 N. Oak Street (843) 448-0035
Fax: (843) 626-6403

Services every day.

South Dakota

Aberdeen

Synagogues

Conservative

B'nai Isaac
202 N. Kline Street 57401 (605) 225-3404 or 7360
Email: beapre@iw.net

Rapid City

Synagogues

Reform

Synagogue of the Hills
417 N. 40th Street 57702 (605) 348-0805
Email: bhshul@rapidnet.com
Affiliated with UAHC. Services Friday evenings at 7.30.

Tennessee

Chattanooga

Museums

Siskin Museum of Religious Artifacts
1 Siskin Plaza 37403 (423) 634-1700
Fax: (423) 634-1717

Organisations

Jewish Community Federation
5326 Lynnland Terrace 47311 (423) 894-1317
Fax: (423) 894-1319

Synagogues

Conservative

B'nai Zion
114 McBrien Road 37411 (423) 894-8900

Orthodox

Beth Sholom
20 Pisgah Avenue 37411 (423) 894-0801

Reform

Mizpah Congregation
923 McCallie Avenue 37403 (423) 264-9771
Fax: (423) 267-9773
Email: admmizpahcong@juno.com

Memphis

Delicatessens

Rubenstein's
4965 Summer Avenue 38122
Closed Shabbat.

Kashrut Information

Vaad Hakehilloth of Memphis
Memphis Orthodox Jewish Community Council,
PO Box 41133 38104 (901) 767-2263
Fax: (901) 761-3788

Mikvaot

Baron Hirsch Congregation
369 Winter Oak Lane 38119 (901) 683-7485

Organisations

Jewish Federation and Community Center
6560 Poplar Avenue 38138 (901) 767-7100

Synagogues

Conservative

Beth Sholom
482 S. Mendenhall Ave. 38117 (901) 683-3591

Orthodox

Anshei Sephard-Beth El Emeth
120 E.Yates Road N. 38117 (901) 682-1611

Reform

Temple Israel
1376 E. Massey Road (901) 761-3130

Nashville

Mikvaot

Sherith Israel
3600 West End Avenue 37205 (615) 292-6614
Fax: (615) 463-8260
Email: SylvL@AOL.com

Organisations

Jewish Federation of Nashville and Middle Tennessee
801 Percy Warner Blvd. 37205 (615) 356-3242
Fax: (615) 352-0056

Synagogues

Conservative

West End Synagogue
3814 West End Avenue 37205 (615) 269-4592
Fax: (615) 269-4695
Email: office@westendsyn.org or exec@westendsyn.org

Reform

The Temple
5015 Harding Road 37205 (615) 352-7620
Fax: (615) 352-9365

Oak Ridge

Synagogues

Jewish Congregation of Oak Ridge
101 W. Madison Lane 37830 (423) 482-3581

Texas

Amarillo

Synagogues

Reform

Temple B'nai Israel
4316 Albert Street 79106 (806) 352-7191

Austin

Organisations

Jewish Federation and Community Center of Austin
7300 Hart Lane 78731 (512) 331-1144
Fax: (512) 331-7059

Synagogues

Conservative

Agudas Achim
4300 Bull Creek Road 78731

Congregation Beth El
8902 Mesa Drive 78759 (512) 346-1776
Fax: (512) 233-004
Email: difriedman@aol.com

Orthodox

Chabad House
2101 Neuces Street 78705 (512) 499-8202
Mikva on premises.

Reform

Temple Beth Israel
3901 Shoal Creek Blvd 78756 (512) 454-6806

Baytown

Synagogues

Unaffiliated

K'nesseth Israel
100 W. Sterling, PO Box 702 77522 (281) 424-8765

Beaumont

Synagogues

Reform

Temple Emanuel
1120 Broadway 7740 (409) 832-6131

Corpus Christi

Synagogues

Conservative

B'nai Israel
3434 Fort Worth Street 78411 (361) 855-7308
Fax: (361) 855-7309
Email: CGDK@aol.com

Reform

Temple Beth El
4402 Saratoga Street 78413 (512) 857-8181

Dallas

The Dallas Jewish community was founded in the decade following the Civil War by predominantly German Jews. The social importance of German Jewish ancestry can still be seen in the Temple Emanu-El cemetery which is home to scores of nineteenth-century headstones bearing German regional names for Eastern European birthplaces.

The JCC sponsors a prestigious Jewish Arts Festival each August along with concerts and gallery exhibitions. A Holocaust Museum has served as a regional focal point for preserving the memory of the Shoah. For more information, see the Dallas Virtual Jewish Community website at www.dvjc.org

Community Organisations

Jewish Federation of Greater Dallas and Community Center
7800 Northaven Road 75230 (214) 369-3313
Fax: (214) 369-8943
Email: contact@jfgd.org
Web site: www.jewishdallas.org
The Campus houses the Dallas Holocaust Center and the Dallas Jewish Historical Society. There is a kosher café on Sundays and lunch service on some weekdays during the fall and winter months (under the supervision of the Vaad Hakashrus of Greater Dallas).

Hotels

Sheraton Park Central
12720 Merit Drive 75240 (972) 385-3000

The Westin Galleria, Dallas
13340 Dallas Parkway (972) 934-9494
Fax: (972) 851-2869
Email: galas@westin.com
Lock-up kosher kitchens under the supervision of the Vaad Hakashrus of Dallas.

Mikvaot

Mikvah Association
5640 McShan 75230 (972) 776-0037

Religious Organisations

Dallas Area Torah Association (Kollel)
5840 Forest Lane 75230 (214) 987-3282
Fax: (214) 987-1764
Email: data@datanet.org
Web site: www.datanet.org

Site

Zaide Reuven's Esrog Farm
(972) 931-5596
Fax: (972) 931-5476
Email: zrsesrog@aol.com
Web site: www.members.aol.com/arsesrog
Dallas' only Esrog tree farm is open by appointment.

Synagogues

Orthodox

Chabad of Dallas
7008 Forest Lane 75230 (214) 361-8600
Fax: (214) 361-8680
Email: shull@airmail.net
Web site: www.chabadcenters.com/dallas

Ohr HaTorah
12800 Preston Road (972) 404-8980

Shaare Tefilla
6131 Churchill Way, off Preston Road 75230
(972) 661-0127
Fax: (972) 661-0150
Email: shaaretefilla@juno.com

Reform

Temple Emanu-El
8500 Hillcrest Road 75230 (214) 706-0000
Fax: (214) 706-0025
Web site: www.tedallas.org

Sephardi

Magen David Congregation
7314 Campbell Road, Dallas, Texas 75248
(972) 386-7166

El Paso

Community Organisations

Chabad House
6515 Westwind 79912 (915) 584-8218
Web site: www.chabadelpaso.com
Also has a mikva.

Museums

El Paso Holocaust Museum and Study Center
401 Wallenberg Drive 79912 (915) 833-5656
Fax: (915) 833-9523
Email: epholo@flash.net
Web site: www.flash.net/~epholo.com
The museum features an impressive collection of artifacts, dramatic displays, pictures and posters depicting the chronological history of Europe during the Nazi era. Open Sunday and Tuesday 1 pm-4 pm or by appointment.

Synagogues

Conservative

B'nai Zion
805 Cherry Hill Lane 79912 (915) 833-2222
Also has a mikva.

Reform

Sinai
4408 N. Stanton Street 79902 (915) 532-5959

Houston

Bakeries

Kroger's
S. Post Oak @ W. Bellfort 77096 (713) 721-7691
Supervision: Houston Kashruth Association.
LeMoulin European Bakery
5645 Beechnut 77096 (713) 779-1618
Supervision: Houston Kashruth Association.
New York Bagel Shop
9724 Hillcroft 77096 (713) 723-5879
Supervision: Houston Kashruth Association.
Randall's Bakery
Supervision: Houston Kashruth Association.
Can be found at eight locations including : Clear Lake, Sugar Land, Highway 6 & Memorial, Fondren & Bissonnet, W. Bellfort & S. Post Oak, Gessner & W. Bellfort, and Holcombe & Kirby.
Three Brothers Bakery
4036 S. Braeswood 77025 (713) 666-2551
Supervision: Houston Kashruth Association.

Butchers

Albertson's
S. Braeswood@Fondren (713) 271-1180
Supervision: Houston Kashruth Association.
Kroger's
S. Post Oak @ W. Bellfort 77096 (713) 721-7691
Supervision: Houston Kashruth Association.

Embassy

Consul General of Israel
Suite 1500, 24 Greenway Plaza 77046

Groceries

Albertson's
S. Braeswood@Fondren (713) 271-1180
Supervision: Houston Kashruth Association.

Kashrut Information

Houston Kashrut Association
9001 Greenwillow 77096 (713) 723-3850
Fax: (713) 723-3852

TORCH - Torah & Outreach Resource Center of Houston
7000 Westview, Suite 121 77055 (713) 957-8993
Fax: (713) 680-9932
Email: torch@torchweb.com
Web site: www.torchweb.com

Mikvaot

Chabad Lubavitch Center
10900 Fondren Road 77096 (713) 777-2000
United Orthodox Synagogues
4221 S. Braeswood Blvd 77096 (713) 723-3850

Organisations

Jewish Federation of Greater Houston
5603 S. Braeswood Blvd 77096 (713) 729-7000
Fax: (713) 721-6232
Web site: www.houstonjewish.org

Restaurants

King David Center
5925 South Braeswood (713) 729-5741

Dairy

Saba's Mediterranean
9704 Fondren (713) 270-7222
Supervision: Houston Kashruth Association.
Pizza, Felafel Fish.

Meat

Nosher's at the Jewish Community Centre
5601 S. Braeswood 77096 (713) 729-3200
Supervision: Houston Kashruth Association.

Vegetarian

Madras Pavilion
3910 Kirby Drive 77098 (713) 521-2617
Supervision: Houston Kashruth Association.

Wonderful Vegetarian Restaurant
7549 Westheimer 77063 (713) 977-3137
Supervision: Houston Kashruth Association.

Synagogues

Conservative

B'rith Shalom
4610 Bellaire Blvd. 77401 (713) 667-9201
Beth Am
1431 Brittmore Rd. 77043 (713) 461-7725
Fax: (713) 461-7773
Email: ebbe@earthlink.net
Web site: www.bethamtx.org
One room and board is available to anyone attending services.
Beth Yeshurun
4525 Beechnut St. 77096 (713) 666-1881
Fax: (713) 666-7767
Email: arthur@bethyeshurun.org
Web site: www.bethyeshurun.org
Congregation Shaar Hashalom
16020 El Camino Real 77062 (281) 488-5861
Fax: (281) 488-3561
Email: Ferderow@blkbox.com
Web site: www.uscj.org.sowest/houstosh

Orthodox

Chabad Lubavitch of Houston
10900 Fondren Road 77096 (713) 777-2000
Congregation Beth Rambam
11333 Braesridge Blvd. 77071 (713) 723-3030
Fax: (713) 726-8737
Email: gez@flash.net
Web site: www.flash.net/~bentzion/br.htm
Home hospitality available. Office hours Monday-Friday 9 am to 2 pm.
United Orthodox Synogogues
9001 Greenwillow 77096 (713) 723-3850
Web site: www.uosh.org
Mikva on premises. Daily minyan and Shabbat services.
Young Israel of Houston
7823 Ludinton Road 77071 (713) 729-0719
Web site: www.youngisraelofhouston.org

Reform

Beth Israel
5600 N. Braeswood Blvd. 77096 (713) 771-6221
Fax: (713) 771-5705
Web site: www.Beth-Israel.org
Congregation Emanu El
1500 Sunset Blvd 77005 (713) 529-5771
Fax: (713) 529-0703
Email: emanuelhouston.org
Web site: www.emanuel.org
Congregation for Reform Judaism
801 Bering Dr. 77057 (713) 782-4162
Fax: (713) 782-4167
Jewish Community North
5400 Fellowship Lane 77379 (281) 376-0016
Fax: (281) 251-1033
Email: jcn@wt.net
Temple Sinai
783 Country Place Dr. 77079 (281) 496-5950
Fax: (281) 496-1537

Lubbock

Groceries

Albertson's (806) 794-6761
Lowe's Supermarket
82nd & Slide Rd
United (906) 791-0220
Good selection for Passover.

Synagogues

Congregation Shaareth Israel
6928 3rd Street 79424 (806) 794-7517
Mailing address: PO Box 93594, 79493-3594.

San Antonio

Delicatessens

Delicious Food
7460 Callaghan Road 78229 (512) 366-1844

Museums

Holocaust Memorial
12500 N W Military Highway 78231
(210) 302-6807
Fax: (210) 408-2332
Email: cohenm@jfstx.org
Institute of Texan Cultures
Hemisphere Plaza, Downtown Riverfront

Organisations

Jewish Federation
8434 Ahern Drive 78216 (512) 341-8234

Synagogues

Conservative

Agudas Achim
1201 Donaldson Avenue 78228 (210) 734-4216

Orthodox

Rodfei Sholom
3003 Sholom Drive 78230 (210) 493 3558
Fax: (210) 492 0629
Email: rodfei@world-net.net
Web site: www.ou.org
Mikva on premises.

Reform

Beth El
211 Belknap Place 78212

Waco

Synagogues

Conservative

Agudath Jacob
4925 Hillcrest Drive 76710 (254) 772-1451

Reform

Rodef Sholom
1717 N. New Road 76707 (254) 754-3703
Fax: (254) 754-5538

Utah

Salt Lake City

Organisations

United Jewish Federation of Utah
2416 East, 1700 South 84108 (801) 581-0102
Fax: (801) 581-1334

Synagogues

Chabad Lubavitch of Utah
1433 South 1100 East 84105 (801) 467-7777
Fax: (801) 486-7526
Email: chabadutah@aol.com
Web site: www.chabadutah.com

For Mikvah appointment call Mrs Sharonne Zippel, Tel: (801) 582-0220.

Reconstructionist

Chavurah B'yachad
PO Box 9115 84109 (801) 325-4539
Email: byachad@aol.com

Reform

Congregation Kol Ami
2425 E. Heritage Way 84109 (801) 484-1501
Fax: (801) 484-1162
Email: clyon@conkolami.org
Web site: www.conkolami.org

Vermont

Burlington

Synagogues

Conservative

Ohavi Zedek
188 N. Prospect Street 05401 (802) 864-0218

Orthodox

Ahavath Gerim
cnr. Archibald & Hyde Streets 05401
(802) 862-3001

Reform

Temple Sinai
500 Swift Street 05401 (802) 862-5125

Virginia

Alexandria

Synagogues

Conservative

Agudas Achim
2908 Valley Drive 22302 (703) 998-6460

Reform

Beth El Hebrew Congregation
3830 Seminary Road 22304 (703) 370-9400
Fax: (703) 370-7730
Email: bethelhc@erols.com

Arlington

Synagogues

Conservative

Arlington-Fairfax Jewish Congregation
2920 Arlington Blvd 22204 (703) 979-4466
Fax: (703) 979-4468
Email: office@arfax.net
Web site: www.arfax.org

Daily minyan and Shabbat services. Includes areas known as Crystal City, Rosslyn and Skyline.

Charlottesville

Synagogues

The Hillel Jewish Center
The University of Virginia,
1824 University Circle 22903 (804) 295-4963

Reform

Congregation Beth Israel
301 E. Jefferson Street 22902 (804) 295-6382
Fax: (804) 296-6491
Email: office@www.cbicville.org

Danville

Synagogues

Temple Beth Sholom
Sutherlin Avenue (804) 792-3489
This building is 95 years old, one of oldest synagogues in the South. Friday evening and holiday services.

Fairfax

Synagogues

Conservative

Congregation Olam Tikvah
3800 Glenbrook Road 22031 (703) 425-1880
Fax: (703) 425-0835
Two miles from Beltway Exit 6W.

Falls Church

Synagogues

Reform

Temple Rodef Shalom
2100 Westmoreland Street 22043 (703) 532-2217
Email: trsfcva@erols.com

Norfolk

Groceries

Meat

The Kosher Place
738 W. 22nd Street (757) 623-1770
Supervision: Vaad Hakashrus of Tidewater.
Meats, deli, prepared foods. Hours: Monday to Thursday, 9 am to 6 pm; Friday, to 3 pm; Sunday, 10 am to 4 pm. Close to colonial Williamsburg and Virginia Beach.

Hotels

Sheraton Norfolk Waterside Hotel
777 Waterside Drive 23510 (757) 622-6664
Supervision: Va'ad.

Kashrut Information

Va'ad Hakashrut
c/o B'nai Israel (757) 627-7358
Fax: (757) 627-8544
Email: rebyosef@hotmail.com

Mikvaot

B'nai Israel Congregation
420 Spotswood Avenue 23517 (757) 627-7358
Fax: (757) 627-8544
Email: bnaioffice@juno.com

Organisations

United Jewish Federation of Tidewater
5029 Corporate Woods Drive, Suite 225,
Virginia Beach 23462 (757) 671-1600
Fax: (757) 671-7613

Synagogues

Conservative

Beth El
422 Shirley Ave. 23517 (757) 625-7821
Fax: (757) 627-4905
Email: office@bethelnorfolk.com

Temple Israel
7255 Granby St. 23505 (804) 489-4550

Orthodox

B'nai Israel
402 Spotswood Avenue 23517 (757) 627-7358

Reform

Ohef Sholom
Stockley Gdns at Raleigh Av. 23507 (804) 625-4295

The Commodore Levy Chapel
Frazier Hall, Building C-7 (inside Gate 2),
Norfolk US Navy Station (757) 444-7361
Fax: (757) 444-7362
Email: chaplain@nsn.cmar.navy.mil
The US Navy's oldest synagogue. Visitors welcome for tour or Erev Shabbat services. Contact Jewish chaplain for Base Pass first.

Richmond

Hotels

The Farbreng-Inn Kosher Retreat Center
1800 SEE Virginia 23233
(804) 740-2000/800-733-8474
Fax: (804) 750-1341
Email: info@chabadofva.org
Kosher retreat center open year round. Under the Hashgacht of Lubavitch of Virginia.

Mikvaot

Young Israel
4811 Patterson Avenue 23226 (804) 353-3831
Fax: (804) 288-4381
Email: adere@juno.com

Museums

Beth Ahabah
1117 W. Franklin Street 23220
Also housing Jewish archives, which are of great historical interest.

Organisations

Jewish Community Federation
5403 Monument Avenue 23226 (804) 288-0045
Fax: (804) 282-7507
Email: www.jewishrichmond.org

United States of America / Virginia

Synagogues

Conservative

Or Atid
501 Parham Road 23229 (804) 740-4747

Orthodox

Keneseth Beth Israel
6300 Patterson Avenue 23226 (804) 288-7953
Fax: (804) 673-9558
Email: kbi6300@erols.com

Young Israel of Richmond
4811 Patterson Avenue 23226 (804) 353-5831
Email: yosefb@juno.com

Reform

Or Ami
9400 N. Huguenot Road 23235 (804) 272-0017

Virginia Beach

Media

Magazines

Renewal Magazine
5029 Corporate Woods, Suite 225 23462
(757) 671-1600
Fax: (757) 671-7613
Email: news@ujft.org
Web site: www.jewishva.org
Published three times per year.

Newspapers

Southeastern Virginia Jewish News
5029 Corporate Woods Drive, Suite 225 23462
(757) 671-1600
Fax: (757) 671-7613
Email: news@ujft.org
Web site: www.jewishva.org
Published every two weeks.

Synagogues

Conservative

Kempsville Conservative
952 Indian Lakes Blvd. 23464 (757) 495-8510
Web site: www.uscj.org/seabd/virginiabeach/

Temple Emanuel
25th Street 23451

Orthodox

Chabad Lubavitch
533 Gleneagle Drive 23462 (804) 499-0507

Reform

Beth Chaverim
3820 Stoneshore Road 23452-7965 (757) 463-3226
Fax: (757) 463-1134
Email: bethchaverim@ddaccess.com

Virginia Peninsula

Bakeries

Brenner's Warwick Bakery
240 31st Street, Newport News 23607
Supervision: Va'ad Hakashrut.

Mikvaot

Adath Jeshurun
12646 Nettles Drive, Newport News 23606

Organisations

United Jewish Community of the Virginia Peninsula
2700 Spring Road, Newport News 23606
(804) 930-1422

Synagogues

Conservative

Rodef Shalom
318 Whealton Road, Hampton 23666

Reform

Temple Sinai
11620 Warwick Blvd., Newport News 23601
(804) 596-8352

Traditional

B'nai Israel
3116 Kecoughtan Road, Hampton 23661

Washington

Aberdeen

Synagogues

Conservative

Temple Beth Israel
1219 Spur Street 98520 (360) 533-3784

Seattle

Jewish Student/Young Adult Center

Hillel, Foundation for Jewish Campus Life at the University of Washington
4745 17th Av. N.E. 98105 (206) 527-1997
Fax: (206) 527-1999
Email: mail@hilleluw.org
Programmes, services, occasional kosher meals for students & young adults, 18-30.

Kashrut Information

Va'ad HaRabanim
6500 52nd Avenue St 98118 (206) 760-0805
Fax: (206) 725-0347
Email: seavaad@aol.com

The Va'ad HaRabanim was organised in 1993. In addition to providing kosher meat, the board provides kosher supervision for many restaurants, bakeries, retail outlets and catering facilities in the Seattle area. For further questions and information, please contact David Grashin at the number above.

Media

Transcripts

The Jewish Transcript
2031 3rd Avenue 98121 (206) 441-4553
Fax: (206) 441-2736
Email: jewishtran@aol.com

Museums

Community Center
3801 E. Mercer Way, Mercer Island 98040
(206) 232-7115

A Holocaust memorial with a bronze sculpture by Gizel Berman has been dedicated here.

Organisations

Jewish Federation of Greater Seattle
2031 3rd Avenue 98121 (206) 443-5400

Stroum Jewish Community Center, Northend Facility
8606 35th Avenue NE 98115 (206) 526-8073
Fax: (206) 526-9958
Email: cherie@sjcc.org

Washington Association of Jewish Communities
2031 3rd Avenue 98121

Restaurants

Chinese Vegetarian

Bamboo Garden
364 Roy Street, near Seattle Center 98109
(206) 282-6616
Fax: (206) 284-2775
Email: bamboogarden@aol.com
Supervision: Va'ad HaRabanim of Greater Seattle.

Dairy

Panini Grill
2118 NE 65 St. (206) 522-2730

Delicatessen

Leah's Deli
65 St. between 21st and 22nd (206) 985-2647
Take-out.

Vegetarian

Teapot Vegetarian House
125 E. 15th Ave. (206) 325-1010

Spokane

Organisations

Jewish Community Council
North 221 Wall, Suite 500, Spokane 99201
(509) 838-4261

Synagogues

Conservative

Temple Beth Shalom
11322 E. 30th Street 99203 (509) 747-3304

West Virginia

Huntingdon

Synagogues

Conservative & Reform

B'nai Sholom
949 10th Avenue 25701 (304) 522-2980

Wisconsin

Madison

Organisations

Madison Jewish Community Council
6434 Enterprise Lane 53179 (608) 278-1808
Fax: (608) 278-7814
Email: mjcc@mjcc.net
Web site: www.jewishmadison.org

Synagogues

Hillel Foundation
611 Langdon Street 53703 (608) 256-8361

Conservative

Beth Israel Center
1406 Mound Street 53711 (608) 256-7763
Fax: (608) 256-9434
Email: office@bethisraelcenter.org
Web site: www.bethisraelcenter.org

Orthodox

Chabad House
1722 Regent Street 53705 (608) 231-3450
Fax: (608) 231-3790

Reform

Beth El
2702 Arbor Drive 53711 (608) 238-3123

Mequon

Synagogues

Orthodox

Agudas Achim Chabad
2233 West Mequon Road 53092 (262) 242-2235
Fax: (262) 242-2268
Email: chabadmequon@aol.com
Web site: www.chabadmequon.org
Also has a mikva

Congregation Anshai Leibowitz
2415 West Mequon Road 53092 (262) 512-1195
Fax: (262) 512-1695

Milwaukee

Community Organisations

Coalition for Jewish Learning
6401 North Santa Monica Boulevard 53217
(414) 962-8860
Fax: (414) 962-8852

Media

Directories

Milkwaukee Jewish Federation
1360 N. Prospect Avenue 53202 (414) 271-2992

Newspapers

Wisconsin Jewish Chronicle
1360 N. Prospect Avenue 53202 (414) 390-5888
Fax: (414) 271-0487
Email: milwaukeej@aol.com

Restaurants

Meat

Kosher Meat Klub
4731 West Burleigh 53210 (414) 449-5980
Fax: (414) 449-5985
Meat sandwiches, delicatessen and kosher groceries are available.

Shelley's Deliworks
4311 West Bradley Road 53223 (414) 365-8560
Fax: (414) 365-8526
Regular meals

Synagogues

Orthodox

Beth Jehudah
3100 North 52nd Street 53216 (414) 442-5730
Fax: (414) 442-6171
Email: bethjehudah@juno.com
Web site: www.bethjehudah.org

Sheboygan

Synagogues

Traditional

Temple Beth El
1007 North Avenue 53083 (920) 452-5828
Email: bethelsheboygan@juno.com

Wyoming

Casper

Synagogues

Reform

Temple Beth El
4105 S. Poplar, PO Box 3534 82602 (307) 237-2330

Cheyenne

Synagogues

Conservative

Mount Sinai
2610 Pioneer Avenue 82001 (307) 634-3052
Gift shop and mikva by appointment.

Green River

Synagogues

Congregation of Beth Israel
PO Box 648 Green River Way 82935
(307) 875-4194

Laramie

Synagogues

Reform

Laramie JCC
PO Box 202 82073 (307) 745-8813
Email: www.uahc.org/wy/wy001

Uruguay

After the *Conversos* in the sixteenth century, there was no known Jewish community in Uruguay until the late nineteenth century, when the country served as a stop over on the way to Argentina. The Jewish population rose in the twentieth century, with immigration from the Middle East and Eastern Europe. A synagogue was opened by 1917. Despite restrictive immigration laws imposed against European Jews fleeing Nazism, 2,500 Jews managed to enter the country between 1939 and 1940. Further Jewish immigration followed, from Hungary and the Middle East, in the post-War period.

There are many Jewish organisations functioning in Urugauy, including Zionist and women's organisations. Kosher restaurants exist in Jewish institutions, and there are a number of synagogues.

GMT - 3 hours	Total Population 3,337,000
Country calling code (598)	Jewish Population 22,800
Emergency Telephone (999)	Electricity voltage 220

Montevideo

With approximately 10,000 families in the capital of Uruguay, Montevideo contains almost all of the country's Jewish community. There is a Museum of the Holocaust in Montevideo, and near the Teatro Solis opera house stands a Golda Meir monument. An Albert Einstein monument can be found in Rodo Park.

Communal Organisation

Comite Central Israelita Del Uruguay
Rio Negro 1308, P. 5 11100 (2) 903-0464
Fax: (2) 900-6562
Email: cciu@adinet.com.uy

Community Organisations

Centro Lubavitch
Av. Brasil 2704, CP 11300
(2) 709-3444; 708-5169
Fax: (2) 711-3696
Email: shemtov@chasque.apc.org

Embassy

Embassy of Israel
Bulevar Artigas 1585-89 (2) 400-4164
Fax: (2) 409-5821
Email: emisuyur@adlnet.com.uy

Groceries

Yavne
Cavia 2800 (2) 908-7869
Fax: (2) 707-0866

Media

Newspapers

Semanario Hebreo
Soriano 875/201 (442) 925-311
Spanish-language weekly. Editor also directs daily Yiddish radio programme.

Mikvaot

Adat Yiereim
Durazno 1183 (2) 711-1686
Fax: (2) 711-7736

Museum

Centro Recordatorio del Holocausto
Canelones 1084, P.3 11100 (2) 902-5750
Fax: (2) 902-5740
Email: centroshoa@conectate.com.uy
Is the home for several Jewish institutions and events are frequently held here.

Restaurants

Kasherissimo
Camacua 623 (2) 915-0128
Fax: (2) 208-1536
Supervision: Chief Rabbi Yosef Bitton.
The restaurant is situated in the Hebraica Macabi building.

Synagogues

Anshei Jeshurun
Durazno 972 (2) 900-8456
Fax: (2) 900-8456

Comunidad Israelita Hungara
Durazno 972 (2) 900-8456
Fax: (2) 900-8456

Uruguay

Social Isralite Adat Yeshurun
Alarcon 1396

Vaad Ha'ir
Canelones 828 (2) 900-6106
Fax: (2) 711-7736
Email: marebis@com.uy

Ashekenazi

Comunidad Israelita de Uruguay
Canelones 1084, Piso 1 (2) 902-5750
Fax: (2) 902-5740
Email: kehila@adinet.com.uy

Conservative

Nueva Congregacion Israelita
Wilson Ferreira Aldunate 1168 (2) 902-6620
Fax: (2) 902-0589
Email: nci@adinet.com.uy

Sephardi

Comunidad Israelita Sefardi
Buenos Aires 234, 21 de Setiembre 3111
(442) 710-179

Templo Sefardi
de Pocitos L. Franzini 888

Tourist Sites

"Memorial to Golda Meir"
Reconquista y Ciudadela
Email: cciu@adinet.com.uy

Uzbekistan

The ancient Jewish community in this central Asian republic is believed to have been founded by Persian exiles in the fifth century. The Jews were subject to harsh treatment under the various rulers of the region, but still managed to become important traders in this area, which straddled the route between Europe and China and the Far East. In the late Middle Ages Jewish weavers and dyers were asked to help in the local cloth industry, and Bukhara became a key Jewish city after it became the capital of the country in the 1500s. Once the area had been incorporated into the Russian Empire in 1868, many Jews from the west of the Empire moved into Uzbekistan. A further influx occurred when Uzbekistan was used to shelter Jews during the Nazi invasion of the Soviet Union; many subsequently set up home there.

The original Bukharan Jews are generally more religious than the Ashkenazim who entered the area in the nineteenth and twentieth centuries. There are Jewish schools in the area, and although there is no central Jewish organisation, there are many Jewish bodies operating on separate levels for the Ashkenazim and the Bukharans.

GMT + 5 to 6 hours	Total Population 24,318,000
Country calling code (998)	Jewish Population 15,000
Emergency Telephone (Police, Fire, Ambulance - 03)	Electricity voltage 220

Andizhan

Synagogues

7 Sovetskaya Street

Bukhara

Synagogues

20 Tsentralnaya Street

Katta-Kurgan

Synagogues

1 Karl Marx Alley

Kermine

Synagogues

36 Narimanov Street

Kokand

Synagogues

Dekabristov Street, Fergan Oblast

Margelan

Synagogues

Turtkilskaya Street, Fergan Oblast

Navoy

Synagogues

36 Narimanov Street

Samarkand

Three thousand Jews live in Samarkand. Many are Bukharan, and live in the special mahala, the quarter designated to Jews.

Synagogues

18 Esayva Street

Tashkent

Embassy

Embassy of Israel
16A Shakhrisabz Street, 5th floor (71) 152911
Fax: (71) 1521378
Email: isremb@online.ru

Synagogues

9 Chkalov Street
Gorbunova Street 62 (71) 1525978
Fax: (71) 1525978
Email: jewish@bcc.com.uz
Web site: www.jewish.uz

Ashkenazi

77 Chempianov Street

Sephardi

3 Sagban Street (71) 40-0768

Venezuela

Settlement in Venezuela began in the early nineteenth century from the Caribbean. The Jews were granted freedom early (between 1819 and 1821), which encouraged more settlement. The community at that time was not religious. At the beginning of the twentieth century, some Middle Eastern Jewish immigrants organised a central committee for the first time. The powerful influence of the Catholic Church meant that few Jews were accepted as immigrants in the pre-War rush to escape Nazi Europe.

After the War, however, the community began to expand, with arrivals from Hungary and the Middle East. The successful oil industry and the excellent Jewish education system attracted immigrants from other South American countries.

Today, most Jews live in Caracas, the capital. Fifteen synagogues serve the country. The Lubavitch movement is present and maintains a yeshivah. Caracas has a Jewish bookshop and a weekly Jewish newspaper. Venezuela has an expanding Jewish community, in contrast to many of its South American neighbours. The oldest Jewish cemetery in South America, in Coro, with tombstones dating from 1832, is still in use today.

GMT - 4 hours — Total Population 24,170,000
Country calling code (58) — Jewish Population 18,000
Emergency Telephone (Ambulance - 545 4545) (Dr. - 483 7021) — Electricity voltage 110

Caracas

Bakeries

Le Notre
Avenida Andres Bello (2) 782-4448

Pasteleria Kasher
Avenida Los Proceres (2) 515-086

Booksellers

Libreria Cultural Maimonides
Av Altamira Edif. Carlitos PB, (near Av. Galapen), San Bernardino (2) 551-6356
Fax: (2) 552-9127
Email: judaico@tecel.net.ve

Contact Information

Chabad-Lubavitch Centre
Apartado 5454 1010A (2) 523-887

Delicatessens

La Belle Delicatesses
Av. Bogotá, Edif Santa María, Local 2, Los Caobos (2) 781-7204
Fax: (2) 781-7182
Kosher delicatessen and mini-market, restaurant and take-away.

Embassy

Embassy of Israel
Avenida Francisco de Miranda, Centro Empresarial Miranda, 4 Piso Oficina 4-D, Apartado Postal Los Ruices 70081 (2) 239-4511; 239-4921
Fax: (2) 239-4320

Groceries

Mini Market
Avenida Los Caobas (2) 781-7204
Take-away.

Hotels

Hotel Aventura
A short walk away from the Union Synagogue, convenient for Shabbat observers.

Hotel Avila
Next door to the Union Synagogue, convenient for Shabbat observers.

Media

Newspaper

Nuevo Mundo Israelita
Av Marques del Toro 9, Los Caobos

Mikvaot

Shomrei Shabbat Association Synagogue
Av Anauco, San Bernardino (2) 517-197

Union Israelita de Caracas Synagogue & Community Centre
Av Marques del Toro 9, San Bernardino
(2) 552-8222
Fax: (2) 552-7628
Email: rabino@brener@eldish.net

Synagogues

Ashkenazi

Great Synagogue of Caracas
Av Francisco Javier Ustariz, San Bernardino
(2) 511-869

Shomrei Shabbat Assoc. Synagogue
Av Anauco, San Bernardino (2) 517-197

Union Israelita de Caracas Synagogue & Community Centre
Av Marques del Toro 9, San Bernardino
(2) 552-8222
Fax: (2) 552-7628
Email: rabino@brener@eldish.net
If notified in advance, they can arrange kosher lunches. There is also a meat snack bar open in the evening.

Sephardi

Bet El
Av Cajigal, San Bernardino (2) 522-008

Keter Tora
Av Lopez Mendez, San Bernardino

Shaare Shalom
Av Bogota, Quinta Julieta, Los Caobos

Tiferet Yisrael
Av Mariperez, Los Caobos (2) 781-1942

Maracaibo

Community Organisations

Associación Israelita de Maracaibo
Calle 74 No 13-26 (61) 70333

Porlamar

Synagogues

Or Meir
Calle Carnevali, Margarita Island (95) 634-433
Mikva on premises.

Virgin Islands (USA)

Jews first began to settle on the island in 1655, taking advantage of liberal Danish rule. They were mainly traders in sugar-cane, rum and molasses, and by 1796 a synagogue had been founded. The Jewish population of 400 in 1850 made up half of the islands' white community. There have been three Jewish governors; one of whom was the first, Gabriel Milan appointed by King Christian of Denmark.

The community began to shrink after the Panama Canal was opened in 1914, and by 1942 only fifty Jews remained. Since 1945, the community has expanded again, with families arriving from the US mainland.

GMT - 4 hours — Total Population 114,000
Country calling code (1) — Jewish Population 300

St Thomas

Synagogues

Hebrew Congregation of St. Thomas
PO Box 266 00804 (340) 774-4312
Fax: (340) 774-4312
Email: hebrewcong@islands.vi
Web site: www.onepaper.com/synagogue
This synagogue was built in 1833, restored in 2000

Orthodox

Khal Hakodesh
(809) 779-2000

Yugoslavia

[Yugoslavia at present comprises Serbia and Montenegro.] The history of Serbian Jewry is both long and comparatively happy, with initial settlement occurring in Roman times. After the onset of Turkish domination in 1389, the community continued to thrive and also prospered under Austrian rule in the eighteenth century. The nineteenth century saw some measures being taken against the Jews after Serbia became independent, but these were quickly redressed in 1889 following the Treaty of Berlin.

After 1918, Serbia was united with Croatia, Slovenia and the other southern Slavic states, into one country, known as Yugoslavia. The community suffered heavily under Nazi domination. The Jews were active among the Yugoslav partisans and, after liberation, many who had hidden or fought with the partisans began to return to their homes. Before the break-up of Yugoslavia, the Jews were allowed contact with other communities, including Israel. Since the Civil War, some Jews have remained in the country, and there is a synagogue and a Talmud Torah school in Belgrade.

GMT + 1 hour — Total Population 10,600,000
Country calling code (381) — Jewish Population 1,800
Emergency Telephone (Police - 92) (Fire - 93) (Ambulance - 94) — Electricity voltage 220

Belgrade

Some 2,000 Jews now live in the capital of Serbia, compared with hardly any during the latter stages of World War Two. There is an Ashkenazi synagogue which follows Sephardi tradition (or nusach), and there is a community centre, although kosher food is not available.

Tourist site

Jewish Cemetery

There are monuments here to fallen fighters and martyrs of Fascism, fallen Jewish soldiers in the Serbian army in the First World War. In 1990 a new monument to Jews killed in Serbia was erected by the Danube, in the pre-War Jewish quarter Dorcol.

Community Organisations

Local Community

7 Kralja Petra Street 71a/11 11001 (11) 624-289

Museums

Jewish Historical Museum

Kralja Petra Street 71a/1 11001 (11) 622-634
Fax: (11) 626-674
Email: muzej@eunet.yu
Web site: www.jim-bg.org

Open daily from 10.00 to 12.00.

Representative Organisations

Federation of Jewish Communities

7 Kralja Petra Street 71a/111,
PO Box 841 11001 (11) 624-359/621-837
Fax: (11) 626-674

Synagogues

Birjuzova Street 19

Services are held Friday evenings and Jewish holidays.

Novi Sad

Tourist site

Jewish Cemetery

There is a monument to the Jews who fell in the War and the victims of Fascism. The synagogue here is no longer open but it's reported to be extremely beautiful, and is currently being converted to a concert hall.

Community Organisations

Community Offices

Jevrejska 11 (21) 613-882

Subotica

Community Organisations

Community Offices

Dimitrija Tucovica Street 13 () 28483

Tourist Site

The Subotica Synagogue built in 1901 and considered one of the finest Art Nouveau buildings in Europe is currently being restored.

Zambia

The Jewish community began in the early twentieth century, with cattle ranching being the main attraction for Jewish immigrants. The community grew, and the copper industry was developed largely by Jewish entrepreneurs. With refugees from Nazism and a post-War economic boom, the Jewish community in the mid-1950s totalled 1,200. The community declined after independence in 1964.

Today, the Council for Zambian Jewry (founded in 1978) fulfils the role of the community's central body.

GMT + 2 hours
Country calling code (260)
Emergency Telphone (Police, Fire and Ambulance - 999)

Total Population 9,715,000
Jewish Population Under 100
Electricity voltage 220

Lusaka

Communal Organisation

Council for Zambian Jewry
P O Box 30089 10101 (1) 229-556
Fax: (1) 223-798
Email: galaun@zamnet.zm

Synagogues

Lusaka Hebrew Congregation
Chachacha Road, POB 30020 (1) 229-190
Fax: (1) 221-428
Email: galaun@zamnet.zm

Zimbabwe

Jews were among the earliest pioneers in Zimbabwe; (formerly Rhodesia) in fact, the first white child born there (April 1894) was Jewish.

The first synagogue in Zimbabwe was set up in 1894, in a tent in Bulawayo. In 1897 a Jew was elected as the first mayor of Bulawayo. The first Jews came from Europe (especially Lithuania), and they became involved in trade and managing hotels. They were joined in the 1920s and 1930s by Sephardis from Rhodes. Some senior politicians in the country were Jewish, including one prime minister.

The 1970s saw the turbulent transition to Zimbabwe and many Jews emigrated to escape the unrest. The community is now mainly Ashkenazi, with an important Sephardi component. Harare has both an Ashkenazi and a Sephardi synagogue; Bulawayo has a Ashkenazi synagogue. There are community centres in both the towns, and schools, although the latter have many local, non-Jewish pupils.

GMT + 2 hours
Country calling code (263)
Emergency Telephone (Police, Fire and Ambulance - 999)

Total Population 11,669,000
Jewish Population 900
Electricity voltage 220/240

Bulawayo

Synagogues

Bulawayo Hebrew Congregation
Jason Moyo Street, PO Box 337 (9) 237-335

Harare

Representative Organisations

Zimbabwe Jewish Board of Deputies
PO Box 1954 (4) 702-507
Fax: (4) 702-506
Email: cazo@zol.co.zw
Hours of opening 8.30 am to 12 noon

Synagogues

Harare Hebrew Congregation
Milton Park Jewish Centre, Lezard Avenue,
PO Box 342 (4) 727-576

Sephardi Congregation
54 Josiah Chinamano Avenue,
PO Box 1051 (4) 722-899

International Access Dialling Codes

In order to phone from one country to another one must use the appropriate International Access Dialling Code.

Most International Access Dialling Codes are 00. The following however are the exceptions.

Australia	0011
Bahamas	011
Belarus	810
Canada	011
Colombia	009
El Salvador	0
Estonia	800
Finland	varies
Hong Kong	001
Japan	varies
Lithuania	810
Mexico	98
Russia	810
Singapore	001
South Africa	09
South Korea	varies
Sweden	varies
Taiwan	002
Thailand	001
Ukraine	810
United States of America	011
Uzbekistan	810
Yugoslavia	99

The procedure is as follows:

FIRST dial the International Access Code for the country you are calling from (as shown above).

SECOND dial the country calling code (as shown on the appropriate page of this Guide) for the country you are calling to.

THIRD dial the area code for the location you are dialling to (some countries do not require a area code).

FOURTH dial the local phone number.

Kosher Fish Throughout the World

AUSTRALIA

Anchovy
Baramundi
Barracouta
Barracuda
Blue Eye
Blue Grenadier
Bream
Butterfly-fish
Cod
Coral Perch
Duckfish
Flathead
Flounder
Garfish
Groper
Gurnard
Haddock
Hake
Harpuka
Herring
Jewfish
John Dory
Lemon Sole
Mackerel
Morwong
Mullet
Murray Cod
Murray Perch
Orange Roughy
Perch
Pike
Pilchard
Red Emperor
Redfin
Salmon
Sardines
Sea Perch
Shad
Sild
Snapper
Tailor
Tasmanian
Trumpeter
Terakiji
Trevally
Trout
Tuna:
  Albacore,
Bluefin
  North bluefin
  South bluefin
  Skipjack
(striped)
  Yellowfin
Whiting
Yellowtail

CANADA

Albacore
Anchovies
Bass
Boston Bluefish
Carp
Cisco
Cod
Flounder
Goldeye
Haddock
Hake
Halibut
Herring
Mackerel
Orange Roughy
Perch
Pickerel
Pike
Pollock
Pompano
Salmon
Sardines
Silversides
Smelts
Snapper
Sole
Sunfish
Tarpon
Trout
Tuna

CARIBBEAN

Bonito
Grouper
Kingsish
Mullets
Muttonfish
Pompano
Roballo
Smelts
Snapper
Red/Yellow
Spanish Mackerel
Trout
Tuna

CYPRUS

Antzouva
Bacceliaos
Barbouni
Cephalos
Glossa
Lavraki
Sardella
Scoumbri
Tonos
Tsipoura

CZECH REPUBLIC

Ancovicka
Belicka
Kambala
Kapr
Lin
Lipan
Losos
Makrela
Okoun
Parmice
Platejs
Platyz
Plotice
Prazama
Pstruh
Sardinka
Sled
Sprota
Stika
Treska
Tunak

DENMARK

Aborre
Ansjos
Bars
Brasen
Brisling
Gedde
Helleyflynder
Hvilling
Ising
Karpe
Knurhane
Kuller
Kulmule
Laks
Lange
Lubbe
Makrel
Multe
Orred
Rodspaette
Sardin
Sild
Skalle
Skrubbe
Slethvarre
Suder

Torsk
Tun fisk
Tunge

FRANCE

Aiglefin
Anchois
Bar Commun
Barbue
Breme
Brochet
Cabillaud
Carpe
Carrelet
Flet
Fletan
Gardon
Grondin
Hareng
Lieu Jaune
Limande
Lingue
Maquereau
Merlan
Merlu
Mulet
Ombre
Perche
Pilchard
Plie
Sardine
Saumon
Sole
Sprat
Tanche
Thon
Truite

GERMANY

Asche
Barsch
Brasse
Flunder
Forelle
Glattbutt
Hecht
Heilbutt
Hering
Kabeljau
Knurrhahn
Lachs
Leng
Makrele
Meerasche
Pilchard
Plotze
Pollack
Sardelle
Sardine
Scharbe
Schellfisch
Schlei
Scholle
Seebarsch
Seehecht
Seezunge
Sprotte
Thun
Weissfisch
Wittling

GREECE

Antjuga
Bakaliaros
Chematida
Chromatida
Gados
Giavros
Glinia
Glossa
Glossaki
Hippoglossa
Kaponi
Kephalos
Kyprinos
Lavraki
Lestia
Papalina
Pentiki
Perca chani
Pestropha
Pissi
Regha
Romvos
Sardella
Sardine
Scoumbri
Solomos
Tonnos
Tourna
Tsironi

HONG KONG

Anchovies
Bigeyes
Carp
Crevalles
Croakers
Giant Perch
Grey Mullet
Groupers
Japanese Sea
Perch
Leopard Coral
Trout
Pampano
Pilchards
Red Sea Bream
Round Herring
Sardines
Scads
Whitefish

ITALY

Acciuga
Aringa
Asinello
Brama
Carpa
Cefalo
Halibut
Limanda
Luccio
Maccerello
Merlano
Merluzzo Bianco
Merluzzo Giallo
Molva
Nasello
Passera
Passera Pianuzza
Pesce
Pesce Capone
Rombo Liscio
Salmone
Sardina
Sogliola
Spigola
Spratto
Tinca
Tonno
Triotto
Trota

JAPAN

Bora
Hirasaba
Hobo
Iwashi
Kadoiwashi
Kanagashira
Karei
Katakuchiiwashi
Kawakamasu
Koi
Maguro-rui
Maiwashi
Masu
Nishin
Ohyo
Saba
Sake masu-rui
Shitabirame
Tara

NETHERLANDS

Aaldoe
Ansjovis
Baars
Blankvoorn

Bot
Brasem
Forel
Griet
Harder
Haring
Heek
Helibot
Kabeljauw
Karper
Leng
Makree
Pelser
Poon
Salm
Sardien
Schar
Schelvis
Schol
Snoek
Sprot
Tong
Tonijn
Wijting
Witte koolvis
Zeebaars
Zeelt

NEW ZEALAND

Hoki
John Dory
Kingfish
Mackerel
Mullet
Orange Roughy
Perch
Piper
Salmon
Smooth Black
Snapper
Sole
Southern Whiting
Terakihi
Trevally
Trout

PORTUGAL

Alabote
Anchova
Arenque
Arinca
Atum
Bacalhau
Badejo
Biqueirao
Carpa
Donzela
Espadilha
Linguado
Lucio
Perca
Pescada
Petruca
Robalo
Rodovalho
Ruivaca
Ruivo
Salmao
Sarda
Sardinha
Sargo
Solha
Solhao
Tainha
Tenca
Truta

SOUTH AFRICA

Albacore Tuna
Anchovies
Butterfish
Carp
Euthynnus Tuna
Haddock
Hake
Herring
Kabeljou
Kingklip
Maas Banker
Mackerel
Pilchards
Red Roman
Salmon
Sardines
Seventy Four
Skipjack Tuna
Snoek
Sole
Steembras
Stock Fish
Stump Nose
Tongol Tuna
Trout
Yellowfin Tuna

SPAIN

Albadejo
Anchoa
Arenque
Atun
Bacalao
Bermejuela
Boqueron
Caballa
Carpa
Eglefino
Espadin
Halibut
Lenguado
Limanda
Lisa
Lubina
Lucio
Maruca
Merlan
Merluza
Perca
Platija
Remol
Rubios
Salmon
Sardina
Solla
Tenca
Trucha

TURKEY

Alabalik
Bakalyaro
Berlam
Caca
Civisiz kalkan
Derepissi
Dil baligi
Gelincik
Hamsi
Kadife baligi
Kefal
Kirlangic
Kizilgoz
Levrek
Morina
Palatika
Pisi baligi
Ringa
Sardalya
Sazan
Som baligi
Tahta baligi
Tatlisu levregi
Ton baligi
Turna baligi
Uskumru

UNITED KINGDOM

Anchovy
Barbel
Bass
Bloater
Bonito
Bream
Brill
Brisling
Buckling
Carp
Coalfish
Cod
Coley
Dab

Dace
Flounder
Fluke
Grayling
Gurnard
Haddock
Hake
Halibut
Herring
Hoki
John Dory
Keta Salmon
Kipper
Ling
Mackerel
Megrim
Mock Halibut
Mullet Grey
Mullet Red
Norway Haddock
Parrot Fish
Perch
Pike
Pilchard
Plaice
Pole
Pollack
Redfish
Roach
Saithe
Salmon
Sardine
Shad
Sild
Smelt
Snapper
Snoek
Sole Dover
Sole Lemon
Sprat
Tench
Tilapia
Trout
Tuna (Tunny)
Whitebait
Whiting
Witch

UNITED STATES OF AMERICA

Albacore
Alewife
Amberjack
Anchovies
Angelfish
Barb
Barracouta
Barracuda
Bass
Bigeyes
Black Cod
Blackfish
Blueback
Bluefish
Bluegill
Bonito
Bream
Brill
Capelin
Carp
Cero
Char
Chub
Cisco
Coalfish
Cod
Crevalle
Dab
Flounders
Fluke
Gag
Grayling
Grouper
Haddock
Hake
Halibut
Herrings
John Dory
Kingfish
Mackerel
Mahi Mahi
Merluccio
Mullet
Parrot Fish
Perch
Pike
Pilchard
Plaice
Pollock
Pomfrets
Red Snapper
Roach
Saithe
Salmon
Sardine
Shad
Sierra
Skipjack
Smelts
Snapper
Sole
Sprat
Tench
Tilapia
Trout
Tuna
Wahoo
Whitefish
Whiting
Yellowtail

Abridged Jewish Calendar

2002 (5762-5763)

Fast of Esther	Monday	February 25th
Purim	Tuesday	February 26th
First Day Pesach	Thursday	March 28th
Second Day Pesach	Friday	March 29th
Seventh Day Pesach	Wednesday	April 3rd
Eighth Day Pesach (Yizkor)	Thursday	April 4th
Holocaust Memorial Day	Tuesday	April 9th
Israel Independence Day	Wednesday	April 17th
Lag B'Omer	Tuesday	April 30th
First Day Shavout	Friday	May 17th
Second Day Shavout (Yizkor)	Saturday	May 18th
Fast of Tammuz	Thursday	June 27th
Fast of Av	Thursday	July 18th
First Day Rosh Hashanah	Saturday	September 7th
Second Day Rosh Hashanah	Sunday	September 8th
Fast of Gedaliah	Monday	September 9th
Yom Kippur (Yizkor)	Monday	September 16th
First Day Succot	Saturday	September 21st
Second Day Succot	Sunday	September 22nd
Shemini Atseret (Yizkor)	Saturday	September 28th
Simchat Torah	Sunday	September 29th
First Day Chanutah	Friday	November 30th

2003 (5763-5764)

Fast of Esther	Monday	March 17th
Purim	Tuesday	March 18th
First Day Pesach	Thursday	April 17th
Second Day Pesach	Friday	April 18th
Seventh Day Pesach	Wednesday	April 23rd
Eighth Day Pesach (Yizkor)	Thursday	April 24th
Holocaust Memorial Day	Tuesday	April 29th
Israel Independence Day	Wednesday	May 7th
Lag B'Omer	Tuesday	May 20th
First Day Shavout	Friday	June 6th
Second Day Shavout (Yizkor)	Saturday	June 7th
Fast of Tammuz	Thursday	July 17th
Fast of Av	Thursday	August 7th
First Day Rosh Hashanah	Saturday	September 27th
Second Day Rosh Hashanah	Sunday	September 28th
Fast of Gedaliah	Monday	September 29th
Yom Kippur (Yizkor)	Monday	October 6th
First Day Succot	Saturday	October 11th
Second Day Succot	Sunday	October 12th
Shemini Atseret (Yizkor)	Saturday	October 18th
Simchat Torah	Sunday	October 19th
First Day Chanukah	Saturday	December 20th

Index

C

D

E

F

G

J

K

M

Q

R

S

Y

Z

Index to Advertisers

ADVERTISEMENT ORDER FORM 2003

Please complete and return Jewish Travel Guide form to us by 1 September 2002

Please reserve the following advertising space in

Jewish Travel Guide 2003:

☐ Full Page	£475	181 x 115 mm
☐ Half Page	£245	91 x 115 mm
☐ Quarter Page	£145	45.5 x 115 mm

(UK advertisers please note that the above rates are subject to VAT)

Special positions by arrangement

☐ **Please insert the attached copy (If setting is required a 10% setting charge will be made.)**

☐ **Copy will be forwarded from our Advertising Agents (*see below*)**

Contact Name: ______________________________

Advertisers Name: ______________________________

Address for invoicing: ______________________________

____

Tel: ____________________ Fax: ____________________

Signed: ____________________ Title: ____________________

VAT No: ______________________________

Date: ____________________

Agency Name (if applicable): ______________________________

Address: ______________________________

____

Tel: ____________________ Fax: ____________________

All advertisements set by the publisher will only be included if they have been signed and approved by the advertiser.

To the Advertising Department
Jewish Travel Guide
Vallentine Mitchell & Co. Ltd.
Crown House, 47 Chase Side,
Southgate, London N14 5BP
Fax: + 44(0)20-8447 8548. E-mail: jtg@vmbooks.com

PUBLISHER'S REQUEST

Update for Jewish Travel Guide 2003

Readers are asked kindly to draw attention to any errors or omissions. If errors are discovered, it would be appreciated if you could give up-to-date information, referring to page, place, etc., and return this form to the Editor at the address given below.

With reference to the following entry:

Page:

Country:

Entry should read:

Kindly list on separate sheet if preferred.

Signed: ______________________ Date: __________

Name (BLOCK CAPITALS) ______________________

Address: ______________________

____

Telephone: ______________________

SEND TO:

The Editor
Jewish Travel Guide
Vallentine Mitchell & Co. Ltd.
Crown House, 47 Chase Side,
Southgate, London N14 5BP
Fax: + 44(0)20-8447 8548. E-mail: jtg@vmbooks.com

Notes

Notes

Notes

NASJ
VIEL
NasjViel